D0395645

THE CENTRAL INTELLIGENCE AGENCY
An Instrument of Government, to 1950

THE
CENTRAL
INTELLIGENCE
AGENCY

AN
INSTRUMENT
OF
GOVERNMENT,
TO 1950

Arthur B. Darling

With Introductions by Bruce D. Berkowitz and Allan E. Goodman

THE PENNSYLVANIA STATE UNIVERSITY PRESS
University Park and London

Library of Congress Cataloging-in-Publication Data

Darling, Arthur B. (Arthur Burr), 1892–1971.
    The Central Intelligence Agency : an instrument of government, to
  1950 / Arthur B. Darling with introductions by Bruce D. Berkowitz
  and Allan E. Goodman.
        p.   cm.
    Includes bibliographical references and index.
    ISBN 0-271-00715-X—ISBN 0-271-00717-6 (pbk. : alk.
  paper)
    1. United States. Central Intelligence Agency—History.
  I. Title.
  JK468.I6D37   1990
  327.1'2'06073—dc20   90–45807

It is the policy of The Pennsylvania State University Press to use acid-free paper for the first printing of all clothbound books. Publications on uncoated stock satisfy the minimum requirements of American National Standard for Information Sciences—Permanence of Paper for Printed Library Materials, ANSI Z39.48–1984.

Printed in the United States of America

Contents

Contents

List of Illustrations

(following page xxvii)

General William J. Donovan
      (Coordinator of Strategic Information, 1941–1945)

Admiral Sidney W. Souers
      (Director of Central Intelligence, 1946)

General Hoyt S. Vandenberg
      (Director of Central Intelligence, 1946–1947)

Admiral Roscoe H. Hillenkoetter
      (Director of Central Intelligence, 1947–1950)

General Walter B. Smith
      (Director of Central Intelligence, 1950–1953)

Publisher's Note

Any publisher today would be grateful to have an author who submitted a manuscript as carefully prepared as this one completed by Arthur B. Darling nearly thirty years ago. It is fortunate for all of us that he wrote so clearly, making very few mistakes, for no substantive editing of any kind was therefore necessary. Only minimal editing was undertaken to ensure consistency of reference and eliminate redundancy in the notes, and in the text changes were made simply to conform the style more closely to current practices in capitalization, hyphenation, italicization, punctuation, and the like. Of course, internal cross-references also had to be changed in the process of converting manuscript to printed book.

This volume contains the complete document as released to the public in November 1989 by the Central Intelligence Agency, with two exceptions. It omits a summary of Darling's work prepared by the CIA's History Staff that covers 224 pages of typescript in the original document. And the index, said in a handwritten note to have been prepared by John Mitchell in September 1954, has been significantly revised and supplemented by the professional indexer hired to edit it, Diana Witt.

Additions to the document made for the purpose of setting it in historical context and clarifying its significance are the introductions, both to the book as a whole and to the separate chapters, prepared by Bruce D. Berkowitz and Allan E. Goodman at the publisher's invitation and also the two memoranda on the CIA's Historical Review Program reproduced in Appendix B.

The publisher wishes to express his thanks to Dr. Berkowitz for undertaking the initial formal review of the manuscript that led the Editorial Committee of the Pennsylvania State University Press to approve its publication at a meeting in January 1990. Both he and Dr. Goodman deserve our gratitude, too, for undertaking the research and writing that produced the fine introductions for this volume. The photographs in this volume were provided through the courtesy of the National Archives.

Publisher's Note

This is the first in what is hoped to be a series of publications by the Pennsylvania State University Press arising from the materials released through the CIA's Historical Review Program. A second volume entitled *General Walter Bedell Smith as Director of Central Intelligence, October 1950–February 1953* by Ludwell Lee Montague, also with introductory comments by Drs. Berkowitz and Goodman, is now in preparation, with publication planned for the spring of 1991.

Introduction

This book is a historical account of how the Central Intelligence Agency was created in the years immediately following World War II. It was written in 1952–1953 by Arthur B. Darling, a professional historian who had taught at Yale and Phillips Academy prior to becoming the CIA's first official historian. The manuscript was classified until November 1989, when it was released under the Agency's Historical Review Program. The text, along with its citations of supporting documentation and interviews, is presented here exactly as written by Darling, with only minor copyediting by the publisher, save for deletions made during the process of declassification and our own introductory comments that precede each chapter.

As this book goes to press, most national security policy experts agree that the Cold War has come to an end. They may have a point. The Cold War was based on three threats to the United States. Originally the threat was the possibility of a large-scale, Soviet-led invasion of Western Europe. Later the ability of the Soviet Union to carry out a nuclear strike against the United States itself became the most significant threat. Later still Soviet expansion in the Third World was added to the strategic calculus.

Today these threats have diminished, if not disappeared. The breakup of the Warsaw Pact, the reduction of Soviet forces west of the Elbe, and the rise of democratic governments in Poland, Hungary, Czechoslovakia, and East Germany have made the first threat militarily infeasible. At the same time, the U.S.-Soviet strategic nuclear balance has settled into middle-aged stability; both sides have little to gain and too much to lose from any imaginable nuclear exchange. And, in the Third World, any remaining role of the Soviet Union as a cause of instability is being overshadowed by home-grown threats ranging from terrorism to narcotrafficking to proliferation of nuclear and chemical weapons.

If these threats are no longer so critical, then one might wonder whether a book set in the early days of the Cold War when the United States was gearing up for containing the Soviet Union and some U.S.

officials thought it essential to preserve an intelligence apparatus to respond to this threat has any relevance today. We think that it does.

First, it is important simply for the historical record to establish an accurate, public record of the origins of the Central Intelligence Agency. Creating a permanent espionage service was a difficult decision for the Truman Administration and the Congress. The United States had no tradition of a standing peacetime intelligence organization, and many leaders thought that such an agency was incompatible with American democracy. Once the decision to create the CIA was made, the new agency initially ran up against resistance by the existing members of the national security bureaucracy when it attempted to exercise the central role in intelligence assigned to it by statute. Darling's study records and documents many of these early decisions, pressures, and events.

No comparable account upon which scholars can rely has previously been available, despite the fact that so much has come to light during the past fifteen years about the origins of the CIA and its early operations. Several hundred pages of Senate testimony taken in connection with the debate over the National Security Act of 1947 have been declassified and released by the Senate Foreign Relations Committee,[1] but this is a partial record at best. The Final Report of the Church Committee, published in 1976, contains a history prepared by Committee staff members provided access to CIA classified records and interviews with then current or retired officials.[2] In the early 1980s the CIA's Office of Training sponsored an unclassified history of the Office of Strategic Services (OSS, the World War II predecessor of the CIA) and William Donovan's efforts to preserve his intelligence organization as World War II drew to a close.[3] Academics and journalists have also produced summary histories based on press reports, interviews, material from some official archives, and published memoirs.[4]

These works have added substantially to the record, but all were written without the benefit of sources that most scholars would con-

---

[1]U.S. Congress, Senate, 80th Congress, 1st and 2d sess., *Executive Sessions of the Senate Foreign Relations Committee, 1947–1948* (Washington, D.C.: U.S. Government Printing Office, May 1976).

[2]U.S. Congress, Senate, 94th Congress, 2d sess., *Final Report of the Select Committee to Study Government Operations with Respect to Intelligence Activities* (Washington, D.C.: U.S. Government Printing Office, April 1976).

[3]Thomas F. Troy, *Donovan and the CIA* (Washington, D.C.: Central Intelligence Agency, 1981).

[4]The most ambitious of these is by John Ranelagh, *The Agency: The Rise and Decline of the CIA* (New York: Simon and Schuster, 1986). Numerous others could be cited.

sider essential to an authoritative history, namely, full access to the official files and records of the CIA and, if possible, interviews with the participants in the meetings and staff sessions connected with the creation and early operations of the CIA. Although much background material concerning the CIA has been released during the past two decades, until now the basic sources—the various memoranda and records of meetings connected with the establishment of the Agency— have not. Darling was provided access to the files of the National Security Council and the OSS. He was also allowed to interview all of the main players in the drama. As is customary in scholarly historical studies, Darling cited these sources in the text. So, although some may quarrel with his interpretation of events (and, as will be seen in a moment, there have been criticisms), the primary evidence is there for all to interpret.[5]

Also, all previous histories of the CIA's early years have been written long after the fact, either by participants who recorded their memoirs or by outsiders who have tried to assemble the story from available records. Consequently, none of these studies and books can really recreate the atmosphere of the times and the attitudes of the officials who took part. In this respect, Darling's study is especially important. Atmosphere and attitudes are perishable and usually require one to interview officials who played key roles at the time in order to get at the meaning behind the material in the archives. By recording these views at the time, Darling preserved a vital and unique record.

In addition, Darling's study makes a major contribution for a second reason that is possibly even more important. The period that Darling examines was the one during which the main controversies over the establishment, responsibilities, and turf of the agency were cast. Many of the controversies persist to this day and underlie debates regarding the operation and organization of the current U.S. intelligence bureaucracy.

Before the establishment of the CIA, U.S. intelligence was primarily the responsibility of components of the military services and the State Department, and these organizations operated primarily to provide only the specific tactical and operational information that their sponsors required. Also, before the establishment of the CIA, there was no organization that could provide the top U.S. leadership with comprehensive intelligence that could be considered independent of the views of the military services and the State Department.

[5]These citations are all included at the end of the text. These documents are currently being reviewed for release under the Historical Review Program and most are expected to be available through the National Archives in the same way as the Darling manuscript is.

As a result, U.S. leaders had never before been required to address many of the basic issues one confronts when a country decides to have a peacetime and centralized intelligence community. Some of these issues include, for example:

What is the proper role of the Director of Central Intelligence?

Should the DCI be insulated from the policy process?

Should the DCI have cabinet rank, so that the intelligence community has equal rank with the Defense Department and State Department?

How much control should the DCI have over the planning and control of U.S. intelligence assets (most of which are operated by agencies other than the CIA)?

Is covert action compatible with the U.S. democratic system? If so, who should carry it out, and how should it be planned and executed?

How does one ensure effective congressional oversight of the intelligence community?

Many of these issues, which were raised in the struggle to create the CIA during this period, were to surface repeatedly during the following forty years, and they continue to generate second thoughts today.

Darling's own views on these matters are clear. He argues that, in the modern era, effective intelligence is as much the product of effective organizations as of brave and ingenious individuals. Therefore, he concludes, centralizing the collection and dissemination of information while coordinating the production of estimates improves the effectiveness of intelligence. This view is foreshadowed in the subtitle of the study. By arguing that intelligence should be an "instrument of government," Darling intended to make two points: by using the term "instrument," he means that intelligence should be a tool, separate from the policymaking process; by using the term "government," he implies that intelligence should not be produced by a single agency, but by the government as a whole.

Even though Darling wrote this history during the time of the Korean War—a conflict that vindicated the position of those who argued that a CIA was needed because the Cold War would inevitably have hot spots—one of the most interesting features of the book is that it hardly mentions outside events at all. Rather, the study is mainly a narrative about politics within the national security bureaucracy and the debate about how to organize intelligence most effectively. In these pages the narrative only makes passing reference to the communist threat.

Much of the CIA's early history appears to have been shaped at least as much by these internal debates (many of which originated in World War II and the role of the OSS, well before a Soviet threat materialized) over how intelligence was to be organized and carried out. As Darling makes clear, there was considerable difference of opinion about what kind of organization was really needed. On one side, the armed services and State Department had been doing their own intelligence collection and analysis since before the war, and their leaders felt that their methods and product were already well suited to their needs. They believed that what they needed most was more resources, not another agency. On the other side, advocates of a CIA—mainly veterans of the OSS, experts outside the community, and dissidents within the armed services and State Department—argued that an independent, centralized intelligence service was needed. Their evidence consisted of the finding from post mortems of why the U.S. government had failed to warn itself about the impending Japanese attack on Pearl Harbor in December of 1941.

The creation of the CIA was also caught in controversies over the unification of the armed services and the problem of defining the role of the State Department in the making of U.S. national security policy. World War II had set in place both a process of unification and a tendency for the President to make foreign policy in the White House rather than leaving it to Foggy Bottom. Postwar events accelerated these trends. As a result, all departments involved in national security policy were determined to stake out their turf in the struggle that eventually led to the National Security Act of 1947. Adding a third player to the national security apparatus—the newly created Director of Central Intelligence—with responsibility for providing the President with information and judgments on both military and political matters made the stakes ever more clear.

A combination of bureaucratic and political factors virtually guaranteed that the early years of the CIA were to be tempestuous. The DCI was outside the departmental structure of cabinet offices. This fact underscored the erosion of the Secretaries' power and the growing influence of the President's staff to determine and set policy. At the same time, the DCI was junior to both cabinet secretaries and (at least initially) to all of the chiefs of staff of the armed services, so he was compelled to negotiate and maneuver with his counterparts; he could not simply assert his authority. And, to make matters even more difficult for the DCI, the CIA initially depended heavily on the Defense and State Departments for most of the information it was supposed to present to the President; later the CIA acquired some collection resources of its own, but still depended on Defense and State for most of its raw intelligence data. It was against this backdrop of personal and departmental politicking that Darling set his narrative.

The study thus sheds considerable light on the practical and political difficulties associated with creating a centralized intelligence function within the U.S. government. Unlike statesmen elsewhere, American leaders had tended consistently to conclude that there was no apparent need for a permanent organization in peacetime dedicated to gathering and analyzing intelligence. When one was created in the wake of World War II, moreover, there remained a substantial body of people who were skeptical about the need for and practicality of it. As Darling makes clear, this skepticism translated into resistance, battles over turf, and only a limited grant of authority to the DCI to command and control the production of intelligence.

Darling's criticism of the military services and the Department of State and his pique at the interdepartmental political games they play is at its sharpest when he discusses the problems associated with developing a meaningful process for coordinating the review of estimates and other intelligence analyses. Such coordination—the system by which draft reports done by one unit are reviewed and debated by the other components of the intelligence community—lies at the heart of an accurate and effective process of intelligence production as Darling saw it. Without the rigor and candor that such outside scrutiny provides, the end product is too likely to repeat conventional wisdom or leave unchallenged key assumptions and the consensus that may have been reached about ambiguous pieces of evidence. Although this theory of review made good sense (and still does), its introduction into the production of national strategic estimates, coupled with assigning the DCI responsibility for mediating between disputes over interpretations of facts by the Departments of State and Defense, was in fact revolutionary.

The study documents how such coordination was resisted at the very outset of the effort to create a centralized intelligence function within the U.S. Government. More significantly, reading Darling's account of the early battles over the authority of the DCI to require such review has a very current and familiar ring. Indeed, some parts of the manuscript read as if they had been written after reflection on the kinds of struggles that such DCIs as Richard Helms, William Colby, and

Stansfield Turner had over coordination, and especially the role that individual agency and service dissent should play in the drafting and approval of estimates.

Despite the comprehensiveness of Darling's account, some qualifications are needed in order to put the history into perspective. Like any other organization—and especially one whose leaders change because of political appointments and staff turnover as individuals find new professional interests—the CIA rarely speaks with a single voice or a fixed mindset. This is especially true of Darling's study.

The CIA Historian is in many respects more like an academic than a government official. The Historian is allowed free run in developing ideas and (within the limits of classification) publishing them. On the other hand, the Historian is usually not "one of the boys." The Historian has no line responsibilities; sometimes (as with Darling) the Historian is recruited from outside the Agency and has no prior experience in the intelligence community.

Most importantly, the Historian does not necessarily establish an official CIA position. Darling's account is "authoritative" in the sense that it is based on hard evidence from original sources. But it is not authoritative in the sense of a National Intelligence Estimate, which would be coordinated among the various offices that contributed to the analysis and would be signed by the Director of Central Intelligence. This is an important point to keep in mind because reporters and scholars are often wont to assign more significance to "official" documents, especially if they were at one time classified.

Ludwell Lee Montague, a long-time intelligence official, described the genesis of the Darling manuscript in his own Agency-sponsored account of the history of the CIA in the early 1950s.[6] According to

---

[6]Ludwell Lee Montague, *General Walter Bedell Smith as Director of Central Intelligence, October 1950–February 1953* (Washington, D.C.: Central Intelligence Agency, 1971), pp. 112–13.

Montague served in the Military Intelligence Division of the U.S. General Staff during World War II. He took part in many of the debates connected with the establishment of the CIA. Montague was a protégé of Smith and served as executive assistant to the DCI during Smith's term. Montague was one of the original members of the Board of National Estimates—the executive body that oversaw the production of National Intelligence Estimates until its dissolution in 1973—and remained on the BNE throughout the 1950s and 1960s.

Montague's study was the second major work declassified under the Historical Review Program and is also available in the National Archives. It will soon be published by the Pennsylvania State University Press.

Montague, the study was initiated in December 1950 when the Deputy Director of Central Intelligence (DDCI), William Jackson, proposed the creation of a History Staff within the CIA to maintain a current history of the agency, as well as handle relations with the press. Chester Hansen, a lieutenant colonel in the Air Force who had previously ghostwritten Omar Bradley's autobiography, *A Soldier's Story,* was appointed its first chief. Arthur Darling assumed the position of CIA Historian when he was asked by Hansen to help establish the History Staff.

Jackson had proposed to Hansen that the History Staff prepare a "historical audit" of the evolution of a national intelligence system. The purpose was to identify lessons learned from the early years of the CIA and its predecessors, the OSS and the Central Intelligence Group (CIG). Jackson had been one of the co-authors of a 1949 Presidential study (the "Dulles—Jackson—Correa Report") that was highly critical of the performance of the CIA in its early years. This study, combined with a series of intelligence failures, led to the reassignment of DCI Rear Admiral Roscoe Hillenkoetter and the appointment of Lieutenant General Walter Bedell Smith.

According to Montague, Darling understood Jackson's instructions to mean that the history should describe the "horrors of the pre-Smith period in order to justify and applaud the reforms of the Smith era."[7] For his part, Smith is said by Montague to have wanted this history to be a "dispassionate chronological history (by which he meant a strictly objective narrative)." Smith's instructions might explain the organization and style of Darling's work, in the sense that the study is rigidly chronological and the text tied virtually paragraph by paragraph to specific document sources.

In the end, Darling's study was neither an elaboration of the Dulles–Jackson–Correa Report nor a dispassionate chronology. Instead, it emphasized the bureaucratic opposition Smith's predecessors had experienced while serving as DCI and, by implication, condemned most of the parties that had opposed or had been critical of them. Unfortunately, one of these was Allen Dulles, another co-author of the Dulles–Jackson–Correa Report, Jackson's successor as DDCI and, after February 1953, Director of Central Intelligence.

One can only speculate why Darling departed from what he understood to be his instructions, namely, to write a history providing the rationale for the reforms being instigated at the CIA at the time. Indeed, it is remarkable that Darling went so far as to be so critical of so

---

[7]Ibid. Montague cites 1952 correspondence to him from Darling as the basis of this conclusion.

many sitting officials, including the man who was DDCI at the time. According to Montague, Smith decided not to retain Darling, who returned to Phillips Academy at the expiration of his leave in December 1953. Montague claims that Dulles felt sufficiently displeased with the study that, when he became DCI, he required individuals to request his express permission to gain access to the Darling manuscript.

This background places into context the CIA History Staff's 1988 comment (which appears on page xxv), alerting the reader that Allen Dulles (DCI from February 1953 to November 1961) did not agree with Darling's conclusions and "restricted access to the history." However, it also must be noted that, according to the current CIA Historian, access was not nearly as restrictive as this comment might imply and that "all of the senior people saw" Darling's study when it was completed and could have had access to it for reference at any time. Of course, circulation of the manuscript would have been limited at the time of its release in any case because of its classification. Also, the CIA tended to produce few copies of such reports; only fourteen copies were made, and this small number would have limited circulation as well. (As much as anything, this reflected the carbon-paper technology of the age.)

In the event, an adaptation of about half of Darling's study was published in the mid-1960s in *Studies in Intelligence,* the CIA's in-house professional journal. *Studies* is classified at the "Secret" level, so at this point it would have been available to all CIA staff employees and most of the rest of the U.S. national security community.

The declassification and release on November 14, 1989, of the Darling manuscript is a result of a clearly stated effort by the CIA to open its historical archives. The aim of the effort, known as the Historical Review Program, is "to provide the American people with a more accurate record and fuller understanding of CIA's role in our nation's history."[8] The program was created at a time when other U.S. government agencies were (and remain) under fire for constraining access to historical records.[9]

The impetus behind the program was a result of a deal struck in late 1983 between DCI William Casey and Senator Dave Durenberger, who

---

[8]Letter to the President, November 14, 1989, from Don W. Wilson and William H. Webster.

[9]See, for example, Karen J. Winkler, "Historians Criticize State Department for 'Distortions' and 'Deletions' in Its Record of U.S. Foreign Policy," *The Chronicle of Higher Education,* April 4, 1990.

was at the time a member of the Senate Select Committee on Intelligence. In retrospect, it is hard to imagine two high officials less likely to reach agreement about the issues involved. The CIA wanted to receive a partial exemption from the Freedom of Information Act (FOIA); the members of the Senate oversight committee wished to make sure that, if one were granted, the Agency would still press on with the review and declassification of its records. Distrust of Casey ran high in Congress, and especially among members of the Senate Select Committee. However, both Casey and Durenberger were devoted amateur historians; prior to becoming DCI Casey had been writing his own book using declassified OSS files.[10] Casey and the Intelligence Committee worked out an accommodation by an exchange of letters in 1983. In October 1984 the CIA got its exemption from FOIA, and in May 1985 DCI Casey reported to Congress that the review and declassification of selected CIA material of historical significance were feasible and would not result in damage to national security.

The Agency decided to start its declassification of historical documents by beginning with the earliest and most significant documents and proceeding chronologically. Thus, studies and records produced by or under the auspices of the Office of the DCI are being declassified first. The process can be time-consuming; clearance for declassification has to be received from each CIA unit and all other U.S. government agencies and departments on whose information the particular study draws. Darling's study is the first product to emerge from the process and required about three years to review. Although this seems lengthy, in fairness the number of sources cited and variety of their origins do suggest that considerable work is required to sanitize a work such as this.

For a once highly classified government document, the manuscript has been released with very few deletions, suggesting that the Agency is serious about allowing as much material as possible to be made available within the constraints of true national security concerns. Only some two hundred lines of text (as counted in the original typewritten manuscript) are missing; these deletions are indicated in the printed text. From the context, it is evident that about half of the excised material pertains to covert-action operations; the rest is more or less evenly divided between references to CIA liaison work with foreign intelligence services and to nuclear energy and weapons intelligence.

---

[10]William J. Casey, *The Secret War Against Hitler* (Washington, D.C.: Regnery Gateway, 1988).

Arthur Burr Darling trained in history at Harvard University under the tutelage of Frederick Jackson Turner, for whom he wrote his doctoral dissertation, "Jacksonian Democracy in Massachusetts, 1824–1848." He defended this dissertation in 1922 before a committee consisting of Turner, Albert Bushnell Hart, and Samuel Eliot Morison. A revised version of this work was published by Yale University Press under the title *Political Changes in Massachusetts, 1824–1848* and was described by one reviewer as a "detailed history of the process by which the political system of Massachusetts was transformed and the isolation of the state was terminated." The reviewer went on to note that the study was "based upon an amazing amount of research among manuscripts, both public and private, and pamphlets, newspapers and documents. . . . The author has constructed a clear narrative of an intricate story and is particularly skillful in his use of excerpts from his sources. His judgments are moderate and seem well founded."[11] These were precisely the qualities that impressed us when we first read the present manuscript.

It is fair to say, though, that Darling is probably better remembered for his excellence—and toughness—as a teacher than for his publications. Among Darling's students at Phillips Academy were President George Bush and the current CIA Historian, Dr. J. Kenneth McDonald. During the 1988 Presidential campaign, Mr. Bush cited Darling as his favorite teacher: "he was tough, demanding, yet exceedingly fair. He knew American history and made it come alive. . . ."[12] And in the bicentennial history of Phillips Academy, Darling was characterized as a teacher who "demanded extraordinarily high standards." While he was "famous for the number of boys who failed their diplomas in June as a result of failing American history," he was also voted "best teacher" for many years.[13]

After receiving his doctorate from Harvard, Darling taught at Yale (which he had previously attended as an undergraduate) from 1922 to 1933. At the end of that year he assumed a position in the Department of History at Phillips Academy (from which he had graduated in 1912). Darling took leave from 1951 to 1953 to serve as CIA Historian, having been recommended by Sherman Kent, one of his former students who was serving as Chairman of the Board of National Estimates. Darling

---

[11]Review by Lawrence B. Evans, *American Political Science Review,* vol. 20 (November 1926), p. 892.

[12]Quoted in the *Washington Post,* October 11, 1988.

[13]Frederick S. Allis, Jr., *Youth from Every Quarter: A Bicentennial History of Phillips Academy, Andover* (Hanover, N.H.: University Press of New England, 1979).

returned to Phillips Academy, from which he retired in 1956. He spent the following year abroad as a Fulbright scholar in Italy and then returned to the United States to live in Washington, D.C. In 1969 Darling moved to Paris, where one of his daughters lived. He died there in November 1971 at the age of 78.

The idea to publish the Darling manuscript originated with Stanley Weintraub, a member of the Pennsylvania State University Press's Editorial Committee. Dr. Weintraub became interested in the project after seeing an Associated Press story about the release of the manuscript in the *New York Times* on November 28, 1989.

The cooperation of the CIA Chief Historian, J. Kenneth McDonald, and members of his staff was invaluable in explaining the background to the study and the process by which it was declassified. We also appreciate the efforts of David Gries, our colleague at Georgetown and the Agency, in making the necessary introductions.

In addition, we are glad to have the opportunity to thank the many persons who provided information or support as we prepared this introduction and the commentary accompanying the text. John Taylor of the National Archives assisted us in reviewing the Darling and Montague manuscripts. Additional material on Dr. Darling and his career was provided by Gail A. Ferris, Director of the Yale University Alumni Records Office; Kathleen A. Markees, Curatorial Associate, Harvard University Archives; and Ruth Quattlebaum, Archivist at Phillips Academy. Dr. Richard W. Leopold provided further commentary on Dr. Darling's historical research, publications, and teaching at Phillips Academy. Stephanie Baird assisted in collecting material from the National Archives.

We also must make special mention of the contribution made by our research associate at Georgetown University, Julie Barnhorst. In addition to tracking down the materials we needed for our research into the background of Arthur Darling and his study, Ms. Barnhorst was our sounding board for ideas and prepared summaries of the manuscript that we used in writing the chapter introductions appearing in this volume. We can truly say that she has been a full partner at every stage in the project.

Finally, we owe a debt of gratitude to Sanford G. Thatcher, director of the Pennsylvania State University Press, for encouraging us to collaborate on another book about strategic intelligence in the American system.

Note

The reader should be aware that Arthur B. Darling's history, *The Central Intelligence Agency: An Instrument of Goverment, to 1950,* has a definite and sometimes controversial point of view. Darling blames the State Department, the FBI, and what he terms the Military Establishment—especially the heads of the military intelligence services—for much of the hardship which the early CIA (and its predecessor, the Central Intelligence Group) endured. He also heavily criticizes the Dulles–Jackson–Correa Report of 1949, which held the Director of Central Intelligence responsible for a major and ongoing failure in intelligence coordination. Reportedly, Allen Dulles (chairman of the Dulles–Jackson–Correa Report) did not concur with Darling's conclusions and, when he became Director of Central Intelligence, restricted access to the history.

History Staff
Office of the Director of Central Intelligence
Central Intelligence Agency
August 1988

"The necessity of procuring good Intelligence
is apparent & need not be further urged.
All that remains for me to add is, that you
keep the whole matter as secret as possible.
For upon Secrecy, Success depends in most
Enterprises of the kind, and for want of it,
they are generally defeated, however well
planned & promising a favourable issue."

George Washington
July 26, 1777

Preface

Two themes run through this historical study. The theory of central intelligence has developed with the growth of the instrument of government. The themes are so interrelated that they are not to be treated separately. When attention is upon the developing theory, the issue is that of individual versus collective responsibility, the rivalry between the Director of Central Intelligence and the chiefs of the departmental services who constituted his board of advisors. They were his counsellors with respect to many affairs of the central organization and in particular the production of national estimates.

When considered from the position of the growing instrument of government, the question is whether the institution should continue as a cooperative interdepartmental activity or should become an independent agency, authorized by law as determined by the Congress rather than subject to direction as recommended to the President by his Secretaries. They were caught between the interests of their departments and their collective authority over the central intelligence organization, first in the National Intelligence Authority and then as the National Security Council.

Thucydides found his task a laborious one. Eyewitnesses of the same occurrences, he said, gave different accounts as they remembered or were interested in the actions of one side or the other. Throughout this study the purpose has been to retain historical perspective, however contemporary the crisis or heated the conflict of interests. The records of the National Security Council were open for this investigation. References in the endnotes show the significant documents and interviews which have been gathered in a permanent Historical Collection for the Director of Central Intelligence.

December 3, 1953   Arthur B. Darling

General William J. Donovan (Credit: Historical Picture Services, Chicago)

Admiral Sidney W. Souers (Credit: National Archives)

General Hoyt S. Vandenberg (Credit: National Archives)

Admiral Roscoe H. Hillenkoetter (Credit: National Archives)

General Walter B. Smith (Credit: National Archives)

THE CENTRAL INTELLIGENCE AGENCY
An Instrument of Government, to 1950

Introduction to Chapter I

The idea that the United States should have a permanent, peacetime intelligence agency was spawned and pursued during World War II by several key individuals, the most notable among them William Donovan. Separate agencies had their own intelligence-gathering systems, to be sure, but no central clearinghouse existed to synthesize the information from all departments.

Donovan's travels in Europe for the U.S. government and his study of British intelligence operations led him to suggest the formation of an office of strategic information in the United States. President Roosevelt agreed and in 1941 appointed Donovan as Coordinator of Information (COI). After U.S. entry into World War II, the COI became the Office of Strategic Services (OSS).

From the beginning, attempts to create a central intelligence organization ran into opposition from the State, War, and Navy Departments. The State Department had traditionally been the source of foreign information, and the Army and Navy maintained their own intelligence operations, which they did not want to give up. Largely to quell the opposition of these departments, the OSS was placed under the jurisdiction of the Joint Chiefs of Staff (JCS).

Even so, as the U.S. war effort picked up, Donovan's OSS matured into a credible organization for collecting and analyzing intelligence, as well as for carrying out special operations and covert action. Within OSS Donovan established a Research and Analysis Branch; X-2 Branch, for conducting counterintelligence; Secret Intelligence Branch, for performing espionage and "human intelligence collection"; the Special Operations Branch, for carrying out sabotage and physical subversion; and other branches focusing on foreign nationalities and psychological warfare.

Although resistance to centralized intelligence authority continued, many government and military officials agreed that a central intelligence organization was necessary to gather all intelligence information from various government agencies and synthesize it for policymakers. These officials not only argued for strengthening OSS's resources and power but also began to promote the idea of a permanent, independent intelligence agency after the war ended.

The prospect of a permanent, peacetime agency that would require the State, War, and Navy Departments to relinquish significant authority over intelligence operations immediately started a turf battle in the national security establishment. Proposal followed proposal as each agency put forth its vision for how to organize intelligence in the postwar era. Each plan, naturally, was skewed toward the advantage of the individual or agency proposing it. The main points of contention in this debate concerned who should have authority over this central intelligence agency; whether it should have the power to collect its own information or only coordinate information from other agencies; and how it should be funded. Donovan and his Deputy Director, John Magruder, drafted a proposal that would essentially have preserved the OSS and established its authority over national intelligence. The services came up with their own plans for a less centralized peacetime intelligence community.

The Joint Intelligence Committee (the body within the Joint Chiefs of Staff responsible for intelligence matters) drafted a plan that compromised the recommendations of Donovan and those of the services in early 1945. This compromise provided for a National Intelligence Authority (NIA) comprised of the Secretaries of State, War, Navy, and the Chief of Staff to the President. Under the NIA a central intelligence agency was to be established with a Director of Central Intelligence (DCI) appointed by the President on the recommendation of the Authority. An Intelligence Advisory Board consisting of the heads of the intelligence services of the Army, Navy, and State Departments would assist the Director.

In developing this compromise plan, the authority of the DCI proved to be a major point of contention. Those who favored a high degree of centralization, such as Donovan, believed that the DCI should have autonomy and should report directly to the President. The military services opposed this, arguing that an autonomous DCI—who would possibly be a military officer—would blur the principle of chain of command. Civilian Defense Department officials had been willing to accept a DCI, but only one who was subordinate to the NIA.

These compromises in the centralized organization of U.S. intelligence and the authority of the DCI did not satisfy Donovan's expectations, and he persisted in trying to gain acceptance of a more centralized, independent, and active agency. Alas, President Roosevelt, who had personally asked Donovan to head the OSS and who had often supported him in his bureaucratic battles, died in April 1945. Germany surrendered in May and Japan in August. As America turned toward peace, Donovan made final pleas to maintain the OSS, but in vain. In September 1945 President Truman signed the OSS out of existence.

These controversies—the need for centralized intelligence analysis, control over national intelligence assets, and the role of the DCI—were to form the basis of most interagency disputes over intelligence in the postwar era.

For example, even today the National Foreign Intelligence Program is planned by the Director of Central Intelligence, but includes technical collection systems operated by military personnel and human intelligence assets from the State Department (most "HUMINT" consists of embassy reporting). These departments view these technical systems and personnel as "theirs" and want to be able to draw on them as necessary. Proponents of centralization, on the other hand, point out that these assets are national resources bought with national dollars. They go on to argue that the national interest requires that these resources be assigned to meet national priorities, rather than those of a particular government organization.

The seeds of controversy over how the U.S. intelligence community should be planned, managed, and operated were planted even before the end of World War II. For the most part, not only have the issues remained the same; the positions argued by each of the players has remained remarkably constant as well.

I

ORIGINS IN WAR

PRECEDENTS

 Precedents for the systematic collection of intelligence about one people by the agents of another lie as deep in recorded history as the first diplomatic mission of good will, or deeper. There doubtless went along some unpretentious person to scout around the town, listening to the talk of plain folk and having a look at things while the resplendent emissary dealt in rhetoric with the King. Professions and intentions do not always coincide. But then intelligence officers in any time know that one who is friend today may be foe tomorrow. War or the mood of war rather than peace is the norm among the nations of the world.

There have been agents abroad for this nation since its founding in revolution. Some of them have been official, some informal, some well withdrawn from public view. All have been there to gather information upon other countries and the attitudes of their governments. The Department of State, by nature and by tradition since its establishment in 1789, has been the collector and purveyor of such knowledge for the President and the Congress. The Army and the Navy of necessity have had their own means of obtaining information about the forces of the enemy whether actual or hypothetical.

No comparable efforts maintained counterintelligence to defend the United States. It may have been a false sense of security behind the oceans. But so great was the flood of immigration from abroad, excepting the Oriental countries, there was little use in trying to intercept foreign agents. They could roam the land at will. Americans in private life and in the Government, one might say, were proud to have foreigners come and see for themselves. It was a matter of policy in the 1880s to instruct visiting statesmen from Latin America with regard to the strength of the United States, as James G. Blaine sought reciprocal trade, a common silver currency with those countries, and the Pan-American Union.[1] Certain officers of a recent foe were conducted from East to West during the summer of 1951 for this Agency to acquaint them with the resources and capabilities of the nation. It may be inferred, if not said, that they were impressed with its wealth and power, and with the good fortune of those from the fatherland now living here.

THE IDEA OF INTELLIGENCE

News does not become knowledge by the mere process of gathering. Certainly it does not become intelligence, as the term must be understood in considering the weapons of war and the instruments of peace. The raw material of information has first to be verified and then appraised for its usefulness. It may be interesting but inconsequential. Subjected to analysis, it may however display elements, though insignificant in themselves, that associate in startling fashion with other bits of information. New evaluations follow. The readjustments of old elements become new syntheses that have significance. And intelligence has been produced for the policymaker. It remains for him to judge whether this intelligence or some other or his own intuitive reaction to events should govern the construction of policy and determine the correct course of action.

There comes to mind at this point the historic work of Alfred Thayer Mahan, who did so much to determine the naval policy of the United States in the Caribbean Sea at the beginning of the century.[2] Mahan's writings upon the influence of sea power in history affected too the judgments of Great Britain, rival if not hypothetical enemy of the United States in that area and the vicinity of the Panama Canal. It is not meant here to imply that Admiral Mahan collected, produced, or employed intelligence in the present meaning of the term. It is intended to show that in advocating policy he made use of comparable materials from the familiar categories of geographic, economic, political, social, and even emotional data. Historical evidence is closely akin to intelligence.

So far attention has been held upon separate intelligence, that is to say, upon knowledge drawn from a single source. But the concept of central intelligence is intrinsic. Definitive information upon a subject seldom if ever comes from a single source; it is usual to learn of the matter from several quarters. And in dealing with human affairs at least, one can be sure that one's information has come through a mold. The effect of human fashioning may be quite unintentional; it will be present nonetheless. It can be very conscious and have all the persuasiveness of a vested interest. There is then clear need to determine the forces which have shaped the material in order to bring it into proper relation with information that has been obtained on the same subject from other sources.

The way in which this coordination and synthesis should be accomplished has been a particular concern of government, especially in this country. The necessity had been fully recognized by 1939. Representatives from the Departments of Agriculture, Commerce, and the Interior were assigned to the Foreign Service as attachés. Their reports were made through the State Department. The military and naval attachés in American embassies and legations were less subject to coordination as their reports were directly to their respective services.[3] The evolution of the method now employed is a major theme in this study. Woven with it is the issue yet to be fully settled. Should there be individual responsibility for estimating the intelligence which is sent to the policymaker, or should the representatives of the several interests involved take collective responsibility for that estimate?

British services and German operations during the First World War made their contributions to American concepts of intelligence. An inspired and subsidized press, stories of atrocities nicely timed, the release of documents like the Zimmerman note to Mexico, sabotage, strikes, and acts of violence within this country revealed associations and made distinctions that are now classic. There were differences between British and German methods of subversion and propaganda in neutral America. The dynamiting attributed to German agents destroyed property. Atrocity stories spread by the British were intent upon corroding thought. Opinion in this country took greater exception to German action against property than to British manipulation of the truth. Both, however, were parts of an attack upon the American tradition of isolation which had persisted since Thomas Paine's exhortation in 1776 to have done with the "wars and quarrels" of Europe.[4] Both gave expert guidance to American participation in the wars of the future.

Espionage is clandestine. The collection of information seems overt, though much of it too is under cover. The decision that espionage is sinister and malignant, while the collection of information is honest and benign, depends upon one's own interest and point of view. As Daniel Webster observed, "In a question of *goring* it makes all the difference in the world who owns the *Bull* and who owns the *Ox*."[5] Propaganda's kinship with the foreign missions of religious faiths is historic. Both engage in purveying information as the truth. But the relativity of truth under pragmatic influences is notorious, at least in international affairs. With the growth of black propaganda in psychological warfare to break the will of the enemy, the cause of truth as the best weapon seems lost. The concepts of intelligence are relative and variable. Duplicity is inherent. Only the national security seems to remain integral and constant.[6]

THE IDEA IN ACTION

The processes of intelligence and their attendant propaganda, sabotage, and guerrilla tactics received tremendous stimulus during the Second World War. Fifth-column activities had become famous in the Spanish civil strife prior to the Nazi invasion of Czechoslovakia and Poland. An interdepartmental committee of the Army, Navy, and Federal Bureau of Investigation in July 1939 sought to control spies, saboteurs, and subversive persons.[7] The overthrow of France in June 1940 and the expulsion of Britain's troops from the Continent at Dunkirk convinced leading Americans that this country must prepare in every way for the eventuality of war. German agents under Nazi direction were already at work in Latin America as their predecessors had been for the Kaiser. The specter of an invasion even of North America possessed some minds. The British fleet had long supported the Monroe Doctrine against foreign encroachment upon Anglo–American dominance in the Western Hemisphere. If Britain fell, there would be no British fleet.

President Roosevelt took the eminent Republicans, Stimson and Knox, into the Cabinet as Secretaries of War and the Navy. Churchill cabled to Stimson "on les aura."[8] Arrangements were made to supply the British fleet with destroyers in return for air and naval bases. Congress revived the Selective Service of 1917 in September. Ambassador Kennedy was making statements that Britain could not stand up to the German attack. The President sent William J. Donovan in July to find out. Donovan was to study too Germany's fifth-column practices. He returned by August 4 to report orally to Secretary Knox and the President upon those practices, Britain's organization for secret intelligence, and what Donovan liked to call "unorthodox warfare."[9] The German activities were spread before the American public in a series of newspaper articles signed by Edgar A. Mowrer and Colonel Donovan.[10] British advices and plans entered from time to time into the development of an American system of intelligence and clandestine operations.

Donovan believed that Britain would stand. He was abroad again before Christmas to make a strategic survey of American economic and political interests in the Mediterranean and the Near East. Many Americans found it hard to discover those interests, though the Navy had once fought Barbary corsairs on the coasts of Africa and put the Marines ashore in Tripoli, and there still were American missionaries, hospitals, and colleges in the Near East. Donovan saw them and a good deal more as he worked with a British officer against the pro-Nazi regent, Prince Paul, in Yugoslavia. The Germans sensed enough of his purposes to keep him from conferring with the French commander, General Weygand.[11]

By March 18, Colonel Donovan was home to report upon the dangers to shipping, the importance of Northwest Africa to the United States, the use of psychological and political warfare, and upon a central intelligence committee which he saw taking form in London under the exigencies of war. At Roosevelt's direction he talked with Secretaries Stimson and Knox and Attorney General Jackson about his concept of an intelligence agency with the accompanying forces of propaganda and subversion. They recommended it to the President.[12] The result was Donovan's proposal on June 10, 1941, that there should be a "service of strategic information." Strategy without information, he said, was helpless. Information collected for no strategic purpose was futile.[13]

With this memorandum, his first written statement on the subject, Donovan laid foundations for the instrument of government which has become the Central Intelligence Agency. Whether or not he was aware of it at the time, he indicated, too, the difficulties that would perplex the administrators of this common service for the departments of the Government.

He suggested that the Coordinator of Strategic Information should have an advisory panel consisting of the Director of the Federal Bureau of Investigation, the heads of the intelligence services of the Army and the Navy, and corresponding officials from other departments concerned. He would draw the personnel of his central agency from the Army and the Navy as well as from civilian sources. He would make sure that the Agency should not displace or encroach upon the departments, although it might collect information independently. It was to analyze and interpret information of many kinds for use by the departments. Above all, it was "to constitute a means by which the President, as Commander-in-Chief, and his Strategic Board would have available accurate and complete enemy intelligence reports upon which military operational decisions could be based."[14]

Donovan would place under the direction of the Coordinator of Strategic Information that psychological warfare which he had observed the Germans using so effectively upon "the moral and spiritual defenses of a nation." He did not include in his memorandum the physical subversion and guerrilla warfare which he had also in mind. They had been discussed with the Cabinet officers; they were implicit in the plan. True to the military character of his whole conception, he proposed that the Coordinator of Strategic Information should be responsible directly to the President.

This led at once to disagreement with the armed services which has complicated relationships ever since between them and the central intelligence service. President Roosevelt's military order of June 25, 1941, as Commander-in-Chief, created the office of Coordinator of Strategic Information and gave him military authority. It aroused so much opposition that the order was rewritten.[15] Another order on July 11, 1941, established the office of Coordinator of Information. The word "Strategic" was omitted from the title. The regular military and naval advisers of the President were carefully guarded against interference with or impairment of their duties and responsibilities by this new aide to the Chief Executive.[16]

Many in the armed services were far from pleased. It still was in effect a military order. Colonel William J. Donovan was of course to be the Coordinator of Information. Senator Taft caught up their feeling, though in an overstatement of the facts: Donovan could "boss the intelligence services of the Army and Navy in the name of the President and have more influence with the President on military and naval strategy than the General Staffs."[17]

Criticism from another quarter was more in keeping with the facts. After a conference on June 18 with Donovan and Benjamin Cohen, counsel for the National Power Policy Committee, regarding Donovan's ideas on a "service of strategic information," President Roosevelt sent Cohen to consult with the Assistant Director of the Bureau of the Budget. Donovan too explained his plans for the future of the organization. From the beginning officials in the Bureau had the impression that he was ambitious to make the powers of his new agency "all-inclusive." He was interested in domestic morale and economic defense, in research upon Latin America, in the negotiations for peace at the end of the European war, in postwar economic planning, and apparently anything and everything else that pertained to the strategic intelligence necessary to the formulation of national policy.

It is not surprising that members of the Bureau of the Budget thought Donovan eager to compete with "many of the old line agencies and most of the defense agencies." It was rather soon for all of the possibilities which his avid imagination conceived. It was altogether too soon to draw the lines and establish the interstices between rival institutions of the Government so that they worked harmoniously to the common end.[18] The criticism was fair at the moment. It did not, however, show due appreciation of the fact that, regardless of his personal ambitions, Donovan was pioneering in the public interest beyond the experiences and assumptions of the moment. He believed that it was his duty as well as opportunity to put all elements of intelligence in one central organization. This, he declared in 1953, was an American contribution in the history of intelligence.[19]

The office of the Coordinator of Information developed so rapidly under Donovan's direction that many elements of a central intelligence service were in operation by the time of the Japanese attack upon Pearl Harbor in December. To broadcast radio messages, issue pamphlets, and spread the propaganda of truth regarding American principles, the Foreign Information Service had begun to take shape even before the President's order of July 11. With its listening outposts, it was also soon obtaining information for the production of intelligence. The Research and Analysis Branch, well established in August, began to collect and evaluate the basic materials for intelligence reports. By October the Visual Presentation Branch was at work upon the techniques of delivering such reports and related data to the departments and services concerned.

An Oral Intelligence Unit was created to interview persons recently arrived from abroad. Foreign nationals within this country came under study to discover what they might reveal concerning the conditions and opinions in the countries of their origin. The collection of information by undercover agents outside the Western Hemisphere had begun upon agreement with the Army and the Navy in October that their clandestine intelligence services should be consolidated under the Coordinator of Information.[20]

There was agreement also with the British. During the First World War an intimate relationship had existed between the two governments on the diplomatic level, resulting in the exchange of information of great value. Now, with the consent of Churchill, Donovan placed a branch office in London. [three lines deleted][21]

There was even planning for the eventuality of war before it came with the disaster at Pearl Harbor. A section in Donovan's office, named "Special Activities—K and L Funds," was established on October 10, 1941, to take charge of espionage, sabotage, subversive activities, and guerrilla units. There had been no formal authorization for them. The President's order of July 11 merely provided for "such supplementary activities as may facilitate the securing of information important for national security not now available to the Government." But the intent was clear. Donovan sent an officer to study British practices in close association with the British Special Operations Executive. It was only a short step into guer-

rilla warfare after the declaration of war. He submitted to President Roosevelt on December 22, 1941, the plan long in mind for an American force
like the British Commandos "imbued with the maximum of the offensive
and imaginative spirit," an excellent weapon of physical subversion to
accompany the black propaganda of psychological warfare.[22] Those who
have been watching recent preparations within the Central Intelligence
Agency for paramilitary action may find ample precedent and good example in the policy of Colonel Donovan. He developed it in action far more
than in theory.

THE OFFICE OF STRATEGIC SERVICES

The burst of war which he anticipated had two effects upon Colonel
Donovan. He pressed the organization of his office to completion so that
he might leave for a command in combat, and he urged that the Coordinator of Information be placed under the direction of the Joint Chiefs of
Staff. They held their first meeting on February 9, 1942, as they prepared
to work with the British officers in the Combined Chiefs of Staff.[23]

Donovan sent a proposal through Secretary Knox to the President that
there be attached to the Navy an independent force of land, sea, and air
raiders, five thousand men, whom Donovan himself would command;
and he suggested a successor as Coordinator of Information. Donovan
was not permitted to take command of American Commandos. He had
instead to develop within his office the forces of physical subversion and
guerrilla warfare. But the Office of Strategic Services, which succeeded
the Coordinator of Information, was placed as Donovan wished under the
direction of the Joint Chiefs of Staff by military order of the President on
June 13, 1942.[24]

Meanwhile, the Coordinator of Information had come under pressures
that were generated by diverse temperaments quite as much as by differences of opinion concerning methods in war. Over Donovan's protests,
the Foreign Information Service was removed from his jurisdiction and
joined with other information services in the new Office of War Information. Donovan believed that the effectiveness of psychological warfare
would be impaired if the control of propaganda directed abroad were
taken from the Coordinator of Information. It is to be noted too that with
the Foreign Information Service went the listening outposts which were
sources of information for the production of intelligence reports by the
Coordinator. But this caused little hardship as the Foreign Broadcast

Monitoring Service of the Federal Communications Commission provided complete summaries of its auditing and the Office of Strategic Services soon enlarged its own system of collecting secret intelligence overseas.[25]

There was a prolonged dispute over psychological warfare. The Joint Chiefs of Staff had created a Joint Psychological Warfare Committee in March, but reorganized it on June 21, 1942, to make Donovan the chairman, as Director of the Office of Strategic Services. The committee was composed of representatives from the Army and the Navy and supported by an advisory committee drawn from the Department of State, the Board of Economic Warfare, the Coordinator of Inter-American Affairs, and the Office of War Information.[26]

For the next six months, plans and proposals, suggestions and exceptions, basic estimates, reports and dissents were tossed back and forth between the Joint Psychological Warfare Committee and its subcommittees on the one hand and the Office of Strategic Services and its subordinate groups on the other without ever reaching the Joint Chiefs of Staff. However stated or argued, specifically or in general terms, the real matter at issue would seem to an outsider to have been whether the Office of Strategic Services were to be an agent directly responsible for the Joint Chiefs of Staff for the conception and conduct of psychological warfare. If the Office of Strategic Services reported to the Joint Psychological Warfare Committee, "OSS" would run the risk of having its projects stopped there by the overwhelming majority representing the Army and the Navy. The armed services did not like any sort of independent paramilitary command. As Donovan recalled in 1953, it was a critical moment in the whole endeavor to establish an American system of central intelligence.[27]

The issue came to conclusion in December 1942. The Joint Chiefs of Staff sent General McNarney and Admiral Horne to inquire into the Office of Strategic Services. They visited the Office separately. Donovan talked with them, showed them papers, and asked them to spend a day watching it in operation. There followed a directive from the Joint Chiefs of Staff on December 22, 1942, abolishing the Joint Psychological Warfare Committee and designating the Office of Strategic Services as the "agency" of the Joint Chiefs of Staff, charged with the military program of psychological warfare.[28]

Donovan received a note from General Marshall saying that he could not let the holiday season pass without expressing gratitude for Donovan's cooperation in the trying times of the past year. Marshall regretted that Donovan, after voluntarily coming under the jurisdiction of the Joint Chiefs, had not enjoyed smoother sailing. Marshall hoped that the new directive would eliminate most of the difficulties.[29]

The Office of Strategic Services gained most of the points for which it had contended. To supervise the military program of psychological warfare and integrate it with military and naval operations, there was established within the Office a new Planning Group composed of one member from the Department of State, two from the Army, two from the Navy, and four including the chairman from the Office of Strategic Services. An advisory committee represented the Board of Economic Warfare, Office of War Information, Coordinator of Inter-American Affairs, the Treasury, and other agencies from time to time as their interests were concerned. After approval by the Director of the Office of Strategic Services, the plans and projects of the Planning Group were to be submitted through the Joint Staff Planners to the Joint Chiefs of Staff for their final approval.[30]

The operations of propaganda, and of economic warfare within the military program for psychological warfare, were reserved to the Office of War Information and to the Board of Economic Warfare respectively. The Joint Intelligence Committee of the Joint Chiefs of Staff was to prepare such special information and intelligence studies as the Joint Chiefs of Staff required.

Elmer Davis, head of the Office of War Information, would have no share in this cooperative effort in psychological warfare. He declined representation on the Advisory Committee of the Planning Group in the Office of Strategic Services. Admiral Leahy had written for the Joint Chiefs of Staff that the Planning Group would be confined to recommendations to them and they would decide upon the propaganda which they wished Mr. Davis to execute. But he saw it differently. There was no purpose to be served in giving advice to another group upon matters which one was already under obligation to the President to formulate and execute. The President, he said, could "hardly be overruled by lesser authority." Davis considered his representative a visitor to rather than a member of the Office of Strategic Services. If Davis thought of the federal principle at all, he had no inclination to let it bind the part of the national effort in war for which he was responsible to President Roosevelt.[31]

The intelligence functions of the Office of Strategic Services were restricted by the directive of December 22, 1942, to those "necessary for the planning and execution of the military program for psychological warfare, and for the preparation of assigned portions of intelligence digests and such other data and visual presentation as may be requested." That was not all. The collection of intelligence by OSS was confined to the special operations of sabotage, espionage, and counterespionage in enemy-occupied or controlled territory, guerrilla warfare, underground groups, and contacts with foreign nationals in the United States.

These restrictions upon the intelligence service of the Office were not permitted to hamper its work for long, on paper. They were removed from the text of the directive by the Joint Chiefs of Staff on April 4, 1943. And by the final revision of the directive on October 27, 1943, the Office's function of collecting information for the production of intelligence was fully restored. But collection is not reception. Obtaining particular information is different from having the right to it in general terms. General Vandenberg and Admiral Hillenkoetter were to find this true again and again as Directors of Central Intelligence.[32]

It had been agreed by both Army and Navy in October 1941, before the attack upon Pearl Harbor, that the "undercover intelligence of the two services" should be consolidated under the Coordinator of Information. As General Miles expressed it, the work was "much more effective if under one head rather than three. . . ." A civilian agency, such as the Coordinator of Information, had distinct advantages, he said, over any military or naval agency in the administration of such a service. At the same time the Army and Navy set up their Joint Army and Navy Intelligence Committee to forestall the Coordinator of Information. Ludwell L. Montague became its secretary on October 14.[33]

Following the agreement with the Army and Navy, Donovan planned at once to put a wireless station and agents in North Africa. But the understanding had contained the reservation that in the event of war the Army and the Navy should have full power to operate undercover intelligence services of their own. After Pearl Harbor, the best that could be obtained in the directives of the Joint Chiefs of Staff was the statement that the military and naval intelligence services and the Office of Strategic Services would "provide for the complete and free interchange of information, evaluated as to creditability of source, required for the execution of their respective missions."[34]

In practice this meant to the intelligence officers of the Army and the Navy no obligation whatever upon them to turn over to Donovan's Office information about operations which they thought should not be revealed. It is to be said on their behalf that they had some reasons to fear that the civilians in his agency were not disciplined in military necessities; the Office of Strategic Services deserved part of its reputation for being a sieve. (When General Donovan read this statement in February 1953, he blurted: "How could you say such a thing! That makes me sore." The military men, he said, were the "leaky boys.")[35] It is also to be said that intelligence reports worth submitting to the policymakers cannot be had if strategic information is withheld from those who have the task of making the reports.

According to one who remarked that he ought to know because he was one of them, men in the armed services looked with suspicion upon the expert economists, geographers, historians, and scientists whom Donovan gathered about him; they "lowered their horns" against those experts, said General Magruder, and they kept their horns down.[36] We might add that there was milling and bawling and pawing the dust, but no stampede.

A case in point was the refusal of the Navy to release its radio "intercepts" to the Office of Strategic Services. Donovan protested on October 22, 1942, that such action would impair his ability to discharge his mission. At the time that he had been willing to refrain from cryptographic work, he had understood that the proceeds resulting from decoding by the Armed Forces would be made available to the Office of Strategic Services. The Office could not carry out the duties specifically assigned to it by the Joint Chiefs of Staff. His undercover representatives in foreign countries were entitled to the protection and help which would come from the interceptions of enemy messages. The Research and Analysis Branch needed the information for its strategic studies. The Office of Strategic Services could not function completely without such important materials.[37]

Donovan's protest got a cool reception in the Joint Intelligence Committee of the Joint Chiefs of Staff. The chairman, General George V. Strong, was unwilling to accept even the obvious provisions in the directive of December 22, 1942, arguing at first that it confined the Office of Strategic Services to the planning and execution of psychological warfare. When Donovan's deputy, General Magruder, pointed out that the Office had much wider functions in the field of intelligence, General Strong abandoned the argument but remained obviously reluctant to yield. This was apparent as the representative of the Navy on the Joint Intelligence Committee read a letter from Admiral King stating that he would not agree to any increase in the dissemination of "intercept material." The attitude of the Committee as a whole was unsympathetic with Donovan's claim; and so his representative there, General Magruder, having in mind "the longer range point of view being able to reconstruct harmonious relations with the Armed Forces," did not press the legal point that the Office of Strategic Services was entitled to such information.[38]

The issue was seemingly closed on January 19, 1943, by the Joint Chiefs of Staff. They ruled that the release of the information was within the province of representatives of the Army and Navy in the Planning Group of the Office of Strategic Services. This, of course, reduced the matter of specific instances and left power with the Army and Navy still to withhold any particular piece of information. They are reluctant to this moment in 1953 to give a central civilian agency intelligence which exposes their capabilities in war. The result has been interference with the flow of raw materials essential to the realistic estimates which should go to the makers of diplomatic policy and military strategy.[39]

Early in 1943 the Joint Chiefs of Staff created the Joint Intelligence Collection Agencies of the Army, Navy, and Air Forces. These too had the appearance of being helpful to the Office of Strategic Services; but they were no more so than the ruling with regard to the Navy's intercepts. The joint agencies were not to engage in initial procurement; they were only to assemble material in the field offices and forward it to Washington. In theory this cooperation should have helped the Secret Intelligence Branch of the Office of Strategic Services. In fact the Joint Intelligence Collection Agencies laid the secret agents of the Office of Strategic Services open to exposure in the field, and delayed their material in reaching the Secret Intelligence Branch in Washington. Such interference gave Donovan's supporters opportunity to argue that the armed services had established the joint collection agencies to thwart OSS and keep it from being the central agency in the national intelligence system. The situation did seem to prove that instead of three or four collecting agencies, there should be a single and exclusive collector in the field of secret intelligence and counterespionage abroad.[40]

The Office of Strategic Services came under another cross fire. After the experience at Pearl Harbor, General Marshall and Admiral King were convinced that something had to be done about combining the intelligence services of the Army and Navy, regardless of any arrangement with the Office of Strategic Services. Their agreement apparently led in the spring of 1943 to a proposal that the Joint Intelligence Committee should be reorganized. It should have a civilian member besides representatives of the Army, Navy, Air Force, and Office of Strategic Services to form a better estimating board for the Joint Chiefs of Staff. This civilian, by reason of exceptional performance, might even become the chairman of the Joint Intelligence Committee.[41] There was resemblance here to the British estimating committee in which the civilian representing the Foreign Office sat as chairman with the military experts.[42]

Each member of the reorganized Joint Intelligence Committee should have access to all of the intelligence in the service which he represented, and presumably he would purvey it to the Committee. How much of the information at his disposal each of them would be allowed to submit still remained to be established. The proposers of the new Joint Intelligence Committee, however, seemed to be confident that such ranking officers could be trusted to decide whether they could release certain information to the Committee without jeopardy to their respective services and at the same time supply the Committee with the proper materials for its estimates.

More important in the plan, and perhaps the telltale, was the suggestion that the Research and Analysis Branch of the Office of Strategic

Services should be linked with the Office of Naval Intelligence and the Military Intelligence Service so far as their functions in foreign intelligence were involved. The idea was that the Research and Analysis Branch would thus become a central agency. Files and personnel transferred from the Army and Navy would be integrated with similar files and persons of the Office of Strategic Services so that there would be a single activity engaged in making strategic surveys.

In following this thought further the plan was to transfer officers and other experts from the armed services to the Research and Analysis Branch, now directly under the Joint Intelligence Committee. The presumption was that the officers would no longer be directly responsible to the Army or the Navy. They would be officers within the central agency. But the fact remained that in the Joint Intelligence Committee itself the Office of Strategic Services would have only one representative while the Army and Navy and Air Forces together would have three. Even if the civilian in the chair agreed with the representative of OSS, they would still be in the minority on the Committee.[43]

General Magruder favored the plan. He reported to Donovan in September that on the whole it recommended steps "very close to our own desires." But he believed that the branches of Secret Intelligence and of Counterespionage too should be elevated to the "strategic level" with Research and Analysis. They belonged in the organization of the Joint Chiefs of Staff if it were to be the "authoritative body of the future superior strategic intelligence service." The three were, after all, the essentials in any central intelligence service.

Magruder was not so willing to mix the intelligence experts of the Army, Navy, and Air Force with the civilians or "scholar experts" in the divisions of Research and Analysis. Each group should retain "its own sense of responsibility"; the results of their separate efforts should be brought together. Otherwise, he said, their efforts would be wasted, and the chiefs of the groups would not demand the best personnel.[44] Military men and civilians since then seem to have been working together in the same group on problems of intelligence more effectively than General Magruder anticipated.

General Donovan did not take to the plan so readily as Magruder. Possibly it looked to Donovan, as it well could, more like an immediate attempt to deprive him of a major service within the Office of Strategic Services and to narrow his activities still further in the field of intelligence. The plan did not materialize.[45]

In the words of a contemporary observer, the Army, Navy, and the Department of State were always glad to use the Research and Analysis Branch of the Office of Strategic Services as a servant. They were not willing to accept it as an equal partner in final judgments. By depriving it of the "sensitive information" which they had within their control, they were able to keep it from being what it was supposed to be, the competent research agency in the political-economic-social field of national intelligence.[46]

Complicated issues between the armed services and the central intelligence service will appear again in this study. General Vandenberg and Admiral Hillenkoetter, as Directors of Central Intelligence, will be found in similar clashes of opinion and trials of strength with advisory boards and committees over the collection and production of intelligence. Psychological warfare too, in all its ramifications, is still at issue among the services and departments concerned with devising and executing its projects. The President's planners of 1953 might examine in more detail than has been given here General Donovan's experience in 1942 with the Joint Psychological Warfare Committee.[47]

Notwithstanding serious blocks to the production of strategic reports and interference with its activities in other ways, the Office of Strategic Services established institutions and practices that are requisite to a national system of intelligence. It accumulated the wealth of experience for its successors to enjoy. Among its legacies to the Central Intelligence Agency were the methods and means of procuring both overt and secret intelligence, the devices of counterespionage, the procedures of research and analysis, and a considerable number of skilled persons.

The foreign groups in the United States, a mosaic of nationalities, were certain to be useful as sources of intelligence. It was important to exploit those who had come from nations under the Nazis and the Communists. It was wise to keep them under surveillance also for subversive activities. The Foreign Nationalities Branch, established to scan the foreign language press and to deal with political refugees and leaders of foreign groups, at first met opposition from the Departments of Justice and State. The Federal Bureau of Investigation was afraid that the Branch would interfere with its work. Members of the State Department were suspicious that the Branch might usurp functions of policymaking. But the Foreign Nationalities Branch demonstrated its value so effectively to the Joint Chiefs of Staff that it was fixed as part of the intelligence system in the Office of Strategic Services. It obtained a large amount of significant information concerning Czechoslovakia, Greece, and Poland.[48]

The Secret Intelligence Branch grew from a small organization with a few overseas units which supplied the armed services with fifty reports in May 1942 to a system of penetration by land, sea, and air, producing five thousand reports a month at its peak. Its "geographic desks" were increased and regrouped to operate more effectively in neutral countries and to gain access into adjacent hostile or occupied territories. The Reporting Board controlled the dissemination of intelligence and directed geographic units which were more carriers than collectors of information. The Branch developed a section to enlist the support of labor in all countries not only for intelligence but for sabotage and subversion. A "ship observer unit" obtained the especially valuable intelligence to be had from seamen, their organization, ship operators, and other maritime sources. A technical section provided information on roads, bridges, aqueducts, weapons, and similar matters of engineering. It maintained daily contact with the "Manhattan Project" in atomic energy.[49]

The counterpart of Secret Intelligence, known as "X-2," developed a network of counterespionage which spread from London to Shanghai through Europe, Africa, the Near East, India, Burma, and China, with each headquarters reporting directly to Washington. And by October 1945 a registry of enemies and subversive persons had been developed in Washington that ran to some 400,000 names. This with the records of the Federal Bureau of Investigation constituted the backbone of Security Intelligence. Moreover, working agreements with the British, French, and others were ready for the future.[50]

The British were willing to let Americans into their organization to learn about Hitler's agents, but not so disposed to have the American intelligence services come into regions where Britain had primary interests. In some instances the reluctance amounted to downright refusal. This appears to have been the case for some time in Northern France, the Low Countries, and Southeast Asia. It is to be said, though, that the situation in the last instance was complicated further by Chiang Kai-shek and Douglas MacArthur.[51]

Before long, geographical understandings were established upon the principle that the Office of Strategic Services would take a leading position in the work of intelligence as the American military forces penetrated certain areas. This was particularly true in Western Europe as the invasion gained momentum. In other regions the British intelligence services continued to dominate, and in some instances made it practically impossible for American intelligence officers to go about their business. In Istanbul and doubtless other places like it, for very good reasons of security or rather the complete lack of it, the British did not care to become involved with American intelligence.[52]

In spite of all this, there was cooperation to a great degree both in London and in New York. The British supplied the Office of Strategic Services with information on occasion when the United States Army and Navy either could or would not do so. To be appreciated as well, the British allowed American officers to observe the interrelationships of their services and the working of their intelligence system, for report to the

Office of Strategic Services and benefit of the American system.[53] The study which William H. Jackson made of the British organization in 1945 and then with Kingman Douglass in 1946 influenced the development of the Central Intelligence Agency.[54]

However valuable in themselves, the first reports of the Research and Analysis Branch under the Coordinator of Information were neither well related to one another nor focused properly upon the needs of the Army and Navy. For this condition, the services were in part responsible until they gave better explanation of what they wanted. Such strategic surveys became the major enterprise of the Branch in 1942. This basic intelligence laid bare at the demand of war the hard economic and geographical facts within the conflict of nations. The strategic surveys of Research and Analysis were the predecessors of the Joint Army–Navy Intelligence Studies which in turn were superseded by the program of National Intelligence Surveys.[55]

The Research and Analysis Branch also provided intelligence upon contemporary events. Information came from outposts of the Branch in such advantageous places for observation as London, Algiers, Cairo, Stockholm, New Delhi, Chungking, Bucharest, Istanbul, Rome, Lisbon, and Athens. This current intelligence had usefulness distinct from the information which came from Secret Intelligence and from the Department of State. Collection by "R&A" was not hampered by the secrecy of one nor by the diplomatic protocol of the other.[56]

The use of photography as well as words was fully appreciated in the Office of Strategic Services and passed on to its successors in the national intelligence system. It had a War Room with maps, charts, and reports. There was a *Daily Intelligence Summary* and a *Political Intelligence Weekly.* Called by whatever name, things indispensable are much the same. The Central Intelligence Agency has similar mechanisms and aids, and they are administered in quite similar fashion. The need is immediate and apparent for supporting services like the recruitment and training of personnel, legal advice, accounting, procurement and maintenance of equipment. The Office of Strategic Services had such supporting services. Improvement and expansion came with experience, but little change in the essential functions. The methods of communication were the best in existence then. They have been improved since with every innovation in the transmission of visual images and sound. The Office of Strategic Services used the three kinds of cover for its agents and operations—governmental, commercial, and professional.[57] The choice today among these types of concealment is determined as then by the peculiarities of the particular situation.

The covert activities of the Office of Strategic Services have been examined in the War Report of the Office and are not to be appraised project by project in this study. But their contribution to the Central Intelligence Agency is a matter of concern here. The Special Operations Branch, in charge of sabotage and physical subversion, was uppermost in the purposes of General Donovan; accordingly it grew from small beginnings in 1941 until it had become a valuable auxiliary to military operations in the theaters of war where it was allowed to participate. Because the Office of Strategic Services could not make arrangements satisfactory to both MacArthur and Donovan, it did not operate in the Western Pacific, though it had a role in China.[58]

Opinions of OSS varied from praise to blame as a matter of course with the predilections and interests of the observers. Agreement appears to have been general outside the Office itself, however, that its Special Operations Branch should be liquidated at the close of the war with other unorthodox or paramilitary enterprises such as the Operations Groups or guerrillas and the Maritime Unit, whose "frog men" have attracted so much attention. This was even more true of the Morale Operations Branch engaged in black propaganda, although a movement began shortly afterward to apply the lessons in this art of war. On March 5, 1946, Patterson, Secretary of War, wrote to Secretary Forrestal of the Navy urging that a body of experts should institute some kind of a system to develop weapons for the psychological warfare of the future.[59]

THE DONOVAN PLAN

Long before the troops of the Allies invaded Germany or the atomic bombs had fallen on Hiroshima and Nagasaki, thoughts were upon profiting in times of peace from experience with the Office of Strategic Services, the Office of War Information, and other intelligence services. Brigadier General John Magruder, while head of Lend Lease in China, had observed in practical operation the need for joint intelligence among the services. Because of his office, he obtained information more easily than the military attaché and others. He therefore suggested that they should cooperate in gathering and verifying intelligence, and he proposed to General Stilwell that the practice might be extended to Washington among the armed services at the highest level. General Stilwell did not believe that it would succeed in Washington. When Magruder returned to the United States in the summer of 1942, however, he conferred enthusiastically with General Donovan and put his ideas on paper. Donovan assured him that the Office of Strategic Services was designed for just that purpose, and invited him to join the organization as its Deputy Director for Intelligence.[60]

The plan which Magruder proposed in August 1942 stressed the imperative need for coordinating all of the agencies concerned with intelligence. The collecting services of the departments obtained valuable information, he said; but not a single one was competent to furnish the complete information which was necessary to "national decisions." There were no "sure and continuous" connections between the intelligence agencies and those who were responsible for making the decisions and plans. He found all of the intelligence services so "compartmented" that the only escape from the situation was to establish a "superior joint intelligence agency." No vital decisions could be made for the conduct of the war without "complete and digested intelligence."[61]

Looking back upon this memorandum, we may well admire the perception with which the author wrote of difficulties that still persist. General Magruder did not then visualize the intricate system for coordinating departmental intelligence with strategic studies made independently by experts in research and analysis. But he did appreciate the necessity for "synthesis" of the information from all services for strategic planning and decisions by those who had to make both diplomatic and military policies. Since the Joint Chiefs of Staff was then at work on problems of intelligence for the Army and Navy, he thought of it rather than of some other central agency for his purposes. But he observed that the Joint Intelligence Committee would have to be reorganized and its functions augmented or it could not operate effectively as the body of advice, coordination, and recommendation to the Joint Chiefs of Staff.

Magruder proposed in August 1942 that in place of the working staff of the Joint Intelligence Committee there should be established a Joint Intelligence Bureau. The new bureau should act as an agency of the Joint Chiefs of Staff. Under its director and deputy director there should be research divisions in the several fields of intelligence, political, economic, military, and others. The product of their effort should be systematically administered by an initiating and reviewing committee. This key committee should make assignments to the working groups, should requisition material from the various departments concerned, and should approve the studies and estimates of the Bureau before they went through the Director's office to the Joint Chiefs of Staff.

The committee of initiation and review within the Bureau was to be composed of representatives from the intelligence services of the departments. But it was clear that Magruder intended that they should not be merely visitors from their respective departments; they were to be members of the Bureau. Although representing separate interests, they were to be gathered into one body with functions expressly delegated in accordance with the federal principle.

Congress itself, with sovereign powers expressly delegated in the Constitution, is the best example of the principle. Though representative of the States, component parts of the Union, Congress exercises powers that are superior to and exclusive of powers retained by the States; the product of its action is national. The concept that the federal principle was applicable within an agency of the Government seems to have been ahead of its time in the fall of 1942. There were of course military men in the Office of Strategic Services, but the idea that they represented the services from which they had come at the same time they worked as members of a central intelligence agency was then highly theoretical.

General Magruder clung to his ideas and strengthened them in dealing with those who obstructed the actual working of the Secret Intelligence Branch and the Research and Analysis Branch of the Office of Strategic Services. He wrote on July 30, 1943, to the Executive Secretary of the Joint Chiefs of Staff a series of observations upon the United States Intelligence Service in which he said as much in so many words.

The Secret Intelligence Branch had reached an impressive stage of development in spite of the fact that it was handicapped by outright resistance in some quarters and by limitations imposed by some well-intentioned officials who lacked familiarity with its objectives and failed to appreciate its value as a national asset.

The Research and Analysis Branch, he said, could be the very core of an agency which could not be duplicated in any other intelligence organization restricting itself to the needs of a particular department. The Branch was uniquely designed to serve a particular need. Its group of highly qualified specialists should be the "servitors" of the Joint Chiefs and have functions befitting their ability to produce. Instead, they were being denied access to information by other agencies in spite of what were believed to be both the terms and the spirit of the direction from the Joint Chiefs of Staff. Magruder wished now in the fall of 1943 to see the Secret Intelligence Branch and the Counterespionage Branch taken up to "the strategic level" and incorporated with the Research and Analysis Branch in a superior intelligence agency under the Joint Chiefs of Staff.[62]

General Donovan looked beyond the immediate exigencies of war even more than his deputy, General Magruder. At the request of General Walter B. Smith, recently Secretary of the Joint Chiefs of Staff and now Chief of Staff of the Allied Forces in North Africa, Donovan wrote on September 17, 1943, to give his ideas in detail upon the creation of a strategic intelligence organization as an integral and permanent part of the military establishment. Donovan had worked with Smith to put the Office of Strategic Services under the Joint Chiefs of Staff. Though produced in war and quite naturally reflecting that fact, Donovan's paper revealed that his thinking ran far ahead into times of peace.[63]

His was a long-range view of requirements. There must be independence from other nations for reasons of security, verification of information, and control. Friends today might not be so cordial tomorrow. Secret means had to be maintained for collecting political, economic, sociological, and psychological data. There should be counterintelligence as a matter of course to protect these primary services. He stressed the use of the radio and the need for independent communications and passport privileges. A separate budget and unvouchered funds were essential.

Donovan advocated a civilian director supported largely by civilian personnel. He explained the importance of research and analysis by those who were expert in critical appraisal, by skilled technicians and specialists on particular regions. And, as was to be expected of him, General Donovan associated these requirements for an intelligence service closely with physical subversion and warfare upon morale. They were all indispensable parts of a national intelligence system.

It may be only coincidence, but it is a striking coincidence, that General Smith later became Director of Central Intelligence and adhered to much the same requirements in administering the affairs of the Central Intelligence Agency, though they were far greater in scope and pace than those of the Office of Strategic Services.[64]

As General Smith had asked, Donovan consulted other officers experienced in intelligence, particularly Colonel Dudley W. Clarke, a friend in the British Army who had much to do with the Commandos. Taking up Clarke's suggestion of the "ideal control" for a strategic intelligence organization, Donovan proposed that it should be included with the Army, Navy, and the Air Force as the "fourth arm" under the jurisdiction of the Joint Chiefs of Staff. The chief of the intelligence organization, or "Strategic Services," would be a member of the Joint Chiefs of Staff. They all, of course, were under the President as Commander-in-Chief.

General Donovan did not then let a question interfere which later wrecked his plan in the committees of the Joint Chiefs of Staff. Whether the chief of "Strategic Services" should be responsible directly to the President or to the Secretary of a department, he said in his letter to General Smith, did not affect the issue. Donovan did not wish to have the strategic intelligence organization placed under the control of one department. The intelligence organization was to serve and support not only the

armed forces but the diplomatic, economic, and propaganda services—
that is to say, the Department of State, the Foreign Economic Administration, and the Office of War Information of those days.

At that time Donovan saw "distracting political consequences" in placing "Strategic Services" directly under the control of the President. If it
should be decided to have a Department of Defense in which all the
"Fighting Services" would be placed, then the strategic intelligence organization should be included on a parity with the others. If no such legislation were enacted, "Strategic Services," or a new intelligence agency to
take its place, could continue under the Joint Chiefs of Staff with a
civilian head appointed by the President.

What led General Donovan to endeavor later to return the Office of
Strategic Services directly under the President is hard to discover in the
documentary evidence. His enemies were certain that he was intent upon
building the proverbial empire. The hypothesis is too simple. One difficulty with it is that he was instantly removable from office at the President's whim as even political appointees were not. Donovan will be found
fairly reasonable in discussing with the Joint Strategic Survey Committee
of the Joint Chiefs of Staff the possibility, though he did not favor the idea,
of placing the Director of Central Intelligence under a board consisting of
the Secretaries of State, War, and the Navy. His opinion seems consistently to have been that the responsibility should be individual; it should
not be "diffused through intermediate echelons." If he had to compromise, he preferred to have the Director under the Joint Chiefs of Staff. He
thoroughly understood the principle of chain of command.[65]

Drawing further upon his staff, General Magruder, and others for ideas
and suggestions, General Donovan stated his views again in October
1944 when public thoughts, though still in the midst of war, were upon
the solemn endeavor at Dumbarton Oaks to establish a United Nations
which might settle international disputes by some means other than
war.[66] It was the time of greatest cooperation between the Soviet Union
and the United States. It was before the Russian armies had driven the
Germans from Poland. It was also before British and American troops had
broken the last great German effort on the western front in the deathly
fog and gloom of the Battle of the Bulge, before they had swept over the
Rhine deep into Germany to meet the Russians on the Elbe, suspicious
friends becoming foes. It was before the uncertain agreements at Yalta
and the rising quarrels over Poland, the Balkan States, and Red China. It
was before the United States had the atomic bomb to drop upon Japan
and to complicate further negotiations with the Soviet Union.

The essentials to any central intelligence service were plain and clear.
There must be an uninterrupted flow of intelligence in peace as in war so

that national policy, military and political, could be based upon knowledge. This was to be obtained by both overt and clandestine means abroad; there should be no clandestine operation within the United States. Moreover, the central agency should have no police powers; nor should it be identified with any law-enforcing body either at home or abroad. This statement should be kept always in mind by those who are wont to accuse "Wild Bill" Donovan of wishing to set up an American Gestapo.

The outstanding purpose of the central intelligence service which Donovan proposed was to collect, analyze, and deliver intelligence "on the policy or strategy level" to the policymakers of the Government as directed by the President. This intelligence was to serve the Army and the Navy as well as the Department of State or any other branch of the Government. He would not interfere with the operational intelligence of the departments. But he did intend to make the principle of individual responsibility for national intelligence starkly clear.

A Director, appointed by the President and under his orders, was to administer this central service and determine its policy with the advice and assistance of a board of representatives from the Department of State, the Army, and the Navy. Donovan did not say "with the advice and consent" of those representatives; he said "advice and assistance." Here was a source of much argument, heated argument, and great difficulty from that time until now.[67]

Charged with the duty of collecting information and producing intelligence for the national defense, the central agency should have its own means of communication and of control over all secret activities, espionage and counterespionage, crypto-analysis, and subversive operations. It would have to use both vouchered and unvouchered funds. It would need as a matter of course, let us repeat, a staff of specialists, professionally trained in analysis, expert in languages, informed about particular regions, possessed of the many skills that were necessary to the working of so complicated an organization.

All of these essentials to a central intelligence service General Donovan believed that he had in the Office of Strategic Services. There was no need to create a new agency. There would be only the task of adjusting the Office of Strategic Services to peacetime conditions and perpetuating it as an instrument of government within the Executive Office of the President. The way to accomplish it now in the fall of 1944 was by means of an executive order to replace the order of June 13, 1942, which had put the Office of Strategic Services under the Joint Chiefs of Staff.[68]

There were conferences about the plan with the President's advisers in the White House. There were discussions with members of the committees of the Joint Chiefs of Staff to whom the proposal would be eventually referred. There were negotiations with representatives of the Foreign Economic Administration, the Bureau of the Budget, and the Department of State. For Donovan was well aware that there were many in the armed services and elsewhere who did not share his views and who had ideas of their own about the kind of intelligence services which the country should have.[69]

The Department of State in particular, as a party of major interest in policymaking, had begun to make provision for a foreign intelligence service within its organization. Donovan had among his papers such a program dated September 30, 1944; he knew that members of the State Department were conferring with persons in the War Department, the Navy Department, and the Bureau of the Budget. And then there was the Federal Bureau of Investigation at work in Latin America as well as the continental United States, guarding its prerogatives and patrolling its jurisdiction. It was apparent that he must have his plan well in hand and properly explained in advance of its presentation to the Joint Chiefs of Staff.[70]

At this juncture, shortly after submitting a preliminary draft to the President,[71] Donovan received from Roosevelt a plan for his "eyes only." The President did not give the name of its author. But Donovan knew that it came from John F. Carter, commentator and author known as "Jay Franklin." His plan has interest for opinions and purposes other than General Donovan's. It afforded Donovan an opportunity to speak his mind forcefully as usual and place credit where it was due.[72]

Carter felt that "the British Intelligence" had already "penetrated" the Office of Strategic Services; its usefulness after the war therefore would be impaired. The British would pursue their own ends; these might not be "synonymous" with American purposes. Carter offered to establish a less expensive and adequately camouflaged central office. [three lines deleted] He would leave the evaluation of reports to the State Department. Carter had formerly worked in the Department.

Donovan dismissed the suggestion. The author's thinking on intelligence, he said, was in the "horse and buggy stage." As for British penetration of the Office of Strategic Services, it was in fact cooperation from which the Office had greatly profited. He might have added that the Office was dependent upon British sources for much of its information. He declared that it had maintained its integrity. In point of fact, he said, the President would be interested to know that "both our Allies and our enemies know less about our inner workings than we do about theirs."[73]

No more was heard from Carter, unless he was one of those who were advocating the expansion of the Federal Bureau of Investigation into an intelligence service overseas. By November 7 word came from the White House to discourage that movement. The Federal Bureau of Investigation was to have no intelligence functions outside of the United States. But talk of it continued. Attorney General Biddle favored it in the spring of 1945. His successor, Tom Clark, proposed a similar measure in the fall of 1945. It was some time before the question was settled and the agents of the Federal Bureau of Investigation finally withdrawn from Latin America.[74]

Donovan's final draft of his plan for a "Permanent World-Wide Intelligence Service" went to the President on November 18, 1944. In it Donovan stressed two requirements. Control of the system should return from the Joint Chiefs of Staff to the President. There should be a central authority reporting directly to the President with responsibility for setting objectives and coordinating the material necessary in planning and executing "national policy and strategy." Though they were in the midst of war, he added, before they were aware of it they would be in the "tumult of rehabilitation." An orderly system of intelligence would contribute to informed decisions. They had in the Government at the time the trained and specialized personnel needed for the task. This talent should not be dispersed.[75]

In the draft of a directive which he enclosed, Donovan proposed that the board to "advise and assist" the director of this central intelligence service should consist of the Secretaries of State, War, the Navy, and other members whom the President might subsequently appoint.[76] This designation of the Secretaries themselves is not to be overlooked. Donovan had no thought here of making the departmental chiefs of intelligence advisors to the director, unless of course they might happen to be named severally by the Secretaries to sit in their places as deputies. We shall find later that the opponents of Donovan's plan advocated the use of the departmental chiefs of intelligence as an advisory board. We shall also find that General Donovan adhered to his idea that such a board of advice should be at the high level of the Secretaries or their representatives.

The proposed executive order for the transfer of the Office of Strategic Services and the directive to accompany it, as finally drafted near the end of November 1944, contained the expected provision for national intelligence, carefully distinguishing it from the operational intelligence of the departments. The directive laid plans for subversive operations abroad and for liaison with the intelligence agencies of foreign governments. It prohibited the use of any police power either at home or abroad. In addition, the directive called for the dissolution of all joint intelligence committees and agencies then operating under the Joint Chiefs of Staff, the War, and the Navy Departments. Their functions, personnel, and facilities

were to be given over to the Office of Strategic Services. In time of war or
unlimited national emergency, its operations were to be coordinated with
military plans and subject to the approval of the Joint Chiefs of Staff;
theater commanders were to have control in their areas. Under other
conditions, there were to be no geographical restrictions upon the operations of the Office of Strategic Services.[77] These last provisions were
certainly not designed to win friends in the Army, the Navy, or even the
Federal Bureau of Investigation. Donovan's plan looked like an invitation
to ordeal by battle before the Joint Chiefs of Staff. So it proved.

A memorandum from Magruder on November 22, 1944, had specifically urged that the executive order be precise and detailed. Otherwise,
he said, the matter would not be "tied up"; the services would "worm out
of generalities." The Joint Intelligence Committee of the Joint Chiefs of
Staff would fit into the plan, once the authority for it was obtained. It
could of course remain responsible to the Joint Chiefs of Staff for correlating and evaluating military intelligence as such, though it were eliminated as a body having to do with the estimates for "national policy and
strategy" which the Office of Strategic Services should provide.[78]

General Donovan was ready by November 27 for the hearing before the
Joint Chiefs of Staff. And so he wrote to General Marshall, Admiral King,
and General Arnold of the Army, the Navy, and the Army Air Forces; to
Lieutenant General Embick, chairman of the Joint Strategic Survey Committee of the Joint Chiefs of Staff and to Vice Admiral Horne, deputy of
Admiral King as Chief of Naval Operations; to Secretary Stimson and
Assistant Secretary McCloy of the War Department; to Secretary Forrestal
and Assistant Secretary Bard of the Navy; and to Mr. James C. Dunn, the
State Department's Officer of Foreign Affairs. To all of these ranking
officers, heads of departments and their assistants, Donovan explained
his plan for turning the Office of Strategic Services into a permanent
central intelligence system and enclosed a copy of his final memorandum
for the President of November 18, 1944. He reiterated again and again in
these letters that he did not propose to interfere with the operational
intelligence services of the departments or seek any police functions for
the central agency. It was to be a coordinating agency. As he closed this
phase of the endeavor, General Donovan declared that it "might be well to
capitalize on our errors of the past two years and put it into effect at
once."[79]

But this was not to happen. The Federal Bureau of Investigation and
the armed services accepted the invitation to combat vociferously and at
length. Shouts of "Gestapo" echoed through the committees and Congress into the press and back again from far corners of the world. The
Department of State proceeded with its own plan, aided and encouraged

by the Bureau of the Budget and the Department of Justice. Another full year passed before a central intelligence service began to operate in times of peace, and then the Office of Strategic Services was no longer in existence.[80]

CONSTRUCTIVE CONTROVERSY

The scene of action shifted to the committee of the Joint Chiefs of Staff in December 1944 as General Donovan went abroad on a tour of inspection. Members of the Joint Intelligence Staff, working committee of the Joint Intelligence Committee, for some time had been dissatisfied with the system of collecting and appraising intelligence. They were discussing issues and problems among themselves in the hope that they might discover common ground for the Army and Navy, the Department of State, Foreign Economic Administration, and the Office of Strategic Services. The Donovan plan disturbed their thinking; it contained a provision agreeable to none of them. This, of course, was the idea that the Director of Central Intelligence should be immediately responsible to the President and subject only to advice from the departments. In the end, the Joint Intelligence Staff had reason to thank General Donovan. His thoughts were so great a shock to departmental minds that the members of the Staff got for their own suggestions an audience which otherwise they might never have received from their superiors in the Joint Intelligence Committee.[81]

A large part of the resistance to the Donovan plan in the meetings of the committees of the Joint Chiefs of Staff grew out of malice toward General Donovan himself. Some remarks were kept from the record, but enough of the bitterness came through to convince any reader that Donovan's proposal would not be accepted as such. There was, fortunately, a body of criticism based upon honest and constructive disapproval. There was agreement too with many of his major principles.[82]

Two separate proposals, called for brevity's sake the "services plan" and the "civilian plan," emerged from the controversy. Both were influenced by the Donovan plan. Both rejected Donovan's suggestion that the head of the central intelligence agency should report directly to the President. They seriously modified, though they did not entirely remove, his concept of individual responsibility. As so well expressed during the argument in the prolonged meeting of the Joint Intelligence Committee on December

22, 1944, the issue lay between "the principle of coordination and the principle of chain of command."[83]

The "services plan" placed authority jointly with the Secretaries of State, War, and the Navy, but did not elaborate upon their conduct as a board. The thought may simply have been that no one of them would be

---

The dissatisfaction of the JIS was not with the "system of collecting and appraising intelligence" (p. 29) of which it was hardly cognizant, but with a process of coordination that required the common consent of six sovereign powers, a process with which the JIS was all too familiar. Thus, the JIS was strongly in favor of vesting a power of decision in a DCI, with a compensating procedure for registering departmental dissents. This was and still is the essential element of the solution eventually adopted.

Darling's description of the "civilian plan" presented to the JIC (p. 29 and p. 31) is actually a description of the final compromise. The "civilian plan" was substantially identical with the Donovan proposal, as Donovan himself noted (p. 32).

All members of the JIS were personally sympathetic toward the Donovan proposal, but the service members were instructed delegates. On that basis, I was the author of the "services plan." The long deadlock was broken when, to my astonishment, General Bissell publicly instructed me to perfect the "civilian plan." I then prepared the final compromise with Gleason's participation and concurrence. It was simply the "civilian plan" with the NIA from the "services plan" inserted into it.

Ludwell Montague
April 23, 1969

---

allowed by the others to have control; all three therefore should operate by unanimous consent. They could watch one another as each looked out for his own interests. The idea that this group should function as a whole, however, was inherent in the authority descending to the Secretaries from the President. Authority is single; it is not divided when shared by several persons. The Secretaries were individually responsible to the President. But he could assign tasks to them individually or collectively at his own pleasure. As indicated in the debate of the Joint Intelligence Committee, the assumption was logical that the three Secretaries would function as a whole.

The real intent of the "services plan" seems nevertheless to have lain in the word "federal" as it was applied to the "intelligence directorate" designed to operate under the Secretaries. This directorate was to have a civilian head from the Department of State and deputies from the War and Navy Departments. It should have powers of inspection, coordination, and planning. It should have no administrative or operating functions; apparently these were to remain with the respective departments. A "single national intelligence service," according to this plan, was "undesirable."

Separate from the Directorate there would be a joint intelligence service to conduct operations of "common concern" to the three departments and, it may be supposed, any other agency or department which had interests involved from time to time. Stress upon matters of "common concern" in this manner accentuated the desire to keep other interests of the departments distinctly their own concern.

Those who favored this plan, mostly representatives of the armed services, wished to have the Joint Intelligence Committee of the Joint Chiefs of Staff continue to provide intelligence estimates, or synthesis of departmental intelligence, on a "strategic level." From their point of view, the fact that the Department of State, the Foreign Economic Administration, and the Office of Strategic Services all had representation in the Joint Intelligence Committee made it possible and fairly easy to develop the committee into a national estimating board.[84]

The "civilian plan" accepted Donovan's principles and methods for the most part. The proposed central intelligence agency for coordination and secret collection should operate with an independent budget. All departments, though maintaining their own operational intelligence, should make available to the central agency whatever materials the director might request. The central agency should have no police functions. In time of war it should come directly under the Joint Chiefs of Staff.

But the advocates of this plan did not make the director immediately responsible to the President. The director, though appointed by the President, would be subject to the "direction and control" of the Secretaries of State, War, and the Navy sitting as a board of authority. In time of war a representative of the Joint Chiefs of Staff would also be a member of this board. Further exception to Donovan's plan appeared in the statement that the collection of intelligence, except by clandestine methods, should be the function of the existing agencies and not of the central intelligence service. Nor would the "civilian plan" allow the agency to engage in subversive operations abroad; they were not to be considered an appropriate function of the proposed intelligence service. We should note also that the "civilian plan" did not give to the central agency the power of inspection which the "services plan" included for its "directorate."[85]

Before he went abroad on December 26, General Donovan sent to President Roosevelt a memorandum upon these two proposals from the Joint Intelligence Staff. The plan of the military members, said Donovan, evaded early action. Worse than that, it approached the problem of national intelligence from the departmental point of view, providing a minimum of centralization. He was surprised at the lack of understanding among responsible officers in the field of intelligence. They did not seem to comprehend, he said, the importance of a central service in which both military and civilian experts would work together to synthesize all available information and to make estimates before the event of political or military developments. The plan of the civilians was another matter. It closely followed his own ideas. Its end in view was a complete system for producing estimates which should aid in the construction of national policy.

Donovan reported to the President that he had appeared at its request before the Joint Strategic Survey Committee, which advised the Joint Chiefs of Staff on political matters. He had done so with apparent willingness to entertain the idea in the plan of the civilians that there should be a board between the President and the director of the proposed central intelligence service. But there is no mistaking that he was unwilling at that time to make such a concession unless it were clearly understood that the director would be free to administer the affairs of the agency. He might be a general manager, with the Secretaries over him as a board of directors. Put in colloquial language perhaps more accurately conveying the thought, this meant that the general manager might be hired and fired by the Secretaries; so long as he was in charge, he was not to be bossed by them. Donovan was determined to get an agency in which there would be real centralization and coordination of the intelligence services under a single administrator ultimately responsible to the President.[86]

The Joint Strategic Survey Committee reported in January along much the same line of thought which Donovan had given to the President, but with the impression that he had been more willing to concede to the "advice and control" of the Secretaries as proposed in the plan of the civilians.

The Committee spoke of a diagram subsequently furnished by Donovan's office to comprehend the possibility of an "Intelligence Directing Board" over the Director.[87] The difference in interpretation did not lay General Donovan's statement open to question. It put different emphasis upon the possibilities of the future. The position which he took in 1945 as Director of the Office of Strategic Services anticipated the practical situation of the Director of Central Intelligence under the National Security Council. Although by the Act of Congress in 1947, the Council had authority over the Director of Central Intelligence and the Agency, the Director had frequent access to the President. The responsibility of the Director to the President in actual working conditions was often immediate and direct. President Truman used the Agency as his personal information service.[88]

Pressure from above seems to have come upon the representatives of the armed services in the Joint Intelligence Committee. The long meeting of December 22, 1944, ended in agreement that the Joint Intelligence Staff should go over the plans and perfect them. No hope was expressed that they ever could be consolidated into one; the idea appears nevertheless to have lurked in the atmosphere. When the representative of the Army suggested that his surbordinate on the Joint Intelligence Staff should help the authors of the "civilian plan" to perfect their inadequate proposals, results came fast.[89]

Within a week there was a single plan which had the merits of General Donovan's original concepts coupled with specific provision that the Secretaries of State, War, and the Navy with the Chief of Staff to the Commander-in-Chief should constitute a National Intelligence Authority. Later the fourth member was changed to be simply a representative of the Joint Chiefs of Staff.[90]

Unmistakably intended to function as a whole, the National Intelligence Authority would be charged with responsibility for all federal intelligence activities related to the national security. Under it there was to be established a Central Intelligence Agency headed by a Director who should be appointed by the President on the recommendation of the Authority.

As a body of advisers to the Director, there was to be set up a board consisting of the heads of the intelligence services of the Army, Navy, Department of State, and other agencies concerned with the national security. This advisory board would be subordinated to the National Intelligence Authority by the directive which established it. Its members, of course, were severally responsible to their Secretaries. There was no indication in the plan that the advisory board was to dictate to the Director of the Central Intelligence Agency. The board was to be only a means for advice from the intelligence officers of the departments.[91]

Thus, the members of the Joint Intelligence Staff, with a good deal of independent thinking and inspiration as well as external pressure, arrived at the principles for a national system of intelligence which represented parties of conflicting interests and yet centralized controls under an authority receiving its power from the Chief Executive of the United States.

The Joint Strategic Survey Committee reported to the Joint Chiefs of Staff on January 18, 1945, that the plan of the Joint Intelligence Staff, now the proposal of the Joint Intelligence Committee, was superior to General Donovan's plan. He would "overcentralize" the intelligence service. He would subject the departmental intelligence agencies to central control without making that control responsible either to the head of a single department or to the heads of all of the departments as a body. The plan of the Joint Intelligence Committee, on the other hand, would hold the Central Intelligence Agency within bounds set by the Secretaries in the National Intelligence Authority.[92]

The Joint Strategic Survey Committee accepted the provision in the plan of the Joint Intelligence Committee that the Central Intelligence Agency should have the power to inspect the operations of the departmental intelligence agencies in connection with its planning function. But to make certain that the use of the power to inspect intelligence operations should not jeopardize military operations, the JSSC amended the plan so that the Authority and the Agency under it should be responsible for protecting "intelligence sources and methods" which had direct and important bearing upon "military operations." Military men evidently at that time did not object to imperfection if it were closely associated with the duty to protect military operations. Restriction upon the right of inspection came later. In addition, it was separated from the responsibility of the Director of Central Intelligence to guard sources and methods of intelligence from unauthorized exposure.[93]

Essential features of the Central Intelligence Agency were clearly in view during the month of January 1945 before the conference at Yalta, the surrender of Germany, and the collapse of Japan. The national system of intelligence, however, was not to come into operation in time of war when a people is more easily governed, it is said, than in time of peace. Donovan's plan was released to the public by someone who has yet to confess. Circumstantial evidence narrowed suspicion to two or three who might have violated the secrecy of the documents. Motive for doing so could easily be found in hatred. Donovan and his Office of Strategic Services had bitter enemies.[94] But no useful purpose is served in speculations here.

The *Chicago Tribune* and the *Washington Times Herald* simultaneously produced Donovan's memorandum to the President and proposal on February 9, 1945. There were headlines and editorials on a "superspy system," "bigger and better spying," and "police state." There were interviews with Congressmen who obliged with accusations of "super-Gestapo" and the like.[95] Then the plan of the Joint Intelligence Committee got into the same newspapers. This rather successfully destroyed the insinuations that Donovan and Roosevelt were establishing a personal regime. But the exposure seemed to dismay the President and the Joint Chiefs of Staff. Another view is that they were glad of an excuse to set the whole question aside.

Reports from the Yalta Conference sent "superspy" off the front pages immediately. The American public was much more interested in news of the troops driving into Germany. Had the Joint Chiefs of Staff wished to settle the issue at that time, they might have completed their study in secret session without much attention from the public and have put aside the rsulting plan for establishment later. Instead, they recalled their papers on Donovan's proposal and the plan of the Joint Intelligence Committee. They made some effort to discover who had released the papers. Donovan persisted in trying to find out, and he continued to urge acceptance of his plan for a central intelligence system. Others who seemed really to care were few.[96]

On April 5, shortly before his death, President Roosevelt sent a brief note asking Donovan to call together the chiefs of intelligence and security units in the various executive agencies so that a consensus might be obtained regarding a central intelligence service. It must have seemed as though he were to go back to the beginning and start again, but General Donovan was nothing if not persistent. He sent letters the very next day to the Secretaries and heads of agencies as suggested, with a statement of his principles, a copy of the President's note, and another copy of his memorandum for the President of November 18, 1944.[97]

To judge from the replies, these familiar papers were news to some of the officials who received them. The objectives were not "sufficiently clear" to permit the Secretary of the Treasury on April 12 to express a "firm opinion." But Henry Morgenthau was certain that the burdens upon the President were already too heavy for him to be directly responsible for the proposed central intelligence agency. President Roosevelt died that day. Postmaster General Walker advised Donovan that "it must be clear that any government intelligence service outside the Post Office Department must operate through the Post Office Department and recognize the absolute jurisdiction of this Department." This must have been news to General Donovan.

Secretary Wickard was content with the existing arrangements between the Department of Agriculture and the Department of State. He saw no reason for a separate office to coordinate intelligence upon foreign conditions and developments. Additional coordination of such intelligence he believed could be and in fact was being secured through the

Bureau of the Budget. Again Donovan must have been rather surprised. He had received much from the Bureau of the Budget on financial matters, plans, programs, but nothing worth the name of foreign intelligence.

Attorney General Biddle replied with terse comment reflecting the interest of the Department of Justice in the Federal Bureau of Investigation. He was satisfied with existing arrangements for the exchange of intelligence among that Bureau, the Office of Naval Intelligence, and the Military Intelligence Service of the Army. He did not wish any change in the "middle of the war," nor did he believe that Congress would grant an appropriation for such a purpose. The intelligence service "should be organized quietly and not in the manner suggested." He favored the idea of a policy committee consisting of representatives from the agencies chiefly concerned—State, War, Navy, Justice, and the Office of Strategic Services. The Attorney General's reply could have left no doubt where he stood. It may have recalled Carter's proposal to President Roosevelt in the preceding fall. General Donovan had placed that in the "horse and buggy stage."[98]

Secretary Ickes replied on behalf of the Department of Interior that the central intelligence service would be a handicap to his department if it were to foreclose in any manner the ability of the department's bureaus to secure intelligence from any source, domestic or foreign, which concerned matters under his jurisdiction. To Ickes, General Donovan replied that he need have no concern. One of the principal objectives of the agency would be to coordinate intelligence for the very purpose of facilitating and increasing the flow of material to the departments.

For the Department of Labor, Secretary Perkins replied that she could not support the proposal to create an "Intelligence Officer reporting directly to the President." She favored keeping the State Department above any other agency in coordinating foreign intelligence except the "narrowly defined military subjects." She favored improved arrangements among the Secretaries of State, War, and the Navy, so that there would be no gaps and no need for coordination by some officer reporting directly to the President.

The reply of Stimson, Secretary of War, on May 1, 1945, was the most significant. General Donovan's plan had received careful consideration in the War Department. It was in entire agreement with his objective. It differed with regard to his methods. From Stimson's point of view, responsibility should not be separated from the authority to discharge that responsibility. Security against foreign aggression was the primary concern of the Secretary of State, Secretary of War, and Secretary of the Navy. All responsibility, therefore, should remain with them. Donovan's intelligence service, moreover, would subject the operations of departmental intelligence to control outside the respective departments. This was not advisable. Secretary Stimson agreed that coordination must be attained, but he did not think that "the coordinating authority should engage in operations." The inevitable tendency, he declared, would be to expand its operating functions at the expense of the agencies which had the responsibilities for operations in intelligence.

Secretary Stimson's position was clear. The methods of coordination, and those combined operations which were necessary, should be determined by the heads of the departments controlling the operating agencies. This coordination was one of the matters to be considered in the general problem of a single Department of Defense. In short, Secretary Stimson did not wish an independent agency with a separate budget. In any event, he said, the Departments of State, War, Justice, and the Navy had examined together the proposed central intelligence service; they were in substantial agreement that it should not be considered before the end of hostilities against Germany and Japan. This statement gave further evidence that the armed services had been more pleased than dismayed in February when the Donovan plan got into the news.[99]

General Magruder advised Donovan that the letter from Stimson left two courses of action. Either Donovan could try to develop political pressures upon President Truman that were stronger than the influence of the departments. Or Donovan might compromise his cherished independence of the directorate of the agency in order to obtain immediate action. Magruder knew that he was recommending what to Donovan was "a pet abomination," compromise; but Magruder felt that it would win many high-ranking officials in the Army, Navy, and the Department of State. It would eliminate the Federal Bureau of Investigation from consideration. It would make the situation less difficult for the President. If it won his support, "he could restore large powers to the director" later in executive orders.[100]

General Donovan, however, would keep trying. He had found some encouragement in the interest of the State Department after the latest version of the so-called compromise plan had come from the Joint Strategic Survey Committee of the Joint Chiefs of Staff. He had been pleased, too, that Admiral Horne had requested a copy of the Joint Intelligence Committee's final paper, presumably for study and report to Admiral King. Donovan had cabled from London that he would like to have his deputies at home pursue these opportunities. They should keep in mind as they discussed the matter that so far as he was concerned the ultimate interests of the country required that the responsibility should be vested in the President and not "diffused through intermediate echelons."[101]

Donovan replied to Secretary Stimson on May 16. The Secretaries were to provide for security against aggression. It was their primary concern. But that did not give them the right, said Donovan, to exercise exclusive control over the proposed Central Intelligence Agency. That was the responsibility of the President, who was Commander-in-Chief in peace as well as in war; the "authority of decision" resided in him. Policy was necessarily dependent upon intelligence. To make that decision, the President was entitled to an intelligence service free from domination by one or any group of the departments.[102] Secretary Stimson's reply, however, had been made on behalf of the Administration. Nothing further was to be done after General Eisenhower took the surrender of the Germans on May 7 until plans had been carried out for the overwhelming defeat of Japan. The atomic bomb was tested at Alamogordo on July 16.

LIQUIDATION FOR OSS

After the surrender of Germany, the Appropriations Committee of the House inquired whether General MacArthur and Admiral Nimitz wished to use the Office of Strategic Services in the Pacific War. For the Joint Chiefs of Staff, without personal comment, Admiral Leahy replied on May 25 and 27, 1945, by quoting from messages of Admiral Nimitz and Generals MacArthur, Sultan, and Wedemeyer who had commands in Far Eastern theaters and from General McNarney and Eisenhower concerning Europe.[103]

General Sultan in the India–Burma theater said that the Office of Strategic Services had furnished most effective assistance but that it was no longer needed. Its present functions would be "more economically and efficiently" accomplished within the War and Navy Departments "through normal command channels."

Admiral Nimitz answered that use of the Office of Strategic Services in the Pacific had been very limited. In his "considered opinion" better results could be obtained if its task were "reassigned to the War and Navy Departments."

General MacArthur's view on the matter was as definite, and characteristic: "No statement," he said, "has emanated from this headquarters nor so far as known from this area in comment on OSS. Any items that may have appeared in the press along this line must be regarded as speculative conjecture. The OSS has not up to the present time operated within this area, I know little of its methods, have no control of its agencies, and consequently have no plans for its future employment." Donovan considered this a "very fair statement" from MacArthur's own point of view.

General Eisenhower wrote that the future of the Office of Strategic Services in the European theater would be subject to certain contingencies. It would be confined of course to the functions of an intelligence-gathering and counterespionage organization. Complete control of its activities by each theater commander would be essential to efficient and smooth operations. But its value in the European theater would "continue to be very high."

General McNarney reported that the Office of Strategic Services had done an "outstanding job" in Italy. So long as conditions there, in Austria, and in the Balkans remained unstable, it was essential to continue the secret intelligence work of the Office in that theater. Its staff in the Mediterranean area could be reduced, but he specifically recommended that trained personnel from the Office of Strategic Services be redeployed to the Pacific.

General Wedemeyer declared that its potential value in the China theater was high. It was training twenty commando groups and intelligence teams there. These groups and others already trained were to be charged with "responsible missions in direct support of contemplated future plans." According to Donovan's memory, they might have accomplished much to appraise the situation in Manchuria before the atomic bomb was used in Japan.[104]

The opinions of such commanders in the Pacific as Nimitz and MacArthur, however, were likely to have more influence in this country than the plans of Wedemeyer for the China theater. After the atomic bombs fell on Hiroshima and Nagasaki, there was little point to arguing here the need for the Office of Strategic Services in China. If the mood of the American people prevailed, there was going to be no theater of war in China.

It may be harder to govern in time of peace than in time of war. It is more difficult still to control a people turning from war to peace. Public relaxation in America with the news from Tokyo Bay took on the aspects of an orgy; the treatment of gasoline rationing that summer's evening, August 14, 1945, was but one response of a people cherishing the belief that government draws its just powers from the consent of the governed. More ominous was the rush to disband America's forces. The fleet went into "mothballs" for a possibility which has since become fact in Korean waters. But there were too many instances where demobilization meant disintegration. Personnel disappeared beyond recall. The ruin of much valuable organization was complete.

The Bureau of the Budget, obliged by the nature of its office to peer into the costs of future events, quickly sensed the change in the American mood following Japan's surrender. Replacing the notice which he had sent on July 17 in regard to expenditures for war, Director Smith of the Bureau advised General Donovan on August 25, 1945, that the "overriding consideration" now in estimating the budgets for 1947 would be to retain full employment and to resume the social and economic progress which had been interrupted by the war.

To this end, there would be no expansion of present "peacetime activities" unless it were to contribute to the "reconversion process and the expansion of industry and trade." The Office of Strategic Services was a wartime enterprise with no "peacetime activities" established in the past. In short, although Mr. Smith did not say, it looked as though General Donovan were going to have a very hard time maintaining his independent agency, however its indispensable functions might be distributed. The Bureau of the Budget itself had been studying for months the problems of an intelligence system and had a plan of its own to propose.[105]

Donovan strove to keep his organization intact. He wrote on September 4 to Samuel Rosenman in the White House that it was absurd to allocate different segments to different departments. The Office of Strategic Services had been established "as an entity, every function supporting and supplementing the other." It was time "to grow up" and realize that the new responsibilities of the American people required "an adequate intelligence system."[106]

The expectation of the American people, however, was clearly that expenditure for war would be stopped with the fighting, and the "boys brought home." Apparently the mood of the Negro spiritual was rather general that there would be "no war, no more." There would be no place now in American policy for sabotage, psychological warfare, and guerrilla tactics. Whatever services were necessary in peacetime for the collection of information and the coordination of intelligence might be had within the established Departments of State, War, and the Navy as so many of the Cabinet officers had written to Donovan in the spring. The Office of Strategic Services should be closed.

Responsible observers took stock as the Office of Strategic Services went out of existence. For the first time in the history of the United States, there had been established an organized network of espionage and counterespionage operating in Europe, North Africa, the Near and Middle East, and the Far East. American scholars had been mobilized to supplement current information with comprehensive surveys and to blend them into intelligence reports for the policymakers of the Government. OSS had demonstrated the usefulness of a central body to process materials from every source of information. Its experiences indicated that a single authority ought to have charge of collecting secret information outside of the United States. Cooperation with the agencies of other governments left much still to be desired, but the value of the endeavor had been shown. The Office of Strategic Services had closely associated secret intelligence with covert operations, economic intrusion, and other subversive practices. The latter perhaps should have been kept separate and administered in a "Department of Dirty Tricks." The immovable fact was that the two were complementary. Each seemed to work better when associated with the other. But the problem of their articulation was not yet solved.[107]

President Truman praised General Donovan on September 20, 1945, for exceptional leadership in a wartime activity. More than this, he could say that General Donovan retired to private life with the reward of knowing that the intelligence services of the Government for time of peace were being erected upon the foundations which he had laid in the Office of Strategic Services. It went out of existence as a wartime expedient commended for many accomplishments. It was entitled to the greater praise of close study by those who had charge of creating and administering the instrument of government which succeeded it.[108]

Introduction to Chapter II

From the close of the war in August 1945 until January 1946, the debate over the organization of national intelligence raged. The decision to dismantle the OSS posed the question of where to place the assets that the service had accumulated during the war, as well as how the new National Intelligence Authority was to function. Meanwhile, the postwar global situation made the need for an effective U.S. intelligence system indispensable.

The Department of State argued that it should run any national intelligence service and was supported by the Bureau of the Budget. The Joint Chiefs of Staff, meanwhile, pressed their plan for an interdepartmental National Intelligence Authority. Donovan continued to argue in vain for a centralized agency above the control of any one department and directly accountable to the President, but he still lacked support, and the dismantling of OSS proceeded as scheduled. The State Department received all personnel and facilities from the now defunct OSS Research and Analysis Branch and the Presentation Branch. All other OSS functions (mainly special forces and espionage operations) went to the War Department, where the Strategic Services Unit was established.

President Truman initially supported the plan for State Department direction of national intelligence. Secretary of State James Byrnes and his Special Assistant, Alfred McCormack, pursued their program aggressively, much to the dismay of the military. Under the State Department plan, leadership and commanding positions were to be reserved for State Department officials under a proposed "Office of Foreign Intelligence." McCormack's role, incidentally, had a certain amount of irony, as he had been the head of the Army's intelligence service during the war and a nemesis of Donovan; McCormack apparently envisioned himself as the postwar intelligence czar and seemed not to care if he reigned from the Pentagon or from Foggy Bottom.

The military continued to promote the JCS plan to counter State, and an obvious collision was impending. During the closing months of the war, the Secretary of the Navy and the Secretary of War each commissioned studies to articulate the military's position. (The reader needs to keep in mind that not only do many of the events that Darling describes in detail encompass just a few months but he also sometimes backtracks in his narrative in order to explain the origins of a particular event.) The Navy study was chaired by investment banker Ferdinand Eberstadt, a friend of Navy Secretary James Forrestal; the War Department study was chaired by Assistant Secretary of War Robert

Lovett. These two reports were to provide the intellectual underpinnings of the JCS proposal in which a National Intelligence Authority was to be supported by a Central Intelligence Agency and headed by a Director of Central Intelligence responsible to the NIA.

This JCS proposal was not only a compromise between Donovan's proposal for a strong DCI and the proposal presented by the military services for a decentralized intelligence community; it also provided a successful response to the State Department's proposal for State Department control over national intelligence. The State Department lost its bid to grab control of the postwar intelligence community when its opponents won the support of President Truman by arguing that the President needed access to all intelligence produced by the national security community, without the State Department acting as an intermediary. Also, the President appears to have wanted his own representative providing him intelligence from the community.

On January 6, 1946, the Secretaries of State, War, and Navy met and agreed to most of the JCS plan. On January 9 Truman accepted the Secretaries' decision; the Presidential Directive implementing the plan was formally issued on January 22. This directive modified the Secretaries' proposal by designating a fourth member of the NIA, in addition to the Secretaries of War, State, and Navy, who would be a personal representative of the President; Truman had in mind his Chief of Staff, Admiral William Leahy. For the post of Director of Central Intelligence, Truman nominated Rear Admiral Sidney Souers, who had been instrumental in developing the JCS intelligence plan.

Despite the President's action, though, some matters remained ambiguous. For example, in principle the DCI enjoyed direct access to the President. Yet the DCI was also a *nonvoting* member of the NIA, responsible for carrying out the decisions of the Authority. This stipulation suggested that the DCI was subordinate to the Secretaries and could not represent views to the President that had not been approved by the NIA. Also, there was no guarantee that the DCI would have access to intelligence data produced by the departments, which he would need to produce estimates.

The new organization established by the directive, designated the Central Intelligence Group (CIG), was to consist of personnel drawn from the various departments. In addition, the provision for the CIG to collect intelligence was omitted from the final directive. The new organization was not to meddle in internal security issues, which were the jurisdiction of the FBI. And, despite the recommendation of the JCS plan, the CIG had no independent source of funding; rather, it was to receive proportional funding from the Departments of State, War, and Navy. All of these factors were to weaken the autonomy and capabilities of the new organization.

II

PLANS IN PEACETIME

PEACEFUL METHODS OF WAR

There was more than economy in mind as Smith, Director of the Budget, corresponded with General Donovan in August 1945 about liquidating the Office of Strategic Services. On the day Smith advised the General in regard to agencies with no peacetime activities, Donovan was explaining to the Director once more the principles which should govern a centralized "United States Foreign Intelligence System." Donovan believed those principles were already at work in the Office of Strategic Services. But since it was to be abandoned, another agency should be set up immediately to take over "the valuable assets created by OSS" and aid the nation in "the organization and maintenance of the peace." Within the week Donovan had a report from Gregory Bateson concerning the effect of the atomic bomb upon "indirect methods of warfare." It made the need for a permanent system of national intelligence peremptory.[1]

Writing from the headquarters of OSS in the India–Burma theater, Mr. Bateson forecast changes in psychological warfare, clandestine operations, and strategic intelligence. The physicists of all countries had been engaged in research leading to the atomic bomb. All major powers were likely to have weapons of the sort within the next ten years. Inadequate hydroelectric power to isolate "heavy water" was more of a delaying factor than lack of uranium; ores containing it were not excessively rare. The atomic bomb would shift the balance of warlike and peaceful methods of international pressure.

The bomb would be powerless, said Bateson, against subversive practices, guerilla tactics, social and economic manipulation, diplomatic forces, and propaganda either black or white. The nations would resort to those "peaceful methods of war." The importance of the work of the Foreign Economic Administration, the Office of War Information, and the Office of Strategic Services, therefore, would be "infinitely greater" than it had ever been. The country could not rely upon the Army and Navy alone for defense. There should be a third agency acting under the Department of State to combine the functions and employ the weapons of clandestine operations, economic controls, and psychological pressures in the new warfare.

DONOVAN'S PRINCIPLES

Two assets of OSS were clear. For the first time in its history, said Donovan, this country had a secret intelligence service gathering information abroad and reporting directly to a central office in Washington. Inseparable from this service, a group of specialists were analyzing and evaluating the information for those who should determine the nation's policies. With these two cardinal purposes, secret collection abroad and expert appraisal at home, Donovan stressed again the familiar points in his plan. Each department would have its own intelligence service to meet its own needs; its materials would be made available to the central agency. This agency would serve all of the departments with supplemental information obtained either by its own collectors or from other services. It would supply its "strategic interpretive studies" to authorized agencies and officials.

The agency should have no clandestine activities within the United States nor any police functions either at home or abroad. In time of war it would be subject to the Joint Chiefs of Staff. But it should be independent of any department since it was to serve all. It should have an independent budget. Again he proposed that it should be administered by a single officer appointed by the President and under his direction. The President might designate a general manager to act as his intermediary, but the agency should be established in the Executive Office of the President. Beyond that Donovan would not go in meeting the criticisms of his plan for a director of central intelligence who should be responsible directly to the President.

Subject to the approval of the President, or the general manager, the director should determine the policy of the agency with the "advice and assistance" of a board representing the Secretaries. With State, War, and the Navy, Donovan now included the Treasury. He still insisted that the board should be only a body of advice and not of authority. This requirement was certain to keep alive the opposition which his proposal had met in the military services throughout the previous year. But to General Donovan the principle of individual responsibility was as indispensable as the need for experts in research and analysis and the maintenance of covert services abroad. None of the three principles should be subject to his "pet abomination," compromise.[2]

As could be expected, Donovan sent copies of his letter to Director Smith and the accompanying principles to the heads of the branch offices of the Office of Strategic Services. The response from Cairo was particularly interesting. Donovan's dispatch arrived in time to give point to the conversation at a dinner with members of Congress who were travelling in the Middle East. One view was like Bateson's, that the Department of State should take over the new intelligence system. But the counterargument was so outspoken that the advocate of the State Department appeared shaken in his conviction. Another thought that the Federal Bureau of Investigation should take charge. This idea was "horrific" to the officer who reported the event, but a better idea than some; at least the Federal Bureau of Investigation was a civilian organization, he said, "a going concern" with an "enviable reputation" among the American people.[3]

PROPOSALS FROM THE BUREAU OF THE BUDGET

General Donovan's "all-inclusive" purposes had met doubts among officials of the Bureau of the Budget in 1941. Now on September 20, 1945, a report tracing the history of intelligence in this country objected to continuance of the Office of Strategic Services and proposed a new organization.

The Office of Strategic Services was commended for blazing "new trails" and for raising the "level of competence" in the whole system of intelligence, but dismissed as a wartime agency which should not be superimposed "on the normal structure of government." The advocates of OSS did not take into account the fact that the "principal operations" of intelligence must be at the point where decisions were made; that is, the operations must occur in the departments. As they were responsible for the decisions and actions, they should propose the intelligence upon which the decisions and actions were based. This, we may recall, was virtually Secretary Stimson's position in the preceding May. Moreover, according to the members of the Bureau who wrote this paper, the Donovan plan did not recognize the leading role of the State Department as a "staff agency of the President." Here, it would seem, was the main point of the report.

It conceded the necessity which Donovan had maintained in every reconsideration of his principles. There must be some machinery for coordinating the intelligence operations in the several departments of the Government. There must be some provision for supplying intelligence reports to the President, and others, who had decisions to make with regard to national policy. National policy invariably cuts across some departmental lines, often rises above and beyond all of them.

For this purpose, the report of the Bureau of the Budget suggested a small "independent central staff" which could rely on the product of the research and analysis in the departments. It should not engage in original research. It should "harmonize" the intelligence which it received from the departments, and reconcile any conflicts among them. Until the President saw fit to have such a small staff in his own office, the Department of State could provide the facilities.

The suggestion did not meet, it ignored General Donovan's contention that no department should control the production of the intelligence reports for the policymakers. The Bureau of the Budget preferred the Department of State as the one best equipped by tradition, function, and experience to provide that service. However grateful were the planners in the Department of State, this suggestion was no more likely to please the Army and Navy than General Donovan's plan.

There were those who preferred some form of his proposal, until the Joint Chiefs of Staff brought out again the plan of their Joint Intelligence Committee for a National Intelligence Authority. Captain W. D. Puleston, former Director of Naval Intelligence, wrote on September 22 to Admiral Horne, Vice Chief of Naval Operations, to protest that officials of the State Department could not be counted upon to deal with officers of the Army and Navy as representatives of "coordinate" branches of the Government. In Puleston's opinion, the central agency should come directly under the Office of the President. Admiral Robinson expressed much the same opinion on October 4. The "Intelligence Branch" should be independent of the departments, he said, and directly responsible to the President.[5]

The details of the new organization proposed in the report of the Bureau of the Budget on September 20 should not detain us. They were significant chiefly for the support which they gave to the organization then taking shape in the State Department. But the officials who wrote the report made so sharp a distinction between security intelligence, or counterespionage, and the positive intelligence obtained from collecting information that some attention must be given to their proposal. They would have the two functions kept apart under the jurisdictions of two separate interdepartmental committees. These committees should devise the plans for and coordinate the work of the several departments in each field.

The nucleus of each committee was to be the Assistant Secretaries of State, War, and Navy. When they sat as the Intelligence Coordinating Committee, the Assistant Secretary of Commerce would attend. When they were the Security Coordinating Committee, the additional members would be the Assistant Secretary of the Treasury and the Assistant Attorney General.

This division into two committees seems unrealistic. The presence of the Assistant Secretary of Commerce alone could hardly insulate the minds of the Assistant Secretaries of State, War, and Navy if their thoughts should move from problems of intelligence-gathering and coordinating to problems of security. It would seem as though one committee for coordination were sufficient. Men of the caliber to be expected in the office of Assistant Secretary might consider the two phases of intelligence in the same meeting on the same afternoon. If one committee were able to coordinate the intelligence operations of the departments, it might coordinate intelligence with security. After all, they were complementary. Like other plans, however, that of the Bureau of the Budget did recognize the reasonableness and efficiency in having a single agency to handle administrative matters and operations of "common concern."[6]

The Bureau of the Budget won the attention of President Truman. On the same day, September 20, 1945, that he wrote to thank Donovan for his services in time of war, the President directed Secretary Byrnes of the Department of State to take the lead in developing the program for a comprehensive and coordinated system of foreign intelligence. The Secretary should form an interdepartmental group to make plans for the President's approval. This procedure would allow arrangement for "complete coverage of the foreign intelligence field"; it would permit assignment and control of operations to meet with "maximum effectiveness" the needs of "the individual agencies and the Government as a whole."[7]

At the same time, President Truman signed the executive order breaking up the Office of Strategic Services in spite of Donovan's protests to Rosenman, Special Counsel to the President, and to Smith, Director of the Bureau of the Budget. The personnel and the facilities of the Research and Analysis Branch and the Presentation Branch went to the Department of State. These, the President had agreed with Secretary Byrnes, would provide resources to aid the State Department in developing their foreign policy. The War Department received the remaining activities, chiefly those in secret intelligence and counterespionage and the subversive practices which were to be ended as soon as possible. To take care of these activities in the War Department, the Strategic Services Unit was established under Brigadier General John Magruder, who had been Donovan's Deputy Director for Intelligence. By October 26, 1945, an organization which at its peak had some 13,000 persons, exclusive of agents and other foreign nationals in special capacities, had been reduced to less than 8,000. All of these measures were in line with the purposes of the Bureau of the Budget.[8]

PURPOSES OF THE JOINT CHIEFS OF STAFF

Much was happening in those few days. The Joint Chiefs of Staff revived, with few changes, the plan for a National Intelligence Authority. Instead of the stipulation that the new central intelligence agency should have an independent budget, the Joint Chiefs of Staff now proposed that funds should be supplied by the participating departments in amount and proportions to be agreed upon by them. Within the limits of these funds, the director of the agency might employ personnel and make provision for supplies, facilities, and services.

The Independent Offices Appropriation Act for 1945 had made it impossible without further legislation to give the central intelligence authority a separate budget. Under this recent Act of Congress no part of any appropriation or fund made available by this or any other act could be expended by an agency or instrumentality, including those established by executive order, after such an agency or instrumentality had been in existence for more than a year, unless Congress had specifically authorized the expenditure of funds by that agency.[9]

The plan was submitted to the Secretaries of War and the Navy by Admiral Leahy for the Joint Chiefs of Staff on September 19. Leahy asked that the Secretaries forward it to the President. We should not overlook the fact that Admiral Leahy himself was Chief of Staff to the President, as well as senior member of the Joint Chiefs of Staff. Ten days later Secretaries Patterson and Forrestal sent the plan of the Joint Chiefs to the Secretary of State. In view of the executive order terminating the Office of Strategic Services, and President Truman's letter to Secretary Byrnes of the same date asking him to take the lead, Patterson and Forrestal assumed that Byrnes would transmit the recommendations to the President for his information.[10]

If one were to draw from this roundabout procedure the inference that up to the moment the President did not know the plan of the Joint Chiefs of Staff, one would be as naive as those who may think the Secretaries of War and the Navy did not understand the President when he asked the Secretary of State to take the lead in developing the intelligence program. Although neither Byrnes nor Patterson had actually seen the plan of the Joint Chiefs before meeting with Forrestal on October 16, the familiar issue was open again between the parties of greatest interest. The armed services, if there had to be a central intelligence agency, were preparing to have that organization develop according to their ideas. Ranking officers in both Army and Navy did not want a central agency; but they liked even less to think that a civilian instrument of government, whether the Office of Strategic Services or the Department of State, would have control over the intelligence system of the nation.[11]

The Joint Chiefs of Staff took note of General Donovan's "principles" in his letter of August 25, 1945, to the Bureau of the Budget. They recognized with him the desirability of coordinating intelligence, conducting activities of common concern in one agency, and synthesizing departmental intelligence on "the strategic and national level." But their thinking in September had not advanced much beyond the conclusions of the Joint Strategic Survey Committee in January 1945. Donovan would "overcentralize" the intelligence service. He would place it at so high a level in the Government that it would control the departmental intelligence agencies. The central intelligence organization ought to be responsible to the heads of the departments. The Joint Chiefs of Staff favored the federal rather than the national principle for the permanent system of intelligence to replace OSS.[12]

Conditions, however, were different from what they had been in January. Though hostilities were ended, the atomic bomb made the future uncertain. President Truman was home from the Potsdam Conference where friction with Russia over Poland, Austria, Germany, and the Far East had become dangerous. The Joint Chiefs of Staff indeed could feel that an efficient intelligence service had become indispensable. It was now "entirely possible that failure to provide such a system might bring national disaster." Committees were at work for both the Army and the Navy, to reconcile their differences and find common ground if they could for a single Department of Defense, and with it a central intelligence service. Meanwhile, a member of the Department of State, specially assigned to the task, went ahead to build upon ideas in the Department and the suggestion of the Bureau of the Budget.

THE PLAN FOR THE STATE DEPARTMENT

During the fall of 1944 considerable thought had been given to establishing an Office of Foreign Intelligence within the Department. Its geographic and functional divisions did not provide a central repository where policymakers could find accumulated knowledge on subjects involving the work of several divisions. Nor was there place in the Department for coordination with other agencies of the Government. The proposed Office of Foreign Intelligence was expected to fill these needs with a planning staff and divisions of research in political, economic, geographic, social, scientific, and related matters.[13]

Now in the fall of 1945 the State Department contemplated not only reorganizing but extending its jurisdiction as it took the lead in developing the program of intelligence for all federal agencies. The Special Assistant to the Secretary of State for Research and Intelligence was to gather the functions of collection, evaluation, and dissemination of information regarding foreign nations which heretofore had been spread among several geographic offices in the Department. There were to be two new offices under his direction, one for intelligence and the other for counterintelligence.

As the Research and Analysis Branch and the Presentation Branch came over from the Office of Strategic Services, their functions, personnel, records, and property were to be absorbed according to the Department's wishes. Any remainder would be abandoned. The other departments and agencies of the Government, as well as the State Department's own field offices, would then be expected to send their intelligence to the Department of State for correlation and synthesis. The relationship of these ideas with the suggestions of the Bureau of the Budget is obvious.[14]

President Truman's letter to Secretary Byrnes enlarged the opportunity for the State Department. The Special Assistant to the Secretary, Mr. Alfred McCormack, came from the Army where he had been Director of the Military Intelligence Service. He brought into the Department Ludwell L. Montague and James S. Lay, who also had military careers as secretaries of the Joint Intelligence Committee of the Joint Chiefs of Staff; both had contributed to its plan for central intelligence. McCormack entered with enthusiasm and conviction upon the work of taking over the whole business of correlating and evaluating intelligence for the makers of policy in the Federal Government. He was certain to arouse opposition in the Army and Navy for fear that he might succeed in establishing control over national estimates in the Department of State.[15]

Secretary Forrestal of the Navy, seeking to develop a central intelligence agency together with the close interrelationship of the Army, Navy, and Air Force which he so earnestly desired, thought of having the heads of the several intelligence agencies to dinner so that they might discuss the matter and perhaps remove some of their differences. A memorandum from Thomas B. Inglis, Acting Chief of Naval Intelligence, on October 10, 1945, gave Forrestal information of what he might expect. Mr. McCormack within the past ten days had declined General Magruder's proposal of an "informal interim committee"; pending action by Secretary Byrnes to initiate proceedings as directed by the President, McCormack preferred "to conduct liaison directly with G-2, MIS, and ONI." Mr. Hoover, said Inglis, was "not in favor of a national intelligence agency." There probably would be "veiled antagonism," too, among some of the other guests. One of them was to be General Bissell. To judge from the record of his participation in the historic meeting of the Joint Intelligence Committee on December 22, 1944, it is doubtful that Bissell's antagonism toward Central Intelligence was veiled. Inglis suggested that Magruder, as head of the Strategic Services Unit, might be included in the dinner party. "It would be an interesting, but perhaps somewhat uncongenial, meeting."[16]

By November the departments were clearly heading into a collision. Forrestal wrote to Patterson on October 13 that they should push the Joint Chiefs' plans vigorously at the White House. The three Secretaries, Byrnes, Patterson, and Forrestal, agreed in principle at their meeting on October 16 that any central intelligence organization should report to them rather than to the President; Donovan's proposal at least was out of the controversy. But Inglis observed on October 18 that whatever Byrnes may have said in the meeting of the Secretaries, McCormack was not keeping the Navy in touch with his planning. Patterson authorized a special committee to study the problem in the War Department under the chairmanship of Robert A. Lovett, Assistant Secretary for Air. We shall examine later the findings of this committee for their influence upon the ultimate development of Central Intelligence. At the moment the Lovett committee was more significant as part of the effort on the part of the Army and Navy to forestall the Bureau of the Budget and the Department of State.

In the next meeting of the Secretaries on November 14, Forrestal asked that they devote their discussion to the proposed Central Intelligence Agency. Byrnes suggested that they endeavor to "integrate and reconcile" the several plans. Patterson had brought Lovett to give his views. Lovett stated that the plan of the Bureau of the Budget appeared to him to fail in three respects: its coordination would be "very loose"; it provided for multiple collecting agencies, which were "bad in clandestine intelligence"; and it treated the problem as though the Secretaries themselves were going to operate the Agency, an impossibility in practice. Lovett advocated the plan of the Joint Chiefs to give the Secretaries authority over a director and an agency under his administration.

Byrnes too did not like the idea of the joint commissions in the Bureau's plan, nor the emphasis upon research and analysis. The scheme seemed to him "too elaborate" and "too big." Without other comment for the record, Byrnes remarked that they all favored a central agency. With Patterson endorsing the suggestion, Byrnes proposed that they have an interdepartmental working committee to get at the problem as quickly as possible before the existing organization disintegrated further. The funds for certain units were available only until the first of January.

The Secretaries agreed to have such a committee. As it was constituted later, its members for the State Department were Donald S. Russell and Alfred McCormack; for the Army, Robert A. Lovett and Brigadier General George Brownell; and for the Navy, Rear Admiral Sidney Souers and Major Matthias Correa, special adviser to Secretary Forrestal. At the close of the meeting on November 14, Secretary Patterson inquired if anyone knew of a good man for the position as Director of Intelligence. Lovett replied that the only name he had heard mentioned was that of Allen Dulles.[17]

Secretary Byrnes's acceptance of a central agency may have been notice to his Assistant Secretary, McCormack, to enter negotiations with the representatives of the Army and Navy upon some basis other than the plan of the Bureau of the Budget. But McCormack did not so interpret the remark of the Secretary of State. When the working committee met on November 19, he insisted that the President's letter of September 20 to Secretary Byrnes directed him to take the lead not only in developing the interdepartmental program for intelligence but also in putting that program into operation. The representatives of the Army and Navy read the President's letter to mean only that the interdepartmental group should formulate plans for the President's approval; he would decide upon the plan to be adopted and the department, agency, or office to put it into operation.[18]

The plan which McCormack would send to the President provided that the Executive Secretary of the coordinating authority over the intelligence services of the department should be named by the Secretary of State and should be an employee in the State Department. Instead of having a central agency made responsible for producing the "national intelligence estimates" for the policymakers of the Government, McCormack would assign that major responsibility to the Estimates Staff in the State Department under the Special Assistant for Research and Intelligence, who was McCormack himself at the time.

The response of the representatives for the Army and Navy was that the Director of the Central Intelligence Agency should be named by the President and should be made responsible to the Secretaries of State, War, Navy, and representatives of the Joint Chiefs of Staff. The Agency would produce the "national intelligence estimates." As neither side would yield, there was nothing to do but ask the Secretaries which concept should prevail.[19]

McCormack gave some ground as he brought his plan for the Department of State to its final form in December. He endeavored to combine the best features in the plan of the Bureau of the Budget with the plan of the Joint Chiefs of Staff. The armed services were to have representatives throughout the proposed central intelligence organization. Leadership and commanding positions within the organization were to be clearly reserved for the Department of State. Upon close examination more can be said for such an arrangement than was accepted then by its critics in the Army and Navy.

If the central intelligence service were to be a really interdepartmental organization rather than the separate entity independent of the departments which Donovan had insisted it should be, all the personnel in the new agency should hold office in one or another of the interested departments. This was the premise upon which McCormack based the structure of his thinking. And within the interdepartmental system the senior department should have the most influential position. This was his interpretation of the letter from President Truman directing Secretary Byrnes to "take the lead in developing a comprehensive and coordinated foreign intelligence program for all Federal agencies concerned with that type of activity." Granted his premise and his interpretation of the President's letter, McCormack had foundation for his kind of a federal system of intelligence.[20]

The real question, however, seems to lie deeper in the maze of departmental privileges and national interests. It is not so much a question of federal union as of integration. But one must not carry the idea too far at this point. It has not yet become a matter of complete fusion in which there are left to the departments no inner recesses of autonomy and decision. We should catch glimpses here of that individual responsibility in a chain of command which Donovan and many following him have advocated for the director of the central intelligence service. We should have in mind also the concept of collective responsibility on the part of the several agencies participating in the services. To this concept many others have adhered. Somewhere between these opposing principles is to be found the ultimate rule for the governance of the national intelligence system.[21]

As he developed his plan for the State Department, McCormack reduced the two coordinating committees from the authoritative position which had been proposed by the Bureau of the Budget. These committees or boards for intelligence and security, both consisting of full-time representatives of those services in their departments, were to have merely advisory capacity.

In the place of two authoritative committees, McCormack accepted on December 3 the single National Intelligence Authority which had been advocated successfully a year before in the meetings of the Joint Intelligence Committee of the Joint Chiefs of Staff. Now, however, McCormack would have the Authority consist of the Secretary of State as chairman and the Secretaries of War and the Navy. Deputies of the rank of Under Secretary or Assistant Secretary might serve with full powers for any member of the Authority. Heads of other departments and agencies might be invited by the Secretary of State to sit in its meetings from time to time. Representatives of the Treasury and the Federal Bureau of Investigation in the Department of Justice would attend to discuss matters of security. McCormack omitted the provision for a representative from the Joint Chiefs of Staff. The Secretaries were adequate to represent the armed services; they would have a two-to-one vote in the proposed Authority. The Department of State should retain the "leadership and final responsibility."[22]

Under the Authority there should be an Executive Secretary appointed by the Secretary of State with the approval of the Secretaries of War and the Navy. If the Executive Secretary were not an official of the State Department at the time of his appointment, McCormack proposed that he should become so before assuming his duties. The intent of this provision cannot be misconstrued.

The executive officer controlling the administration of the central intelligence service was to be an official of the Department of State. Express declaration that the Executive Secretary would be responsible to the Authority as a whole did not alter the fact. While in office he would be so obligated; but if he were to lose the confidence of the Secretary of State, he would not be likely to remain in office as the Executive Secretary of the Authority.

His deputies and members of his staff might come from the Departments of War and the Navy. The personnel might be obtained from other agencies than those represented in the Authority. The administrative services, other than the provisions for pay and personnel, would be furnished by the State Department.

To gain acceptance of his plan, McCormack was willing finally to have the Executive Secretary in the precarious situation of being an employee of the Department of State but removable at the will of the Departments of War and the Navy. He agreed that the Secretary might be dismissed by a two-thirds vote of the Authority. The idea that the Executive Secretary should be subject to the influence of the Secretary of State had lost meaning. And yet the Army and Navy had gained no more than a smashing right of veto. Constructive policies would be hard to obtain from an Executive Secretary so entangled.

Besides the advisory boards for intelligence and security, there were to be lesser coordinating committees. The names of some are indicative of the breadth of services which the McCormack plan for the Department of State comprehended. As in the proposal of 1944 for an Office of Foreign Intelligence within the Department, there should be committees on politics, economics, geography, science and technology, biographical records, military affairs, and other divisions under the National Intelligence Authority.

Throughout the cluster of committees the Department of State was to have the chairmanship in practically every instance except, of course, military intelligence, controlled by the armed services; physical security, where the Federal Bureau of Investigation should have charge; and communications. In the last committee, the chairmanship was to rotate among the Departments of State, War, and the Navy. Again there is no mistaking that McCormack's central intelligence organization, although interdepartmental in many respects, was to be the interest and concern primarily of the Department of State. It was by tradition and function, as the Bureau of the Budget held, the "staff agency of the President" for the making of foreign policy.[23]

To put the best face possible on the McCormack plan, the State Department was to be only first among equals. This was not the way it looked to the Army and the Navy. Their view was comparable to Latin American opinion of Pan-Americanism in the days of James G. Blaine. *Primus inter pares* meant that the North American Secretary of State would make a resounding speech on equality among the nations of the Western Hemisphere and then would settle himself in the chair, to listen perhaps while others talked but to dominate the proceedings.[24]

McCormack accepted from the War Department on December 15 a provision that recommendations for the intelligence program or any operating plan to carry out such a program should be submitted for concurrence or comment by the appropriate advisory board before the recommendation went to the Authority. This was designed to assure the representatives of the Army and Navy, Treasury, or Federal Bureau of Investigation a hearing and to keep the Executive Secretary from overriding their opinions if they should disagree with him.[25]

When a member of the advisory board did not concur, he was to have the right to submit his view to the Authority with the recommendation from the Executive Secretary. If the advisory board were to concur with the Secretary's recommendation, he might initiate action without having to wait for approval by the Authority. How such an arrangement could provide for concerted action and at the same time protect minority rights within the agency was to be debated again and again as the Central Intelligence Group developed into the Central Intelligence Agency.[26]

Although members of the Army and Navy still may not think so, the lamest provision in McCormack's plan was that for strategic intelligence, Donovan's intelligence for "national policy and strategy," what is known today as coordinated national intelligence estimates. McCormack wished to have this production centralized not in the National Intelligence Authority but in the Department of State where some beginnings had already been made. He proposed that the State Department's estimates staff should include working representatives of the Army and Navy. His presumption seems to have been that the flow of raw materials to such a processing staff would be steady and complete.

The Research and Analysis Branch, now in the Department of State, might render its services effectively and supply the basic intelligence which its strategic surveys had provided in the days of the Office of Strategic Services. But the presumption did not have support from the experiences of the Office of Strategic Services with the reception of military and naval intelligence. It took more than a request to obtain for a civilian intelligence staff "complete and free interchange of information" with the armed services. It still does. Nor did McCormack make adequate provision for supplying the Special Estimates Staff with the secret intelligence from abroad that is so vital to national estimates.[27]

Toward the end of the discussion of his plan, McCormack conceded that there should be a director of operations under the Executive Secretary. This director would handle secret intelligence and security matters, if the Authority should decide that such hidden operations could be performed more effectively by a centralized organization than by the departments. Personnel, funds, and facilities should be provided by the departments in amounts and proportions accepted by them and approved by the Authority, and based upon relative responsibilities and capacities.

How such complicated decisions would be reached with dispatch and what the Executive Secretary would do if the Director of Operations, who seemingly would be semi-autonomous, should take exception in specific instances to the Secretary's general planning, were questions that were not explained in McCormack's proposal. In fairness to him, one must say that he had no chance to elaborate upon his idea regarding the Director of Operations. The Secretaries of State, War, and the Navy reached agreement at that time to ask the President to put the plan of the Joint Chiefs of

Staff into effect, practically as it had been revised in September pending the liquidation of the Office of Strategic Services.[28]

McCormack stated that the system which he proposed for the production of national estimates did not preclude similar operations in the Authority. It would have mechanisms, he said, which could lead to centralizing such activities in the many fields. This might happen either by vesting responsibility for a particular field in a single agency or by bringing together the working units of several agencies in a joint organization under the direction of the Authority. In the meantime, the Special Estimates Staff of the Department of State could take care of the needs of the policymakers. He was certain that the Staff met the urgency of the moment.[29]

It would seem in retrospect, however, that McCormack's plan amounted to hindrance and delay in establishing the "service of strategic information" which Donovan had proposed in his first memorandum on June 10, 1941, and which had been accepted by many others as the ultimate objective of a central and coordinated intelligence service. The Joint Chiefs of Staff had not favored Donovan's scheme as a whole, but they had recognized with him that the time was at hand. There must be no further delay in providing strategic intelligence from every possible source for the guidance of those who made national policy.[30]

ANTICIPATIONS IN THE ARMED SERVICES

Secretary Forrestal of the Navy had appointed Ferdinand Eberstadt in June to make a special study of the proposed merger of the War and Navy Departments. The Eberstadt report, published on October 22, 1945, held that the national security would not be improved by unifying the Army and Navy under a single head. One civilian secretary could not administer successfully the huge and complex structure which would result from such a merger. Longing for the "one-man decision" minimized the benefits to be had from "parallel, competitive, and sometimes conflicting efforts." A unified military structure in other countries had accomplished the "subordination of civilian to military life—to their own and other nations' grief."

Certainly this was not to be desired in the United States. On the other hand, neither was a system of competitive and conflicting efforts which did not respond to new conditions rising out of war. Experience and knowledge were inadequate for the "increased international commitments," both political and military, which were being assumed under the charter of the United Nations, the Act of Chapultapec for inter-American defense, and military occupation of Germany and Japan in widely separated parts of the world. Nor was it any easier to forecast the "repercussions on world peace" from the scientific discoveries and advances in engineering during the war.

The Eberstadt report called for the organization of the military forces into "three coordinate departments"—Army, Navy, Air—and their close association with the Department of State in a National Security Council. There should be established also a Central Intelligence Agency to supply the "authoritative information on conditions and developments in the outside world." Without it, the National Security Council could not "fulfil its role" nor the military services "perform their duty to the Nation."[31]

Mr. Eberstadt had named Captain Souers of the Navy a committee of one to write the section of the report on military intelligence. As Assistant Director of Naval Intelligence in charge of plans, Captain Souers had helped in the work of the Joint Intelligence Committee of the Joint Chiefs of Staff and had attended the meeting on December 22, 1944, when the "services" and "civilian" plans had been debated. Since then he had been actively interested with General Magruder of the Office of Strategic Services, and others in both Army and Navy, who wished to establish a permanent central intelligence system. Souers opposed the Donovan plan because he felt that the Director of Central Intelligence should serve not only the President but also the members of his Cabinet who were responsible for the national security. Now, as the Eberstadt report appeared in the fall of 1945, Souers was opposing the McCormack plan because it would put the intelligence system under the domination of a single department.[32]

Captain Souers's chapter in the Eberstadt report passed rapidly over the nature, organization, and handling of intelligence in the United States before the war, the British system, the career of the Coordinator of Information, and the Office of Strategic Services. He concentrated upon the efforts of the Army and the Navy as they endeavored to combine their intelligence services and obtain "coordinated" and "synthesized" intelligence for the use of the Joint Staff Planners of the Joint Chiefs of Staff.

The Joint Intelligence Committee had been formed for that purpose. It was able through its subcommittees, he said, to coordinate requests for industrial intelligence, technical information, topographical studies, the joint Army–Navy intelligence studies, files of incoming reports and documents pertaining to German equipment, hostile trends, and other matters of interest to the Chiefs of Staff. Souers commended the Joint Intelligence Collection Agencies for their procurement of information in the field and their distribution of intelligence to Theater Commanders and the Joint Intelligence Agency Reception Center in Washington, where it was "reevaluated, synthesized, and transmitted" to the Joint Staff Planners, interested agencies, and the departments.[33]

Thus, the whole field of strategic intelligence had become a collaborative effort embracing the Office of Naval Intelligence, Military Intelligence Services, Assistant Chiefs of Air Staff (Intelligence), the Weather Service Division of the Army Air Forces, the United States Army, the Office of Chief of Engineers, Office of the Surgeon General, the Coast and Geodetic Survey, Hydrographic Office, Joint Meteorological Committee, Board of Geographical Names, and the Office of Strategic Services. No doubt they were all embraced, but Souers would agree that even under the stimulus of war the interchange of information among them had been neither free nor complete.

Upon the return to peace, such collaboration as there had been in collecting and distributing military intelligence would practically cease to exist. Moreover, Souers would concede that strategic intelligence involves more than military and naval information. None of the agencies which he named, with the possible exception of the Board of Geographical Names in the Department of the Interior, can be called civilian in the sense that the Department of State is instantly understood. The Department of State was significantly absent from the list. And, in this discussion of strategic intelligence, Souers did not mention the Research and Analysis Branch of the Office of Strategic Services.

Strategic intelligence requires knowledge of economic, social, and political forces within the structure of a nation that are not so readily ascertainable in swift reconnaissance as in deliberate research. For that very reason, the Joint Intelligence Committee of the Joint Chiefs of Staff, as Souers remarked, could not be considered a permanent organization. It might be reorganized to include permanent representation of all agencies which were concerned with intelligence, both military and civilian. If it were so organized, it would cease to be merely the instrument of the Joint Chiefs of Staff.[34]

The complete merger of the intelligence services of the State, War, and Navy Departments was no more feasible to Captain Souers than consolidation of the departments themselves into one. Each of them had need of intelligence operations peculiar to itself and exclusive of interference by any other department. The inevitable conclusions therefore were that each department should maintain its own intelligence service and that each should participate in the joint undertaking of a central intelligence organization. This should coordinate all intelligence relating to national security, maintain activities of common concern which should not be reduplicated in the departments, and synthesize departmental intelligence "on the strategic and national policy level."[35]

Souers recommended that there be established a Central Intelligence Agency and urged that courses of instruction be given "at appropriate levels of military education in order to indoctrinate officers with the importance of the function of intelligence to our national security." There was need. The experiences of General Grow in 1952 indicated that there still was need.[36]

Souers did not argue in the Eberstadt report for the establishment of the Secretaries of the departments as a National Intelligence Authority above the Agency and the Director of Central Intelligence. But here was the battleground at the end of October 1945 between the armed services and the civilian agencies concerned with the "comprehensive and coordinated foreign intelligence program" which President Truman had instructed Secretary Byrnes and his interdepartmental committee to devise. We should keep in mind that Secretaries Patterson and Forrestal had sent the plan of the Joint Chiefs of Staff to Secretary Byrnes on September 29. Byrnes had accepted the concept of the Authority in the meeting of the three Secretaries on October 16.[37]

Secretary Patterson, engaged in considering various proposals to unify the armed forces and to create new instruments of defense, appointed a committee of representative officers to examine the problem of intelligence in the War Department and to determine the kind of central intelligence organization which the Department should advocate. There was involved in this question the disposition of the personnel, facilities, and assets of OSS which had been assigned to the War Department by the President's order of September 20, 1945. Patterson sent a memorandum to the President on October 22 to report that the functions of OSS, chiefly clandestine activities, had been kept separate in the Strategic Services Unit of the War Department as the "nucleus of a possible central intelligence service" which might result from the study under the leadership of the Secretary of State. Patterson's memorandum, prepared in SSU, called attention to the fact that a decision must be reached at once in regard to its "future disposition" as the funds available for it would not last beyond December 31. He recommended that Congress be asked to approve continuance of the clandestine activities of SSU for the balance of the fiscal year 1946.[38]

The committee appointed on the same day under the chairmanship of Robert A. Lovett, Assistant Secretary of War for Air, gathered testimony by means of a questionnaire and written reports within the War Department. There were formal interviews with persons specially qualified to speak upon the subject of intelligence. Among these were Major General Clayton Bissell, Assistant Chief of Staff, G-2; William H. Jackson, who had reported upon the British system; and Kingman Douglass, who had been representative of the Army Air Forces at the Air Ministry in London; Lieutenant General Stanley D. Embick, member of the Joint Strategic Survey Committee; David K. E. Bruce, who had been prominent in OSS; and Alfred McCormack from the State Department.

The Lovett Committee invited the Director of Naval Intelligence and Mr. Hoover of the Federal Bureau of Intelligence to express their views and make recommendations. Both declined to appear. Why they did so was not explained. The committee had to report without benefit from their presence, but their views must have been known. Hoover was on record, with the Navy at least, as opposed to a national system of intelligence. Commodore Inglis was working for the Navy against the Bureau of the Budget and its plan for the Department of State.[39]

The record of the testimony before the Lovett Committee, unfortunately, was not in the archives of the Agency when this account was written. Intermediaries for the Agency did not obtain the papers in the War Department. But the opinions of some who appeared before the committee can be fairly surmised. It would be interesting to read General Bissell's remarks on Central Intelligence but unnecessary to do so in order to state here that he was hostile. It is likely that General Embick expressed again what he thought when the Joint Strategic Survey Committee made its report to the Joint Chiefs of Staff, on January 18, 1945, and the Joint Chiefs repeated on September 19 with regard to the Donovan plan. Mr. McCormack's thoughts and purposes could not have been much different from those he was asserting at the time in his effort to place the central intelligence service in the Department of State. William H. Jackson gave his ideas on November 14 to Secretary Forrestal.[40]

In view of Jackson's participation in the Intelligence Survey Group of the National Security Council in 1948 and his subsequent role as Deputy Director of Central Intelligence under General Walter B. Smith, it is proper to examine at some length his proposals in the fall of 1945. His reports in the previous spring to Generals Donovan and Bradley on the British system of coordinating intelligence doubtless influenced his views, said Jackson, but he would recommend a substantially different system for "achieving coordination of intelligence functions" in the American Government.

Like many others that fall, Jackson started his argument with the atomic bomb. The new weapon would not relieve the United States of the need for armed forces. On the contrary, they would have to be kept in first-class condition. The bomb made necessary even greater effort to obtain "informed and reliable estimates" on the capabilities of potential enemies. The military services, therefore, should retain and improve their intelligence organizations, but not as independent and isolated agencies.

There must be a "comprehensive and integrated" system of intelligence. If the "lessons of Pearl Harbor" were not proof of the urgent necessity for the coordination of the departmental intelligence activities, the use of atomic energy and the threat of scientific discoveries to come "must now supply that proof beyond shadow of doubt."

Upon these assumptions, Jackson set his case for "imposing intelligence responsibilities on the military services within the scope of their missions" and for "compelling the coordination of intelligence functions under one national intelligence system." The ideas of imposition and compulsion should not escape our notice. It was the fall of 1945 when the coercive mood of war was still prevailing among thoughtful men, although the public seemed bent upon relaxing to the point of weakness. Congress was about to investigate the disaster of Pearl Harbor to make sure that it should not happen again. The intent with regard to the national system of intelligence, whatever form it might take, was to establish it permanently with the sanction of law. When we come again to Jackson's ideas regarding the coordination of intelligence functions and activities in the summer of 1948, we shall find the international situation quite as tense. We shall not find him advocating coercion so much as leadership in the central agency and cooperation on the part of the departmental services.[41]

Jackson recommended in the fall of 1945 that the authority over the "integrated intelligence system revolving around a central intelligence agency" should be vested in the Department of Defense if it were created; or in the National Security Council if the proposal in the Eberstadt report to Forrestal were adopted; or, if the military organization remained as it was, in the Secretaries of State, War, Navy, and the Assistant Secretary of War for Air, at the moment Robert A. Lovett. This, one need only mention, was not Donovan's plan. Moreover, Jackson would move the Director of the Central Intelligence Agency farther down the scale of responsibility than the Joint Chiefs of Staff proposed.

The "active direction" of Jackson's central intelligence organization in 1945 would be in a "Directorate of Intelligence" consisting of the chiefs of intelligence in the Army, Navy, Air Forces, a representative of the State Department, and, when their interests in national security were involved, other departments such as the Treasury and the Department of Justice, which of course included the Federal Bureau of Investigation. Under the "general supervision" of this governing board of departmental intelligence officers, the Director of the Central Intelligence Agency would manage the services of "common usefulness" and, under direction from above, maintain the coordination of the national system in its "four aspects": collection of information, evaluation and collation of that information, centralization of common services, and production of "general estimates of a broad strategic nature." Although Jackson could not get completely away from Donovan's principles, Jackson's Director of Central Intelligence was reduced to an office manager. The Director's only initiative was that of suggestion to the Directorate.

Jackson would not have the central agency supersede or interfere with the machinery of the departmental services for collecting information. He would in fact not allow the central agency to engage in clandestine collection. That, with foreign counterintelligence, should be reserved to the Department of State. Officers of the Army, Navy, and Air Forces should be assigned to work with the State Department in secret intelligence. Interception by radio should be given to the central agency, and it might do its own collection "above-cover" in the fields of economic and scientific intelligence. It will be found later, however, that the State Department objected to interference by the central intelligence organization in those fields of collection.[42]

In the "aspects" of evaluation and collation and of "general estimates of a broad strategic nature," Jackson sought working arrangements that would ensure close articulation of the departmental services and the central agency, each performing its proper function. The intelligence service of the Air Forces, for example, would evaluate and collate information directly related to the enemy's capabilities in the air. But there would be a "free flow of the collated material" to other services concerned and to the central agency where a staff of qualified military and civilian personnel would "assemble and draft" the general estimates of a strategic nature. If a department disagreed with an estimate in whole or in part, there should be the right of dissent, even after full discussion in the "Directorate" composed of the departmental chiefs of intelligence. Thus, Jackson anticipated the issue between individual and collective responsibility for the coordinated national intelligence estimates of the Agency.[43]

In the meantime, the Lovett Committee completed its investigation and submitted a report on November 3. General Magruder had made a notable contribution from his experience in OSS, his thinking upon central intelligence in theory and in practice, and his responsibility in the War Department as Director of the Strategic Services Unit. His first memorandum went to Lovett on October 20. In it Magruder restated the principles of the Donovan plan with which he himself had been actively concerned in the preceding fall and winter. But Magruder set aside one principle which Donovan would not yield. Magruder accepted the concept of authority in the plan of the Joint Chiefs of Staff.[44]

There should be a national intelligence organization under a Director responsible to the Secretaries of State, War, and the Navy as a group. This central agency should serve as the instrument of all parts of the Government concerned with national security or foreign policy. It should coordinate the intelligence activities of the departments for them. It should be the central agency for comprehensive analysis and synthesis of information concerning foreign countries. All of the departments and other agencies of the Government therefore should be required to deposit their pertinent information with the central organization and to do so promptly upon its request. But this requirement was not to interfere with their own departmental intelligence services. It was designed to accomplish the pooling of their product for the benefit of the policymakers. The central agency should be the national instrument for procuring foreign intelligence by clandestine means, both espionage and counterespionage. Collection by overt means should continue to be the function of the State Department, the military and naval attachés, and other agencies. The central agency should not engage in clandestine collection within the United States. It should have no police power. By this time Magruder must have been able to repeat the points by heart. But he did not speak of an independent budget in this memorandum.[45]

Within a week General Magruder made an extensive report at the request of Secretary Lovett. Magruder's mastery of the subject ranged from the record of the Office of Strategic Services, its achievements and its shortcomings, through the existing functions of the Strategic Services Unit, to recommendations for the future that were comprehensive and definitive. The situation was acute, he said, in view of the fact that the United States had taken a pivotal position in world affairs. The Government could no longer afford to rely on information obtained from other countries. It could not depend upon "haphazard contributions" from its own departmental services. It must have intelligence available from every source with the least possible delay and in the form most likely to be of service to the makers of national policy.

There must be a central intelligence organization. Every safeguard was required to keep it from becoming the instrument of policy of a single department. The central agency itself must be completely denied any policymaking function in order that its objectivity might be preserved; otherwise it might "succumb to the inevitable temptation to tailor its reports" to support a policy in which it had an interest. There are those who fear that the temptation still exists despite all efforts to submerge particular interest in the national security.[46]

Only a separate agency, said Magruder, solely concerned with intelligence matters could be successfully made the repository of powers and functions delegated to it by the interested departments. It was apparent that the War Department would hesitate to rely upon a branch of the

State Department for clandestine intelligence of a military nature. He might have said, too, that the Department of State would be skeptical with regard to any diplomatic, social, economic, or similar information purveyed to it by a division of the War Department.

By tradition and esprit de corps the departments are mutually and reciprocally aloof. Cooperation was an ideal much professed, less often practiced. The difficulty was going to be to get them all to share, and share alike, in respect for and confidence in the Central Intelligence Agency as their common servant. This would be even more arduous if it should happen that the agency were to have superiority over any one or all of the departments in a particular area of thought or action.

General Magruder proposed such an exclusive jurisdiction. From past experience he argued that the agency of the future must have sole responsibility for the procurement of foreign intelligence by clandestine means. It was an operation so highly professional that it should be undertaken only by experts. The problem of placing and maintaining agents in foreign countries with proper safeguards both for them and for the information which they obtained was so complex that it had to be centralized in a separate unit acting for the United States Government.

The professional hazards were so great that no country could afford to increase them by allowing uncoordinated operations in various agencies. Moreover, clandestine operations involved constant breaking of rules. To put it broadly, he said, such operations were necessarily extra-legal and sometimes illegal. The departments, whether War, Navy, or State, could not afford to house such extraordinary operations. Clandestine intelligence should be assigned to a separate and central instrument of government not only because its service was common to all of the departments but because the operations should on occasion be unknown to them. William H. Jackson did not weigh these arguments in his proposal that secret collection should be the function of the State Department.[47]

In what might be considered a lecture to fellow officers of the Army, General Magruder proposed that the central intelligence agency should be vested with authority to require cooperation by the departments in making available the products of their intelligence activities. Experience has demonstrated that cooperation did not occur "on a voluntary level." Real or imagined reasons of security, pride of ownership, and simple interdepartmental jealousy, he said, interfered with effective accumulation and use of the materials necessary for strategic intelligence.

Taking up the problem of comprehensive analysis and synthesis, the production of national estimates, still a much disputed subject, General Magruder used the American assembly line for illustration. The intelligence system, he said, resembled a costly group of factories, "each manufacturing component parts" without an assembly line to turn out the finished article. He was right about the cost. The illustration was good, but it was incomplete. He did not mean to imply that the process was purely mechanical.[48]

The synthesis of ideas does something more to the component parts than join them according to an engineer's drawing. Whatever the state of affairs in mathematics, in the synthesis of ideas the whole can be different from the sum of the parts. The endeavor to fuse them may produce something quite unexpected. Other forces may have come to bear upon one or more of the parts after the fact-finding for the synthesis has begun. There are emotional disturbances among nations but vaguely understood even by the experts in mob psychology. There are elusive factors and imponderables in the process of estimating. Political considerations scarcely relevant to the facts of the case have entered into the construction of estimates upon the capabilities and intentions of other countries, more particularly into dissents from the estimates of the Agency. The "Oriental mind" is not the only one with inscrutable ways.[49]

General Magruder stressed that the central agency must concentrate upon foreign intelligence and stay out of the business of clandestine procurement within the United States. There must be no ground upon which the Agency could be used as a political tool by the party in power. For the same reason, the central intelligence organization should have no police power. Secret intelligence and police together make possible a "Gestapo."[50]

The proposed central intelligence agency should have an independent budget even though it were under the authority of the Secretaries and committed to services of common concern to the departments. The costs of intelligence were high; no money value could be assigned to its accomplishments. Clandestine intelligence required secret accounting; the publication of salary lists would jeopardize the success and safety of operations. The budget of the agency should be considered by Congress without detailed inquiry into the expenditures.

Magruder closed his report to Lovett on October 26 with suggestions showing how the intelligence services in the War Department might continue to function "with perfect freedom" in their own fields where the military men were experts and the civilians were laymen. The Strategic Services Unit should be maintaind as it was, until definite decision had been reached in regard to a central intelligence agency. If there should be no agency, then SSU should revert to the control of the Assistant Chief of Staff, G-2, and should operate as a unit under his jurisdiction. But Magruder believed that integration of its personnel and activities into the Military Intelligence Service would neutralize the peculiar assets of SSU and "minimize its effectiveness."[51]

On October 31 Magruder compressed his views into two recommendations for Secretary Patterson. The Strategic Services Unit, if retained in the War Department under G-2, should include all other clandestine activities controlled by that office. The War Department, however, should favor the establishment of a central intelligence service including the activities of SSU along the lines of the plan advocated by the Joint Chiefs of Staff. There should be one exception. The new agency should have an independent budget as the Joint Intelligence Committee had proposed.[52]

After general condemnation of the uncoordinated efforts at clandestine intelligence and counterespionage during the war, but with some appreciation of OSS as well as of G-2, the report of the Lovett Committee came to specific points. There were jealousy and mistrust among the intelligence services of the Government and between a "surprising number of officers and civilians" engaged in those activities. The lack of trained and experienced officers in both military services contributed to the unsatisfactory situation. No serious effort had been made to treat intelligence as a career. There must be a national intelligence organization, "competent and alert to the extreme of possibility," manned by permanent personnel of the highest caliber, trained as specialists in the components of modern intelligence. To this end there evidently had to be an approach different from that of departmental units, once engaged in uncoordinated activity, now in "haphazard demobilization."[53]

The Lovett Committee unanimously concluded that its views were more nearly in agreement with the proposal of the Joint Chiefs of Staff than with the Donovan plan or other suggestions which had been offered. The committee therefore recommended the creation of a National Intelligence Authority over a Central Intelligence Agency. The Director of the Agency should be responsible to the Authority and sit as a nonvoting member in its meetings. To ensure continuity, the Director should be appointed for a term of at least six years.

The committee developed the idea in the plan of the Joint Chiefs of Staff that the Director should consult with the departmental chiefs of intelligence. The Intelligence Advisory Board should consider all important questions, and the Director should obtain its opinion before delivering estimates to the President or any member of the Cabinet. If there were differences of opinion between the Director and members of the Board, his decision should be controlling and their opinions should accompany his report. McCormack was willing to include this provision in his plan for the State Department.[54]

The Lovett Committee modified the plan of the Joint Chiefs further by proposing, as General Magruder wished, that the new agency should be the sole collecting agency in the fields of foreign espionage and counterespionage. The third change of the Lovett Committee was also suggested by General Magruder. The new agency should have an independent budget, and its appropriations should be granted by Congress without public hearings, even though it were necessary to obtain additional legislation.

Then Lovett appeared before Secretaries Byrnes, Patterson, and Forrestal in their meeting on November 14. Lovett gave them a summary of the report from his committee and spoke particularly of its conception of the "reading panel," the Intelligence Advisory Board in its capacity as an estimating body. Besides the military intelligence services, the principal civilian agencies should be represented. Lovett especially included the FBI because it had the "best personality file in the world." He added for the interest of the Secretaries that the FBI was expert in producing false documents, an art which "we developed so successfully during the war and at which we became outstandingly adept."[55]

Lovett emphasized that the Intelligence Board would be expected to study and evaluate facts, not to shape policy. The reports of the Board would represent the combined views of its members. Dissident views would be included. The failure of the German Intelligence Service to allow presentation of dissenting opinions, he believed, was largely responsible for its breakdown. The British Service was superior; its organization permitted the divorce of factual findings from political creed. Even the Italian system was better than the German. The four ranking German Intelligence Officers had been executed for political reasons. The result was that German intelligence authorities were "afraid to interpret facts" contrary to Nazi policy. That was why the Germans had failed to anticipate the American landings in North Africa. The advantage in the system which he proposed lay in the fact, he said, that conclusions would be reached not by one man but by a board; it would avoid "the danger of having a single slanted view guide our policies." Thus, Robert Lovett joined in advocating collective responsibility for national intelligence estimates with William H. Jackson, who was writing to Secretary Forrestal on the same day.[56]

THE PRESIDENT'S DECISION

When McCormack accepted the National Intelligence Authority provided in the plan of the Joint Chiefs of Staff, representatives of the Army and Navy realized that they could lose their grip upon the negotiations unless they countered with some other issue. McCormack was carrying out Secretary Byrnes's instructions that he should "resolve the issues" with the Secretaries of War and the Navy. McCormack himself became an issue. It was not that he refused to listen to particular objections, although the impression lingers that he was high-handed. He might have gained more if he had been less imperious. It was because he intended to dominate for the Department of State in the organization of the central intelligence service. Critics within the Department took exception to his insisting upon a separate office for intelligence and research which he would direct. It was over the latter question that he resigned from the Department of State on April 23, 1946.[57]

General Magruder expressed the opinion of the military men with his accustomed poise and candor. There was "general agreement" in the Army and Navy about "the urgency of doing something as quickly as possible," but they felt that the McCormack plan was "inadequate and administratively unsound." It placed "undue weight in the State Department." Magruder's sense of humor came also into play. Just a few months before there had been only "scattered voices crying in the wilderness." His, we will recall, was one of them. Now "many, many people" were urging the necessity of a central intelligence agency and adopting "the slogan as a new and original cause." The Congressional investigation of "Pearl Harbor" was having an evident effect upon public opinion.[58]

Admiral Souers brought an influential voice into the military and naval chorus. He prepared the first draft of a memorandum from Admiral Nimitz to the Secretary of the Navy. The Fleet Admiral did not favor the State Department's plan; the proposal of the Joint Chiefs of Staff was "more likely to assure sound national intelligence" and to prove "more satisfactory to the Navy." The idea of central intelligence was pleasing now to Nimitz, who had not cared much for OSS during the war. The product of the new Agency would reflect the best judgment of the experts from all of the participating departments; it would not be dominated by any one of them. He recommended that the President should select the Director from the Army, the Navy, or the Marine Corps.[59]

The reasons given for the choice of the Director from the armed services were these: a nonpolitical administration would thus be ensured and its intelligence estimates would be unbiased and objective; the Director would be subject to military discipline, continuing after his retirement; he could be required to avoid publicity. Besides, the plan of the State Department was objectionable because the Secretaries of War and the Navy might not be informed of the intelligence furnished the President by the State Department. There was more to the memorandum, but these statements should be enough, without debating their merits, to show that Souers and Nimitz, with Leahy and others, were parties to the plan that the Department of State should not take over where the Office of Strategic Services had left off.[60]

Admiral Souers feared at one time that the Army might desert the Navy and accept terms with the State Department. An elaborate arrangement was in the making to incorporate much of the Joint Chief's plan for a central organization with the McCormack plan and to provide for assignment of an Army or Navy officer to the State Department in case the President should select him to be the chief executive. Army men were talking of reservations which might be made if the McCormack plan were accepted. At the request of President Truman, Souers submitted a memorandum on December 27, 1945, stating his objections to the McCormack plan and explaining why he thought that the interests of the President would be better protected under the plan of the Joint Chiefs of Staff.[61]

Souers objected to McCormack's plan because it did not give the Army and Navy equal access to the President with the State Department. The evaluation of information was not an exact science, he said, and so every safeguard should be imposed to keep any one department from having the opportunity to interpret information to support "previously accepted policies or preconceived opinions." McCormack had indicated in interviews that he did not favor a central agency.

The plan of the Joint Chiefs, on the other hand, placed the National Intelligence Authority on a higher level than any department. The President would appoint an outstanding man of ability and integrity to be Director. Through pooling of expert personnel in the Central Intelligence Agency there would be more efficiency and economy. There would be summaries and estimates approved by all of the participating agencies for those who needed them most: the President himself, his Cabinet, and the Joint Planners. Finally, the plan of the Joint Chiefs contemplated "a full partnership" among the three departments and operation of the Central Intelligence Agency "on a reciprocal basis." The suggestion fitted neatly into the recommendations of the Eberstadt Committee for reorganization of the Army, Navy, Air Force, and their closer association with the State Department in a National Security Council.

Admiral Souers ended his memorandum for the President, to his own amusement when he read it again in the spring of 1952, with the declaration that he was not a candidate for the job of Director "and couldn't accept even if it were offered" to him. It was offered, and he did accept it for six months, until he could construct the new organization and obtain his successor as Director of Central Intelligence.[62]

The representatives of the Army and Navy were not obliged to press upon McCormack their formal rejection of his plan. Admiral Souers, personal friend of the President, and Admiral Leahy, his Chief of Staff, favored the interdepartmental plan of the Joint Chiefs. There is no reason to suppose that President Truman himself did not prefer an arrangement which promised to bring all of the departments more effectively together in a common enterprise. In any case, though the full story may not yet be known, Secretary Forrestal of the Navy waited upon the Secretary of State as Brynes momentarily returned to Washington from Moscow before setting out again for the meeting of the United Nations Assembly in London, and more wrangling with the Russians.

The tale still going the rounds is that Forrestal said to Byrnes: "Jimmy, we like you but we don't like your plan. Just think what might happen if another William Jennings Bryan were to succeed you in the State Department." With Under Secretary Royall acting for Patterson, the Secretaries met in the Shoreham Hotel on Sunday, January 6, 1946, and agreed upon the plan of the Joint Chiefs of Staff. They omitted the provision for a representative of the Joint Chiefs of Staff in the National Intelligence Authority.[63]

In the conference at the White House attended by Samuel Rosenman (Special Counsel to the President), Admiral Leahy, Commodore Vardaman (Naval Aide to the President), and Admiral Souers on January 9, Director Smith of the Bureau of the Budget still argued for the plan of the State Department. But President Truman said at the end of the conference that the proposal of the Secretaries was what he wanted, and he asked that representatives of the Bureau of the Budget and of the Department of Justice, together with Admiral Souers, now to become the first Director of Central Intelligence, should make such changes in the directive as were necessary to conform with legal and budgetary requirements.

Comparison of the proposal by the Secretaries and the President's Directive as finally issued on January 22, 1946, revealed interesting differences. The fourth member of the National Intelligence Authority was restored, but instead of attending for the Joint Chiefs of Staff he was to be the "personal representative" of the President. This was designed to place on the board of authority Admiral Leahy, President Truman's Chief of Staff. This had been proposed the previous year in the plan of the Joint Intelligence Committee.[64]

The provision conformed in some degree with General Donovan's original concept that the central intelligence organization should be connected with the Executive Office of the President. The head of the new intelligence organization would have immediate access, if not to the President himself, to his "personal representative" in the National Intelligence Authority. The Director would not have to approach the President through the Secretaries of the departments. It seemed a fair working compromise of the opposing principles of "coordination" and of "chain of command."⁶⁵

The wording of the President's Directive did not make the unity of the proposed national intelligence system so evident as had the plan of the Joint Chiefs of Staff. The new agency of the Authority was named the Central Intelligence Group and described as consisting of persons assigned from the respective department by the three Secretaries. These persons were "collectively" to form the Group. It was an assemblage, not a unified institution. They were to be under the Director of Central Intelligence. He was not one of them. The point is so obvious that its significance can be easily overlooked. The Director was to be designated by the President and held responsible to the National Intelligence Authority. He would sit in its meetings as a nonvoting member.

The last provision did not have the meaning which at first glance it may seem to convey—that the Director was to be a mere servant of the National Intelligence Authority, to hear but not to have a voice in its deliberations. The Authority was, of course, integral; it was to operate by unanimous opinion. Although this was not specifically slated, it was thoroughly understood. There could hardly be a split decision that was binding against the expressed views of the President's "personal representative" on the board.

It is generally held that the change of the name for the new central intelligence organization from Agency to Group was made because the word "Group" would have to suffice pending an Act of Congress to place the new organization on a statutory basis. There were legal connotations to the word "Agency" which, according to the Bureau of the Budget, made its use impossible until such legislation had been obtained. In the light of recurrent controversy and friction, however, one would suspect that the collective concept then had more adherents within the Group than the idea of its unity.

The head of the new organization, on the other hand, was not Director of the Central Intelligence Group. He was entitled Director of Central Intelligence. The designation has been explained as being necessary merely because the unit was not to be called an agency. The explanation is not so significant as the latent meaning within the title. The very phrase, Director of Central Intelligence, neither qualified nor confined to a particular institution, is heavy with connotations of power and responsibility in the whole field of central intelligence beyond that institution.⁶⁶

There were stipulations within the President's Directive to support this view. Although subject to the existing law and to the direction and control of the National Intelligence Authority, the Director of Central Intelligence was to have duties and functions which in themselves expressed power as well as responsibility. He should plan for coordinating the activities of the intelligence agencies in the three departments. To the extent approved by the Authority, he could inspect the operations of the departmental intelligence agencies in connection with his planning. He should recommend to the National Intelligence Authority the establishment of policies and objectives of the "national intelligence mission." He should accomplish the correlation and evaluation of intelligence for strategic and national policy and its dissemination within the Government. And, in doing this, he was to have full use of the staff and facilities of the intelligence agencies in the three departments. He should perform such other functions and duties related to intelligence as the President and the National Intelligence Authority directed from time to time.

All of these duties and functions, though controlled by the President and the National Intelligence Authority, gave to the Director of Central Intelligence more than mere administrative control over the Central Intelligence Group. Whether or not he would be successful in exercising that superior power beyond the Group remained to be seen in the first days of the new national intelligence system.

The Director of Central Intelligence had also to perform services of common concern for the benefit of the intelligence agencies of the departments, where those services could be performed more efficiently by the central organization. This decision was to be made by the National Intelligence Authority. The Presidential Directive explicitly reserved to the intelligence services of the departments their right to collect, evaluate, correlate, and disseminate their own departmental intelligence.

There was significantly omitted the stipulation that the Director of Central Intelligence should perform the service of directly procuring intelligence. This the Joint Chiefs' plan had included as a service of "common concern." General Magruder had argued cogently that secret collection of intelligence abroad should be the exclusive function of the central intelligence organization. Why then should the provision have been omitted from the President's Directive? To include it would have revealed to the public no secrets of method, source, or content. The wording was so mild that it could have stirred little opposition at home among those who detest spies. Certainly no foreign government would be deceived by the omission. A fairer inference seems to be that the advocates of the Central Intelligence Group were anxious to get the new system established and at work.

The exclusive right to collect secret intelligence was one issue which could be set aside for the time while the Director and the Group undertook to coordinate the intelligence activities of the departments and to provide the first correlated summaries and estimates, current and strategic intelligence, for the makers of policy. Magruder, Lovett, and others wished to place the clandestine activities of SSU in the new central intelligence organization. William H. Jackson was one who thought then that secret intelligence and counterespionage should be functions of the State Department; he considered the possibility with Allen W. Dulles again in the spring of 1948. Members of G-2 and the Military Intelligence Services, doubtless others in the Office of Naval Intelligence, and J. Edgar Hoover of the FBI were opposed to giving the Central Intelligence Group the exclusive right to collect secret intelligence abroad. They did not wish to be denied the right to continue acquiring secretly whatever they wished to find for themselves. It would take time to settle the issue. It was not finally settled in 1953. Experienced observers in the military services and the Agency think that it never will be settled in terms that give the sole and exclusive right of collecting secret intelligence overseas to the Central Intelligence Agency.[67]

The President's Directive of January 22, 1946, retained the provision of the Joint Chiefs of Staff for an Intelligence Agency Board which should include the heads (or their representatives) of the principal military and civilian intelligence agencies of the Government, as determined by the National Intelligence Authority. This Board should give advice to the Director of Central Intelligence, obviously in the interest of the various intelligence agencies which its members represented. We should note that there was no statement, nor even implication, that the Director could not act unless he had the consent of the Advisory Board. Neither should one forget General Donovan's troubles with representatives from other agencies. His successors were bound to have similar experiences.

General Magruder's surmise in May that the Federal Bureau of Investigation might cease to be a factor was wishful and wrong. The plan of Attorneys General Biddle and Clark to make the FBI the center of the national intelligence system did not materialize. But the President's Directive of January 27, 1946, under the eye of the Department of Justice, took care to stipulate that, in addition to the denial of police and law-enforcing power to the Central Intelligence Group, there should be a provision against interfering with "internal security functions." Moreover, the Directive stated that nothing in it could be construed to authorize the Central Intelligence Group to make investigations within the continental limits of the United States and its possessions except as provided by law and the directives of the President. The Federal Bureau of Investigation was entrenched in control of security intelligence within the United States.[68]

Anyone who still thought that the Government intended to set up an American Gestapo should by this time have given up his fears. But those who were to put the Central Intelligence Group to work with the Federal

Bureau of Investigation were on their way to trouble. Distinctions between secret intelligence or espionage and security intelligence or counterespionage are easy to make upon paper. They are difficult to maintain in practice. The two functions interlace. They are dependent upon each other. To divide them arbitrarily according to geographical areas and assign them to separate administrations ignored the fact that the exercise of one without careful association with the other was likely to jeopardize the secrecy of both. Admiral Souers and succeeding Directors of Central Intelligence were to have a merry time with J. Edgar Hoover of the FBI.

Introduction to Chapter III

Souers as DCI recognized the latent power in his position, yet also was aware of the continued resistance to the Central Intelligence Group in various departments and the lack of Congressional authorization for it. Thus, Souers pursued a relatively conciliatory style of leadership. He believed in the principle of collective input to form the CIG.

Souers intended to organize ad hoc committees to study specific issues, yet he found it difficult to acquire personnel from the departments and often could not get the people he wanted. Supervisors tended not to recommend the best men for the job, as such a transfer would be a loss to their own department. In addition, the individual departmental intelligence services were not inclined to give up their intelligence information in peacetime any more than they were in wartime.

There was another type of information that the departments would not release to the CIG: information concerning U.S. military and diplomatic plans. Secretary of State James Byrnes in particular was reluctant to brief the CIG on foreign policy matters. The lack of such information created difficulties in knowing what kinds of intelligence U.S. officials needed and also made it difficult to put intelligence into context. To some degree, the intelligence community still has difficulty acquiring access to such information. CIA analysts, for example, are sometimes unaware of the latest U.S. arms control proposals (admittedly, less so during routine negotiations than when top U.S. leaders make personal overtures to their foreign counterparts), and they rarely are allowed access to U.S. military operational planning.

Souers assigned responsibility for coordinating departmental intelligence to the CIG's Central Planning Staff. In addition to assessing U.S. intelligence capabilities and requirements and assisting the DCI in disposing of assorted intelligence organizations left over from the war, the Central Planning Staff was also given the task of arranging and coordinating interdepartmental studies.

Alas, the CIG lacked the resources for its task, or even the ability to draw on resources from the State Department and military services, and so it was not surprising that it soon began to falter. One notable study that came to be known as the Defense Project illustrated the problem. The Defense Project was initially proposed as a response to rising Cold War tensions and was supposed to produce high quality intelligence on Soviet capabilities as rapidly as possible. Initially proposed in March 1946, this study was not ready for publication until March 1948 and was not actually complete until early 1949. Even on such a critical task the CIG was unable to carry out its mission effectively.

Meanwhile, U.S. officials had to decide what to do about a remaining legacy of the OSS, the Strategic Services Unit (SSU). The National Intelligence Authority had taken over the personnel and assets of the SSU (remnants of OSS special operations and espionage organizations) in April 1946 until its liquidation. This liquidation was to be completed by June 30, 1946. John Magruder, who had been appointed director of the unit, wanted to keep at least parts of the SSU and put them under the DCI's control, as he believed that it had developed valuable liaison relationships with foreign intelligence services and intelligence sources. Others were not so sure, saying that liaison activities could best be conducted through diplomatic channels and that many of the OSS's sources had been compromised.

Souers established an interdepartmental committee to study the issue. The committee recommended that the Unit should be "pruned and rebuilt," but retained and operated as part of the CIG. The remnants of the SSU eventually became the CIA's Office of Special Operations.

Today liaison activities with foreign intelligence services remain controversial. Most foreign intelligence agencies do not have strict oversight requirements and guidelines for conduct such as those under which the CIA operates. Also, the need to conceal U.S. relationships with foreign intelligence services has sometimes been given as a reason to withhold information from Congressional oversight committees. Even so, almost no one today questions in principle the legitimacy of the CIA in maintaining such relationships; the fact that the CIG had to compete for this turf reflects the tenuous position it held at the time.

Souers served as DCI for only six months. In his outgoing message to his successor, he pointed out the need to overcome the problem of acquiring personnel, particularly qualified personnel, from the various departments to staff the CIG. He also noted that increased and independent funding was necessary and recommended Congressional legislation to legitimize the Group and grant it funding. Lieutenant General Hoyt Vandenberg of the U.S. Army Air Forces took over as DCI in June 1946. According to Darling, Vandenberg immediately went on the offensive to give the CIG the power it needed to fulfill its mission.

III

THE CENTRAL INTELLIGENCE GROUP: BEGINNINGS UNDER SOUERS

A SMALL BODY OF EXPERTS

The first Director of Central Intelligence was well aware of the latent power in the President's Directive. Admiral Souers wished to see the duties and responsibilities of the Director mature under the guidance of the Secretaries and the personal representative of the President in the National Intelligence Authority. But Souers also knew that many in the Army, the Navy, and the Department of State were still resisting every thought of a central intelligence organization which might overpower their own intelligence agencies. High officials, though accepting the Authority, the Director, and the Group, were doubtful of them because there was no supporting legislation by Congress. They rested only upon a directive by the President to the Secretaries of State, War, and the Navy. It might even be said that the President's power to establish the central intelligence organization was a power in time of war which would expire with the return of peace. Souers appreciated that it was no time to foster misgiving or animosity. No obstacle should lie in the way of Congress as it approached the reorganization of the national military establishment in which the central intelligence system would have a part.[1]

Admiral Souers's immediate end in view was to get the Central Intelligence Group established and in operation as a small body of experts drawn proportionately from the departments and serving them under their supervision and control in the National Intelligence Authority. The power of the Director of Central Intelligence inherent in his duties and responsibilities should wait until later for adequate and proper development. Souers did not accept Donovan's principle that the Director of Central Intelligence should be independent of the Secretaries, equal if not superior to them, and responsible directly to the President. Souers believed that such independence would not place the Director close to the President; it would tend in fact to isolate the Director from the President. The Director would discover that a great part of the time he and his agency would be shut off from the President by the interests and representations of the departments. Through their prestige and functions they were likely to have greater power—at least of obstruction. Sabotage in government, even of a President's directives, has been suspect before this.

As a practical matter, in politics and the science of government, such an extraordinary officer as the Director of Central Intelligence needed the company of other officials. On occasion he might find their opposition almost as useful as their assent. His position might become clearer and stronger, at least it would command attention, because it had to be formally opposed. An independent Director of eminence and exceptional force might reach the President regardless of isolation and sabotage. But even such a Director would have to keep everlastingly at it, and he would always have a hidden war on his hands. The time for a Director of Central Intelligence with those attributes and traits was not at the start of the new organization in February 1946. It might not survive the impact.

It was Admiral Souers's nature to remove issues rather than to create them. He did not seek a fight for the fight's sake. But neither did he choose diplomacy with no end in view. Like Eberstadt, he did not care for the "one-man decision" at the expense of benefits which might be obtained from "parallel, competitive, and sometimes conflicting efforts." He read the President's Directive explicitly; he himself had shared in writing it. The persons assigned from the departments were "collectively" to form the Central Intelligence Group. The draft on February 4 of the first directive to himself from the National Intelligence Authority therefore declared that the Group should be organized and operated as "a cooperative interdepartmental activity." There should be in it "adequate and equitable participation" by the State, War, and Navy Departments and by other agencies as approved by the Authority. The Army Air Forces should have representation on the same basis as that of the Army and Navy. There was likely to be a Department of Air.[2]

Those in the Bureau of the Budget and the Department of Justice who watched legalities were not satisfied with the President's Directive. The draft of an executive order, approved by the Acting Attorney General, J. Howard McGrath, was ready in February to replace the Directive. The view of the National Intelligence Authority was that no impediment so far had been encountered in carrying out the President's Directive. But there was no objection to having an executive order as well, if its effect were to "confirm and formalize" the status of the Authority as a "cooperative interdepartmental activity, rather than a new or independent agency requiring legislation for its existence."[3]

Further discussion and study of the question continued through the spring. By May 23 all parties appear to have been satisfied that the President's Directive had legal standing without an executive order. The order was returned to the Attorney General's Office, and the issue closed. Until superseded the following year by the Central Intelligence Agency, established by Act of Congress, the Central Intelligence Group rested upon the President's authority under the Constitution, with no particular reference to his war power.[4]

To satisfy President Truman's wish that the Central Intelligence Group should bring all intelligence activities into cooperation and harmony, Admiral Souers planned to have the composition of the Intelligence Advisory Board flexible. Its membership should depend upon the matter under discussion in each instance. In addition to the four permanent members, the chief intelligence officers from the Departments of State, War, Navy, and the Air Forces, the first directive of the Authority therefore stipulated that the Board should include representatives from other agencies of the Government at the Director's invitation. This gave room for the Federal Bureau of Investigation to have a representative present if the Central Intelligence Group were to take up questions of internal security and other matters in which the Bureau had an interest, such as the collection of intelligence in Latin America.[5]

Having the same purpose in mind, Admiral Souers preferred in the beginning to name ad hoc committees to study and report on specific problems. They would represent the permanent departmental members of the Intelligence Advisory Board, with a chairman drawn from the Group to act as "coordinator" of their particular interests. In theory this procedure promised cooperation and harmony, if at all possible. The practical difficulty of obtaining the representatives from the departments to man the ad hoc committees and to accomplish their work in time was discouraging. Souers soon turned to his Central Planning Staff for the work.[6]

MEN AND DIRECTIVES

It was going to be none too easy to apportion all appointments among the departments and secure at the same time persons both competent and inclined to enter the central intelligence service. But Admiral Souers did not find it hard to allot key positions. Kingman Douglass, who had been a representative of the Air Force at the Air Ministry in London and knew much about the British system, became Assistant Director and Acting Deputy Director. Souers appointed Colonel Louis J. Fortier Assistant Director and Acting Chief of Operational Services. He had served on the Joint Intelligence Staff for the Army. Captain William B. Goggins came from experience with intelligence in the Navy to head the Central Planning Staff.

Souers obtained James S. Lay, Jr., from the State Department to be Secretary of the Authority and of the Intelligence Advisory Board. Lay had been Secretary to the Joint Intelligence Committee of the Joint Chiefs of Staff. Ludwell L. Montague also came from the State Department to head the Central Reports Staff. He had been Secretary of the Joint Army–Navy Intelligence Committee in the fall of 1941, then Secretary of the Joint Intelligence Committee of the Joint Chiefs of Staff and a senior member of its Joint Intelligence Staff for the Army throughout the war. Both Lay and Montague had participated in the discussions which had contributed so much, with Donovan's "principles" and Magruder's thinking, to the eventual formulation of the President's Directive. They had been chosen by McCormack for his organization of the central intelligence system under the State Department. Both were expert in the work which the new Central Intelligence Group was to undertake, qualified to aid Souers immediately, as they did, in writing the directives of the National Intelligence Authority. The Group had begun to take form on January 25.[7]

The draft of the first directive to Souers in February followed the general design of the President's Directive of January 22. But there was one clause in the draft so filled with past controversy and so indicative of more to come that it deserves examination in detail. It did not appear in the directive as finally adopted by the National Intelligence Authority.

Article 7 of the draft submitted by Admiral Souers stipulated that the Director of Central Intelligence should have "all necessary facilities, intelligence, and information in the possession of our respective departments, including necessary information as to policies, plans, actions, capabilities, and intentions of the United States with reference to foreign countries." At Souers's own suggestion, the clause concerning the capabilities and intentions of the United States was stricken from the draft in the first meeting of the Authority on February 5, 1946. There were no comments in the minutes. Why it was omitted was left to conjecture. But one can reconstruct the event with some assurance.

The provision had been included at the start, it is very likely, because the drafters appreciated that knowledge of this nation's own capabilities is essential to considering what its enemy may do. At the first intimation, however, that the specific statement regarding capabilities and intentions might stir resistance in the armed services over their right to withhold "operational" matters, Admiral Souers preferred to remove the statement with no argument. The beginning of the Group was precarious enough without inviting trouble that could be postponed. For much the same reason doubtless, Souers did not use his right to inspect the operations of the departmental intelligence services.[8]

It is easy to presume that those who had been so reluctant to allow the Office of Strategic Services and its Research and Analysis Branch to have access to "intercepts" were no more willing now to supply the new Director of Central Intelligence with knowledge of the capabilities and intentions of this country. According to Admiral Souers, however, the Army and the Navy both understood that he was entitled by the President's Directive to have all intelligence in their possession. From their point of view, he said, information about "policies, plans, actions, capabilities, and intentions of the United States" was not intelligence. In their thinking, the concept of intelligence had to do only with information about foreign countries; it did not include knowledge of domestic concerns. The new Central Intelligence Group was expected to purvey its intelligence to the departments. The reverse was not entirely true. They did not believe that they had to deliver to the Central Intelligence Group every sort of information about themselves, least of all "operational" information.[9]

It still seems to be the particular reservation of the Army and Navy that they are not obliged to reveal their capabilities and intentions to the estimators in the Central Intelligence Agency. Policies, plans, and intentions are certainly to be distinguished from capabilities. What one intends to do is different from what one can do. It is as true, however, that if a person tells what he is able to do, he may disclose his purpose. The Army and Navy are not readily disposed to separate their capabilities from their intentions. Critics have also said that they are prone to confuse the capability of an enemy with his intention.

Close examination of the clause in article 7 of the first directive to Admiral Souers, even as it was put in final form by the National Intelligence Authority, nevertheless reveals that the Authority gave to the Director of Central Intelligence the right to have "as required in the performance" of his authorized mission, "all necessary facilities, intelligence, and information" in the possession of the departments. This distinguished "intelligence" and "information." But the word "all" cannot be misconstrued: it is comprehensive. It applies to both "intelligence" and "information."

Article 7, moreover, is to be read with article 2 of the directive in its final form. Article 2 stated that the Central Intelligence Group was to "furnish strategic and national policy intelligence to the President and the State, War, and Navy Departments." The Group was also to furnish such intelligence, as appropriate, to the State–War–Navy Coordinating Committee, the Joint Chiefs of Staff, and other governmental departments and agencies having "strategic and policy functions related to the national security."[10]

Knowledge of the nation's own "capabilities" enters into the intelligence which is necessary to determine the policy for maintaining the nation's security. One may argue that the information withheld by the armed services from the estimating board of the central intelligence organization goes to the policymakers at the highest level. The answer is that if this practice is allowed, the national estimates which the policymakers request from the estimating board fall short. Those estimates cannot approximate the definiteness which the policymakers have a right to expect. The requirement of an effective national estimate is that it shall be compounded from all facts to be had in every available source.[11]

Article 3 of the first directive to Souers also pertained to "strategic and national policy intelligence." It stipulated that "all recommendations" should be referred to the Intelligence Advisory Board "for concurrence of comment" prior to submission to the Authority. If a member of the Board did not concur, the Director was to submit "the basis for his nonconcurrence" together with his own recommendation. If the Board approved the Director's recommendation unanimously, he might put it into effect without action by the Authority. The Lovett Committee had proposed such a procedure for national estimates to safeguard the interests of the departmental intelligence services as they came under the coordinating power of the central intelligence organization. William H. Jackson's letter to Secretary Forrestal contained a similar provision.

It was essential that the makers of national policy should know the several interpretations of the facts in the board of correlation and appraisal, if those views had substance and relation to the facts. The procedure was to become established practice in estimating. But before then the stipulation in article 3 that "all recommendations" of the Director should be referred to the Intelligence Advisory Board was to be the center of controversy between the Director and the Board over the administration of the Group and its successor, the Central Intelligence Agency. The chiefs of departmental intelligence endeavored to make themselves the governing board of the "cooperative interdepartmental activity." If they had their wish, it was not to be an "independent agency."[12]

Secretary Byrnes, just returned from London, presided over the first meeting of the National Intelligence Authority on February 5, 1946. Byrnes wished to make it clear at once that the Department of State was responsible for reporting to the President on matters of foreign policy. The idea had been clear since the founding of the department in the organic legislation of 1789. Moreover, throughout the discussion of the proposed central intelligence organization, it had been reiterated that the organization should not make policy. But Secretary Byrnes would reserve for the Department of State what the President himself had designated as an immediate service to be performed by the new Central Intelligence Group expressly for him. Instead of the piles of cables, dispatches, and reports on his desk, President Truman wanted a daily summary that was comprehensive. He wished to be rid of the mass of papers, and yet to be certain that nothing significant had been left out.

Admiral Souers endeavored to reassure Secretary Byrnes that the President expected the Director of Central Intelligence only to have the cables and dispatches digested; there was no intention that the information should be interpreted to advise the President on matters of foreign policy. The Secretary nevertheless pressed the point that it was his function to supply the President with information upon which to base conclusions. Admiral Leahy entered the discussion as the personal representative of the President; information from all three departments, said Leahy, should be summarized in order to keep the President currently informed. Byrnes replied that Admiral Souers would not be representing the viewpoint of any one department; any man assigned to the Group from a department would be responsible to Admiral Souers.

Where this left Souers at the moment is anybody's guess. Somehow he was expected to avoid a dilemma. He was not to interfere with the prerogative of the State Department and yet he was to combine its information with the information of the other departments and provide President Truman with a "single summary."[13]

Secretary Byrnes felt so strongly about the matter that he appealed to the President personally on behalf of the Department of State. According to the recollection of Admiral Souers, the argument ran along the line that such information was not intelligence within the jurisdiction of the Central Intelligence Group and the Director. President Truman conceded that it might not be generally considered intelligence, but it was information which he needed and therefore it was intelligence to him. The result was agreement that the daily summaries should be "factual statements." The Department of State prepared its own digest, and so the President had two summaries on his desk. At least they were better than the pile of cables, dispatches, and reports which had confronted him.[14]

COORDINATION—THE DEFENSE PROJECT

The Central Planning Staff was to be sensitive to the interests of all the departments. It should assist the Director in preparing recommendations with regard to policies and objectives for the whole "national intelligence mission." This was the statement in the second directive of the National Intelligence Authority on February 8 with the concurrence of the Intelligence Advisory Board. And for this purpose Admiral Souers advised Captain Goggins on March 4 that, "as a general rule, the Central Planning Staff should take the active leadership in arranging and conducting interdepartmental studies." There was no inference, however, that in doing so the Staff might use the Director's right of inspection.[15]

One of its members should participate and act as coordinator in all meetings concerning foreign intelligence related to the national security. A representative of the Federal Bureau of Investigation was standing by, of course, to take part in proceedings as a member of the Intelligence Advisory Board, if not of the particular committee, whenever the interests of his Bureau, foreign or domestic, seemed to be involved. As the use of ad hoc interdepartmental committees proved difficult, the Central Planning Staff was soon loaded with orders for investigation and report upon a variety of subjects that were intricate and sweeping.

Besides having a hand in the business of the executive order which was prepared but not used to confirm the President's Directive, the Central Planning Staff undertook on March 21, 1946, at Souers's direction to make a broad survey of all clandestine collection of foreign intelligence by agencies in the Government. This followed the intensive study of the Strategic Services Unit by the ad hoc committee which we shall consider in a moment.[16]

On March 28 the Central Planning Staff received instruction to put its Information Branch to work upon a survey of the coverage of the foreign language press in the United States. The next day the Information Branch was assigned also an interim survey of the collection of intelligence in China. On April 20 the Intelligence Branch of the Planning Staff was directed to examine the problem of the Joint Intelligence Study Publishing Board and to determine whether there should be any change in its supervision and control; the Publishing Board was then under the Joint Intelligence Committee of the Joint Chiefs of Staff.[17]

The Central Planning Staff inherited a share with the State Department in the study of the Foreign Broadcast Intelligence Service which the Federal Communications Commission had once conducted to monitor foreign news and propaganda. As the Service was being liquidated by the Commission, the facilities were taken over by the War Department on December 30, 1945, for the remainder of the fiscal year. The War Department wished to have the monitoring service placed somewhere in the new central intelligence organization. Some said that this eagerness sprang from a desire to be rid of expense and personnel. Those who remembered the difficulties with the collection of intelligence during the war could readily agree that the monitoring of foreign broadcasts was manifestly one service of "common concern." It might well be operated by a central office for the Departments of State, War, the Navy, the Air Forces, and other agencies interested in its product.[18]

But Souers was not eager to expand the administrative services of the Central Intelligence Group. His ad hoc committee of March 5, 1946, reported and he recommended on April 26 that the War Department should continue to operate the service with a new organization; this meant personnel which had been thoroughly screened for security. The War Department demurred, on May 8, on the ground that the State Department was the chief user of this "predominately nonmilitary intelligence function." The matter was discussed the next day by the Intelligence Advisory Board.[19]

It was at this point that members of the Central Planning Staff were directed to consult with representatives of the Assistant Chief of Staff (G-2) and the Special Assistant to the Secretary of State. The result was that the latter, now William L. Langer in place of Alfred McCormack, agreed on behalf of the Department of State that it should support the budget of the Foreign Broadcast Intelligence Service. The War Department should continue its operation, at least during the fiscal year 1947. For the time being this was the working arrangement. Eventually the opinion prevailed that the Central Intelligence Group should take over the whole function of monitoring foreign propaganda and broadcasts for all departments and agencies concerned with the national security.[20]

The Central Planning Staff meantime had been assigned other tasks.

Its Information Branch was directed on May 31 to make an informal survey of the intelligence available in the United States from colleges, foundations, libraries, individuals, business concerns, and sources other than those of the Government. On June 4 the Information Branch received instructions to study the exploitation of American businesses with connections abroad which might produce foreign intelligence. On June 6 the Support Branch was told to look into the problems of psychological warfare. And on June 7 the Central Planning Staff was called upon to make an interim survey of the adequacy of the intelligence facilities related to the national security. This was to be a preliminary to a conclusive study on the coordination of all agencies under the National Intelligence Authority.[21]

The Central Planning Staff set for itself a chore of tremendous possibilities. It was the elaboration of a "complete framework of a system of interdepartmental intelligence coordination" to be contained in a series of studies for the Director of Central Intelligence. They would include the essential elements of information in a national system, the coordination of counterintelligence and security, intelligence research, the collection of information by means of a coordinating board, a scientific committee, and other interagency committees upon military, economic, political, and geographical matters.[22]

The files of these papers are still available should anybody care to read them. They give the impression that the Central Planning Staff did a considerable amount of work for the Director of Central Intelligence. There is evidence also of much talk on paper, with multiple copies. There are references, annexes, and addenda in great plenty; forms, routing sheets, lists of appurtenances to the trade that seem inconsequential; even a space survey for the Central Reports Staff. One cannot care much whether there were more or less than ninety square feet per person, large and small, in the rooms to be allotted to the Reports Staff. One is more interested, as was the Reports Staff, in the decision of the Planning Staff that it should not approve the plan of the Chief of the Reports Staff for reorganizing his office. This was bound to create other business perhaps not contemplated but to be expected in the beginning.[23]

As he put his Central Planning Staff together, Admiral Souers received an overture promising interdepartmental cooperation immediately and in a most significant enterprise. Colonel J. R. Lovell of the Military Intelligence Service proposed on March 4 that it sponsor a plan for producing "the highest possible quality of intelligence on the USSR in the shortest possible time." The intelligence services of the Army, Navy, Air Forces, and State Department should have equal representation in the planning and working committees of this endeavor, soon to be known as the Defense Project. It should be under the coordination of the Central Intelligence Group. Admiral Souers accepted the offer at once.[24]

According to an observer of the event, the Central Intelligence Group was then a "vast reservoir of good will" toward all kinds of interagency projects. We should note also that this was the spring of 1946. The exchange of accusations in the Council of Foreign Ministers was becoming more and more angry as the time approached for the peace conference of twenty-one nations at Paris to make terms for Italy, Germany, and Austria, Finland, Hungary, Bulgaria, and Rumania. Iran's case against Russia was before the Security Council of the United Nations in New York. Tito was noisy over Trieste. Franco in Spain was jeopardizing amicable relations with the Soviet Union, France, and Britain. General Marshall had returned from China to report that the situation in Manchuria was critical. On March 5 Winston Churchill made his historic address in Fulton, Missouri, and challenged the Soviet statesmen to raise their Iron Curtain.[25]

There should be no surprise that exceptional men had forebodings and sought to learn everything about the Soviet Union in the shortest possible time. It was tragic that so few persons in Washington could use the Russian language well enough to begin to accomplish the purpose of the Defense Project.[26]

The Planning Committee had met twice by March 11 and drawn up a proposal. The Central Intelligence Group should take over active sponsorship as soon as it could obtain the necessary personnel for the work; in the meantime, it would furnish only a coordinator. As the agreement reached final form on May 9 in a directive of the Central Intelligence Group, unanimously approved by the Intelligence Advisory Board, the Planning Committee should have its own chairman and secretary. The coordinator from the Group should meet with the Committee when appropriate. But his function would be primarily to secure the assistance of the Group with problems before the representatives of the Army, Navy, Air Forces, and State Department. In case of disagreement within the Committee, the Coordinator would submit the question to the Director of Central Intelligence for decision. Thus, the task of coordinating if not reconciling opinions would pass on to the head of the new central intelligence organization. The responsibility, however, was more fearsome in prospect than in fact. It would be some time before there could be any great decisions possible. The evidence had first to be accumulated.[27]

It was the Working Committee, under the chairmanship of the secretary of the Planning Committee with the coordinator from the Central Intelligence Group acting in advisory capacity, that had the first and most important job. It was to compile a veritable encyclopedia of "all types of *factual* strategic intelligence on the USSR." This Strategic Intelligence

Digest was to be distributed to the member agencies and the Central Intelligence Group. From it they would prepare Strategic Intelligence Estimates as required to meet their own needs, and when requested by the Director of Central Intelligence. Whenever "the national interest" required it, the Central Intelligence Group too could prepare estimates from the Strategic Intelligence Digest. But such estimates, apparently, could be used or ignored by the member agencies as they were inclined.

There was no attempt here to establish a single national intelligence estimate which should govern the thinking on the subject by all agencies concerned. The Defense Project was essentially to find and to arrange the facts systematically. This alone would be something of a triumph, if successful. Members of the Army, Navy, and the State Department had talked often of cooperating in the common cause of intelligence, and accomplished little.[28]

The Central Reports Staff of the Group was too small at that time to undertake this extraordinary project. The departments were not supplying the personnel which they were supposed to provide. But the inadequacy of the Reports Staff is not the sole explanation why this plan to accumulate a great body of intelligence upon the Soviet Union and to produce estimates from it for the policymakers was not then assigned to the estimating staff of the Group. The plan originated in the Military Intelligence Service. Its advocates looked to the Group for editorial assistants on the Working Committee as well as a coordinator. But the military men considered the project primarily their own affair. The Group had still to establish its right to means of its own for procuring and processing the raw materials of intelligence. Its central facilities had yet to become so useful to the departments that their intelligence officers would rely upon the Group for services of "common concern."[29]

The first task of the Working Committee on the Defense Project was to review the papers of the Joint Intelligence Staff of the Joint Chiefs of Staff concerning the Soviet Union. This took a couple of months. By June 4, however, an outline had been made and allocations planned. The use of task forces, or interdepartmental committees, was rejected on grounds of security; an agency's files would have to be opened to those who were not under its control. Instead, the work was assigned by subject to particular agencies. For example, the Military Intelligence Service was charged at first with preparing certain economic and political data. Later the plan was revised so that the greater portion of the political material was allotted to the State Department. But it had as much trouble as the Army in producing the desired information.

Colonel Lovell's original hopes were disappointed. The Project could not be finished by September. It was far from complete in December when work stopped, pending the decision of an interdepartmental committee upon a program of National Intelligence Surveys to take the place of the Joint Army–Navy Intelligence Studies. This program changed the policy of the Central Intelligence Group toward the Defense Project; it had ceased to be merely a question of coordination. Though the most important, it would be only one of several surveys to be produced by the Group. When resumed in April 1947, the Project was still an interdepartmental activity, but it was no longer centered in the Pentagon as a major interest of the Military Intelligence Service.[30]

The official date of publication for the Strategic Intelligence Digest was March 1, 1948. But it was nearer the beginning of 1949 before all three bulky volumes were complete. In the opinion of the representative from the Central Intelligence Group who took over the chairmanship of the Working Committee in April 1947, the delays and shortcomings of the agencies engaged in the Defense Project had been largely responsible for putting the Central Intelligence Group into the business of economic and political research.[31]

REPORTS AND ESTIMATES

By direction of the National Intelligence Authority on February 8, a Central Reports Staff was to assist the Director in correlating and evaluating intelligence related to the national security and in disseminating within the Government the resultant "strategic and national policy intelligence." Admiral Souers followed the directive with an administrative order on March 4. The Staff, of course, had already gone to work during February and had produced the first daily summary for the President. There were in what was then called the Current Section seventeen persons apportioned among the Departments of State, War, and the Navy. They were established in the Pentagon under Mr. Montague, with the expectation that they would be joined shortly by other persons assigned from the Departments to form the Estimates Section or Branch.

The purpose from the start was to have the Central Intelligence Group take over the major function of producing the strategic estimates for the formulation of national policy as Donovan had proposed. But it was not yet decided that the Group should have a division comparable to the old Research and Analysis Branch of the Office of Strategic Services. There was doubt that the Group ought to engage in initial research. Many believed that it would do well to remain a small and compact body which should receive from the several departmental agencies the materials of intelligence and produce from them the "strategic and national policy intelligence" for the policymakers. The Department of State was still uncertain whether or not it should continue its office of Research and Intelligence as Mr. McCormack expected to have it. He wanted to retain there the function of making intelligence estimates for the policymakers of the Government. Events, however, were to determine otherwise.[32]

Now on March 4 Admiral Souers's administrative order, prepared by Montague, elaborated the organization and functions of the Central Reports Staff within the Central Intelligence Group. It should have a chief who would be responsible to the Director of Central Intelligence for the preparation, substance, and dissemination of all intelligence reports produced by the Group in accordance with the President's Directive of January 22 and the directives of the National Intelligence Authority. The first task of this chief and his staff was to be the daily summary which President Truman so much desired. There was also in this administrative order a provision of great interest. The ideas which it embodied are still valid for the production of national intelligence estimates.[33]

As Montague wished to have the Staff constructed at that time, there should be four Assistants delegated to him as Chief by the permanent members of the Intelligence Advisory Board. The distinction from other persons in the Central Reports Staff was to be that these four Assistants should not be responsible to the Director of Central Intelligence; they should be assigned to the members of the Intelligence Advisory Board and held responsible to them, although serving full-time with the Chief of the Central Reports Staff. The purpose was to have the Assistants represent in the Staff the interests of their respective departments, through their superiors on the Intelligence Advisory Board, and also to represent the Central Reports Staff in its relations with those agencies. Montague had acquired these ideas from his experiences as representative of the Army on the "Senior Team" of the Joint Intelligence Staff.[34]

Serving with the Chief of the Reports Staff on full time, the Assistants would aid him in formulating directives to the subdivisions of the Reports Staff. They would share in drafting requests from the intelligence agencies of the departments. They would review all summaries, estimates, and studies which were prepared by the subdivisions of the Reports Staff, and they would make the recommendations for the appropriate dissemination of such papers. With the Chief of the Reports Staff, the Assistants were to effect such reconciliation of conflicting departmental estimates as could be obtained.

If they could not remove disagreement and reach unanimous concurrence, the responsibility would rest upon the Chief. He would determine in accordance with the weight of the evidence and opinion the position to be taken in the report. This would be the estimate of the Central Intelligence Group. Substantial dissents would be submitted to the National Intelligence Authority with the estimate of the Group, as provided in the first directive of the Authority. But they would clearly be opinions in dissent from the official estimate of the Group.

Thus, Souers and Montague hoped to establish a panel of intelligence experts drawn from the departments who would continue to understand and represent the interests of those departments, but at the same time through their continuous work in the Reports Staff would become experts, too, in the business of central intelligence and the production of national estimates. The benefits to accrue from the continuity and momentum which might be gained from such an estimating board were left unknown. The ideas were put on paper but were not tested. Difficulties in obtaining personnel and in meeting other more immediate and pressing duties of the new Central Intelligence Group prevented the establishment of such a board within the Reports Staff. The system has yet to be fully tried.[35]

Within a month of its formal activation, the Central Reports Staff entered another phase of its development. Montague proposed on April 1 a revision of the administrative order to make possible two things. First, experience with the allotment of personnel by the Departments of State, War, and the Navy demonstrated that there should be more flexibility within the proportion agreed among the departments. The right persons for particular positions were not to be had from the departments according to any ratio previously established. The difficulty grew worse with the necessity of apportioning within each grade. Navy captains, Army colonels, and civilian P-8s were not equally available in number or competence. The principle of proportion should be maintained, but deviation from it permitted so long as there was no substantial change in the budgetary obligation of the departments. This was in fact accepted practice in the Civil Service.[36]

We should note at this point the predicament of the whole Central Intelligence Group with respect to personnel. The Secretaries had been directed by the President to assign persons to the Group. The assumption was, of course, that they would supply the Group with able persons as soon as possible. To make the general statement that they minimized the obligation is doubtless to do injustice in some cases, perhaps many. A reading of correspondence upon this matter in the spring of 1946, and conversations with some who were present and responsible for recruitment at the time, lead to the conclusion that there were many recommendations for office in the Central Intelligence Group which were not bona fide nominations.

Some persons concerned were not really available because they were headed toward more important positions in their own services and could not remain long in the Central Intelligence Group if they came at all. Six months was often the limit. Or they appeared on the lists of suggestions for the Group because they had become surplus—good fellows, fine friends, nice to have around, but with no future in the service to which they had given so much of their lives. The name of the best man available was often left off the list even though he himself might be willing, even glad of the chance, to take office in the Central Intelligence Group.[37]

It was neither easy nor desirable to select the personnel of the new staffs, branches, and sections of the Group from such lists. Admiral Souers and his successor, General Vandenberg, were not able to do much about solving the problem so long as they were obliged to request personnel from the departments and hope for the best. Whether or not they minimized their responsibility, the departments failed to provide adequate personnel for the Central Intelligence Group. Why General Vandenberg sought an independent budget and the right to hire and fire his own personnel is clear.[38]

The second change in the Central Reports Staff was intended to provide it with specially qualified persons as it set up its Estimates Branch. Further development along functional lines might become desirable, but more immediate was the necessity for enlargement according to geographical regions. Montague did not wish to construct the Estimates Branch itself on geographical divisions. Supporting services were necessary. The plan was to have five sections of that nature: Western Europe–Africa, Eastern Europe–USSR, Middle East–India, Far East–Pacific, and Western Hemisphere. The persons in each section were to be closely apportioned with regard to their grades and their departments.

Such a geographical arrangement was dictated by the facts of world affairs. It would seem as though there could have been little exception taken. Although some deviation in numbers and grades had to be made from the authorization in the second directive of the National Intelligence Authority, the net result in expenditure was likely to be an actual reduction of the budget. Nevertheless, it was over this proposed reorganization of the Central Reports Staff that there occurred within the Group one of those more amusing, and trying, disturbances from which administrators in governmental agencies might profit if they would.[39]

The Central Planning Staff took exception in the Council of the Group to so "basic" a change in the Central Reports Staff. It "should not be acted upon without detailed study." This, of course, it had received from its own Chief and, through his representations, from the Director of Central Intelligence, too. The matter was referred, however, to the Central Planning Staff for review. While the Chief of the Reports Staff waited, the Deputy Chief of the Planning Staff directed its Policy and Review Board to study the situation. Montague was ready to proceed by April 3; Nicholas set his deadline for the ninth. On April 12 the officer in the Planning Staff delegated to examine Montague's plan for enlarging the Reports Staff called him by telephone in the evening to find out what it was that should be investigated.

But under the dateline of that same day a memorandum went from the Chief of the Planning Staff to the Director of Central Intelligence. The memorandum stated that, pursuant to instructions, the plan for the Reports Staff had been reviewed by the Planning Staff and had not been approved. Several reasons were given. For one, the plan meant an influx of personnel, subject to no scheme of organization. Montague's plan had a scheme of organization; it might not have proved a good scheme, but it was a scheme. For another reason, "no clear necessity for the paper" was seen. This must have been the case—in the Planning Staff.

For a third reason, "any handicaps due to rigidity" under the original administrative order of March 4 could be obviated by instructions to the Chief of the Reports Staff authorizing "such flexibility of assignment and use of personnel" as he deemed necessary. It would, of course, maintain "the functions outlined in paragraphs 4 to 6, inclusive," of the original administrative order. This was more authority than Montague had sought. After so great a concession with regard to interpreting the administrative order, it would seem odd that the Chief of the Planning Staff should object to revising the order itself. But so it was.

Montague put into the record on April 16 a memorandum that was deflating. Admiral Souers had approved the recommendations in the Council's meeting on April 2 and had decided that Montague should draft a revision of the administrative order. The draft had been referred to the Central Planning Staff for review, with respect not to the merits of the Director's decision but to the question whether Montague had expressed that decision adequately. The report of the Planning Staff came so late, and yet so close to the telephone call from its officer, there could be no pretense that the report was based on "inquiry into the realities of the subject or upon profound study." Constructive advice regarding the organization and operation of the Reports Staff would be welcome, but this was "more hindrance than help in an already difficult situation."[40]

Montague recommended that the Central Planning Staff be discharged from further consideration of the proposal; henceforth, except when issues of major policy were involved, it should be kept out of matters concerning the internal administration of coordinate subdivisions of the Central Intelligence Group. The Council unanimously agreed on April 18 and recommended that Admiral Souers approve the ruling that the chiefs of the component parts of the Central Intelligence Group should be responsible for the organization and administration of their respective subdivisions as they deemed necessary and appropriate. And then Montague's plan for the Central Reports Staff was approved.[41]

THE COUNCIL

The Council of the Central Intelligence Group had been in operation for some time. Colonel Fortier proposed to Admiral Souers on March 15 that the three Assistant Directors and Acting Deputy should meet daily. As the four senior officials under the Director of Central Intelligence, they might participate in supervising general plans, the policies, studies, and output of the Group. The idea suited Admiral Souers's purposes exactly. Such a Council could discuss problems presented to it by the Secretary; it could be empowered to make definite recommendations. Or it could sit as a body of special consideration in case the Director were to seek advice. And finally it could keep in touch with what was happening within the organization to overcome some of the looseness which a "cooperative interdepartmental activity" was very likely to have.

At the first meeting on March 18, with Mr. Douglass in the chair, Colonel Fortier, Mr. Montague, Colonel Nicholas representing Captain Goggins, and Mr. Lay, Secretary, discussed the functions of the Group and entered at once upon other matters which would concern it. Admiral Souers himself was not present. It was his plan to attend weekly on Tuesday, but he wished his assistants to meet each day, or as frequently as required, in order to understand one another's problems. Before long Colonel Harris, Administrative Officer, joined the Council. The practice grew of meeting for half an hour to an hour and a half in the morning, according to the business brought to their attention in the Status Report of Secretary Lay, or the amount of friction which developed over dissensions and rivalries. Mr. Douglass in the chair had a thorough testing for patience.[42]

The Council was so active in carrying out the original idea of supervising general plans and surveys that it stirred Captain Goggins of the Planning Staff finally to make a formal presentation to Admiral Souers on May

13. The Council that morning had objected to two of the Planning Staff's papers. Certain members could see solutions which in their opinions were better, and the Council went ahead to direct the Secretary to "implement" its own ideas in one of the cases. It left the status of the other "unknown" to Captain Goggins at the time.

This type of action, said Goggins, was improper. And he did not think that it was in accordance with the Director's wishes. Four members of the Council had no responsibility for planning; their "frequent specious objections" seriously delayed final action on matters which had already been "exhaustively considered" by the Planning Staff. Unless the Director intended to give the planning function for the Group over to the Council, said Goggins, the practice of having the planning papers reviewed by the Council should cease.[43]

It was just short of a month since Goggins and his Deputy, Nicholas, had taken exception to Montague's plan for the Central Reports Staff. One should not blame Goggins; it was not pleasant to have the plans of his office thwarted by another body within the Group. But like the case of the Central Reports Staff, in which the Council had also overruled Captain Goggins, the episode revealed the usefulness of a separate body of deliberation, to review the enterprises of the central intelligence organization and to see that they were more cooperative than competitive.

The decisions of the Council on occasion were of more than internal concern. Relationships with the Department of State, the Army, the Navy, and other federal agencies interested in the problems of central intelligence came up for discussion. In the meeting of March 28 the Council took notice of the fact that the Department of State had under consideration the reorganization of its intelligence service; the Central Intelligence Group should study the effect of any change in the Department of State upon its own part in the "national intelligence mission." The Council suggested to the Director that he might approach the Secretary of State with the information that the Central Intelligence Group was about to undertake a study which might determine the most effective and efficient allocation of responsibility for research and intelligence among the various departments. This would lead to discussing the contribution which the departments should be expected to make to the Group and to each other. It would be a matter for recommendation to the National Intelligence Authority.[44]

Such deliberation in the Council of the Group is noteworthy because it reveals the growing sense of individuality which the Council, if not the whole Group, was beginning to have. And this was true even though its members had come to the new institution from the established departments whose traditions and taboos were not readily thrown off. We may wonder if interdepartmental acceptance and support for the Central Intelligence Group might not have been accelerated if the Council had been maintained within it. The Council met almost daily. The Intelligence Advisory Board had but four meetings during Admiral Souers's regime. Instead, such acceptance as there was seems to have been through the more diffused interests of the Intelligence Advisory Board and in such standing committees as the Interdepartmental Coordinating and Planning Staff, which will concern us later. Secretary Lay explained the organization and purposes of the Council to General Vandenberg when he took charge of the Central Intelligence Group in June. But the Assistant Directors were not brought into conference in any way comparable to the procedure under Admiral Souers. General Vandenberg and his Executive, Colonel Wright, came with other plans. Wright interpreted his position to be that of a military chief of staff with responsibility in the chain of command for all phases of the work in the Central Intelligence Group. This interpretation was not conducive to maintenance of the Council as a body of deliberation and advice to the Director.[45]

ESPIONAGE AND COUNTERESPIONAGE

It was imperative that Admiral Souers should not delay over the disposition of the Strategic Services Unit. By the executive order of September 20, 1945, the Secretary of War had to discontinue the Unit as soon as its functions and facilities could be placed in a new central intelligence organization or in the War Department. Meanwhile, General Magruder was to release personnel and bring an end to those activities which were not to be retained in time of peace.[46]

Some who had been of great service while the United States aided Russia in war against Germany were no longer desirable as hostility increased toward the Soviet Union and its satellites. The operations of many more had become so well known during the war that they had lost their usefulness in secret intelligence. Magruder kept at the task of liquidation throughout the fall of 1945 and into January 1946 until the number of military and civilian personnel had fallen from over 9,000 to nearly 3,000. It was a difficult task to perform without loss of essential persons. But the time was rapidly approaching when there would be no funds left in the appropriation by Congress.[47]

The Secretary of War on January 29, 1946, directed that the Strategic Services Unit should be closed by June 30. Any of its records required by the Director of Central Intelligence were to be transferred to the Office of the Secretary of War and "placed under the operational control of the Director of Central Intelligence." Title to the records remained to be settled later. The papers of the Secret Intelligence Branch included thousands of reports, processed and indexed, from four years of work by the Office of Strategic Services. There were diaries, histories, records of operations, files of United States scientists, specialists in many fields of knowledge, and an extensive bibliography of espionage. There was a roster kept of departing personnel who might be recovered if the new organization were not too long delayed.[48]

General Magruder strove to make clear to his superiors that the assets of the Strategic Services Unit were indispensable for the procurement of intelligence in peacetime. His memorandum on January 15 to Major General S. Leroy Irwin, Interim Activities Director, showed the irreparable loss that would occur if the plans and properties as well as the personnel of the Unit were not maintained.[49]

The Secret Intelligence Branch had stations in seven countries through the Near East and four in North Africa that were already converted to activities in peacetime. There were continuing activities with the armies in Germany, Austria, China, and Southeast Asia. Plans were being completed for operations in the Far East, and studies were in process elsewhere. Selected persons from the old subversive branches had been transferred into the Secret Intelligence Branch to be ready for the future. The Counterintelligence Branch (X-2) had some 400,000 dossiers on individuals. It was still at work against the operations of foreign intelligence services and secret organizations, especially in cooperation with the Counterintelligence Corps of the Army. Magruder was bringing the Secret Intelligence Branch and the Counterintelligence Branch into closer administration for eventual consolidation. Communications though reduced, technical services, special funds, a training program, and other parts of the old Office of Strategic Services were still in existence.[50]

As the new Central Intelligence Group got under way, General Magruder sent a memorandum to the Secretary of War on February 4, 1946, answering criticisms of the Strategic Services Unit and recommending that there be immediate action by the National Intelligence Authority to appraise the value of the Unit. Again on February 14 he urged that the Authority place the Unit under the Director of Central Intelligence and set the date for transferring its assets, plans, personnel, and properties. Had there been only the thought that the Strategic Services Unit should be turned over to the Central Intelligence Group as soon as feasible, there should have been no further delay. But there was more than one opinion on the matter.[51]

At a meeting held in the War Department on February 8, representatives of the intelligence services were still discussing which facilities and functions of the Strategic Services Unit should be kept and, of those retained, which should be operated by the Central Intelligence Group and which by the departments or other existing agencies. There was a question whether the Group should take all of the personnel and the plans of the Strategic Services Unit and place them at the center of the national intelligence system. There was strong doubt that the Central Intelligence Group should have exclusive collection of foreign intelligence by clandestine means, as Magruder was advocating.

It was agreed in the meeting at the War Department that "an authoritative group" should make a study and that prompt decisions should be reached. By the first directive of the Central Intelligence Group on February 19, 1946, therefore, Admiral Souers, with the concurrence of the Intelligence Advisory Board, established an interdepartmental committee to study the problem of the Strategic Services Unit. Souers promised separate action by the Central Intelligence Group to survey all "existing facilities for the collection of foreign intelligence by clandestine methods." The Director of Central Intelligence was ready to proceed.[52]

The interdepartmental committee, with Colonel Fortier as chairman, met continuously until March 13. During a period of less than a month, the committee listened to General Magruder and his principal subordinates, inspected files, obtained opinions on the value of the Strategic Services Unit from other agencies and the departments which used its product, and heard testimony from ranking officers in the Office of Strategic Services overseas. The members themselves made individual studies of branches and divisions in its organization.[53]

The Fortier Committee heard that the bulk of the information for intelligence purposes came from friendly governments. A large amount of material, such as economic and commercial statistics, was obtained from activities other than secret collection. These facts gave support to an opinion already expressed that the Strategic Services Unit, as it was, should not be taken over by the Central Intelligence Group.

Another reservation appearing frequently in the investigation was that the personnel of SSU had not been adequately screened. The Office of Strategic Services had grown so fast in the emergency that many who did not belong in the intelligence service of the country were there, and quite willing to remain the rest of their lives. The objectives of the war had determined the selection of others; a considerable number, once useful in working with Soviet officials, should not be retained now that conditions had changed. To be safe, all individuals of the Unit should be cleared again before given places in the Central Intelligence Group. And there was the fact that a high percentage of the clandestine personnel of the Strategic Services Unit had become exposed during the course of the war. It would be necessary to replace them gradually, without their knowing by whom they were replaced.[54]

The conclusions of the Fortier Committee were nevertheless in favor of the Strategic Services Unit. It was a "going concern" for operations in the field of foreign intelligence. It should be "properly and closely supervised, pruned and rebuilt," and placed under the Central Intelligence Group. Conflicts with other intelligence-gathering agencies such as the Foreign Service, the Military, Naval, and Air attachés, and the Federal Bureau of Investigation were not in the province of the committee to discuss. The inference was obvious that the Central Intelligence Group should not suffer on their account.

The Fortier Committee proposed that the Secretary of State, the Director of the Federal Bureau of Investigation, and the Director of Central Intelligence should reconsider the division of "analogous functions" on a geographic basis which then existed between the two organizations. [three lines deleted] There should be clear demarcation, too, between the military services and the SSU under the Central Intelligence Group. Clandestine operations should be closely coordinated by the Group, leaving the more overt collection of intelligence to other agencies of the Government.[55]

The committee suggested that the Strategic Services Unit under the Group should do what was already in the minds of the advocates of the Defense Project in the War Department. The Unit should concentrate upon the current activities of the Soviet Union and its satellites. Plans should be made to penetrate key institutions for possible aid to military operations by the United States. Liaison with the intelligence agencies of other countries should be developed for the same purpose. [three lines deleted]

Liquidation should continue substantially as it had been proposed by General Magruder. The Director of Central Intelligence, however, should take over the responsibility and complete authority for it; such personnel and facilities should be transferred to the Central Intelligence Group as he wished to have, and upon terms of new employment which he should provide. Counter to the arrangement in the President's Directive of January 22, 1946, the Fortier Committee did not hesitate to recommend that in time the Central Intelligence Group should have an independent budget and funds of its own. Meanwhile, the War Department should continue to supply the amounts needed for the liquidation of the Strategic Services Unit and its current operations. Budgetary provisions for the fiscal year 1947 had already been accepted.

The Fortier Committee proposed that, besides redistribution of personnel in the field and reduction of the administrative staff in Washington, there should be closer coordination of the SSU under the Central Intelligence Group with the research and other activities of the Government. The committee had not been authorized to examine the Research and Analysis Branch of the Office of Strategic Services, which had been transferred to the State Department. But the Branch was "closely geared to the secret intelligence branches as their chief customer and their chief guide" in the selection of sources and the evaluation of intelligence. Their files were interrelated, and their activities interwoven. They had much business in common, and they were likely still to have.[56]

The inference to be drawn from these facts was quickly drawn when the State Department altered McCormack's program for Research and Analysis in the Department. General Vandenberg soon thereafter expanded the Central Reports Staff of the Central Intelligence Group into an Office of Reports and Estimates as he also established the Office of Special Operations to take over clandestine functions of the Strategic Services Unit.[57]

General Magruder, who had declined to be considered for the office of Director of Central Intelligence, was about to retire from his duties as head of the Strategic Services Unit. After his clear and urgent statements, recourse to an interdepartmental survey must have carried some implication that his recommendations were not likely to succeed. But with the Fortier report, Magruder and his successor, Colonel Quinn, were encouraged to continue making plans as if the Strategic Services Unit adjusted to peacetime requirements, by whatever name it might be called, were going to be the primary, if not exclusive, governmental service for the clandestine collection of intelligence abroad. By the end of May, as General Vandenberg was about to become Director of Central Intelligence, there was ready a comprehensive program for world coverage with the assistance of the departments carefully specified in each case.[58]

Following the report of the interdepartmental committee, and agreement between Admiral Souers and Secretary Patterson of the War Department, the National Intelligence Authority issued a directive on April 2, 1946, to take over the administration of the Strategic Services Unit pending final liquidation. The Director of Central Intelligence was now to give the orders to the Director of the Unit. The Director of Central Intelligence would determine which funds, personnel, and facilities of the Unit were required in performing its services to the Group. They would then be transferred from the Unit to the appropriate section of the War Department. Secretary Patterson reserved for the Department the right to determine what portion of its funds, personnel, and facilities could be made available to the Central Intelligence Group.[59]

On the next day a memorandum for the Director of the Strategic Services Unit notified him that final liquidation of the Unit would be postponed another fiscal year, until June 30, 1947. In the meantime, he was to proceed according to instructions from the Director of Central Intelligence or his designated subordinate. The way was fully cleared for Colonel Fortier as Chief of Operational Services in the Central Intelligence Group to take over use of the plans, persons, and properties from the Strategic Services Unit—such assets, of course, as the Director of Central Intelligence chose to take. Any others would be absorbed into the War Department or abandoned. There was unrest that spring among the employees of the old Office of Strategic Services still left in the Strategic Services Unit. The number of able persons who were willing to stay shrank toward the vanishing point.[60]

The provisions in the directive of April 2 for transferring assets of the Strategic Services Unit to the War Department, and Patterson's reservation that the Department should determine the portion which could be made available to the Central Intelligence Group, need more careful explanation. They seem roundabout and cumbersome. They were, but they were not futile. They were legally necessary. Had the intention been to shift the Strategic Services Unit as a whole from the War Department to the Group, as the Research and Analysis Branch had been placed in the State Department, merely another executive order like that of September 20, 1945, would have sufficed. But that was not the intention.

The Strategic Services Unit, as a legal body, was on the road to extinction. It was necessary in dealing with personnel to bring to an end the appointment of everybody in the Strategic Services Unit. To those who might be desired in the Central Intelligence Group, new appointments would be issued. Thus, the enormously difficult problem of "reduction in force" would be eliminated. Otherwise, priorities, preference for veterans, and the whole intricate regulation of the Civil Service would have made practically impossible swift and effective liquidation of the Strategic Services Unit.[61]

The plans, records, and properties of the Unit were to be handled differently. There were funds, such as rupees in India, that were not to be turned back to the Treasury but were to be retained, like a stockpile of coal for future use. There were physical properties which might be welcomed in other agencies but which should be available first to the Central Intelligence Group. The equipment, techniques, codes, and other facilities of communication came through intact. The technical question of title, under the circumstances, was subordinate to the use of the assets by the appropriate agency. The Economy Act of 1933 prevented the transfer of property without reimbursement.[62]

The way out of this complicated situation was to ensure that, in agreement with the Secretary of War, the Director of Central Intelligence should have the use of such assets as he wanted, and the National Intelligence Authority would allow him to have. The remainder, surplus to the needs of the Central Intelligence Group, could then be disposed of as the War Department saw fit. So long as the Director of Central Intelligence enjoyed operational control and full use of those assets, it would be to the very practical advantage of the Central Intelligence Group, the War Department, and the public interest. Since then the passage of time and the inferential approval of the National Security Act of 1947 would appear to have vested title to the properties in the Central Intelligence Group. The Act of 1947 transferred the "personnel, property, and records" of the Group to the Central Intelligence Agency.[63]

CONTRIBUTIONS OF THE ADVISORY BOARD

After accepting Admiral Souers's program for the Strategic Services Unit on April 2, 1946, the National Intelligence Authority did not meet again formally until it assembled on July ‚17 to confer with General Vandenberg about his reorganization of the Central Intelligence Group. The Secretaries and Admiral Leahy, personal representative to the President, were content to rely upon the Intelligence Advisory Board and Admiral Souers, personal choice of President Truman, to establish and maintain the new central intelligence organization as a "cooperative interdepartmental activity."[64]

The Intelligence Advisory Board also held but occasional meetings. There appears to have been little need to debate "all recommendations" of the Director before they went to the Authority. The Board discussed on February 4 the proposed policies and procedures to govern the Group but made no important comment. It was evident that the departments could send whom they chose to the meetings of the Board. The Director and the permanent members of the Board had only to be consulted.[65]

The second meeting on March 26 produced decisions of no particular moment. The policy of liquidating the Strategic Services Unit interested but did not disturb the Board. The men who composed it had made their decisions elsewhere. As the representative of the Army, General Vandenberg wished to be certain that the United States forces in China would not be left during the transition without intelligence service to replace the Unit there. He was reassured by Admiral Souers. Production of the weekly summary by the Central Reports Staff had been delayed for want of personnel from the departments. This report should have given notice to their representatives on the Advisory Board. Possibly it did. The next subject of conversation was an agreement for exchanging appropriate papers with the Joint Intelligence Committee of the Joint Chiefs of Staff. It offered no difficulty. The Director should choose the papers that would benefit the Joint Intelligence Staff of the Joint Intelligence Committee. The Advisory Board concurred.

The fourth question before the Board touched upon the problem of secret intelligence lying at the foundations of the whole structure. General Vandenberg remarked that applications were coming from persons who wished to be special agents abroad. Admiral Souers preferred not to confuse the existing operations of the Strategic Services Unit with the permanent program. Until it was established, he thought, the agencies should continue their own operations. Vandenberg, however, gained from Souers agreement that "all such operations should be under a single directing head." Mr. J. Edgar Hoover was present; he could have been sure that they did not mean the head of the Federal Bureau of Investigation. Here was one expression of opinion giving promise of more lively meetings of the Intelligence Advisory Board.[66]

The third meeting of the Board on April 8, 1946, found Kingman Douglass in the chair as Acting Director of Central Intelligence. Alfred McCormack for the Department of State presented the fact that the Bureau of the Budget had reduced the amount requested by the Secretary of State for the intelligence work of the Department in 1947. This, coupled with uncertainty in the Department whether to continue its work in research and analysis, brought the Advisory Board of the Central Intelligence Group straight to the question which had already been raised in the Council of the Group. Admiral Inglis for the Navy and General Vandenberg for the Army both favored transferring the function of research and analysis from the Department to the Group, if the Department did not wish to retain it.[67]

Here was another promise of things to come. McCormack's plan for the State Department failed, and he resigned on April 23, 1946. Within four months there was an Office of Research and Evaluation in the Central Intelligence Group. Admiral Inglis and General Vandenberg were not then in entire agreement concerning its organization and functions.[68]

The last meeting of the Intelligence Advisory Board with Admiral Souers as Director of Central Intelligence came on May 9, 1946. There was discussion of the request from General Vandenberg on behalf of the War Department that the Department of State should take over the Foreign Broadcast Intelligence Service. The matter was referred to the Central Planning Staff for consultation with the proper officials in the Army and the Department of State. The Advisory Board listened to the plan for the Defense Project, but made no suggestions worth mention. Again the intelligence officers present had done their deciding elsewhere. Admiral Souers advised that the Director of the Federal Bureau of Investigation wished to have his name on the list for the daily summary; Souers would submit the request to the Secretary of State, he said, as the distribution for the summary had been established by the National Intelligence Authority. And the Board considered the method of clearing personnel for duty with the Group.[69]

The suggestion of Admiral Inglis that there should be an interdepartmental screening committee for the purpose did not meet approval. Instead, each department was held responsible for clearing the persons whom it assigned to the Group. Its security officer would then have the right of review, with final decision in every case resting with the Director of Central Intelligence. The method did not prove satisfactory, and so the directive was rescinded on October 4, 1946. The Group undertook full responsibility for clearing its personnel.[70]

There was one more meeting of the Intelligence Advisory Board with Admiral Souers in the chair as General Vandenberg became Director of Central Intelligence on June 10, 1946. It was a meeting to attend to unfinished business rather than to hear the new Director state his policies, though they were already taking shape and becoming known. For one, at this meeting General Vandenberg accepted the plan that the Foreign Broadcast Intelligence Service should be operated by the Central Intelligence Group with the administrative assistance of the War Department. The operation was to begin, of course, only when the Group should have funds to disburse on its own account. But these the new Director intended to have as soon as he could get them.[71]

The members of the Advisory Board listened at some length to a discussion of the weekly summary, of which a preliminary issue had appeared on June 7. Dr. Langer of the State Department emphasized that it ought to be done by people of "responsibility and weight." Mr. Montague's reply for the Central Reports Staff amounted to the conclusion that it might be done—as soon as the specialists whom the Reports Staff needed had arrived from the departments which were supposed to provide them.

General Vandenberg proposed that the weekly summary continue under the "common observation" of the members of the Advisory Board. They agreed. And so, after approving eventual coordination of the acquisition of foreign publications under the supervision of the Librarian of Congress, the Intelligence Advisory Board came to the end of its short and relatively uneventful career with Admiral Souers as Director of Central Intelligence. It was to have new experiences in the near future.

Admiral Souers expressed his appreciation of the "unstinted coopera-

---

October 16, 1974

Memorandum for: The Record
Subject: Appointment of General Vandenberg as DCI in 1946

1. General Hoyt S. Vandenberg became Director of Central Intelligence and head of the Central Intelligence Group on June 10, 1946, in succession to Admiral Souers. Previous to his becoming DCI, General Vandenberg was G-2 of the War Department.

2. Reference is made to Chapter III of The Central Intelligence Agency: An Instrument of Government, to 1950 *in the DCI Historical Series, and in particular to page 103 of that chapter. There it is stated that Souers "took great satisfaction in turning his duties over to General Vandenberg. . . . He had recommended a successor for his public appeal and personal attributes."*

3. It remains in the back of my mind that there were other reasons for Souers's replacement. He was basically a conciliator, particularly knowing the background of the establishment of CIG after so long a fight. He did not want to push the other departments too far too fast. Vandenberg was a man of action who wanted CIG to move faster into asserting its role, even though he was in G-2 at the time. I was told that Vandenberg had taken this matter up with the President and had urged more direct action by CIG. Shortly after, he was handed the job as DCI.

Walter Pforzheimer

---

tion" by everyone. He took great satisfaction in turning his duties over to General Vandenberg. As he reminisced in 1952, there was no doubt in his mind that he did. He had been reluctant to take the office. He had sought others for it in his place at the start. He had recommended a successor for his public appeal and personal attributes.[72]

The first Director of Central Intelligence left a Progress Report, dated June 7, 1946, to summarize his administration and point to the immediate needs of his successor. Responsible officers in the departments had cooperated wholeheartedly in meeting his requests for personnel, he said; but the process had been slow because of demobilization in the armed forces and the very specific requirements of the Central Intelligence Group. Souers had given priority to the Central Planning Staff as a necessary "prelude to accomplishment." Concentration now should be upon the Central Reports Staff.[73]

The primary function of the Group was to prepare and distribute "definite estimates" upon the capabilities and intentions of foreign countries. As the Group required the best qualified personnel, it had been slow in filling the complement of the Reports Staff. This had also delayed the solution of the relationship to be established with the departments, the State–War–Navy Coordinating Committee, the Joint Chiefs of Staff, and other agencies in regard to the production of such "national policy intelligence."

Souers hoped that it would be obtained now at an early date. He called attention to the appointment of consultants to the Director of Central Intelligence, a policy which he considered to be of great importance. Dr. H. P. Robertson was scientific consultant. Mr. George Kennan was to become the special adviser on the Soviet Union.

There had been some relief in the administration of the Group by the part-time use of persons and facilities in the Strategic Services Unit. Greater need would appear when the "centralized operations" began, as the functions of the Unit were taken over by the Group.

Admiral Souers listed the interdepartmental problems which the Central Planning Staff had undertaken to solve or to advance in the stages of study and planning. He stressed in particular the function of the Central Intelligence Group in supporting the budgets for departmental intelligence. "Coordinated representation to the Bureau of the Budget and the Congress," he said, promised to be "one of the more effective means for guarding against arbitrary depletion of intelligence sources at the expense of national security." It was an interesting suggestion, leading far into the future of the national intelligence system. But it was hardly a suggestion to appeal to the chiefs of departmental intelligence if it meant curtailing the appropriation of one agency for the benefit of another. Coordination of that nature had no appeal then. Nor has it enjoyed much since.[74]

General Vandenberg was more concerned at that time with getting a budget which would ensure the survival and effective operation of the Group itself. His General Counsel advised him on June 13 that the Group had no power to expend Government funds; and thanks to the Independent Office Appropriation Act of 1945, the Group would be without unvouchered funds from the departments after January 22, 1947. It would even be questionable whether they could furnish personnel and supplies from vouchered funds. The Act forbade making funds available to any agency in existence more than a year without a specific appropriation by Congress.[75]

The final paragraphs of Admiral Souers's Progress Report bore down upon the administrative, budgetary, and legal difficulties of the Central Intelligence Group and came to positive conclusions on behalf of General Vandenberg. The relationship with the National Intelligence Authority and the Intelligence Advisory Board was sound. But the Group was suffering because the reduction of the departments' funds and personnel kept them from supplying the Group with the facilities which it had to have. It could recruit no personnel from civilian life. Without enabling legislation, it could make no contracts for essential services. It was now ready to monitor foreign broadcasts, to collect foreign intelligence by clandestine methods, to produce intelligence studies of foreign countries, to establish a central register of information, and to engage in the basic research and analysis in economics, geography, sociology, and other subjects of common concern to all departments. The National Intelligence Authority and its Central Intelligence Group should have "enabling legislation and an independent budget" as soon as possible, either as part of a new national defense organization or as a separate agency.[76]

Introduction to Chapter IV

Vandenberg held the office of DCI for about twice the time of his predecessor, Souers—about one year. Like his predecessor, he was to leave
frustrated over the lack of independence and power for the CIG.
Vandenberg had almost continual conflict with military intelligence officers over the authority of the DCI to carry out independent collection,
coordination of intelligence collection by the various departments and
the Group, and, in general, the place of the DCI and the CIG in relation to the military services.

Vandenberg took over as DCI on June 10, 1946, and "hit the ground
running." Within ten days he issued a memorandum asserting that the
DCI should be permitted to have the Central Intelligence Group collect
intelligence and carry out independent research and analysis. To support these activities, he proposed that departmental funds be transferred to the CIG. Vandenberg planned for the DCI to be independent
and for the CIG to be the truly central organization in the national
intelligence system. The reaction was predictable, given the record
since 1941, when the OSS was first proposed: the military services and
State Department immediately objected.

Vandenberg did succeed in getting some of his ideas enacted. The
revised version of his memorandum, which became the Fifth Directive
of the National Intelligence Authority on July 8, 1946, permitted the
DCI to assess the adequacy of intelligence analysis and, when the departments agreed, to centralize such analysis in the CIG. Vandenberg
also acquired the prerogative for the CIG to carry out "federal" espionage and collection of information from foreign media.

Darling was sympathetic to Vandenberg's efforts to gain more control
over national intelligence and portrays him as one of the "heroes" of his
narrative (as, will be seen, was Hillenkoetter, the third DCI to serve
and the third to leave frustrated). Although Darling is probably correct
in his assessment of the resistance the military services and the State
Department presented to Vandenberg, two points should be remembered. First, Vandenberg—a line military officer who had distinguished
himself in World War II and who would eventually become Air Force
Chief of Staff—was accustomed to a strictly defined, smoothly operating chain of command. He expected an intelligence community to operate in a similar fashion. Second, the degree of centralization that
Vandenberg proposed was considerably beyond that envisioned by any
of the top intelligence figures of the time, save for William Donovan.

Indeed, all of Vandenberg's successors as Directors of Central Intelligence up to Stansfield Turner (1977–1981) would fight the same battle over who would plan and direct U.S. intelligence assets, and all would encounter approximately the same amount of resistance by the military services. No DCI had the authority Vandenberg proposed until William Casey took office, and even today the military services and the intelligence community play a game of tug-of-war over turf and dollars.

In September Vandenberg gained ground over the administration of the funding for the CIG. Although the funding would still consist of proportional contributions from the various departments, the money would now go into a working fund that the DCI was to allocate as he chose.

One key feature of Vandenberg's regime was the new Office of Special Operations headed by Colonel Galloway. This new office was to focus specifically on collecting foreign intelligence. Galloway instructed his staff to have minimal contact with personnel from State, War, and Navy in order to prevent OSO activities from being exposed.

Under Galloway, Captain Goggins was Deputy and Kingman Douglass was "B" Deputy and Chief of Foreign Commerce. Galloway was concentrating on European affairs, particularly the allied zones in Germany; Goggins was to oversee the Far East, where tensions were increasing over Korea and Communist China was expanding its operations in Manchuria. Douglass and William Jackson were on a special mission, the results of which were not fully revealed until the tenure of General Smith as DCI in the early 1950s. Their report, the Douglass–Jackson report, revealed the ineffectiveness of the Strategic Services Unit in competition with the intelligence services of the Army, Navy, and FBI and argued for a single collecting agency.

Vandenberg fought to gain CIG authority over collecting intelligence. He began by challenging the authority of the FBI in Latin America. Although the FBI defended its activities in Latin America as counterintelligence measures intended to protect American security, the Fifth Directive of the NIA, which was passed in the wake of this debate, gave the DCI the right to conduct all organized federal espionage and counterespionage. J. Edgar Hoover gave way on Latin America but retained for the FBI the exclusive control over the investigation and analysis of subversive activities within the United States.

The struggle over the CIG's authority came to a head again with the FBI and the military over its creation of a "central contact control register." This register would keep records of all persons or groups, especially businesses, contacted for overt collection of foreign intelligence within the United States. The military objected to this encroachment upon their rights to keep their contacts secret. The Intelligence Advisory Board denied the CIG the exclusive right to brief and interrogate, and the competition among the intelligence services therefore continued. When Kingman Douglass left the CIG in the fall of 1946 and General Sibert took over collection of clandestine and overt intelligence, the staff of the "B" Deputy and Chief of Foreign Commerce was renamed the Commercial Contact Branch and was placed in the new Office of Operations. This Contact Branch was responsible for collecting foreign intelligence in the United States. The Foreign Broadcast Information Branch and the Foreign Documents Branch were joined with it.

To coordinate the intelligence work of the departments, Vandenberg abolished the Central Planning Staff and replaced it with the Interdepartmental Coordinating and Planning Staff (ICAPS). Like its predecessor, instead of fulfillng its mission, ICAPS took more interest in the internal operation of the CIG, such as the production of estimates by the Office of Research and Evaluation (ORE).

The Office of Research and Evaluation (later known as the Office of Reports and Estimates) saw hard times under Vandenberg. J. K. Huddle was appointed Assistant Director in charge of the ORE, which replaced the Central Reports Staff in July 1946. Colonel Ludwell Montague, who had worked with McCormack in the State Department and had been Chief of the Central Reports Staff, became Chief of Intelligence Staff within the office to produce estimates. The first estimate requested covered the foreign and military policy of the Soviet Union. "ORE 1," as it was called, was produced singlehandedly according to Montague, as it was requested on a Friday and due the following Tuesday and no experienced staff was in place to assist him.

Open warfare between the departments followed the submission of this first estimate as the military wanted to pass muster on all CIG estimates. The estimates system was not working for the main reason that the intelligence officers of the departments were not willing to assist the Group. In addition, the staff of the estimates division was at half strength, the Interdepartmental Coordinating and Planning Staff criticized the Office's work, and disputes arose between the regional branches and the intelligence staff in the ORE. The regional branches did not understand why the Intelligence Staff at CIG had the final say. The Western Europe Branch therefore filed a memorandum detailing the organizational defects of the ORE. For all these reasons, the Intelligence Staff was abolished. Huddle left for another post in the Foreign Service and Assistant Director McCollum took over for him. The regional branches reported directly to him. Montague and his staff were tasked to form the Global Survey Group.

Further action was taken on the issue of intelligence collection when the NIA issued Directive No. 7 in January 1947. Primary responsibility for collection still remained with the departments, with the exceptions of the secret intelligence collection by the CIG's Office of Special Operations, the Foreign Broadcast Intelligence Branch collection, and the Contact Branch in the Office of Operations. A special exception was also given for intelligence collection in China, which the NIA's Eighth Directive in February 1947 sanctioned.

Vandenberg addressed the NIA on February 12, 1947, on the issue of the authority of the DCI, and while the Authority reasserted the power of the DCI in word, in fact the controversy over the power given the DCI and the IAB to control the CIG continued and was inherited by Hillenkoetter. At this same meeting Vandenberg suggested abolishing the Joint Intelligence Committee, which duplicated the IAB. (Page 159: "The permanent members of the Advisory Board were the Joint Intelligence Committee of the Joint Chiefs of Staff.") The Authority agreed, but passed the matter to the Joint Chiefs of Staff for its approval. The JCS voted to keep but reorganize the JIC. By this time, however, the proposed merger of the armed forces moved to the forefront and blocked any final decision on the JIC.

Finally, Vandenberg asserted the CIG's authority into the area of scientific intelligence. Concerned with the development of atomic energy abroad, Vandenberg wanted to form a special section for scientific intelligence within the Office of Scientific Research and Development, which Souers had established. The Chairman of this Office was Vannevar Bush. A Joint Research and Development Board had been established in July 1946 by Secretaries Forrestal and Patterson. At a meeting in December 1946 the technical advisers of this Board agreed that the CIG should be in charge of scientific and technical intelligence. On January 23, 1947, the Scientific Branch in the Office of Reports and Estimates was formally established. This Branch was to collaborate with the Joint Research and Development Board and other departments to prepare estimates on scientific capabilities and intentions of foreign countries. On April 18, 1947, a directive was issued authorizing the DCI to coordinate intelligence relating to foreign developments of atomic energy. The Nuclear Energy Group in the Scientific Branch would prepare estimates on foreign capabilities and intentions in the field of nuclear energy and represent the DCI on the Atomic Energy Commission, which had been established in August 1946.

IV

THE CENTRAL INTELLIGENCE GROUP: VANDENBERG'S REGIME

EXECUTIVE AGENT

 The new Director of Central Intelligence brought to the Group the prestige of high rank in the Army, prominence before the public, and forthright determination to take responsibility. Lieutenant General Vandenberg and Admiral Souers agreed that the time had come when the Group should perform certain operations in the national system of intelligence. The initial organization and planning had been done. It was time to develop the power latent in the duties which the President had assigned to the Director of Central Intelligence.[1]

Experiences of the past six months on the Intelligence Advisory Board had convinced General Vandenberg that if he were to fulfill those duties, he must be able to get the persons necessary for his work without having to wait upon the will of the departments to supply them. He must have "operating funds" which he could expend as he chose without dependence upon or accountability to some other agency. He was certain that the Central Intelligence Group could not meet its primary obligation to produce strategic intelligence unless it had better arrangements for collecting the raw materials of such intelligence. It must have the means to conduct the initial research and analysis necessary for the production of estimates. The Group should not have to rely entirely upon the contribution of the departments.[2]

Vandenberg wished the Director of Central Intelligence to be the executive officer of the National Intelligence Authority. While the President kept him in the office, he would have command of its functions. This was quite different from thinking of the Central Intelligence Group as a "cooperative interdepartmental activity." We meet again as in the days of the Office of Strategic Services the fundamental concept of individual responsibility in conflict with the principle of collective responsibility. Members of the Intelligence Advisory Board, representing the intelligence services of the departments, were immediately aware of the change.[3]

As Vandenberg expressed it, the Board had the right to give him advice, either in concurrence or in dissent. He would accept such counsel, listen to argument, and consider new facts; but he would make up his own mind and determine the position of the Group. He would not block dissent. But it was not to be the official position of the Group, not even if it were the unanimous opinion of the Advisory Board. His superiors in the Authority might prefer the dissent. It was their right. But so long as he was Director of Central Intelligence, at the pleasure of the President, Vandenberg intended to make the final decision within the Group. He was individually responsible through the Authority to the President.[4]

There was solid ground in the President's Directive for this interpretation of the powers of the Director. But acceptance of it by the chiefs of intelligence on the Advisory Board was most unlikely. Theirs was the countertheory of collective responsibility. The Group was to them a cooperative interdepartmental enterprise in which, for all matters of deliberation and decision, they were the representatives of the departments and therefore the equals of the Director. If he was not their executive secretary, he was no more than their chairman.[5]

REORGANIZATION—THE FIFTH DIRECTIVE

Vandenberg's memorandum of June 20 explaining his purposes created such a stir that it was revised before the meeting of the Board on June 28. The original text with his signature declared that "to discharge his vital responsibilities," the Director of Central Intelligence "should not be required to rely solely upon evaluated intelligence from the various departments." He should have authority to undertake within the Central Intelligence Group such basic research and analysis as in his opinion might be required to produce "the necessary strategic and national policy intelligence." This would require the "centralization" of activities concerning more than one agency; existing organizations of the State, War, and Navy Departments, including their "funds, personnel, and facilities," would be "integrated into the Central Intelligence Group as a central service."[6]

There was no mention of the Intelligence Advisory Board in the original text. Criticisms ranged accordingly from insistence that a single member of the Board should have virtually the right of vetoing the Director's choice of subjects for research to the requirement that he must consult the appropriate members of the Board whenever he planned central activities of "common, but secondary interest" to more than one department.[7]

The right of an individual member to veto would have destroyed the function of the Director of Central Intelligence, as it would have ruined the Board itself. The requirement that the Director must consult regarding activities of "common, but secondary" interest placed him at the mercy of the intelligence officers in the departments. Under such conditions there would be very few instances where they thought an activity so secondary that it could be wholly relinquished to the Central Intelligence Group. We are to hear more of this requirement later.[8]

Vandenberg well understood the meaning of the "turmoil" over his proposals. He regretted that the original version had caused it. He accepted revisions designed to make the research and analysis in the Group supplementary to work of the departments. He discarded altogether the stipulation that departmental funds, personnel, and facilities would be "integrated" into the Group. His primary purpose, he told the Board, was to get the staff necessary to do the job of assisting the Departments of State, War, and the Navy. He wished to find where their intelligence activities stopped short; he wanted to meet the deficiencies and fill the gaps. But he did not give up his intention to have the Central Intelligence Group engage in the initial research and analysis requisite to the production of "strategic and national policy intelligence."[9]

As he spoke for the Department of State, Dr. Langer must have had memories of the Research and Analysis Branch in the Office of Strategic Services. Then research and analysis had been closely tied with clandestine collection. The Branch had been both guide and customer of Secret Intelligence. But now Langer, who had succeeded McCormack, presented the case of the State Department's division of Research and Intelligence. Langer doubted that it was necessary for the Central Intelligence Group to engage in extensive research and analysis. When the departments could not do the work, specific authorization might be given to the Group. The Director of Central Intelligence should undertake only such research and analysis as might be necessary to determine what functions were not being performed adequately "in the fields of national security intelligence."

Langer saw danger to the "solidarity of the Board" in negotiations by the Director with individual members. He feared that the Board would "pass into eclipse"; it must be maintained, he said, to give moral support to the Director. But he appreciated the difficulty, if not uselessness, in endeavoring to distinguish primary from secondary interests in an enterprise. The Group should assume those activities in research and analysis which might be accomplished better by a central agency. Langer had to defer in the end to the individual member; the Board could not act by a vote of the majority. The decision was to be made by the Director and the appropriate member or members of the Intelligence Advisory Board. This was the provision as it was finally adopted and included on July 8, 1946, in the fifth directive of the National Intelligence Authority.[10]

There were decided opinions for and against the compromise between the Director and the Advisory Board. One extreme view was that he should have left research and evaluation entirely with the departments. But if he had done so, any office which he might have created in the Group to bring their products together would have been no more than a stapling device to put the departmental papers in one bundle. There would have been no analysis of the materials. There could hardly have been synthesis into a national estimate. That job would have been left to the policymakers, as the Director of Central Intelligence was not supposed to leave it.

Another view was that he should have insisted upon taking over the function as a whole from the Department of State, which had received the Research and Analysis Branch from the Office of Strategic Services. If Vandenberg had been allowed to do so, any work of that nature remaining in the State, War, or Navy Departments, and elsewhere, would have been merely a limited service, to verify and support the information which the department had received. The Central Intelligence Group would have had the task of doing the research into underlying geographical, economic, and social factors for all of the departments and agencies of the Government interested in intelligence. The Group would have rendered them a common service. It would have supplied itself with the requisite materials for producing "strategic and national intelligence" as directed by the National Intelligence Authority.

Even if the State Department had been willing to allow the Group to engage in extensive evaluation of geographical, economic, and social factors, which was most unlikely, such an undertaking would have required a staff and equipment beyond existing facilities of the Group or any that it could hope to obtain from the Departments of State, War and the Navy for some time to come. Though possessed of the whole right, General Vandenberg would not have been able to use it. He would have had still to rely, as he believed he could not, upon the evaluated intelligence from the departments to supplement the information which the Group obtained for itself from its collecting offices.

If the Group had taken no part of the function of research and analysis, so runs another argument, there would have been no investigation anywhere that would have been adequate for the production of strategic intelligence. The State Department had abandoned the McCormack plan to concentrate research and analysis and had dispersed it among the geographical divisions of the department. The War and the Navy Departments were engaged in nothing like the work of the old Branch in the Office of Strategic Services. Though respecting the scholarship evident in the armed services, one must concede that it was present in neither the amount nor the steady application to research and analysis that were essential to the production of national estimates.[11]

The Defense Project, inspired by Colonel Lovell in the War Department, was a huge undertaking of great moment. But it was transitory at best, and it was not comparable to the plan for the production of strategic intelligence by the Central Intelligence Group. Even though the Defense Project was an interdepartmental enterprise, in a sense under the supervision of the Director of Central Intelligence, he could not choose the subjects for research and analysis. He could merely settle disputes among the members engaged in the Project. However successful it might have been in obtaining strategic intelligence for effective national estimates of the capabilities and intentions of the Soviet Union, it would only have proved that the Director of Central Intelligence should have under his administration a permanent organization for research and analysis.

Being a practical man inclined to action, General Vandenberg withdrew the provisions in his first draft which seemed so obnoxious that they might defeat his purpose. He accepted changes to mollify the Advisory Board. But he retained the principle. There was to be within the Central Intelligence Group the research and analysis which it had to have regardless of duplication and overlapping with the departmental services. It is naive to think that he was artless because he did not delay over problematical aspects of his situation. He took what he could get then. If that were established, more would come in time.

Vandenberg and his Executive, Colonel Wright, had large plans for the Group as they came over from "G-2" in the War Department. The Group was to be the truly central organization in the national system of intelligence. The new Office of Research and Evaluation was to process all of the material that came into Washington, with a staff of researchers and analysts that might rise to two thousand persons. DeForest Van Slyck, deputy to Montague in the Central Reports Staff at the time, recalled the situation of July 1946 with both exasperation and amusement. The idea was altogether good that the Group should do the estimating; but it could not get enough qualified persons to do the reflective writing required in the weekly summaries, let alone to undertake the grandiose scheme of Vandenberg and Wright for research and synthesis.[12]

Following the check by the State Department, representatives of the Army and Navy also made reservations which were adopted by the Board and included in the fifth directive of the Authority. Vandenberg had asked that the Director of Central Intelligence should be authorized to act as the "executive agent of this Authority in coordinating and supervising all federal foreign intelligence activities related to the national security." As changed by the Advisory Board on June 28, the directive stipulated that the Director of Central Intelligence should merely act as the agent of the Authority in coordinating such activities.

There were two significant omissions. The word "executive" was dropped before the phrase "agent of this Authority." The word "supervising" disappeared. Exception had been taken to Vandenberg's original phrasing because it seemed to infringe upon the responsibility of the members of the Intelligence Advisory Board; each was supposed to be responsible for executing within his own department the recommendations of the Authority. The Director might engage in "coordinating"; but he might not in "supervising" the intelligence activities of the departments. The Director's right of inspection was involved in this affair. How to coordinate those departmental activities without inspecting and supervising them was a question which prolonged the dispute between the Director and the Board for months. Admiral Hillenkoetter had not yet solved the problem in 1949 when the Dulles Report called for leadership in the endeavor without the power to coerce.[13]

As Magruder had so effectively urged, Vandenberg wished to have all espionage and counterespionage for the collection of foreign intelligence abroad conducted by the Director of Central Intelligence. But the directive as revised by the Advisory Board on June 28 carefully stated that the Director of Central Intelligence should conduct only those "organized federal" operations which were outside the United States and its possessions. This of course was designed, first, to assure the military intelligence of services that they might continue departmental operations in collecting intelligence for their own purposes. Presumably those operations were not "organized." Second, the provision was to guard the Federal Bureau of Investigation in performing its duties within the area and jurisdiction of the United States.

The fifth section of Vandenberg's draft dealt with the funds, personnel, and facilities of the Group. The departments upon his request were to provide such funds and facilities to the extent of available appropriations and within the limits of their capabilities. At the earliest practicable date, he would submit a supplemental budget. The revision in this section of the directive by the Intelligence Advisory Board made sure that the departments should continue to have the decision in regard to the funds which they apportioned to the Central Intelligence Group.

The proposed directive as it had thus been amended by the Intelligence Advisory Board went to the members of the National Intelligence Authority individually on June 29. The Secretaries of State, War, and the Navy approved it without change. But Admiral Leahy objected to Vandenberg's use of the word "agent" in the paragraph concerning the coordination of foreign intelligence. This word, he said, might imply unwarranted freedom for the Director of Central Intelligence. General Vandenberg agreed that the possibility of such an interpretation was not desirable. The paragraph was reworded so that it authorized the Director of Central Intelligence to "act for" the Authority in coordinating such activities. With this last change, Vandenberg's proposal became on July 8 the fifth directive of the National Intelligence Authority and took its place next to the President's Directive of January 22, 1946, as most important in the instructions to the Director of Central Intelligence.[14]

General Vandenberg had not obtained all that he sought in this first endeavor to reorganize the Central Intelligence Group so that the Director might perform "operations and functions" implicit in his duties and responsibilities. But he did have authority now to determine what activities in research and analysis were not being performed adequately and to centralize them in the Group with the consent of the department concerned. He could act for the Authority in coordinating all departmental activities in intelligence, though he could not supervise them. He could perform two services of common usefulness: he was to conduct all organized federal espionage and counterespionage abroad for the collection of foreign intelligence and all federal monitoring of the press and broadcasts of foreign powers. He had a clearer statement regarding the allotment of funds from the departments and the supplemental budget which he desired. He was equipped to go before the National Intelligence Authority on July 17, 1946, in its first meeting since he had taken office and argue there that the Director must have independent funds and the right to hire his own people.[15]

In his opening remarks Vandenberg called attention to the conclusions in the Progress Report of Admiral Souers. Vandenberg explained that each intelligence agency was working at the moment along the lines of primary concern to its own department. The departments, he said, might be interested in much the same thing, but from different points of view and often with separate purposes. It was therefore the business of the Central Intelligence Group to find the needs of all and endeavor to satisfy them. This would require an adequate staff and independent funds; it was extremely difficult to secure the necessary personnel by requisition from the departments. The Director of Central Intelligence should have the right to hire his own staff. This, he knew, would mean that the Central Intelligence Group should eventually become an agency in the Government established by Act of Congress.[16]

Secretary Byrnes demurred on the ground that the National Intelligence Authority had been intentionally created to avoid any need for an independent budget. The statement was historically inaccurate. The Authority, composed of the Secretaries, had been conceived as a better institution than the single Director proposed in Donovan's plan. The conception was not involved with the budget. Nor was the question of the budget uppermost when the Army and Navy pushed the Authority to keep the State Department from taking charge under McCormack's plan. But Secretary Patterson agreed with Byrnes and explained that the amount of money spent upon Central Intelligence should be concealed for reasons of security.[17]

General Vandenberg interposed that such considerations ought to be balanced against the administrative difficulties they caused. For him the important thing was to have an effective and efficient organization. At this point Admiral Leahy, representative of the President, remarked that it had always been understood that the Central Intelligence Group eventually would broaden its scope. He was about convinced, he said, that the Authority should now endeavor to obtain its own appropriations. They should be small, of course, as the three departments would continue to furnish the bulk of the appropriations.

Patterson still thought that the administrative problems might be solved under the existing arrangement. Byrnes too thought that the departments might find a way to give the Group whatever money it had to have. There was further discussion in which Langer for the State Department joined to endorse Admiral Leahy's suggestion that funds might be separated from actions concerning personnel. The money might be appropriated from the funds of the departments without an independent appropriation for the Group; but the Director of Central Intelligence, for reasons of security as well as efficiency, might be given full charge of selecting and directing his personnel.

The discussion went on to consider the relationship with Congress and its eventual legislation. General Vandenberg stressed that the Group was not an agency authorized to disburse funds. Even if it had sufficient funds from a department for a particular purpose, it would be obligated to maintain disbursing officers and auditors in all three departments besides the necessary accounting staff in the Group. Thus, four fiscal operations were required where one really would suffice. All of this pointed to the necessity for making the Central Intelligence Group an agency authorized to control its own purse. Secretary Byrnes undertook to discuss the matter with officials in the Bureau of the Budget and report back to the National Intelligence Authority.[18]

General Vandenberg then made a brief report on his progress to date. The Group was about to take over the Foreign Broadcast Intelligence Service and all clandestine activities in foreign intelligence. He had set up an Office of Special Operations. He expected soon to have in good working order other Offices for Collection, Dissemination, and Research and Evaluation. The Group was receiving requests almost daily to assume other functions now being performed by various committees of the State, War, and Navy Departments. [three lines deleted] He was establishing an Interdepartmental Coordinating and Planning Staff.[19]

As this significant meeting of the National Intelligence Authority came to an end, it was in the mood of Secretary Patterson, who felt that all of General Vandenberg's immediate problems should be solved if the Secretary of State could obtain help from the Bureau of the Budget. Vandenberg put it more explicitly. He needed money, the authority to spend it, and the authority to hire and fire. But he must have left the meeting with his mind turning over the remarks of Admiral Leahy.

The Admiral was convinced that the Group should have funds for which it did not have to account in detail. The President, however, had authorized him to "make it clear": the Director of Central Intelligence was "not responsible further than to carry out the directives" of the National Intelligence Authority. The President would hold the Cabinet officers "primarily responsible for coordination of intelligence activities." Were the Secretaries then to see to it that their decisions in the Authority were obeyed in their departments whether or not those decisions were popular? General Vandenberg, anyhow, was to know that he should not become another General Donovan seeking an independent directorate.[20]

In immediate consequence of Vandenberg's urging, a letter from the National Intelligence Authority on July 30, 1946, to the Secretary of the Treasury and the Comptroller General requested the establishment of a "working fund" for the Central Intelligence Group. This fund was to contain the allotments from the Departments of State, War, and the Navy and to be subject to the administration of the Director of Central Intelligence, or his authorized representative, for paying personnel, procuring supplies and equipment, and the certification of vouchers.[21]

Upon approval of the fund, a second letter to the Comptroller General, signed by each member of the National Intelligence Authority, gave the authorization on September 5. The Director of Central Intelligence now had "full powers" to determine the "propriety of expenditures" from the working fund, under the policies established by the Authority. He was to arrange with the Comptroller General the procedures, practices, and controls necessary for proper accounting. Once the allotments from the departments were in the working fund, Vandenberg had authority and the resources to maintain a staff and facilities for the Central Intelligence Group upon his own responsibility as Director of Central Intelligence. But he still could not be sure that his allotment from a department would not be cut. He protested to Congressional committees that the Central Intelligence Group should have an independent budget.[22]

OPERATIONS: COVERT AND OVERT

The Group had a military character in spite of Admiral Souers's efforts to make it a cooperative activity representing the State Department as well as the armed services. He had been successful in obtaining some men with experience as civilians although they had been in the Army or Navy during the war. But for the most part he was obliged to rely upon those who thought of the Army or Navy as a career. The distinction between regular and reserve officers, if seldom expressed, was always present. The Agency still reverberates with talk of the colonels who arrived with General Vandenberg and took over from others who possessed military records, but who for one reason or another did not measure up to his expectations.

Maturer minds will not linger upon the military aspect of the matter. There doubtless were varied reasons for changing personnel. But neither should the criticism be ignored altogether. It entered as a fact into the deliberations of Congress upon the legislative provisions of the future for central intelligence in the national system of security, just as it had embittered the argument between the State Department and the armed services prior to the establishment of the Central Intelligence Group by the President.[23]

Colonel Fortier was relieved from duty as Assistant Director and Acting Chief of Operational Services on July 11, 1946. Colonel Galloway became Assistant Director for Special Operations. Captain Goggins was moved from his post at the head of the Central Planning Staff to be Galloway's Deputy. Kingman Douglass, no longer the Acting Deputy Director of Central Intelligence, became "B" Deputy and Chief of Foreign Commerce under Colonel Galloway. Upon the understanding that there should be no one between himself and General Vandenberg, Colonel Wright had come from the position as Vandenberg's Executive on the General Staff, "G-2," to be his Executive to the Director in the Central Intelligence Group. Colonel Dabney accompanied Wright as his Assistant Executive. For the time, there was no Deputy Director of Central Intelligence. Colonel Wright received this appointment on January 20, 1947.[24]

November 15, 1974

Memorandum for: Chief, Historical Staff
Subject: General Brigadier Louis J. Fortier

1. On p. 115 of Arthur Darling's history, there appears the sentence "Colonel Fortier was relieved from duty as Assistant Director and Acting Chief of Operational Services on July 11, 1946." General Fortier died on November 6, 1974, at the age of 82 (Washington Post, November 8, 1974).

2. During much of the period General Fortier was in CIG, he and I shared an office. In the course of his duties, he offered me the directorship of FBIS, which CIG had just acquired and was a can of worms. I was smart enough to decline on the grounds that I was a better staff officer than line officer, and eventually Colonel K. K. "Red" White was hired for the job. His firm hand was just what was needed. Professor Darling writes of the relief of General Fortier in the context of the influx of officers who came in with General Vandenberg, headed by Colonel E. K. Wright. That is a part of the story.

3. Fortier had had a lengthy career in intelligence. He had been in Paris attending the Ecole Supérieure de Guerre when the Germans moved on Yugoslavia, and Fortier was sent there as MA at once. He did an outstanding job in trying to save the royalist government, and then returned to G-2 in Washington. He also had a role in setting up the JIC. But Fortier wanted combat with his basic field artillery arm and finally got it. He was sent to Europe, where he rose to be the Division Artillery Officer (DivArty) of the 94th Division under General Harry Malony in General Ernest Harmon's XXII Corps. Fortier was promoted to Brigadier General, and when the Division ended up in Czechoslovakia at the end of the war, he became Division Commander for a short time. At the end of the war, the DivArtys were among the first to be busted back to

their permanent rank, and Fortier became a Colonel. This rankled him
until his retirement from the Armed Forces after the Korean War, when
he returned to his General's rank in retirement.

4. Fortier could be a delightful guy, and he was a good friend to me.
But he was a snob and could be terribly arrogant. He had been born
on the right side of the tracks in New Orleans, where his family was
an old and distinguished one in civil affairs. He was a graduate of
Tulane. He looked down on officers who had come up from the enlisted
ranks, as having "the smell of the stable" upon them. His wife was also
social, and they were both terribly unhappy at his being busted back to
colonel. He looked down his patrician nose at those colonels who had
never made general. Furthermore, he prided himself on his knowledge
of tank warfare, learned under General Harmon. Colonel E. K. "Pinky"
Wright, on the other hand, thought he was a pretty good tank man. He
was on Bradley's staff at 12 Army Group.

5. One could easily imagine the immediate clash of personalities between Fortier and Wright. The latter had only very limited experience
in intelligence. Many a time, Wright would come into our office on one
matter or the other, and he and Fortier would get into lengthy talks on
tank warfare or the like, with Fortier always patronizing Wright until
you could see the latter's hair rise on the back of his neck. And Fortier
would always talk about "Ernie" [Harmon], or other generals by their
first names.

6. It was obvious that Fortier was not long for the CIG world, the
way he handled Pinky Wright, if for no other reason. Wright was
terse; Louis was verbose. It was unfortunate, because Fortier had
much to contribute, and he was pro-CIG. Sharing his office, I began to
worry how much Wright's dislike of Fortier would rub off on me. Then
Fortier was relieved, as of July 11, 1946, and sent off to help set up
the intelligence program at the newly formed Armed Forces Staff College at Norfolk. He subsequently joined General Willoughby's G-2 Staff
under General MacArthur for the Korean War and then retired.

7. When Colonel Fortier left CIG, he left me his overstuffed brown
leather chair (an OSS legacy) which is still in the Historical Intelligence Collection, and his two-pen, Shaeffer penholder—a tremendous
status symbol in those days! It is still on the Curator's desk. When
Fortier was relieved, Wright came into the office when I was alone,
said that he and General Vandenberg were terribly busy at the time
but that he would advise me of my future assignment in two weeks'
time. (I spent a worried two weeks.) Two weeks to the day, Wright
came into the office, or sent for me, I forget which. He said that he
and General Vandenberg had reviewed my background and experience,

*and had decided that I would handle CIG's legislative and Congres-
sional matters. Thus was the Legislative Counsel born. Previous to
that, I had sent the DCI (I thought it was Admiral Souers, but it probably was General Vandenberg) some notes on the possibility of Congressional interest in CIG. The notes had borne fruit.*

> *Walter Pforzheimer*
> *Curator Emeritus*
> *Historical Intelligence Collection*

The Director of the Strategic Services Unit, Colonel Quinn, who had
succeeded General Magruder, now found himself also under Colonel Galloway as Executive for Special Operations. Perhaps this was so that Galloway could give Quinn orders more readily pending the ultimate extinction of the Strategic Services Unit. Meanwhile, the Secret Intelligence
and the Counterespionage (X-2) Branches of the Unit had been consolidated in a temporary organization of the War Department, named the
Foreign Security Reports Office for want of a better title. The head of this
office, Stephen B. L. Penrose, formerly in the Office of Strategic Services,
became "A" Deputy under Galloway at the request of Colonel Quinn. As
the liquidation of SSU progressed, Penrose logically would have charge of
secret intelligence and counterespionage within the Office of Special
Operations of the Central Intelligence Group. This did not mean that the
Army would discontinue its own activities in espionage. The question was
still being discussed in 1951.[25]

Thus, leading officials were reassigned during the summer of 1946 and
provision made for major operations in collecting foreign intelligence by
the new Office of Special Operations. Colonel Galloway admonished his
subordinates in OSO that they were to reduce to the minimum their
associations with members of the Departments of State, War, and the
Navy; and these were to be only through the Control Officer. They were
to have nothing except official business with the other offices in the
Group. Their activities were to be kept as much as possible under cover.[26]

The conception of OSO which Vandenberg, Wright, and Galloway had
was that the new office should be as free as possible from connections
which might expose its affairs. They believed that the operations of the
Group should be kept apart from the observation and influence of the
departmental chiefs of intelligence in the Intelligence Advisory Board.
The operations of the Group were different from other services of "com-

mon concern" to the departments. And yet the Office of Special Operations should be in close touch with the agencies of the Government which used its product. It was therefore authorized on October 25 to receive requests for information or action directly from those agencies through its own Control Officer.[27]

In this way OSO, in a semi-autonomous relation, could maintain direct liaison on secret operations with other parts of the Government. If Vandenberg and his assistants could prevent it, their endeavor in collecting foreign intelligence by clandestine means was not to gain the reputation for "freewheeling" and self-exposure which he ascribed to the Office of Strategic Services.[28]

Schedules were established in July and arrangements made for taking over the personnel, undercover agents, and foreign stations of the Strategic Services Unit during the fall. On September 12 Vandenberg notified the Secretary of War that all activities of SSU would end as of October 19. There were delays in clearance for reasons of security. There was a shortage of persons to do the clerical work involved. By April 11, 1947, however, the services of all civilians had been terminated. Military personnel had been transferred or reassigned. Foreign missions and stations had ceased to be installations of SSU. There were funds adequate to meet outstanding obligations. Some claims and inquiries would continue, a few indefinitely, but persons on duty with the Central Intelligence Group were familiar with them. Colonel Quinn had completed the liquidation of the Strategic Services Unit.[29]

Colonel Galloway applied himself to European affairs as the United States and Britain economically joined their zones in Germany. Captain Goggins concentrated upon the Far East and left soon for Tsing Tao, where he arranged with the Commander of the Seventh Fleet to support the old mission of the Office of Strategic Services, known as External Survey Detachment #44. This General Vandenberg had been anxious to keep for the Army in China as the Strategic Services Unit went out of existence. The usefulness of the organization, for both overt and clandestine intelligence in China, Manchuria, and the hinterland which it could penetrate, was greater now than ever as the Communist Chinese increased their Manchurian operations in the summer of 1946 and tension grew over Korea.[30]

Stopping in Tokyo on the way home, Captain Goggins reached tentative agreement for cooperation between the Central Intelligence Group and General MacArthur who, we will recall, once had no room in his plans for the Office of Strategic Services. [four lines deleted]

Captain Goggins had to postpone for later discussion the issue whether or not these installations of the Central Intelligence Group should be under the command of General MacArthur and Admiral Cooke of the Seventh Fleet. Vandenberg declined because the units of the Central Intelligence Group were not military activities. He was directly responsible to the National Intelligence Authority. He could not take orders from MacArthur and Cooke.[31]

While Captain Goggins visited the Far East as General Vandenberg's representative, Kingman Douglass and William H. Jackson undertook a special mission for Vandenberg on July 27. [nine lines deleted][1]

In addition [several words deleted] Douglass and Jackson were to learn if General Sibert, chief of intelligence on General McNarney's staff, could be assigned to the Central Intelligence Group. The thought was that General Sibert should become the Deputy Director under Vandenberg, and eventually might succeed him as Director of Central Intelligence. Sibert was to have charge of all collection, both clandestine and overt.[33]

[entire paragraph of seventeen lines deleted][34]

The full results of the Douglass–Jackson mission in August 1946 did not come until later in the administration of the Central Intelligence Agency by General Smith. But the report at the time had value for the Group under General Vandenberg. It showed the ineffectiveness of the Strategic Services Unit in competition with the intelligence services of the Army, Navy, and Federal Bureau of Investigation. There was need for a single collecting agency [four lines deleted].[35]

Douglass and Jackson returned with a careful description of the Joint Intelligence Board which had been organized [one line deleted]. The Board has been called the first institution of its kind actually to administer services of common usefulness to other departments and governmental agencies. Its organization has influenced similar institutions here.[36]

[one or more paragraphs consisting of twenty-nine lines deleted][37]

With the dissolution of the Office of Strategic Services, the Joint Chiefs of Staff had lost their hold upon the American intelligence organization. Their Joint Intelligence Committee continued, but it kept aloof from rather than worked with the Central Intelligence Group. Here was one lesson to be learned from the British system. General Vandenberg endeavored to apply it before he left office as Director of Central Intelligence.[38]

As Douglass, Jackson, and Quinn worked [several words deleted] in London, and Goggins negotiated in Tsing Tao and Tokyo, General Vandenberg himself undertook to settle with J. Edgar Hoover and the Federal Bureau of Investigation affairs concerning this hemisphere. According to Vandenberg's memory, Mr. Hoover was irate; but he yielded to the request that the Bureau withdraw from Latin America. It would confine its activities to security intelligence within the United States and possessions as anticipated in the fifth directive of the National Intelligence Authority on July 8, 1946.[39]

Hoover complied so swiftly in fact that he was preparing to remove his men, their equipment, and records from the Dominican Republic and Costa Rica by August 16 and from Haiti, El Salvador, and Honduras soon thereafter [two lines deleted]. A hurried meeting of the National Intelligence Authority, with Acting Secretary of State Dean Acheson in the chair, was held on August 7 to consider Hoover's action. The State Department had understood that the Federal Bureau of Investigation was obligated to remain in Latin America, if necessary, until June 30, 1947. The Authority directed that a letter should go to the Attorney General asking him to keep the personnel of the Bureau in Latin America [two lines deleted]. Such a letter went over the signatures of the four members of the Authority. Hoover slowed his withdrawals, but insisted that the Group should not employ men who had been working for the Bureau in Latin America.[40]

The episode was not simply a clash of personalities. There was sharp feeling, but that was not all. The Office of Strategic Services had been excluded from operating in the Western Hemisphere. The whole area had been reserved for the Federal Bureau of Investigation on the grounds that the primary concern there had been protection of the United States against subversive practices. It was the field of counterespionage and security intelligence. For the same purposes the Bureau had been allowed liaison stations in Spain, Portugal, France, and Britain. Donovan had sought to remove geographical barriers and to gain worldwide operations. But even in the Office of Strategic Services itself the distinction had been kept between secret intelligence and counterespionage. It was not until Magruder took over the Strategic Services Unit that the two functions began to merge.[41]

They were consolidated in the Foreign Security Reports Office preparatory to incorporation in the Office of Special Operations of the Central Intelligence Group. But there still remained the habit of thought that counterespionage was a defensive measure against subversion; it was counterintelligence rather than aggressive intelligence, a safety device rather than a weapon of attack. To those accustomed to think of it in such terms, counterespionage or security intelligence should continue to be the business of the Federal Bureau of Investigation, especially in those geographical areas where the agents of the Bureau were established.

General Vandenberg did not think so. It was his conviction that, as head of the national intelligence agency, he could not do his job if some other organizations were engaged in the same work. One was likely to expose the other. In his opinion, Hitler's system of intelligence had been easy to penetrate because the parts of it so often interfered with each other. Either Vandenberg or Hoover should withdraw from the field. Since the National Intelligence Authority in its fifth directive on July 8, 1946, had decided that the Director of Central Intelligence was to conduct all organized federal espionage and counterespionage, the Federal Bureau of Investigation should give way to the Central Intelligence Group in Latin America.[42]

The Federal Bureau of Investigation interfered in another activity assigned to the new Office of Special Operations until General Vandenberg with the aid of Admiral Leahy made clear that the Group would not encroach upon the jurisdiction of the Bureau. [seven lines deleted][43]

The value of information about foreign countries from American businesses, institutions, and individuals with connections abroad had long been recognized. The problem of correlating and reducing the overlapping efforts of the agencies in the Government with real or fancied interests in the information had not been persistently attacked. Never has Jimmy Durante's universal judgment been more apt: everybody wanted to get in this act; no one seemed willing to let anyone else do the work for the rest of them. Many of the investigators talked of "exploiting" the businesses. This is a matter of terminology, to be sure; but the usual meaning of the word is sinister. And the behavior of some interrogators has been of that nature, where as a matter of fact the business under examination was seeking to do the Government a favor, provided that its trade secrets were not divulged to its own enemies or competitors. The attitude of policing rather than inquiry to obtain help has often characterized this activity.[44]

General Vandenberg took up the report of the Central Planning Staff. His directive as first prepared on July 22, five days after the meeting of the National Intelligence Authority, provided that the Director of Central Intelligence should maintain a "central contact control register" of the persons and groups interviewed or to be approached. This logically would accompany the use of American businesses, institutions, and individuals as sources of intelligence regarding other countries. It was an obvious service of common concern to the agencies in the Group and others of the Government. It afforded nonetheless, for those who would, an opportunity to object.

The word "control," coupled with the authorization of the Director to maintain the register, gave him power. Another provision would have field offices of the Central Intelligence Group to do the work of collecting this particular kind of "foreign intelligence information." The Departments of State, War, and the Navy were to make available the persons and facilities which the Director might require and to take with him the steps necessary to carry out the policies and procedures. Through the first draft of the directive ran the idea that the Director should supervise as well as direct and coordinate the activities.[45]

It was not enough for the departments that they could give the Director counsel through their chiefs of intelligence on the Intelligence Advisory Board and check him through the Secretaries in the National Intelligence Authority. As the Department of State had restricted Vandenberg's direction and control over research and analysis, the Departments of War and the Navy insisted now upon revising the draft of this directive on overt collection. The Navy had a register of its own. In April, when Vandenberg had been chief of intelligence on the General Staff, the Army had appeared to favor "central control of contacts"; it would eliminate the confusion and embarrassment when two or more agencies tried to use a source of information simultaneously. That practice was, moreover, annoying to those who were interviewed. But in August the Military Intelligence Division opposed the idea that the Central Intelligence Group should have control of the register.[46]

Kingman Douglass summed up the contentions and desires of the armed services and the situation for Vandenberg on August 26 as they prepared to meet the Intelligence Advisory Board. The Army and Navy had not liked the powers of direction and supervision delegated to the Director of Central Intelligence in the original draft; these were functions of their own Secretaries and Chiefs of Staff. To remove their obstruction on this account, the words "direct" and "supervise" and "control" had been taken from the directive. The word "coordination" now stood alone and untrammeled, though it was hard to perceive how there could have been coordination without at least some supervision of the collecting agencies. The services had to be satisfied, too, that the Director would not have final authority in requisitioning military and naval personnel and facilities. The departments should still determine "availability." The Navy could be assured, said Douglass, that there would be no interference with its own "Special Observer Plan."[47]

Douglass expected that the chief arguments in the meeting of the Board would be aimed at the establishment of interagency field offices and at the monopoly of "briefing" and interrogation which the Central Intelligence Group sought. But it was essential that the amount of briefing should be kept to a minimum; only those who had been completely checked for security and discretion should be told what the intelligence services were endeavoring to learn. The representative of the Group would be in the best position to know the specific requests of the departmental agencies and then to interrogate in the interest of all rather than one.

As for the field offices in liaison with local headquarters of the Army, Navy, and Air Forces, serious objection was to be expected—especially from the Army—because the participating agencies would lose control over their personnel to some degree. On the other hand, they were not as well equipped as the Group to do the work. [four lines deleted] The armed services had more to gain than to lose, Douglass said, by cooperating in the enterprise. Moreover, it would ensure coordination "on the working level in the field," where it was essential. Without interagency offices, the competition which was now so undesirable would continue.

Douglass was none too hopeful. He expected "various other unrelated objections for no other reason than to defeat the general purpose" of the directive. There were officers in the Army who had plans for "a G-2 exploitation in this field." It did not include coordination with any other department.[48]

The meeting of the Intelligence Advisory Board on August 26, 1946, was taken up mostly with the objections of the Federal Bureau of Investigation. The representatives of the armed services seemed to be on the side of Vandenberg. But more was to happen before the meeting closed. There was some discussion of the central register, now separated into two parts: one was to be the depository of all foreign intelligence acquired by the Government, a tremendous undertaking even in prospect; and the other, a careful record of the companies and persons interviewed by the intelligence agencies. There was an exchange of views on whether the "contacts" should or should not be registered. The final opinion was that they should be unless they insisted upon secrecy. And then came an end to the hopes of Vandenberg and Douglass that they might get the Intelligence Advisory Board to accept the "monopoly" of briefing and interrogation by the Central Intelligence Group on behalf of all agencies concerned.[49]

William A. Eddy, Langer's successor on the Board for the State Department, suggested and the Board agreed that they should change the paragraph with regard to briefing private persons about to go abroad. It had stated that the briefing should be performed "only by representatives of the Central Intelligence Group." It now provided that the briefing should be done "by the agency making the contacts." If agreeable to the person interviewed, however, a representative of the Group was to be present, and upon request by a participating agency, technical specialists furnished by that agency would also take part.[50]

It is wrong to conclude from this restriction by the Advisory Board that the Central Intelligence Group was denied the right of overt collection in this country. What was denied to the Group was the exclusive right of briefing and interrogating. The chance of eliminating competition among the intelligence services of the Government was gone for the time being. Vandenberg might have taken the matter to the National Intelligence Authority. But there was no point in doing so at this stage in the development of overt collection. The departments were not yet ready to give up their own facilities and rely for such a service of common concern upon the Central Intelligence Group under General Vandenberg.[51]

The Group was not deprived of the right to have a Contact Branch with field offices for collecting information in this country about foreign countries. The fact that the directive, as finally accepted by the Intelligence Advisory Board on October 1, 1946, did not in so many words grant the right of collection does not prove that the Group had no right. The directive provided for field representatives of the Group who should maintain liaison with the intelligence officers in local headquarters of the Army, Navy, and Air Forces "through the medium of local interagency offices"; they would effect for the Director of Central Intelligence the coordination of such overt collection.[52]

It was a loose and indirect statement, but its meaning was evident. Any intelligence which the Director's field representatives obtained in liaison with the local officers of the services was the legitimate byproduct of that coordination. All foreign intelligence acquired by the Government was to be deposited in the central register maintained by the Group. [three lines deleted][53]

These were the more serious obstacles. Vandenberg sent his memorandum of August 21, 1946, to Hoover and received a reply two days later by special messenger. At the same time, Hoover expressed his opinions to Admiral Leahy, personal representative of President Truman in the National Intelligence Authority. If Hoover's views had prevailed, the Central Intelligence Group might have been unable to exploit the rich source of positive intelligence upon world affairs which lies in American business abroad and the travel of American individuals everywhere.

Hoover called Vandenberg's attention to section nine in the President's Directive. It specifically withheld "investigations inside the continental limits of the United States and its possessions," except as provided by law and directives of the President. No one questioned that the restriction applied to the Group and Director; the issue turned upon the meaning of the word "investigations." Mr. Hoover took it to envelop the work of General Vandenberg's field offices and agents in liaison with the intelligence officers of local military, air, and naval headquarters.[54]

Mr. Hoover disapproved. He would accept uniform procedures established by the Director of Central Intelligence. He would engage to transmit promptly any foreign intelligence gathered by the Federal Bureau of Investigation in the course of its investigations of American businesses. But he would not accept control by the Central Contact Register. The Bureau should be exempt from such clearance, because it had to work on a daily basis. Instead, the Group should obtain clearance from the Bureau. After all, it had the right of making the "investigations" within the country. Until Congress or the President changed the terms of the concept, Mr. Hoover would decide what they were.

To Admiral Leahy, Hoover described Vandenberg's proposal as an "invasion of domestic intelligence coverage" assigned by law to the "sole responsibility" of the Bureau. If the proposed directive of the Group should go into effect, he said, it would lead inevitably to "confusion, duplication of effort in intolerable conditions to the detriment of the national well-being." Admiral Leahy did not think so. He replied on September 4 that a careful reading of the directive failed to find for him where it invaded the responsibility of the Bureau. By this time the meaning of the word "investigations" was suffering under the tension.[55]

James S. Lay, Secretary of the Group, the Board, and the Authority, had submitted a memorandum for the Director of Central Intelligence on September 3 to show the changes in the position of the Federal Bureau of Investigation as presented before the Advisory Board on August 26 and to provide answers to Hoover's objections. His representative on the Board had indicated that he would agree to the activities of the Group's field offices in the United States if they confined themselves to "business concerns"; he would still object to the inclusion of other groups and persons for fear that the activities of the Group would conflict with the operations of the Bureau.

The answer to Mr. Hoover in all cases was that the "investigations" which he had in mind were for the internal security of the country. Those which the Group wished to conduct were normal methods of collecting intelligence which the Army and Navy had employed within the country and out of it for years. Lay suggested that Hoover might be assured that the Group would consult with the Bureau on the "advisability of contacts of other than American business concerns." This should preclude "any danger of conflict."[56]

The next letter from Hoover to Vandenberg, on September 5, 1946, narrowed the anxiety of the Bureau to foreign language groups, other organizations, and persons in whom it was "primarily interested because of its responsibility in covering Communistic activities within the United States." The issue was beginning to clear. Mr. Hoover would not be concerned with how the Group should check with the Bureau "in connection with contacts made with American business concerns doing business abroad"; normally he would not care either about scientists, students, and other private persons travelling abroad. He would be satisfied if the provision relating to "other nongovernmental groups and individuals with connections abroad" were eliminated from the directive, so that the Bureau would be free to attend to Communist activities without hindrance.

The tension over "investigations" within the United States rapidly subsided so far as it involved the Federal Bureau of Investigation and the Central Intelligence Group. Mr. Hoover approved on September 23 the changes which General Vandenberg made at his request. There was no need even to stipulate that the Bureau had the primary interest in foreign nationalities groups within the United States. The statement was stricken from the draft of the directive. Vandenberg reported to the Intelligence Advisory Board on October 1, 1946, that he had reached agreement with Director Hoover of the Federal Bureau of Investigation. The Group would not interfere with the Bureau's control over subversive activities in this country. And so the directive of the Central Intelligence Group with regard to the overt collection of foreign intelligence within the United States was adopted that day. It had the unanimous consent of the Intelligence Advisory Board and the Director of the Federal Bureau of Investigation. General Vandenberg proceeded to organize the Office of Operations.[57]

Meanwhile, Kingman Douglass had withdrawn from the Group. General Sibert was to take charge of all collection, both clandestine and overt. As he came to do so, however, Vandenberg listened to the pleas that secret collection should be kept separate under Colonel Galloway in the Office of Special Operations. The staff of his "B" Deputy and Chief of Foreign Commerce, renamed the Commercial Contact Branch, was placed in the new Office of Operations to do the work of collecting foreign intelligence in this country. With it there was joined the Foreign Broadcast Information Branch to take over that service from the Army. The Foreign Documents Branch was added later in December. General Sibert became Assistant Director for Operations on October 17, 1946.[58]

RESEARCH AND ESTIMATES

It is well to recall the mandates under which General Vandenberg took the primary obligation of the Central Intelligence Group before examining his procedure with regard to estimates upon the capabilities and intentions of foreign countries for the policymakers. By the President's Directive of January 22, 1946, the Director of Central Intelligence was to accomplish the correlation and evaluation of intelligence relating to the national security, and he was to disseminate the resulting "strategic and national policy intelligence" within the Government. This he was to do under the National Intelligence Authority, but he was to have full use of the staffs and facilities in the intelligence agencies of the departments.

The first directive of the Authority on February 8, 1946, then instructed the Director to furnish that intelligence to the President, the State, War, and Navy Departments and, as appropriate, to the State, War, and Navy Coordinating Committee, the Joint Chiefs of Staff, and other agencies of the Government with strategic and policymaking functions related to the national security. The Central Intelligence Group was to utilize all available intelligence. It should note in its reports any substantial dissent by a participating agency.

The second directive of the Authority on February 8, 1946, stipulated that the Departments of State, War, and Navy were to assign personnel to the Group upon the requisition of the Director; and it stated that he should have a Central Reports Staff to assist him in accomplishing the correlation, evaluation, and dissemination. The fifth directive of the Authority on July 8, 1946, authorized the Director, in performing these functions, to undertake such research and analysis as the departments were not performing adequately and as, in his opinion and that of the appropriate member or members of the Intelligence Advisory Board, the Central Intelligence Group might accomplish more efficiently or effectively.[59]

These provisions should be carefully studied and remembered. They formed the complete authorization to General Vandenberg by the President and the National Intelligence Authority with regard to the production of "strategic and national policy intelligence." Donovan had perceived the vital importance of strategic information in June 1941. It was imperative again in the summer of 1946 as the Working Committee of the Defense Project in the Pentagon endeavored to amass the best intelligence possible on the Soviet Union in the shortest period of time.[60]

The instructions to Vandenberg were complex, but they were clear. Their limits were defined. The area of his operation was marked off. He had the nucleus of his organization already at work in the Central Reports Staff producing current intelligence with the daily and weekly summaries. The chief of the staff, Montague, was experienced in strategic intelligence and prepared to establish a national estimating board of representatives from the intelligence agencies of the departments as soon as qualified persons could be obtained to give their full time.[61]

The situation was propitious. But there were dangers. Whenever new personnel began to come, they might arrive too rapidly and in too great number to be properly assimilated into the organization. They might continue to think of themselves as departmental rather than national. The supply of information might prove difficult to get in both quantity and quality from the intelligence agencies of the departments, the collecting offices of the Group, and elsewhere. It was easy to say that persons and materials should be available at the request of the Director of Central Intelligence. Delivery was another matter.

Quite apart from their personal ambitions and antipathies peculiar to governmental enterprise, there were political encumbrances without and within the Group. The departments were determined to have equal rights, though they might be remiss in fulfilling their obligations to supply the Group with skilled personnel and adequate facilities. Their mood varied with the importance of an issue to themselves, from wary cooperation to studied reluctance to open warfare. These were meanings never absent from the word "coordination." General Vandenberg deferred to them when he asked the Secretaries of State, War, and Navy to nominate his Assistant Directors.[62]

As the Department of State had something of a vested interest in producing the intelligence essential to national policy, Vandenberg stood ready to let it choose the head of the new Office of Research and Evaluation. He offered to retain the chief of the Central Reports Staff in the position. Montague had come to the Group from McCormack's organization in the State Department. But Vandenberg's Executive, Colonel Wright, felt that Montague did not properly represent the department; the selection should be made from its Foreign Service. Montague had learned his intelligence in the Army.

Vandenberg yielded to this argument, and the State Department sent Mr. J. Klahr Huddle to be the Assistant Director in charge of the Office of Research and Evaluation. The Deputy Assistant Director had therefore according to custom to be selected from some other department. Montague was too much of a representative of the State Department for that post, and so Captain A. H. McCollum of the Navy received the appointment. Montague remained in the Office as Chief of the Intelligence Staff to carry on the production of estimates. For this purpose the Assistant Director assured Montague that he was in fact, though not in name, the Deputy. This, however, as we shall presently observe, was not made sufficiently clear to save him from trouble with others in the Office.[63]

Besides this encumbrance from interdepartmental politics, there were within the Group, as apparently there must always be in governmental services, the planners who think upon policy and talk about policy though they have no experience in the actual work for which they are planning. At first Vandenberg had some idea of letting those do the planning who would have to do the work. But the idea did not long remain undefiled.

The Office of Research and Evaluation was to meet the same sort of interference from the Interdepartmental Coordinating and Planning Staff that the Central Reports Staff had experienced from the Central Planning Staff.

General Vandenberg issued the order on July 19 that the Office of Research and Evaluation should replace the Central Reports Staff. Montague, acting as Assistant Director of the new office for the time being, was to arrange the details. At practically the same moment, Vandenberg called upon him also to produce its first estimate on the foreign and military policy of the Soviet Union.[64]

The preliminary organization of the new office on August 7, 1946, amounted to little more than continuation of the Central Reports Staff with a program for enlargement as funds and personnel became available. There were to be added a Library, an Information Center, and a Plans and Requirements Staff. This staff would do further organizing in consultation with other staffs and branches in the Office. The Information Center was to have charge of receiving the materials of intelligence for the Office and of sending out the products of its research and evaluation. The Library of the Group was to be in the Office of Research and Evaluation at first, presumably to have its resources at hand for the persons with the most use for them. It was moved later to the Office of Collection and Dissemination. The branches of Eastern Europe and the Middle East were temporarily consolidated. Montague's administrative order expressly stated that the Reports Staff would direct and coordinate the activities of the regional branches in producing strategic and national policy intelligence.[65]

The first estimate deserved its fame as "ORE 1." The findings of July 23, 1946, still have significance with regard to Soviet intentions and capabilities. Vandenberg made his request to Montague on Friday; he wished to have the estimate on the following Tuesday morning. There was no adequate staff in the Office. The Central Reports Staff had not been able to get from the departments the persons to put its Estimate Branch into operation. There were not enough available even to assign the editorial assistants needed by the Defense Project. Montague himself was the only one in the Office of Research and Evaluation with extensive experience in estimating. His work on the Joint Intelligence Staff for the Army served him well in this emergency. Fortunately, there was material available in reports and papers from the Joint Intelligence Staff as brought up to date in connection with the Defense Project in the Pentagon.[66]

An ad hoc committee which had undertaken the problem for the Joint Intelligence Staff was not making use of the material accumulated in the Defense Project. The task came down upon Montague himself, if it were to be done that weekend. He spent Saturday until 9 P.M. and Sunday into Monday at 3 A.M. studying the reports and papers, reading cables from George Kennan in Moscow, drawing the determinant factors together, and formulating the conclusions which Monday at 2 P.M. he submitted to representatives of the departments and the Joint Chiefs of Staff. Following their comments, Montague spent the rest of Monday until midnight revising his paper and checking it with the report of the ad hoc committee. The clerical work was finished and the estimate delivered to Vandenberg on Tuesday afternoon.

The summary of "ORE 1" stated that the Soviet Government anticipated an inevitable conflict with the capitalist world, and so it endeavored to increase its own strength and to undermine that of its antagonists. At the same time, the Soviet Union needed to avoid the conflict indefinitely; it had therefore to avoid provoking reaction by a combination of major powers. In matters essential to its security, Soviet policy would prove adamant; it would be grasping and opportunistic in others, but flexible in proportion to the nature and the degree of the resistance which it encountered.

The Soviet Union would insist upon exclusively dominating Europe east of the line from Stettin to Trieste and would endeavor to extend its predominant influence over all of Germany and Austria. In the remainder of Europe, the Soviet Union would seek to prevent regional blocs from which it was excluded. It would try to influence national policies through the political activities of local Communists.

The Soviet Union wanted Greece, Turkey, and Iran within its security zone. Local factors favored such friendly governments, but the danger of provoking Great Britain and the United States in combination was a deterrent to overt action. The Soviet objective was to prevent the use of China, Korea, or Japan as bases of attack upon the Soviet Far East, and so the Soviet Union sought an influence in those countries at least equal to that of the United States.

The military policy of the Soviets was to maintain an armed force, primarily large masses of ground troops, capable of ensuring security and supporting foreign policy against any combination of hostile powers. The Soviets were impressed with Anglo-American strategic air power and sought accordingly to create fighter defense and long-range bombing forces; they would obtain as quickly as possible guided missiles and the atomic bomb. The estimate advised, too, that they had it within their power to develop a considerable submarine force.[67]

This was a masterly demonstration of what could be done by a single person in correlating, evaluating, and producing strategic intelligence. It was coordination of a sort, too, but not the kind that Montague wished to have. From his experience on the Joint Intelligence Staff for the Army, he had proposed that full-time assistants in the Central Reports Staff should both represent their respective departments and work with the chief of the Reports Staff at the same time upon the syntheses of departmental intelligence to produce national estimates. The chief might have the decision which would be the estimate of the Group when approved by the Director of Central Intelligence. But substantial dissents from that estimate would be submitted with it to the policymakers, as stipulated in the first directive of the authority.[68]

Opportunity came in October to restore the arrangement which had been provided on paper for the Central Reports Staff. Admiral Inglis, Chief of Naval Intelligence, objected to the fact that "ORE 1" gave no indication that the intelligence agencies or the departments had concurred prior to its dissemination. There was no issue with Montague. He agreed. The point was that the permanent members of the Intelligence Advisory Board represented those agencies. Inglis maintained that, in approving the estimates of the Group, the Board should employ the voting system used by the Joint Intelligence Committee of the Joint Chiefs of Staff.[69]

What Admiral Inglis was seeking to entrench was the exclusive right of each department to give its concurrence or dissent through the chief of its intelligence service. He wished to have the daily and weekly summaries of the Office of Research and Evaluation, its factual publications, distinguished from its formal estimates. These should not be left to the judgment of the Navy men in the Office; they should be reported severally to the Chief of Naval Intelligence. He should have at least two or three days to consider each paper. Inglis was willing in case of delay to let the estimate go forward with a statement that the dissent, or concurrence, should follow from the department. He was willing to have a part-time representative of the Navy assigned to the estimating staff. But that officer, he said, should be only a "messenger" to the Office of Naval Intelligence. He should not exercise the right of dissent.[70]

At its best, such a system meant that the proposed estimate received painstaking and diligent review by the chief intelligence officer in the department. At its worst, it was merely obstructive, time-consuming, and baffling to the researchers and analysts in the Group. In any case, it did not provide what Montague and others of experience in estimates at the working level sought to establish—representation and responsibility for the departments at the working level. With the Inglis plan, there was likely to be no real fusion of departmental intelligence into a national estimate. The proposal of Admiral Inglis laid the process open to dissents from the departments as they saw fit. In that event there might be no synthesis.

The plan of Montague was to have the men who took part in making the estimate exercise the right of dissent on behalf of their respective departments, subject of course to review by their superiors on the Intelligence Advisory Board. He believed that as they worked day after day with the evidence, giving their full time to the business, they would make more effective synthesis of the materials. They did not have to lose their sense of responsibility to their departments because they became expert in the common concern of all of them. The chances were good that they would make better estimates, and dissents, in shorter periods of time.[71]

Taken up by General Vandenberg, Montague's plan went to the Advisory Board on October 31. It was debated at length; or, we should say, the debate ranged for some time over many phases of the relation between the Director and the Board. Others we shall consider in a moment. At first glance, it seemed as though Montague's plan was adopted and put into operation by administrative order on November 1, 1946. Close examination revealed that it was not.[72]

Each member of the Advisory Board was to designate a personal representative as liaison in the estimating divison of the Office of Research and Evaluation. He was to concur or to present dissenting opinions as directed by his chief. He was to be afforded "complete opportunity to participate in all phases of the development of estimates." But this was far from what Montague proposed. The participation might take the officer's full time, if he and his chief so desired; but it was optional, not mandatory, that he give his full time to such participation in producing estimates. Whether or not the plan should become effective depended upon the willingness of the departments to have it succeed.[73]

When Montague came to take stock on April 15, 1947, at the end of Vandenberg's administration, it was apparent that the departments had been more than wary in their cooperation. It looked as though there had been open warfare upon the effort of the Office of Research and Evaluation in the Central Intelligence Group to produce "strategic and national policy intelligence." The members of the Advisory Board appointed their personal representatives as requested. But the record showed that none of these men gave his full time to the work of estimating. Only one, in fact, held an office in the Group. They were, as Admiral Inglis wished, no more than messengers to the chiefs of intelligence in the departments.

The average lapse of time between submission of estimates and receipt of concurrence or dissent from the departments was seventeen days. Montague reached the conclusion that the procedure hindered substantive agreement as well as caused unnecessary delays. It is no wonder that in February Vandenberg had urged again that he should be named the executive agent of the Secretaries of the departments, and his decisions accepted accordingly as emanating from them.[74]

Another survey of the twenty reports and estimates which had been fully coordinated by August 1947, as the Group became the Agency under the National Security Council, brought out the degree of difference in the performance of the several departments with respect to medians, averages, and extremes. The Air Force had scored the best record with seven, eight, and fourteen days respectively. The Navy came next with eight, nine, and seventeen. The Army lagged with eight, eleven, and twenty-seven. The State Department had the worst record; its median was eleven days, its average fourteen, and its extreme fifty-five.[75]

The last case merits special attention. [two lines deleted] It was submitted to the departmental representatives on May 20, and received the concurrences of the Navy, Army, and Air Force on May 28. A dissent from the State Department arrived on June 10. This was surprising, as prior comments from the Department had not foreshadowed it. There had been some changes in personnel; but more than that, another section of the Department in the meantime had given a contradictory opinion to the State–War–Navy Coordinating Committee. Frequent conferences between June 23 and July 14 brought the dissent of the State Department to its final form, substantially as it had been on June 23. If this presentation of the case strikes the reader as absurd, the papers are accessible in the files of the Agency.[76]

The story of the estimating functions in central intelligence has been carried into the summer of 1947 to show that the Office of Reports and Estimates had not effectively produced national estimates with substantial dissents up to that time. The failure was due in largest part to the fact that the intelligence officers of the departments were not ready, if they were willing, to make the work of the central agency swift and definitive. Such concerted interdepartmental action was remote from their experience. It certainly was not according to tradition except in the dire circumstances of war, and even then it took the leadership of exceptional men to accomplish it with the minimum of procrastination and exchange of views. But there were other handicaps besides the propensity of the departmental officers to hinder the formulation of the national estimates in the Office of Research and Evaluation.

For months it could not undertake the research and evaluation which Vandenberg intended it to have. For example, Galloway inquired on August 1, 1946, concerning the evaluation of the reports in the Office of Special Operations from the Strategic Services Unit. A directive went to Montague. He had to reply that the Office of Research and Evaluation at that time had neither the persons nor the working files for appraising such information. The Reports Staff was at half-strength and equipped only for reporting current intelligence and attempting to synthesize departmental estimates. The Group would have to ask that the intelligence service of the Army should continue to grade these secret materials so essential in the formulation of national estimates.[77]

How much longer the Group would have to remain at this disadvantage was unpredictable. By the end of the year Huddle, Assistant Director in charge of the Office, now called the Office of Reports and Estimates at the request of the Department of State, reported to General Vandenberg that it was still operating at only 20 percent of its proposed strength. It was not until June 1947 that the Office of Special Operations began to have a file of evaluations from the Office of Reports and Estimates. And even then the work put a strain upon its facilities.[78]

After the new Assistant Director, Huddle, came to the Office of Reports and Estimates from the State Department, Montague and his deputy, Van Slyck, remained at the head of the Reports Staff, now called the Intelligence Staff. They were to concentrate upon producing the current summaries and the synthesis of national estimates. This was agreeable to them, and it might have been reasonably effective if others in the Office and elsewhere in the Group had been advised that the Intelligence Staff had full authority for those purposes. But there were difficulties with the regional branches of the Office. There was persistent obstruction by the Interdepartmental Coordinating and Planning Staff.[79]

Beyond personal antagonisms, the issue between the regional branches and the Intelligence Staff was that unending dispute among those who know the facts and those who endeavor to reflect upon them. There is no implication here that a single person cannot attain both knowledge and judgment and present his ideas in good literary form. But there is a disparity between the processes of accumulating knowledge and of appraising it.

The expert in an area of knowledge is expected to form judgments from his mastery of the facts and to express those judgments intelligently. It does not follow that in so doing he has arrived at the definitive judgment, that there can be no other besides his own. He certainly is not expected to be an expert in all fields of knowledge which may have some association with his.

Neither is the estimator supposed to know everything. But he is expected to subject the knowledge and the judgment of the expert to scrutiny and reflection and to correlate it with intelligence from other sources. It is the duty of the estimator to make the synthesis.

This was the issue between the regional branches and the Intelligence Staff in the Office of Reports and Estimates. It was blurred with animosity and bickering over editorial changes of text; one may question an author's fact often with impunity, it would seem, never his style. But the issue was so important in the development of central intelligence that we should ignore the personalities as we look into the controversy.

The Intelligence Staff maintained that it was to have the "final review" in the Office upon the finished product, except of course the decision with regard to it by the Assistant Director himself, who in turn was responsible to the Director of Central Intelligence. This was the opinion which the new Assistant Director held throughout the period of controversy. He failed, however, to make this authorization clear to the heads of the branches in the Office and to others in the Group who were concerned in one way or another with the controversy. General Vandenberg apparently took no part. He was pleased with "ORE 1" and well aware of the experience and skill which made it possible. But he seems to have left the subsequent difficulties of the estimators on his staff to his administrative subordinates.[80]

The number of the branches in the Office increased. By October 1946 a new chart appeared showing the relationships among them, the Intelligence Staff, and the Assistant Director's Office. The Staff was placed to one side, with the line going straight from the branches to the Assistant Director's office.[81]

The explicit understanding of the Chief of the Intelligence Staff with the chartmaker and the Assistant Director, however, was that the Staff as in the past should have supervision over and final review of the reports and estimates coming from the several branches. Otherwise there could have been little if any synthesis within the Group. On the merits of the case we may say that if the Staff had not been there, General Vandenberg would have had to establish some office for the purpose. It was essential to the production of "strategic and national policy intelligence."

Whether or not the heads of the branches felt free to ignore the Chief of the Intelligence Staff because he had been demoted from Acting Assistant Director of the Central Reports Staff in the Souers organization by the Vandenberg administration is one of those personal inquiries which historians are to set aside. Let us not be unaware of it, however, as we pass to the next event in the dispute between the expert in research and the estimator of his product for submission to the policymaker.

On behalf of the Western Europe Branch and others mentioned but not designated, someone prepared a memorandum on organizational defects in the Office of Reports and Estimates and recommendations for their correction. From internal evidence we may be fairly certain that it was written in February or March 1947; its ideas had been taking form long since. From the location of the original, it is likely that the memorandum reached the Chief of the Interdepartmental Coordinating and Planning Staff. It may have gone farther to the Deputy Director of Central Intelligence. Perhaps it reached General Vandenberg, though we have no indication that it did. One cannot be confident that the Assistant Director in charge of the Office had a chance to see it. It is certain that the Chief of the Intelligence Staff did not.[82]

The memorandum opened with the statement that morale in the branches had been deteriorating for some time because of the Intelligence Staff. It should be disbanded at once and its duties reallocated. "Sound intelligence theory and practice," said the author of the memorandum, required that intelligence should pass directly from the experts in the branches to those who used it. The expert must be relied upon for "incisive intelligence." To allow a group of men who spent but little of their time in studying the subject to censor, change, or suppress the conclusions of the expert, he said, was to stultify the product for both quality and timeliness. It was to be assumed, until proven otherwise, that the expert possessed the background, current information, the talent, and the will to produce the forecasts which were timely and directly useful in both short- and long-range operations of the Government.[83]

The Chief of the Intelligence Staff was not aware of the memorandum of the Western Europe Branch. But he was aware of the friction over the so-called editorial and substantive functions; and so, to bring the issue to an end, he submitted to the Assistant Director on April 17, 1947, a memorandum upon the authority and responsibility of the Staff and the branches.

From his point of view, there should be no separation of the functions. Both should be exercised in the branches as well as in the Staff. The distinction between them, he maintained, was that the personnel of the branches as specialists in their particular fields should amass the significant evidence and prepare the reports; the members of the Staff were responsible for supervising and coordinating that activity of the several branches. The Staff rather than the branches should make the decision with regard to the estimates. The Office, he said, could not accomplish its purpose unless the Staff and the branches were in close collaboration. He asked that the Assistant Director call a meeting on April 25 to settle the matter.[84]

The rejoinder on April 21 from the Western Branch, which the Chief of the Intelligence Staff did not see, was that he had failed to appreciate the role of the chiefs of the geographical branches. They were more than specialists in the Office at one end of the scale with him at the other. They were authorities in daily contact with the problems of their areas with "the widest possible, coherent overall viewpoints." In comparison, the information of the Intelligence Staff was "only general and necessarily superficial." The rhetorical question was: would the Assistant Director wish to stake his reputation on the former or on the latter type of authority?[85]

Mr. Huddle left no categorical answer whether he would or he would not, so far as we have yet been able to discover in the files of the Group. He replied to the Chief of the Intelligence Staff on April 23 that the subject had long been considered. He would attempt soon to have the respective authority and responsibility delineated in a general instruction. He did not wish a general discussion of the theme at that time. A pencilled note on a copy of Montague's memorandum of April 17 recorded that no meeting occurred on Friday, April 25, but the matter was discussed on Monday, April 28, in a meeting of the branch chiefs. This Montague himself called. His own papers contain the notes of a statement in that meeting to make clear his position. And then he went on a month's temporary duty in Europe.[86]

When he returned he found that Huddle had left the Group for a post in the Foreign Service. Admiral Hillenkoetter had become Director of Central Intelligence in place of General Vandenberg. Acting Assistant Director, Captain McCollum, had adopted the new plan of organization for the Office of Reports and Estimates. The Assistant Director was to assume the duties of the Chief of the Intelligence Staff. It was abolished. Its three divisions—Basic Intelligence, Current Intelligence, and an Estimates Group—were responsible to the Assistant Director. But a line ran straight past them from the branches to his office. On one side there was space for a "Global Survey Group" in which the Chief of the Intelligence Staff and his deputy were laid to rest.[87]

COORDINATION AND CONTROL

The President's Directive gave the Director of Central Intelligence with his planning the right to inspect the operations of the intelligence services of the departments. This was of course to be done only with the approval of the Secretaries of the departments and the personal representative of the President, who constituted the National Intelligence Authority. Their first directive to him stipulated that arrangements should be made with the members of the Intelligence Advisory Board. But it was far too early in the development of central intelligence to expect any of them to give his consent. The thought that the Director might invade the precincts of the departments was revolutionary. The provision was for the future. It still is, so far as it relates to physical inspection. Admiral Souers made no move in that direction. He kept his Central Planning Staff at work, instead, preparing studies and recommendations on paper that the chiefs of intelligence in the departments might consider. The Staff took upon itself the related but additional function of planning for other staffs and offices within the Central Intelligence Group.[88]

As a result of this activity, which proved irksome to others, Vandenberg came to the directorship inclined to let them make their own plans and set their policies for his approval. It was in this mood that he broke up the Central Planning Staff on July 20, 1946, and distributed its members among the Offices of Special Operations, Collection, Dissemination, Research and Evaluation. The heads of the new offices were directed to organize them by administrative orders. But Vandenberg's struggle with the Intelligence Advisory Board over the fifth directive of the Authority convinced him that he still should have a representative staff to prepare the way in future dealings with the Board.[89]

He established the Interdepartmental Coordinating and Planning Staff for that purpose. Its membership represented the departments, with its chief from the Department of State. Its title indicated clearly what it was to be. Vandenberg intended, no more than Souers, to stress his right of inspection. He was having trouble because he insisted upon his individual responsibility. It seemed wise therefore to have representatives of the Board work with him before he formulated his opinions and reached his decisions; the chief intelligence officers of the departments then would know in advance what entered into his thinking. In short, ICAPS was to have been a working staff within the Group for the Intelligence Advisory Board representing the departments. Like the Central Planning Staff preceding it, ICAPS gained more of a reputation for action inside the Group than for coordinating the activities of the departments.[90]

The Central Planning Staff had conceived of a whole series of interdepartmental coordinating committees which should handle matters of foreign, scientific, military, political, economic, geographical intelligence, and possibly others. This grandiose scheme was abandoned with the explanation that such committees and boards were not necessary; all personnel in the Group were authorized and encouraged to establish relations and to consult with persons of similar positions in other intelligence agencies. This, as we have seen, was not true of the members of the Office of Special Operations. But it was applicable to other offices and staffs in the Group. One interdepartmental coordinating committee was sufficient.[91]

The "mission" which the Chief of the Interdepartmental Coordinating and Planning Staff set for it, and which seems to have been unchallenged by the Director or his Executive, would have kept a dozen committees engrossed. If ICAPS had come near to accomplishing its declared purposes, several offices and staffs elsewhere in the Government would have been excess baggage. It was to act for the Director in coordinating the intelligence activities of the State, War, Navy, and other departments. In doing this, it was to ensure that the facilities of each department were ample, that each was covering its proper fields of intelligence, and that its methods, procedures, and controls were adequate for the collection, integrated research and evaluation, and dissemination of strategic and national policy intelligence.[92]

The most optimistic advocate of central intelligence could not have imagined in August 1946 that the intelligence services of the departments would tolerate such supervision and control. It would have meant inspection of the most vigorous and persistent nature. But of course no realist in the business, perhaps not even the Chief of ICAPS, anticipated that he could subject the departments to such control. The members of the Staff were to confer, to discuss, to propose plans and measures, to engage in liaison with the intelligence officers of the departments.

The Chief of ICAPS intended to exercise a much more effective right of inspection and direction within the Group. He instructed himself to maintain continuous supervision over the planning and coordination of its intelligence activities. And General Vandenberg, who had given the impression at first that he would let the offices do their own organizing and policymaking subject to his approval, seems to have put no check upon the internal activities of ICAPS. In any case, it was allowed the right of constant inquiry and suggestion, if not dictation, to other offices with regard to their "policies, plans, and procedures."[93]

The Chief of ICAPS at once sent a memorandum to the heads of the Offices of Collection, Research and Evaluation, and Dissemination requesting information on the Peace Conference scheduled to open in Paris on July 28. What steps had been taken by the State, War, and Navy Departments to provide reports? What steps had been taken to disseminate the information when it had arrived in Washington? The offices should consult with agencies of the departments, find out, and report to ICAPS. Why the Chief did not send his inquiries on behalf of the Group directly to the intelligence officers of the departments is a fair question. General Vandenberg had established ICAPS to work with the Intelligence Advisory Board.[94]

The Chief requested on August 5 that the Office of Research and Evaluation undertake a general study of the periodic and special reports of the intelligence agencies of the Government. Upon receipt of the request the Office was to inform ICAPS of the date when the study would be completed. Montague had just produced "ORE 1" between a Friday and a Tuesday, but he was hardly familiar enough with all of the intelligence reports, both periodic and special, by all of the agencies of the Government, to answer offhand when he would complete the study of their "general content and scope"—if it had been within his province to do so. He replied on August 9 that the task fell within the jurisdiction of the Office of Dissemination, which had already issued one directive upon the subject.[95]

There were other attempts on the part of ICAPS to keep the Office of Research and Evaluation (Reports and Estimates) "on its toes." The Executive to the Director stopped one memorandum asking it for a report on a lurid story out of China. But the effort to manage its program of production succeeded. In this there seems to have been an understanding, if not agreement, with those in the branches of the Office who opposed its Intelligence Staff with regard to estimating.[96]

The Office of Dissemination had begun a study of the daily and weekly summaries at the end of July to determine if they met the requirements of the President and others who received them. There was question whether they should not be divided according to recipients and classification of materials. Certain matters were for the President and Cabinet members only; other officers might receive daily reports on less restricted materials.

This preliminary investigation brought about by December 9 an adequacy survey which found that the summaries of current intelligence were generally considered good. But there were specific queries and suggestions which gave the Chief of ICAPS an opportunity to criticize. He made the most of it to submit on January 13, 1947, a program of production for the Office of Reports and Estimates. The argument in detail is not necessary here. Its outstanding features were that the Office should have a current intelligence staff giving its whole time to the work; that the Office should issue monthly "situation reports" on the several geographic and strategic areas of the world; and that there should be created within the Office a group drawn from the personnel of its branches to prepare for "National Intelligence Digests."[97]

The Chief of the Intelligence Staff had already submitted a report to the Assistant Director on December 17, 1946, on the production of intelligence by the Office of Reports and Estimates. It was handicapped by the lack of personnel qualified and equipped for the work; but it had kept up the daily and weekly summaries, initiated a special series of evaluations and interpretive comments upon current reports, and carried on the series of deliberate and coordinated estimates which had begun with "ORE 1." Five of these had been published, and six were in various stages of preparation. Five more were planned.[98]

This was a fair record of accomplishment within six months since the establishment of the Office. By the middle of January, when ICAPS offered its criticism, the Office at the direction of General Vandenberg was undertaking also to make oral presentations of the world situation weekly to the personnel of the Group and visitors from other intelligence agencies. One participant has recalled that it became customary in the Group to estimate from the attendance who were the most idle. Attendance from ICAPS, he said, was "exceptionally faithful."[99]

Now that the Office was under fire from ICAPS, the Chief of the Intelligence Staff wrote again to his Assistant Director on January 29, 1947, to counter the interpretation by ICAPS of the adequacy survey. The impression is strong from an examination of the survey itself that the Chief of the Intelligence Staff read the report more accurately than his opponent. Comments upon the summaries had been complimentary for the most part; there had been no demand for a substantial change in them. There was no reason to distinguish the President from his Secretaries and their intelligence officers as recipients of the reports from the Central Intelligence Group.[100]

The Chief of the Intelligence Staff accepted the idea of "situation reports." Their origin from a request of the Navy was in fact separate from the criticism of ICAPS; they had much to be said for them as another form of knowledge between basic intelligence and current information. But the resources of the Office were still inadequate. The work involved in such periodic and accumulative production was tremendous. If the Office could get the staff for it, he said, the revision and issue of subsequent reports should not be done rigidly month by month. They should be governed by events.

To the suggestion that the Office of Reports and Estimates should assign persons from the several branches to the production of National Intelligence Digests—basic intelligence on the grand scale of the Defense Project in the Pentagon—there was the same answer which Souers had given at the inception of the Project. The Group was not yet ready for the undertaking. Its Office of Reports and Estimates did not have the staff for the work, nor the immediate prospect of obtaining it.[101]

The Chief of ICAPS, however, insisted upon forcing the Office of Reports and Estimates to undertake the enlarged program of production and urged that the Assistant Director set deadlines. These were so close that they were preposterous. The Office had fifteen key persons in its six regional branches at that time and only two more in prospect, where a total of seventy-seven had been authorized. But this was a relatively minor point in the controversy. The crux of it was that a planning staff was dictating a program worse than unrealistic in terms of possible achievement. It was distorting the original and true purpose of the Office of Reports and Estimates, successor to the Central Reports Staff.[102]

As soon as equipped, the Office might produce basic intelligence, taking charge of the Defense Project and the Joint Army–Navy Intelligence Studies, and in time developing an elaborate series of National Intelligence Surveys—as the Agency is doing today. It might continue, and improve, its service of current intelligence with daily and weekly summaries, bulletins, and special estimates. It might engage in providing what has been called Staff Intelligence, special reports as required by the Director and situation reports according to regional, national, or functional plans. All of these the Office might do when it had the staff, facilities, quarters, and departmental support for such enterprises. But they were contributory, and they were subordinate, to the primary purpose of the Group which Admiral Souers had stated in his Progress Report. The purpose was the production of "definitive estimates of the capabilities and intentions of foreign countries" as they affected the security of this nation.[103]

The decision of General Vandenberg, recorded on March 25, 1947, by his Deputy, General Wright, favored the plan of ICAPS for production by the Office of Reports and Estimates. He spoke of a "reasonable balance" and recognized the immediate problems of space, staff, and support for the remainder of the fiscal year. But he threw his influence on the side of ICAPS. The proposal of the Office, he said, was lacking the long-range view and it was not sufficiently specific. The Assistant Director in charge should submit his program for the next quarter to the Chief of ICAPS by June 1. The Chief would submit his "comments and suggested revisions or additions" to the Director before June 15. The Assistant Director apparently could then take the revised program and like it.[104]

The production program which Captain McCollum as Deputy Assistant Director had submitted on May 29 for the Office of Reports and Estimates did not lack the long-range view; nor was it deficient in specification on paper. The Chief of ICAPS ordered one of his men to make a tour of inspection in the Office of Reports and Estimates by July 10 to see how it was progressing. The Chief of the defunct Intelligence Staff could look on from the Global Survey Group with perspective, some humor if he chose, and leisure.[105]

Throughout the discussion we should note that the Chief of the Intelligence Staff had not lost sight of the fact that the primary function of the Central Intelligence Group and its subdivisions was to produce national intelligence estimates, the intelligence for "national policy and strategy" which General Donovan had conceived at the start and the framers of the President's Directive of January 22, 1946, had stated explicitly.[106]

Others lost sight of it or preferred to discount it in considering the importance of departmental activities or the particular concerns of regional and special branches within the Group. To this reversal General Vandenberg himself made some contribution when he insisted upon taking over the function of research and evaluation and greatly enlarging the Group as an independent producing agency. This meant duplication in spite of all protests and intentions to have it otherwise. This meant, too, intensified efforts to defend the prerogatives of established services. The close interdepartmental cooperation so indispensable to the production of strategic intelligence for the policymakers was not to be had under such circumstances. Here was a "mission" which might have absorbed more of the time and energy of the Interdepartmental Coordinating and Planning Staff.[107]

The Interdepartmental Coordinating and Planning Staff was not divided into functional sections or branches. Its members formed working groups and received assignments from time to time, each submitting a weekly report of his activities, conferences, and accomplishments. The result was a flow of papers that impressed the reader until he observed how often the same subject reappeared from week to week as unfinished business and recognized, too, that some of these were old friends from the days of the Central Planning Staff. The candor of one weekly reporter deserves whatever immortality this study can give him. He wrote on October 14, 1946, that he had made "no progress worthy of reporting." A week later he had finished the organization charts, but there was "no other progress of note," he said, "except in frustration."[108]

At the end of the year the Chief had called for an annual report and got a list of projects from "a" to "k" which had been "instituted, planned, and completed" by the Interdepartmental Coordinating and Planning Staff. There were additional lists of undertakings completed but awaiting approval, others nearing completion, and still others in the "planning stages." Anyone experienced in the ways of governmental reporting would know at a glance that ICAPS had neither instituted nor planned nor completed these undertakings alone. But the report itself admitted that some of the work had been done by other offices in the Group. What ICAPS contributed was called "guidance." Its participation, though claimed, could not even be called guidance in the case of the establishment of the Contact Branch in the Office of Operations.[109]

The Chief of the Interdepartmental Coordination and Planning Staff was on much surer ground when he considered the difficulties which the

Staff encountered in endeavoring to plan and coordinate with the departments for the Director of Central Intelligence. These were the difficulties which General Donovan, General Magruder, Colonel McCormack, Admiral Souers, and others had experienced whenever they sought to bring the intelligence officers of the departments together. These men seemed not to understand each other's problems. They did not like to turn "operational" information over to civilians. They shied away from the centralization of common functions. They deplored, but they did little to eliminate, duplication of effort. They were unwilling to give up their own activities. They came to interdepartmental meetings poorly prepared to discuss matters which had been for some time on the agenda. And there were frequent changes in announced policy. Any concurrence which had been approached was then no longer valid. The whole negotiation went back to the beginning.[110]

The Intelligence Advisory Board did not accept ICAPS in the role of working staff as Vandenberg wished. Instead, the Board sent ad hoc committees to confer with it, and these specially appointed representatives carried back to the members of the Board what they found ICAPS pondering for the Director. The procedure did not make for speed or decisiveness in coordinating the intelligence activities of the departments. It certainly did not expedite the formulation of policies and procedures by the central agency in which they had a common concern.

THE BATTLE WITH THE BOARD

The Director of Naval Intelligence offered on September 6, 1946, a plan for merging the "static intelligence functions" of the State, War, and Navy Departments in the Central Intelligence Group. By "static intelligence" Admiral Inglis meant political, economic, sociological, topographic, and technical information such as composed the Joint Army–Navy Studies, papers prepared for the Joint War Planners of the two departments, and the Defense Project then under way in the Pentagon. This subject of "common concern" had been discussed before. The chief obstacle in the Group was the lack of personnel and equipment. It made sense to have the work done centrally if for no other reason than to eliminate the waste of public funds upon duplication.[111]

The matter came before the Advisory Board on October 1. The representative of the State Department, Mr. Eddy, caused some distraction by declaring that his department was not willing to turn over to the Group its responsibility for obtaining economic and political intelligence. The representative of the War Department, General Chamberlin, caused more distraction by wondering if it were not possible to "parcel out functions on the basis of primary responsibility." Each would furnish finished intelligence, he said, to others and they could "rework it to meet their particular needs." In other words, there would be no central operation.

Admiral Inglis answered the objection of the State Department by stating that he was talking about processing, not collection. He might have recalled, to General Chamberlin, Langer's point in the meeting of June 28 that any distinctions between primary and secondary interests were extremely difficult. But the Board rambled on, discussing whether the departments wished to conduct the Group as a "middle man" and whether or not one department used the same kind of political and economic intelligence as another.

Admiral Inglis reduced it to simple terms. Each department should retain its own operational intelligence. It should supply the raw materials of static intelligence to the Group, which would do the processing very much like a publishing house, and turn the product over to the departments. They could then put it in a different "final form," if so desired by their "customer," and assume the responsibility for its dissemination. The Advisory Board, however, came to no conclusion at this meeting. A special committee was to make further study of the problem for the Director and the Board.[112]

This committee of personal representatives met on October 8. It too ranged the fields of intelligence near and far from the question at issue: should the Central Intelligence Group undertake to produce basic intelligence for the departments from materials supplied by their intelligence services? The Office of Naval Intelligence offered to transfer its personnel engaged in strategic intelligence to the Central Intelligence Group if other agencies participated in similar fashion. But the Military Intelligence Division of the War Department declined on the ground that it would lose direct control over intelligence functions related to its problems of staff and command. The representative of the State Department emphasized again its "inescapable responsibilities," particularly those concerned with political and economic intelligence.

The special committee observed that positive results could be obtained in some fields. It suggested recourse to bilateral agreements between the Group and the departmental agencies, and asked to be relieved. The Group on its own responsibility made further study of the problem of basic intelligence in the following winter and spring. A member of the Office of Reports and Estimates became chairman of the Working Committee of the Defense Project in March 1947. The Joint Army–Navy

Studies were taken over by the Group on October 1, 1947, as it began its program of National Intelligence Surveys.[113]

The second major issue before the Advisory Board in October 1946 was that of national estimating. We have already carried it into the summer of 1947 in order to show why the primary function of the Central Intelligence Group failed to develop as both Admiral Souers and General Vandenberg intended that it should. Admiral Inglis had been as determined and as clear in his opposition to the Montague plan for national estimates with substantial dissents as in his advocacy of basic intelligence studies by the Group. Through the whole debate within the Board, Admiral Inglis consistently looked upon the Group as a cooperative interdepartmental enterprise and upon the Director of Central Intelligence as subject to more than the advice of the Intelligence Advisory Board.[114]

The third problem of importance before the Advisory Board was the collection of intelligence. It became entangled with production and dissemination as the debate progressed. The State Department proposed on October 18 that in an effort to eliminate duplication it should assume complete responsibility for the overt collection of intelligence in foreign areas upon all political, economic, social, and cultural matters. There of course would be some overlapping. The departments would assist each other. But the State Department would be responsible for these matters. It would share with the armed services the collection of scientific intelligence.[115]

The Military Intelligence Division of the War Department matched this proposal with a plan to coordinate the intelligence activities of the three departments. It was not so much an answer to the State Department, however, as notice to General Vandenberg, Director of Central Intelligence, that the Secretaries and not the Director would manage the intelligence activities of the departments. Vandenberg had heard Leahy say much the same thing in July.[116]

The War Department intended not only to have the departments retain determination of their primary interests but also do their own research, evaluation, and analysis on those subjects. Collection in the field would follow the same lines of primary interest. Matters of principle would be coordinated between the departments in Washington. But in the field the coordination of collection would be the function of the "Chief of Mission," presumably for each department.

Regardless of source, reports would be sent directly to the agency primarily concerned. Estimates too would be the responsibility of each agency; they would provide information on their respective subjects to other agencies as the needs required. Communication would be direct from one agency to another, and not through the Central Intelligence

Group. Each would collect information and maintain files on persons within their primary responsibility; a central file should be maintained for common reference. Each agency should contribute chapters of a Strategic Intelligence Digest like the Defense Project. Apparently this would be maintained as an interdepartmental activity.

The central agency, thus carefully segregated from the departmental activities of "primary responsibility," was nevertheless to maintain supervision over interdepartmental cooperation and production. No explicit indication was given regarding the authority which should determine which department had such "primary responsibility" in case two or more claimed it. The inference is that the Secretaries, and the President's personal representative, Admiral Leahy, would make that decision. It would have to be done by unanimous opinion, hard to get unless the President's personal representative revealed the President's mind as Leahy had to Vandenberg in July.[117]

This plan from the War Department came before the Advisory Board on November 26, together with the proposal from the State Department, the draft of a directive for the National Intelligence Authority which had been prepared by ICAPS, and specific reservations by General Vandenberg. The directive, if adopted by the Authority, was to be accompanied by a directive to the Group providing definitions and arrangements in detail to put into effect the whole scheme for coordinating collection. Vandenberg's reservations before the Board covered the secret activities of the Office of Special Operations and the overt collection by the Foreign Broadcast Information Branch and the foreign information obtained by the Contact Branch from American businesses and travellers. What had been drawn into the central organization Vandenberg was not disposed to put back into the field of departmental activity and control.[118]

The draft prepared by ICAPS brought the proposals of the State and War Departments together and added provisions for coordinators in foreign areas as well as the Director of Central Intelligence at Washington. The stress was upon maintaining him as the chief coordinator of the whole system of collection and the Group under him as the central intelligence organization. The duties of the coordinators for the agencies in the field were precisely indicated according to the situation in the areas. The coordinators might be the chief of the diplomatic mission or the senior military commander—or in some cases both; then the Director of Central Intelligence with the approval of the Advisory Board would designate someone to supervise them. We shall find this provision missing from the final directive. The omission will have significance in the affair at Bogotá in April 1948.[119]

By agreement among the departments, the factors of primary responsibility would be assigned in careful detail: to the State Department, political, cultural, sociological, economic, and international matters; to the War and Navy Departments, their respective military and naval concerns; and scientific intelligence to each agency according to its particular interests. A specific list was constructed to fix the allotments and reduce misunderstandings and conflicts of interest to a minimum.

Admiral Inglis commended ICAPS for its fine paper, but wished to have another week to study it. General Vandenberg asked if it might not be approved as a guide. The controversial parts might be set aside to be considered later. He felt that there should be no further delay. General Chamberlin too praised the paper; but he still wished to assign fields of primary responsibility for activities besides those of collection. He thought that ambassadors as political officers went abroad without training in intelligence; certain principles should be defined for their guidance. And so the Board agreed to have another ad hoc committee which should study with ICAPS and bring back another report to the Board. A companion piece should also be prepared on the coordination of production and dissemination of intelligence. By this time any idea which Vandenberg may have had that ICAPS was the representative working staff of the Advisory Board in the Group must have left him.[120]

The ad hoc committee and ICAPS met on December 3, 1946. They defined "area" to mean a country which had a station of the Foreign Service. They recommended that the word "coordinator" be dropped and "senior U.S. representative" be used. Reference to theater commanders should be omitted, because coordination in occupied areas was temporary. They listened to another division of intelligence into categories, this one by the representative of the Army. The name was different, but the nature of the category seemed much the same: "factual" took the place of "basic"; "current" did not change, but "staff" replaced "departmental." The production of "strategic and national policy intelligence," so essential to the policymakers of the Government, did not enter the discussion. One cannot escape the conclusion that the representatives of the departments were not present to advance the case for the Director of Central Intelligence and the Central Intelligence Group.[121]

The draft of ICAPS as modified by the ad hoc committee and without the supplementary directive of the Group went to the Intelligence Advisory Board on December 17 in what proved to be its last meeting with General Vandenberg as Director of Central Intelligence. He explained why the directive for the Group had not been submitted to the Board. The ad hoc committee had gone over it with ICAPS. Directives within the Group did not require the approval of the Intelligence Advisory Board. The recommendations of their ad hoc committee had been accepted.

There should be no further need for extensive discussion. The State Department's request was urgent. The directive of the Authority regarding collection should be completed and put into effect.[122]

But there was further discussion on into the afternoon. Should collectors in the field make their reports on duplicating pads, or should they not? Should political intelligence be separated in the allocations from economic intelligence? Had they not been bracketed in the State Department for years? Other questions also took time and led to no significant conclusions. They seemed like obstructionist tactics in defense of vested interests.

Mr. Eddy asked on behalf of the State Department that the section in the directive to the Group concerning the allocations of primary responsibilities be incorporated in the directive of the Authority. General Vandenberg consented. With it was included the provision that collectors in the field might send copies to their own agencies when they transmitted materials directly to the field representatives of the agencies most concerned.[123]

Such a procedure vitiated the distinction between primary responsibility and secondary interest. If both agencies had the same access at practically the same moment, what did it matter if one were considered superior to the other? The procedure was certain, however, to eliminate any coordination or control by the central intelligence organization of the departments. It is questionable that the Group could even be thought a "cooperative interdepartmental activity" as it was thus passed by and ignored. But then collection was not yet accepted as a matter of common concern.

Since the Board had adjourned without taking a vote, the final draft of the directive went to the members individually. By the end of the month all had approved without further change. It was issued on January 2, 1947, as Directive No. 7 of the National Intelligence Authority.

It allocated primary responsibility to the departments for collection within broad categories. It then allowed the collectors in the field to send copies of all materials regardless to their own agencies. The senior representative of the United States in each area with a foreign service post was made responsible for coordinating all collection in that area. There was no supervision over him by the Director of Central Intelligence in Washington. All facilities for collection were to be utilized within budgetary limitations to their maximum in order to avoid duplication and overlap. How this self-contradicting feat could be accomplished the directive did not say. It should provoke laughter. But its consequences were not humorous. Coordination by the "senior U.S. representative" in the field was to prove no coordination at all.[124]

Directive No. 7 stipulated that there should be free and unrestricted flow of information between the departments to meet the secondary needs of each. Common sense would be applied to ensure individual initiative and favorable contacts by collecting agents. No interpretation of these principles and objectives should negate the basic principle that all departmental representatives abroad were individually responsible for the collection and transmission to Washington of all intelligence material useful to their departments and the "national intelligence mission." But the directive contained no statement of the authority and the sanction under which violations of these instructions would come to judgment. They were useful as ideas, perhaps, but little more.[125]

There was no mention in the directive of the Central Intelligence Group nor of the Director of Central Intelligence. The permanent members of the Advisory Board had obtained control over the collection of intelligence for the departments, excepting the secret intelligence of the Office of Special Operations and the collections of the Foreign Broadcast Intelligence and the Contact Branch in the Office of Operations. Vandenberg let the directive pass. He had no veto over the actions of the Advisory Board. He might have withheld his approval formally. But there was no point in arguing further with the chiefs of intelligence in the services. He took his case up to the Secretaries in the National Intelligence Authority.[126]

Now that the general matter of collection had been settled for the time being, the specific question of collection in China perhaps could be answered. It had been proposed as an area for trying out the coordination of collection by the intelligence agencies of the departments. As a member of the Advisory Board under Admiral Souers, General Vandenberg had urged that the Strategic Services Unit be kept at work [one or two words deleted] until it could be replaced. The Central Planning Staff had begun to study the problem. Admiral Goggins had gone to the Far East during the summer to make arrangements with General MacArthur and Admiral Cooke. Vandenberg was in correspondence with General Willoughby [one line deleted]. It was time to make the specifications for the activity within the Communist area.[127]

The Office of Reports and Estimates had prepared a draft of the intelligence requirements for China on October 1 at the request of ICAPS. The Office formulated a tentative policy for the United States under the headings of peace, unity, democracy, nonintervention, rehabilitation, and foreign trade. It laid out the fields of subject matter according to the policies and actions of the three parties concerned: the Central Government, the Chinese Communist Party, and the Soviet Union. A fourth field of intelligence contained developing situations in the strategic areas of China.

Under these classifications there were details with regard to trends of policy, military dispositions, industries, crops, and other matters which need not be elaborated here.[128]

From this beginning ICAPS had developed, in conference with another ad hoc committee for the Advisory Board, the draft of a directive to be issued by the National Intelligence Authority. It did not include basic intelligence. It omitted scientific information on the assumption that there would be little in the area. It focused upon current intelligence. Little exception was taken in the Advisory Board's meeting on November 7, except that the text was changed to make the words "essential elements" become "current essentials" and "requirements" give way to "objectives." But General Chamberlin stopped acceptance and issue as a directive until he could see the contents of the directive for collection which should be based upon these requirements for China.[129]

It was not until January 8, 1947, not until after the Authority's directive on collection had been issued, that General Chamberlin came again to the question of intelligence on China, and then he gave his views to General Vandenberg. The Authority's directive on collection, he said, and the plan for coordinating the production of intelligence by the department, which seemed about to be approved by the Advisory Board, appeared to make "the China experiment" unnecessary. Chamberlin thought that it should be withdrawn or at least postponed for consideration "to insure that it be brought into full consonance with the broader directives."[130]

Vandenberg knew those "broader directives" too well ever to accept such an invitation. It meant sending the project for intelligence upon China into oblivion. He replied on January 23, 1947, that the Chamberlin proposal indicated a "misunderstanding of the national intelligence program" as it was being developed by the Central Intelligence Group with the "advice and the assistance of the representatives of the Advisory Board."[131]

Vandenberg then unfolded the argument that we should expect. The Director of Central Intelligence was endeavoring to develop the plans in the President's Directive of January 22, 1946, a year before. They laid the foundations of a central intelligence system which should furnish the President and the departments with "strategic and national policy intelligence." These plans came under the three general heads of collection, research and evaluation, and dissemination. They were designed to facilitate departmental intelligence as well as national intelligence. But it was allocated by the President to the Director of Central Intelligence alone. He had therefore to determine its requirements and procedures for collection, research, and dissemination.

General Vandenberg became peremptory. He requested that General

Chamberlin concur in the immediate release of "NIR China" and that he issue directives to the individuals already named by him to assist the Group in preparing a similar paper on the Soviet Union and the Near East. To cap this ultimatum, Vandenberg stated that he was withdrawing the "implementing directive to NIR China" and referring the problem to his Assistant Director for Collection and Dissemination within the Group. He would issue such requests regarding collection as might be necessary. On February 12, 1947, "NIR China" appeared as the eighth directive of the National Intelligence Authority, with the concurrence of the Intelligence Advisory Board and without further comment from the members of the Board, the Authority, or anybody else, at least that we have been able to discover.[132]

This was the day of the historic ninth session of the Authority. It met to discuss the problem of correlating intelligence upon foreign developments of atomic energy and to hear a report from the Director of Central Intelligence. Secretary Patterson made a brief statement on the transfer of personnel and files from the Atomic Energy Commission to the Central Intelligence Group, and then the members of the Authority heard General Vandenberg pass quickly over the accomplishments of the Group since his last remarks to them on October 16, 1946, concerning the budget for 1948. Vandenberg concentrated upon his present difficulties.[133]

They grew from uncertainty with regard to the "directive authority" of the Director of Central Intelligence. He found it adequately stated in the President's Directive of January 22, 1946, and the fifth directive of the Authority on July 8, 1946. He was to "act for" the Authority in coordinating foreign intelligence activities. The interpretation of the agencies, he said, was coordination "by mutual agreement"; and in some instances this had taken from six to eight months. He requested authority to act as agent for the Secretaries of the departments. The alternative was that the Central Intelligence Group should forward its directives to the members of the Authority for issuance from their own offices. This would be cumbersome, and it would involve great loss of time for all concerned.

The production of "strategic and national policy intelligence" by the Group, its primary purpose as the central intelligence organization of the Government, was further hindered by uncertainty among the agencies over its definition. Vandenberg asked the Authority to approve the definition established in the thinking of the Group ever since it had taken over the ideas of Donovan and Magruder. Such intelligence was that collected from every available source, both covert and overt, and then verified, appraised, and synthesized in estimates for the benefit of the policymakers of the Government.[134]

After listening to General Vandenberg's statements, Secretary Patterson saw no alternative to approving his request, provided that any aggrieved agency might appeal his action to the Authority itself through the Secretary of the department concerned. Vandenberg acknowledged such a right as inherent. Admiral Leahy agreed with Patterson. The change altered only the stress of Leahy's statement in the preceding July. Secretary Forrestal gave his consent. Mr. Eddy, member of the Advisory Board who was also present with Secretary Marshall for the State Department, assumed that normally any directive would have prior discussion by the Board. Vandenberg assented.[135]

The Authority approved the statement that the Director of Central Intelligence should "operate within his jurisdiction as an agent of the Secretaries of State, War, and the Navy," and delegated the necessary authority to him so that "his decisions, orders, and directives" should have full force and effect as emanating from the Secretaries. Any aggrieved departmental agency might have access to its own Secretary and through him to the Authority.

And then to make General Vandenberg's satisfaction complete, the Authority authorized the definition: "Strategic and national policy intelligence is that composite intelligence, interdepartmental in character, which is required by the President and other high officers and staffs to assist them in determining policies with respect to national planning and security in peace and in war and for the advancement of broad national policy. It is in that political-economic-military area of concern to more than one agency, must be objective, and must transcend the exclusive competence of any one department."[136]

It would seem as though these decisions should have been final. They were not. Admiral Inglis, for one, persisted in taking the first directive of the Authority literally. The Intelligence Advisory Board should have "all recommendations" of the Director for study and concurrence or dissent, prior to submission to the National Intelligence Authority. If Inglis had his way, the Board would govern the Director even though he was the executive agent of the Secretaries and "his decisions, orders, and directives" had force and effect as emanating from them. Admiral Hillenkoetter inherited a bitter controversy from General Vandenberg.[137]

INTELLIGENCE AND MILITARY PLANNING

Vandenberg brought the relationship between the Central Intelligence Group and the Joint Chiefs of Staff before this same meeting of the

National Intelligence Authority. The arrangement which had existed between the Office of Strategic Services under General Donovan and the Chiefs of Staff must have been in the minds of all, especially General Marshall, who now sat in the chair as Secretary of State. Admiral Leahy too could well remember when he had presided as senior member of the Joint Chiefs of Staff and considered opposing plans for a new central intelligence organization. Secretaries Patterson and Forrestal were thoroughly conversant with the origins of the Central Intelligence Group. They had taken part in its construction. All were concerned at the time with the legislation for merging the armed services and establishing the National Security Council.[138]

[five lines deleted] There had been representation of the State Department, the Foreign Economic Administration, and the Office of Strategic Services in the Joint Intelligence Committee of the Joint Chiefs of Staff during the war. But the presence of civilians in military councils was not generally acceptable to the Army and the Navy.[139]

Admiral Inglis, Chief of Naval Intelligence and member of the Intelligence Advisory Board, had proposed to General Vandenberg on August 12, 1946, that a channel be established between the Central Intelligence Group and the Joint Chiefs of Staff. They were working upon subjects of common interest such as atomic energy and making parallel reports. There should be a method of handling such papers for the benefit of both. Useless duplication was to be eliminated.

Inglis planned to have the Joint Intelligence Staff of the Joint Intelligence Committee serve as the staff also of the Intelligence Advisory Board. At first glance this plan looked good. The permanent members of the Board, chief intelligence officers of the departments, were the Joint Intelligence Committee of the Joint Chiefs of Staff. At that time the State Department was still represented on the Joint Intelligence Committee. Additional members of the Advisory Board could appoint ad hoc representatives to the proposed Intelligence Advisory Staff whenever their affairs were considered.[140]

But General Vandenberg was aware of the flaws in the Inglis plan. Moreover, he had other ideas regarding the representation of the Central Intelligence Group in the organization of the Joint Chiefs of Staff. General Donovan or his representatives had sat in their Joint Intelligence Committee as well as taken orders from the Joint Chiefs. Vandenberg replied to Inglis on September 4. The Central Intelligence Group was designed to represent the interests of the State, War, and Navy Departments adequately and equitably. A full-time staff for the Advisory Board, said Vandenberg, implied that the Board would have to act unanimously. Its recommendations could be submitted to the Authority at that time even though a member of the Board did not concur. He urged Inglis to join in sponsoring a study of the problem by ICAPS together with the Joint Intelligence Staff. This placed Vandenberg's working committee on a par with the staff of those who were the permanent members of both the Intelligence Advisory Board and the Joint Intelligence Committee of the Joint Chiefs of Staff. In the light of subsequent events, there is little doubt that Admiral Inglis appreciated the adroitness of Vandenberg's response.[141]

Before Inglis could make another move, ICAPS working with Lay, Secretary of the Authority and the Group, had prepared a counterplan. It would establish the Director of Central Intelligence as the chief adviser on intelligence to the Joint Chiefs of Staff and therefore rank him above the Joint Intelligence Committee. The Director would meet with the Chiefs of Staff as he sat, without a vote, in the meetings of the National Intelligence Authority. He would submit appropriate matters to the Joint Intelligence Committee of which he should be chairman, as in practice he was presiding officer of the Intelligence Advisory Board.[142]

Since these bodies were identical in permanent membership, their secretaries would be merged to ensure coordination, though they were kept in separate sections especially to protect certain affairs of the Joint Chiefs of Staff which for reasons of security ought not to be divulged in other parts of the Central Intelligence Group. And finally, under this plan, the subcommittees of the Joint Intelligence Committee together with its Joint Intelligence Staff would be combined with the Group to create a compact and efficient intelligence organization serving both the Joint Chiefs of Staff and the Secretaries of the departments constituting the National Intelligence Authority.

This plan too had merit. But the military and naval authorities saw in it features which they were reluctant to accept. Colonel Carter W. Clarke, Deputy Director of Intelligence on the War Department's General Staff, summarized the weakness as he saw it for General Chamberlin. The Director of Central Intelligence was to be chief intelligence adviser to the Joint Chiefs of Staff, but they would have no authority over him. He would be responsible still to the National Intelligence Authority. An external agency which the Chiefs did not control, said Clarke, would come between them and their subordinates. This violated the usual chain of command; it was a fundamental in the Army that intelligence was a function of command. Colonel Clarke did not discuss for General Chamberlin, however, the point that the Secretaries who were the Director's superiors in the National Intelligence Authority were also the superiors of the Chiefs of Staff. It was possible that the Secretaries might employ the Director as their adviser to the Joint Chiefs of Staff upon matters of intelligence.[143]

In further conversation Colonel Clarke remarked for himself that the Joint Intelligence Committee should be abolished, though one good reason for keeping it was its relationship with the British committee. Clarke believed that the Director of Central Intelligence should be a member of the Joint Chiefs of Staff, and he felt sure that General Eisenhower would agree. Clarke was doubtful of the Navy. If the Director of Central Intelligence were included with the Joint Chiefs of Staff, he said, the Central Intelligence Group would then be in an echelon above the Joint Intelligence Committee. In that case there would be little use for the Joint Intelligence Committee apart from the Intelligence Advisory Board. The permanent membership was identical.[144]

At this juncture on September 25, 1946, Vandenberg took the matter before the National Intelligence Authority. First of all he set the scene by stating plainly that the Central Intelligence Group could not produce national intelligence unless it had all of the information available to the Government. He was getting complete coverage, he thought, from the State Department and the Navy; but he was not obtaining access to the President's messages, General Marshall's, nor the War Department's "OPD eyes only" messages. He would like to have a trained officer from the Group placed in the message center of each department, to review and transmit under necessary restrictions those items which had value for intelligence. Secretary Patterson thought such an arrangement could be made. Vandenberg could have added that he was obtaining secret intelligence through the Office of Special Operations which he might have received from the War Department's G-2. The inference that it was deliberately withheld is unavoidable.[145]

Against this sharp background Vandenberg pointed out that the Joint Intelligence Committee of the Joint Chiefs of Staff was duplicating work of the Central Intelligence Group. The coordinating activities of the Committee often conflicted with similar activities of the Group. The studies of the Committee got priority in the intelligence agencies of the War and Navy Departments because the Chiefs of Staff were the immediate superiors of the heads of those agencies. It had been suggested, he said, that the Group should be combined with the Joint Intelligence Staff. Secretary Patterson responded that he saw no reason why the Staff should not be disbanded. Admiral Leahy agreed with Patterson and remarked that he had so stated to the Joint Chiefs of Staff.[146]

This was the situation as the Intelligence Advisory Board met on October 1, 1946. It is hard to believe that the departmental chiefs of intelligence present had not heard in fairly accurate terms what Vandenberg had said at the meeting of the Authority on September 25. There were random comments upon the plan offered by Vandenberg, and objections in small detail. But the real cause for hesitance on the part of the military men became obvious with the question from General Chamberlin whether it would be acceptable to the planners for the Joint Chiefs of Staff. He wondered whether they would be willing to let an outside agency know their thoughts. He knew well, in fact, that the planners would not. It would require orders from higher up to develop such willingness. General Vandenberg knew that, too. He suggested further study. General Chamberlin agreed. He would like, he said, to discuss the problem with General Eisenhower.[147]

When the Intelligence Advisory Board met on November 7, Admiral Inglis had a new proposal from the Navy. It modified Vandenberg's plan by confining the members in the Joint Intelligence Committee to representatives of the armed services. Thus, it eliminated the membership of the State Department, but it left the Director of Central Intelligence as one of the committee and its chairman. Its name would be changed to Joint Intelligence Board. The Joint Intelligence Staff would remain, but without a representative from the State Department. The State Department should have its contact henceforth only through the Intelligence Advisory Board and the National Intelligence Authority. Inglis believed those connections would be adequate for the State Department. He thought also that the Director of Central Intelligence should be responsible to the Authority in peacetime and become responsible to the Joint Chiefs of Staff only in time of war. It was evident then, as he admitted later, that Admiral Inglis had been in touch with higher authority in the Navy. The Chief of Naval Operations proposed a similar plan to the Joint Chiefs of Staff on December 9.[148]

General Chamberlin brought to the meeting of the Advisory Board on November 7 five principles from his discussion with General Eisenhower. He too had misgivings about civilian participation in the committees of the Joint Chiefs of Staff. It must remain essentially a military agency. But he would hesitate, as Admiral Inglis and his superiors apparently would not, to change the existing arrangements for coordination with the Department of State. The second fundamental in Eisenhower's thinking, said Chamberlin, was that the Director of Central Intelligence had duties beyond the scope of the Joint Chiefs of Staff; this fundamental should be observed. Third, there should be no obstacle between the President and the Chiefs of Staff in wartime. Fourth, no civilian agency should be interpolated between the Chiefs of Staff and their agencies engaged in making war plans. Fifth, and of the same nature, no agencies which were not strictly military should have access to military plans.[149]

To an outsider, this appears to be the continuing problem of today even though the interpolating agency, CIA, is controlled and manned, in large part, by men of military experience. The plans upon which a commander bases his estimate of probable success have to be jealously guarded. And yet no estimating board can give him a realistic appraisal of eventualities without knowing the capabilities and intentions of its own side. The board should know at least as much as the enemy is likely to know. There ought to be no real dilemma caused by civilian participation in the formulation of war plans. After all, the Secretaries of the departments themselves by tradition are civilians. It can hardly be said that they should be kept in ignorance of war plans.

General Vandenberg accepted the principles declared by Chamberlin for Eisenhower, but said that the Central Intelligence Group proposed to have a "watertight compartment" for military secrets. The war planners should have the best intelligence available; the Group therefore should work closely with the planners. The talk went on and on but reached no conclusion. General Chamberlin disavowed personal opposition to Vandenberg, but doubted the wisdom of mixing with the Joint Chiefs of Staff the head of an agency which reported to civilian authority. That is to say, the National Intelligence Authority consisting of the three Secretaries and Admiral Leahy was a civilian authority. So was the President, although the Constitution made him Commander-in-Chief of the Army, Navy, and the state militia when called into the federal service.

Admiral Inglis observed that the Director of Central Intelligence reported to the National Intelligence Authority, and so Inglis would assign additional duties to the Director for the Joint Chiefs of Staff. But he did not discuss the fact that the Authority was made up of Secretaries and the President's personal representative who were superiors of the Joint Chiefs of Staff. Vandenberg brought the discussion finally to an end by proposing further work upon the problem by staff members. Another ad hoc committee therefore was named to deliberate with ICAPS. They might bring in majority and minority reports.[150]

This committee agreed on December 3 that each agency should submit its own plan. The proceeding came to naught. In the meantime, the Joint Intelligence Committee had endorsed what had been Admiral Inglis's original plan to use the Joint Intelligence Staff as the Intelligence Advisory Staff of the Intelligence Advisory Board. Let us repeat once more that the permanent members of the Advisory Board were the Joint Intelligence Committee of the Joint Chiefs of Staff. Vandenberg saw no point in discussing the matter further with Admiral Inglis, General Chamberlin, General Samford, and Mr. Eddy. He took the question to the National Intelligence Authority on February 12, 1947.[151]

General Vandenberg stated his position to Secretaries Marshall, Patterson, Forrestal, and Admiral Leahy. Those who had created the Central

Intelligence Group, he understood, had in mind that the Group would replace the Joint Intelligence Committee. This, however, had not occurred; nor had any working relationship been achieved. The two organizations continued with parallel responsibilities; there was no effective coordination. There was constant friction with the intelligence agencies of the War and Navy Departments over priorities. The duplication was unnecessary. He recommended that the Joint Intelligence Committee be abolished. The Central Intelligence Group should provide the necessary intelligence for the Joint Chiefs of Staff.

Secretary Forrestal inquired if the plan to replace the Joint Intelligence Committee with the Central Intelligence Group had been taken up with the Joint Chiefs of Staff. Vandenberg was sure that it had, through the members of the Advisory Board. He could have said Joint Intelligence Committee. Mr. Eddy, present for the State Department, thought it important to abolish the Committee and to have all interdepartmental intelligence under the Group. Without further comment the Authority agreed that the Joint Intelligence Committe should be abolished and its functions assumed by the Central Intelligence Group, but withheld decision until the Joint Chiefs of Staff should discuss the matter. Admiral Leahy was to consult with them.

What the Joint Chiefs were likely to decide had already been indicated. On December 9, 1946, the Chief of Naval Operations, Admiral Nimitz, declared that the time had come to reorganize the Joint Intelligence Committee upon the principle that it should consist only of representatives from the military services. Coordination with other agencies, he said, should be had through the Central Intelligence Group. The wartime representation of the Foreign Economic Administration and the Office of Strategic Services had come to an end. Only that of the State Department remained. It should be removed from the Joint Intelligence Committee. The Joint Chiefs of Staff approved this concept of the Committee on February 21, 1947, and there the matter rested for months as all were far more concerned with actions in Congress over the merger of the Armed Forces and the National Security Council.[152]

When the question arose again, General Vandenberg was no longer Director of Central Intelligence and was soon to be a member of the Joint Chiefs of Staff. Admiral Hillenkoetter had become Director of Central Intelligence. One suggestion was to be that if the Director were a civilian, his Deputy should represent him in the councils of the Joint Chiefs of Staff. The deputy to a civilian presumably had to be a military person. The possibility that two civilians might head the nation's central intelligence organization was inconceivable.[153]

SCIENTIFIC INTELLIGENCE

The British had shared their information with the American services during the war, especially in regard to the V-weapons of Germany. There had been a reading panel of the Army, the Navy, and the Office of Scientific Research and Development within the organization of the Joint Chiefs of Staff to keep up with discoveries in electronics and new weapons. The "Manhattan Engineer District" was represented in London to coordinate information on atomic energy. [three lines deleted] The Office of Strategic Services supplied technical and scientific intelligence. It had brought to this country foreign experts in air flow and electronics. It kept General Groves informed regarding German progress with atomic fission.[154]

The atomic bombing of Hiroshima and Nagasaki made certain that the secret collection of scientific intelligence would continue regardless of any public controls which the United Nations might establish. All nations would seek atomic weapons in self-defense, and they were likely to obtain them. The spread of scientific knowledge was only a matter of time. Thanks to espionage, the Soviet Government acquired the information on the atomic bomb sooner than anticipated. The nations were bound to intensify their scientific research. They were likely to hesitate even less than in the past over seizing the advantage of the surprise attack. The thought of a Pearl Harbor with atomic weapons was shattering.

General Donovan urged retaining the Office of Strategic Services as the permanent system of foreign intelligence because all nations would increase their secret activities. The Joint Chiefs of Staff understood, too, though they did not care to perpetuate the Donovan regime. Admiral Souers took the initiative, soon after the Central Intelligence Group had been established, to coordinate scientific intelligence with the Office of Scientific Research and Development. He directed the Central Planning Staff to look into the problem. He obtained Dr. H. P. Robertson as his scientific consultant. The Secretaries of State, War, and the Navy through their coordinating committee, predecessor of the National Security Council, investigated Japanese research in nuclear energy and deliberated upon policy with regard to controlling it as the atomic tests against naval vessels were made at Bikini in the summer of 1946. On August 1 Congress passed the act creating the Atomic Energy Commission.[155]

Anticipating that the Commission would take over the "Manhattan Engineer District" from the War Department, General Vandenberg had a directive prepared to place within the jurisdiction of the Central Intelligence Group those intelligence activities which were related to foreign developments of atomic energy. Vandenberg knew from his experience with the fifth directive in July that his plan would never get by the Intelligence Advisory Board with the phrases in it regarding "control and supervision." He accepted the looser concept of "coordination." The papers were ready for the Authority on August 13. Secretaries Patterson and Forrestal approved. Admiral Leahy wished only a few editorial changes. But Acheson, Acting Secretary of State while Byrnes attended the peace conference in Paris, would not permit the directive to issue. Instead, Acheson called a meeting of the National Intelligence Authority for August 21.[156]

Secretary Patterson opened the discussion. It seemed senseless to him that the small division in the office of General Groves engaged in collecting information about foreign activities in the field of atomic energy should be kept apart from the Central Intelligence Group. The division was not concerned with the production of atomic energy in this country; there was no reason to leave it under the Atomic Energy Commission. Secretary Forrestal agreed, if the Commission were not denied the information. Admiral Leahy favored the plan of the directive. Vandenberg assured them that it was designed to provide and not to deny information; he would certainly furnish the intelligence to the Atomic Energy Commission as directed by the Authority. But Acheson demurred. He would not interfere with the organization which was searching for uranium ore. In any case, they should wait until President Truman had appointed the Commission and it could establish its policies. He had reason to believe that the President would so prefer.[157]

Secretary Patterson, however, persisted in saying that the matter was already within the province of the Authority, and it was urgent. The Atomic Energy Commission would only delay the transfer while attending to matters of more importance to itself. Admiral Leahy gave Patterson further support. And so Secretary Acheson suggested that Leahy clear the directive with the President. This Leahy agreed to do by telegraph, with a note to commit the Authority to any change in the future which the Atomic Energy Commission might desire. The President replied on August 23 that he wished to postpone action until he had returned to Washington. There followed delay until December as the appointment of David Lilienthal to the chairmanship of the Commission aroused opposition. In the meantime, ICAPS became much interested in coordinating the intelligence of several agencies on guided missiles and the requirements of scientific intelligence concerning Russia.[158]

As General Vandenberg sought to transfer the collection of foreign intelligence on atomic energy from the "Manhattan Engineer District" to the Central Intelligence Group, he was endeavoring also to obtain a close relationship with the Joint Research and Development Board which Secretaries Patterson and Forrestal had established on July 3, 1946. President Truman had been inclined to continue the Office of Scientific Research and Development which had done so well during the war under the chairmanship of Vannevar Bush. But the opinion of Bush prevailed that the Office had come to the logical end of its career and should go out of existence, much as the Office of Strategic Services and other wartime agencies had done. He himself and members of the old organization were willing to stay at the request of the Secretaries and carry on those functions and programs of the Office which were considered worthwhile.[159]

The new Joint Board was not exactly a continuation of the old Office. The Board was to be more concerned with planning than with operations which had engaged so much of the Office's time. The Office had been an independent executive agency like the Office of Strategic Services, the Foreign Economic Administration, and others which had been closely associated with the Joint Chiefs of Staff from policymaking to working levels. The new Joint Board was directly responsible to the Secretaries of War and the Navy. The old Office had collected intelligence with regard to foreign activities in science, as had the "Manhattan Engineer District." The new Joint Board was interested in arranging with the new Central Intelligence Group for its intelligence while it concentrated upon its planning for the Army and the Navy.

It was in this spirit that the Technical Advisors of the Joint Research and Development Board held a preliminary meeting on October 23, 1946. At their next meeting, on November 20, they had an estimate from the Office of Reports and Estimates to read and consider on the capabilities of the Soviet Union for developing the atomic bomb, guided missiles, heavy bombers, fighters, radar, and submarines during the next ten years. It was, as it said, at best "educated guess work." But it was impressive as coming from representatives of the Army and Navy and the coordinator of the Defense Project; it has since proved surprisingly accurate. With this substantial evidence before them of the work which the Central Intelligence Group was preparing to do, the Technical Advisors then listened to Dr. H. P. Robertson, scientific consultant of Admiral Souers and General Vandenberg, explain the organization of the Group, discuss the problems in the field of scientific intelligence, and suggest ways of mutual assistance between the Group and the Joint Board.[160]

The third meeting of the Technical Advisors on December 6, 7, and 8 brought together General Vandenberg, Allen W. Dulles, and General Donovan for a thorough discussion of foreign intelligence. Unfortunately, there was no stenotypist present to make a record of their remarks. From the recollections of a member of the secretariat who was present, we may gather that Mr. Dulles gave his experiences during the war in the Office of Strategic Services at Berne, Switzerland. General Donovan repeated with his usual fervor the principles which he advocated and the criticisms of the Central Intelligence Group which he had made in the issue of *Life* for September 30, 1946. He did not like the National Intelligence Authority as a board of control. The Director of Central Intelligence should be responsible directly to the President, with the Secretaries of the departments serving as advisers and not as superiors of the Director. [161]

General Vandenberg reviewed his difficulties with the Intelligence Advisory Board. He was at that time, as we have seen, at odds with the chief intelligence officers of the Army and the Navy over the authority of the Director in relation to the Advisory Board, the requirements and the coordination of collection by the departments and the Group, and the place which the Director and the Group should have with the Joint Chiefs of Staff. [162]

The result of this three-day conference in December 1946 was agreement that the Joint Research and Development Board should find a head for the section in the Central Intelligence to have charge of evaluating scientific and technical intelligence and should help him obtain the experts necessary for his work. It was further agreed that there should be a statement of the scope of the term "scientific and technical intelligence," a general plan for securing coverage of foreign developments in science, and a definite relationship between the Board and the Group. [163]

Vannevar Bush and General Vandenberg issued their program for cooperation in the field of scientific intelligence on January 10, 1947. It provided that the Scientific Branch in the Office of Reports and Estimates of the Group should assume the initiative and responsibility for developing a national program of scientific intelligence. The head of the Branch should serve as adviser on scientific intelligence to the Director of Central Intelligence. He should have direct access to the activities of the Joint Research and Development Board pertaining to his work.

It would be the duty of the Branch to formulate the requirements of scientific intelligence in collaboration with the Board and the Army, Navy, Air Forces, State Department, and other agencies. The Branch would be responsible for the plans and the coordination necessary to adequate collection. It would prepare estimates on the scientific capabilities and intentions of foreign countries. It would correlate these scientific estimates with those in other fields of intelligence for the production of strategic intelligence.

The Central Intelligence Group undertook to provide the Joint Research and Development Board with the intelligence to meet its needs, particularly foreign items of specific interest. On its part, the Board undertook to cooperate in supplying the Group with qualified personnel, special facilities, and close day-to-day liaison on scientific matters.[164]

General Vandenberg endeavored to arrange a meeting of the National Intelligence Authority for January 6 prior to the adoption on January 10 of the agreement with Bush. The meeting was not held. Nor had the person been obtained to head the Branch when it was formally established on January 23, 1947. Pending the arrival of the new chief of the Scientific Branch, Vandenberg wrote to Bush on March 13 to say that he was appointing an acting chief within the Group who should report to the chairman of the Joint Board and should make himself and the Branch as a whole fully available. It was a long while, however, before the Branch was equipped to perform the functions stipulated in the program of cooperation between the Central Intelligence Group and the Joint Research and Development Board.[165]

Meanwhile, the Authority at its meeting on February 12 heard a brief report by Secretary Patterson on the arrangement for the Atomic Energy Commission to retain the information concerning uranium deposits and approved the transfer of the files and personnel in the intelligence division of the "Manhattan Engineer District" to the Central Intelligence Group. The transfer was completed on February 18. The directive which authorized the Director of Central Intelligence to coordinate all intelligence related to foreign developments of atomic energy, however, was not issued until April 18, 1947.[166]

Those who were transferred from the "Manhattan Engineer District" to the Central Intelligence Group became the Nuclear Energy Group in the Scientific Branch of the Office of Reports and Estimates on March 28. They were instructed to conduct and coordinate research and evaluation of nuclear intelligence. They were to prepare estimates of the capabilities and intentions of foreign countries in the field of nuclear energy. They were to represent the Director of Central Intelligence in dealing with the Atomic Energy Commission, to attend to its needs for intelligence, and to be, as it should specify, the point of contact between the Commission and intelligence agencies of the Government. This was a very large order. How it was fulfilled will be discussed in subsequent chapters.[167]

Introduction to Chapter V

Vandenberg realized that as long as the DCI was a nonvoting member of the National Intelligence Authority, he would have no real power. He also wanted to gain legitimacy for the Central Intelligence Group, as well as the authority to control personnel, funds, contracts, and operations. His problem was that the post of Director of Central Intelligence and the Central Intelligence Group were based only on the President's letter to the Secretaries of State, War, and the Navy. To gain the authority he envisioned for the DCI and the CIG, he would need an act of Congress.

The legitimization of the Director of Central Intelligence, a central intelligence organization, and the concept of national intelligence came about in a two-step process. The first step was the passage of the National Security Act of 1947, which provided Congressional authority to the position of DCI and established the Central Intelligence Agency. The National Security Act also defined and established a legal basis for the responsibilities of the DCI and CIA. The second step was the passage of the Central Intelligence Agency Act of 1949, which served as "enabling legislation" for the Agency, in effect filling in many of the details of how the CIA would operate after the National Security Act had established the general principles.

Vandenberg directed the CIG General Counsel, Lawrence R. Houston, to draft a bill to be submitted to Congress on the statutory position he desired for the CIG. In this draft Vandenberg specifically omitted any provision for the Intelligence Advisory Board, which consisted of the chief intelligence officers from the Army, Navy, and State Departments and which had frustrated his control of the CIG. Vandenberg considered the departments' unwillingness to cooperate and surrender departmental intelligence and personnel vital to national intelligence the greatest obstacle to a unified and effective national intelligence organization.

Vandenberg's efforts to strengthen the DCI and the CIG coincided with efforts throughout the U.S. national security community to create the organizations necessary to meet the new challenges that were emerging with the onset of the Cold War. Prior to World War II, the United States lacked—in addition to a national strategic intelligence agency—both a unified military command structure and a top-level council that combined the diplomatic, military, economic, and intelligence components of government. Some of these organizations had been established during the war (the OSS and the Joint Chiefs of Staff are both examples), but their legitimacy had lapsed with the onset of peace.

In January 1947 Truman approved the decision of Secretaries Patterson and Forrestal to support legislation consolidating the military and establishing a council of national defense and a central intelligence organization. The White House Drafting Committee produced its own version of a national defense establishment. Although the drafting committee considered omitting any mention of a central intelligence organization, lobbying by Vandenberg and his Executive Assistant (later Deputy DCI) Brigadier General E.K. "Pinky" Wright won them over. The draft released to the press in February 1947 stated that there should be a Central Intelligence Agency run by a Director of Central Intelligence under a National Security Council. The National Intelligence Authority and the Central Intelligence Group would cease to exist, as their basic functions were to be taken over by the National Security Council and the Central Intelligence Agency respectively.

President Truman sent the bill for a national defense establishment to Congress on February 26, 1947. In the hearings that followed, the debate focussed on whether the DCI should be a military person or a civilian, how long the tenure of the DCI should be, to whom or what the CIA should be accountable, and whether the CIA should be allowed to collect its own intelligence independent of the military intelligence organizations. More often than not, Vandenberg prevailed over his critics in the military services, who fought a losing battle to maintain their effective control over U.S. intelligence.

The National Security Act was passed by Congress and approved by President Truman on July 26, 1947. This law established the basic organizational structure on which the United States was to rely for the duration of the Cold War and even to this day. In the process of setting up this structure, the Central Intelligence Agency was created and one more step was taken in the development of a national centralized intelligence community.

The declared intention of the National Security Act was "to unify direction of the separate military departments under civilian control." It chartered a National Security Council, which was to consist of the Secretaries of State and Defense and other Secretaries and appointees of the President. The Act also established a Central Intelligence Agency, which was to operate under the authority of the NSC and was to be headed by a Director of Central Intelligence. The DCI could be recruited from either the military or from civilian life and was to be appointed by the President and confirmed by the the Senate. The Act also stated that the mission of the CIA was "coordinating the intelligence activities of the several Government departments and agencies in the interest of national security"—the language Vandenberg had sought to establish the primacy of the DCI and CIA.

The National Security Act made several significant contributions to the central intelligence community and the new Agency. Not only would the DCI continue to coordinate, evaluate, and disseminate intelligence information, but he would also be responsible for advising the NSC on intelligence and national security matters. The Act granted the CIA the status of a national intelligence service, stating that it was to perform "additional services of common concern" to the departments. The National Security Act also eliminated some of the obstacles that Souers and Vandenberg had faced in attempting to act as the country's top intelligence official; it made no provision for the Intelligence Advisory Board. Instead, the DCI was permitted to appoint an advisory committee and advisory personnel as he saw fit.

Possibly most important, the National Security Act added permanence to the post of DCI and the notion of a national intelligence community. Because the DCI and CIA were now based on law, and not merely executive action, the President could not unilaterally expand, limit, or revoke the duties and responsibilities of the Director and the Agency. Not that such Presidential action was a real threat; the problem had always been that the DCI had to fight for his authority in Executive Branch battles with the military services, the FBI, and the State Department. Now he had leverage from outside—the authority of Congress—to press his case. Any would-be encroacher would not only have to obtain a Presidential order to limit the DCI; he would also require new legislation from Congress, which also had added its imprimatur to a national intelligence community.

The final measure necessary to establish the CIA as a Congressionally authorized body was enabling legislation, or the detailed listing of functions and responsibilities assigned to the Agency and its head, the DCI. One key issue concerned the appropriation and accountability of funds for secret intelligence operations. The Bureau of the Budget and Congress had not previously needed a routine system for dealing with unvouchered funds during peacetime. Ultimately the Congress agreed that "objects of a confidential, extraordinary, or emergency nature" were to be accounted for "solely on the certificate of the Director."

With the enactment of the Central Intelligence Agency Act of 1949 on June 20, 1949, the CIA now had full authorization for procurement of personnel, supplies, services, and other facilities. Even so, as would soon be clear, an act of Congress was a necessary, but not sufficient, condition for the emergence of a strong DCI. Although the military services and the State Department could not do away with the DCI and CIA, they did not necessarily have to cooperate with them either.

V

ACTION BY CONGRESS, 1947–1949

NATIONAL SECURITY

 The movement to gather the armed services in a system of national defense carried with it the idea of a central intelligence agency. Disaster to men and ships in Pearl Harbor convinced as nothing else could that all branches of the Government must share their knowledge of hostile capabilities and intentions completely and with dispatch. Experience with the British in the Combined Chiefs of Staff and their Combined Intelligence Committee proved the value of concerted effort. The American services had to meet the British with their own Joint Chiefs of Staff and Intelligence Committee. Since the Foreign Office was closely associated with the British Navy and Army, it was natural that the Department of State and also the extraordinary agencies of war, the Foreign Economic Administration and the Office of Strategic Services, should participate in the Joint Intelligence Committee and its working staff. Progress from the cooperation of allied forces in the field to success under the unified command of Eisenhower gave impetus toward permanent unification. A flurry of bills in the committees of Congress endeavored to apply these experiences in reorganizing the means of common defense and providing the future weapons of national security.[1]

Robert P. Patterson, Under Secretary to Stimson, declared before the Woodrum Committee of the House on April 16, 1944, that he was "wholeheartedly in favor of consolidating the War Department and the Navy Department into a single department of armed forces." Patterson had been constantly impressed by the need to eliminate duplication and conflict in administration. The Army and Navy should not compete for the supplies of war. In total war there must be total mobilization of industry. There must be controls, priorities, allocations of materials and facilities. All of these complicated matters required direction. "Cooperation," he said, "is never as good as command in time of war."[2]

Secretary Forrestal of the Navy also saw the need to reconstruct the armed services. But there were distinctions to be sturdily maintained for the Navy, by nature as well as tradition separate from and rival to the older service. These were as imperative to men of the Navy as the insistence of the Marines upon distinction from the Navy itself. Forrestal turned for an impartial survey and report to Ferdinand Eberstadt, a civilian of much experience during the war. But it was significant that in his letter on June 19, 1945, Forrestal should ask Eberstadt to answer the question whether the unification of the War and Navy Departments under a single head would improve our national security. If not, might there be some other way?[3]

Eberstadt's finding, with the aid of many experts, was something less than unification. There should be three coordinate services, War, Navy, and Air Force, each with a civilian Secretary in the President's Cabinet. They should be drawn together with the Secretary of State and the Chairman of the National Security Resources Board in the National Security Council. Within the jurisdiction of this Council, and beside the Joint Chiefs of Staff, though separate from them, there should be a Director and a Central Intelligence Agency reporting to the National Security Council.[4]

It was too soon to be more specific regarding the central intelligence organization. When Eberstadt made his report to Forrestal on September 25, 1945, Donovan's Office of Strategic Services was just expiring. The Bureau of the Budget and the State Department were starting their drive to place the foreign intelligence service in the State Department. The Joint Chiefs of Staff were bringing out again the plan which had resulted from the debate over the "services" and the "civilian" plans and which had been exposed to public view in February, amid shouts of "super-spy" and "Gestapo."[5]

As the Lovett Committee in the War Department worked over the proposal of the Joint Chiefs during the fall of 1945, and representatives of the Army and Navy maneuvered to keep the Department of State from taking the central intelligence system, the Senate's Committee on Military Affairs held hearings upon bills which provided for a single department of armed forces, or military security, or common defense. The titles varied with the preferences of their authors. The proposals came to much the same conclusion: there should be a consolidation of the armed services in one department of the Government. In most there was room for some kind of a federal intelligence agency.[6]

PLACEMENT OF THE GROUP

The new intelligence organization was not intended to be the "fourth arm" which Donovan had described to General Walter B. Smith in September 1943, with a place beside the Army, Navy, and Air Force and its head a member of the Joint Chiefs of Staff. Nor was it to be Donovan's independent civilian service responsible solely to the President or to a General Manager in the Executive Office. It was not to be the State Department's coordinating committees under the McCormack plan or some compromise of that plan. It was to be the President's information service, with a Director responsible to an Authority composed of the President's Secretaries and his personal representative. The task of those who were putting this organization to work under the President's Directive of January 22, 1946, was not easy, as Congressional committees considered bills for consolidating or unifying or coordinating the ground, sea, and air forces in the national military establishment.[7]

It was not certain that the Central Intelligence Group would function as a truly interdepartmental activity at the same time that its head, the Director of Central Intelligence, exercised the power as well as the responsibility which the President intended the Director to have. The intelligence officers of the services who constituted the Intelligence Advisory Board did not respect the position of the Director of Central Intelligence as a nonvoting member of the National Intelligence Authority with direct access to the President. The Advisory Board made this very apparent to General Vandenberg through the summer and fall of 1946. His successor, Admiral Hillenkoetter, was to learn it also from his Intelligence Advisory Committee under the National Security Council.[8]

The process of change was double. While enduring pressure from the established services, as it still is, the central intelligence system was moving also from executive to statutory foundations. This had been the intention of its creators. There was ample authority for the Central Intelligence Group to be a coordinating body as originally conceived under the constitutional powers of the President. But he could establish and abandon such an interdepartmental organization as he wished. For this reason, if no other, it was essential to transfer the organization to a statutory basis; its funds and properties should be firmly set upon law. If the organization were to engage in operations of any sort, it should have continuity and insurance against the whim of this President or the next. There was an additional advantage in its establishment by Congress on Capitol Hill. The Central Intelligence Agency would be less open to accusation as another "Gestapo," an instrument of tyranny in the White House.

The difficulty was to preserve and to improve the President's organization as it became the creature of Congress. Early bills in the spring of 1946 provided but loosely for establishing a Central Intelligence Agency with a Director who might be appointed from either civilian or military life. Often the functions of the Agency were not distinguished from those of the Director. More time was given to the Director's salary and to protecting his military privileges in case he were to come from one of the services than to the powers which he might develop while performing the duties and meeting the responsibilities of his office. As often, there was no clear delineation of the jurisdictions of the departmental intelligence agencies in relation to the jurisdiction of the central agency. Francis Parkman on the Central Planning Staff took considerable pains with a critical examination of one of these bills for Admiral Souers. In this case, a significant omission had been the clause of the President's Directive providing the right of inspection by the Director in the intelligence operations of the departments.[9]

Admiral Souers's final report as Director of Central Intelligence on June 7, 1946, urged legislation by Congress and an independent budget for the National Intelligence Authority and its Central Intelligence Group, either as a separate agency or as part of the system of national defense. General Vandenberg's counsel advised him on June 13 that the administrative authority of the Group at that time was "purely a coordination function with no substance or authority to act on its own responsibility in other than an advisory and directing capacity."[10]

The Group had no power to take action in regard to personnel, payrolls, and vouchers, travel, procurement of supplies for itself, or contracts. It had no independent power to expend vouchered or unvouchered funds; it was dependent upon the Departments of State, War, and the Navy for its funds and bound by the restrictions governing them. The Secretary of War, for example, might give the Director of Central Intelligence unvouchered funds to expend at his discretion, "but even so the certification of the voucher would have to be done by the Secretary." Moreover, the Group was so hampered by the Independent Offices Appropriation Act that its funds from the departments would practically end within another year. In short, there would have to be specific appropriations by Congress.[11]

According to the memory of his counsel, General Vandenberg asked for the draft of a bill "by tomorrow," much as he called upon the Chief of the Reports Staff to produce "ORE 1" on the capabilities and intentions of the Soviet Union over a single weekend. The draft was forthcoming in due time. It served as the enabling bill of December 1946 when the drafting committee of the Army, Navy, and the White House came to prepare legislation for the National Defense Establishment and the National Security Council.[12]

The proposal from Vandenberg's counsel reflected Donovan's principles and Magruder's reasoning, the purposes of the President's Directive, and experiences in the Office of Strategic Services of the men who drafted it. It profited, too, from the difficulties of the Central Intelligence Group under Souers. Persons skilled in intelligence were hard to obtain from the departments. The collection of foreign intelligence by separate agencies had proved ineffective. There ought to be coordination of the work of the several agencies and centralization of the processes of analyzing, evaluating, and disseminating the information for the makers of national policy. There should be provision for other measures in the field of foreign intelligence to defend the nation.[13]

The President would now appoint his personal representative in the Authority with the consent of the Senate as he did the Secretaries according to the requirements of the Constitution. The Director was expressly designated the head of the Agency; his duties were not set apart from those of the Agency as they had been from those of the Group in the President's Directive. It was the Agency which now, under the supervision and direction of the Authority, should exercise by law the familiar duties of correlating and evaluating intelligence, making plans for coordination, providing services of common concern, and performing other functions as directed by the President or the Authority.

This concept of the Agency was somewhat different from that of the Group. Persons provided by the departments constituted the Group. The Agency, however, would be an institution unto itself. The personnel would hold offices in it; they would not comprise it. They would be less independent of the Director and, by so much, less representative of the departments from which they came.

Under the bill proposed for Vandenberg, the departments were to retain their own intelligence services, except as relieved of certain activities by the Agency at the order of the Authority. They were to make their intelligence freely available to the Agency. They were to extend to it the use of their facilities and services, and they were to participate in its projects as similarly directed. Their own intelligence operations were to be open to the Director's inspection in connection with the planning of the Agency.

It would be his duty to protect the sources and methods of intelligence. It is well to remember that this provision in regard to the protection of sources originated with the military men during the discussion of January 1945. If they were to allow the proposed Director of Central Intelligence to inspect their intelligence operations, he was to undertake to safeguard their military operations against exposure.

The proposal of Vandenberg's counsel stated that the Agency, like the Group, should have no police powers, no right to subpoena, no powers or functions of law enforcement, either within or without the continental limits of the United States. There should be no ground whatever for suspicion that the United States was setting up a Gestapo to terrorize the American people. Nor should the Federal Bureau of Investigation have any cause to worry that its jurisdiction over internal security would be curtailed.[14]

Out of recent experience came the provision that the Agency should procure, train, and supervise its own employees. The hope was that in time it would not have to depend upon the assignment of military and naval personnel for tours of duty in the intelligence work of the Agency. The bill also sought general authority from Congress so that the Agency might procure services, supplies, and equipment, handle financial matters, transfer funds, pay allowances and expenses for transportation, and make similar expenditures upon the certification of the Director. Within appropriations by Congress, he would be free to employ persons and spend money for specified purposes, without regard for the Act of Congress regulating travel and subsistence. He might have expenditures of a confidential nature accounted for solely upon his certificate as sufficient voucher. Any part of the act held invalid was not to affect the rest of it.

This was the measure which Houston, General Counsel of the Group, and Lay, Secretary of the Authority, took into conference with Clark M. Clifford, Special Counsel to the President. Lay had made some verbal changes from his experience in helping with the construction of the original charters of the Authority and the Group. Clifford, evidently unfamiliar with the details in the Fifth Directive of the Authority which General Vandenberg had obtained on July 8, 1946, and the development of the offices within the Group, was surprised by the magnitude of its organizations and operations. He had thought the Group a small activity for coordinating the intelligence of the departments and little else. After examining this bill he remarked that it seemed good to him. It is to be noted especially that it contained no provision for an Intelligence Advisory Board composed of the chief intelligence officers from the Army, the Navy, and the Department of State. The omission was deliberate.[15]

THE WHITE HOUSE BILL

The American press carried dispatches from London, dated October 4, 1946, announcing that the British Army, Navy, and Air Command had been brought together under a Minister of Defense. The new arrangement would put in his control such interservice organizations as the Joint Intelligence Bureau [two lines deleted]. How much this action in Britain influenced procedure here is undetermined. There is no question that the British decision drew attention. It may have accelerated a movement which had been developing for some time toward a compromise of the opposing plans of the War and Navy Departments. General Collins had presented another plan in the fall of 1945 from the Joint Chiefs of Staff to place the three coordinate services of Army, Navy, and Air Force under a Chief of Staff of the Armed Forces who in turn should be responsible to a Secretary under the President as Commander-in-Chief.[16]

In any case, President Truman received and approved a letter, jointly signed by Secretaries Patterson and Forrestal on January 16, 1947, announcing that they had agreed to support legislation establishing a council of national defense, a national security resources board, and a central intelligence agency. The armed services should come under a secretary of national defense; but each, reorganized as a department, should have its own secretary. There should then be a war council of the secretaries and military heads of the services, a joint chiefs of staff, and a full-time joint staff of the three services. The Secretary of National Defense should be vested with authority under the President to establish common policies and programs.[17]

A drafting committee for what may be called the White House bill consisted of Charles S. Murphy, Administrative Assistant to the President, General Lauris Norstad for the Army, and Admiral Forrest Sherman representing the Navy. Their task was to fill in the details of the act for the National Defense Establishment and the National Security Council according to the principles in the joint letter of the Secretaries. A major concern from the point of view of the White House, if not the armed services, was the disposition of the National Intelligence Authority and the Central Intelligence Group operating under the President's Directive. On January 23 General Vandenberg sat in conference with the drafting committee and made his views and wishes unmistakable. He was by that time at the end of his endeavor to work with the Intelligence Advisory Board and about to request that the Secretaries in the National Intelligence Authority make the Director of Central Intelligence their executive agent.[18]

The preliminary draft of the White House bill included practically without change the sections on intelligence from a Senate bill such as Francis Parkman had criticized in May for the Director of Central Intelligence. Having just come to his office on January 20, Murphy was not aware that an enabling bill for the Group had been discussed with Clifford. Murphy suggested that it should replace the proposed sections on intelligence for the initial discussions. This eliminated most of the suggestions which Vandenberg's legislative adviser was prepared to offer. But his proposal that mention should be made in the declaration of policy with respect to centralized intelligence received support from Admiral Sherman.[19]

General Vandenberg stated emphatically in this meeting on January 23 that he was opposed to having the Agency or the Director participate in the policymaking of the Government. Their function was to provide the intelligence necessary for the makers of policy. But he was insistent that the Director should attend the meetings of the National Security Council. General Norstad offered objections from the experiences of the Joint Chiefs of Staff with observers. Admiral Sherman suggested that the Director might normally be present at the discretion of the Council. In this Vandenberg concurred, and so the matter rested for the time being, with the provision that the Joint Chiefs might attend sessions of the Council upon the same terms.

Vandenberg explained his difficulties in going to the Authority with so many problems. It would be worse, he thought, if the Director were obliged to seek guidance and direction from the much larger Council contemplated in the bill. He was assured by its drafters, however, that the intent of the act would be to have the Central Intelligence Agency operate independently in large measure; it would come under the Council's direction only on specific matters as the Council from time to time might desire. There was no intention that the Agency should have to ask continually for approval. Upon this understanding Vandenberg withdrew his proposal that, in regard to the administration of the Agency, the Director should receive guidance only from the Secretaries of State and Defense and the personal representative of the President in the proposed Council.

Vandenberg closed his remarks before the drafting committee on January 23 with comments on the difficulties of clandestine operations. They must be supported, he said, by legislation which authorized the use of unvouchered funds. Personnel had to be subject to discharge upon the merest question of loyalty. Concerning these necessities there was entire agreement in the committee and assurance that provision for them would be included in the bill.[20]

It was the final sense of the meeting that the Director of Central Intelligence should report to the proposed Council. Vandenberg declared that neither the President nor he wanted another agency "freewheeling" around the Government. But the Agency should have sufficient power to perform its own functions without having to seek specific approval from the Council for each action. It is to be noted again that no provision was being made within the Agency for an Intelligence Advisory Board representing the departments.[21]

The corrections were submitted to the drafting committee that same day. On the next, January 25, Vandenberg's legislative officer, Walter L. Pforzheimer, prepared an additional paragraph at Murphy's suggestion specifically providing for the dissolution of the Authority and the Group and the transfer of personnel, property, and records from the Group to the Agency; unexpended balances of the Group should be available and authorized in like manner to the Agency. And then later on January 25 Murphy announced that the drafting committee had decided to omit from the bill all but the barest mention of the proposed Central Intelligence Agency.

General Norstad and Admiral Sherman, after thinking over the discussion of January 23 and conferring with their superiors in the War and Navy Departments, concluded that the time was not right for so complete and detailed a proposal as the enabling bill of the Group. Reasons given to Vandenberg's legislative officer were that substantive portions of it were too controversial and subject to attack by other agencies. One can imagine that the omission of an advisory board composed of intelligence officers from the departments was as distasteful to many in the Army and Navy.

It was said also that the general authorities which the Group sought for managing its properties, funds, and expenditures would invite objections and cause delays in passing the National Security Act. The Group might later justify its requests in its own bill, given more time in hearings before the committees of Congress. There was indeed point in avoiding argument over detail for the Central Intelligence Agency, as the ambitions of the Marine Corps were being held in check. The enabling measure was good. The act for the Central Intelligence Agency which eventually became law gained from the experiences of the next two years.[22]

The decision to set the enabling act aside was not meant, however, to stop further suggestion by General Vandenberg and his advisers in the Group. Admiral Leahy reassured Colonel Wright, acting in the absence of Vandenberg abroad. Wright therefore requested that the drafting committee include in the brief section of the National Security Act allotted to the Central Intelligence Agency two specific provisions: there should be a Deputy Director; and, as the President's Directive had made the Director a nonvoting member of the National Intelligence Authority, it seemed proper to have him placed in a similar relationship with the National Security Council. Wright urged upon Murphy a paragraph to make the Director of Central Intelligence on all matters pertaining to national intelligence "Advisor to the Council." In this capacity he might attend the meetings of the Council at its discretion, though taking no part in its decisions.[23]

Murphy agreed, but Norstad and Sherman overruled him. The provision for a Deputy Director was too controversial, and so was that making the Director the Intelligence Advisor of the Council. Those who conferred for the Army and the Navy held that the function of advising the Council was inherent in the office of the Director. It was not proper, they said, to provide by law that the head of one agency subordinate to another should sit in the superior body. As everyone in the services must know who has attended councils in the official capacity of technical adviser, there is a difference between sitting in and sitting with a superior council.

Wright's proposal to Murphy clearly marked the difference. The question whether the Director of Central Intelligence was to be allowed in the same room with the National Security Council was relatively inconsequential. It was not the presence of his body but of his thoughts that should have significance. It is hard to adapt to this situation the historic fear of Alexander Hamilton's personality which is said to have gripped the First Congress when it forbad him to appear in person and argue for his financial measures as Secretary of the Treasury. The idea that the Director should advise and recommend to the Council persisted. Though cast somewhat differently, it reappeared in the Senate bill which became the National Security Act of 1947.[24]

Colonel Wright and his advisers were not to be stopped by adverse opinion in the Army and Navy. Murphy's feelings would not be hurt, he said, if they took the matter to the White House. This Wright did in a memorandum to Clifford, Special Counsel to the President, on January 28, 1947. What Clifford replied is not in available records. But the bill released to the press from the White House, on February 26, was terse and conclusive.[25]

It stated that there should be under the National Security Council a Central Intelligence Agency with a Director of Central Intelligence at the head, to be appointed by the President. The Director should receive $14,000 a year; if a military person, his perquisites, privileges, and benefits should be safeguarded. When he took office, the functions of the National Intelligence Authority would be transferred to the National Security Council. The Authority would cease to exist. The functions of the Director of Central Intelligence, and the functions, personnel, property, and records of the Central Intelligence Group would be transferred respectively to the Director of Central Intelligence and to the Central Intelligence Agency. The Group would cease to exist. Its unexpended balances and other monies available or authorized should be available to the Agency and authorized in like manner.

This was all that the bill from the White House did say. In its brevity, however, one statement was complete. Unlike the proposal from Vandenberg's counsel and the eventual Act of Congress, the White House bill kept the functions of the Agency distinct from those of the Director of Central Intelligence. The separation does not appear to have been inadvertent. It recorded the meaning of the President's Directive of January 22, 1946, as interpreted by both Admiral Souers and General Vandenberg. It had bearing upon the subsequent controversy over powers inherent in the expressed duties and responsibilities of the Director of Central Intelligence and upon the question whether the Agency were an interdepartmental activity or an independent instrument of government.[26]

HEARINGS

President Truman sent the bill for the National Defense Establishment to Congress on February 26, 1947. There followed a parade of ranking officers and officials before the Senate's Committee on the Armed Services and the Committee of the House of Representatives on Expenditures in the Executive Departments. Secretaries Patterson and Forrestal, Generals Eisenhower and Spaatz, Admirals Nimitz and King, General Vandegrift of the Marines, all made prepared statements and answered questions. General Norstad and Admiral Sherman spoke as members of the drafting committee. Vannevar Bush and William J. Donovan offered testimony from their experiences during the war. Representatives of veterans and reserve officers appeared before the committees. There were remarks, too, from officeholders and private citizens who asked to be heard.

Major attention, of course, centered upon the proposed merger of the Armed Forces, the authority of the Secretary of Defense, and the National Security Council. But there was accompanying interest in the plan for the Central Intelligence Agency. This grew more intense as representatives of the armed services sought to restrict its operations and certain Congressmen looked into the bill for evidence that the President might be able to turn the Agency into a Gestapo.

Representatives of the Central Intelligence Group, it is to be said, exploited the word at appropriate moments to entrench the idea that Gestapo was one thing which the Agency would not be. It would have no police power, no right to subpoena, no authority of law enforcement, no functions pertaining to the internal security of the nation. These marked the secret police of a totalitarian state tyrannizing its own people. Without them the Group and its successor, the Central Intelligence Agency, would be instruments of espionage, counterespionage, and even subversive practices against other countries, but not against their own.[27]

The questioning of Admiral Sherman on April 1 by Senators Tydings, Byrd, and Saltonstall, with General Vandenberg present, brought to light political if not legal weakness in attempting to perpetuate the President's Directive of January 22, 1946, by Act of Congress without expressly stipulating the functions of the Group which should become those of the Agency. There was a seeming void, even though the provisions of the Directive and its limitations would be incorporated by reference in the Act of Congress. To those who were not familiar with the President's letter to his Secretaries and the subsequent directives of the National Intelligence Authority, the silence of the Act of Congress on the functions of the new Agency and the Director of Central Intelligence was forbidding. The President might abrogate to himself unforeseen power. Representative Clarence J. Brown of Ohio expressed this fear completely on June 12, 1947, to Walter L. Pforzheimer, legislative counsel of the Group. There was no guarantee that the enabling bill might later be sent to Congress; the Administration, said Brown, might conveniently forget to do so. Safeguards should be written into the Act of Congress with the delineation of the Agency's function.[28]

Under these circumstances Vandenberg's staff took care to give proper tone to his statement before the committees of Congress. He went straight to the political issue and thence through all doubts and misgivings to the inevitable conclusion that the United States should never be caught again as at Pearl Harbor without an effective central intelligence organization.

General Vandenberg's first point was that ever since the President's Directive of January 22, 1946, his predecessor, Admiral Souers, and he had been looking to the time when they could obtain permanent status for the Central Intelligence Group by Act of Congress. There must be a permanent system. The oceans had shrunk until Europe and Asia were as close as Canada and Mexico. The interests, intentions, and capabilities of the nations on those land masses must be known to our national policymakers if we were to be forewarned against aggression in an era of atomic warfare. Those who felt that there was something un-American about espionage should realize that all intelligence was not sinister. Fully 80 percent of it came from the great open sources of information. Before the attack upon

Pearl Harbor these had not been properly utilized. Since then many intelligence agencies had sprung up. It was fashionable for the departments and services of the Government to engage in collecting intelligence. But it was not adequately coordinated, analyzed, and disseminated.

There was need for one central organization to perform those functions for the benefit of all. This the Central Intelligence Group was endeavoring to accomplish without injury to the legitimate activities of the several departments and their agencies. With a final survey of the functions of the Director of Central Intelligence and the operations of the Group, Vandenberg put the President's Directive of January 22, 1946, into the record and urged upon Congress adoption of the bill. The understanding would be that enabling legislation for the Agency should follow in due course.[29]

It was an effective presentation of the Central Intelligence Group as the beginning of a permanent system of national intelligence for times of peace as well as war. But it was not satisfying to all elements in Congress. It did not convince the members of the armed services who believed that the central organization duplicated their work and usurped functions properly belonging to them. There was difficulty in getting through Congress the provision in the President's Directive that the Director should perform "services of common concern" for the departmental agencies, particularly with regard to the collection of intelligence. Representative Brown and others would not be content until the duties of the Central Intelligence Agency under the National Security Council were stipulated in the Act. There was much discussion in committees, on the air, and in the press about the danger in having a military head of the Agency.

Representative James W. Wadsworth of New York remarked in the House Committee on April 29 that the bill evidently anticipated the appointment of military men as Directors of Central Intelligence. This he thought unwise. Secretary Patterson replied that the appointment was discretionary; special provisions had to be included, he said, in case military men should be selected. To date the Directors had come from the Navy and the Army. It would be unwise, he maintained, to exclude from the post such men of experience with foreign intelligence.[30]

This was not the usual approach to the question whether civilians should be Directors of Central Intelligence. All of them had been military or naval officers. Though an eminent lawyer, William J. Donovan was also an outstanding soldier; however versatile, he was hardly to be considered a civilian in the sense which the question implied. Admiral Souers was a civilian inasmuch as the Navy was not his profession; but he had acquired his experience in intelligence as a reserve officer. No one had come to the post from a career in the Department of State.

The issue was raised again with General Eisenhower on May 7, 1947. Representative Fred E. Busbey of Illinois asked if it would not be better to have a permanent civilian head of the Central Intelligence Group than the succession of military and naval officers. Admiral Hillenkoetter had just succeeded General Vandenberg as Director of Central Intelligence. Eisenhower, who as Chief of Staff of the Army had requested the return of Vandenberg to eventual command of the Air Force, gave his candid opinion that frequent change was wrong. They should leave a Director in office for three years, he said, unless there was an emergency or some necessity for a change. To Representative John W. McCormack of Massachusetts on the following day, Eisenhower elaborated the point. The position required a man with considerable training in intelligence. If they could obtain the right civilian, he would be content to keep the civilian in office indefinitely and provide him with technical assistance. He agreed that they should have greater stability.[31]

Senator Leverett Saltonstall of Massachusetts was willing at one time to go so far as to have a properly qualified civilian hold the office of Director of Central Intelligence for life "just like Mr. Hoover of the F.B.I." Allen W. Dulles took a similar position later in an executive session of the House Committee. General Donovan and his Assistant Director in the Office of Strategic Services, Charles S. Cheston, stressed their familiar principles. The Director must be a civilian. He ought to have an independent budget. He should report to no committee or council but to an individual, such as the Secretary of Defense.[32]

On this last point Donovan's opinion was fixed. The Director of Central Intelligence should be responsible immediately to the President or his representative. Donovan did not like the idea of a National Security Council over the Director any more than he had favored the National Intelligence Authority. The fact that the State Department might be handicapped if the Director reported only to the Secretary of Defense did not appear to disturb Cheston and Donovan. General Vandenberg, however, pointed out that the Central Intelligence Agency would not be the sole intelligence agency. If it were, it might be made responsible exclusively to the Department of Defense. But so long as it was to be the central organization among departmental agencies, and Vandenberg believed that it should, its Director ought to be responsible to a council which represented those agencies as well as governed the central activities.[33]

Admiral Hillenkoetter was influenced by the views of Donovan and Cheston to agree that if he were offered the position as Director at the head of the new Central Intelligence Agency, he would accept it as a career. With that idea in mind his counsel prepared an amendment to the bill which would give Admiral Hillenkoetter the post for fourteen years.

But nothing was done about it. Upon reflection it seemed preferable to leave the choice of the Director from military or civilian life to the President with the consent of the Senate, just as he appointed his Cabinet. He should have a free hand with regard to the tenure of the Office.[34]

It had originated as a personal instrument of President Truman. He enjoyed calling Admirals Leahy and Souers his snoopers. The Group was his personal information service. The Director of Central Intelligence had duties and responsibilities quite different from those assigned to the head of the Federal Bureau of Investigation. Although the Director of Central Intelligence did not actually make policy, he came close to doing so as personal appointee and adviser to the President on matters of intelligence. This was characteristic of the office during Hillenkoetter's administration and the two years of General Smith's tenure. Though formally responsible to the National Security Council, the Director of Central Intelligence had ready access to the White House and talked often with the President himself. The possibilities in this fact were not lost upon the intelligence officers of the armed services and their superiors in the departments.[35]

The Army's intelligence service did not want the Director of Central Intelligence to have charge of collection. The opposition shown in the conflict between Vandenberg and his Advisory Board appeared again before the House committee. Representative Wadsworth remarked, as they questioned General Vandenberg in executive session, that collection would be one of their main issues. Witnesses for the Military Intelligence Service opposed even clandestine collection by the central agency. It should be restricted to coordinating the work of the departmental intelligence agencies and to evaluating and disseminating the materials which they purveyed to it. It might engage in some research as a "service of common concern" to the departmental agencies. It should not interpret its functions to include the right of independent, least of all, exclusive collection.[36]

One of these witnesses for G-2, Peter Vischer, would go so far as to deny the Agency the powers which the Director possessed under the President's Directive to perform services of common concern and other functions that the President and the National Intelligence Authority should designate. Vischer would retain the provision that the Director should plan for coordinating the activities of the intelligence agencies of the departments. There was nothing wrong with it, he said; he knew, because he himself had written it. He had worked with Souers, Montague, Lay, and others on the draft of the First Directive of the National Intelligence Authority.

Vischer then gave his version of the Fifth Directive. The Authority had no right to surrender the function of clandestine collection to the Director of Central Intelligence. Representative Judd punctured this statement. It was not "surrender"; it was "delegation" of the power to act for the Authority. The Secretaries and Admiral Leahy could take it back anytime. Vischer asserted that the Secretary of War had agreed before he asked G-2, who had objected. The implication was that Secretary Patterson at least had exceeded the proprieties. But the answer to Vischer was obviously that through the chain of command General Chamberlin, Assistant Chief of Staff, G-2, received instructions from, and did not give them to, the Secretary of War.

Vischer's further remark was that G-2 was saying only the other day his orders were "that this thing should be abolished" and those were his orders "until some higher power, perhaps the Congress," changed them. Representative Wadsworth closed this phase of Vischer's testimony with the comment: "I think it fair to say that perhaps you have given an impartial explanation of what happened." Possibly the tone of Wadsworth's voice hardened on the word "perhaps."[37]

Brigadier General H. Kroner then testified against collection by the Agency. It would be unwise to empower the Agency to "overburden itself with operations," especially collection, however "romantic" and interesting to those who engaged in it. The Agency, he said, should keep to its "main strategic mission," the production of "evaluated information." Kroner, a former chief of the Military Intelligence Service, gave additional testimony which indicated that the Agency might not be able to produce such complete and comprehensive information for the policymakers if the Army continued as it had during the war. He explained with evident satisfaction how a strategic intelligence service of the Army had been set upon so high a level of "privacy" that its findings were known only to the War Department, the Department of State, and the President. A subsequent witness, Admiral Inglis, vouched for this on behalf of the Navy. It had stumbled upon this strategic service of the Army by accident and against the wishes of the Army. The information was never made available to the Navy.[38]

The Army was operating the exclusive service, we should note, at the same time that General Marshall and Admiral King were trying to bring their intelligence agencies together and to work with the Office of Strategic Services through the Joint Chiefs of Staff. The failure of these agencies to cooperate effectively with one another during the war was very much in the minds of the House Committee and the witnesses before it in the spring of 1947.[39]

On the one hand were the spokesmen for G-2 who wished to avoid in the future the distressing relationship which had existed between the Office of Strategic Services and the intelligence agencies of the armed services. They would do this by confining the new Central Intelligence Agency and the Director strictly to the business of coordinating the work of the agencies and of evaluating the intelligence which they chose to release to the central body. On the other hand were General Vandenberg, Allen W. Dulles, and Admiral Inglis testifying that experience had proved that the armed services should leave the collection of secret intelligence to one central organization holding its officers and their informants closely in hand. It should receive all other information essential to evaluating and disseminating the finished product for the policymakers in the departments and appropriate councils of the Government.[40]

Vandenberg explained the weaknesses in the system of contracts which had been used by the Army for collecting secret intelligence. It was inadequate. It was too easily penetrated by the enemy's agents. But he understood as well why the intelligence officers of the armed services were so averse to giving top secrets to men in another service. Their discretion could not be assured by court-martial, if necessary. Vandenberg hoped that in a few years the "flow of information" would be established as the Army, Navy, and Department of State accepted the Central Intelligence Agency into the system of national defense. The thought seems to have been that the departmental agencies would become more interested in filling the central pool of intelligence than in guarding the sources of their information and keeping their operations to themselves.[41]

The opinions of Vandenberg and his associates had greater weight in the committees of Congress than those of the spokesmen for G-2. Representative Brown agreed that the Agency ought to have charge of clandestine collection. Representatives Wadsworth and Manasco were particularly impressed that the British were moving, with their Joint Intelligence Board for services of common usefulness, toward centralized intelligence as the American agencies appeared to be withdrawing from it. When the section of the unification bill on the Central Intelligence Agency came finally to enactment in July 1947, it contained the provisions of the President's Directive of January 22, 1946, that the Agency should perform "services of common concern" for the departments and such other functions related to intelligence as the National Security Council should from time to time direct.[42]

Representative Brown's insistence throughout the hearings accomplished its purpose. Congress abandoned the device of incorporating the President's Directive by reference. Instead, the National Security Act contained specific statements regarding the functions of the new Agency. These came into the Senate bill as amendments by the House Committee; they were known as the Hoffman–Norstad amendments largely because Representative Hoffman was chairman of the committee and General Norstad's assistants appear to have written them. They were modeled upon the provisions in the enabling bill from the counsel's office in the Group. But there were changes from that measure, and from the President's Directive itself, which are to be closely examined in the light of Vandenberg's experiences as Director of Central Intelligence. They may serve as guides for appraising Admiral Hillenkoetter's difficulties.[43]

SPECIFICATIONS

The National Security Act became law with President Truman's approval on July 26, 1947. Its declared intent was to unify direction of the separate military departments under civilian control. The principal assistant of the President in all matters relating to the national security was to be the Secretary of Defense. He should establish general policies and exercise general direction. He should eliminate unnecessary duplication and overlapping; he should supervise and coordinate the budget estimates of the departments and agencies in the National Military Establishment. He was to sit with the Secretary of State and other Secretaries and appointees of the President in the National Security Council where all domestic, foreign, and military policies relating to the national security should be integrated for advice to the President.

Under the direction of this extraordinary body for making high policy there was placed a Central Intelligence Agency headed by a Director of Central Intelligence to be appointed from either military or civilian life by the President with the advice and consent of the Senate. The Secretary of Defense and the Director of Central Intelligence, by reason of their mutual concern with matters "relating to the national security" and the armed services, were to have a particular relationship that was not fully embodied in the Act of Congress. James Forrestal, who became the first Secretary of Defense, thought of the Agency as second only to the Council among the essentials of the National Security Act. The need for the Agency, he said, "should be obvious to all of us."[44]

The Central Intelligence Agency, administered by the Director of Central Intelligence, had the duty to perform stipulated functions as directed by the National Security Council for the express purpose of "coordinating the intelligence activities of the several Government departments and agencies in the interest of national security." This final clause in the declaration of purpose is so often stated, and so easily taken for granted, that its import may be overlooked. The unity of the purpose is mandatory.

National security is not divisible. It is not subject to individual discretion, nor pliable under departmental interpretation. It is not to be jeopardized by professional jealousies and competition. The armed services and civilian agencies are not to war upon one another. Some had behaved during the war, it was said, as though the others were greater enemies than the Japanese and Germans.[45]

The National Security Act gave the Central Intelligence Agency a wider field of recommendation and advice to the makers of national policy than the Director and the Group had been assigned under the President's Directive of January 22, 1946. The Directive had authorized recommendations of "overall policies and objectives" to accomplish the "national intelligence mission." The Act made it the duty of the Agency to advise the Security Council in matters concerning the "intelligence activities" of the departments and agencies related to "national security." The term "national security" is broader than "national intelligence mission."

Moreover, the power to advise the Council was distinguished and strengthened by separation in the Act from the power to make recommendations for the "coordination" of those departmental "intelligence activities." The Director of Central Intelligence, at the head of the Agency, now had clearer authorization to take the initiative in suggesting "intelligence activities" for the departments and agencies of the Government. It was conceivable that he might recommend activities for one that would not be "coordinated" with those of another. He might propose, for example, that the Atomic Energy Commission provide intelligence which should be withheld from "coordination" at every level below that of the President and his closest advisers in the National Security Council.[46]

The new Agency received the Group's functions of correlating, evaluating, and disseminating intelligence within the Government. The departments and other agencies should continue to collect, evaluate, correlate, and disseminate their own intelligence. That there should be no further misunderstanding or misgiving on this score, the word "departmental" was inserted in the text. With this statement came the familiar proviso that the Agency should have no "police, subpoena, law-enforcement powers, or internal-security functions," to allay the fear that the President and his Director of Central Intelligence might turn the Agency into an American Gestapo. It also assured the Federal Bureau of Investigation again that it would have no interference from the Agency in checking subversive persons and practices within the country.[47]

Another proviso in the same section continued the responsibility of the Director of Central Intelligence for protecting the sources and methods of intelligence from unauthorized disclosure. Whether this gave him authority in other intelligence services than the Agency was not made clear in the text. The presumption is fair that there was no longer any intention, if there ever had been, to extend the Director's surveillance into other agencies. It was logical to do so and in fact it might be necessary if he really were to protect the sources and methods of intelligence. But the view that there was no such intention is supported by the restrictions which Congress now placed upon the Director's right of inspection.

The right of the Director to inspect the operations of the departmental intelligence agencies in connection with his planning had originated under the requirement that, in exercising the right, the Director must protect sources and methods with direct and important bearing upon military operations. The right to inspect and the duty to protect, however, had been separated as they came into the President's Directive. The statement of the duty no longer referred expressly to military operations; it stipulated that the Director should be responsible for "fully" protecting intelligence sources and methods.[48]

From one point of view this change enlarged the Director's opportunity as well as his responsibility. But from another the removal of the specification with regard to military operations, taken with the separation of the duty to protect from the right to inspect, weakened both functions; it laid them open to adverse interpretation by those who did not wish to have the Director of Central Intelligence wield so much power. Neither Admiral Souers nor General Vandenberg used the right of inspection. They had trouble enough in getting the departments to send the product of their intelligence activities to the Central Intelligence Group without antagonizing them by probing into their operations.

The Act of Congress restricted the right of inspection to the product of the departmental agencies. Only their intelligence relating to the national security should be "open to the inspection" of the Director of Central Intelligence. And to make doubly certain that he should not hamper the Federal Bureau of Investigation, "such information" would be made available to him by the Bureau only upon "written request" to its Director. The intelligence services of the Government were still to supply their information to the Central Intelligence Agency for correlation, evaluation, and dissemination to the proper authorities and policymakers of the Government in the interest of national security. There were no provisions in the Act for priorities and other facilities to ensure delivery of the departmental intelligence to the Central Intelligence Agency.[49]

The Director of Central Intelligence received a special grant from Congress with regard to his subordinates in the Agency. The requirements of the Civil Service, while protecting the rights of the Government's employees, made it difficult for the administrative heads of offices to remove persons who were incompetent, improperly placed, or in some cases even menacing to the public interest, without causing delay and attracting attention. In such an organization as the Central Intelligence Agency the results could be disastrous. General Vandenberg had explained his need in secret operations to remove any officer or employee who might be under no more than the suspicion of disloyalty. Representative Manasco put into the Act the measure which had been prepared by the legislative counsel of the Group. The Director was empowered, in his discretion, to terminate employment in the Agency without affecting the right of the persons concerned to employment elsewhere in the Government.[50]

Congress gave the Agency the much discussed function of performing for the benefit of existing intelligence agencies "such additional services of common concern" as could be accomplished more efficiently by the central organization. The National Security Council should determine what services were in that category and when they should be turned over to the Central Intelligence Agency. After the hearings before the committees of the Senate and the House of Representatives in which the problem of collecting intelligence, both overt and secret, was a major issue, there could be no doubt that Congress intended the Agency to have the right of collection notwithstanding objections from the Army.

Any thought that Congress compromised the right of the Agency, by failing to state the right in so many words, is mistaken. The compromise lay in the choice of words and not in the intent of Congress to put the essential authority into the phrase "common concern." Congress avoided publicity for the institution by clothing it with the phrase. The collection of intelligence is a service of common usefulness, especially in its clandestine aspects. It should be undercover to be successful.[51]

The Fifth Directive of the old National Intelligence Authority, subject to the control of the new National Security Council, had been validated by Congress. General Vandenberg was entitled to satisfaction with the outcome. Generals Donovan and Magruder also had reason to be gratified. Their pioneering in these fields of intelligence had been accepted for the permanent organization of the national system of intelligence. Clandestine collection was included with research and analysis as essential, even though they were not exclusive, functions of the Central Intelligence Agency.[52]

There is less certainty with regard to the stipulation in the Act, carried over from the President's Directive, that the Agency should perform "such other functions and duties related to intelligence affecting the national security" as the National Security Council might from time to time direct. There is no question that the provision was put in the Act, as it was in the Directive, to allow flexibility and enlargement within the bounds of original intent and of reasonable interpretation in the light of experience. But the executive discretion of the National Intelligence Authority under the President's Directive was a different thing from the legislative authorization of the National Security Council by the Act of Congress.

The President might expand, limit, suspend, or revoke at any time the duties and responsibilities of the Director and the Group under his directive. He might interpret his own order as he himself saw fit. The provisions in the Act of Congress could be altered only by the process of amendment or repeal; they require the change of not one mind but many minds. Meanwhile, the interpretation of the law was not to be had so much from those who administered it as from those who made the law. Congress could establish standards and fields of operation for other instruments of government. It could not delegate its own legislative power to any other branch or institution. These considerations must enter into any discussion of the authority which Congress gave to the President and the National Security Council over the Director of Central Intelligence and the Agency of which he was made the head.

From one point of view Congress itself had distinguished the provision with regard to "other functions and duties" from the four preceding it in the same section of the Act. They pertained to the intelligence activities of the departments and of the central agency as such; it was concerned with matters which were merely "related to intelligence affecting the national security." This was a loose term which not only supported the inclusion of clandestine collection and research and analysis among the duties of the Agency as "services of common concern"; it gave room for the "unorthodox warfare" which General Donovan believed essential to a fully developed system of intelligence. The Council might direct the Agency from time to time to engage in psychological activities, economic manipulation, sabotage and subversion, paramilitary actions, and covert operations generally, so long as they produced some intelligence "affecting the national security." The Council therefore should exercise more guidance over the Director and the Agency in such operations than in purely "intelligence activities." It was this expansive interpretation which prevailed in the Council when it came to establishing the Office of Policy Coordination in the Agency and the Psychological Strategy Board.[53]

An opposing interpretation was built upon the same premise that Congress had distinguished "other functions and duties" from the "intelligence activities" of the departments and the Agency. This interpretation maintained, however, that Congress had not delegated to the Council the legislative function of defining the term "national security." If the Director or the Council or any other administrative body had the power to do so, there would be practically no limitation upon the "functions and duties" which could be assigned to the Agency short of organized warfare. Almost every action produced intelligence of a sort. According to this view, the intent of Congress must be examined before assuming that the National Security Council had authority to direct the Agency to undertake other functions and duties than those which were clearly indicated in the Act. The key to the mind of Congress would be quickly found when the Director of Central Intelligence went to Congress for the necessary appropriation. There would be no doubt then whether those in control of Congress intended that the Agency should engage in a particular activity.[54]

The National Security Act placed the Director of Central Intelligence in a different legal relationship with the President and his Secretaries. The Director was no longer head of a Group drawn from the several departments by order of the President. The Director was to be head of an independent agency in the Federal Government having its own personnel, property, and records when those of the Central Intelligence Group were transferred to the Central Intelligence Agency as the Group ceased to exist. The duties and responsibilities of the Director were no longer subject to change solely at the pleasure of the President. They were designated and established now in organic legislation by Congress. The President could not, of his own volition, abolish the office nor reduce the functions of the Director, though he might possibly increase them. Here enters again the question whether Congress gave the President, his Secretaries, and other appointees in the National Security Council expansive power by stipulating that the Agency should perform "other functions and duties" as the Council might from time to time direct.

But, regardless of its legal aspects, the relationship between the Director of Central Intelligence and the President, for all practical purposes, remained the same. The President still could dismiss the Director if he did not like him or the way in which he conducted his office. The power of the Council to direct the Agency had no authorization from Congress that was independent of the President's authority. The Council was advisory to him. He could reject as readily as accept its advice. If he had time and inclination, the President could maintain full control over the Director and his administration of the Agency. It would continue to be his personal information service at the center of the Government, no matter how much the departmental intelligence agencies might prefer to have it elsewhere.

To their displeasure, a feature of the President's Directive creating the Group was notably missing from the National Security Act. It made no provision for the Intelligence Advisory Board. General Vandenberg had found the Board a source of obstruction and delay rather than of constructive advice from the departmental chiefs of intelligence. The institution had been deliberately omitted from the enabling measure of the Group and from the White House bill. In its place the Act of Congress authorized the Director of Central Intelligence to appoint an advisory committee and to employ part-time advisory personnel as he deemed necessary in carrying out his functions and those of the Agency. The intelligence officers of the armed services, however, would not believe that the Intelligence Advisory Board had been destroyed. The Act did not forbid such an interdepartmental board as they desired. They were determined to make the first directive from the National Security Council to the Agency establish it.[55]

THE ENABLING MEASURE

Opposition to the Central Intelligence Agency subsided noticeably in Congress once the National Security Act had passed. The expectation was that the Agency would present its enabling bill in the next session to supply the details which had been omitted from the Act. The bill would take its place on the legislative calendar. It would suffer the postponements and obstructions to be expected in partisan maneuvering over appropriations. But it eventually would become law. In the meantime, the members of the outgoing National Intelligence Authority notified the Comptroller General that they had authorized the Director of Central Intelligence to administer for another year the "working fund" provided by the Departments of State, War, and the Navy. The General Accounting Office continued with the Agency the understanding which had governed its relations with the Group. The Agency was to conform as nearly as possible to normal procedures until further legislation by Congress should make exceptions fitting the special needs of the Agency. It was clear to everyone concerned that the Group could not have been in operation at all without the cooperation of the Comptroller General and the General Accounting Office.[56]

Uncertainties were at a minimum with regard to the vouchered funds which had been earmarked by the committees of Congress for the Group and put in the "working fund." The Treasury Department and the Bureau of the Budget, as well as the Authority, had approved the arrangement. Auditors from the General Accounting Office, especially assigned for the purpose, examined vouchered expenditures within the Group. The problem was to handle unvouchered funds properly. They must be kept secret; even the provision for them by Congress should not be known. The

Director had "Special Funds' officers" personally responsible to him for their administration. His certification took the place of itemized vouchers to show that they had been properly expended. And yet there ought to be an external control of some sort over unvouchered funds. It was not sound practice in accounting to let the man who authorized an expenditure validate also the legitimacy of the expenditure.

The law officers of the Agency conferred with representatives of the Bureau of the Budget and the Comptroller General to find the correct formula for expressing in the statute the practices of budgeting and accounting which should be employed. Mr. Lindsay Warren, Comptroller General, although fully appreciating the necessity of special procedures for the Agency, could not personally approve so sweeping a delegation of authority as that of the right of the Director to account for secret expenditures solely on his certification. Warren was willing that unvouchered funds which the National Security Council approved should be exempt from the normal restrictions upon expenditure. But the Bureau of the Budget held that such approval in advance was more properly the function of the Director of the Budget. To this the Comptroller agreed and the proposal went to Congress. The Senate's committee, however, thought otherwise and exempted the Agency from any control by the Bureau of the Budget over the amount of the expenditures which should be unvouchered. It did seem more a function of accounting after an expenditure than of budgeting an amount before its disbursement. The House of Representatives failed to pass the measure in that session. It was necessary for the Secretaries to extend the "working fund" of the Agency for a second year.[57]

The events in the spring of 1948 which caused so much tension in the State Department, the National Security Council, and the Agency over psychological warfare against Communists around the world apparently had no effects upon the enabling measure in Congress. The war scare stirred by General Clay, the Italian election, the Berlin blockade and airlift, even "Bogotá," did not speed the legislative process. Representative Brown talked of investigating the Agency and altering the National Security Act, but nothing came of his threats except publicity for the Agency. The enabling measure remained in committee until the last days of the session, and then there was no time left to do anything about it. The approaching national conventions may have caused some distraction among Congressmen wondering whether Dewey were going to be the next President. The story that the radical Congressman from New York, Marcantonio, stopped the measure is interesting for itself. But Marcantonio was not responsible for defeating the Agency's enabling bill in the session of 1948.[58]

Marcantonio's accomplishment was to attract attention to a provision in the measure that an officer or employee of the Agency might be assigned for special instruction by labor associations. The Congressman from New York, looking for something to criticize, concluded that the Agency was trying to bore into the labor unions, and he so informed an official of the Congress of Industrial Organizations. This officer called the general counsel of the Agency to inquire if it were true. He said that he was not alarmed; he would just like to know. Mr. Houston replied that if the Agency were trying to penetrate the CIO, it certainly would not go about the business in that way. Both laughed over the telephone and agreed that if the Agency might wish to have labor organizations cooperate with it, the Congress of Industrial Organizations should be quite pleased.[59]

The enabling bill had to go over to the next session of Congress, but at least the procrastination and interruption which are customary in the legislative process did not interfere. The Comptroller General again withheld his personal objection to granting the Director of Central Intelligence blanket authority over unvouchered funds. The "CIA Act of 1949" became law with President Truman's approval on June 20.[60]

The National Security Act of 1947 was amended in the same session to alter the National Security Council as the Department of Defense took the place of the National Military Establishment. The Secretary of Defense was no longer "principal assistant" to the President in all matters relating to the national security, but simply in matters concerning the Department of Defense. The Secretary of State was restored to his traditional leadership in the Executive Branch under the President. Truman had never interpreted the Act of 1947 otherwise. The Secretaries of the Army, the Navy, and the Air Force were removed from the Council and the Vice President given a place. There were no material changes from the Act of 1947 with regard to the duties of the Director of Central Intelligence or the functions of the Agency under the direction of the National Security Council.[61]

By separate Act of Congress the Central Intelligence Agency now had full authorization for procurement of supplies, services, and other facilities. The Director of Central Intelligence and his designated subordinates could negotiate purchases and make contracts without advertising their purposes. Expenditures could be made on education and training, travel by employees, shipments of their household effects, and related matters. The Agency was granted the extraordinary authority to approve the entry into the United States of certain aliens and their families, without regard to other laws. In these admissions, however, the Attorney General and the Commissioner of Immigration were to concur. The number of persons was limited to one hundred a year. The Agency might employ three outstanding men in the scientific field of foreign intelligence.

A general authority allowed the financing of the Agency's affairs by interdepartmental transfers of appropriations to and from the Agency, notwithstanding other legislation which would interfere. In lieu of annual appropriations for specific categories of expenditures the Agency was given a general authority for those purposes. The list included some items which made other agencies of the Government envious and critical, but unable to do more than complain of the Agency's intrusion into their domains.

Finally, the "CIA Act of 1949" contained in its section 10(b) the statement that expenditures upon "objects of a confidential, extraordinary, or emergency nature" were to be accounted for "solely on the certificate of the Director." So far as can be determined from the statement itself, the power was absolute. But no one, least of all the Director of Central Intelligence, thought so. The understanding in the committees of Congress, the Bureau of the Budget, the Office of the Comptroller General, and the Agency was that so great power was overshadowed by the even greater responsibility attendant upon it. The Director was to certify only those expenditures from unvouchered funds which applied to the unique purposes of the Central Intelligence Agency.

The limitation which Congress placed upon the Director of Central Intelligence was well expressed by an exchange of letters between General Smith as Director and Mr. Warren as Comptroller General in the fall of 1951. Congress preferred to hold the Director of Central Intelligence singly and solely responsible for the proper use of public money for clandestine purposes, but to hold him responsible in close relationship with the watchdog over appropriations, the Comptroller General. Smith asked if he might be authorized under the extraordinary powers granted by Congress, by his freedom from statutory controls over expenditure and accounting, to raise the pay of the Agency's employees retroactively. Warren answered that he was certain the sponsors of the Act in Congress had not contemplated use of the "broad authority" of the Agency in disregard of control with respect to "normal administrative or operating problems," such as confronted any agency of the Government. The Central Intelligence Agency had no authority "contingent only on the availability of funds."[62]

Introduction to Chapter VI

Although some thought it was the State Department's "turn" to have leadership of the CIA since officers from both the Navy and Air Force had already held the job, others were not ready for a civilian DCI and Allen Dulles, State's candidate, was passed over for Roscoe Hillenkoetter of the Navy.

Hillenkoetter came into office in May 1947 facing the continued resentment of the armed services. The Intelligence Advisory Board—which the service chiefs strongly favored—had been slated by Congress to expire, and the DCI was now to be the executive agent of the Secretaries of State, War, and Navy. This situation allowed him to advise the National Security Council without first consulting a board of the departmental intelligence chiefs.

The departmental intelligence chiefs, however, were determined to hold on to their authority. Even while the National Security Act was being developed by the Executive Branch and Congress to assert the role of the DCI more clearly, the service intelligence chiefs behaved as though the DCI were their equal, if not their subordinate. Being a realist, Hillenkoetter was reluctant simply to assert his authority, knowing that even if he was DCI, he still needed the cooperation of the departmental intelligence services, since they remained in possession of most of the real capabilities of the intelligence community. Thus, months followed in which the DCI tried to negotiate and maneuver in order to establish his position.

Matters finally came to a head on December 8, 1947, at a meeting called by the new Secretary of Defense, James Forrestal (Forrestal had assumed his post just two months earlier, as the National Security Act was put into effect). The meeting included the secretaries of each military service, their chiefs of intelligence, a representative from the State Department, Admiral Souers (now NSC Executive Secretary), and Hillenkoetter. At this meeting Forrestal sharply reprimanded Admiral Inglis and General Chamberlin, intelligence chiefs from the Navy and Army respectively, for thwarting the DCI. Forrestal made clear that he wanted the CIA to be the central agency for intelligence information and the DCI to have authority over the departmental intelligence organizations.

Armed with the backing of the Secretary of Defense, Hillenkoetter submitted his proposal for NSCID 1 to the National Security Council, outlining the duties of the DCI and his relationship to the Intelligence Advisory Committee in the production of intelligence. Under NSCID 1 the IAC would consist of the intelligence chiefs from the Departments of State, Army, Navy, Air Force, JCS, and Atomic Energy Commission. The DCI was required to submit statements of "substantial dissent" by members of the Committee when submitting national intelligence or recommendations to the President. The DCI was expressly assigned the production of national intelligence, using existing resources and departmental intelligence. In spite of the greater authority given the DCI, he still was restricted from inspecting departmental intelligence operations.

The greatest catastrophe of Hillenkoetter's tenure, notwithstanding all of the ongoing turf battles, was directly related to these early steps to institute the new intelligence organization. On April 9, 1948, during the Ninth International Conference of American Republics in Bogotá, Colombia, Jorge Gaitan, the leader of the left wing of Colombia's Liberal Party, was assassinated and large-scale rioting broke out between the Colombian conservative factions (who dominated the army) and liberals (who were backed by the police force). More than a thousand people were killed or wounded. Hillenkoetter was held responsible for not warning the Department of State about potential violence and the political crisis that accompanied it.

All of the prevailing conditions conspired to make the intelligence failure seem as bad as possible. Since Secretary of State George Marshall had attended the conference, critics of the CIA were able to argue that the Agency had failed in even the most basic task of keeping a high U.S. official from traveling to a foreign location in which his life might be endangered. Also, the 1948 presidential campaign was under way, and President Truman's opponent, Thomas Dewey, claimed that the Truman Administration had allowed U.S. intelligence capabilities in Latin America to lapse.

In the subsequent special hearings in Congress (incidentally, the first Congressional investigation of an intelligence failure by the CIA) the facts showed that the Agency was not totally to blame. The Agency had received word that tensions were growing in Colombia and had informed the State Department of this fact. Then, shortly before the conference, the Agency received a report that "Communist-inspired agitators" might try to stage an incident directly against the Secretary of State.

Hillenkoetter did not pass this particular report to the State Department in Washington. He felt constrained by NSCID 2, which allowed the "senior U.S. representative" in an area to decide whether a particular intelligence report from their region should be released. In this case, the U.S. ambassador to Colombia and the State Department's officer responsible for preparing for the conference decided not to forward the information to Washington, fearing that doing so might unduly alarm U.S. officials and other delegates.

When these facts became known, Hillenkoetter was exonerated by the Committee and received a strong statement of support from the Committee chairman that advocated the importance of an unfettered CIA. Nevertheless, the "Bogotá incident" was to become synonymous with "intelligence failure" in the early days of the intelligence community.

VI

HILLENKOETTER'S ADMINISTRATION: INTELLIGENCE

A CAREER

 The man to succeed General Vandenberg at the head of the President's information service had been under consideration for some time. Though often credited with the choice, Admiral Souers took no part in selecting Admiral Hillenkoetter. Admiral Leahy had not shared in the choice of General Vandenberg. There was no disagreement between the personal representatives of the President; they merely were not consulted in the respective instances. Each was curious to know later what happened in the other case.[1]

Admiral Leahy while Ambassador at Vichy from 1940 to 1942 had formed a high regard for his naval attaché's skill with the French underground. Hillenkoetter was expert in helping patriots escape into Africa and in acquiring information from both French and German sources. "He never got caught." He had been so successful earlier for Ambassador Bullitt in Moscow and in Paris that the State Department wished to keep him. The Navy, according to Leahy, had to recall Hillenkoetter into service so that he might learn about ships. Later in 1942 Hillenkoetter organized the Intelligence Center at Pearl Harbor for Admiral Nimitz and won his commendation. Donovan tried to get Hillenkoetter to take charge for OSS in the Pacific, but the Navy would not release him. Since then he had returned to Paris where he was engaged in collecting intelligence when ordered against his wishes to take charge of Central Intelligence at Washington.[2]

Admiral Leahy and Secretary Forrestal recommended Hillenkoetter to their fellow members of the National Intelligence Authority when the Army asked to have Vandenberg returned for high command in the Air Force. It was on February 17, 1947, that the Authority and the President approved the assignment of Hillenkoetter, recently made a Rear Admiral, to be Director of Central Intelligence when Lieutenant General Vandenberg should leave the office. The date is to be noted. It was but five days after Vandenberg had been named executive agent for the Secretaries of State, War, and the Navy by the National Intelligence Authority, an event which was to have a decided effect upon Hillenkoetter's administration of the Central Intelligence Group and its successor, the Agency. Nine days after the assignment of Hillenkoetter, President Truman sent to Congress the bill for the National Military Establishment and the National Security Council.[3]

From the point of view of the Agency, it may well be said that General Vandenberg should not have been called back to military service at that time. He had been in charge of the Central Intelligence Group less than a year; its new offices were not in full working order. He was just establishing in the minds of the Secretaries of the departments that the Director of Central Intelligence ought to be their executive agent. He had not convinced the chiefs of intelligence in the armed services or the State Department that the Director was an officer above and apart from their control. They were not yet accepting the distinction which exists between advice and consent. As Vandenberg left and Hillenkoetter came in the spring of 1947, the Intelligence Advisory Board was still endeavoring to have the business of the Director come before the Board for concurrence or dissent on its way to the Authority.[4]

General Eisenhower, responsible in large part for the recall of Vandenberg to the Air Force, may have known little or nothing of these matters concerning the Central Intelligence Group. But he readily agreed in the spring of 1947 that frequent change was wrong; there should be stability in the office of Director of Central Intelligence. Three years at least, Eisenhower then thought, should be the term of service, subject of course to exigencies.[5]

The question why the Department of State was not given the appointment of the third Director of Central Intelligence raises many conjectures. It was, so to speak, the State Department's turn to have the office; the first two Directors had been chosen from the Navy and the Army. There was in fact a plan fostered in the State Department to make Allen W. Dulles the first civilian Director of Central Intelligence. Robert Lovett had mentioned him to the Secretaries in November 1945. His effective work for the Office of Strategic Services in Switzerland during the war attracted attention. He was publishing a book on his experiences. His views had been sought on scientific intelligence by the Technical Advisors of the Joint Research and Development Board. He was soon to give testimony before Congress upon the need for central intelligence and its possibilities as a civilian career.[6]

No answer to the question can be final. There were personalities involved. President Truman's own ideas and opinions of men were at work as he abandoned the Office of Strategic Services, let Donovan return to his law practice, and established the Central Intelligence Group; in its first days Secretary Byrnes caused a disturbance which led President Truman to emphasize the fact that the Group was his personal information service and Admirals Leahy and Souers his personal representatives. Congressional antipathies toward the Department of State were endemic for many reasons. Among these the suspicion that radical persons infected the Department was certainly one. But more to be credited than such hostility toward the State Department was the influence of the Army and the Navy. In this Admiral Leahy had a large share. They were uneasy as the central intelligence organization came under a new Director and moved from executive order to institution by law.[7]

The chiefs of intelligence were determined that the Intelligence Advisory Board should have governing functions. They were annoyed that Vandenberg should insist upon being their superior, certainly not their servant. With this reaction against the Director of Central Intelligence went the purpose to keep the office in the armed services, at least away from the Department of State. There was persistence, and there was presumption, in the efforts to put in the successive bills before Congress during 1946 and 1947 the stipulation that Army and Navy men, and Marines, might hold the office of Director of Central Intelligence.

The Joint Chiefs of Staff were moving at the same time toward eliminating the State Department's representation from their Joint Intelligence Committee. The coincidence of events is never to be overlooked. There were many interrelating factors in the opinion often expressed that the time had not yet come when a civilian should take the office of Director of Central Intelligence under the National Security Council.[8]

Into this situation stepped a man of experience in collecting secret intelligence abroad and with a reputation for skillfully doing it. Though reluctant to leave his post in France, he was willing to make a career of the Central Intelligence Agency which Congress was about to establish among the permanent instruments of the national government. It was as important an addition to the federal system in its time as the Interstate

Commerce Commission in the 1880s or the Federal Reserve System of 1913.[9]

Comparisons are dangerous. But those who recall the disaster at Pearl Harbor will be inclined to agree. The merits of federal control over interstate commerce, currency, and banking to promote the "general welfare" in accordance with the Constitution have long since been recognized. The need was as great for providing in the "common defense" centralized authority over the collection of intelligence and its distribution without delay to the responsible heads of government.[10]

Admiral Hillenkoetter was convinced of this. He would forego his career in the Navy to devote himself to establishing the new instrument of government upon its legislative foundations. It is one thing, however, to be an intelligence agent in the field and another to manage the affairs of an institution. It is yet another task to control, without antagonizing, agencies which still consider themselves rivals of one another and competitors with the central agency even though the law says that they no longer are.[11]

There was no specific provision in the National Security Act perpetuating the Intelligence Advisory Board for the armed services and the Department of State. The Director of Central Intelligence was free to have as he wished an advisory committee or part-time individual advisers or both. But Hillenkoetter was a newcomer among the admirals and generals. He was made at once sharply aware of the animus toward Vandenberg for insisting that the Director be the executive agent of the Secretaries of State, War, and the Navy. The letter of farewell to Vandenberg from the Intelligence Advisory Board was too ironic to be thought amusing. His "splendid work" claimed "the admiration of all." The Board's regret at his departure was "tempered with the hope" that its members might have "the good fortune" to be associated with him again.[12]

Military men let Hillenkoetter know, too, that the Army and Navy had been in existence a long while; he was merely head of a civilian agency but recently established. Vandenberg had urged that the Director of Central Intelligence should be designated in the National Security Act "Advisor to the Council." General Norstad and Admiral Sherman found this suggestion too controversial to accept on behalf of the Army, Navy, and Air Forces. The concept remained, however, in the function of the Agency under the Director of Central Intelligence to advise the National Security Council on intelligence matters pertaining to the national security. Admiral Hillenkoetter had authority from Congress to advise the Council if he chose without consulting first a board containing the intelligence chiefs of the armed services, unless of course the National Security Council should direct him to do so. This direction the intelligence chiefs, members of the expiring Intelligence Advisory Board, were determined to obtain.[13]

The new Director of Central Intelligence furthermore inherited complicated relationships with the Joint Chiefs of Staff, the Research and Development Board in the National Military Establishment, and the Atomic Energy Commission quite apart from it. Both of them had to do with scientific developments which the Joint Chiefs must take into account when formulating military strategy. The production and delivery of scientific intelligence—vital to all three, Joint Chiefs of Staff, Research and Development Board, and Atomic Energy Commission—would have been difficult enough to accomplish had there been complete cooperation among the departmental intelligence services and the central intelligence organization, as there was not. Within the Group the problem of scientific intelligence and the Nuclear Energy Group, recently taken over from the Atomic Energy Commission, lay between the Offices of Reports and Estimates and Special Operations.[14]

Matters were still to be arranged in detail with the Federal Bureau of Investigation, particularly with regard to counterespionage. They would concern the Office of Special Operations in the Agency for some time to come. In fact, they would constitute a problem of intelligence so long as Hoover was head of the FBI.[15]

Admiral Hillenkoetter had to remove turbulence and disagreement within the Group due to the ceaseless rows among the ambitious or querulous men who are found in any company engaged in a common enterprise whether it is academic, commercial, or governmental. Perhaps the medical and legal professions, because of their highly developed codes of ethics, are free from the curse. It would seem unlikely. Even so, the Central Intelligence Group did not have that good fortune.

There was friction between the Interdepartmental Coordinating and Planning Staff and the Office of Reports and Estimates. The conflict between the Branches and the Intelligence Staff had brought the Office of Reports and Estimates to reorganization in less than a year after its establishment in place of the Central Reports Staff. Boundaries between the Office of Operations and the Office of Special Operations were still to be marked at every point. Within the Office of Special Operations, just completing the absorption of the Strategic Services Unit, there were plans to further the change of secret intelligence, counterespionage, and covert operations from functional to geographic organization. The consolidation of clandestine efforts overseas was to go much farther in the administration of General Smith along lines which General Donovan had laid in his "principles."[16]

Something had to be done to stop the interminable bickering and delay over every issue with the Intelligence Advisory Board. General Vandenberg had established the Interdepartmental Coordinating and Planning Staff to work for him with the Board. But it had effectively thwarted that purpose by sending successive ad hoc committees to deal with ICAPS. The battle with the Board continued as Hillenkoetter took up the task of revising the directives of the old National Intelligence Authority and the Central Intelligence Group for the National Security Council. In view of the great amount of work which had been done through the previous year, this should have been a relatively simple task. It proved to be far from that.[17]

FIRST MEETINGS AND RECOMMENDATIONS

When Admiral Hillenkoetter took responsibility as Director of Central Intelligence on May 1, 1947, Admiral Inglis closely supported by General Chamberlin was pressing measures in the Intelligence Advisory Board counter to the wishes of General Vandenberg. One of these would disperse the production of intelligence among the agencies according to the dominant interests of the departments, as in the case of collection. To complicate the issue, controversy over air intelligence was rising between the Navy and the Army Air Forces which were about to become a separate department under the National Security Act. The Navy wished to keep its own air intelligence.[18]

Another measure called for redefining "strategic and national policy intelligence" notwithstanding the fact that an explicit formula had just been established by the National Intelligence Authority. The production of this final intelligence—coordinated national estimates for the makers of policy—was the responsibility of the Director of Central Intelligence. Admiral Inglis, however, would have it certain that the control of "operational" intelligence was still reserved to the armed services. In other words, the Director should have to produce his national estimates without access to items of military intelligence, however pertinent to those estimates, if the service chose to withhold that knowledge from his estimating staff. Inglis maintained that "strategic" intelligence and "national policy" intelligence were separate and distinct. To General Donovan who originated the phrase, and to others who had followed him in central intelligence, they were one and the same thing.[19]

The third measure to greet Admiral Hillenkoetter as he came to his meeting with the Intelligence Advisory Board on May 15, 1947, was

Admiral Inglis's plan to have all recommendations of the Director of Central Intelligence to the National Intelligence Authority pass through the Intelligence Advisory Board. The agenda for a meeting of the Authority should be referred by the Director beforehand to the Board together with copies of all papers to be considered. Members of the Board should informally express concurrence or submit comments to the Director for submission by him to the Authority. On important matters of the agenda any member of the Board might request a formal meeting of the Board to discuss the subjects before they were submitted to the Authority.[20]

The accompanying paper on behalf of the Director emphasized that the Board was advisory to him. He was responsible not to the Board but to the Authority as directed by the President in his letter to the Secretaries on January 22, 1946. The Director was not at liberty to reveal to the Board all of the recommendations which the Authority requested of him. This of course was so true of budgeting and expenditure that the departmental intelligence chiefs, though curious, never sought to interfere in the matters, thus seriously questioning their right in regard to other affairs. The paper for the Director had been under consideration within the Group ever since Admiral Inglis had submitted his plan on February 20, 1947, following the decision of the National Intelligence Authority to make the Director of Central Intelligence the executive agent of the Secretaries of State, War, and the Navy.[21]

The men present at the meeting on May 15, 1947, were those who had opposed Vandenberg through the summer and fall of 1946, or their representatives, several of whom had served on the ad hoc committees which had thwarted the purpose of ICAPS. And it seems fair to say that any who had been infrequent in attendance at those sessions or who were newcomers upon the scene had been thoroughly informed of what had gone before. With few exceptions each and every one of them was familiar with the issues in detail and with the interest of his own service and department in particular. Admiral Hillenkoetter would appear to have been the least well informed of the group, and he soon gave evidence that he too had learned much of past events.[22]

The new Director of Central Intelligence endeavored to maintain the position of his predecessor that the Director should have supervision over the production of intelligence by the several agencies. The Advisory Board, however, agreed to successive phrasings which left out specific reference to the Director and stipulated merely that the work in question should be done. The minutes of the meeting do not state that Admiral Hillenkoetter expressed disapproval, but neither do they record his assent.[23]

The purpose of the President's Directive and the supplementary directives of the Authority obviously was not to deny the Advisory Board the

right of giving the Director advice contrary to his opinions. Neither was
the intent to oblige him to accept the opinion of the Board. Although
Hillenkoetter let an action of the Board pass for the moment without
disapproval, he still had the right to recommend his own ideas to the
Authority, provided that he also sent the proposals of the Board.[24]

The hope had been that there would be few split opinions, that differences would be removed in the deliberations of the Board with the Director, and that the Authority would receive from the Director and his advisers considered and concerted judgments. These would be the result of
true coordination. It was ideal to talk of thus resolving problems and
reconciling opposite views. But the right of decision had to belong either
to the Director or to a majority of the Board. In terms of political science,
sovereignty must reside somewhere, either in the will of an individual or
in the tyranny of a majority.

The issue was clearly drawn. Admiral Hillenkoetter inherited from General Vandenberg the view that the action of the Director of Central Intelligence was the official action of the Group regardless of dissents. Admiral
Inglis, General Chamberlin, and other chiefs of intelligence in the departments clung to the opinion that the departments had inherent right to
make the Intelligence Advisory Board their working staff under the National Intelligence Authority which their Secretaries constituted with Admiral Leahy, personal representative of the President. In accordance with
this theory, the Board was entitled to know the agenda of the Authority in
advance of its action. Secretary Forrestal had come to this conclusion by
June 26, 1947, when the Authority met for the last time.[25]

The theory had been given some support by Admiral Leahy. In the
preceding July he had admonished Vandenberg that the President held
the Secretaries primarily responsible for coordinating intelligence activities. Leahy had advised Vandenberg to drop the word "agent" and put in
its place the phrase "act for" the National Intelligence Authority. Since
then, however, Admiral Leahy had modified his position to endorse
Vandenberg's designation as executive agent of the Secretaries. Now in
the meeting of the Authority on June 26, 1947, Leahy stood by Vandenberg again. When interviewed upon the subject on July 3, 1952, Leahy
still favored the idea that the Director of Central Intelligence should be
individually responsible. There should be room for dissent, he said; the
policymakers had the right to accept the dissent. Leahy made no distinction between "estimates" and other affairs of the Agency. The Director of
Central Intelligence alone was responsible for the opinion of the Central
Intelligence Agency. This applied to "coordination" as well as other affairs
of the Agency.[26]

In the historic final meeting of the National Intelligence Authority on

June 26, 1947, Admiral Hillenkoetter stated to Secretaries Marshall, Patterson, Forrestal, and Admiral Leahy that the Director of Central Intelligence did not need the authority which they had given to General Vandenberg on February 12 to act as the executive agent of the Secretaries of State, War, and the Navy. Its revocation, Hillenkoetter said, would create better feeling with the agencies represented on the Intelligence Advisory Board. If he should need the authority in the future, he would be the first to request its reinstatement. Both General Chamberlin and Admiral Inglis were present to hear the declaration.[27]

Secretary Patterson, who had favored the grant with a right of appeal by an aggrieved agency through its Secretary, would offer no objection to the withdrawal if the authority were no longer needed. But Admiral Leahy remarked that he saw no reason for withdrawing it, though he would agree if Hillenkoetter wished to have it revoked. As a matter of fact, it had never been used. Secretary Marshall was concerned to know if the withdrawal would adversely affect the relationship between the central organization and the departmental agencies. Hillenkoetter replied that, on the contrary, he expected the relationship to improve. Marshall appeared to be satisfied. Secretary Forrestal, whose assent in February had been fairly reticent, came out now with a positive statement. The Director's authority to issue orders in the names of the Secretaries, he said, made the Central Intelligence Group appear as a Gestapo and caused unnecessary friction. Further discussion was not recorded. It was agreed to withdraw the authority of the Director of Central Intelligence to issue his decisions, orders, and directives in the names of the Secretaries of State, War, and the Navy and to act as their executive agent.[28]

Secretary Patterson then asked Admiral Hillenkoetter if the section on the central intelligence organization in the National Security Act were satisfactory to the Group. Hillenkoetter replied that it was and, in answer to Secretary Forrestal, remarked further that General Donovan, Mr. Cheston, and Mr. Dulles, of the old Office of Strategic Services, approved of the present organization of the Central Intelligence Group. General Donovan's criticism of the National Intelligence Authority comes to mind, and his proposal that the Director of Central Intelligence should be responsible to no group or council but to the Secretary of Defense. The remarks of Mr. Dulles before the House Committee did not indicate entire approval on his part. But in general terms there was agreement among these eminent men in the field of intelligence that the law would improve the nation's system of intelligence. Other matters before the Authority in its last meeting were the transfer of the Map Division from the State Department to the Agency, unfavorable publicity, and a general report by Hillenkoetter for Vandenberg.[29]

Admiral Inglis followed up the advantage which Admiral Hillenkoetter had given him. Inglis argued at length for his plan on July 17, 1947, in Hillenkoetter's second meeting with the Intelligence Advisory Board. There were present the usual representatives of the intelligence services and the aides who served on their ad hoc committees. Mr. Eddy, for the State Department, took the side of the Director. But General Chamberlin, and General McDonald for the Air Forces, supported Admiral Inglis. The Advisory Board was intended to be something more than an advisory council; it had authority to commit the departments to action; it brought their intelligence services into cooperation with the central agency. The success of intelligence in government, declared General Chamberlin, was dependent entirely on cooperation. At this point Admiral Inglis might have remembered recent testimony before the House Committee to show that there had not been cooperation during the war between the Army and the Navy on certain matters of intelligence.[30]

General Chamberlin called for an ad hoc committee to draft a new paper. General McDonald supported him, and so an ad hoc committee of the familiar persons took over once more the job of trying to reconcile the fixed views of the intelligence chiefs of the services and the Director of Central Intelligence. There appeared again the names of Edgar, Treacy, Davis, and Mussett.[31]

There was much discussion in the same meeting about the origin of the concept of "strategic and national policy intelligence." Admiral Inglis kept perfectly clear that he was willing to accept the concept so long as control over "operational" intelligence was not taken from the armed services. It was finally agreed that his proposal should be adopted until the Joint Chiefs of Staff had finished reorganizing their Joint Intelligence Committee. Then the definition of "national" as distinct from "departmental," of "strategic" as distinguished from "operational" intelligence, might be obtained to the satisfaction of most, if not all, parties of interest.[32]

At the next meeting of the Intelligence Advisory Board on July 31, five days after the President had approved the National Security Act, Admiral Hillenkoetter obtained the concurrence of the Board in asking that the National Security Council, when formed, should continue all of the directives under which the Group and the Board were functioning, until the Council made such changes as it saw fit. According to the Act, its provisions should go into effect one day after the Secretary of Defense took office or the sixtieth day after the date of the approval of the Act, whichever came earlier. This gave time for the Intelligence Advisory Board and its ad hoc committee to finish its business in regard to control of the Director. The result was one more directive of the National Intelligence Authority under the President's Directive. Forrestal became Secretary of

Defense on September 17, 1947, in the midst of rising tension over Russian activity against the Marshall Plan for Europe.[33]

The report of the ad hoc committee reconciled the views of the Director and the Board by finding for the most part in favor of the Board. It should have some governing power. All recommendations by the Director to the National Intelligence Authority and its successor, the National Security Council, should be submitted to the Board in writing, with the necessary papers and with voting slips for concurrence, dissent, or request for a meeting of the Board. Its members should have seven working days to consider the subject. The Secretary should send to the members of the Board any recommendations, proposals, or other papers which any member might originate. A recommendation by two or more members of the Board should be submitted with the opinion of the Director to the Authority or the Council. The thought that every recommendation would have taken at least seven days to get by the Board ought to have dismayed even the ad hoc committee.[34]

The suggestion of the ad hoc committee on that part of the Fifth Directive which authorized the Director to act for the Authority "in coordinating all Federal foreign intelligence activities related to the national security" met resistance from both the Army and Air Forces. It involved control over matters of espionage and counterespionage which the Army was not yet willing to concede in any form to the Central Intelligence Agency. This part of the ad hoc committee's plan for control by the Board was therefore deleted.[35]

General Hillenkoetter allowed the report of the ad hoc committee upon Admiral Inglis's original proposal, thus modified, to become the Eleventh Directive of the National Intelligence Authority on September 11, 1947. It was but nine days before he took office under the provisions of the Act of Congress, and the National Intelligence Authority ceased to exist. Why Hillenkoetter did not withhold his approval of a measure placing the Director under the restrictions of his Advisory Board is not to be explained by a desire to reverse Vandenberg's policy. Hillenkoetter had under consideration at the time a program for continuing the essentials of that policy. He stood ready to accept advice and to safeguard the right of dissent; he would not yield the Director's independent right of making recommendations to his superiors in the National Security Council.[36]

Perhaps it would have been to his ultimate advantage if Hillenkoetter had settled the issue then and there. But he found tempers so high and feelings so hard that, as he put it later, he preferred to indulge in a little "chicanery" and let the Eleventh Directive go through. After all, he said, both sides must have known that it would not remain determining. He hoped that in time everybody would cool. Whether or not the Director of

Central Intelligence was called the executive agent of the Secretaries was no longer of great consequence. He was about to become the head of the Central Intelligence Agency under authorizations set in law by the Act of Congress.[37]

On the same day, September 11, 1947, Admiral Hillenkoetter sent to the Secretaries of State, War, the Navy, and Admiral Leahy, personal representative of the President, a memorandum of suggestions for the first meeting of the National Security Council. It was too soon to address the Secretaries as the Council, for the Council had yet to be established according to the Act, and he himsef to take office under the new authority. It was not too soon, however, to anticipate the requirements of the Act that the Director of Central Intelligence should give advice and make recommendations with regard to matters of intelligence related to the national security.[38]

In this memorandum of September 11 to the Secretaries and Admiral Leahy, with a copy for Admiral Souers who was named the Executive Secretary of the Council on August 17, Hillenkoetter suggested that the Director of Central Intelligence and his associates in the Agency should prepare their reports on the new directives within the sixty days following the establishment of the Council. This administrative detail had not been discussed with the Intelligence Advisory Board. It hardly seemed necessary to do so, even though the Eleventh Directive provided that all recommendations from the Director of Central Intelligence should be cleared through his Intelligence Advisory Board before going up to the Authority or its successor, the Council. But Admiral Hillenkoetter went on to suggestions of policy which also had not been discussed with the Intelligence Advisory Board. At least we have yet to find evidence that they were.

One was that there should be a subcommittee of the National Security Council to act as the National Intelligence Authority had acted in control and supervision over the Director of Central Intelligence and the Central Intelligence Group. The idea had been discussed in the hearings of Congress. Dulles especially had advocated a small governing authority over the Director and the Agency. Donovan of course still insisted upon having one responsible officer, the Secretary of Defense, between the Director and the President. Hillenkoetter suggested that the subcommittee to furnish "the active direction" might be merely the Secretaries of State and Defense. His alternative was that it should consist of these Secretaries and the Secretaries of the Army, Navy, and Air Force. But he preferred the first suggestion because the Department of State would not be overshadowed by the military establishment. And then he proposed that the Director of Central Intelligence should sit with the National Secretary Council as "observer, counsel, or adviser" to keep in touch with the thoughts of the Council and to answer its direct questions.[39]

There was some uncertainty in August whether the Director should continue the Intelligence Advisory Board. By September 19, however, the members of the Board had been informed that Hillenkoetter intended to use his authority under the National Security Act and have such an advisory committee as he deemed necessary in carrying out his functions and those of the Central Intelligence Agency. He told them that he wished also to readjust the Interdepartmental Coordinating and Planning Staff so that it might work with a standing committee of the new Intelligence Advisory Committee. This one working committee for the departmental intelligence chiefs would take the place of successive ad hoc committees. Members of the Standing Committee would remain in their respective agencies but be ready on occasion to go over to the Agency and confer with ICAPS. It too would be composed of representatives from the departments; but these men as officers in the Agency would not always be able to vote according to the wishes of their departments. Again the hope was that the Standing Committee for the Advisory Committee and ICAPS for the Director of Central Intelligence somehow would be able to reconcile differences and reach "coordinated" recommendations. But it did not work out as Hillenkoetter hoped. The Standing Committee was to behave like its predecessors, the ad hoc committees of the old Advisory Board.[40]

Hillenkoetter sent formal recommendations on September 19 to the National Security Council for its first meeting on September 26. All of the directives of the Authority and the Group should continue in full force until changed. The Agency should have sixty days in which to make revisions for submission to the Council. He presented his plan for the new Advisory Committee in a separate memorandum. Then on the following day, September 20, 1947, Admiral Hillenkoetter took office as the Director of Central Intelligence under the National Security Act, in the midst of rising fear of Soviet propaganda and talk of retaliation.[41]

THE INTELLIGENCE ADVISORY COMMITTEE

Hillenkoetter's general counsel advised him on July 29, 1947, that under the National Security Act, just approved by President Truman, the Director as head of the Agency was "solely responsible for the performance of the Agency's duties." He therefore could go to the Council without wait-ing upon advice from a committee. Any committee which he chose to have would be his own. Its membership might be supplied from the respective intelligence services, but they would sit at his request. They might take adverse opinions to their own departmental heads, who consti-tuted the Council with other appointees of the President. But the Direc-tor's advisory committee would in no sense be a governing board to con-trol his thought or action. There was no idea that the members had first to give their consent before he could proceed.[42]

Building upon the President's letter of January 22, 1946, and section 303 in the National Security Act of 1947 which made provision for advis-ers, either as committees or individuals, Admiral Hillenkoetter asserted in his memorandum of September 19 to the Council that he was not obli-gated to continue the old Intelligence Advisory Board. He might have a committee which for all intents and purposes would continue the Board; but it would be more subject to the Director's control. He therefore re-quested that the National Security Council should authorize participation by members from the several departments in what he named "the Direc-tor of Central Intelligence's Intelligence Advisory Committee." He would have representatives of the State Department, the Army, Navy, and Air Force, and also of the Atomic Energy Commission to serve as the perma-nent members of the committee. Others would come at his invitation.

The Director would supply the secretariat for the committee. It should meet on his call as chairman. Its communications would be kept in care-ful order. Any disagreement between the Director and a member of the committee would be formally recorded so that the opinion of the member would accompany the Director's recommendation to the Council. The Director would prevent discussion of any matters which members had not yet studied with the related papers and with the opinions held in their respective departments if it were possible to obtain them. He wanted a concerted opinion before making a recommendation to the National Secu-rity Council. In deference to the wishes of Admiral Inglis and General Chamberlin, Hillenkoetter's proposal also carried provision that recom-mendations from two or more members of the Advisory Committee would be sent by the Director to the Council.[43]

The first response to Hillenkoetter's suggestions of which we have any record came on September 23 from Robert A. Lovett, Acting Secretary of State. Secretary Marshall was attending the Assembly of the United Na-tions in New York. Lovett favored the idea of a subcommittee of the Secretaries of State and Defense to handle the affairs of the Central Intelligence Agency for the National Security Council. He wished to add the personal representative of the President in order to retain an authority comparable to the old National Intelligence Authority. The Director should be present as a nonvoting member. It would also be desirable to have him present in the meetings of the National Security Council.

Lovett stated that the Director should consult with an advisory board to ensure "prior consideration by the chiefs of the intelligence services" in regard to matters which should come before the Council. This made clear that the Department of State wished there to be an advisory board for coordination at the so-called working level. The Secretaries ought to have the benefit of such deliberations when they discussed matters of intelligence in the National Security Council. There was, however, no indication in this memorandum to Hillenkoetter that Lovett wished to subject the Director of Central Intelligence to a governing board composed of departmental intelligence officers.[44]

The second reaction to Admiral Hillenkoetter's program came in the National Security Council on September 26. It adopted his recommendations that the old directives remain in full force and sixty days be allowed in which to make the necessary revisions of them, for submission to the Council. The Intelligence Advisory Board therefore continued to have legal standing until it should be replaced by action of the Director and the Council. The Council decided that the Director should attend all of its meetings as observer and adviser. It authorized him to submit the Agency's budget for 1949 to the Bureau of the Budget. No action, however, was taken with regard to establishing the subcommittee to direct the Agency. Possibly, too, the Council formed at that time no opinion of Hillenkoetter's proposal for an advisory committee under the provision of the National Security Act. There is no statement in the published record. But there is evidence elsewhere that there could have been considerable discussion of these suggestions from the Director of Central Intelligence in the first meeting of the National Security Council.[45]

Secretary Royall of the Army wrote on October 6 that the subcommittee was "incompatible" in his view with the purpose of the National Security Council. It was supposed to operate as an "entity," he said, on all matters within its "cognizance"; the Director of Central Intelligence should expect "broad directives" from the Council.[46]

This statement to Admiral Hillenkoetter might have been construed as an invitation to the Director to manage the Agency as he saw fit, looking to the Council only for direction in large matters of policy. But it was quite apparent that the Secretary of the Army did not so intend. Royall was taking exception to the suggestion of a small governing board consisting of the Secretaries of State and Defense to the exclusion of the Secretaries of the Army, Navy, and Air Force. His demurrer was closely related to other things to come. Admiral Souers knew this well and prevailed upon Admiral Hillenkoetter to withdraw the suggestion on October 17.[47]

The records of the National Security Council show that Hillenkoetter's suggestion of a new advisory committee came under revision in the office of the Executive Secretary. Both Admiral Souers and his assistant, James S. Lay, were experienced in the Central Intelligence Group from its beginning. Together they changed the wording in several places with Admiral Hillenkoetter's consent. The Director was made to recommend and not to request. His memorandum as revised did not speak of the "several" but of the "respective" departments. Hillenkoetter's forthright declaration that it was the Director's advisory committee was softened to read: "the Intelligence Advisory Committee proposed by the Director of Central Intelligence."

Souers eliminated the provision that recommendations from two or more members of the Intelligence Advisory Council were to be sent to the National Security Council by the Director. Souer's did so on his own responsibility as Executive Secretary of the National Security Council. His point was that the chiefs of intelligence already had proper access to the Council through their superiors, the Secretaries of the departments.[48]

This provision in the Inglis plan is not to be confused with the stipulation that the dissent of a member or members of the Board should be submitted to the Security Council with the opinion of the Director. Such a dissent was supposed to be substantial in character, and it was to be agreed upon in the deliberations of the Board with the Director. There was no reason for the chiefs of intelligence to approach the Security Council through the Director of Central Intelligence on other matters, except to put him to the annoyance of having to relay their desires contrary to his own wishes. As Hillenkoetter remembered it, after some discussion be flatly refused. It was erroneous to think that such a provision would give to the chiefs of the departmental agencies more positive control over his thoughts and actions.[49]

Approvals of the plan for the advisory committee proposed by Admiral Hillenkoetter, as modified by Souers and Lay, came back to the Executive Secretary from Forrestal, Secretary of Defense, on October 10; Symington, Secretary of the Air Force, on October 17; Lovett, Acting Secretary of State, and Hill, Chairman of the National Security Resources Board, on October 20. No replies from the Secretaries of the Army and of the Navy are to be found in the same file of the Council. But there is a memorandum from the Secretary of the Army for the Executive Secretary. It was sent on November 26, 1947, through the office of the Secretary of Defense. Forrestal's special assistant kept a copy and forwarded the memorandum with a note that the Secretary of Defense had not yet seen it.[50]

The Secretary of the Army opposed Hillenkoetter's plan. Royall declared that the Director of Central Intelligence had been required by the first directive of the National Intelligence Authority to refer "all recommendations" through the Intelligence Advisory Board; the Board therefore performed not only the service of advising the Director of Central Intelligence but also the duty of ensuring that there would be "full departmental coordination of all matters before they were submitted" to the National Intelligence Authority. Royall insisted that the new Intelligence Advisory Committee should be of the same nature.[51]

It was due notice that the Army would support General Chamberlin and Admiral Inglis rather than Admiral Hillenkoetter. On Wednesday, December 3, a formal statement came from the National Security Council to the Director of Central Intelligence enclosing Secretary Royall's memorandum of November 26 and requesting that the Director of Central Intelligence comment on it for "concurrent consideration." Hillenkoetter did so within the week before the Secretaries of War, Navy, the Air Force, the departmental chiefs of intelligence, Souers, and Forrestal in the Office of the Secretary of Defense. Hillenkoetter remembered the conference vividly, he said, as one of the moments in his life. He could recall the words almost as they were spoken. But let us bring to the same point the pertinent story of the NSCIDs before we enter into the historic occasion.[52]

It was evident by this time in another quarter that the intelligence services of the armed forces were entrenching against Hillenkoetter as they had in the preceding fall against Vandenberg. Members of the Interdepartmental Coordinating and Planning Staff and of the Offices in the Agency had gone systematically to work revising and consolidating the directives of the old Authority and the Group according to the instruction from the National Security Council on September 26. The directives of the Council, to be known as NSCIDs, were to lay the principles; directives issued by the Director of Central Intelligence, called DCLs, would carry the relevant administrative orders. Those orders of the Authority and the Group which had lost meaning or become obsolete, either through events or changes caused by the Act of Congress, were abandoned. For one example, we may recall the directive providing for the survey of the Strategic Services Unit. Such housecleaning need not detain us.[53]

Drafts of new measures were ready by October 16 and submitted for discussion within the Agency on October 20. Three days later revisions had been completed and forwarded to the deputies, assistants, and legal counsel of the Director for further suggestion. The measures were practically in order for submission to the Intelligence Advisory Board as Acting Secretary Lovett had advised. There had been no concealment of this activity within the Agency. The Director had sent a memorandum to the department on October 9 with regard to the initial directive which the National Security Council should issue to the Central Intelligence Agency.[54]

The reply from W. Park Armstrong, Jr., Acting Special Assistant to the Secretary of State and representative of the Department on the Intelligence Advisory Board, reflected indirectly the displeasure in the departments because of this activity in the Agency. It was the only reply received. Armstrong gave also a direct view of the tension between the State Department and the members of the military establishment. He proposed that the new directives should define intelligence to conform with the concept of national intelligence which had been approved on February 12, 1947, by the National Intelligence Authority. This would hardly please Admiral Inglis.

Armstrong moreover urged that the Director's right of inspection be restored to include the operations of the intelligence agencies as well as their materials. It had been so provided in the President's Directive of January 22, 1946. But Armstrong would go farther and have the Director determine the causes of "omissions, inadequacies, or duplication" and propose to the Council "corrective measures." Such ideas could never be pleasant for the chiefs of intelligence in the armed services. There were suspicions in the Agency that Armstrong directed his remarks on the Director's right of inspection at his own department where chiefs of geographical areas opposed his work in research and intelligence as they had McCormack's.[55]

Armstrong's letter, however, was not aimed solely at the military branches of the Government or his rivals in the State Department. The Department had in common with the armed services antipathies toward the Central Intelligence Agency. His proposal in regard to the Director's right of inspection carried with it repeal of the section in the Fifth Directive authorizing the Group to undertake research and analysis. Armstrong would have "centralization of functions" only when, by agreement among the departments and the Agency, such functions could be "most beneficially and effectively accomplished on a central basis." His contention was that the intelligence agencies of the departments should produce "finished intelligence" in the fields of their dominant interests; the Director of Intelligence should exercise his right of inspection to see to it that they did. Then the Agency would not produce national intelligence from "source materials" which it had processed for itself. It would derive national intelligence from that "finished" departmental intelligence.[56]

Along the same line of reasoning Armstrong proposed to abandon the directive of February 12, 1947, in which the Central Intelligence Group had laid the national requirements for the collection of intelligence on China. These when classified as economic, social, political, scientific, and military were considered matters of primary interest to the respective departments and not the immediate concern of their central agency. With this suggestion Armstrong could count upon entire agreement from General Chamberlin.[57]

The reply to Armstrong from the Agency on November 3 was lacking somewhat in candor. It said that almost everything he desired had been incorporated in the drafts which would be complete and ready for delivery to the chiefs of intelligence of the departments on November 10. There was no provision in the drafts for abandoning, as Armstrong implied, research and analysis of "source materials" in the Agency and for having recourse only, as he suggested, to the "finished" intelligence of the departments for the construction of national estimates. The directive with regard to the national requirements for collection in China, too, was to be incorporated in a new NSCID. But then Armstrong was to have another chance in the Advisory Board and, as it proved, in yet another ad hoc committee if he wished to press his case for the State Department against the central agency and against the armed services.[58]

Telephone calls went out to the members of the Intelligence Advisory Board by November 13, inviting them to a meeting with the Director of Central Intelligence on November 20, 1947, when they should discuss with him the proposed directives of the National Security Council and of the Director of Central Intelligence. These were to go to the Council on November 26 as directed by the Council in its first meeting on September 26.[59]

The conference of the intelligence chiefs with Admiral Hillenkoetter on November 20 was notable, but not for analysis and criticism of the proposed directives of the Council and the Director. The chiefs spent time arguing whether or not they were the Intelligence Advisory Board. It was idle discussion. The National Intelligence Authority had gone out of existence as Hillenkoetter took office under the National Security Act on September 20, following Forrestal's induction as Secretary of Defense on September 17. But the Intelligence Advisory Board did not die with the Authority. The Board remained to function after the National Security Council's decision on September 26 that the old directives should continue in full force at least sixty days.[60]

The Intelligence Advisory Board continued to exist so long as the First and Eleventh Directives remained in effect. Admiral Hillenkoetter may have befogged the issue by pointing to the fact that there no longer was an Authority to which the Board might report. But he himself accepted the Advisory Board as such when he accepted its request that the proposed NSCIDs and DCIs should be referred to an ad hoc committee for discussion with ICAPS.[61]

The meeting of the Intelligence Advisory Board on November 20, 1947, was notable for the demeanor of its members. Coming upon them for the first time in such a meeting as this with the Director, one might think that, being relatively uniformed, they were piqued because he had taken them by surprise and, being conscientious men who did not like to be unprepared for their duty, they were provoked because they were not ready. We have followed these men and their aides on successive ad hoc committees, however, through a year of meeting and maneuvering over the duties and responsibilities of the Director of Central Intelligence, the facilities and functions of the central intelligence organization of which the Director was head, and the relationship which he was supposed to maintain with the intelligence agencies of the departments.

The thought is hard to resist that the members of the Board were present on this occasion not to cooperate in an enterprise of common concern but to take exception to this, to be hesitant over that, and above all to stall and delay. They had been given not just ten days since receipt of the memorandum of November 10 to consider the proposals. They themselves had been engaged with almost all of these matters as members either of the Advisory Board or of its ad hoc committees for more than ten months.[62]

Instead of pressing his case, Armstrong announced that the Department had not been able to arrive at a "firm position" on the directives. Secretary Marshall was leaving for London; Mr. Lovett had the matter in hand, but the Department could not be committed as yet. Hillenkoetter hoped that, as heads of the intelligence agencies, the members of the Board might be able at least to get through the first four directives having to do with the duties and responsibilities of the Director, collection, production, and the objectives of national intelligence. But Armstrong insisted that, as the matters were coming before the National Security Council, the head of each intelligence agency must have the position of his department established before he could speak finally.

This was turning the function of the advisory committee upside down. If this were the true interpretation, the Department of Central Intelligence could not seek the advice of his advisory committee with regard to his recommendations to the Secretaries in the Council until they themselves had made up their minds on what they wished their intelligence officers to advise the Director to advise them. Admiral Inglis cut straight to the point. As Chief of Naval Intelligence, he said, he was not the "mouthpiece of the Secretary." What Inglis had to say in the meetings was his own opinion.

Admiral Inglis did not like his present situation. The Agency had produced these papers "on its own initiative and its own authority"; they should have been considered by the Board as they were formulated. Had they been new papers, there would have been more strength in his argument. But they were revisions of things with which Inglis himself had been conversant for much more than a year.[63]

General Chamberlin added to Admiral Inglis's remark that the system used by the Agency was difficult for them. Chamberlin had other things to do as chief of intelligence for the Army. He could not turn his responsibility off or on "at somebody else's command." As far as he himself was concerned, he said, he had come "unprepared to discuss these papers." His subordinates, though, had worked on them and found many things to challenge. There were "important differences of principle," he said, that had never been approached, nor were they included in past directives. What those principles were General Chamberlin did not specify.

Later on, however, he revealed a marked difference in principle between Admiral Inglis and himself over expressing their views in the advisory committee. General Chamberlin objected to a procedure in the committee which might "drive a wedge" between the chief of intelligence in a department and his superior, the Secretary; it completely destroyed "command principles." He would be inclined, he said, "to keep quiet at all times" because he would be afraid that an action in the committee would be appealed over his head.[64]

General McDonald for the Air Force unleashed a statement. Analysis of the proposed directives had revealed to him, he said, that it was going to be necessary for him to recommend many changes. It would be impossible to cover the directives that afternoon; no attempt therefore should be made to go into either the philosophy or the composition of the directives. There should be an ad hoc committee "for the purpose of reconciling views." And so there was another such committee, made of the familiar aides who by now must have been expert on the philosophies, the details, and most assuredly the conflicting views. This was to become known as The Ad Hoc Committee.[65]

Admiral Gingrich, who was relatively new, having come on the Board to represent the Atomic Energy Commission, went to the heart of the situation. "One point I might mention, Hilly," he said, "there doesn't appear to be any provision in these first two directives here for an Intelligence Advisory Committee, or Board, such as is executed under our old setup." Hillenkoetter replied that the law gave him the power to appoint an advisory committee. It would seem that all present must have known that he had submitted his plan on September 19. The members of the Board in any case were not to be diverted from their intention to have the National Security Council direct him in establishing the committee as they wished. The matter went to the ad hoc committee. Six days later Secretary Royall submitted his objections to Hillenkoetter's plan on behalf of the Army.[66]

No one could have been surprised at the revisions of the drafts by the ad hoc committee. The changes, often small in detail, were persistently designed to restrict the Director, to make him defer to the Intelligence Advisory Committee, and to remove his supervisory authority over the departmental intelligence agencies. This purpose is best shown by examination of the draft of NSCID 1 concerning the duties of the Director and his relations with the Advisory Committee. The Committee, consisting of the intelligence chiefs from the Departments of State, Army, Navy, and the Air Force, the Joint Chiefs of Staff, and the Atomic Energy Commission, was to advise the Director on "all recommendations and advice" to the National Security Council and upon his own directives or administrative orders for carrying out the directives of the Council. He should "act for" the National Security Council "through the Intelligence Advisory Committee." The coordination of intelligence activities should be accomplished "by recognizing primary departmental requirements and by supporting the intelligence agencies." Whatever coordination meant, it did not mean on this occasion consent by the will of a majority after reasoned discussion. Under the cloak of the Committee, the will of an individual agency, reasoning or capricious, appeared to hold sway.[67]

The Director was to disseminate intelligence subject to the security regulations of the agency in which the information had originated. He was to perform services of common concern as determined with the Advisory Committee. He was to obtain personnel from the departmental agencies in agreement with the intelligence chief of the organization concerned. He was to arrange with the respective intelligence chiefs for "surveys and inspections of departmental intelligence activities."

Here the ad hoc committee made a slip. But it was soon corrected. Although Armstrong for the Department of State recommended inspection of departmental intelligence activities by the Director of Central Intelligence, the chiefs of intelligence for the armed services could not endure such interference with their operations. When the measure came from the meeting of the Intelligence Advisory Board on December 8, the words "intelligence activities" had given way to "intelligence material." But after much discussion, control by the Department was not restored. This too was rectified before the provision was finally incorporated in NSCID 1 as issued by the Council on December 12, 1947.[68]

The Council extended the Director's right of inspection, "for the coordination of intelligence activities," only to the "intelligence material" of the federal departments and agencies by arrangement with their heads. Their operations "relating to the national security" were not open to survey and inspection by the Director of Central Intelligence. Those activities are not now open to his inspection. The value of centralized inspection of intelligence activities, as originally provided in the President's Directive of January 22, 1946, is still too much for the departments to grasp.[69]

Admiral Hillenkoetter notified the ad hoc committee on November 25 that he could not accept as a whole its revisions in the drafts of the NSCIDs. He called another meeting of the intelligence chiefs for December 8 to consider the changes which he would make in the proposals of their ad hoc committee, and he sent those changes to them on December 1 so that they might bring to the meeting whatever statements of nonconcurrence they might choose to submit.[70]

Records are not available for all of the determining events between the action of the ad hoc committee on November 24 and the meeting of the intelligence chiefs again with Hillenkoetter on December 8. But memories of some who participated are still keen. There is recorded evidence to show why the chiefs of intelligence were in a different mood from that of November 20. And the minutes of the meeting on December 8, stenotyped but never circulated, have come to light.[71]

Hillenkoetter went to Forrestal when he learned of Secretary Royall's opposition on November 26 to the plan for the new Intelligence Advisory Committee. Forrestal had approved the plan in October. There followed some days of telephoning and conversation, and then Forrestal called a meeting of the Secretaries and their chiefs of intelligence, a representative of the State Department, and Souers. Hillenkoetter was there to explain his plan for the operation of the Central Intelligence Agency under the National Security Act. We should remember Forrestal's declaration to Congress in the preceding spring that the Agency, after the Security Council, would be the most important institution in the forthcoming Act.[72]

As Hillenkoetter recalled the episode in the office of the Secretary of Defense, Forrestal asked for no opinions when Hillenkoetter had finished his statement but turned to Admiral Inglis and General Chamberlin on one side of the table. Forrestal did not include the representative of the State Department in his glance. Nor, apparently, was the member of the Air Force in his line of fire. He spoke directly to Inglis and Chamberlin: "You are not going to interfere with this thing," he said. "It is going to run as Hillenkoetter says. Do you both understand that now?" Hillenkoetter was quite sure of that last question and of the remark to him later by

Admiral Inglis: "He talked to us like a couple of plebes. I guess that makes us your servants now."[73]

The record is not yet clear whether this meeting came before or after Forrestal received a note written on Friday, December 5, by Vannevar Bush, head of the Research and Development Board. It seems likely that Bush's letter arrived shortly after the Secretary of Defense had told the military and naval chiefs of intelligence what they were not to do. In any event, the statements by Vannevar Bush, chief adviser to the Secretary of Defense on scientific matters, added weight to Hillenkoetter's authority when he met with the chiefs of intelligence again on Monday, December 8, to discuss their differences over the NSCIDs.[74]

Bush declared with effectively restrained language that the Central Intelligence Agency was not in good position to provide scientific intelligence to the Atomic Energy Commission. The Intelligence Advisory Committee was divided; Mr. Souers, said Bush, should be warned of the situation. To amplify his statement, Bush included memoranda from officers in his organization who were in even closer touch. His chief of intelligence reported that under the leadership of the State Department's representative the ad hoc committee was seeking more authority for the Intelligence Advisory Committee. The director of his program division reported that the intelligence chiefs wanted an executive order apart from the directive of the Council to establish the Committee as the "governing committee" of the Agency. In this situation the officer responsible for scientific intelligence in the Agency was "completely stymied." Bush urged that someone "at the highest level" should determine the relationships between the Agency and the "operating" services so that the production of "information, detailed intelligence, and integrated strategic intelligence" could proceed.[75]

Hillenkoetter read this statement in the meeting of December 8. The response of General Chamberlin was that he was not conscious there was any question whether the Intelligence Advisory Committee was to be a controlling or an advisory board. "I frankly admit," he said, "it is an advisory body"; others might have a different opinion. He felt that he had authority to commit his own department "on certain things" in agreement with other members of the Committee and carry out the decisions "loyally without any command to do so." Thus, the Committee could eliminate a lot of "minutiae," but it would still be an "advisory committee."

The position was tenable, and it was logical after the admonition from the Secretary of Defense that the Agency was going to run as the Director of Central Intelligence said. But there had been some evolution in the thinking of the representative from the Army since the meeting on July 17 when he stated that the Advisory Board was "a little more than an advisory body" and the meeting on November 20 in which he maintained that the right of appeal by the Director to the Secretary of a department over the head of its chief of intelligence destroyed "command principles."[76]

There was action in the meeting of December 8 which the stenotypist could not record. The memory of Hillenkoetter's general counsel who was present is certain on that score. Although the record is one of friendly words in half-finished sentences, Hillenkoetter's demeanor was as strong as Houston ever saw him use. Houston sat where he could observe faces and catch fleeting expressions. As General Chamberlin's overtones conveyed his acknowledgment that "Hilly" was "the boss," Houston saw an aide of the General "turn white." Admiral Inglis sat shaking his head in an unmistakable "no."[77]

The representative of the Navy had attended nearly every meeting of the Intelligence Advisory Board from its beginning under Souers in February 1946. Admiral Inglis had insisted all along that in most respects the Group, and then the Agency, should be a cooperative departmental activity. To the statement by Vannevar Bush that the Agency would be either "almost completely self-sufficient" or "a small coordinating body" surrounded by strong departmental agencies, Admiral Inglis's response now was that there could be a "middle ground" for the Agency. As an "integrated operating agency," he said, it should have as little interference from the Advisory Committee as possible; the Committee should be "purely advisory, and absolutely nothing more." But in the relationships between the central agency and the departmental intelligence agencies the Intelligence Advisory Committee should go beyond advisory capacity; it had something to do with "liaison, coordination, and implementation." That was his "philosophy," he said, "for whatever it was worth."[78]

There was further discussion in general terms. But the remainder of the meeting on December 8 was given for the most part to examining in detail revisions which the ad hoc committee had made in the NSCIDs of the Agency. For the time being, the Director of Central Intelligence had his way. With the exception of the change regarding inspection of "intelligence material" which we have considered and the inclusion of a phrase regarding "national policy" intelligence that was later deleted, NSCID 1 went to the Council practically as it had been recast in the Agency on December 1. Hillenkoetter sent with it on December 9 the suggestion that the Council might name the Director of Central Intelligence as chairman of the Intelligence Advisory Committee to "emphasize" that it was an advisory body "to help the Director" and not a "Board of Directors or Board of Management."[79]

THE DIRECTIVES

The National Security Council adopted four NSCIDs on December 12, 1947. Two others were delayed until the Secretary of Defense should decide the issue between the Navy and the Air Force over air intelligence. Still others remained to be considered later in the spring and summer of 1948. One was delayed until January 1949.

The first intelligence directive of the Council established duties and responsibilities for the Director of Central Intelligence, according to the purposes enunciated in the National Security Act. The directive prescribed the relationship between the Central Intelligence Agency of which he was the head and the several intelligence organizations for which the Intelligence Advisory Committee should give him advice. The Committee was to be composed of the intelligence chiefs, or their representatives, from the Departments of State, Army, Navy, and Air Force, the Joint Chiefs of Staff, and the Atomic Energy Commission. The Director was to invite the representatives of other intelligence agencies to sit with the Committee when matters related to the national security concerned them. There was place for the Federal Bureau of Investigation as in the Intelligence Advisory Board under the Authority.[80]

The directive did not stipulate, as Hillenkoetter had suggested, that the Director should be the chairman of the Advisory Committee. The omission may have been considered by some of his associates as a defeat for Hillenkoetter. From another point of view, it was quite the contrary. A responsible officer should not be a voting member of his own advisory body. He need not be its chairman to listen to its counsel.

The first directive, however, did require, as had the directives of the National Intelligence Authority, that in making recommendations or giving advice to his superiors on the Council the Director should transmit a record of the concurrence or nonconcurrence of members of the Advisory Committee. Where there was disagreement among the heads of departments in the National Military Establishment, the Director should refer the matter to the Secretary of Defense. When approved by the Council, recommendations of the Director should issue as directives from the Council to the Director, and the intelligence chiefs respectively should be responsible for ensuring that such orders when applicable were "implemented in their organizations."

The Director was to act for the Council in issuing supplementary directives (known as DCIDs). Whenever one or more members of the Advisory Committee disagreed with the Director over one of these directives, it should be sent with statements of nonconcurrence to the Council for decision as in the case of recommendations or advice by the Director to the Council. The procedure was much the same as under the old directives of the National Intelligence Authority. Difficulty would arise, as it had in those days, over the variable meanings possible in the words "agreed," "substantial," and even "dissent."[81]

With regard to the production of "national intelligence" which was expressly assigned to the Director of Central Intelligence as it had been in the President's Directive, the Director was to make use of existing intelligence facilities and to utilize departmental intelligence. So far as practicable he should not duplicate departmental activities and research. But there was no statement in the directive, as many had wished and some still think wise, to keep the Central Intelligence Agency from engaging in original research and analysis of the materials.

In disseminating his "national intelligence" to the President, the Council, the intelligence chiefs of the agencies, and others whom the Council might designate, the Director of Central Intelligence was to send with his own view "an agreed statement of substantial dissent." The inference seems possible that, if there had to be a split opinion, there should be only one dissent agreed among the members of the Intelligence Advisory Committee. Such agreement proved hard to get. Subsequently the provision allowed several differing opinions.[82]

Other sections of NSCID 1 pertained to relations directly between the several intelligence chiefs and the Director of Central Intelligence. In arranging for inspection of "departmental intelligence material," he was authorized to pass by the intelligence chiefs to the heads of the departments or agencies concerned. The coordination of intelligence activities was to be done with recognition of "primary departmental requirements"; they should receive the cooperation and support of the Central Intelligence Agency. But although much had been said in the meeting on December 8, there was nothing in NSCID 1 to require the Director to wait upon the consent of the intelligence chiefs concerned with those activities. The same was true of the Director's power to perform services of "common concern"; they were to be determined by the National Security Council. The Director was to disseminate "intelligence or intelligence information" to the Federal Bureau of Investigation and other departments or agencies as the security regulations of the originating agency permitted, when he himself thought such dissemination appropriate. He was to make arrangements with the departments and agencies for the assignment of personnel to the Central Intelligence Agency; he did not have specifically to negotiate through the intelligence chief concerned. In short, the individual chiefs of intelligence were not to possess, under the rule of the National Security Council, many of the privileges and rights of exemption which they had enjoyed in the days of the Group as a "cooperative interdepartmental activity" under Admiral Souers and had fought to maintain against encroachment by the directives of General Vandenberg.[83]

Three remaining paragraphs in NSCID 1 merit special attention for the interpretation which military authorities put upon them as the Joint Chiefs of Staff dissociated their intelligence system from civilian membership. These paragraphs stipulated that the intelligence organizations of the departments and agencies should maintain with the Central Intelligence Agency and with each other "a continuing interchange of intelligence information and intelligence available to them." But there was a saving clause, "as appropriate to their respective responsibilities." It would be interpreted by the organizations for themselves. Their files, too, were to be available for consultation under their own security regulations. They were to provide "within the limits of their capabilities" such intelligence as the Director of Central Intelligence or any of the other departments and agencies should request. General Gruenther's commentary upon these provisions in NSCID I will appear shortly as we take up again the relationship between the Central Intelligence Agency and the Joint Chiefs of Staff.[84]

The National Security Council on the same day accepted NSCID 4 concerning the objectives of national intelligence. Divorced from the geographical areas of collection and the kinds of intelligence such as political, economic, and military in which the departments had or arrogated to themselves proprietary rights, these objectives were relatively easy to determine. The changes were minor which the ad hoc committee made in the draft prepared in the Agency. It was agreed that the Director of Central Intelligence in collaboration with the several agencies should make a comprehensive outline of the objectives in foreign countries.

Priorities for both collection and production, however, were another question. They should be determined from time to time with regard for current importance by the Director and the agencies under the guidance of the National Security Council. As the directive issued from the Council, it stipulated that the guidance should be furnished by the "NSC Staff," composed of the Executive Secretary and representatives from the departments who should be designated by the members of the Council. In case of disagreement in the Staff, the Council was to decide.

There was no provision in case the Council should not decide. Presumably these men at the highest level in the Government would never leave so important a matter as priorities without establishing some preference. But coordination by the Secretaries, political officers, is harder to obtain than one may think. They are relatively unfamiliar with factual detail and are inclined accordingly to depend for advice upon subordinates who are specialists in their fields. In any case, if the Council should not decide, the issue would rest of course upon the ultimate responsibility of its chairman, the President.[85]

The directive with regard to wireless and radio monitoring, NSCID 6, offered no difficulties once it passed the ad hoc committee. It had met resistance chiefly from the Navy. The Office of Operations in the Agency had wished precise safeguards for its "service of common concern," the Foreign Broadcast Information Branch. The Agency wanted to keep the problem within a DCID supplementary to NSCID 1. But, rather than delay over small points, Admiral Hillenkoetter let the matter be handled in NSCID 6. The wording of it, though not what the Office of Operations preferred, did provide that the Director of Central Intelligence should conduct all federal monitoring of foreign propaganda and press broadcasts required to meet the needs of the department and agencies. And he was to disseminate such information to the departments and agencies with authorized interests in it. Press broadcasts might be narrow in scope. The words "foreign propaganda" gave ample room for the Agency to operate without interfering with the Navy's interceptions.[86]

The fourth intelligence measure adopted by the National Security Council on December 12, 1947, had to do with espionage and counterespionage outside the United States. They were "top secret" matters which had embroiled the Office of Strategic Services with the armed forces and were still to cause misunderstanding and much trouble as the Army, the Navy, the Air Force, and the Central Intelligence Agency worked often at cross purposes when there should have been the closest cooperation. The difficulty is not to be ascribed merely to departmental rancor and jealousy.

We have considered General Magruder's analysis of the problem and his proposal that the central intelligence organization should have exclusive control over the collection of secret intelligence by means of espionage and counterespionage abroad. We have observed General Vandenberg's successful endeavor to have such authority established in the Fifth Directive of the National Intelligence Authority. But we have seen, too, that the Army continued its secret intelligence operations in foreign countries, and did so in some instances without informing even its fellow armed service, the Navy, in regard to the activity or its accomplishments.[87]

The Fifth Directive of the Authority had given the Director of Central Intelligence authority to conduct "all organized Federal espionage and counterespionage operations" for the collection of secret intelligence abroad. The word "organized" had left the field open by inference for unorganized or "casual" operations. Close definition had also distinguished the work of the Counterintelligence Corps of the Army from the activity of the Office of Special Operations in the Central Intelligence Group. Collection of foreign intelligence by the Corps was supposed to be incidental to its function of protecting the American forces. It was to be hoped, but not presumed, that such clandestine information would eventually reach the Central Intelligence Group either in its stations overseas or in Washington. The relationship between the armed services and the Group was further complicated by the use of reserve officers from the Army and the Navy in the secret operations of the Group.

First efforts in the Agency to draft a DCID which should protect the military services and yet allow the Agency to use such officers led to discussion of the whole problem. Under pressure from the services through the ad hoc committee, the plan for the DCID gave way to another directive for adoption by the Council, NSCID 5. General Chamberlin insisted upon sharply distinguishing espionage from counterespionage so that the Army might continue to operate in counterintelligence. With this conceded, and the provision that all other NSCIDs and DCIDs should be construed to apply solely to "overt intelligence activities" unless otherwise specified, NSCID 5 was accepted by all parties.[88].

As issued by the Council, its fifth intelligence directive stipulated that the Director of Central Intelligence should conduct all organized federal operations in espionage outside the United States and its possessions for the collection of "intelligence information required to meet the needs of all departments and agencies concerned" except for "certain agreed activities" by other departments and agencies. What these activities were the directive did not say. No one familiar with the operations of the Central Intelligence Agency or of the armed services, however, was in doubt.

The directive stated separately that the Director should conduct all organized federal operations in counterespionage outside the United States and its possessions "and in occupied areas." This was to provide for protecting the interests of the United States where its armed forces were still maintained. In addition to "certain agreed activities," it was stipulated expressly in this paragraph that counterintelligence activities of any military command or installation were not to be precluded. The Director of Central Intelligence was also to be responsible for coordinating overt with covert activities in collecting intelligence. He should disseminate such intelligence to the departments and agencies authorized to receive it. Though carefully worded, NSCID 5 had loopholes which gave the Office of Special Operations many experiences with other agencies during the administrations of both Hillenkoetter and Smith.[89]

The directives concerning overt collection and production which had caused Vandenberg so much trouble in the previous year had been delayed past the meeting of the National Security Council on December 12, 1947. The dispute between the Navy and the new Department of the Air Force over air intelligence was stubborn. Secretary Forrestal, after much reluctance, finally abandoned hope that the differences could be reconciled and a solution found in the discussions of the intelligence chiefs with the Director of Central Intelligence. Coordination failed at the "working level." The Secretary of Defense had to decide the issue. Forrestal declared on January 3, 1948, that the Air Force should be assigned "the dominant interest" and the Navy should be allowed to continue producing the intelligence it required. This he called "staff intelligence." He had been assured by Admiral Souers, Executive Secretary of the Council, that the Navy was objecting primarily to object; it would persist until the Secretary of Defense exercised his authority under the National Security Act. When he did so, the measures, NSCID 2 and NSCID 3, were adopted by the Council on January 13, 1948.[90]

The first of these directives had to do with the coordination of collection activities abroad, except of course those involved with espionage, counterespionage, and the "agreed activities" specified in NSCID 5.

Despite the failure of coordination in the field during the abortive Dominican revolutionary expedition from Cuba in the previous summer, no effort had been made in the Agency to apply the lesson and to reopen the question whether the Director of Central Intelligence rather than the "senior U.S. representative" in each foreign area should "coordinate" collection activities there. The members of the Intelligence Advisory Board were fully informed of the Dominican affair, but they appear to have given little thought to this fiasco in cooperative responsibility. In view of the distressing experience at Bogotá in the following spring, it would have been better if the issue had been decided in favor of the Director of Central Intelligence before the Council adopted NSCID 2 in January 1948. But all parties appear to have been willing at that time to leave overt collection of intelligence abroad without centralized supervision and control.[91]

Hillenkoetter's drafting officers had endeavored to give the Director some authority where economic and scientific matters concerned more than one department but were "of primary concern to none." This was to be done only "upon specific approval by the National Security Council." The proposal, however, did not survive the operation of the ad hoc committee. In its place there appeared the provision that each agency should collect economic, scientific, and technological intelligence "in accordance with its own needs." And so it was left in the text of NSCID 2 as adopted by the Council.[92]

The remainder of NSCID 2 was practically a repetition of the Seventh Directive of the National Intelligence Authority, which Vandenberg had opposed the year before and from which he had appealed his case to the Authority. A collector in the field was still to transmit his "intelligence information" to the representative there of the agency most concerned and send copies to his own agency as he pleased. This may have been coordination; it certainly was not control.

There was to be no "unproductive duplication and uncoordinated overlap." There were to be "full flow of intelligence information" and "full utilization" of "individual initiative and favorable contacts." No interpretation should "negate the basic principle" that all departmental representatives abroad were individually responsible for collecting and transmitting pertinent information to their respective departments. There was to be "free and unrestricted interdepartmental exchange of intelligence information" to meet the "recognized secondary needs" of each department and agency.[93]

Needs obvious in one department but unrecognized by another were not included. Clearly there was no intention to have NSCID 2 depart from the loosely articulated system of overt collection which the departments had maintained against Vandenberg's efforts to establish supervision and control. If Hillenkoetter is to be blamed for this, the National Security Council is entitled to share the criticism with him.[94]

The directive pertaining to the coordination of production, NSCID 3, also adopted on January 13, 1948, established the definitions and the categories of intelligence which henceforth were to govern activities and separate responsibilities. Dominant interests in producing intelligence were to coincide with those in collecting it. The whole scheme of production, however, was to be "subject to refinement through a continuous program of coordination by the Director of Central Intelligence" as the system of collection was not.[95]

Since the definition of "basic," "current," "staff," "departmental," and "national" intelligence may be studied in the texts themselves, no paraphrase is given here. But distinctions should be noted with some care. Basic intelligence, the product of fact-finding and analysis, best exemplified in the "National Intelligence Surveys," is permanent and static by nature. It is to be distinguished from current intelligence, which has value for the moment but which may prove in time less important and even no longer useful.

Staff intelligence is prepared by a department or agency to satisfy its own requirements. No matter how many others are engaged in collecting the same information, the idea is fixed that an agency has a right to collect staff intelligence for itself and even keep that intelligence to itself. But in this exclusive enterprise it does not feel that it should be confined to the use of materials obtained within its own system of collection. It expects, in fact assumes, that it has a right to receive information from other agencies and the departments. In short, the process is not reciprocal. When reluctant to release certain information, an agency is likely to think of it as staff intelligence exclusively for its own use.

Departmental intelligence is distinguished from staff intelligence primarily because the departments choose to have it so. Whether basic, current, or staff intelligence, departmental intelligence presumably is always available to the Central Intelligence Agency for use in its national estimates and for distribution to other agencies when that intelligence is pertinent to their work in maintaining the national security.

National intelligence by definition in NSCID 3 is therefore "integrated departmental intelligence" covering the "broad aspects of national policy and national security." It concerns more than one department or agency. It transcends the "exclusive competence" of a single department or agency or the military establishment. That is to say, it includes the intelligence of the State Department and other nonmilitary agencies of the Government. The Director of Central Intelligence is expressly designated as the one who produces and disseminates national intelligence. He is to receive materials from the departments and agencies by agreement with them, in accordance with their dominant interests and their capabilities to produce such materials and, we should add, their willingness to give it to him.

Since the adoption of NSCID 3 in January 1948 there has been no legal ground for questioning the authorization of the Director of Central Intelligence to produce and disseminate national intelligence. But there still have been many occasions when the several intelligence agencies of the departments have made it hard for the Director to do so. The issue of individual versus collective responsibility for national estimates has remained in a state of suspense. This may have been fortunate for the development of the theory of central intelligence and the growth of this Agency. It has not always worked for the production of the best possible national estimates.[96]

The NSCID to continue the "exploitation" of American businesses and individuals within the United States for intelligence on affairs abroad had been under consideration since August. There were several reasons for the delay. The ad hoc committee made an issue of the Agency's desire to put the details of the regulation in a DCID based upon NSCID 1 and the responsibility of the Agency for matters of "common concern." Admiral Souers had urged on behalf of the Council that its directives be kept few in number and their administrative details put in DCIDs. But the captains and colonels of the ad hoc committee insisted upon a separate NSCID 7. The idea appears to have been that the intelligence agencies of the departments thus would be in closer relation to the Council and less subordinate to the Director of Central Intelligence. The draft had to be referred back to the working committee and the Office of Operations.[97]

And then the representative of G-2 raised a question for the Army whether the Intelligence Advisory Committee ought not to have some power of revision, just in case there should be need in time of war. Hillenkoetter gave the perfect answer: all directives, NSCIDs and DCIDs, were drawn to establish procedures which should be changed in practice. The directives were "not irrevocable"; they were subject to developing circumstances. General Chamberlin offered no further objection. By February 9 all concurrences had come from the Intelligence Advisory Committee. The Council adopted NSCID 7 on February 12, 1948.[98]

Kingman Douglass and others who had struggled with the colonels and captains over the same problem in August and September 1946 must have been pleased when they read NSCID 7. It gave the Central Intelligence Agency charge of collecting foreign intelligence from American businesses and individuals within the United States. It stipulated that the Agency should make the rules, establish the procedures, set the standards, manage the field offices, arrange for the contacts, obtain the agreements, inform the departmental agencies, and disseminate the information acquired. The departmental agencies might assign representatives to the field offices, but they would be under the direction of "the CIA managers." The departmental agencies could expect full service from the Central Intelligence Agency, but it in turn was to receive, "to the maximum extent possible," the information which they obtained as a byproduct of their nonintelligence activities.[99]

The directive regarding biographical data on foreign scientists and technologists, NSCID 8, issued on May 25, 1948, caused no particular disturbances among the departmental agencies. It assigned primary responsibility to the Central Intelligence Agency but left to the departmental agencies the right still to collect, analyze, and abstract such material. The directive on communications intelligence, however, was involved in a prolonged and complicated deliberation over the relation to be maintained between the Director of Central Intelligence and the Agency, on the one hand, and the United States Communications Intelligence Board, on the other. NSCID 9, closely held under "limited distribution," was not issued by the National Security Council until July 1, 1948. NSCID 10, concerning the collection of data on foreign science and technology, in which the State Department claimed a "primary interest," was delayed until January 18, 1949.[100]

SCIENTIFIC INTELLIGENCE

The Nuclear Energy Group, established in the Scientific Branch of the Office of Reports and Estimates on March 28, 1947, marked time with little accomplishment as the Atomic Energy Commission and the Central Intelligence Group endeavored to find a working arrangement between themselves. The Scientific Branch engaged energetically for months in other projects according to the agreement with the Joint Research and Development Board but produced little to satisfy the need for intelligence on the scientific "capabilities and intentions" of the Union of Soviet Socialist Republics.[101]

There were papers on guided missiles, plans for intelligence requirements concerning the Soviet Union, arrangements for security, a visit from the liaison officer of JRDB to ascertain the information in the possession of the Branch which he would like to have sent to the Board. [eleven lines deleted]

Critics chose to lay the blame for this situation upon the Central Intelligence Group and Admiral Hillenkoetter. They were failing to coordinate the activities of the departmental agencies in scientific intelligence. This criticism presumed that the agencies were yearning for the Director's leadership, as they were certainly not if the past experience of Vandenberg and Hillenkoetter were any indication. This criticism presumed, too, that the raw materials of scientific intelligence were within reach. Obviously they were not. The collection of scientific intelligence still is one of the most difficult activities of the Agency to accomplish with any volume, accuracy, or speed. To Hillenkoetter the problem was primarily one of obtaining the necessarily skilled personnel both at home and in the field.[102]

The Office of Collection and Dissemination endeavored in August 1947 to make by geographical location a survey of the persons and offices available in the Departments of State, War, Navy, and Air Forces for collecting scientific intelligence. The State Department stalled over definition of "satisfactory capability" and over phases in the scientific information involved; besides, its officer was not ready to make any commitment regarding the assignment of "reporting personnel in our foreign missions" to that sort of work. This, we should notice, was before the Department of State delayed the adoption of NSCID 10 on the ground that the Department had the "primary interest" in the collection of data on foreign science and technology.

The Navy did not think itself equipped to collect scientific intelligence except [several words deleted]. The Army and the Air Forces reported that they could take care of such intelligence for their own purposes. None of the armed services expressed much interest beyond their own requirements, though all recognized the need for improved national collection. To the suggestion that the Central Intelligence Group, then becomiing the Agency, might select and pay scientific attachés who should be controlled by the State Department, OCD expected these reactions: the Department would decline on the ground that it had enough to do; the Army would prefer its own scientific net; the Navy and the Air Force would be indifferent.

In the meantime, members of ORE had met with representatives of the JRDB on July 17. They were to obtain by September 1, with such means and information as were available, some idea of the scientific and technological capabilities of the Soviet Union which would affect the "defense economy" of the United States by 1949. In line with this project, quite apparently approved if not instigated by Secretary Forrestal, there came a letter on July 31 from Karl T. Compton addressed to Forrestal as Secretary of National Security. Forrestal was about to take office on August 17 as the first Secretary of Defense.[103]

Compton recalled for Secretaries Marshall and Forrestal the special committee which Secretary Stimson had asked in the late spring of 1945 to estimate how long it would take Russia to construct an atomic bomb. We should notice that the inquiry was before the American bomb was tested at Alamagordo and dropped upon Hiroshima and Nagasaki. The scientists and manufacturers present at that meeting concluded that it would take at least five years, presumably with "full blueprint information." On thinking it over, with the knowledge that the Russians now had the aid of German scientists, engineers, and manufacturers, Compton brought the estimate to the minimum of "Potsdam plus three years," or the summer of 1948. He personally felt that it might take longer. The Russians' first atomic explosion came in the fall of 1949.

But Compton's discussion of the problem in July 1947 was convincing to Secretary Forrestal. There should be closer scrutiny and estimating. He sent Compton's letter to Nimitz and to Hillenkoetter on August 11. Forrestal called upon the Navy to collaborate with the Agency in a restudy of the "Russian Atomic Bomb Time Schedule." Hillenkoetter replied on August 18. He had to say that, although the matter was urgent, the information in the Agency was scanty and of doubtful merit. There was none to change the estimate which had been sent to Admiral Inglis in May.[104]

The Central Intelligence Group had a plan by April 14 for cooperation with the Atomic Energy Commission. The Group proposed that the chief of its Nuclear Energy Group should be the adviser on nuclear intelligence to the Chairman of the Commission and to the Director of Central Intelligence. The Nuclear Energy Group should exclusively represent the Director in all contacts with the Commission. On its part the Atomic Energy Commission should arrange to give the chief of the Nuclear Energy Group access to personnel, activities, and records within the Commission that were necessary to his work for the Commission and the Central Intelligence Group. The assumption was that the Central Intelligence Group must be kept informed of nuclear research and development in the United States in order to handle effectively its task of producing foreign intelligence. The plan called upon the Commission to reveal its activities and records to the Group but did not provide that the Group should expose its sources of information to the Commission.[105]

Finding the plan of the Central Intelligence Group for collaboration unsatisfactory, Lewis L. Strauss of the Atomic Energy Commission asked Admiral Souers, then in retirement, to undertake a comprehensive investigation and report. A major obstacle between the Commission and the Group was that of "sources." The Commission wished to know the origins of all intelligence so that it could determine the authenticity and significance of the information. The Group, on the other hand, was obliged to protect its sources of information against discovery, or there would be none. [three lines deleted][106]

Admiral Souers made his report on July 1, 1947. He did not approach the problem directly through the controversy over sources of information. Instead, he explained for the benefit of the Commission the origin and responsibility of the National Intelligence Authority. He examined then the peculiar responsibilities of the Commission for its own "operational intelligence." This pertained to the exploration and procurement of the raw materials for atomic energy; it was necessary that the Commission should control the export of equipment and materials used in the search and should maintain the security of the information about them.[107]

Souers constructed with care the role of the Atomic Energy Commission in aiding the development of "strategic and national policy" intelligence. It should be the policy of the Commission to avoid duplication [two lines deleted]. Particularly in its scientific and technological guidance, the Commission should look to the Group for "coordinated estimates" of political and economic factors while the Commission concentrated upon the field of atomic energy as such. The Commission should have "direct contact" with other intelligence agencies, especially with the Federal Bureau of Investigation, which had exclusive responsibility for all investigations within its jurisdiction. Unless the Commission maintained those contacts, there would be "failure to recognize" items of interest to the

Commission; and that interest was reciprocal. There must be a "rapid interchange" of information for the benefit of all parties concerned in the development of national intelligence.

To this end Souers recommended that the Atomic Energy Commission should have permanent membership in the Intelligence Advisory Board. The National Intelligence Authority quickly adopted the recommendation. Admiral Hillenkoetter adhered to it throughout his administration of the Group and the Agency.[108]

Within the Atomic Energy Commission itself, Souers saw need for a Director of Intelligence who should be responsible to the General Manager. Under the administration of the Director there should be an organization to "permeate" the installations and plants of the Commission in order that scientific intelligence acquired through the Central Intelligence Group might be evaluated and applied immediately in the work of the Commission. For this reciprocal relationship with the Group the Commission's Director of Intelligence should be its member of the Intelligence Advisory Board. Admiral John E. Gingrich held this post until succeeded by Dr. Walter F. Colby.[109]

Souers's recommendations were put into operation by the Commission. But the issue between the Atomic Energy Commission and the Central Intelligence Agency over "sources" was not yet settled. An agreement was not reached until after the Scientific Branch of ORE had been reorganized [two lines deleted].

Vannevar Bush, head of the Research and Development Board, approached the problem of scientific intelligence with a point of view less interdepartmental than that of Souers, who was now Executive Secretary of the National Security Council. Senator Hickenlooper had urged in a letter to the departments on August 7, 1947, that there should be cooperation among the several agencies in the matter of intelligence on nuclear energy. This suggestion led to the appointment of representatives from the Departments of State, War, the Navy, and the Atomic Energy Commission and to a proposal from Admiral Hillenkoetter that there should be a Joint Nuclear Energy Intelligence Committee at the "working level" under the coordination of the Central Intelligence Agency. This working committee would manage the whole business of collecting, correlating, and evaluating, ascertaining requirements, preparing estimates, and disseminating scientific intelligence.

Nothing came of the proposal. For the Navy, Inglis objected on the ground that dissemination was a matter of policy which should not be controlled by a committee at the "working level." But Vannevar Bush returned from a meeting of the Joint Congressional Committee on Atomic

Energy, where the whole subject had been under discussion, to express his views on December 5 in writing to Secretary Forrestal.

Bush had indicated in the meeting that morning, and he judged that Forrestal agreed, that the Congressional Committee should turn to the Central Intelligence Agency itself for intelligence on nuclear energy and scientific matters in general. Bush feared that the Agency was not yet in position to meet this call because of the confusion within its councils. We have already observed the admonition which Forrestal gave at this moment to Admiral Inglis and General Chamberlin, and the use which Hillenkoetter made of Bush's letter to Forrestal in the next meeting of the Director with the Advisory Board on December 8.[110]

Bush's director of programs in RDB, Ralph L. Clark, reported that Wallace R. Brode, chief of the Scientific Branch in the Agency, was "completely stymied" by the controversy between the Board and the Director. Brode could not recruit and organize his staff, let alone provide useful intelligence to RDB and other agencies. Apparently the situation was worse than that, for Brode himself was not fully cleared in some field of science to the satisfaction of someone with influence. Circumstantial evidence points to the field of nuclear energy.[111]

By a general order on January 14, 1948, Admiral Hillenkoetter reorganized the Scientific Branch of ORE to place upon the Assistant Director, Theodore Babbitt, "full administrative and operational responsibility" for the Scientific Branch, with specific exceptions. For these Brode was directly responsible. It was obviously but another way of saying that he was no longer in charge of the Scientific Branch. He was to maintain and supervise "liaison" with other agencies. He was to advise the Director. But he was not to administer the nuclear intelligence program of the Agency now under the "closer coordination and supervision" of the Assistant Director for Reports and Estimates. This order lasted only until March 5 [three lines deleted]. Then Babbitt and Brode resumed their normal relationships as respectively head of the Office of Reports and Estimates and chief of its Scientific Branch.[112]

Repercussions of this affair were heard to the disadvantage of Admiral Hillenkoetter in the Intelligence Survey Group, which by this time had begun its investigation of the Agency for the National Security Council. But the more important consequence of the readjustment in the Agency with regard to intelligence on nuclear energy was Admiral Hillenkoetter's meeting with representatives of the Atomic Energy Commission and its Military Liaison Committee on April 2, 1948. It was a special conference to consider a proposal for improving the evaluation of foreign intelligence in the field of atomic energy.[113]

Lewis L. Strauss, who had asked Souers to make his study for the Atomic Energy Commission, opened the discussion by reviewing the unsatisfactory situation and then stating the desire of the Commission. It wanted a better channel of information between the Commission and the Agency. If agreeable to the Agency, the Commission would employ a scientist qualified to have access to all foreign intelligence available to the Agency, "including the sources." There was the issue fully in view. The Commission would delegate responsibility to this person and rely upon his evaluation of the intelligence, including the sources. He would thus obtain knowledge of them, appraise them for expertness, honesty, and significance, and then keep their names to himself. This procedure would satisfy the Atomic Energy Commission. [two lines deleted]

Admiral Hillenkoetter [two lines deleted]. He agreed at the meeting to the proposal in general, undertook to discuss it with the intelligence chiefs of the Army, Navy, and Air Force, and followed his tentative agreement with formal acceptance on April 12, 1948, on behalf of the Central Intelligence Agency.

[three lines deleted] He appreciated also the offer of the Commission to assist with evaluating the material, particularly the nomination of Dr. Walter F. Colby for the job of appraising the sources. Colby, then serving the Agency on a part-time basis, should devote full time to the work, as an employee either of the Commission or of the Agency. Hillenkoetter had no preference on this matter. Dr. Colby eventually became the Director of Intelligence in the Commission and its representative on the Intelligence Advisory Committee for his work with the Central Intelligence Agency.[114]

Thus, progress had been made by the summer of 1948 toward constructing a system of national intelligence for the field of nuclear energy and atomic fission. There was still much to be done in other areas of scientific intelligence. The investigating committees of 1948 were to find that the Agency was short of achieving what had been set on paper. They would find also that the departmental intelligence services contributed to the delay. There was reargument of old issues in scientific intelligence between the armed services and the Office of Scientific Intelligence in the Agency as this account was being written in 1953.[115]

THE JOINT CHIEFS AND CIVILIANS

The fact that the Joint Chiefs of Staff were to be represented in the Intelligence Advisory Committee did not justify optimism concerning their future relationships with the Agency. They had decided in the previous February to eliminate civilian membership from their Joint Intelligence Committee. This meant that representation of the State Department would cease; it gave notice that any plan to include a member of the Central Intelligence Agency would meet disfavor. In such circumstances there was a natural reluctance on the part of military men to become involved in the affairs of the Agency; participation might lead to commitments jeopardizing secrets that were theirs exclusively according to their views on the matter. But the Joint Chiefs had been courteously willing to hear the suggestions of the Director of Central Intelligence. They sent their plan for reorganizing the Joint Intelligence Committee and its Joint Intelligence Staff to Admiral Hillenkoetter on June 23, 1947.[116]

The plan dropped the representatives of the State Department from both Committee and Staff. It stipulated that the Committee should "give maximum support to integration of governmental intelligence activities through the medium of the Central Intelligence Group." How this was to be done, however, was not stated. The Committee, and its Staff, were furthermore to "utilize the structure of the Central Intelligence Group in procuring information, intelligence, and assistance from governmental agencies and activities other than the military agencies." This presumably was to be done, with the consent of the Director of Central Intelligence, through the military and naval officers who were already on his staff in the Group or the customary liaison officers appointed for such purposes.[117]

It was not much of an opportunity to reverse the thinking and penetrate the organization of the Joint Chiefs of Staff, but Hillenkoetter took advantage of it to offer a counterproposal prepared for him by ICAPS. As referred to the chiefs of the departmental agencies in the Intelligence Advisory Board on July 11, 1947, Hillenkoetter's plan for the Joint Intelligence Committee of the Joint Chiefs of Staff replaced the representative of the State Department with the Director of Central Intelligence. He should not be a member of the Committee, however, but merely an "adviser and observer" who should receive the papers of the Committee to ensure the "closest collaboration" between the Joint Intelligence Committee and the Central Intelligence Group.[118]

For liaison, and even that "maximum support to integration" of intelligence activities which the Joint Chiefs desired, Hillenkoetter's plan was better than their proposed revision. The Director himself would take part in their Committee. But his further suggestion that the Deputy Director should act in place of the Director of Central Intelligence if he were a civilian does not merit consideration. It is inconceivable that anyone, whether military or civilian, could remain deputy to the Director if he concealed anything from his superior. If he were kept in office, there would be two Directors of Central Intelligence, one entrusted with military secrets and the other not, an impossibility under both the President's Directive of January 22, 1946, and its successor, the National Security Act of July 26, 1947.[119]

The plan submitted by Hillenkoetter for the Central Intelligence Group would supplant the Joint Intelligence Staff with a Secretary to the Joint Intelligence Committee. The Secretary would have assistants. The work of the Staff, such as the preparation of intelligence studies for the Joint Chiefs of Staff according to their requirements, would then be transferred in large part to the Central Intelligence Group. Departmental intelligence would still be submitted directly from the War and Navy Departments to the Joint Intelligence Committee. Its Secretary and his assistants would have charge of those matters which were inappropriate for the Group to handle. Hillenkoetter argued that the Joint Chiefs of Staff would thus receive intelligence "national in scope" without any barrier between themselves and their departmental agencies to impede the "flow of strictly military intelligence."[120]

The chiefs of intelligence did not linger over this proposal for the Central Intelligence Group. From their replies it is apparent that all of them sought and received instructions from their superiors. Mr. Eddy, for the State Department, was the first to answer. He concurred on July 15 in the principles of the proposal and suggested further interlocking of the Group with the Joint Intelligence Committee in practice. Eddy would have this done by increasing the duties of the representatives of the departmental chiefs of intelligence in the Office of Reports and Estimates. These representatives were supposed to assist in preparing interdepartmental estimates. They could also form an advisory staff to the Intelligence Advisory Board. We should remember that the chiefs of intelligence constituted both the Joint Intelligence Committee of the Joint Chiefs of Staff and the Intelligence Advisory Board under the National Intelligence Authority.[121]

Such close articulation was far from the thoughts of the other members of the Intelligence Advisory Board. They represented the armed services. Mr. Eddy was to withdraw from the Joint Intelligence Committee. They, or succeeding representatives of the Army, the Navy, and the Air Force, would stay on the Committee.

Admiral Inglis replied to Hillenkoetter on July 17. He was frank to say that he had once proposed that the Director of Central Intelligence should advise the Joint Chiefs of Staff and sit as chairman of their Joint Intelligence Committee. He had thought then that strictly military intelligence might be insulated within the Central Intelligence Group. But his ideas had not been in accordance with the views of higher authority in the Navy. We have seen that Admiral Nimitz as Chief of Naval Operations favored on December 9, 1946, exclusion of the civilian services from representation in the Joint Intelligence Committee.[122]

With the decision of the Joint Chiefs to adopt the proposal of Nimitz, there was nothing for the Chief of Naval Intelligence to do but state his personal position for the record and present the case for his orders. Inglis declared that, in a military organization, intelligence was a function of command; military authority therefore had to maintain direct control over operational intelligence. For reasons of security, nonmilitary persons had never been given access to military plans, he said; the authority over such persons was insufficient for the purpose. As for estimates, those of the Joint Intelligence Committee would be "national in scope," he declared, since they would include pertinent contributions from the Central Intelligence Group. In short, if this meant what it seems to mean, all materials from the Department of State entering into the construction of national intelligence would have to come to the estimators in the Joint Intelligence Committee by way of the contributions from the Central Intelligence Group.[123]

The declaration of Admiral Inglis explains why he persisted throughout the summer and fall of 1947 in maintaining that operational intelligence should remain in the control of the armed services. His statements made clear once more the misgiving which so many military men have when they think of civilian collaboration in their affairs. But his arguments confirmed, rather than destroyed, the fact that those who make national estimates should have access to knowledge of the capabilities and intentions of their own country. The question remained whether the Joint Intelligence Committee of the Joint Chiefs of Staff or the Central Intelligence Agency or the Director of Central Intelligence or some other authority could perform the function.[124]

General Chamberlin's executive officer wrote for him on July 21 that he could not concur with the Group's plan to reorganize the Joint Intelligence Committee. The Joint Chiefs must have control of their intelligence agencies. There was no objection to the Director of Central Intelligence sitting as an observer in the meetings of the Joint Intelligence Committee, provided that he were a member of the armed forces; but as most of the meetings were concerned with military problems, he said, there was no need for instituting such a procedure. One might conclude, from this statement for Chamberlin, that the central intelligence organization had very little to do with military matters, until one recalled the work of the Coordinator of Information, the Office of Strategic Services, and the Strategic Services Unit, predecessors of the Central Intelligence Group. No one in the Agency today, with any knowledge of its covert operations, would have the notion.

General McDonald's rejection followed on July 25. The plan of the Group ignored, he said, the fundamental principle that a "staff intelligence responsibility" existed within every planning organization. And so the Joint Chiefs of Staff required within their organization an agency capable of producing intelligence rather than one which merely transmitted intelligence which had been produced. Ignoring General McDonald's inadequate description of the Central Intelligence Group, which at that time was an agency collecting, producing, and disseminating intelligence, let us point out that he too was ignoring a fact. Whatever its shortcomings, the plan which Hillenkoetter sponsored for the reorganization of the Joint Intelligence Committee comprehended use of the Group by the Joint Chiefs of Staff for producing certain kinds of "staff intelligence." Others were to be kept from the Group. But then, to General McDonald, intelligence was "not an exact science." Let us leave his nonconcurrence on that note.[125]

Admiral Hillenkoetter resubmitted his plan for the Joint Intelligence Committee on August 7, 1947—this time directly to the Joint Chiefs of Staff. It was his right to go over the heads of the departmental intelligence agencies. The National Security Act had become law. Both the Joint Chiefs of Staff and the Central Intelligence Agency were now upon statutory foundations. Their positions were comparable. Although Hillenkoetter was only a Rear Admiral, as Director of Central Intelligence he was by law on practically the same level of responsibility as the Joint Chiefs of Staff. The Director as head of the Agency was adviser to the President and the National Security Council on matters of intelligence specified in the Act of Congress. The Joint Chiefs were the principal military advisers to the President and the Secretary of Defense. The interests of the Agency and the Joint Chiefs of Staff were involved. It was time to determine relations and procedures.[126]

The plan of the Joint Chiefs for reorganizing the Joint Intelligence Committee, wrote Hillenkoetter, did not ensure the cooperation and coordination that were to be desired between the intelligence agencies which supported the Security Council and the President, on the one hand, and the Joint Chiefs, on the other. He suggested that a special military group within the Agency might help the Agency and the Joint Chiefs of Staff to work together on matters concerning operational intelligence which gave the Joint Chiefs anxiety when they thought of dealing with civilians.[127]

There the matter stood in the fall of 1947 as the Group became the

Agency, Hillenkoetter sought his own advisory committee, and his drafting officers prepared the NSCIDs. And then he received notice from the State Department on November 5 that it had withdrawn its representation from the Joint Intelligence Committee and Staff as of October 31; henceforth the proper channel for joint action between itself and the Joint Chiefs with regard to intelligence should be through the Director of Central Intelligence and the Agency. The State Department requested the Director to establish such "liaison and coordinating relations." There were several ways this might be done. The Department preferred use of the Standing Committee which Hillenkoetter had suggested as a means for keeping the Intelligence Advisory Committee in touch with ICAPS.[128]

Hillenkoetter had a reply ready on November 19, the day before his meeting with the Intelligence Advisory Board to discuss the first NSCIDs. In this letter to Armstrong he said that arrangements were being made for him to be on the Joint Intelligence Committee; correspondingly the Deputy Director for the Joint Intelligence Group within the Joint Staff was to become a permanent member of the Intelligence Advisory Committee which Hillenkoetter proposed to establish. The next day General Todd attended the meeting of the Intelligence Advisory Board in that capacity, and again on December 8. In fact, he or his representative continued to do so for months to come. But Todd was not comfortable in his situation. He was hesitant to designate a representative on the ad hoc committee to correct the NSCIDs of the Agency. He did not feel that his superior, General Gruenther, Director of the Joint Staff under the Joint Chiefs of Staff, would care to do so.[129]

Later, in February 1948, when asked to appoint a representative on the Standing Committee, General Todd declined. He would sit in the Intelligence Advisory Committee, but he had no desire to be involved in the affairs of the Agency "on the working level." His decision was sound. He could attend the meetings as an observer and reporter to General Gruenther, Director of the Joint Staff, responsible to the Joint Chiefs of Staff. But the Joint Intelligence Group over which Todd presided was composed of equal numbers of officers from the Army, Navy, and Air Force. He therefore could take no position at variance with that of any one of the services. And, if they were in agreement, there was little use in his expressing the same opinion. The Joint Intelligence Group in reality had no mind of its own. Any dissenting faction could go straight from the Group to its chief of intelligence in the Intelligence Advisory Committee of the Agency or in the Joint Intelligence Committee of the Joint Chiefs of Staff.[130]

Although Admiral Hillenkoetter attended meetings of the Joint Intelligence Committee, as a matter of courtesy, [one line deleted] he never took part as had General Donovan and his deputies. If Hillenkoetter had done so, he would have walked right into the place of the Office of Strategic Services in the Joint Intelligence Committee, near the foot of the table. It was hardly the place for the man supposed to be the Coordinator of Information or the Director of the Office of Strategic Services or the Director of Central Intelligence.[131]

There are those who think that this aspect of the situation should have troubled Hillenkoetter and that he should have insisted upon a stronger position of leadership. To him, however, the place in the Joint Intelligence Committee offered an opportunity to look after the interests of the State Department and of the Atomic Energy Commission in matters of intelligence. He was not so concerned with deference to his rank as Director of Central Intelligence. And he did not wish to antagonize the chiefs of intelligence any more than he was doing at that time. If they sat in his advisory committee under the Act of Congress, he would sit as an observer and servant, in a sense, when they constituted the Joint Intelligence Committee by order of the Joint Chiefs of Staff. But his letter to Armstrong in the Department of State was held up for successive weeks until December 22 and never sent.[132]

The Joint Chiefs of Staff on December 4 issued a plan for liaison between its Joint Intelligence Group and the Central Intelligence Agency. The Agency would provide the Group with intelligence from "nonmilitary government agencies." In turn, the Agency would be informed with regard to "intelligence estimates." These familiar words convey the idea that the Agency was not to receive information upon the capabilities and intentions of the armed forces of this country.[133]

Hillenkoetter might have rejected the plan and broken diplomatic relations, as it were, with the Joint Chiefs of Staff at that juncture. If he had done so, he certainly would have met with Forrestal, Secretary of Defense, and the chiefs of intelligence between December 3 and December 8 in a less favorable atmosphere. He had the advantage in that crisis, and he kept the advantage through the meeting of December 8 with the intelligence chiefs. It continued even through the meeting of the National Security Council on December 12 which adopted the first NSCIDs.

Hillenkoetter chose to take what he could get for the Agency at the time. He accepted the plan of the Joint Chiefs on December 22 and sent word to the State Department on December 26 that he had appointed a military representative of the Agency and an assistant to act as liaison officers with the Intelligence Section of the Joint Intelligence Group of the Joint Chiefs of Staff. These officers would attend the meetings of the Joint Intelligence

Committee when it was dealing with intelligence estimates. In this manner they would "ensure the flow of intelligence material" between the Joint Staff and the nonmilitary agencies of the Government.[134]

The arrangement, however, was not satisfactory for the production of "national intelligence" in the Central Intelligence Agency. General Gruenther made this unmistakable to all who read his memorandum of December 12 to the Director of Central Intelligence regarding NSCID 1 and, in particular, its paragraphs pertaining to the interchange of intelligence and access to files among the departmental agencies and the Central Intelligence Agency. Gruenther, at Hillenkoetter's request, confirmed Todd's statements in the meeting of December 8 that the Joint Chiefs of Staff had a special position to maintain. They could not distribute their papers freely. Their security required that documents prepared within their organization should not be available to the departments and agencies outside, said Gruenther, unless there were specific authorization by the Joint Chiefs with the approval of the President.

The departments and agencies, however, would not be deprived of any materials of intelligence because they were denied the papers of the Joint Intelligence Group, Gruenther went on to argue. The Group was not a collecting agency. Those materials of intelligence, he said, would be obtained through the collecting agencies of the departments. He did not elaborate upon the saving clauses in NSCID 1 which left discretion and exception with the departmental agencies according to their responsibilities, capabilities, and security regulations.[135]

Admiral Hillenkoetter accepted General Gruenther's comments of December 12. There was little else that Hillenkoetter could do as the National Security Council adopted the first NSCIDs on the same day. Admiral Souers, Executive Secretary to the Council, noted upon his copy of the memorandum from Gruenther that Hillenkoetter was "apparently agreeable to this concept." So had Souers been as Director of Central Intelligence. So would General Smith later be.[136]

Although the Director of Central Intelligence had authority to produce national intelligence estimates, he did not control all of the resources essential to producing them. He still had to rely upon the departmental intelligence agencies for vital information, particularly with regard to the capabilities and intentions of the armed services of his own country. [three lines deleted] They had yet to place as much confidence in the Office of National Estimates with respect to knowledge of their own capabilities of resisting Soviet aggression. The Agency was in the position of knowing more about the strength of the potential enemy of this country than about its power to meet that enemy at a particular place and a given moment.[137]

BOGOTÁ

One who has viewed an election south of the Rio Grande, from the vantage point of lying on his belly beneath gunfire across a plaza, may conclude that the affair of April 9, 1948, was just another burst of Latin American temperament. This was not true of Congressmen, columnists, and patriots of the press who thought simultaneously of "another Pearl Harbor" and of the Panama Canal so close to Colombia. They were quick to ascribe it all to agents from the Kremlin.

Politicians who aspired to be President found Harry S Truman responsible, not for the assassination of Jorge Gaitan, to be sure, but for failure to know about it in advance. Governor Dewey, in a special broadcast to voters in Nebraska, declared that during the war the United States had the finest intelligence service ever developed, operating all over South America under J. Edgar Hoover. "After the war," said Dewey, "Mr. Truman ordered that entire service discontinued. He cut off our ears and put out our eyes in our information services around the world." The Governor evidently was not troubled at the time with knowledge of the facts concerning the institution and development of the Group and the Agency since the war, nor with the real reasons why the agents of the FBI were replaced by representatives of the CIA in Latin America.[138]

The President added his bit to the confusion by stating in a news conference that he was as surprised as everybody else. He had information that there might be picketing and demonstrations against the Pan-American conference. But he had no indication, he said, that anybody was going to get shot in Bogotá.[139]

There had to be a scapegoat and so, without waiting to separate facts from fears, some to attract attention and others perhaps to avoid it nominated the Director of Central Intelligence and the Agency for that honor in American life. Admiral Zacharias, once Deputy Director of Naval Intelligence, was positive that he knew what was wrong and offered his services to Congress. They were declined. On the air, however, Zacharias criticized the Agency for lacking qualified personnel and failing to make use of overt intelligence. The American delegation went to the conference, he said, without an "overall plan for raising the standard of living in Latin America."[140]

Stephen J. Spingarn, for the Counterintelligence Corps of the Army, wrote a paper explaining why the Agency had not done its job properly. It "*may* have competently discharged" its functions of collecting information in Colombia. There was question whether its evaluation of that information was good. Spingarn was certain that it "did *not* have the ability to get its information in properly evaluated form rapidly to the top policymaking officers concerned." The ineffable conclusion for the reader was that Hillenkoetter tried hard to do well but he lacked that something which intelligence officers properly trained, in the Army, were more likely to possess.[141]

Representative Brown, who had taken so important a part in the hearings during the previous spring and had made a definite contribution to the establishment of the Agency, declared to the press that Congress intended to have an effective intelligence system and he would find out why it did not have one. There would be an investigation of the Agency immediately. "Surely our State Department officials," he said, "would have insisted on the South American conference being held elsewhere if they had been informed a bloody revolution was impending in Bogotá and Colombia, and that they and other Americans would be forced to barricade themselves to perserve their lives. . . ." When he did find out what had happened, Mr. Brown's manner of speech and the tenor of his remarks were different. His apology to Admiral Hillenkoetter was gracious.[142]

The facts were these. The Ninth International Conference of American Republics met in Bogotá, Colombia, on March 30, 1948. From the beginning of the year, warnings had been coming into the Central Intelligence Agency that a campaign of anti-imperialism would be aimed at the United States, that there might be an attempt by Liberals to overturn the Conservative Government in Colombia, and that Communists were interested in the plans for demonstrating against the United States during the conference. Finally on March 23, a week before the conference was to begin, there came a dispatch saying that "Communist-inspired agitators" would attempt to "humiliate" the Secretary of State upon his arrival "by manifestations and possible personal molestation." Admiral Hillenkoetter did not send this message on to the Department of State. Why he did not, and what he thought of that "mistake," we shall discuss in a moment.[143]

There was no attempt to molest Secretary Marshall at Bogotá. The first ten days of the conference were peaceful. The delegation of the United States was not doing well with its plan for hemispheric solidarity nor stirring much enthusiasm over its economic views. The offer of a loan from the Export–Import Bank of $500,000 was greeted by the delegates with silence. And then on April 9 Jorge Gaitan, leader of the left wing of the Liberal Party who had withdrawn all Liberals from the Government in March, was assassinated.[144]

It is established now that one José Sierra killed Gaitan because he had successfully defended in court that morning the murderer of Sierra's uncle. But the assassination of a political leader started rioting that virtually became war between the army, which stood by the Conservative

Government, and the police of Bogotá, who were loyal to the Liberals. Mobs wrecked churches, public buildings, and the Capitolio where the International Conference was in session. The damage to the city was estimated at $150,000,000. The Confederation of Workers of Colombia, in which Communists had influence, called a general strike. But a new government, consisting of six Conservatives, six Liberals, and one nonpartisan, gained control on the next day and adopted an anti-Communist policy.

The conference resumed its meetings on April 14. Secretary Marshall told the delegates that international communism was responsible for the rioting. Harriman, then Secretary of Commerce and present at the conference, stated that Communists had exploited if they had not started the uprising; it looked to him like a swift Communist operation carried out on the European subversive plan with which he was familiar. This became the view accepted generally. The rioting, however, had not been directed against the United States. Although casualties, conservatively estimated, numbered more than a thousand dead and wounded, no member of the American delegation nor any other national of the United States was injured.[145]

When the warning that Secretary Marshall might personally be molested came into the Agency at Washington, Admiral Hillenkoetter's first thought was to take it at once to Under Secretary Lovett in the State Department. To do so, however, would violate the directive NSCID 2 stipulating that the "senior U.S. representative" in an area should "coordinate"—that is to say, release—the intelligence collected there. The advance agent of the State Department, Orion J. Libert, in Bogotá to prepare for the International Conference, decided that this dispatch should not be delivered to the State Department in Washington. Ambassador Willard L. Beaulac agreed with Libert. They did not want to alarm the delegates unduly. Adequate protection, they were sure, would be given by the police. It is to be said also that Marshall had known of the earlier warnings from Bogotá, before leaving Washington, and had expressed himself in "salty language" against letting any threats interfere.[146]

Still, this was direct information [one line deleted] that the life of the Secretary of State might be in danger. It is easy to imagine what the reaction would have been in this country if George Marshall instead of Jorge Gaitan had been assassinated in Bogotá. As Hillenkoetter recalled the affair in 1952, he should have taken the dispatch to Lovett. Hillenkoetter made a "mistake," and it was, he said, entirely his own.[147]

The Director of Central Intelligence as head of the Agency by Act of Congress was ultimately responsible for coordinating intelligence and distributing it to the departments and agencies under the direction of the

National Security Council. This direction had been given for all normal purposes in NSCID 2. It was questionable that Congress ever intended to have the Director bound in critical situations by such a directive. But Hillenkoetter gave that point no particular thought. He was the responsible head of the Agency. He should violate the directive, if necessary, and take the consequences personally. There were other considerations which entered into his thinking and influenced him against his own judgment to make what he considered the wrong decision.[148]

Hillenkoetter and his advisers talked at length over matters not generally known then or since regarding the experiences of the Central Intelligence Agency in Central and South America. The Agency had just been established there in place of the FBI. With the exception of Ambassador James Bruce in Argentina, said Hillenkoetter, the diplomatic representatives of the United States were not giving much support to the Agency, and "in many places" the attitude amounted almost to "hostility." To improve the relations [two lines deleted] Hillenkoetter decided to defer to the request of Beaulac and Libert and not take the warning to Lovett. "By following the Ambassador's request, we could build up some credit for ourselves." If it were to be done again, he would violate the directive and ignore the resentment of the diplomatic officers in the field.[149]

The irony of the affair was that, except for Lovett's private comment to Allen W. Dulles, Hillenkoetter was not elsewhere criticized for the failure which he charged against himself. The omission may be ascribed in part to the fact that knowledge of NSCID 2 was well confined to the Agency, the Council, and the departmental intelligence services. It was no time for chiefs of intelligence to blame the Director of Central Intelligence for failing to exercise supervision over collection in the field when they had been largely responsible for denying him that power in the directives of the National Intelligence Authority and the National Security Council. The Council too could share the blame, for it had accepted the draft of the directive without provision for such authority.[150]

Walter Lippmann, for once, was off the target when he chided Hillenkoetter for talking as if the public had a right to expect the Central Intelligence Agency to "appraise" the situation in Colombia. Hillenkoetter was talking about the coordination, correlation, and evaluation of intelligence, the production of estimates; he was not talking, as Lippmann seems to have concluded, about the construction of policy from those estimates. If to "appraise" means to "determine the worth" of intelligence, it was the duty of the Agency under the Act of Congress to appraise the information from Bogotá and to deliver it without delay to the department most in need of it, in this case the Department of State.[151]

Representative Brown summoned the Director of Central Intelligence on April 15 before a special subcommittee of the House. Brown's purpose was "to explore this matter vigorously" to determine why intelligence reports did not reach their proper destination "in time for protective action." As he listened to Hillenkoetter's testimony, Brown learned of NSCID 2 and Libert's action in Bogotá under that authorization from the National Security Council. Brown did not remark that coordination by the "senior U.S. representative" in the field had proved itself once again no coordination at all, as it had in the abortive Dominican affair during the fall of 1947. But then he may not have heard of that fiasco in cooperative interdepartmental enterprise.[152]

Instead, Brown concentrated his attention upon the facts concerning the action of the State Department in relation to the Central Intelligence Agency. And he reached conclusions as a member of Congress who took satisfaction now in what the framers of the National Security Act had intended to do. It was not the intent of Congress, he said in the committee meeting, to give any agency of the Government "the right of censorship" or control over the activities of the Central Intelligence Agency.[153]

Brown warmed to his theme in his statement for release to the press. "Our Central Intelligence Agency," he declared, "must be protected against censorship or intimidation by any arm of the Executive Branch." Ten days later he was warmer still. He was thinking of legislation to free the Agency from such control. "Otherwise," he declared, "one might as well turn the intelligence agency over to the State Department and let those dumb clucks run it."[154]

Brown may not have known at the time, but that was just what certain officers in the State Department were planning to do with regard to propaganda, economic manipulation, and other covert operations overseas against Communism. As Hillenkoetter received public exoneration in the affair at Bogotá, and private apology from Brown for having contributed to the attack in the press upon his administration of the Agency, Hillenkoetter faced inquiry at the request of Forrestal, Secretary of Defense, and a concerted plan by the Department of State and the National Military Establishment to guide and control the Central Intelligence Agency.

Introduction to Chapter VII

As the international situation grew tense in 1947 with Communist aggression and subversion increasing, pressure mounted in the National Security Council to counter Communist actions. A consensus developed among top U.S. leaders to implement covert action—operations taken to influence foreign leaders, organizations, and situations while concealing the role of the U.S. government—against Communist forces in Europe and elsewhere. At the time one of the main forms of covert action envisioned was psychological warfare, including such "black propaganda" operations as radio broadcasts supported by the United States but operated by a front organization.

The early controversy over covert action focussed not so much on whether such operations should be carried out but on which agency should carry them out and which official should supervise them. Covert operations were not part of the original mandate for the CIA. Such operations had little to do with the collection, analysis, and dissemination of information, and Hillenkoetter initially resisted them. Hillenkoetter and his legal counsel, Lawrence Houston, interpreted the National Security Act of 1947 literally and saw no explicit authority allowing the DCI or the CIA to carry out covert operations. Hillenkoetter also thought that operations such as propaganda, which depend on publicity, would compromise the Agency's clandestine intelligence activities.

White House and State Department officials, however, had another view. They thought that the CIA was the organization best equipped to carry out covert actions and that the National Security Act gave the Agency the authority to do so; they referred to the clause authorizing the DCI to "perform such other functions and duties related to intelligence affecting the national security as the National Security Council may from time to time direct." Thus, the NSC decided to initiate covert operations abroad under NSC 4-A, issued on December 17, 1947. This directive assigned covert psychological operations to the CIA, much to the displeasure of the DCI. The directive also displeased the Department of Defense officials, since covert action included sabotage and paramilitary operations, which traditionally had been military functions. Logistically, covert psychological operations were placed in the CIA's Office of Special Operations, becoming the Special Procedures Group.

While State Department officials did not want responsibility for carrying out covert action, they did want to control the planning and conduct of covert action. George Kennan, Director of the State Department's Policy Planning Staff, argued that covert action was another instrument of foreign policy and that it should therefore be controlled by the State Department. Kennan wanted a separate group of six or seven people under NSC to manage what he called "political warfare." (This disagreement burgeoned into full-scale opposition between State and the Agency, culminating in the Dulles Report of January 1949.) Meanwhile, international events such as the fall of Czechoslovakia, the Berlin blockade in April 1948, and the Bogotá affair were demanding action, and so NSC 4-A went into effect, even as Kennan and his aides argued for its replacement.

Hillenkoetter found himself in a difficult position, being asked to carry out—and accept responsibility for—potentially embarrassing actions, while also being pressed to surrender the ability to plan and supervise them. For the DCI, it was potentially the worst of both worlds.

The system was overhauled on June 18, 1948, when NSC 10-2 was adopted, reorganizing the covert operations system according to State's plan. NSC 10-2 established an Office of Special Projects, which later became the Office of Policy Coordination (OPC), to carry out covert operations. For the sake of security, OPC was to operate independently of other components of the Agency and coordinate its activities with the clandestine intelligence activities of the Office of Special Operations. The Chief of OPC would be nominated by the State Department even though he reported to the DCI. Hillenkoetter obviously did not like this arrangement, and he could not bring OPC under effective control by the DCI.

VII

HILLENKOETTER'S ADMINISTRATION: COVERT OPERATIONS

THE OPPORTUNITY

 Admiral Hillenkoetter had thrust upon him at Christmas 1947 a responsibility and a duty to perform which he did not want in the Central Intelligence Agency. He took part in the preparations. He did not object to the assignment of the task to him. He was reluctant nonetheless to involve the affairs of the Agency with the enterprise. The paper of the National Security Council on the subject, NSC 4-A, returned to its files. The directive to the Director of Central Intelligence, one of but three copies, remained closely guarded in the Director's office, where members of his own staff who did not "need to know" could gain no access to it.

The directive was issued in such a way that it could be rescinded and recalled to the files of the Council without attracting attention. [three lines deleted] Few indeed below the Secretaries and others in the Council, except the members of the staff and of the Agency who shared in drafting and those who were to carry out the directive for Hillenkoetter, had any knowledge of its existence. Other agencies were not concerned, though they were to be kept informed of activities directly affecting them. The third copy of this directive to the Director of Central Intelligence went to George F. Kennan, Director of the Policy Planning Staff in the State Department. It was peculiarly interested in the enterprise. He was to take a dominating role in all phases of the "cold war" with Communism.[1]

The reason for so great secrecy was altogether clear. Not only was the Union of Soviet Socialist Republics condemned in the directive for its "vicious" psychological operations against the United States. The Director of Central Intelligence was charged with planning and conducting under cover a similar attack upon the Soviet Union and its satellites. The attack would have been popular with many, if known. But there were citizens of this country at that time who would have been aghast if they had learned of NSC 4-A, as the public heard in February 1945 about the plan for a permanent intelligence system and cries rang out of Gestapo. Though seemingly fewer in number, there still are those who deplore the use of "black" propaganda and the related arts of political interference, economic intrusion, and physical subversion behind the Iron Curtain and in states within the striking range of Soviet power. To some, and they are pragmatists, the "national security" would be better served if the United States never marred professions of truth with actions that belie it.[2]

The international situation grew worse in the summer and fall of 1947. Petkov, agrarian leader in Bulgaria, was sentenced to death. A so-called free government appeared in northern Greece, and a Soviet veto in the Security Council blocked action by the United Nations to deal with Greek affairs. Russian troops were reported along the Iranian border as negotiations for oil wore on. Violence and bloodshed swept India and Pakistan with the end of British rule. Efforts to withdraw both Russian and American troops from Korea were failing. Italy and France trembled with strikes fomented by Communists. It looked as though they might legally gain control of Italy after the British and American troops withdrew in December. Britain entered an economic crisis. The situation in Europe grew tense as the Marshall Plan got under way and the Cominform appeared in an endeavor to wreck it.

In this atmosphere President Truman attended the conference on hemispheric defense at Rio de Janeiro, Forrestal took office as Secretary of Defense ahead of schedule, and Secretary Marshall proposed that the United Nations have a "little Assembly" to avoid the Soviet veto in the Council and to keep constant watch upon conditions threatening the peace of the world. Vishinsky charged the United States with seeking to dominate the world and, on September 18 before the Assembly of the United Nations in New York, accused John Foster Dulles and other prominent Americans by name of being "war mongers."[3]

General Donovan's reaction to this "political and psychological war" upon the United States was to urge that something be done about it. He had associated "unorthodox warfare" with clandestine intelligence since observing the German success with "fifth column" activities in 1940. He appears not to have been so convinced as others that the Germans had failed with secret intelligence because they had joined it with subversive operations. He wrote to Admiral Hillenkoetter on September 18, "This is a great opportunity for your organization."[4]

Donovan's ideas were that the Director of Central Intelligence should have complete control of psychological warfare, both black and white propaganda. The officer in charge of operations might be appointed as a special assistant to the Secretary of Defense, but he would actually be responsible to the Director of Central Intelligence. This fact would be known to the fewest possible persons. Donovan had many times before insisted that the Director of Central Intelligence should be independent of the departments and answerable only to the President or his "General Manager," now under the National Security Act of 1947 the Secretary of Defense.[5]

Admiral Hillenkoetter did not consider it a great opportunity. The Agency had enough to do in getting itself established under the National Security Act and the directives of the new Council. There were the old issues of collection and production; coordination left to senior representatives in the field was no coordination at all as the Dominican revolutionary affair was proving at the moment. The departmental chiefs of intelligence were trying to make their advisory committee the governing board of the Agency regardless of the Director's wishes or his rights under the Act of Congress. Hillenkoetter had also to maintain representation of some kind with the Joint Chiefs of Staff for the Agency, the Department of State, and the Atomic Energy Commission; the military advisers of the President and the Security Council were removing the last civilian from their Joint Intelligence Committee. Besides, there was the inheritance from Vandenberg's regime of confusion and wrangling between members of the geographical branches and the staff of estimators within the Office of Reports and Estimates.[6]

THE AUTHORITY OF THE COUNCIL

In addition to these practical matters, Admiral Hillenkoetter received the advice of legal counsel on September 25 to support his own reluctance. It was questionable that he could accept General Donovan's suggestion that he join secret intelligence with psychological warfare. As Houston read the National Security Act, the provisions with regard to "services of common concern" and to "other functions and duties related to intelligence affecting the national security" were not to be interpreted loosely. They were to be construed with the intentions of Congress at the time of their enactment.

According to his memory of the debates and the hearings in Congress, its members had been interested primarily in creating an agency which should coordinate intelligence. There had been no "thought in the minds of Congress" of giving the Director and the Central Intelligence Agency authority to engage in "subversion and sabotage." There had been no intention, said Houston, to grant the Agency broad powers of operation. The effort to obtain specific authority for secret collection overseas had been defeated. There had been representation against it from the Army. Instead, Congress adopted "as a compromise" the provision that the Agency should perform "services of common concern" which should be determined by the National Security Council.

One may point out that other functions of the Agency were to be similarly controlled by the Council. The restriction was no more than had been placed upon the Director and the Group by the President's Directive of January 22, 1946. The Director of Central Intelligence had been subject then to the orders of the National Intelligence Authority. But the limitation was no less. Houston found it adequate to maintain that Congress did not intend to grant expansive operational authority to the Director and the Agency. There was evidence also, he said, in the "off-the-record hearings" on appropriations, that the functions of the Agency were not to be interpreted out of context or apart from the history of their enactment. Houston advised Hillenkoetter that if the Agency were to engage in covert psychological operations, even though directed by the Council to do so, Congress should have to be informed beforehand and its approval obtained for both the functions and the expenditure of funds.[7]

This was not the view of the President's advisers in the National Security Council on November 14, 1947, when they decided to open a counterattack upon Soviet propaganda; nor were they wholly convinced that Donovan had the right idea. For their campaign with the truth it was proper to wait upon Congress and seek publicity, though they also invited some delay. But for covert operations the urgency was too great. The British and American forces would be out of Italy before Christmas. The Communists might take over. [several words deleted][8]

The Council was not reluctant [two lines deleted]. "National security" was not confined geographically to the homeland on the North American continent and American possessions overseas; it reached into the economy and the political organization of states anywhere which might become hostile to the United States. In short, there was no time to lose in seeing to it [several words deleted] as the Marshall Plan passed through Congress and ECA competed with the Cominform for control of Europe.[9]

The National Security Council's eventual decision to place covert operations under the Director of Central Intelligence rested upon an interpretation of the National Security Act, and of the Council's relation thereunder to Congress, which was quite different from the opinion of Hillenkoetter's legal counsel. The divergence is best observed in reference again to the provision in the Act. It stipulated that one of the duties of the Agency should be "to perform such other functions and duties related to intelligence affecting the national security as the National Security Council may from time to time direct."[10]

Members of the Council and its Staff interpreted this provision as establishing a quasi-legislative function for the Council in accordance with the general prescription, or standard, of "intelligence affecting the national security." That is to say, Congress gave the Council of Secretaries and others appointed by the President, and under his chairmanship, definite power to expand the jurisdiction of the Central Intelligence Agency in conformity with that prescription, within of course only the administrative branch of the Government. But within that area the Council might add to the functions and duties of the Central Intelligence Agency certain functions and duties which were exercised in other agencies, even in the departments. The Council might create new functions for the Agency. The conception carried with it logically the right of the Council to set up institutions which should aid, guide, and direct the Agency on behalf of the Council in performing those additional duties and functions. Thus, the "panel of guidance" found justification and its successor, the Psychological Strategy Board, has legislative origin.[11]

This interpretation of the National Security Act separated the provision regarding "other functions and duties" from the preceding four which pertained to "intelligence activities" of the departments and the Central Intelligence Agency. The fifth, though caught in the general prescription of relation to "intelligence affecting the national security," might be interpreted to authorize operations which were to be distinguished by their nature from the incidental intelligence which they produced. For those who sought it, the distinction gave to the Council greater control over the Director of Central Intelligence and the Agency with respect to these operations.[12]

Put in military terms, the assignment to the Director of an additional duty in "operations" brought him more under the direction of the operating departments, those of State and Defense as distinguished from the National Security Resources Board and others with representatives in the National Security Council. The operating departments, as a matter of course, were to give the Director guidance with regard to policy or, in military language, strategy. He should therefore expect to be guided also in tactics so far as necessary to prevent conflict with others in purpose and performance.[13]

In any vocabulary, military or civilian, the meaning of "to guide" is "to direct." The degree and the timing of the direction are the decisive factors. This Admiral Hillenkoetter knew well before he undertook covert psychological operations for the National Security Council. It was going to be practically impossible for the strategists to tell him *what* they wished him to do without insisting also upon telling him *how* he should do it.

For Donovan, the situation would have offered no extenuating circumstances nor called for complicated decisions. It would simply have been impossible. Either the Council gave orders, or it did not; there could be no guidance without direction. When the governing board said *what,* it also said *how,* leaving more tactical details to the officer in charge. That is why, it would seem, he insisted upon having the Director of Central Intelligence fully in charge and answerable in a chain of command through the Secretary of Defense to the President.[14]

INTERDEPARTMENTAL PLANNING

The work of the State–War–Navy Coordinating Committee on psychological warfare reached appropriate culmination at this juncture. Patterson, Secretary of War, had suggested to Secretary Forrestal of the Navy in March 1946 that qualified persons, both military and civilian, should study this art of war for future use. Since then a body of ideas and a plan for an organization had been accumulated in more than a year and a half of interdepartmental discussion and report. All that remained was to decide who should direct and control. Here, as usual, was the rub.[15]

The planners of the Joint Chiefs of Staff distinguished a peacetime from a wartime organization, but both were military. The Intelligence Division of the General Staff was ready by May 22, 1946, with a plan which should belong to the Army. Experience with the Office of Strategic Services, said the report, had not been good; in any future emergency the Department should avoid the situation of World War II in which civilian agencies had been forced upon theater commanders. There had been conflicts of authority and lack of control over "training standards and performance." Reasons why military men should know more than civilians about these matters were not given.

It was this plan which prompted Sullivan, Assistant Secretary of the Navy for Air, to recommend on June 4 that the State–War–Navy Coordinating Committee should appoint its own ad hoc committee on psychological warfare. Sullivan assumed that it would "continue under nonmilitary control" in such a way as to "assist and not interfere" with military plans.[16]

By December 10, 1946, the work of the Office of Strategic Services in "morale operations" and of the Office of War Information in propaganda had been reviewed. Objectives and distinctions between "white" and "black" activities were established. The ad hoc committee concluded that planning, the training of personnel, and the perfection of techniques should be under "central leadership." In peacetime this leadership should be taken by an interdepartmental subcommittee of the State–War–Navy Coordinating Committee, with the approval of the Joint Chiefs of Staff as well as the National Intelligence Authority. In time of war there should be a Director of Psychological Warfare at Washington under a central committee responsible to the President. It would consist of representatives from the State, War, and Navy Departments and from the Central Intelligence Group. In the field theater commanders would be practically independent of the central oranization, though accompanied by an adviser from the State Department. Over the whole system in time of war the Joint Chiefs of Staff would exercise "final approval" subject to reversal, it is fair to assume, by the President and the Council.[17]

At the risk of diverting attention too long from the situation of Hillenkoetter in the fall of 1947, let us underline the preference of this ad hoc committee in December 1946 for the Central Committee over the Director of Psychological Warfare. It could not have escaped the notice of General Vandenberg, who was having his troubles at the moment with the departmental chiefs of intelligence on the Intelligence Advisory Board. Possibly the preference was due in large part to that controversy. Although much can be made of the difference between advice upon matters of intelligence and guidance in psychological operations, the conflict between collective and individual responsibility is the same in each case. If the experience of the theater commander was to be the criterion, military men far more than civilians should have been expected to insist upon the sole responsibility of the man in charge of an operation, or administering an office, especially in time of war.[18]

It is to be noted also that in the plan of December 1946 the Department of State, not the Central Intelligence Group, was to have the psychological adviser on the staff of the theater commander. The Group was to provide the Central Psychological Warfare Committee with the intelligence necessary to its plans and policies. Beyond that the role of the

Group was no more than to be a participant in the Committee. There was no suggestion that the Director of Central Intelligence should also be the Director of Psychological Warfare to put those plans and policies into effect.[19]

To State–War–Navy Coordinating Committee adopted the plan of December 1946 on April 29, 1947, and set up the temporary "peacetime" organization as Hillenkoetter took office in place of Vandenberg. Known as SSE from its covering title of Special Studies and Evaluation, this subcommittee prepared another plan during the increasing anxiety of the summer. It was this proposal which came before the Secretaries of State, Defense, Army, Navy, and Air Force as they met for the first time in the National Security Council and considered the ominous news from Italy.[20]

The conclusions of SSE on September 30, 1947, were that in time of war, or the threat of war as determined by the President, the Director of Psychological Warfare, instead of the Central Committee, should be at the head of the organization. An interdepartmental committee would serve as the policy and planning board under the Director. But there was to be no mistake about his authority, and no argument whether there were individual or collective responsibility. The Director should be empowered to provide "unified direction and authoritative coordination" of the nation's psychological warfare. He was to use established agencies in performing their appropriate functions and employing such persons as he himself deemed essential. This statement that the Director could tell the departments whom to employ in the work under his supervision is startling. But so the text of the report by SSE seems to read.[21]

Training with the Departments of the Army, Navy, and Air Force should begin as soon as possible. As neither the Department of State nor the armed services nor the Central Intelligence Agency had the funds and the staffs to cope with planning and conducting psychological warfare, the organization should be provided with manpower, funds, facilities, materials, and access to the intelligence essential to its task. The propaganda which foreign groups were using against the United States, upon "carefully designed plans of military character," made the situation urgent.[22]

The military men in SSE may have decided to make the Director so powerful because they expected the organization shortly to come under the Joint Chiefs of Staff as the troops withdrew from Italy and the situation grew taut at Trieste. It would be easier to give orders to a Director than to a Committee. Besides, the Committee was likely to be under the influence of its chairman from the Department of State.

Donovan's ideas appeared to be on the ascendency. The inference to be drawn was that the several departments and agencies should stop conferring, drop their rivalries, pool their available resources, and take action.

Moreover, it should be executive action. There should be neither the delay nor the publicity attendant upon legislation and appropriation of funds by Congress. In determining that there was the threat of war, the President would recognize the existence of a critical state of affairs and take steps to maintain national security. Defenders of the Constitution might argue at some other time that Congress, not the President, had the power to declare and provide for war.

Admiral Souers, incoming Executive Secretary of the National Security Council, had been busy with the problem as close adviser to the President and to Forrestal, Secretary of Defense. By the Act of Congress the Secretary of Defense was to be the "principal assistant of the President in all matters relating to the national security." Though respecting Donovan's ideas, Souers was not devoted to them. He was particularly concerned that the new Council and the Central Intelligence Agency under its direction should have their proper responsibility. He was in touch daily by telephone and personal conferences with Admiral Hillenkoetter as they worked upon the NSCIDs, the plan for the Intelligence Advisory Council in the Agency, and other proposals from the Agency to the Council. Developments not fully recorded in memoranda or letters were coming fast.[23]

On September 24, 1947, prior to the first meeting of the Council, Hillenkoetter sent to Souers the proposed text of a recommendation on psychological warfare which he understood Souers wished to make. Referring to the plan adopted by the State–War–Navy Committee in April, Hillenkoetter's memorandum for Souers urged that the National Security Council take "immediate steps" to establish a "central organization" which should conduct "vitally needed psychological operations"; the activity of foreign states led the United States to the necessity of similar action. There should be interdepartmental representation at the "policy-forming level" under the "guidance" of the Council. Thus, the essential principles as Souers conceived them were to be laid before the Secretaries in the first meeting of the Council.[24]

Souers's assistant executive secretary suggested that the proposal should first be coordinated informally with the policy staffs of the departments, and possibly the Joint Chiefs of Staff. Unless someone, perhaps Secretary Forrestal, brought the matter up, it should be held until the Council had formed its staff.[25]

Hillenkoetter's memorandum for Souers did not elaborate upon the functions which the Central Intelligence Agency should have in the proposed "central organization." As Hillenkoetter remembered in 1952, he was personally opposed to involving the Agency with psychological warfare and other subversive operations. He agreed with his Assistant Director for Special Operations, Colonel Galloway, that the experience of OSS in combining secret intelligence with propaganda had been "unfortunate." But Hillenkoetter's personal beliefs did not govern his response to the requests of his superiors. He took part in formulating the proposals which they desired. He suggested corrections and additions. And then he carried out his orders whether he liked them or not. "I shall admit," he said of OPC in 1952, "there could not be a great deal of opposition when one's bosses, in this case the NSC, were insistent upon setting it up."[26]

There were good reasons why the Agency should keep out of psychological operations and related subversive practices. But forces were converging upon it to make the task practically impossible to avoid. Roused by the blasts from Soviet orators and press and by the report of SSE, the Army planners declared that the time had come to put the "wartime" organization into effect. Learning of this decision from his representative in SSE, Hillenkoetter wrote to the State–War–Navy Coordinating Committee on October 22 to approve the report and suggest that the new Psychological Warfare Agency should be made accountable to the Joint Chiefs of Staff. It was in line with his belief that psychological operations, as military rather than intelligence functions, belonged in a separate organization.[27]

Much as they might agree with him in theory, others saw the practical advantage of placing covert activities in an agency which already had a system of clandestine operations and possessed unvouchered funds. There would be no immediate need to go to Congress for separate appropriations. There was danger of injuring the collection of secret intelligence by involving it with black propaganda and other subversive practices, but the risk was worth taking to relieve the departments of activities which they would not dare to own. And then there was the very practical view that the Agency had inherited from OSS a group of technicians in subversion and sabotage who could get at once to work. Even some members of the armed services appear to have been persuaded that the Central Intelligence Agency might take over the business, provided that it received guidance from military minds. But always, of course, the theater commander must have control in his area. This was to remain the subject of endless negotiation and debate.[28]

Another report on November 3 to the State–Army–Navy–Air Force Coordinating Committee avoided designating the Central Intelligence Agency. The proposal now was that there should be a coordinating board (representing the departments and the Agency) over a director and a group of full-time representatives from each department and agency. The board should be responsible to the National Security Council or to the Secretaries of State and Defense as a "Committee of Two." This last suggestion was like the proposal of Hillenkoetter with regard to the Director of Central Intelligence.[29]

James S. Lay, Assistant Secretary of the Council, examined this plan on the same day and made suggestions which appeared in the next proposal. It would not be appropriate, he said, to have the National Security Council take charge. Except for its authorization by Congress to direct the Central Intelligence Agency, it had no powers other than to advise the President. The "Committee of Two" was an informal body with no functions of supervision. The State–Army–Navy–Air Force Coordinating Committee, on the other hand, did have such functions. It was already supervising two interdepartmental organizations; it could take on a third.[30]

By similar reasoning, of course, the National Security Council could have been justified in expanding its own supervisory function at that time. It could have done so with more assurance than SANACC, which enjoyed for its authority only a working agreement among the Secretaries; the Council was authorized by Congress to direct the Central Intelligence Agency to perform "other functions and duties." It was this expansive power which the Council employed later when establishing OPC under special "guidance." Neither Souers nor Lay, however, was ready during those first days of the National Security Council in November 1947 to urge so positive an action upon the Secretaries, who were unfamiliar with their power to make and to administer policy collectively in defense of the nation.[31]

Secretary Forrestal himself was not certain what it meant to be "the principal assistant of the President in all matters relating to the national security." With regard to the Army, Navy, and Air Force, he knew fairly well; he made it plain that their chiefs of intelligence were not to serve as the governing board of the Central Intelligence Agency. Within the Council, in case of a division of opinion, it was agreed that the Secretary of Defense should be a sort of arbiter. But how far his mandate as "principal assistant" to the President took him into affairs of the State Department "relating to the national security" he had yet to discover. Forrestal found that it did not take him far. President Truman did not care for this provision in the National Security Act. When it was revised in 1949, after Forrestal's death, the Act made the Secretary of Defense "principal assistant of the President" merely in matters relating to the Department of Defense.[32]

Lay took exception to the proposal of a group with separate funds and staff. It would be just another agency whose director would usurp functions of the State Department and whose request for funds would jeopardize covert psychological operations. He suggested instead that there should be a board of policies and plans responsible to the State–Army–Navy–Air Force Coordinating Committee. The board could be composed of departmental officials who were already in charge of psychological matters and foreign information. Together the departments which they represented could supply the necessary funds. The Assistant Secretary of State for Public Affairs, he proposed, should be the chairman of the board.[33]

There was another proposal from SANACC following Lay's suggestion. But in the meantime both had been thrown into a different setting by conclusions on November 4 in the War Council of the National Military Establishment. Secretary Forrestal and his associates, the Secretaries of the Army, Navy, Air Force, and the Chiefs of Staff of the armed services, were not in accord with Donovan. They did not believe that the Director of Central Intelligence should conduct psychological warfare, both black and white, under the direction of the Secretary of Defense. They held, with the National Security Council, that propaganda of all kinds was primarily the function of the State Department in times of peace. They therefore proposed that the Director of Central Intelligence and a military representative selected by the War Council should serve merely as consultants to the Assistant Secretary of State who had charge. The members of the War Council agreed that he ought to deal in both black and white propaganda abroad; he would obtain the fullest advantages from clandestine operations. The issue was squarely before Secretary Marshall at the next meeting of the National Security Council on November 14.[34]

DECISION BY THE COUNCIL

So far there had been no stress upon clandestine psychological projects. Open propaganda and the truth seemed adequate in time of peace; underhanded procedures were reserved for actual warfare. But now there was no longer peace even if there was not actual war with the Soviet Union and its satellites. It was time for the President to talk of the "threat of war" and for his Secretaries to consider retaliating in kind with subversive propaganda. Beyond that lay political, economic, and eventually physical action abroad. The first step was to separate such clandestine operations from open propaganda, more euphemistically entitled "overt foreign informational activities." Secretary Marshall did not want the State Department concerned directly with sinister practices which, if exposed, would embarrass the Department in its campaign of honesty. Those practices should be conducted elsewhere, subject to concealed and not too remote "guidance" from the Department of State. The Council decided that "two related but separate purposes" should be accomplished. Covert psychological operations should be initiated abroad. They should be "carefully coordinated" with the overt informational activities. The Staff of the Council was directed to submit reports.[35]

The first of these, NSC-4, as adopted by the Council on December 17, 1947, and approved by the President the next day, placed overt "foreign information measures" under the Assistant Secretary of State for Public Affairs. This was essentially the same as the last proposal from SANACC. Hillenkoetter had agreed to it on behalf of the Central Intelligence Agency, suggesting that there was no need for a director of operations under the Assistant Secretary; the personnel detailed from the participating agencies as his staff of assistants were his own responsibility. With this correction NSC-4 went into effect and the Department began putting together its organization. The Voice of America commenced officially in these circumstances. President Truman signed the Act of Congress on January 27, 1948.[36]

The second report to the Council, known as NSC 4-A, came to the Central Intelligence Agency where members of Hillenkoetter's staff made changes for discussion by the Staff of the National Security Council before final adoption by the Council. There is no printed record of NSC 4-A. It is in the minutes of the fourth meeting of the Council on December 17, 1947, as "Tab B." It consists of a note from the Executive Secretary to the Council and the draft of the directive to the Director of Central Intelligence before its final form. NSC 4-A went to the Agency as the National Security Council advised the President on Italy. He should adopt a policy of support for the existing government and a program to combat Communist propaganda there, with information and with "all other practicable means, [several words deleted]. On November 24 President Truman approved the policy and the program "under the coordination of the Secretary of State.[37]

Neither the Central Intelligence Agency nor the Department of Defense was happy over the decision of the Council to assign covert psychological operations to the Agency. In time the State Department too was much displeased. The importance of NSC 4-A in the history of Central Intelligence and relationships between the collection of secret intelligence and subversive activities overseas is not to be underestimated, especially at the date of this writing in January 1953 when some of those activities have been badly exposed. Editors and commentators are calling the attention of the incoming Administration to that fact. It has announced a new commission on psychological strategy in the "cold war."[38]

Admiral Hillenkoetter thought in November 1947, and he still did in December 1952, that black propaganda depended for its success upon publicity where it was employed; clandestine intelligence should escape observation. He insisted that close association of the two was likely to ruin the latter; and to him it was by far the greater asset in any kind of war. From his experience in France during the Vichy regime and German occupation, Hillenkoetter was certain as well that guerrilla tactics and resistance movements yielded wholly inadequate returns. To such opinions General Donovan quite as emphatically did not hold. The friendship of the two former heads of Central Intelligence was enlivened by frequent discussion of these matters and continued disagreement.[39]

The National Security Council took the position of General Donovan, but only in part. It assigned the task of initiating and conducting covert operations against the Communist powers to Admiral Hillenkoetter as head of the Central Intelligence Agency, for the very reason that such activities were related to clandestine collection of intelligence. But he was to expend only "available funds," keep the operations within "normal activities" of the Agency and "consistent with U.S. foreign policy," and see that they were "closely coordinated" with the overt activities of the Assistant Secretary of State for Public Affairs. If these restrictions were to be interpreted literally, there could be little initiative on the part of the Director of Central Intelligence. He could not launch out upon a wide course of action in the manner of General Donovan, subject only to the orders of the President or the Secretary of Defense. If covert operations had to conform at every turn with the "foreign information measures" of the State Department, Hillenkoetter was stopped before he could start.[40]

The framers of the directive to the Director of Central Intelligence, in the Agency and in the Council's Staff, were responsible for an indictment of the Union of Soviet Socialist Republics which had not appeared in the first draft. Psychiatrists will understand why the draftsmen labelled Soviet propaganda "subversive and immoral" and changed to the adjective "vicious." Others may wonder whether they might not have called it just diabolically clever. If the directive was to remain as secret as the Council intended it to be, the draftsmen were only talking to themselves, the members of the Council, its Staff, the Director of Central Intelligence, and his subordinates who were to carry out his orders. But so it was written. So it remained when adopted on December 17, 1947, by the Council, perhaps awaiting the day of exposure to posterity.[41]

Hillenkoetter did not need to convince himself that Soviet practices warranted similarly dirty actions by the United States. They were fair enough in war. They belonged in the armed services, not in the Central Intelligence Agency; but he could not put them there. They had been assigned to him; he could only object to restrictions and request additions to his directive from the Council. For one, there was at first a provision, as in the NSCID on collection, that clandestine operations should be coordinated with the senior diplomatic and military representatives in each area. This provision gave way to the more workable arrangement that those officials should be kept informed of operations directly affecting them. For another, the necessary safeguard was included that nothing in the directive could be construed to require the Agency to disclose its "secret techniques, sources, or contacts."[42]

The matter of "guidance" remained subject to dispute long after the Council issued the directive to Hillenkoetter. As soon as the "planners of the Military Establishment" had a look at the proposal to put the Agency in charge of "black activities," they concluded that the activities should be "restrictively controlled" by the military establishment; there should be a panel designated by the Council to represent the Army, Navy, and Air Force and to approve all policies and major plans.[43]

Hillenkoetter would agree with the planners that "black activities" were military operations, but hardly that they should be assigned to the Agency and then directed from the Pentagon because they were military operations. He himself was heavily engaged with the armed services elsewhere that week, following Secretary Royall's memorandum of November 26; Admiral Inglis and General Chamberlin were shortly to learn from Secretary Forrestal that Hillenkoetter, not the Intelligence Advisory Committee, would direct the Central Intelligence Agency. Hillenkoetter left the battle over the panel of guidance to his deputy, General Wright, who instructed the representative of the Agency to tell the Staff of the Council that the Agency was and had to be "the sole agency to conduct *organized foreign clandestine* operations." Whatever body might "indicate the type" of black operations, the Central Intelligence Agency alone would have to "determine *how* the material" was distributed.[44]

Explanation came back to the Agency from Admiral Souers on December 5 that the panel would not concern itself with operations, once they had been approved. Proposals would usually be accepted by the panel, he thought, because they would also have been discussed by the National Security Council. In any case, the Director would have the right of appeal to the Council itself if the panel were to reject a plan the Director wished to adopt. The "panel of guidance" which Souers had in mind, and which he still advocated in December 1952, would be a board of advice and affirmation with respect to policy. It would not have authority to direct. That power would remain with the Council.[45]

This view, it must be said, does not seem to have been the conception of the military planners when they talked of a panel, nor the idea which officials in the State Department later developed in practice. There was, moreover, an inherent weakness. The Secretaries were busy with many other affairs. The quip that reports of the Staff were read only in taxicabs is too sharp, but it is revealing. The Secretaries were likely to turn to subordinates for information and let their own judgments be governed accordingly. The guidance then would not come from the Secretaries, or even the Under Secretaries, on the high level of policymaking; it would come from specialists at the working level who had foremost in mind the interests of their own departments and agencies. However ideal, it was too much to expect that the Council would sit as a judicial body. It was inherently a political institution. Its "guidance" in psychological warfare was likely to slide from determination of broad policy into management of detail.

Notwithstanding the reluctance in the Agency, Souers on December 16 recommended to the Council that there should be a panel consisting of representatives from the State Department, the Army, Navy, and Air Force and, at the suggestion of General Gruenther, an "observer" for the Joint Chiefs of Staff. Gruenther was as hesitant to take part in this body of supervision or guidance for the Central Intelligence Agency as in its Intelligence Advisory Committee and subordinate Standing Committee. The Joint Chiefs of Staff were shaking themselves free from all civilian encumbrances possible.[46]

But when the directive of December 17 came to Hillenkoetter from the Council, there was no provision in it for a panel to guide him or to govern his choice of operations in covert psychological warfare upon the Soviet Union and its satellites. There was the statement that the Director of Central Intelligence was charged with ensuring that "appropriate agencies of the U.S. Government, both at home and abroad," were kept informed of those operations which directly affected them. It looked like a victory for the Agency over the military planners and even over Souers. Before we jump to any conclusion, however, other factors need to be brought into account.[47]

The record of what actually was said in the Council is not available for this study. Such memoranda are the President's, as opinions which under the Constitution he may require of his Secretaries in writing. Secretary Marshall was not present at the meeting. Under Secretary Lovett represented him. But, according to Souers's memory, both Marshall and Royall, for the State and the War Departments, were opposed to establishing a panel of representatives from the several departments to guide the Director of Central Intelligence in psychological operations overseas.[48]

Marshall did not favor an interdepartmental arrangement which might compromise the State Department as he endeavored to advance the rehabilitation of Europe by economic cooperation and open support of existing

governments. The Secretary of State was obliged to coordinate the open
with the covert policy [one or two words deleted] but that could be done
with less danger of exposure for the Department, as it was done later,
through his Under Secretary, Lovett, the chief of the Planning Staff,
Kennan, and his aides.[49]

Royall, against the desires of the military planners, did not want the
"panel of guidance," because he saw no reason for an intermediary between the Council and the Director of Central Intelligence. He gave the
impression that as Secretary of War he did not wish the responsibility or
the bother. He could argue, as he had earlier in the fall, against making
the Director responsible to a subcommittee of two, the Secretaries of State
and Defense, with regard to matters of intelligence. The Council as a
whole should make broad policy, leave its execution to the Agency, and
hold the Director responsible. There was inconsistency in Royall's position, however, as he was contending at the same time that in all matters
of intelligence the Director should consult the Intelligence Advisory Committee before submitting his recommendations to the Council.[50]

As the directive came to Hillenkoetter on December 17, 1947, the
Central Intelligence Agency was assigned the task of conducting covert
psychological operations against the Communist power, to "ensure their
secrecy and obviate costly duplication." The Director of Central Intelligence was also "charged with ensuring" that these operations were "consistent with U.S. foreign policy and overt foreign information activities."
In doing so, it was to be expected that he would confer with officials in the
Department of State; but there was no stipulation that he was obliged to
defer to them. His was the explicit responsibility. He was obligated to no
other officer or group except the National Security Council. It may be that
the Council did not so intend, but so its directive reads.[51]

The Director appeared to have a free hand as well as full responsibility
so long as he achieved the purposes of this special assignment in coordination with the Department of State to the satisfaction of the Council.
Presumably no one might override his decisions regarding covert operations except the Secretary of State supported by his colleagues in the
National Security Council or by the President himself, of course, if he had
been informed of what was happening. The chances were good that the
President might not be told specifically, to save him from having to lie in
press conferences.[52]

It seemed that Admiral Hillenkoetter, though ordered against his own
judgment to involve the Agency in a dirty task, could engage in it practically as he saw fit so long as he did not get caught. If he did, he could be
certain that he would be disowned, his work repudiated and perhaps
abhorred; it would be contrary to the foreign policy of this country and the

clean activities of the State Department. If all this were true, Admiral Hillenkoetter was liable to criticism when he did not use his power to the limit and brush aside all interference except that of the Secretary of State and the Council. But when he came to choosing his own men and developing the first projects, Hillenkoetter discovered that he did not have a free hand.[53]

Neither the armed services nor the Department of State intended that he should have it. There was in NSC 4-A no "panel of guidance" to control the Director of Central Intelligence; its advocates were not in agreement upon the extent of control which it should exercise. Simple differences between "what" and "how" were not clear. But they did agree that there ought to be some guidance other than broad policy determined by the National Security Council. Negotiations were soon under way to obtain another directive from the Council. There was present also criticism by some that Hillenkoetter was doing nothing. The opinion seemed to be strengthened rather than offset by the misgivings of others that he was doing too much. It is no wonder that he himself came to think that the Agency was meshed in the rivalries of the Department of State and the National Military Establishment. The outcome of this interdepartmental maneuvering was NSC 10-2 and the establishment of OPC.[54]

THE SPECIAL PROCEDURES GROUP

Hillenkoetter on December 22, 1947, instructed Colonel Galloway, Assistant Director in the Office of Special Operations, to organize a "foreign information branch." This became the Special Procedures Group. They took stock of their psychological activities and agents [several words deleted] on January 2. They obtained Thomas G. Cassady, who had been with Donovan in OSS, to begin covert political and psychological operations at once and to prepare for the more subversive actions which might eventuate in the "cold war." Cassady wrote to Donovan on February 17, 1948, that he would not be surprised to find Cassady in Washington "giving some aid to the organization which you so brilliantly founded and directed." By February 25 Cassady asked Galloway to notify the stations of the Agency throughout Europe and the Near East that it had been authorized to engage in covert psychological operations which might "include all measures of information and persuasion short of physical." [three lines deleted] It may be that the impact of Donovan's policy and his spirit caused misgiving in the armed services and the Department of State.[55]

[thirteen lines deleted][56] Cassady was hesitant in March to make any investment of funds until reassured, for he knew that the Department was to take over the American Zone in Germany from the Military Administration. But he was reassured, so he thought, and told to go ahead with the preparations.

Cassady was given to understand at the time that Under Secretary Lovett approved in principle but did not wish to know much about the project. As Cassady remembered in the following August, Lovett said that the less the Department knew about the details, the better its strategic position would be. [four lines deleted] How the Special Procedures Group distributed the propaganda was to be the Agency's own affair. On this matter, however, Hillenkoetter remembered in 1952 that he became quite "indignant" with Kennan, Director of the Department's Policy Planning Staff.[57]

The major project of the Agency for distributing propaganda against the Soviet Union and its satellites was developing with the advice and cooperation of experts in the Navy. [eight lines deleted][58]

When officials in the State Department considered the [several words deleted] project on April 26 and 27, Cassady was told that the time was not opportune for such a campaign. It would be all right for him to continue physical preparations, but the Department did not want any "incitive" propaganda just then. According to Hillenkoetter, Kennan did not want to hurt "Russian feelings." The Berlin blockade and air lift were operating at the time.[59]

Cassady replied to Kennan's subordinate that the Agency did not intend to produce anything so strong as the pamphlets used [one line deleted]. These leaflets for the Soviet people, Cassady said, would speak of "brotherly love," offer "sympathy with their hardships," hold out "the hand of fellowship to the masses, etc." He further declared that he did not see how the proposal differed from what Murphy was actually doing at the time for the Department. To this Cassady received "no response or comment." To his remark that the [one word deleted] project would be no more provoking to the Soviet authorities than the radio station and printing establishement [one or two words deleted] the reply was: "in the light of present circumstances, State might like to reconsider their position on that." Cassady understood this to mean that the officials in the State Department thought "they could obstruct any activation of that plan."[60]

Cassady's surmise on April 27 was accurate. George Kennan and his assistants in the Planning Staff of the Staff Department, John Davies and Henry Villard, met on April 30 with Allen W. Dulles and his aide, Robert Blum, to discuss the progress of the Intelligence Survey for the National Security Council and to consider the ways in which that investigation touched upon political warfare. In Blum's report of the conference, the Survey Group, "privately and off the record," was beginning to think that the collection of secret intelligence "should be divorced from CIA." It should belong in an organization set up to deal with other kinds of secret operations.

Kennan replied that the State Department would not want to take secret intelligence into its organization. The new grouping would be too big and cumbersome. But the Department was looking to the development of a small project, six or seven persons under the National Security Council, who should direct political warfare. The Department, he said, was "very much opposed to giving CIA responsibility for political warfare, contacts with resistance groups," and similar matters. The Agency, he feared, might conduct those activities independently of "national policy considerations." Kennan wanted a director of the "small project" who was "a person of very high standing and with a broad appreciation of national policy matters." Five days later Kennan called the attention of the Council to Allen W. Dulles as a man of outstanding qualifications.[61]

When Cassady reported back, Galloway instructed him to proceed [one line deleted]. So far as he was concerned, said Galloway, Cassady might "ignore State in the matter"; still, they should inform General Wright. Hillenkoetter and Wright agreed with Galloway, but decided that the Agency would be in a stronger position if they submitted a copy of their first pamphlet [several words deleted]. If the State Department refused to approve it or a revision of it, or still another draft, and finally were "uncooperative," the Director's Office would take over the controversy. It would seem as if this were a small amount of indignation. But then Cassady could go ahead with his preparations. [half of a line deleted][62]

When we come again to this project, we shall find that, from the point of view of the Director and the Agency, the situation was even more exasperating. The preparations for covert psychological operations had been investigated on behalf of the National Security Council, and the organization subjected to attack. Secretary Forrestal, growing impatient as international affairs became more critical, called upon the Council on March 26, 1948, to find out what was being done under NSC 4 and NSC 4-A. There was no doubt that the affairs of the world were in crisis. The Russians began their Berlin blockade on April 1. It was by no means yet certain that the air lift could break the blockade. Communists had taken Czechoslovakia by coup d'état. [two lines deleted] Communists were active in Latin America, endangering the life of Secretary Marshall at Bogotá.[63]

These events without question had their part in the movement to replace NSC 4-A with NSC 10-2. But every causal relationship or motive for action is not so manifest. Hillenkoetter's covert organization and performance were examined by the consultants of the National Security Council, of whom Kennan was one; and they had the assistance of George V. Allen, Kennan's subordinate as Assistant Secretary of State for Public Affairs in charge of overt "foreign information measures." There was no comparable investigation of Allen's organization and performance, none at least in which Hillenkoetter or anyone else in the Agency participated. Such discrepancy may have been due to thoughtlessness. But those responsible for it laid themselves open to a different conjecture. As late as June 8, 1948, Allen was still calling for "earnest cooperation" by the departments in setting up his own consultative group and interdepartmental coordinating staff. By that time the covert organization of the Agency was undergoing change.[64]

The "review" which Allen wrote in April for the consultants stated that the Agency had made satisfactory progress in screening personnel for qualifications and security. As first drafted, Allen's report then "admonished" the Director of Central Intelligence to concentrate upon anti-Communist democratic forces in foreign countries and to project these operations as rapidly as possible. The word "admonished" was replaced with "advised" before submission to the Council on April 26. But the report was still hard to take, in view of the operations which had been completed with considerable success [one word deleted]. Cassady was leaving shortly to advance others [several words deleted].[65]

It is quite likely that Allen did not know of the [one word deleted] activities of the Central Intelligence Agency. He may indeed have heard little about the preparations of the Special Procedures Group to penetrate the Soviet world with broadcasts from Germany, [one or two words deleted] leaflets [several words deleted] subversive literature [several words deleted]. Other officials in the Department of State were not so uninformed of the plans for "messages of love, brotherhood, and Mickey Mouse watches." Allen's report was what Souers called it in 1952, a "coat of whitewash." But it appears to have been no more a cloak for Hillenkoetter's seeming delay in applying NSC 4-A than an excuse to promote a plan in the Department of State which, with the aid of the military establishment, resulted in NSC 10-2.[66]

GUIDANCE AND REFORM

Another report arrived opportunely on April 7, 1948, from SANACC. It concurred in the decision of the Joint Chiefs of Staff that a Psychological

Warfare Organization should be established before there was war. One opinion of this latest report was that some persons were trying to make places for themselves. Close to this thought lay comment that the proposed National Security Information Agency should not be under the "lily-fingered treatment" of the State Department; it should belong either to NSC or to SANACC. Another observer held that SANACC was working "at cross purposes" because NSC 4-A was so secret; other departments and agencies did not know of its existence. Anyway, the Staff of the National Security Council on April 19, 1948, made the report from SANACC the basis for discussing several suggestions. Among them was the idea that there should be a new section in the Central Intelligence Agency. Its civilian head would be deputy to the Director but, in case of disagreement with him, should have direct access to the National Security Council. It was the germ of NSC 10-2.[67]

On May 4, 1948, there came from the State Department's Policy Planning Staff a paper whose author was not named. Its erudition and style were Kennan's. It called for the inauguration of organized political warfare upon the "logical application of Clausewitz's doctrine in time of peace." "We have been handicapped," it said, "by a popular attachment to the concept of a basic difference between peace and war." There was "reluctance to recognize . . . the perpetual rhythm of struggle, in and out of war." Upon these premises, which few would question, there was placed an assumption which many in the armed services, it is certain, would dispute even though the War Council had taken much the same position with regard to times of peace. Both overt and covert political warfare, said the representative of the Policy Planning Staff, should be directed and coordinated by the Department of State. The reader need not be misled by the use of the words "political warfare" instead of "psychological operations." For all practical purposes the phrases are interchangeable here. It better suited the argument to use "political" rather than "psychological"; political matters are by tradition the particular concern of the Department of State. "Political warfare" was the phrase used in the talk with Allen W. Dulles on April 30 when Kennan said that the State Department was opposed to giving the responsibility to the Agency.[68]

The writer on May 4 for the Policy Planning Staff candidly remarked that some three months before it had begun "a consideration of specific projects in the field of covert operations, where they should be fitted into the structure of this Government and how the Department of State should exercise direction and coordination." Possibly Hillenkoetter did not know at the time that the third copy of this directive of December 17, 1947, from the Council had gone to Kennan, Director of the Policy Planning Staff. But Hillenkoetter and Cassady had learned before long that the Special Procedures Group of the Agency could expect direction as well as coordination from the Department of State. To Cassady it was "obstruction."[69]

The time was "ripe," said the author of the paper for the Policy Planning Staff, to have a "directorate" within the Government for political warfare; "one man must be boss," he declared, and "answerable" to the Secretary of State. But the officer should not be in the Department. He should have concealed funds and cover elsewhere. The secretariat of the Council was the "best possible" cover; this would permit also a "direct chain of command" from the Secretary of State. The director should have a staff of eight—four chosen by the Secretary of State and four by the Secretary of Defense. And there should be a consultative board of the Council. All current operations of the Central Intelligence Agency would come under the control of this board. The draft of a directive from the Council accompanied the paper. The new officer would be known as "Director of Special Studies."[70]

The paper of May 4 and the proposed directive from the Policy Planning Staff had no ambiguity for the Director of Central Intelligence. Hillenkoetter was neither diverted nor convinced by the use of "political warfare" instead of "psychological operations." He sent a memorandum to the Executive Secretary of the Council the next day to oppose the plan on behalf of the Central Intelligence Agency. The "chief of current activities" should be the officer to direct such studies. If the Council still wished to have a separate Director of Special Studies, he should head only a clerical staff for making plans. Or the Council should rescind NSC 4-A and take the Director of Central Intelligence and the Agency out of the business of covert psychological operations altogether. The Council could set up another operating agency under the Director of Special Studies. Hillenkoetter did not like responsibility without authority.[71]

Following his objection, the Council's Staff revised the draft of May 4 to give the Central Intelligence Agency representation on the staff of the proposed Director of Special Studies. The Staff incorporated some of the terms in the directive of December 17, 1947, to the Director of Central Intelligence. Lay sent a memorandum of Hillenkoetter's comments and their influence upon the Staff to Robert Blum, assistant to Forrestal, Secretary of Defense. Blum was by this time also executive secretary to the Intelligence Survey Group of the Council, better known as the Dulles Committee. Forrestal was not interested merely in the progress of the Agency under NSC 4-A.[72]

Hillenkoetter opposed even more explicitly the directive as it had been revised by the Staff. It would cause "dangerous duplication" of assigned functions. The Agency, he asserted, had made "considerable strides." It was obligated to expenditures; it had firm commitments for psychological

operations outside the United States over a "long period of time." He
urgently recommended that they should not be jeopardized. His experience, he declared, was that combat or tactical operations must be separate from strategic planning in psychological warfare. In other words, if
the Agency were obliged to undertake the operations, which he himself
preferred to have done elsewhere, it should continue to enjoy the authority as well as the responsibility which it had under NSC 4-A.[73]

Hillenkoetter stood his ground through successive attempts to give the
Department of State its Director of Special Studies and meet the request
of the Joint Chiefs of Staff that there should be a Psychological Warfare
Organization to plan before there was a war. One of these proposals
would not rescind NSC 4-A but would rewrite it so that the Director of
Special Studies came between the Director of Central Intelligence and
the National Security Council for some purposes but not for others. The
idea is difficult to express clearly. The best that one can say is: the Director of Special Studies was to give the Director of Central Intelligence
"guidance," and yet stay out of his way while the National Security Council directed him to "conduct" the operations. Who would time the vanishing act of the Director of Special Studies was not determined.[74]

Hillenkoetter may have merited criticism for loose and uncertain statements on some occasions. This was not one of them. He replied that
NSC 4-A should not be changed. The Central Intelligence Agency
should do the planning for wartime as it conducted its current operations. The National Security Council and the Joint Chiefs of Staff should
decide when there was an emergency demanding such preparations for
war. The proposed directive, if enacted, would "establish a staff function
providing for *AUTHORITY* in a delicate field of operation—without the
RESPONSIBILITY."[75]

[seventeen lines deleted][76] This may not have been subordination of
the DCI to the DSS; it certainly was not freedom from his control. Nor did
it meet Kennan's assertion of May 4 that "one man must be boss" and
"answerable" to the Secretary of State.

The argument of the Staff for this complicated arrangement was that
the Director of Special Studies with his representative staff of assistants
would utilize other agencies besides the Central Intelligence Agency. But
there was no necessity for an intermediary to do that. The Council had
only to expand its interpretation of the clause in the National Security Act
giving it power to direct the Central Intelligence Agency to perform "other
functions and duties." Then, too, the Council might have brought its own
powers of "coordination" more fully into play. As for reconciling departmental views, there was no need for one more director with an advisory

board. The Council could have authorized the Director of Central Intelligence to make the endeavor.[77]

At this moment the Intelligence Survey Group came directly into the affair. It was evident that Dulles and his associates had been kept in touch through Lay and Blum. Dulles had conferred with Kennan on April 30 regarding secret intelligence and political warfare. Dulles now wrote to Souers that the plans for covert operations before the Council had "immediate bearing upon the conduct of secret intelligence operations"; the Survey Group would be pleased to submit an "interim report." And this they did on the following day. When interviewed in December 1952, Admiral Hillenkoetter thought that there was no connection between the movement to replace NSC 4-A with NSC 10-2 and the Dulles Report upon the weaknesses in his administration of the Central Intelligence Agency. One is not so sure after reading this "interim report" of May 13, 1948, and taking note of events which followed closely upon it.[78]

The "interim report" maintained that a central planning and coordinating staff was essential and that centralized control of covert operations was equally important. The proposed Director of Special Studies and his staff would be too removed from the operations; these, for reasons of effectiveness and security, were not to be "farmed out." The Director had to keep in intimate touch with details. He therefore should be responsible for all forms of activity, and the chiefs of branches should report to him. He himself should report to the Council or to the Director of Central Intelligence if that official were in charge of collecting secret intelligence. At that time the Dulles Survey Group was still considering whether the Central Intelligence Agency should engage in the collection of secret intelligence.[79]

[most of one line deleted] and the "interim report" of the Survey Group were before the Council in its eleventh meeting on May 20. Some idea of the discussion there may be obtained from the response to both papers by Hillenkoetter as he submitted another proposal for the Central Intelligence Agency on May 24. The State Department's "demands for a directing hand" regarding propaganda and the underground resistance to be supported, he said, would be satisfied by a "high-level liaison officer" for covert operations; it was something which had not yet been tried. The implication was that so far liaison between the Department and the Agency had been conducted at too low a level. Cassady's experience seemed to bear this out.[80]

Hillenkoetter proposed again that NSC 4-A should be maintained. But there could be two groups concerned with covert operations. The Central Intelligence Agency should continue in charge of black propaganda and related practices. The Joint Chiefs of Staff should control the planning of sabotage, physical subversion, and the like; these were operations for wartime or the verge of it. In war or an emergency both groups would come under military commanders. The Special Procedures Group (which he did not mention by name) could be removed intact from the authority of the Director of Central Intelligence to that of the Joint Chiefs of Staff. Hillenkoetter believed this would please the Joint Chiefs. It would answer the objections of the Secretary of the Army; Royall evidently had opposed establishing a new agency or turning the Council into an operating body. And from conversations with senators and representatives, Hillenkoetter believed that the plan which he now proposed would be in line with the intentions of Congress. He had recently been in closed session with a subcommittee of the House because of the Bogotá affair and had heard sharp opinions on the subject.[81]

The Joint Chiefs of Staff discussed the Hillenkoetter plan. General Gruenther attended a meeting for them in Secretary Forrestal's office on May 28 as Admiral Hillenkoetter briefly stated the view of the Central Intelligence Agency. Gruenther remarked that the Joint Chiefs seemed to favor having secret operations conducted with clandestine intelligence by the Agency; but they were doubtful of its ability to handle the task. He asked if Hillenkoetter were willing to have an advisory panel [several words deleted]. Hillenkoetter replied that he would accept it. His concept of advice, though, was not that of management.

Gruenther and Hillenkoetter withdrew when they had finished their exchange. Souers, Executive Secretary of the Council, came for the latter part of the meeting. Forrestal, Secretary of Defense, Lovett, Under Secretary of State, and Allen W. Dulles, chairman of the Intelligence Survey Group, were present throughout, and so was Robert Blum. Apparently he prepared the memorandum of the meeting, dated June 1, which went to the Council before its next session on June 3.[82]

After Gruenther and Hillenkoetter left, Forrestal and Lovett agreed upon the following understandings. The head of the Office of Special Operations in the Agency should be replaced. Responsibility for both secret intelligence and covert operations should be assigned to the Agency under the new head of the office. This "new office" should have considerable autonomy within the Agency; and the head of the office should be authorized, in case of differences arising between him and the Director of Central Intelligence, to appeal directly to the National Security Council. Dulles was then asked if he would accept the position. He did not think so, but would give his final decision in a few days. Others, whose names were not put in the minutes, were considered.[83]

At the request of Forrestal, Lovett, and Dulles, Souers prepared an alternative [one word deleted] for the Council. His proposal stipulated that a "highly qualified" person recruited outside the Agency, and approved by the Council, should head the "Special Services Unit." He should have access to and receive "policy guidance" from the State Department and the National Military Establishment. Thus, Souers's original conception of a "panel of guidance," which Secretaries Marshall and Royall had kept from NSC 4-A, reappeared before the Council. If the plan were adopted, the State Department, the National Military Establishment, and the Central Intelligence Agency jointly should request funds.[84]

If Admiral Hillenkoetter was not informed of the understanding that his Assistant Director, Colonel Galloway, should be removed and the position offered to Allen W. Dulles, Hillenkoetter was given immediate opportunity to comment upon Souers's "alternative [one word deleted]." Hillenkoetter did so on June 4 in a paper for the Staff of the Council and said that he himself would come as the member from the Agency when the Staff worked on his proposal. Following the pattern of Souers's "alternative," Hillenkoetter suggested that the "highly qualified" person to head the new Office of Special Services within the Agency should be chosen from within or outside the Agency, and he should be nominated by the Director of Central Intelligence. There should be an Operations Advisory Board, with its military members "fully accredited by the Joint Chiefs of Staff."[85]

This was Hillenkoetter's specific answer to Gruenther's inquiry. Hillenkoetter meant a board comparable to the Intelligence Advisory Committee. He did not want a "panel of guidance" such as Souers desired. Hillenkoetter further stipulated that the funds should be in the budget of the Agency and that the directives of the new office should be prepared by the Director of Central Intelligence. But on the same day the Council was tentatively approving the principles of Souers's "alternative [one word deleted]." There was little chance that Hillenkoetter's reservations for the Director and the Agency would be retained as he had submitted them.[86]

There were changes before Hillenkoetter's paper went to the Staff on June 8. The Operations Advisory Board, renamed Committee, should consist of two members, one chosen by the Secretary of State and the other by the Secretary of Defense, as Souers proposed. In case of a disagreement with the Director of Central Intelligence, the matter would go to the Council. Hillenkoetter's stipulation that the Director should prepare the directives was omitted. There was a specific statement ending NSC 4-A.[87]

Additional changes by the Staff appeared in the memorandum which Lay sent to the consultants of the Council—Kennan for the State Department, Wedemeyer for the Army, Struble for the Navy, and Norstad for the

Air Force. The name had become Office of Special Projects. There was no statement whether or not the chief of the new office should be chosen from persons in the Central Intelligence Agency. The significant provision was that he should be nominated by the Secretary of State, and not by the Director of Central Intelligence. He was to be "acceptable" to the Director and approved by the Council. Still, he was to report directly to the Director of Central Intelligence.[88]

Unless the Director and the man chosen by the State Department proved remarkably compatible in personality and held much the same views on the projects and their performance, the situation for both was likely to be intolerable. If the Advisory Committee did not accept the Director's view, he would have to take his case to the National Security Council. Although his subordinate in the new office was to report directly to him, the Director would have difficulty in giving orders unless the Advisory Committee approved. The Director's right of "acceptance" was short of both initiative and authority.

Admiral Hillenkoetter saw through the maneuvering to put the State Department in control and said so in two forthright letters on June 9, 1948. One went to Lay for the Council and the other to Lay personally for himself and for Admiral Souers. Hillenkoetter sent copies of each to Major General Todd for General Gruenther and the Joint Chiefs of Staff.[89]

To the Council Hillenkoetter objected that the draft directive of June 8 was confusing and inconsistent; it was weaker than the plan of June 4. There were more restrictions upon the Director of Central Intelligence. If he were out of town, would the work of the new office stop, or would it "freewheel," or would the Acting Director have charge? There was no reason, in his opinion, for treating the Office of Special Projects differently from the Office of Special Operations. It would seem, he said, that either the National Security Council had confidence in the operation of the new office by the Agency, or it did not. If the Council had such confidence, it should make "a general declaration of policy" and leave the operation of the Office of Special Projects to the Agency. If the Council did not have confidence in the Agency, then it "should not be expected or directed" to operate the Office of Special Operations either, in any manner. This was twelve days after the decision in Forrestal's office that Galloway should go and after the offer of the position to Dulles on the understanding that, in differences with the Director, the head of the enlarged office should have the right to appeal directly to the Council.

To Lay and Souers, Hillenkoetter wrote: "I should like to suggest that, since State evidently will not go along with CIA operating this political warfare thing in any sane or sound manner, we go back to the original concept that State proposed. Let State run it and let it have no connection at all with us." Hillenkoetter foresaw "continued bickering and argument" if they were to "try to keep a makeshift in running order." His prophecy of 1948 was fulfilled in subsequent events.

While blaming Hillenkoetter for "confusion as to the responsibility of the DCI," William H. Jackson found during his survey of OPC in the spring of 1951 that there was "no clear distinction or common understanding" with regard to the operations of the administration as a central "service" which should give administrative support and should exercise the functions of review, audit, and inspection of the Office. Excellent work had been done, he said, to minimize these difficulties. But the personal intervention of an able officer was a "spotty, makeshift type of symptom-treatment." It did not "attack the causes of the malady." With this judgment Hillenkoetter would certainly have agreed, although he might not have accepted Jackson's list of causes.[90]

What the consultants thought of the revised paper, now known as the draft of June 10, was not reported in the file available for this study. But there was comment from the Army on June 15, 1948. As should be expected, the military men put their stress upon the time of war when the Joint Chiefs of Staff should have charge. They called specifically for "policy guidance" by the Operations Advisory Committee and submission of disagreements to the Joint Chiefs rather than to the National Security Council. For the National Security Resources Board, Daniel C. Fahey proposed that the departments and agencies concerned should give the advice with respect to economic warfare. Such a clause was included in the revised draft sent to the Council on June 15 as NSC 10-1. With certain deletions and amendments by the Council it became NSC 10-2 on June 18, 1948.[91]

OPC

The National Security Council directed that an Office of Special Projects be created within the Central Intelligence Agency. The name was changed later to Office of Policy Coordination, to ensure plausibility while revealing practically nothing of its purposes. The activities of the new office were to be correlated with the espionage and counterespionage of the Office of Special Operations by the Director of Central Intelligence. He was to keep the two offices separate and to let neither interfere with the other. This undertaking, which Hillenkoetter had disliked from the start, proved so difficult to accomplish that before long another movement to reform the Office of Special Operations got under way. This time it was to "integrate" the clandestine intelligence of OSO with the covert operations of OPC, but not to restore those functions as they had been in the days of Galloway and Cassady under NSC 4-A.[92]

The scope of the Agency's covert operations short of physical subversion was specifically enlarged by NSC 10-2 to include economic warfare and "preventive direct action." Sabotage, antisabotage, demolitions, evacuations, aid to guerrilla action and underground resistance, support of anti-Communists in threatened countries, all came within the province of OPC. It might not include in its operations armed conflict by recognized forces, espionage and counterespionage, nor "cover and deception for military operations."

Plans for wartime should be made in coordination with the Joint Chiefs of Staff. The Director of Central Intelligence was to ensure that such plans were "accepted" by the Joint Chiefs "as consistent with and complementary to approved plans for wartime military operations." Doubtless the statement was clear to those who wrote it, as meaning that the Director would be responsible for making plans which would be acceptable to the Joint Chiefs. If he did not at first succeed in persuading the Joint Chiefs, he could try again. He had no authority to force acceptance. In time of war, or whenever the President directed, there would be no such problem. All plans for covert operations would be coordinated at once with the Joint Chiefs of Staff. The responsibility would be theirs. By later amendment, operations in active theaters of war came under the theater commanders. They would receive their orders through the Joint Chiefs of Staff, unless it were otherwise directed by the President.[93]

The Operations Advisory Committee, clearly delineated in NSC 10-1 to furnish "authoritative policy guidance," was not included in NSC 10-2. Instead, there was the less explicit statement that the Director of Central Intelligence should be responsible for "ensuring, through designated representatives of the Secretary of State and of the Secretary of Defense," that covert operations were planned and conducted consistently with the foreign policy of the United States, military policy, and overt activities. Disagreements were to be referred to the National Security Council.[94]

From his point of view, Admiral Souers obtained the "panel of guidance" which he had been advocating, although the phrase "policy guidance" did not appear in NSC 10-2. The Director of Central Intelligence, he maintained, was to be responsible for planning and conducting covert operations. The representatives of the Secretaries of State and Defense would be monitors; but, in case of disagreement, the Director would have as much right as they to take the matter before their superiors in the

National Security Council. Moreover, the chief of the new office must be acceptable to the Director and report directly to him. For purposes of security and flexibility in operations, the office would function independently within the Agency "to the maximum extent consistent with efficiency." But this did not mean independence of the Director. It would be the Director who decided when the maximum had been reached. The provision was there to ensure that the office would not be hampered by other components of the Agency. The special position thus accorded, however, did leave room for "continued bickering and argument," as Hillenkoetter said, over financial arrangements, accounting, and administrative control.[95]

Admiral Souers discounted the fact that the Director of Central Intelligence had full obligation but incomplete powers. He minimized the possibility that the Director's opponents might take advantage of the fact. If they tried to do so, it would be incumbent upon the Director not to give in for the sake of peace. He should stand his ground and fight for his rights. Once he had obtained "guidance," he was to be in command of the covert operations, subject only to the final authority of the National Security Council and the President. Souers expected the power of the Dirctor to develop in time, with strong leadership in the Agency and vigorous presentation before the Council.[96]

To Admiral Hillenkoetter, this interpretation of NSC 10-2 was not realistic. The representatives of the Secretaries of State and Defense were a board of strategy which not only could advise but could direct the Director of Central Intelligence. In theory, he might choose to reject their instructions and go to the Council for support. In practice, if he did, he would appear before a body of authority in which his opponents' superiors were the most influential members, excepting the President himself. The occasions would be rare when the President disregarded the views of the Secretaries of State and Defense to favor those presented by the Director of Central Intelligence.

Hillenkoetter believed that NSC 10-2 made a bad situation worse. He was responsible under NSC 4-A for operations which he did not want the Agency to conduct. But he had full authority then, so long as he kept in close touch with the Department of State. His was the responsibility to the Council. He had full control over his subordinates in a chain of command. He could direct them as he saw fit. Now under NSC 10-2 he could not choose his own chief of operations; he could merely accept someone offered to him by the Department of State. And it soon proved that the Department did not wish him to retain the man whom he already had in charge of covert operations. Cassady had to go. Hillenkoetter was obliged to accept the nominee of the chief planning officer in the State Department. It amounted to that, for all practical purposes. The Department had a veto far stronger than the Director's power of refusal.[97]

In Hillenkoetter's opinion, the Department of State and the National Military Establishment insisted upon placing OPC in the Agency because neither wanted the other to have it. Both sought the cover of the Agency for it because neither wanted the responsibility. If it failed, they could disown it. Besides, the Agency was popular with Congress at the moment and could obtain funds more easily than the State Department. And yet both Department and Establishment wanted to control. The Department had the lead, but the Establishment was not far behind. The Joint Chiefs of Staff would take charge in time of war. Meanwhile, as the Department and the Establishment kept an eye on each other, they made certain that the Agency should not be free to run its own affairs. The Office conducting covert operations was to be as independent of the Director as they could make it. Hillenkoetter felt himself caught in the summer of 1948 between the Department of State and the armed services in their habitual struggle for power.[98]

There is another conjecture regarding the motives of the Department of State, although the evidence is incomplete. It is possible that there was more anxiety, for the moment, over the activity of the Special Procedures Group under Cassady than desire to defeat the armed services. Cassady was expanding operations in the manner of Donovan. [ten lines deleted] Members of the State Department may well have concluded under these circumstances that the Department should nominate and control the head of the new Office of Special Projects, or Policy Coordination, in the Agency. After all, psychological operations and political activity were much the same; they could be damaging to "national policy." Perhaps they were, as Kennan had feared in his talk with Dulles on April 30. Cassady was conducting his political warfare independently.[99]

In any event, Admiral Hillenkoetter knew by June 10, as the revision of his plan went to the consultants of the Council, that he was not to write the directives for the new Office of Special Projects, nor to have the kind of Operations Advisory Board he desired, nor even to choose his own chief of operations. He advised Cassady on that day to finish with the commitments which were irrevocable and to undertake nothing new. [two lines deleted] Commander Williams in charge of the operation [one or two words deleted] stood by waiting orders and losing the advantage [one or two words deleted]. More than a month passed before Cassady was able to learn how NSC 10-2 of June 18 was to be administered.[100]

Meanwhile, Drew Pearson heard that there was a plan to reach the people of Russia with literature dropped [one or two words deleted] and appropriated the idea, and of course exposed the project to the public and to the Russian police—if they had not already discovered it. This may have added cause for the State Department to withdraw support and then to reject the plan altogether. It was liquidated during the first days of August as Cassady prepared to leave the Special Procedures Group after another trip to Europe and Frank G. Wisner got ready to come over from the Department of State and take charge under the mandates of NSC 10-2.[101]

The research and experimentation for the project, however, were not lost to the Agency. They were put to use later, when the State Department no longer opposed the idea of [several words deleted]. The radio equipment [one or two words deleted] too, after months of idleness, came into use by Radio Free Europe.[102]

The Department of State and the National Military Establishment were slow to reach agreement upon the man who should head the new office in the Agency under Hillenkoetter. It was not until August 6 that Wisner sat in a meeting at Souers's office to discuss the "method of operation and general 'modus vivendi'." Those present besides Souers, Hillenkoetter, and Wisner were Kennan, who was certain to be the first representative of the State Department under NSC 10-2; Colonel J. D. Yeaton, selected by Forrestal to represent both the Military Establishment and the Joint Chiefs of Staff; and Robert Blum, from Forrestal's staff. Let us again note that Blum was busy at this time with the survey of the Agency which produced the Dulles Report.[103]

The meeting was so important to Wisner that he prepared a "memorandum of conversation and understanding" from the notes taken by himself, Yeaton, and Blum. As initialled by those present for deposit in the file of the National Security Council, the memorandum stated that it comprised "an accurate record of the conversation" and their views of "the manner in which the activity shall operate." Wisner was set for eventualities. As Hillenkoetter recalled in 1952, he was too, but not for all of the events which came out of the summer of 1948.[104]

The "memorandum of conversation and understanding" reveals that Kennan took charge of the meeting. He opened with the declaration that political warfare was an instrument of foreign policy. It was therefore the particular concern of the Department of State and the National Military Establishment. Certain attributes placed it in the Central Intelligence Agency; but its "policy direction and guidance" properly belonged to the Department and the Establishment, and so the chief of the Office of Special Projects must have "fullest and freest access" to their representatives. He himself would want "specific knowledge of the objectives of every operation and also the procedures and methods employed in all cases" where political decisions were involved.

Souers "indicated his agreement" with Kennan's thesis and "stated specifically" that it was the intention of the Council to have the Department and the Establishment "responsible" for the "conduct of the activities" of the Office of Special Projects. The State Department should have "preeminence," he said, in time of peace; the Establishment would succeed to the "preeminent position in wartime."

Hillenkoetter must have recalled, as he listened to this exchange of views and expression of purposes, that he had been assured of command and the right to determine how he should conduct operations once he had been told what his superiors wished to have done. It was now his turn to comment. He remarked that the new office would be given "scope and flexibility" within the Agency, just as the old Office of Special Operations was afforded a large measure of "freedom and autonomy." He accepted Kennan's statement regarding political warfare and the necessity of its "guidance" by the State Department. But he "insisted that it was essential for the State Department to accept the political responsibility" of providing that guidance in specific cases. This, he said, the Department had not always done in times past. Kennan agreed that it should do so and stated that he himself would be "accountable."[105]

Wisner enlarged upon Kennan's first declaration. It would be necessary for the head of the Office of Special Projects, he said, to have "continuing and direct access" to the Department and the Military Establishment "without having to proceed through the CIA administrative hierarchy in each case." Hillenkoetter "agreed to this point." But he also said that "it would be necessary that he be kept informed in regard to all important projects and decisions." According to the memorandum, "Mr. Wisner concurred."

It is well that we should pause here, not to speculate upon inflections in the voice of an incoming subordinate, but to examine the statement of his superior. By NSC 10-2 the Director of Central Intelligence, not the head of the new office in the Agency, was responsible for "ensuring" that covert operations were planned and conducted in a manner consistent with foreign and military policy and with overt activities. The head of the office was to "report directly" to him. Representatives of the State Department and the Military Establishment were to participate with the Director. Their differences would be referred to the Council. The Council might overrule the Director. But it does not appear that the Council intended to give the head of the new office any discretion in reporting. In the light of subsequent events, it would have been more advantageous for the Director of Central Intelligence if Hillenkoetter had not allowed the word "important" to remain in the "memorandum of conversation and understanding" with regard to "projects and decisions."[106]

Blum asked what would become of Mr. Raymond Murphy, whose work for the State Department had attracted the attention of Cassady. Kennan said that he thought Murphy might come under the chief of the new office. Hillenkoetter doubted that it would be "desirable," but was willing to leave the matter to the head of the office. Blum then raised the question of foreign nationality groups in the United States and the difficulties of dealing with them for operations overseas. He thought that the difficulties had been due to restrictions by the FBI. Hillenkoetter did not think they had been too difficult. Kennan proposed a public "American Freedom Committee" to work with foreign nationality groups. Suggestions of that nature had already been made.

When the opportunity came again for Wisner to speak, he said that the new head would require "broad latitude" in selecting his "methods of operations." He might use large numbers of Americans overseas; he might prefer to work through foreign groups. He should not be committed to "any existing methods." Hillenkoetter assented. Wisner further suggested that he would need assistance from other departments and agencies. Hillenkoetter replied that there was a "general spirit of cooperation." All seem to have agreed that Kennan and Yeaton should be responsible for soliciting such help and that major troubles regarding it should be referred to the Council. Then "Mr. Wisner stated to Admiral Hillenkoetter that there were a number of internal organizational matters concerning which he felt there should be some discussion and clarification. . . ." But those, he said, could be "more appropriately" discussed between themselves. The conference closed upon agreement that there should be a memorandum circulated for "concurrence."

When Robert Blum was asked in 1953 if there were need to have this conference and signed "memorandum of conversation and understanding" because there were ambiguities in the directive of the National Security Council, his answer was yes. The ambiguities, he said, had been deliberately placed in NSC 10-2 to cover the determination of the Department of State to guide and control the new Office of Special Projects in the Central Intelligence Agency. It was natural that the Assistant Director, who was coming from the State Department and who knew that he was "answerable" to the Department, should wish to have the arrangement clear before he took charge. There should be an understanding, and in writing preferably, if he were to receive his orders from one superior and report to another. Blum saw a difference between the regulations in the Act of Congress concerning the intelligence functions of the Agency and the provision with regard to "other functions and duties" which the Council should assign to the Agency. He did not make the distinction, he said, as a point of law. There ought to be, therefore there was a difference.

The Council should have powers to put the Director of Central Intelligence under restrictions with regard to psychological warfare and related subversive practices.[107]

The Office of Policy Coordination came into operation by general order on September 1, 1948. Wisner held his first meeting with his staff of assistants on September 8. Among them was J. E. Baker, who had been left in charge of the Special Projects Group after the departure of Cassady. Cassady's deputy, R. E. Dulin, who had gone to Europe at the beginning of August, was not included with Wisner's assistants. M. K. Ruddock, recently in the Office of Reports and Estimates, became Acting Deputy Assistant Director. As Wisner was free, according to the "understanding" of August 6, to depart from existing "methods of operations," no further stress was put upon developing the assets and activities of the Special Projects Group abroad [several words deleted].[108]

The new office launched instead upon planning for expansion into the future. The first organizational chart, dated September 17, 1948, divided the functional activities of the office into major groupings to conform with the terms of NSC 10-2: psychological warfare by press, radio, and other devices; political warfare [two lines deleted]; economic warfare including monetary and fiscal operations; preventive direct action such as the support of guerrillas, sabotage, and related subversive practices; front organizations and war plans. There were elaborations in more detail by the time of the third staff meeting on October 19, but as yet the problem of geographical division and operation had not been attacked. The determination of budgets for ensuing years was accordingly hard.[109]

By another general order, dated September 14, 1948, Hillenkoetter drew the budgeting and accounting of the new Office of Policy Coordination closely under his central administration. He also removed the Special Funds Division which had been placed in the Office of Special Operations during July 1947. The Eberstadt Committee, whose findings are to be examined in the next chapter, recommended the reduction of "overhead." The Bureau of the Budget required the elimination of administrative duplication. But, apart from these justifications, Hillenkoetter was within his right according to the instructions of the Council in NSC 10-2. The Office of Policy Coordination was to operate "independently of other components" of the Agency, for security and "flexibility of operations." OPC was to do so to the "maximum degree consistent with efficiency." But it was the Director of Central Intelligence who was to make that decision. Hillenkoetter's judgment was that his responsibility to Congress for the use of vouchered and unvouchered funds made it incumbent upon him to maintain central control over the financing of those operations.[110]

The general order established a Budget Office under the Executive for

Administration. Within that office were set two branches, one for overt, the other for covert budgeting and expenditure. Where practical the administrative elements for support of the covert activities of both OSO and OPC would be physically near the operating offices. From Wisner's point of view, the general order deprived the offices of their control over the resources necessary for their operations. He made it a matter of formal representation to Hillenkoetter.[111]

The centralized control which Hillenkoetter thus had placed over all clandestine activities of the Agency, both secret intelligence and covert operations, black propaganda, and related subversive practices, caused discussion in the Eberstadt Committee for the Hoover Commission and in the Dulles Survey Group for the National Security Council. Both of them were now coming to the end of their surveys and were preparing their reports.[112]

With this centralization of control over budgeting and finance, there was a movement to join the Offices of Special Operations and the new Office of Special Projects, or Policy Coordination. It may prove interesting in the course of the investigations to discover why it was that many who opposed the centralization of financial control should advocate the "integration," perhaps better called the "reunion," of secret intelligence and covert operations under a single administration. One point will be clear from the start. The advocates of "integration" will not be found favoring revision of NSC 10-2 to the extent of restoring NSC 4-A and the directive of December 17, 1947, to Admiral Hillenkoetter.[113]

Introduction to Chapter VIII

In 1948 and 1949 two important investigations of national intelligence organizations were carried out. One, the Eberstadt Committee's report to the Hoover Commission on the Organization of the Executive Branch of the Government, was sponsored by the Congress. The other, the Dulles Report of the Intelligence Survey Group, was initiated by the National Security Council.

The Hoover Commission had been established by Congress to carry out a wide-ranging examination of the efficiency of the federal bureaucracy. The Commission in turn appointed a task force chaired by Ferdinand Eberstadt to examine the intelligence community. As noted earlier, Eberstadt had previously directed a study of the system of national defense and security in 1945 for James Forrestal that was influential in the establishment of the post of Director of Central Intelligence and the structure of the postwar intelligence community.

Congress held hearings of the Eberstadt Committee from June through September 1948. The fundamental issues the Committee examined included the tenure of the DCI; whether the DCI should be a civilian or military officer; the effectiveness of scientific intelligence collection; duplication by various departments; the management of covert operations in wartime; CIA relations with the FBI and JCS; and the role and effectiveness of the Intelligence Advisory Committee.

The Eberstadt Committee began with the assumption that the CIA should be the central evaluator and coordinator of intelligence, reflecting the views of its Congressional sponsors. As one might expect, most of the Commission's conclusions were consistent with this view. After investigating the administration of covert operations and clandestine intelligence, the Eberstadt Report supported integration of all clandestine operations in the CIA under the NSC's supervision. In wartime the operational services would be transferred to the JCS. It also favored a civilian DCI with a long term in office. It emphasized the importance of developing an intelligence corps to develop and keep trained personnel, as well as the need for other agencies—that is, the departmental intelligence services, the State Department, the FBI—to cooperate with the CIA in order for it to fulfill its mission.

The main criticisms the Eberstadt Report directed toward the intelligence community concerned the estimates system. The task force believed the existing system failed to respond to policymakers' needs and lacked access to all relevant information. The Commission did not see

any need to form an Intelligence Advisory Committee to approve estimates (this would have run contrary to the views of Congress, which
wanted a strong DCI); the members of the Commission did, however,
believe that a separate Intelligence Evaluation Board concentrating exclusively on comprehensive, forward-looking estimates would improve
the quality of support that the intelligence community provided to its
customers. The Report also recommended minor internal reorganization of the CIA, such as raising the Scientific Branch to the level of an
Office under an Assistant Director.

The Eberstadt Report concluded that the general framework of the
intelligence system was good, but all departments and agencies had to
improve their efforts to make the system more effective. It recommended making the suggested changes immediately and then freeing
the Agency from scrutiny for a two-year period. This suggestion went
unheard as the NSC and the Secretaries found support for their criticisms of the CIA in the Dulles Report.

The Intelligence Survey Group proved much less friendly to the
newly created intelligence community. Unlike the Eberstadt task force,
the Group was a creature of the Executive Branch, where opponents of
the CIA and the notion of centralized intelligence remained and sought
to press their case.

The Group was chartered by the National Security Council to study
and assess the changes in the U.S. intelligence system following the
reorganizations since the end of the war and the passage of the National Security Act. It was originally directed to assess the departmental intelligence services as well as the CIA and the operation of the
national intelligence community. However, the services declined to cooperate with the investigation and, in any case, the members of the
Group were by inclination more concerned with national intelligence.
As a result, it focussed almost exclusively on the internal management
of the CIA. According to Darling, the Dulles Report (often referred to
as the "Dulles–Jackson–Correa Report") was closely linked to the efforts by the State Department to have covert operations put under its
guidance.

The Intelligence Survey Group was officially established by the National Security Council on January 8, 1948. The Group consisted of
Allen Dulles as Chairman, Matthias Correa, and William Jackson. They
were assisted by Robert Blum, an assistant to Defense Secretary James
Forrestal, who acted as Executive Secretary. Dulles concentrated on
intelligence collection, Jackson on evaluation and correlation (that is,
Reports and Estimates, ICAPS, departmental services), and Correa on
dissemination, administration, and management. The DCI and his ad-

visers were to be assessed last; Blum was especially interested in evaluating the competence of the top staff.

The conclusions of the Group were presented to the NSC in January 1949. The Dulles Report criticized the departmental intelligence services for a lack of cooperation but, more pointedly, charged the top officials of the CIA with a lack of leadership. This criticism led to the departures of Galloway, the head of the Office of Special Operations, and Wright, the DDCI, in December 1948 and May 1949 respectively. Dulles was suggested as a replacement for Galloway by Forrestal in a newly enlarged Office of Special Operations combining secret intelligence, covert operations, and subversive activities. Wright's position as Deputy Director remained vacant for the remainder of Hillenkoetter's tenure.

One key criticism illustrated the difficult position in which Darling believed the Report put Hillenkoetter. The Dulles Report strongly criticized the production of national estimates and intelligence coordination. The report asserted a minimum standard for national estimates: such estimates needed to incorporate all available data, needed to have a coherent point of view provided by the DCI, and needed to have the support of all top U.S. intelligence officials. However, as Darling pointed out, to meet this standard the DCI needed the cooperation of the department intelligence services, and, despite the executive orders and legislation establishing the authority of the DCI, this cooperation had not been forthcoming. Quite the contrary, the departmental services had tried at every turn to stymie the DCI.

The CIA was allowed to respond to the Dulles Report. Hillenkoetter had ready answers for many of the specific criticisms in the Report. For example, to the charge that the CIA was overadministered, Hillenkoetter argued that personnel, support, and budget matters in a clandestine organization needed to be centralized in order to monitor operations and prevent improper activities. The Dulles Report claimed that CIA personnel turnover was too high; Hillenkoetter quoted statistics showing it was lower than in most government agencies. The Dulles Report charged that the CIA had too many military personnel; Hillenhoetter showed that fewer than two percent of the Agency's personnel were in uniform. Still, the overall thrust of the Report was difficult to refute; after all, a number of intelligence failures had occurred and, blameless or not, the DCI was the official designated to be responsible.

According to Darling, the Dulles Report failed to recognize that the DCI lacked the independent authority needed to provide the leadership the Group claimed he failed to produce. Also, Darling implied a strong connection between the Report and the efforts of the State Department to place CIA's covert operations under the guidance of State and the military services. Darling plainly thought that the Report was unfair in this respect, and this was likely one reason why Dulles did not like Darling's study and possibly why Dulles limited its circulation.

VIII

INVESTIGATION, 1948–1949

THE SHADE OF SILENCE

 Criticisms which might have been aimed at the component parts of the national system of intelligence converged upon the Central Intelligence Agency. The departmental intelligence services were relatively unscathed. It was natural that the youngest organization in the system should suffer most under direct fire. The Agency did not have the entrenchments of the departmental services, and it was not yet able to lay an effective counterbarrage. Moreover, it was exposed to crossfire at the center of the system. No one of the older intelligence services wished to have it there; it might grow strong enough to dominate all of them. The Central Intelligence Group had been established as a "cooperative interdepartmental activity" largely because the Army and the Navy had joined forces to keep the Department of State from absorbing the permanent intelligence organization.[1]

The United States would have a truly national rather than a federal system of intelligence if the duty of the Agency to make recommendations for coordinating the intelligence activities of the departments were to become the power to coordinate those activities, the power to use coercion rather than wheedling. But as one observer of the present scheme of individual joined with collective responsibility has put it, any attempt to give such power to the Director of Central Intelligence would cause a "civil war." The armed services would not concede the right of the Director to inspect their activities and to require full information about their "operational intelligence" or the "capabilities and intentions" of this country. Although the observer did not say, one may suspect that military men would stop calling one another "Fancy Dans" and slug it out with the "civilians" in the Central Intelligence Agency.[2]

The Hoover Commission on Organization of the Executive Branch of the Government planned at first to utilize the information about the Central Intelligence Agency which the Intelligence Survey Group of the National Security Council should gather. To this end John F. Meck, Executive Secretary for Hoover, wrote to Admiral Hillenkoetter on April 16, 1948, asking that the pertinent materials be sent to Harvey Bundy and James G. Rogers, members of Hoover's committee on foreign affairs. Bundy had been personal counsel of Secretary Stimson in the War Department. Rogers had been in OSS during the war. The information would be known only to Hoover, Bundy, Rogers, and Meck. Thus, security would be maintained at the same time that the information aided the Hoover Commission in its investigation and report to Congress.[3]

By June, however, the plan of the Hoover Commission placed the affairs of the Central Intelligence Agency within the jurisdiction of the "task force" under Ferdinand Eberstadt, who was examining the whole national security organization. Thus, a broader view of the problems of intelligence might be obtained. Eberstadt had included central intelligence in his study of national security during 1945 when he recommended three "coordinate services," Army, Navy, and Air Force, under the Secretary of Defense. As he continued relationships with the Survey Group of the National Security Council and used some of its materials, Eberstadt would conduct separate hearings and accumulate other evidence on his own responsibility to the Hoover Commission established by Congress.[4]

The purpose of the Intelligence Survey Group was narrower from the start than that of the Eberstadt Committee. The National Security Council set up the Survey Group primarily to take stock within the central intelligence organization as its directives were revised and it was transformed into an independent agency by Act of Congress. The authorization of the Survey Group, however, was soon enlarged by the departments concerned in the action of the National Security Council; the Group might inquire into the work of the departmental intelligence services. There were reservations concerning operations abroad and communications; there was the usual statement about the security regulations peculiar to each service. But the intent was clear. The Survey Group, like the Eberstadt Committee, was supposed to have access to the departmental intelligence services as well as to the Central Intelligence Agency. Their shortcomings, quite as much as its errors and weaknesses, were pertinent to a study of the national system of intelligence.[5]

The focus nevertheless was upon the Central Intelligence Agency. Neither committee of investigation gave as much time and effort to scrutinizing the intelligence services of the departments. For varied reasons, one of which would appear to have been reluctance if not resistance on the part of the departmental authorities, the structure and the performance of their intelligence services received neither the inspection nor the criticism comparable to those given the Central Intelligence Agency. The result was a concentration upon its failures disproportionate to its deserts.

Both committees reached significant conclusions about central intelligence in the federal system. The Eberstadt Report must have had weight with some who read it, particularly those concerned with making the Agency effective. Ideas were applied from it whether or not those who used the ideas knew that they came from the Eberstadt Report. It seems not to have been read by many. It was almost immediately eclipsed by the report of the Intelligence Survey Group. Better known as the Dulles Report, this was honored with its companion, the McNarney Report or NSC 50, by many in the Agency as no less than messianic. Others persist in taking a different view.[6]

One explanation of the seeming futility of the Eberstadt Report is that it was a report to Congress upon which Congress took no action. It would be interesting to think about the changes which Congress might have made in the structure and the functions of the Central Intelligence Agency if the leaders in the House and Senate had taken up the polite, but explicit statements in the Eberstadt Report concerning the need for improvements in the departmental intelligence agencies, together with Representative Brown's assertion that Congress had not intended to give any department the right of censorship over the Central Intelligence Agency. But speculation upon what might have been is idle. Congress did not act on these suggestions. The so-called CIA Act of 1949 had little connection with the investigations of the Agency in 1948 or with the clamor over Bogotá.[7]

Without discarding altogether the explanation that the Eberstadt Report suffered eclipse because Congress ignored it, one may say that the Dulles Report attracted and held more attention because of its origin and the determination of the investigators to look into the fitness of the "principal personnel" in the Agency. Such a purpose is implicit in any investigation of an institution of government. But in the case of the Survey Group and the Agency, if the intention was secondary at the beginning, it quickly became prime. Moreover, the survey by Dulles and his associates was closely related to the plan before the National Security Council to place the covert operations of the Agency under the guidance of the State Department with the aid of the National Military Establishment.[8]

The Eberstadt Report went to Congress where influential men thought well of the Central Intelligence Agency—some of them far better of it in fact, when they came to appropriations, than of the Department of State. In such a comparison, it has been said, Admiral Hillenkoetter enjoyed downright popularity. The Dulles Survey Group reported to the National Security Council where sat representatives of the State Department, the Army, and the Navy, long since provoked by the efforts of both Vanderberg and Hillenkoetter to act as Directors of Central Intelligence with only the advice, and not the consent, of the departmental chiefs of intelligence in the Intelligence Advisory Council. The Dulles Report afforded men who were vexed with Hillenkoetter, for one reason or another, an opportunity and incentive to put their annoyance into action.[9]

EBERSTADT'S FINDINGS

The hearings of the Eberstadt Committee opened with descriptions of the National Security Council and the Central Intelligence Agency by Souers and Hillenkoetter on June 8, 1948, and continued from time to time through the summer months into September when the Committee listened to statements from the administration and several offices in the Agency. Hillenkoetter himself appeared again to answer questions. These were for the most part the inquiries common to all discussions of central intelligence since the debates of 1945 and 1946 over the rival plans for a permanent organization.

The Eberstadt Committee wanted to know whether the Director should be a civilian and should remain long in office; how scientific intelligence might be more adequately obtained; if there were unnecessary duplications by the departmental intelligence services and the Agency, especially by the State Department and the Agency in respect to political intelligence; what should be done in time of war about secret intelligence, counterespionage, and other covert operations of the Agency; what should be its relation generally with the Joint Chiefs of Staff; whether the Intelligence Advisory Committee was fulfilling its purpose; and if associations were happy between the Agency and the FBI.[10]

Matters of major interest in the Eberstadt Report built upon these inquiries. It placed the Central Intelligence Agency at the "apex of a pyramidal intelligence structure." This was certainly not where many in the departmental intelligence services were placing it. But, although the Report called them "important," it declared that neither they nor CIA could operate independently "with success"; they were all "interdependent." The Agency must necessarily be at the center both as a "coordinator" and as an "evaluator" to work with the service agencies and others outside the National Military Establishment. It could not be dominated by any one department; it must accomplish the allocation of responsibility for collection and research among the Government's agencies and meet its own responsibility for central evaluation "free from departmental prejudice, control or bias, whether real or imagined." The Agency then should properly be centered, as it was, under the direction of the National Security Council representing all of the departments.[11]

The administration of the Agency should remain the personal responsibility of the Director of Central Intelligence. He could be held accountable by the Security Council. The Eberstadt Committee disagreed with General Donovan; there was no practical gain in having the Director pass by the Secretaries in the Council and report directly to the President. Apart from burdening the President himself with one more obligation, it did not seem likely to the Committee that the Director's effectiveness as a "coordinator" or "evaluator" would be increased by putting him "on a White House level." His estimates would receive no more attention from the departments. His attempts to coordinate and allocate responsibilities would fare no better.

The Eberstadt Committee recognized the crux of the whole matter. "Efforts to impose directives concerning the internal workings of a department upon officials of the level of the Secretary of State or Secretary of Defense," it said, "are not likely to meet with success." The Director of Central Intelligence would have "initially at least" to exercise the coordinating function of the Agency upon "a more or less negotiated basis." In short, he might do the negotiating; he could not do the coordination. That had to be accomplished by the Secretaries in the Council. Ultimate responsibility lay with them, subject to the will of the President. Congress had made the Council a body of collective authority over the Agency, such as the National Intelligence Authority had been over the Director and the Group by order of the President.[12]

The Secretaries should accept that collective authority as binding upon their respective departments. They should cooperate in carrying out any recommendation of the Director of Central Intelligence which they themselves as the Council approved, even though their departments individually might not like it. Until the Secretaries did so, there was no honesty in asserting that the Central Agency ought to coordinate the intelligence activities of the departmental agencies. In the absence of authorization by the Council, the Agency could not coordinate those activities, nor determine "priorities." It was not proper to indict the Director of Central Intelligence because he failed to submit ideas wh. departmental chiefs of intelligence would accept; they had nothing . their consciences more compelling than academic interest. There were negative forces at work in abundance to safeguard particular and propri- etary interests. The departmental chiefs had a right to expect that their superiors in the Council would make the decisions in the "chain of command." It is, though, a fair query whether they understood at that time such collective responsibility.[13]

Coordination without recourse to command is hard to obtain at any level. The recent maneuver of the Joint Chiefs of Staff to pass their differences on to the Secretary of Defense or, if necessary, to the Presi- dent for settlement has given as clear a demonstration as could be asked to show the failure of concerted action where one might expect it most easy to obtain. The Chiefs of Staff at the top of the military structure, it would seem, should be most sensitive to the national need, in time of war or peace, as well as informed concerning the requirements of their respec- tive branches of the military establishment. If they cannot settle their differences in the national interest, one is led to wonder who can. It is an argument for individual responsibility and "chain of command."[14]

The Eberstadt Report did not indict Hillenkoetter or the Agency. The Committee commented instead upon the institutions and methods by which the Agency was articulated with the several departmental intelli- gence services. There was first and most important the Intelligence Advi- sory Committee which, the Report said, had been established originally as a sort of "forum" to deal with problems arising as the Agency discharged its duties in coordinating the intelligence activities of the departments. This interpretation did not tally with the concept of Admiral Inglis and others in regard to the original Intelligence Advisory Board. It was to them a body with the right to know in advance the agenda of the National Intelligence Authority and to pass upon *all* recommendations from the Director to the Authority. Nor did the Eberstadt Committee support Inglis and his allies in the argument that the new Intelligence Advisory Commit- tee should function as a governing board in the Agency when in- terdepartmental concerns were involved. It was only with respect to par- ticipation in considering "substantive intelligence" that the Eberstadt Committee recommended that the Intelligence Advisory Committee should meet more frequently.[15]

The Director's Interdepartmental Coordinating and Planning Staff, ICAPS, and the Standing Committee of the Intelligence Advisory Commit- tee received attention for their work upon procedural matters and their effort to maintain connections between the Agency and the departments. But the Eberstadt Report did not go into their origins nor examine causes of their failure to develop as interlocking committees in which issues might be explored and measures drafted, conflicting views reconciled or abandoned, coordination practiced at the so-called working level. One senses that the Eberstadt Committee appreciated the relative futility of the effort at this level if the men in authority above it were not prepared to take concerted action.[16]

It is true that there have been accomplishments in government thanks to the dynamism of obstruction and delay. Ingenious suggestions have broken from deadlock to pass the lethargic, the unwary, and the uncomprehending along the best diagonal that could be found between vested interests and contending forces. But the process, however irresistible in time, is a slow one. The thought of Pearl Harbor ought to condemn it, when the national need is great.[17]

The Eberstadt Report took note of the many ad hoc committees, the liaison sections in the Office of Collection and Dissemination of the Agency, the associations developing between regional branches of the Office of Reports and Estimates and their "opposite numbers" in the State Department, the Army, the Navy, and Air Force; the arrangements between the Agency and the FBI for sharing foreign intelligence useful to each; the individuals such as the Chief of the Map Section, who held office in the State Department also, and the economists and scientists under consideration for similar posts. But all of these devices for interrelation were too isolated or sporadic or otherwise limited to provide anything but hope for the future. They might grow in use until the habit of cooperation reduced the task of coordinating departmental and central activities in one system of national intelligence.[18]

Hillenkoetter had assured Eberstadt that relations between the Agency and the FBI now were "close" and were not "strained" as they had been. But Eberstadt and his associates did not think that the arrangements were adequate between the two institutions, both so much concerned with the nation's security. Eberstadt had invited J. Edgar Hoover to discuss matters with the Committee. Hoover declined on the ground that he knew too little of the Agency's activities.[19]

The modesty of the statement could not have been deceiving. The public row over the replacement of the FBI in Latin America by the CIA had not subsided. Dewey had been making the affair an issue in his campaign for the presidency. The head of the Federal Bureau of Investigation, or his representative, had sat in the Intelligence Advisory Board during the formative days of the Central Intelligence Group under Souers. There was a movement to restore the representation in the Intelligence Advisory Committee. Moreover, Hoover had been consulted and informed during the summer and fall of 1946 when Vandenberg established the Office of Operations to collect overt intelligence in this country from businesses, travellers, and others with connections abroad. Mr. Hoover may have been unfamiliar with the Agency's correlation and evaluation of intelligence to produce national estimates. He was not so ill-informed about its endeavors in collecting intelligence and coordinating departmental activities that he could make no contribution in the Eberstadt Report to Congress. If Eberstadt obtained insufficient evidence on the difficulties between the FBI and CIA, the Director of Central Intelligence was not solely to blame.[20]

Following the theme of counterespionage for security at home and intelligence abroad, the Eberstadt Committee considered the possibility of placing the whole operation in the hands of the Director of Central Intelligence. But the Committee did so only to reject the idea in the Report. It would really give basis for the charge that an American Gestapo was taking shape. It would eliminate the FBI, an established organization and tradition, and would burden another organization, the CIA, which was not equipped for the assignment. Admiral Hillenkoetter, already saddled with covert operations under "guidance," must have been pleased, and possibly amused, when he read the pronouncement in the Eberstadt Report that such a "transfer of responsibility" would create more "problems" than it would solve.[21]

Hillenkoetter could not have been too displeased, either, with the plan of the Eberstadt Committee for clandestine operations, although he himself preferred to have sabotage, physical subversion, and similar paramilitary operations conducted elsewhere; and he would not have liked to see the collection of intelligence removed with them from the Agency. The Eberstadt Report declared that all clandestine operations should be "treated together as a single unit." It rejected the British precedent for placing those activities under the Secretary of State. William H. Jackson's ideas of 1945 regarding secret intelligence, redistributed during the past summer, did not appeal to the Eberstadt Committee. Nor did it wish those activities placed under the Secretary of Defense as Donovan preferred. The arguments for using the Secretaries were "mutually exclusive." Their departments in the executive branch of the Government were too much at odds with one another. The operations should remain in the Central Intelligence Agency under the direction of the National Security Council where both the State Department and the Military Establishment were represented. There the Secretaries might be brought to agreement in the presence and under the pressure of other officers.[22]

If war came, the "operational services," including both open and covert collection of information, might be transferred to the Joint Chiefs of Staff in the "wartime chain of command." For that event, all of the operations should be grouped under a Deputy Director who should have "considerable, though not unlimited independence." In time of peace the Deputy would be responsible to the Director of Central Intelligence. In time of war the Deputy might report, if necessary, directly to the Joint Chiefs of Staff.[23]

There was notable similarity between this plan and Hillenkoetter's suggestion to Secretaries Lovett and Forrestal on May 29 in the presence of General Gruenther. Eberstadt's anticipation of recent mergers in the covert offices of the Agency under a Deputy Director (Plans) is striking.[24]

The Eberstadt Committee appreciated that the Agency and the Joint Chiefs of Staff should work together quite as closely in evaluating as in collecting intelligence or in clandestine operations. The Agency, said the Report, was intended to be "the major source of coordinated and evaluated intelligence" for the construction of national policy. It was "the logical arbiter of differences" between the services on the evaluation of intelligence. Assumptions by the Chiefs of Staff "both for planning and operational purposes" should be formulated with the participation of the Agency; at least, those assumptions should be reviewed by it. But so far the Agency had fallen short of this objective. It did not "enjoy the full confidence" of the national security organization, nor of other agencies which it served. With certain "encouraging exceptions," the Agency had not yet played "an important role in the determinations of the National Security Council."[25]

Eberstadt and his associates may not have heard of the efforts which both General Vandenberg and Admiral Hillenkoetter had been making in the past two years to keep the place of the Office of Strategic Services for the Central Intelligence Group in the Joint Intelligence Committee of the Joint Chiefs of Staff. If the Eberstadt Committee knew of the efforts, it did not choose to blame anyone for their failure. The Report merely took the side of the Agency on the issue and declared that "consideration" should be given to including the Director of Central Intelligence in the membership of the Joint Intelligence Committee. The Intelligence Advisory Committee should meet more frequently to discuss questions of "substantive intelligence." Eberstadt and his associates understood that the membership of the two bodies was nearly identical. There ought thus to be "an interchange of intelligence opinion between the principal intelligence officers of the Government." This in itself would "ensure a closer relationship" between the Agency and the Joint Intelligence Committee of the Joint Chiefs of Staff.[26]

To accomplish its purpose, the Agency must solve its major problem which, like that of most agencies, was one of personnel. There had been too rapid expansion under Vandenberg with consequent mistakes in procurement. Time, experience, and training were necessary. But these were matters of internal administration, not of external direction. Good intelligence, said the Eberstadt Report emphasizing a "truism," depends upon good personnel; the supervision must be "imaginative and vigorous." The Committee was convinced that the Director must have continuity in office; he must be selected primarily for competence. "Other things being equal," a civilian was to be preferred.[27]

The Eberstadt Report declared that the Director of Central Intelligence should be a civilian because the position required "a broader background and greater versatility and diplomatic experience than is usually found in service personnel." The point was reinforced with the statement that the "best qualified and most competent officers" would not accept the position, if to do so meant permanent retirement and the "end of the road to important command or operational responsibility." The Eberstadt Committee discounted perhaps too much the practical argument that a military man would command more confidence from the armed services, against whose resistance the Agency could hardly expect to succeed regardless of the brilliance of its leadership or the skill of its personnel.[28]

The argument is to be discounted as readily that relations with the State Department would benefit if the Director were a civilian "known and respected by the Secretary of State and his assistants." By the same line of reasoning, so would the relations profit if a military man had that respect. Although the tradition of the State Department is civilian, it requires too much credulity to suppose that Secretaries of State react without thought against military men. There were warriors before General Marshall among ranking officers in the Department. The Eberstadt Report gave only passing attention to the point.[29]

The principal argument against the choice of a civilian as Director of Central Intelligence, said the Report, was the difficulty of getting a good one, with the requisite force of character, knowledge of history and politics, and acquaintance with military matters and the machinery of the Government. The pay was low in comparison with the remuneration of industry and the professions. The reward was anonymity. The Committee rejected the suggestion that the Director might succeed without experience if he were competent in administration. He must be familiar with the technique of intelligence. The result would be ideal if intelligence were treated as a profession in itself and the man at its head were its master.[30]

The departmental intelligence services also had their problems of mediocre personnel to solve. They had lost many of their skilled and experienced persons after the war. Selection and replacement had been haphazard, the product "often of inadequate caliber." The Report did not recommend the Army's method for improving the Counterintelligence Corps in Germany. Apparently the remedy had been to order "all CIC personnel to wear uniforms, live in barracks, and report for regular Army meals." Thus, they were "to keep in contact with the local population and to catch spies!"

More damaging to the system of national intelligence, though, was the practice of dropping into the intelligence services officers who were "not particularly wanted" elsewhere. Thus, "capable, experienced, and thoroughly devoted personnel," specialists in intelligence, had seen their organizations and system too often "ruined by superior officers with no experience, little capacity, and no imagination." Military misfits were to be found not solely in the Central Intelligence Agency, where many of its critics believed such persons were prevalent. The Eberstadt Report recommended that selection and training systems should be inaugurated. The services should provide "an intelligence corps—or at least an intelligence career."[31]

Turning to the cardinal matter of producing intelligence for the makers of national policy, the Eberstadt Committee declared that the intelligence services under the Joint Chiefs, the State Department, and even the Federal Bureau of Investigation "must do their proper share." The military services must "rid their intelligence estimates of subjective bias." Partly because of natural interest in their own affairs, partly because of competition for appropriations, the estimates of hostile potentialities varied with the services making them. In one case there were so many inconsistencies in a single paper of the Joint Intelligence Committee that its estimate was worthless for the planners. "Out of this mass of jumbled material," said the Eberstadt Report, "and harassed often by the open and covert opposition of the older agencies, CIA has tried to make sense. That it has not always succeeded has not been entirely the fault of CIA." We shall not find the opinion of the Dullas Survey Group coinciding wholly with this judgment.[32]

The estimates of the Agency were criticized in the Eberstadt Report on two principal grounds. They were not responsive to the requirements of the policymakers and received insufficient consideration by them. Related to this weakness, and in large measure accountable for it, was the fact that the estimates of the Agency were made without access to all relevant information. This was particularly true of plans, activities, and decisions in the military services, withheld for reasons of security because they were "operational in nature." The State Department also tended to rely upon its own "judgment and information" without consulting the Agency.

Criticism of the Agency's estimates, then, lost perforce some of its pertinence. If the Agency was to perform its function of evaluating and correlating intelligence "relating to the national security," the function of producing the national intelligence estimates, "it must be aware of, and participate in, the thinking" of the departmental intelligence services, the working committees of the Joint Chiefs of Staff, the State–Army–Navy–Air Force Coordinating Committee, and the National Security Council. Effective intelligence, said the Eberstadt Report, was possible only when it was "closely linked with planning and policymaking." In short, the Agency must be the central organization of the national intelligence system.[33]

Duplication to some degree was to be justified, particularly in political reporting. The Agency and the intelligence division in the State Department worked with different objectives and different priorities. But the Eberstadt Committee now recognized, as Donovan had insisted to Rosenman on September 4, 1945, that it was a mistake to split OSS after the war, assigning part of its functions to one department, the remainder to another. Creation of the Central Agency had largely remedied the mistake, but it lingered in the duplication of research and analysis by the State Department and the Agency in the economic and political field.[34]

The Report supported the Agency's need to engage in research and analysis. The feasibility of shifting a large part of the State Department's intelligence division to the Agency should be studied. If this move were found impractical or undesirable, unnecessary duplication might then be eliminated by "progressive coordination, interchange of personnel, and the allocation of specific responsibilities" to the several agencies under directives from the National Security Council. The Eberstadt Committee suggested that analysts from the Agency might be placed in the "message centers and secretariats" of the departments. They would sift out the "really important material" for routing to the Agency. This procedure would require fewer persons. Moreover, it would save time, a most important consideration in the production of coordinated national estimates.[35]

The Eberstadt Committee declared that the greatest need of the Agency was an Intelligence Evaluation Board. There should be a "small group of highly capable people, freed from administrative detail, to concentrate upon intelligence evaluation." As Hillenkoetter himself had testified on September 10, the Director and his assistants were obliged to give so much of their time to administration that they had little for analysis and evaluation. A small group of "mature men of the highest talents," with access to all information, "might well be released completely from routine and set to thinking about intelligence only." Colonel Truman Smith had proposed to both Eberstadt and Dulles such a board of three to five experts and had mildly criticized Admiral Hillenkoetter for not having one. It should be immediately under the Director, said Smith, with only advisory status.[36]

We have here again essentially the plan for the Estimates Branch of the

Central Reports Staff in the Central Intelligence Group. It is also the concept of the Intelligence Staff in the Office of Reports and Estimates, before reorganization in 1947 put the most experienced estimators to one side in the Global Survey Group and left the estimating to the several geographical branches in the Office. There is missing from the proposal of the Eberstadt Committee, however, any reference to selection of those experts from the department which should both supply the materials for evaluation and use the resulting coordinated national estimates.[37]

Sherman Kent was writing in his *Strategic Intelligence* at this time that "the single most important principle of successful intelligence" was the "closeness" of its producers to its consumers. There should be a "partnership of the departments." One may comment further that it would be good if the departments behaved like partners, if they shared their assets as well as their liabilities.[38]

Why this idea in the original plan of the Central Reports Staff of the Group should have been omitted from the Eberstadt Report is not clear. The Committee made no argument against representation of the departments on the Evaluation Board; it did not assert, on the other hand, that the institution should be exclusively staffed and maintained within the Agency. And yet the silence on this important matter does not seem inadvertent.

Conditions had changed since the days of the Group when the personnel in its branches had to be apportioned among the departments contributing to the "cooperative interdepartmental activity." But those conditions had not changed so much that the interest of the departments in correlating and evaluating intelligence to produce estimates could be overlooked. The Agency may have become the "logical arbiter" of departmental differences on evaluation, as the Eberstadt Report said, and thus may have attained a superior position. But another suggestion in the Report seems as revealing; the Intelligence Advisory Committee, representing the departments, should meet more frequently to discuss "substantive intelligence." This, perhaps, was a hint of things to come.[39]

Whatever the inner thoughts of the Eberstadt Committee, it did not state to Congress that the Evaluation Board of the Agency should correlate the intelligence of the departmental services with other information and produce the intelligence for "national policy and strategy" which had been the aim of Central Intelligence since Donovan formulated its first principles. There was no statement that the Agency should send its national intelligence to the policymakers through the Intelligence Advisory Committee as a sort of clearing house for the departments. It remained for the Dulles Survey Group to make these suggestions to the National

Security Council, preparing the way for the present Office of National Estimates and its National Estimates Board.[40]

The Eberstadt Committee recognized the difficulties of the State Department in providing [one word deleted] communications and other facilities for the personnel of the Agency abroad. The Department could be easily compromised by discovery, and yet the Agency had to rely upon the departments for the greater part of those indispensable services. It was the Dulles Group, however, which made the investigation and the interim report leading to better arrangements between the Department and the Agency.[41]

There were some changes needed in the internal structure of the Agency, said the Eberstadt Committee. For one, the Office of Collection and Dissemination, which was receiving a good deal of criticism for oversize, confusion of functions, and misdirection of efforts, "probably should become purely a reference service" including the map services which were then in the Office of Research and Estimates. The liaison functions of OCD might be split off to form a separate section for its business with other agencies. There could be some reduction of "administrative overhead" in general. There was evidence of administrative interference in matters of primarily operational concern, such as "budgetary controls." But the Eberstadt Committee recognized all of these affairs as internal problems which were the responsibility of the Director and his assistants.[42]

When it came to scientific intelligence, the Eberstadt Committee stressed what everyone was thinking from his own point of view. Existing arrangements for collecting and distributing information on both nuclear energy and general scientific matters were ineffective. Something had to be done.

The agreement which Vandenberg for the Central Intelligence Group had made in January 1947 with Bush of the Joint Research and Development Board, and Hillenkoetter had endeavored to fulfill, was not satisfactory. The failure was due in large part perhaps, as Bush said, to the fact that the clients of the Group lacked confidence in it. The Atomic Energy Commission had installed its own intelligence system after a study and report in July 1947 by Souers and had arranged in the spring of 1948 for an expert to appraise the "sources" of the Agency's information. But the relationship thus established with the Central Intelligence Agency had yet to please both parties. The Commission did not want to have the source of any information withheld from it; the Agency was obliged in some cases to protect foreign agencies [two lines deleted].[43]

The State Department's insistence upon controlling the collection of scientific and technical data from foreign experts delayed the adoption of

NSCID 10 and added to the confusion. The armed services were stubborn against releasing scientific intelligence which had any connection with bombs or other weapons. It was most "operational in nature." The issue was still unsettled in May 1953.[44]

Within the Agency the chief problem was to obtain scientists of the first order who could forego the rewards of their professions in pay and recognition to accept the moderate salary and the namelessness which employment in the Agency required. The political opinions of some had been considered too radical for clearance. And then there was the perplexing difficulty of including nuclear energy with general science in the same administrative unit, where they seemed properly to belong, without entangling matters of great secrecy which must be kept separate.[45]

The Eberstadt Report declared that failure to appraise scientific advances in hostile countries might have "more immediate and catastrophic consequences" than failure in any other field of intelligence. The Committee might have included friendly countries as well. Failure to keep in close touch with scientific discoveries everywhere could bring disaster. After Hiroshima those seeking aggrandizement, or security, were likely to strike first and explain later, if at all. What was needed, said the Eberstadt Report, was a "central authority responsible for assimilating all information concerning developments in the field of science abroad and competent to estimate the significance of these developments." This agency must have access to "all available information" bearing on the problem. It must be able to provide "intelligent direction" in collecting such information.

Responsibility for evaluating scientific intelligence included information about biological and chemical warfare, electronics, aerodynamics, guided missiles, and others. Medical intelligence was still nonexistent. At the moment the responsibility was spread among several agencies. They should be brought more closely in touch with each other. The Scientific Branch in the Agency was not in position, as constituted, either to evaluate intelligence or to stimulate its collection. There was too much "red tape" and subordination to administrative officials. The Branch should be raised to the level of an Office and placed under an Assistant Director. The Eberstadt Committee understood that Hillenkoetter was awaiting the recommendation of such a qualified person by Karl T. Compton, who had succeeded Vannevar Bush at the head of the Research and Development Board.[46]

At the close of its report on intelligence in the national security organization, the Eberstadt Committee commented upon two legislative proposals before Congress directly concerning the Central Intelligence Agency. One had to do with its funds and expenditures. The other was concerned with its security and prosecution of its violators.

The Committee took note that the budget of the Agency was a guarded secret. Amounts requested through the departments were reviewed by representatives of the Bureau of the Budget and controlled by appropriate committees of Congress in closed session. The Eberstadt Report might also have recorded that the funds, both vouchered and unvouchered, were administered under supervision by the Comptroller General and the General Accounting Office that was gratifying both for its appreciation of the Agency's extraordinary needs and for its care of the public's money. The bill before Congress would establish the procedures and authorities in law. The Eberstadt Report supported the measure as providing the "administrative flexibility and anonymity that are essential to satisfactory intelligence"; it warned merely that some of the provisions seemed to "involve undesirably broad grants of power" to the Agency. Congress should examine carefully and modify if necessary, but should act upon the measure as soon as possible. It had been under consideration by Congressional committees since 1947. It became law in the next session of Congress on June 20, 1949.[47]

The Agency, the Federal Bureau of Investigation, and other services had periodically suggested stronger legislation to protect them from espionage. The necessity of proving intent to injure the Government prevented the conviction of a person who otherwise might have been proved guilty of injuring it. Besides, there was need to safeguard the agencies against dangerous disclosures by indiscreet and irresponsible persons. How to accomplish these purposes without infringing upon civil liberties and traditional freedoms was part of the problem. The Eberstadt Committee recognized the desirability of better protection but did not think that it was to be obtained by legislation alone. The Federal Bureau of Investigation, the Counterintelligence Corps of the Army, the Agency: all should strengthen their own counterespionage. It was a "difficult art"; it had "not always been well protected in this country." But, the inference was clear, it could be.[48]

When this was written on April 15, 1953, Senator McCarthy had just sent a questionnaire to the Central Intelligence Agency, among others, for information regarding expenditures upon the press and radio. The press was reverberating, and so were halls in the Agency; McCarthy was about to "move in on the Agency." The conjecture of the Eberstadt Committee still seemed good. The art of counterespionage was difficult, and not "well practiced in this country." Nor had Congress passed remedial legislation.[49]

As it came to the end of its labor, the Eberstadt Committee was firm in the opinion that "there must be major improvement in all of our intelligence services." It could not be achieved overnight. There should be proper selection of personnel and a program for their training and assignment, particularly in the Army. The general framework of the national organization was good; pertinent agencies were aware of its assets and liabilities, its virtues and shortcomings. The National Security Council, which had properly concerned itself with the Central Intelligence Agency, should now give "more thought and attention" to its relations with other intelligence agencies. Working through the Secretaries of State and Defense, the Council should encourage the improvement of those services.[50]

The suggestions of the Committee which were accepted, and those of the Dulles Group too, should be put into effect promptly. When such action had been taken, the Central Intelligence Agency and other intelligence services in the Government ought then to be given a "period of internal development free from the disruption of continual examination and as free as possible from publicity." Congress might have another examination in two or three years by a "watchdog committee," or preferably a committee "akin to the Dulles group," to prevent stagnation. But what the Agency needed for a while was quiet. "Intelligence can best flourish," said the Eberstadt Report, "in the shade of silence."[51]

This is not what the Agency enjoyed in the next two years. The National Security Council did not concentrate upon encouraging improvement in the departmental intelligence services through the good offices of the Secretaries of State and Defense; nor did the Secretaries bend their particular efforts in that direction. They turned to the findings of the Dulles Survey and of its companion, the McNarney Report, against the Agency. The Director of Central Intelligence was not left to make changes according to the suggestions of the surveys in the light of his own experience and "the shade of silence."

THE INTELLIGENCE SURVEY

The atmosphere surrounding the Dulles Group differed from that of the Eberstadt Committee. The Dulles Report was made, issued, debated, and some of it adopted in the midst of prolonged tension between the Department of State and the Central Intelligence Agency. They quarreled over the operation and control of psychological warfare and other subversive activities, the failure of coordination in the field at Bogotá, the collection of scientific and technical intelligence, [several words deleted] even the internal organization and procedures of the Agency.[52]

Members of the military establishment were not averse to participating from time to time in the contest. Although they cared little for the State Department, they were seldom on the side of the Agency. It was an opportunity for every one in the Government who disliked the idea of a central intelligence organization. Its critics could revive their arguments, renew their alliances, and move to the attack. The question was far from settled in departmental minds whether the Intelligence Advisory Committee could merely advise the Director of Central Intelligence at his pleasure or had the right to supervise his work and withhold consent. There was the fact that the Agency was duplicating some of the efforts of the departmental services. They could always charge that its Office of Reports and Estimates was failing to produce the kind of "strategic and national policy intelligence" which was supposed to be the major purpose of the Central Intelligence Agency.[53]

Admiral Hillenkoetter shared in the origin of the Intelligence Survey. Others may have had the same thought. But the Director of Central Intelligence was among the first to suggest in the fall of 1947 to the new officer of the Government, the Secretary of Defense, by Act of Congress "principal assistant to the President in all matters relating to the national security," that they should take stock of the central intelligence system as it entered a new phase. Hillenkoetter had come to the organization when it was still a "cooperative interdepartmental activity" under the President's Directive. He was engaged in revising its orders and instructions, the NSCIDs, as it became an "independent agency" set by Congress under the authority of the National Security Council. In the transition from executive to statutory foundation, it was proper that there should be a thorough examination of the effort and experience during the past two years. There should be a searching for flaws, inadequate performances, misplacement of emphasis and energy. We should remember, too, that the Agency was about to undertake covert operations that would complicate its administration.[54]

Members of the National Security Council and its staff had more than a legal interest in the reappraisal of the intelligence system. Some observers expected Admiral Souers, Executive Secretary, to become virtually the director of the Council, because he was personal friend and adviser to the President on matters of intelligence and security. If Souers were to do so, he would assume direction of the Agency as well, on behalf of the Council. Hillenkoetter, to Souers's distress, appeared to think that this might happen. Souers made it plain at once that he had no intention of letting it happen. Hillenkoetter was the Director of Central Intelligence. He himself was an executive secretary, and no more, to the highest officers of the Government as they engaged in a new enterprise.[55]

The National Security Council was to be an extraordinary Cabinet in which the President's chief assistants discussed in common all phases of the national safety and sought to give him the best possible advice. For this purpose it was requisite that the intelligence system of the country should be closely placed under the direction of the Council. As he had been the first Director of Central Intelligence, Souers was particularly eager to have the Agency succeed in the new order. He brought to his assistance James S. Lay from a unique experience in central intelligence. Lay had been a member of the Joint Intelligence Staff under the Joint Chiefs during the war, then Secretary of the National Intelligence Authority, and more recently head of the projects division in the Office of Reports and Estimates of the Central Intelligence Group.[56]

The Secretary of Defense, too, entering upon an untried course as arbiter and coordinator among the Army, Navy, and Air Force, gathered but not unified in the National Military Establishment, was anxious to have the Central Intelligence Agency work effectively in the national security organization. Forrestal had shared with Patterson, Leahy, Souers, and others in the negotiations which brought the Central Intelligence Group out of the welter of conflicting purposes and rival plans. One of Forrestal's first actions as Secretary of Defense was to accept on October 10, 1947, Hillenkoetter's proposal for an advisory committee under the National Security Act. Forrestal admonished General Chamberlin and Admiral Inglis later in December that Hillenkoetter and not they, the Director of Central Intelligence and not the Intelligence Advisory Committee, was to run the Central Intelligence Agency.[57]

First ideas leading to the Intelligence Survey for the Council are best examined in the interchange of communications which occurred about the same time among Lay and two aides of Secretary Forrestal, John H. Ohly and Robert Blum. The NSCIDs were just coming from the Agency and the ad hoc committee of the departmental chiefs of intelligence. The plan was nearing completion in the Council to make the Director of Central Intelligence responsible for black propaganda and subversive action in the "cold war" against the Soviet Union.[58]

[two lines deleted] Blum's assignment now for the Secretary of Defense was the Central Intelligence Agency in relation to the National Security Council and certain aspects of clandestine intelligence overseas. He had been roused by Hanson Baldwin's article of October 18, 1947, "Where the United States is Weak," to suggest to Forrestal that there should be an investigation. Forrestal asked Blum to submit to Souers and Hillenkoetter the digest of Baldwin's article which Blum had made. This he had done on November 25.[59]

Lay sent a memorandum to Ohly, Special Assistant to Forrestal, on December 4, indicating that Hillenkoetter might prepare a report to the

Council. The attached list of possible subjects for treatment included the usual matters of organization and personnel, the many categories of intelligence—political, economic, scientific, military, and the like—plans for coordination with the departmental agencies, and coverage of the Soviet Union. Ohly referred the memorandum to Blum. He replied on the next day, adding to the list specific problems of collaboration with friendly governments, counterintelligence, duplication, conflicts within the Agency, and similar questions. But Blum felt that such a report would be more encyclopedic than critical. If the Agency were to report, he said, then the other intelligence services too should give an accounting. It would be better to obtain a "qualified independent group" to draft the questionnaire, appraise the several reports, and make the recommendations to the National Security Council.

Ohly made his contribution to the discussion on December 8. The interrogations, he wrote, would have two separate purposes. They would inform the President and Council. They would show the weaknesses in the Agency and the whole system. Ohly observed that the flow of information was insufficient back and forth between the Federal Bureau of Investigation and the Central Intelligence Agency. Within the Agency he saw three principal "sources of difficulty." There was no proper concept regarding the nature of intelligence to guide the collecting agencies; too much effort was "scattered over a large number of heterogeneous projects of minor significance." For another, organizational and personal jealousies were rife. For the third, Ohly pointed to the military personnel in "nearly all the key jobs in CIA." This personnel had no "special aptitude for or learning in intelligence matters." It lacked imagination, energy, and broad perspective. There were in it "persons about to go into retirement" for whom the Army could find "no post commensurate with their ranks." He believed that such military domination was at variance with the concept of Congress that the Agency should be largely civilian. He declared that the effect of such domination upon able civilians in the lesser positions was most unfortunate. Variations of this point with regard to the military blight upon civilian endeavor appear again and again in the history of intelligence.[60]

There is little on paper in the files of the Agency and of the Council between the interchange of these memoranda and the action of the National Security Council on January 13, 1948, establishing the Intelligence Survey Group. But there should be no doubt that there was talk in both places as well as in the Office of the Secretary of Defense. Hillenkoetter had gone ahead with his own plan of investigation; he had invited Sherman Kent from Yale University on December 23, 1947, to look into the working of the Office of Reports and Estimates. Kent had been in the Research and Analysis Branch of OSS and then in the State Department after the war. He was at this time writing his book on *Strategic Intelligence*.[61]

After three intensive days in the Agency, Kent made a quick report, dated February 9, that went to the heart of the matter. The Agency was supposed to coordinate the intelligence activities of the several departments and other agencies in the interest of national security. The most important, that is the substantive, share of this work would fall naturally to the Office of Reports and Estimates. The Council's intelligence directives, said Kent, were inadequate for the purpose; NSCID 1 appeared in fact to afford the departmental intelligence services "the weapons and strategic position" for resisting "any intrusive coordinative activities by ORE." The Office too was short. Its oversize, loose administrative organization, and personnel would keep it from doing the "large coordinating job" even if it were given a clear mandate from the National Security Council.[62]

Kent's name appeared on a pencilled list in the Agency with those of Dulles, Correa, and Jackson who were chosen to make the survey for the Council. It would have more than passing interest to know why he was not selected.[63]

Political considerations entered into the choices for the Intelligence Survey Group. Although Allen W. Dulles had "rather fixed and preconceived ideas" regarding the organization for peacetime, he was an obvious appointment to the chairmanship by reason of his experience in OSS, his personal enthusiasm for central intelligence, and his party affiliations. The central intelligence organization was a favorite creation of the Democratic President, one in which Truman seemed to take more pride than in the National Security Council. Dulles was an outspoken Republican, eager to go "on Dewey's train."[64]

Souers considered Dulles an admirable choice, for his politics if no other reason. He would help to keep the Central Intelligence Agency out of the public eye, where Dewey soon tried to put it for political advantage against the President. It was the election year. Souers, for one, fully anticipated it. The Agency was an institution serving the public which ought not to receive public attention.[65]

Matthias F. Correa was nominated to the Survey Group as a Democrat. He had served the Democratic Administration as Assistant to the Attorney General and then District Attorney in New York. He had experience in counterintelligence during the war against black marketing in Italy. He had been in the Navy Department under Secretary Forrestal. Correa, with Souers, represented the Navy on the Brownell Committee of the three Secretaries when it worked over the several plans for a central intelligence organization, and the McCormack plan of the State Department gave way to the plan of the Joint Chiefs in the President's Directive.[66]

Of William H. Jackson's politics, according to the report on January 16 in the file of the Council, "close friends" said that they did not know whether he was "a Republican or a Democrat." Record of a telephone call on January 22 indicated that he was a personal friend of Forrestal, sought by Forrestal, and ready to undertake the assignment for the Secretary of Defense. It was "not clear" to Jackson whether the Group was appointed by the Council or by Forrestal, until Blum told him on February 2 that the Group would report to the Council through Souers. [three lines deleted][67]

Robert Blum sent another memorandum on February 12, 1948, to Ohly, Special Assistant to Forrestal. Secretary Royall of the Army had commented upon the duplication in the intelligence of the Army and the Navy and suggested that the Central Intelligence Agency might look into the problem. The authority of the Director of Central Intelligence, said Blum, was not "firmly recognized" enough at the time for him to do so. Such a survey should be made, though, and it should include the Air Force; the Secretary of Defense might ask the three chiefs of intelligence to make the study as an internal affair of the National Military Establishment. But it would be better to request that the investigating group of the Council should make suggestions from its forthcoming survey. "This need not be decided now," wrote Blum. Perhaps not, but those might not fully agree who had been following Vandenberg's efforts, and then Hillenkoetter's, to obtain directives for the effective "coordination" of departmental intelligence. It would have to be decided sooner or later, and it would require something more compelling than the recommendation of the Intelligence Survey Group.[68]

It still did in 1953. Duplication was still troubling the Army and Navy, the Air Force, the Agency, and the Department of State. General Collins, Chief of Staff in the Army, proposed merging the intelligence services of the Army, Navy, and Air Force in one military intelligence organization. But he was not prepared to go the whole distance. Each service, he said, should retain its own force for field and "close" intelligence. How General Collins would interlock this military organization with the State Department and with the Central Intelligence Agency was not elaborated in the press.[69]

On the day following Blum's memorandum to Ohly, February 13, 1948, Souers wrote formally to Dulles, Correa, and Jackson, confirming that they were to make a survey of the Central Intelligence Agency for the National Security Council and authorizing them to proceed. The memorandum would serve as an order to the Director of Central Intelligence and to the intelligence chiefs of the departments represented on the

Council to furnish the necessary information and facilities. The enclosed resolution of the Council on January 13 would constitute the limitations upon the Group as well as its guide. It should report to the Council its findings and recommendations with regard to the adequacy and effectiveness of the Agency, the value and efficiency of its activities, and their relationship to those of the departments and other agencies. But the Group was not to have access to "details concerning intelligence sources and methods." This reservation should not be overlooked, as it was on one occasion during the survey.[70]

A week later, on February 20, 1948, Blum recorded a conversation with Souers. The investigation was to be a "survey" and not a "detailed audit." A large staff to examine operations was neither necessary nor advisable. The costs were to be handled by the Agency like the expenditures of the National Security Council, which did not have funds of its own. And "unless something very unfavorable" was discovered, said Souers, it could be assumed that Hillenkoetter was to be retained as Director; "therefore, he should be brought fully into the picture."[71]

Blum conferred with Hillenkoetter and his deputy, General Wright, on the same day. They urged that the Dulles Group should come for a week to interview persons in the Agency, rather than endeavor to talk with them on weekends. The Group might see what the Agency was obtaining, but the general problem of communications should be outside the investigation. Hillenkoetter urged that secret operations, other than collection, should not be emphasized; they were known to only a few persons, and it was questionable whether the Agency was authorized to engage in them. Hillenkoetter was alluding to the work of Cassady and the Special Procedures Group in the Office of Special Operations under NSC 4-A. Blum asked about Kent's "brief investigation." Hillenkoetter replied that the report would be made available to the Survey Group. But Kent, he said, had not turned up very much, and he did not think it would be necessary for Blum to see Kent.[72]

Souers wrote again to Dulles, Correa, and Jackson on February 26, putting on record what had been evident for some time. At the "request" of the Survey Group, Robert Blum was to be its executive secretary on loan to the Council from the Office of the Secretary of Defense. Additional staff members might be cleared for the work. Compensation and expenses would be paid out of funds available to the Council from the Central Intelligence Agency. The Group was to submit from time to time recommendations on individual problems; those concerning the Agency would have priority over those involving other agencies. The survey should be completed and the final report submitted by January 1, 1949. Souers would undertake to seek the cooperation of those departments and agencies which were not represented on the Council. But most important in this communication of February 26, 1948, was the statement that the survey would include an examination of departmental intelligence activities in order to make recommendations for their "effective operation and overall coordination."[73]

This was the hope. It was March 17, however, before Souers could tell the members of the Survey Group that they might look into departmental activities, under certain conditions. As Blum had remarked in December to Ohly, if the Agency were to be investigated, the departmental intelligence services too should be examined. Souers agreed, but he did not believe that the Council had collectively the right to authorize such an examination within the departments; it was the responsibility of the individual Secretaries. Only they could direct the departmental agencies to comply with the request of the Intelligence Survey Group. Souers undertook to confer with Lovett in the State Department. Jackson discussed the matter with Forrestal, and he promised to place it before the War Council of the National Military Establishment, consisting of the Secretaries and the Chief of Staff in the departments under his chairmanship.[74]

Forrestal brought from the War Council, apparently, the formula which he reported to Souers on March 3. The Group might not engage in "actual physical examination" of departmental intelligence operations outside of Washington. Nor could it look into the "collection of communications intelligence." The Group and its staff would be subject also to "security clearance" by the departments. The familiar ring of the last statement should have forewarned the Dulles Survey Group. Perhaps it did.[75]

So the matter went to the Secretaries of the departments. Sullivan replied for the Navy on March 10 that its departmental intelligence might be examined by the Survey Group, according to the Navy's rules of "security clearance." Marshall responded on March 12 that the appropriate officers in the State Department would be instructed to "cooperate fully." It was there that the Dulles Survey Group got most of the information which it acquired outside the Central Intelligence Agency.[76]

Souers reported to the Council on April 7 that the Group was ready to begin its survey in the departmental intelligence services, and he requested that the Secretaries advise the respective intelligence chiefs so that they might be prepared to cooperate. On April 26 Admiral Denfeld, Chief of Naval Operations, informed Souers that the Office of Naval Intelligence had been notified "to cooperate fully." Search in the files of the Council and the Agency has not brought to light similar papers from the Army and the Air Force.[77]

Although the evidence is incomplete, it supports the conjecture that the Dulles Survey Group encountered much reservation on the part of the intelligence agencies of the armed services when it came to specific questions. In any case, the Dulles Report stated that the Survey Group had placed its emphasis upon the contribution of those agencies to national intelligence in their relation to the Central Intelligence Agency. "On the basis of this study" the Survey Group did not consider itself qualified to submit recommendations regarding "either the details of the internal administration of the Services or of their methods of collecting information and producing intelligence." Neither the Dulles Group nor the Eberstadt Committee was successful in bringing the departmental agencies fully into the accounting. This was unfortunate if the surveys were to be considered comprehensive studies of the intelligence system in the national security organization.[78]

The Intelligence Survey Group organized in successive meetings in New York and Washington. On February 21 Dulles and Jackson met with Blum at Jackson's apartment in New York. Correa was not present. Dulles and Jackson discussed the general scope of their undertaking, agreed that they should keep out of politics, concluded that they should extend their investigation throughout the year, and decided to make individual recommendations from time to time. There were two such "interim reports." Dulles declined to make a third.

Two days later in Washington, on February 23, Jackson and Blum met with Forrestal and Souers in Forrestal's office. Dulles was absent, and Correa still not in attendance. But in this meeting the understanding was established that the survey should include the departmental services, with the consequences we have just observed. And then in New York again at Dulles's home on February 26, with Correa present and the Group fully constituted, came the allotment of particular tasks. Dulles was to be concerned with the matter in which he was most experienced and interested, the collection of intelligence, both overt and clandestine. Jackson was to follow his own special interest in problems of evaluation and correlation which should take him into the Office of Reports and Estimates, ICAPS, and the departmental services. Correa drew the assignment of the Office of Collection and Dissemination and the Office of Administration and Management in the Agency. They agreed that the Director and his Advisory Council should be left to later consideration.[79]

It was not long, however, before the "overall agreement" of the Agency took precedence. A memorandum on it prepared by Blum on March 12 appears to have been in Jackson's mind during the next meeting at Dulles's home in New York on April 3. There was also comment by Blum on March 18. The head of ICAPS, Prescott Childs, "regarding whose ability there seems to be some question," wrote Blum, was a member of the "inner circle" of persons who were running the Agency. This small group, he said, consisted of the Deputy Director, Wright, the Executive, Ford, the head of OGD, Olsen, and Shannon, then head of the Office of Administration and Management, as well as Mr. Childs. Why Blum did not include Colonel Galloway, Assistant Director in the Office of Special Operations, is something of a mystery. But then March 18 was early both in the investigations by the Survey Group and in the effort of the State Department to replace NSC 4-A. It was not until May 28 that the decision was reached in Forrestal's office to remove Galloway from OSO and offer the enlarged place to Dulles.[80]

Jackson spent some time in Washington before the end of March, talking with men of experience in advantageous positions. Among them were General Sibert, head of the Office of Operations in the Agency, whom Kingman Douglass and Jackson had been instrumental in bringing to the Central Intelligence Group in the fall of 1946; General Todd, who attended so many meetings of the Intelligence Advisory Board as deputy to General Chamberlain and then to General Gruenther; George R. Fearing, who had worked on the NSCIDs for the State Department; and Ludwell L. Montague, at this time chief of the Global Survey Group in the Office of Reports and Estimates. No memoranda of these conversations have been retained among the papers of the Survey Group in the file of the National Security Council. Their influence upon Jackson together with his own predilections may be surmised in part, however, from the manner in which he stated his views and the location of his emphasis in the discussion at Dulles's home on April 3.[81]

As Blum reported it for the record, Jackson "seemed to have the feeling" that the Survey Group should arrive at "decisions on fundamental issues and on qualifications of principal personnel" before looking into "operational details or individual problems." There is little doubt that Blum, Executive Secretary, set down the statement with pleasure; he believed that changes in the "principal personnel" of the Agency were of first importance. Dulles and Correa, on the other hand, appear to have been less certain at that time. They declared that they would be "delinquent" if they did not try as soon as possible to correct "certain critical deficiencies." It was a "matter of highest priority" to Dulles to look into the subversive activities of the Agency, its contacts with resistance groups abroad and foreign nationalities at home. In short, Allen Dulles wanted to discover what was happening under NSC 4-A, although he may not then have known the directive of December 17, 1947, to Hillenkoetter by that name.[82]

Correa raised one fundamental issue on April 3. He questioned whether a single intelligence organization should engage in both collecting and coordinating intelligence. Jackson had written in November 1945 that the central agency should not itself "handle collection"; he had proposed that both secret intelligence and counterespionage should be placed under the control of the State Department. Allen Dulles considered this idea with George Kennan on April 30 when preparing the interim report on secret intelligence and covert operations. But Kennan did not favor bringing secret intelligence as well as political warfare into the "project" to be dominated by the Department.[83]

Members of G-2 would have been pleased to think that the Agency might have to go out of the business of collecting secret intelligence, whether or not the State Department took it over. General Magruder would have been dismayed. There is no predicting General Donovan's choice of words, but he would have left no one in doubt that coordination without command of independent resources meant nothing. The Central Intelligence Agency should be much more than a coordinating body for the several departmental agencies. Although the Survey Group suspended judgment for a while, it came to the same conclusion.[84]

PERSONALITIES AND INTERIM REPORTS

Blum followed up Jackson's statement of purpose on April 3 with a letter to him, dated April 12, enclosing interviews which Blum had obtained "on the general subject you are interested in." He had talked with McCollum, Van Slyck, and Ruddock in the Office of Reports and Estimates and with Ennis in the Intelligence Division of the Army, who had worked on the ad hoc committee of the Intelligence Advisory Board. The "degree of unanimity" on the subject, both inside and out of the Agency, said Blum, was "striking." On the same day he recommended to Dulles, Correa, and Jackson that the Survey Group should make a preliminary report by June 1. At the head of the list of topics Blum placed the competence of the Agency's "top staff." For his own assignments he suggested the Agency's function of coordinating intelligence activities, its "managerial setup," and investigation in the Office of Special Operations.[85]

Both General Wright and Admiral Hillenkoetter remembered later that they personally became provoked with Blum. It could have been about this time. When he came to the Office of Special Operations in May, he was asked what he wanted to know. Wright had taken exception to his inquiring why certain former employees had left the Office. Galloway now insisted that Blum state his question and name his person "each time." Blum's reply was that he had been assured "free access"; Hillenkoetter had said that he could "see everything." The upshot of it was that Galloway telephoned to Hillenkoetter and got Wright. Wright saw Hillenkoetter and called back that Blum might discuss "operations" with anyone, but he was not to discuss "sources" or the methods in which the material was obtained.

The reply was quite in line with the action of the Council in January establishing the Survey Group. Blum apparently did not think so at this time. He informed Wright of his "understanding that the Survey Group did not intend that any limitations should be put upon any freedom of access to OSO." Hillenkoetter had assured Dulles and him on "at least three occasions, the latest of them yesterday." Blum felt accordingly that it was "inappropriate" for him to argue the matter, as in fact he was doing; he would refer it to the Survey Group. So the issue was closed. It was at the end of the month that Forrestal and Lovett discussed the removal of Galloway in the presence of Souers, Dulles, and Blum.[86]

Meanwhile, Correa and Dulles, less interested for the time being in the "qualifications of principal personnel," had been at work upon "certain critical deficiencies." Correa had been looking into the arrangements concerning atomic energy. He had available for his use materials which Blum gathered to show the relations of the Agency and the Atomic Energy Commission, security in the Commission, and its dissatisfaction with the intelligence obtained from the Agency. It was at this moment that Strauss met with Hillenkoetter to agree upon an officer who should appraise the sources of the Agency's scientific intelligence. The eventual conclusions of the Dulles Group differed little from those of the Eberstadt Committee, or those of Hillenkoetter for that matter, with regard to the great need for improvement in the collection and coordination of scientific intelligence. Allocation of blame for failure was something else.[87]

[entire paragraph of fifteen lines deleted][88]

We should observe Blum's statement with care. It gives to Bogotá a stress which is different from Hillenkoetter's own recollection of his "mistake" in endeavoring to develop good will with the representatives of the State Department in Bogotá by withholding the famous dispatch from Lovett in Washington. The facts are not in dispute that it was Representative Brown who demanded an investigation of the affair and who released the documents to the press. It was Brown who spoke of "dumb clucks" in the State Department.[89]

When Dulles talked with Hillenkoetter about matters in the Agency [most of one line deleted], presumably on April 16, Hillenkoetter agreed with him that public controversy with the State Department over Bogotá was regrettable; [several words deleted]. The next day Dulles found Secretary Lovett in the Department disturbed that the Agency seemed to be trying to build an "empire" abroad. Lovett thought that the Agency had been "seriously at fault" in failing to notify the Department at Washington regarding the information from Bogotá. But Lovett too had no inclination to let that mistake interfere with settling [one line deleted].[90]

[a paragraph, or paragraphs, totalling thirty-three lines deleted][91] [92]

For the Department, Under Secretary Lovett signed a memorandum to the Executive Secretary of the National Security Council on May 20, declaring the willingness of the Department to accept the "general validity" of the observations and the specific recommendations in the interim report. It remained for Souers, Executive Secretary of the Council, to bring the separate acceptances of the Department and the Agency into mutual agreement without making further action by the Council necessary. This was accomplished by August 9, 1948. The principles were established, and the issue settled as much as any issue of the sort can ever be settled between rivals who have to work together.[93]

Blum was disturbed by the hearings on Bogotá. He wrote to Dulles on April 20, 1948, that he was going to look into Admiral Hillenkoetter's files. What there was to learn beyond what he already knew from the hearings Blum did not suggest. Instead of alluding to NSCID 2 as perhaps he might have, from Brown's outburst against "censorship," Blum gave Dulles an account of Robert S. Allen's recent gossip on the air. Secretary Marshall had complained "two months ago" to President Truman about Admiral Hillenkoetter; but the Admiral was "from Missouri," and so nothing had been done. Allen linked the forthcoming report of the Survey Group with this dissatisfaction. As Blum recalled the episode on March 10, 1953, he was still certain that Bogotá had contributed to the recommendation that Hillenkoetter should be removed as Director of Central Intelligence. Hillenkoetter did come off rather well after Brown had finished with his investigation, but the State Department, said Blum, was not happy.[94]

In this letter of April 20 to Dulles, Blum reported also that he had borrowed the manuscript of Kent's book on *Strategic Intelligence* and had the chapter about central intelligence copied for the Survey Group. Blum added that, when Dulles had looked at it, he might pass it along to Jackson and Correa. To collate the chapter of the book with the Dulles Report for contradiction and agreement would make an interesting bit of historical research. There is no specific citation of the book in the Dulles Report.[95]

To Jackson on April 23 Blum wrote again urging that there was "need for pressing on to recommendations on certain fundamental questions." Meanwhile, Larocque and Sprague of the staff were to examine the Office of Operations and the Office of Reports and Estimates. And then came that revealing conference in the State Department, on April 30, of Dulles and Blum with Kennan, Davies, and Villard on the progress of the Intelligence Survey and the ways it touched upon political warfare.[96]

The importance of this conference, with the Survey's Interim Report #2 on secret intelligence and covert operations, has been considered in discussing the movement to place the Agency under the guidance of the State Department and the National Military Establishment by NSC 10-2. The State Department, said Kennan, was "very much opposed to giving CIA responsibility for political warfare"; it might be conducted independently from "national policy considerations." The relation of the conference in the State Department on April 30 to the investigation of "principal personnel" in the Agency was as real. Blum went from the conference to his inquiries in the Office of Special Operations and his contretemps with Wright and Galloway.[97]

The trend was complete by the first of June. Secretaries Forrestal and Lovett had decided in the presence of Souers, Dulles, and Blum that Galloway should go and had offered to Dulles the post of director over both secret intelligence and covert operations, including subversive activities. By June 4 Blum was writing to Dulles, Correa, and Jackson that they were ready for their first comprehensive report on the Agency. In deciding upon the type of the report, he said, they should know more clearly "the premises" underlying their work. Blum offered these:

> For example, it now appears that even though it is generally recognized that Admiral Hillenkoetter is not entirely satisfactory as Director of Central Intelligence, there is no readiness to replace him at present. On the other hand, there is a willingness approaching enthusiasm to dispense with the services of Wright (and presumably certain others with him) and Galloway. If this is the case, then we may want to work directly with Hillenkoetter in bringing about necessary reforms within CIA and in the relations between CIA and other agencies.

This was the case, at least in regard to Hillenkoetter, as Souers had informed Blum in February.[98]

Blum pressed on, as he had urged Jackson. In a memorandum, dated June 9, for Jackson's forthcoming visit, Blum wrote: "You and Allen Dulles will want to meet with Forrestal and Lovett in order to disuss the general problem of CIA, particularly the apparent need for changes in principal personnel." The National Security Council was to consider the latest proposal regarding special operations on June 17. It might be desirable, suggested Blum, to meet with Forrestal and Lovett before that session of the Council. In any case, he himself would be "briefing Forrestal on this matter," even if the Survey Group took no further action. Blum then laid before Jackson things to do and the names of persons whom he should interview. These included Generals Bolling, Gruenther, and Cabell as well as Mr. Armstrong in the State Department. Then there were "people" in the Office of Reports and Estimates to see. There were also "courtesy calls" to be made upon Hillenkoetter and Soeurs.[99]

Preparing the way for the essential charge in the Dulles Report against the administration of the Central Intelligence Agency, Blum wrote at this time in his paper on the Intelligence Advisory Committee: "The basic weakness reaches back to the unwillingness of the IAC members to give their full cooperation if they are to be purely advisory and the absence of strong CIA leadership which would be necessary to overcome this unwillingness and make IAC effective." Those who have studied Vandenberg's efforts and Hillenkoetter's difficulties with the Advisory Board will agree that there was lack of full cooperation. They may also remark that it required something more than leadership and "mutual agreement," as stated in the Dulles Report; it took authority, which the Director did not fully possess, to overcome unwillingness on the part of the departmental chiefs of intelligence who constituted the Intelligence Advisory Board and its successor, the Intelligence Advisory Committee.[100]

In defense of the departmental chiefs, it is to be said that the chain of command for them ran upward through the Chiefs of Staff, not through the Director of Central Intelligence, to the Secretaries of the departments who sat in the National Security Council. On one historic occasion in December 1947, Secretary Forrestal settled the issue and left no doubts in the minds of Admiral Inglis and General Chamberlin that Hillenkoetter was running the Agency. The moment was impressive, for those present. Its influence seems not to have endured. Certainly it did not reach the Secretaries in the National Security Council.[101]

Jackson's interviews in June 1948 had particular significance in the light of the letter which he had written to Forrestal on November 14, 1945, and which Jackson produced for redistribution at this time. In this letter he had summarized his views on the necessity for "an American system of intelligence." He approached the problem then with the objective, on the one hand, of "imposing intelligence responsibility" upon the military services within their respective fields and, on the other hand, of "compelling the coordination of intelligence functions" under one national system.[102]

The force behind this coordination was to come from the Department of Defense or the National Security Council, if either were created, or from the Secretaries of State, War, Navy, and the Assistant Secretary of War for

Air, if the existing military organization were left unchanged. The point
was that there would be authority, wherever it might reside and whether
or not it were single or collective.

Under this authority Jackson had proposed in the fall of 1945 that
active direction of the central intelligence organization should be in a
"Directorate of Intelligence" consisting of the departmental chiefs of intelligence. They would have "general supervision" over the director of the
Central Intelligence Agency. It would be his business to run various
facilities and services of common usefulness to the departments; and
"through the Directorate of Intelligence," subject to the superior authority just indicated, he would maintain the coordination of the national
system in its four aspects. To Jackson these were collection, evaluation
and collation, centralization of common services, and the production of
general estimates. There is no mistaking that in 1945 Jackson subordinated the proposed Director of Central Intelligence to the several chiefs of
departmental intelligence. They were to be his governing board.

It was upon the last of the four functions, the production of coordinated
national estimates, that Jackson concentrated his interest during his investigations as a member of the Intelligence Survey Group in 1948. It is
likely that his views of 1945 on assigning secret collection and counterespionage abroad to the State Department had some part with Correa's
inquiry in reopening for a while the issue whether the Central Intelligence Agency should engage in collection, and possibly some influence
on the conference between Dulles and Kennan on April 30. The whole
letter of November 14, 1945, however, was useful in reaching the attention of leading officers in the intelligence services of the departments and
putting the central intelligence organization from their standpoint in its
proper place for discussion.[103]

Jackson interviewed General Bolling, Deputy G-2, as General Chamberlin was in Europe. Colonel Carter Clarke, among the ablest in the Army's
intelligence service, was also present. Both thought that G-2 was doing
too much intelligence work, because no one else was willing. It should be
done by the Central Intelligence Agency. They cited, for example, the
study of petroleum. Both thought that the Joint Intelligence Committee of
the Joint Chiefs of Staff would welcome the Director of Central Intelligence as its chairman.[104]

Colonel Clarke had declared in September 1946 during Vandenberg's
negotiations that the Director should be a member of the Joint Chiefs of
Staff. Most assuredly Clarke had not been speaking at that time for other
members of G-2. It is as doubtful that Bolling and Clarke were expressing
now any but their own views. We have seen how the Joint Chiefs removed

civilian representation from their committees, refused Hillenkoetter's offer in 1947, and reduced the representation of the Central Intelligence Agency to military liaison.[105]

General Bolling "minimized" personalities and the friction between the chiefs of intelligence and the Director of Central Intelligence. "As a matter of fact," wrote Jackson, "the interview was not, in effect, profitable" except as it revealed the sincerity of Bolling and Clarke in wishing to help the Survey Group. When they came before the Group during its formal hearings on November 22 and 23, 1948, Bolling and Clarke offered criticism of the Office of Special Operations, but with no cases to prove their points. Their commendation of the Office of Operations was opinion equally unsupported by evidence.[106]

Jackson's conversation with General Gruenther, to which Robert Blum listened, turned about the "synthesis of intelligence opinion." The Joint Chiefs relied, of course, on their Joint Intelligence Committee for estimates bearing upon military plans. But Gruenther thought that the Joint Intelligence Committee should go to the Central Intelligence Agency rather than to the Department of State for "political" intelligence. Why Gruenther thought so Jackson did not record.[107]

They talked of putting the Joint Intelligence Group of the National Military Establishment in the Central Intelligence Agency at the "working level" of the Office of Reports and Estimates. But at this point Gruenther was not enthusiastic. He thought of "chain of command," with the customary military reactions. He agreed, however, that it was advisable to have the Director of Central Intelligence become a member of the Joint Intelligence Committee, even its chairman; the State Department also could have representation in the Committee. Then it might well prepare the "national intelligence estimates," as it had done during the war.[108]

Jackson and Gruenther discussed what would become of the function of the Central Intelligence Agency to correlate and evaluate such national intelligence. But there was no apparent hesitance on their part over the fact that it was a function designated by Congress in the National Security Act of 1947. The National Security Council had been authorized to direct the Agency in performing the duty, but hardly to abolish the function or to transfer it to another instrument of the Government without further authorization by Congress. Afterward, when Jackson and Blum talked the question over, they concluded that the "real McCoy in the national estimates field" would emerge where the personnel had the qualifications. It might be either the Joint Intelligence Committee or the Central Intelligence Agency. There was still no deference to the authority of Congress on the matter.[109]

Jackson's next interview seems to have been with Babbitt, head of the

Office of Reports and Estimates in the Agency. His deputy, Captain Winecoff, was present. Jackson gained little information, he said, that he had not already obtained from the report by Sprague. There was a brief discussion of communications intelligence; but Babbitt's statement on this delicate subject differed somewhat from Colonel Clarke's, and so Jackson would see Clarke again. Then Jackson had a few minutes alone with Babbitt and asked him what influence he had in the choice of his new deputy. Babbitt's recommendation had been disregarded. Captain Winecoff had been assigned according to the custom of selecting a naval officer as deputy to the head of ORE, who in turn was chosen by the State Department. Jackson took note that Winecoff had "no intelligence experience whatever"; and he "did not appear to have any aptitude at the work." He would return to the Navy after an "indefinite tour of duty with CIA." It was Babbitt's recollection in March 1953 that Jackson had come into the investigation of the Agency with his mind made up in regard to what should be done.[110]

Then Jackson had a talk with Armstrong, who had succeeded Eddy as representative of the State Department on the Intelligence Advisory Board and knew its business from beginning to end. Jackson found Armstrong possessed of the usual criticism that the Agency was duplicating work which belonged elsewhere, in particular political intelligence, by tradition the primary interest of the Department of State. Armstrong did agree that there were "tag ends" which needed to be caught up; he was surprising in his opinion that the bulk of economic intelligence should be done in the Central Intelligence Agency. "Incidentally," wrote Jackson, "his views and that of Babbitt were all in precise accord on these points." Jackson felt that another interview with Armstrong was desirable. "In the meantime he welcomes (or so he said) a study of State Department intelligence by Mr. Sprague or any other representative of the Survey Group." Sprague later made a report for Blum on the Office of Intelligence Research in the Department of State.[111]

In the morning of June 16 Jackson went with Dulles for the meeting with Secretaries Forrestal and Lovett which Blum had proposed and arranged. Blum's memorandum to Forrestal on the fifteenth stated that he had asked "no one else to be present." This presumably left out Souers, who had been in the meeting of May 29 when the plan for removing Galloway and enlarging the Office of Special Operations had been discussed. Correa was not in Washington. Blum himself would be "available and on call." Apparently he was called, for there was a memorandum of the discussion which Blum showed to Correa on June 21 and with which Correa was in "entire agreement," according to the letter which Blum wrote to Dulles on June 22.[112]

The memorandum may be in the Forrestal papers. It is not in the papers of the Survey Group which Blum sent to the files of the National Security Council at the end of his work on the Dulles Report. One may state with certainty, however, that the "need for changes in principal personnel" in the Agency was among the subjects of discussion. This is apparent from the "premises" which Blum offered to Dulles, Correa, and Jackson on June 4 and from the agenda which Blum gave to Jackson on June 9. There is indication also of what happened in the meeting on June 16; for Blum wrote on July 24 to Jackson on Nantucket Island that they should "reconsider the question of personalities which has been in abeyance since the meeting in Forrestal's office."[113]

As we turn from this phase of the investigation and report by the Intelligence Survey Group, we should note that Thomas G. Cassady was about to be removed from the Special Procedures Group which he had established in the Office of Special Operations under NSC 4-A. General Wright remembered in 1953 that it was distressing to ask a man to leave who had dropped his own business at some sacrifice to undertake the work and had done it well. Colonel Galloway left the Office of Special Operations and the Agency in December 1948. General Wright withdrew in May 1949 for service in the Far East. He was not replaced as Deputy Director so long as Admiral Hillenkoetter remained Director of Central Intelligence.[114]

The Intelligence Survey Group might have produced a third interim report to the National Security Council on biological warfare. It was considered second only to atomic warfare among the evils of the future. It was as related to the conflict of interests among the departments and the Central Intelligence Agency as the [several words deleted] dispute about subversive operations under NSC 4-A. Dulles declined on the ground that the subject lay in "highly technical fields" where the Group was not competent. There were reasons, however, why the Survey Group might have investigated biological warfare in the summer of 1948 and reported upon the failure of intelligence concerning Soviet developments in this art of war.[115]

Secretary Forrestal, intense upon all things that touched the safety of the nation, followed a report from his Research and Development Board with a request to Souers on May 22, 1948, that biological warfare should be given "high priority" and brought to the attention of the Dulles Group. Forrestal sent a memorandum to Hillenkoetter asking him to "take every step possible to provide the maximum reliable intelligence" in the field and to report upon "our present state of knowledge" regarding the activities and intentions of potential enemies.[116]

Admiral Hillenkoetter replied on May 28 with a statement from the

Scientific Branch of the Office of Reports and Estimates. It was fair to assume that Soviet scientists were developing biological weapons. Unclassified publications showed that scientists were investigating biological warfare in Britain and the United States; Soviet experts could be expected to follow these efforts closely. Captured German and Japanese documents indicated Soviet activity during the war; there was no reason to suppose that it had ceased. The publications of many scientists in the Soviet Union proved that they were capable of research in biological warfare. And there were scraps of information such as the desire of the Soviet authorities to purchase in the United States equipment for the manufacture of penicillin; it could be turned easily to the production of biological agents for war.[117]

These facts, and others, indicated capability and pointed to the likelihood that the potential enemy was getting ready for biological warfare. But the nature and extent of that preparation and the intention of the Soviet authorities with regard to its use were altogether different matters. The Agency had no specific information. Medical research and developments for biological warfare were so intimate that one could hardly be distinguished from the other; installations to produce vaccines were so like those for making biological weapons that espionage agents would have difficulty in detecting the latter, even if they were able to penetrate. [twelve lines deleted] The implied criticism of the Agency was candid. The commendation of the military men, however, could have turned no heads. The truth had been stated at the beginning. "Only meager information" had been obtained regarding the activities and intentions of the potential enemy.[118]

The Agency could not produce effective intelligence when so little information on the subject was to be had. The control of its sources, except in those fields of clandestine intelligence where the Office of Special Operations was at work, lay outside the authority of the Director of Central Intelligence. Again let it be said that his power of coordination did not extend beyond the power to recommend to the National Security Council. The power of coordination in each foreign area resided in the "senior U. S. representative" there according to the directive of the Council known as NSCID 2. In relations with foreign intelligence services [several words deleted] there was mutual appreciation. [two lines deleted]

Facts appeared a year later that might have served in an interim report from the Survey Group to sharpen the attention of the National Security Council during the summer of 1948. The Office of Scientific Intelligence recommended by the Eberstadt Committee and established in December 1948 came under aggressive management. This offended many and helped to create its own opposition; but it produced a report on the "inability of OSI to accomplish its mission" that provides useful information here.[119]

Intelligence on biological warfare was particularly difficult to obtain because the size of research laboratories and producing centers, in contrast with the installations for atomic warfare, were so small that detection could be had by only the most direct penetration. [ten lines deleted][120] The points in the story for this discussion are two. The American specialists in biological warfare were not sure that they had obtained all of the testimony [several words deleted]. The proceeding was impeded by fractional interests and cross-purposes, even within the Agency. It was a telling example of the weakness in a system of intelligence which had to be concerned with the difficulties of coordinating information before there was a sufficient supply of it to coordinate.[121]

Even more worth the criticism and actions of the National Security Council in 1948 was the delay over fixing the guide for the collecting agencies. It is not to be assumed that the Director of Central Intelligence could set the requirements in this instance, as he had not been able to do with respect to the directives of the Central Intelligence Group prior to the Act of Congress, nor the NSCIDs and DCIs since; the process was one of slow and often ponderous discussion among representatives of the several departmental intelligence services and those of the Central Intelligence Agency.[122]

[one line deleted]An interdepartmental committee got to work in the middle of 1948 near the time of Forrestal's request and Hillenkoetter's report; but after two sessions a draft, approved by all except the Chemical Corps, was blocked. The representatives of the Corps argued that the form of the "requirements" should be that of the War Department's own "basic intelligence directive." And for this directive they all would have to wait, because the Intelligence Section of the Chemical Corps was "currently revising" it with respect to biological warfare, at the request of the Intelligence Division of the War Department's General Staff. When the Chemical Corps produced the draft some time later, it satisfied neither the interdepartmental committee nor the Intelligence Division of the General Staff. [two lines deleted][123]

The investigations of 1948 were enlivened by public discussion in spite of the efforts to keep the affairs of the Central Intelligence Agency out of the political campaign. Besides Dewey's accusations that Truman ruined the best system of intelligence in the world when he removed the FBI from Latin America, there appeared five articles remarkably informed on the frictions, the weaknesses, and mismanagement in the national system. Hanson Baldwin, writing in the *New York Times* from July 20 to July

25, continued and enlarged upon the theme of the piece in October which had roused Blum to activity in Forrestal's office.[124]

Baldwin's articles showed familiarity with much of the work by the Dulles Survey Group to date. He repeated the refrain of Bogotá perpetuating some of the discord of inadequate reporting and willful opinion on that affair. To make the articles more annoying to Hillenkoetter as well as to Blum, and anybody else concerned with the system of intelligence, whether in the departmental services or in the central agency, Baldwin was a member of the Eberstadt Committee investigating the national security organization for the Hoover Commission on the Executive Branch of the Government.[125]

Blum wrote to Jackson on July 24 that Baldwin had demonstrated either his "complete irresponsibility" in obtaining "information and misinformation" on confidential matters or his "lack of even an elementary understanding of security." Blum feared that the "whole business" would be laid at the "doorstep" of the Survey Group, as indeed it was. Childs, representative of the Agency on the staff of the National Security Council, told Lay, assistant to Souers, that the Eberstadt Committee had not yet inspected the Agency whereas the Dulles Group had "extensively" covered it. Hillenkoetter, according to Blum, was "very angry" with Baldwin. "Perhaps by this time," Blum reported to Jackson, "he has been induced to transfer some of his annoyance to us." Eberstadt was disturbed. He told Blum that he was undecided whether to drop Baldwin from his committee. Baldwin remained, and made his contribution to the findings of the Eberstadt Committee. Among these were the conclusions that the departmental intelligence services should take their share of the blame and that Congress should have a "watchdog" committee of its best members closely in touch with the national system of intelligence.[126]

Staff work in the Dulles Survey Group continued through August and September. But as the Eberstadt Committee held its significant hearings on the Central Intelligence Agency, the principals of the Dulles Group had practically finished their labors. Blum wrote Jackson on October 16 that drafts were in process on the comprehensive report scheduled for January 1, 1949. There were still some gaps such as OSO, Communications, and FBI. There were persons still to be seen, among them Secretaries Royall and Symington of the Army and the Air Force, Wisner in OPC, and Colonel Carter Clarke again.[127]

The formal hearings of the Survey Group on November 22 and 23 produced much the same criticisms of the Agency and comment on central intelligence that had already been received. Among those who appeared were Admiral Inglis of the Navy, Armstrong for the State Department, General Cabell representing the Air Force, Bolling and Clarke from the Army, Colby of the Atomic Energy Commission, and Compton and Hafstad for the Research and Development Board. Hillenkoetter respectfully declined Dulles's invitation of November 12 to attend and make suggestions, although Hillenkoetter would gladly appear or send others to answer questions and give "further clarification on any points." The time left was short. But then the Agency would have more effective comments to make after it had seen the Dulles Report.[128]

ANSWERS FROM THE AGENCY

Admiral Hillenkoetter sent the Dulles Report to the heads of the offices for their comment and set himself to study its findings as he had read and profited from the Eberstadt Report. Upon receiving the replies of the assistant directors and their advisers, Hillenkoetter took responsibility for the views of the Agency, rejected some of the opinions from his assistants, and incorporated the rest in the "Comments" for the National Security Council. As he looked back in the fall of 1952, the Dulles Report would have been better, he said, if Dulles, Jackson, and Correa had done more of the investigating within the Agency for themselves.[129]

On his part, Hillenkoetter studied the comprehensive rather than particular conclusions and recommendations in the Dulles Report. He was concerned with the relations of the Agency and Congress, the Civil Service Commission, the Bureau of the Budget, and the General Accounting Office under the Comptroller General. It was in Hillenkoetter's province to discuss the obligations of the Director of Central Intelligence to his superiors in the National Security Council. The accusation that the Director and his associates in the administration of the Agency did not understand its "mandate" was for Hillenkoetter himself to meet, if it were to be answered at all. In view of the concentration of the Survey Group upon the need for change in "principal personnel," we should expect a rebuttal in the "Comments" of the Agency. Some echo of Blum's "premise" must have penetrated the Agency during the spring or summer of 1948.[130]

The approach of the Dulles Report to the relations of the Agency with Congress, the Civil Service Commission, the Bureau of the Budget, and the General Accounting Office was to assert that the Agency could not be expected to conform to normal administrative practice. The situation "must be understood" by Congress and the Bureau of the Budget; administrative arrangements which might not be so efficient or economical were necessary in the Agency. For one, secret operations should not be administered from a central office; they required "their own separate administration." The Central Intelligence Agency was "overadministered" in the sense that administrative considerations had been allowed to guide and, on occasion, "even control intelligence policy to the detriment of the latter." The Report was voicing convictions in the Agency, the Department of State, and doubtless the military establishment that covert operations, though conducted under the cover of the Agency, should nonetheless be subject to guidance and control elsewhere. The issue was whether the Director's command over the Assistant Director in the Office of Policy Coordination was nominal or real under NSC 10-2.[131]

Hillenkoetter answered that the administration of the Agency had developed along two determining lines. The first was that matters of personnel, services of support, and budgets should be centralized to serve all components of the Agency. Second, controls were established to maintain those budgets, ensure against illegal transactions, avoid waste and duplication in expenditure, and adhere to standards required by security, the Civil Service Commission, the Bureau of the Budget, and the General Accounting Office. No agency, he said, regardless of its nature, and "most emphatically" none that handled confidential funds of the Government, could possibly avoid such controls. Congress and the Bureau of the Budget of course should understand the peculiarities of the Agency. Actions in 1946 and subsequent events, which we have observed, indicated that responsible persons in both places had understood and proceeded accordingly. In practice, said Hillenkoetter, the Agency had to justify its demands and give reassurance that it was careful with public funds. It had no right to expect "a blank check and a free hand."[132]

In seeming inconsistency, Hillenkoetter stated later on that either a centralized or separate administration would work. There had been a separate administration for covert operations until the Eberstadt Committee recommended the reduction of "overhead" and the Bureau of the Budget required the elimination of administrative duplication. For those reasons, centralized administration had been instituted. It had saved over sixty positions and so far had produced few complaints. The last remark did not take much into account the protests from the Offices of Special Operations and Policy Coordination.[133]

Hillenkoetter did not yield to the complaints of his assistant directors, Wisner and McCracken, that the covert offices should have independent financing and separate administrative services of support. Hillenkoetter stood by his general order of September 14, 1948, creating a central Budget Office under the Executive for Administration with a Covert Branch to handle both budgeting and accounting. A year later, by another general order on September 20, 1949, internal reorganization separated budgeting from accounting; covert operations were more distinct from overt affairs. But there was no appreciable departure from the principle of centralization under a single administrative officer responsible to the Director.[134]

To remove ambiguity, three factors should be kept clear. First, when Hillenkoetter said that separate administrations would work, he was not conceding that there should be "a lump sum" for operations and "complete latitude" with regard to employees, travel, and new projects. Such action without controls, he said, could not be permitted when government funds were involved. Hillenkoetter's statement that separate administrations would work did not imply that there should be no auditing. No one responsible for operations, he declared, should be "his own final authority and judge in the utilization of funds and personnel."

Hillenkoetter's concession was not to be construed as abdication of powers which he could not yield without also giving up his office. He was not surrendering his responsibility for the affairs of the Agency, overt or secret, administrative or operational, as Director of Central Intelligence. It is not irrelevant to remind ourselves that although he was subject to direction from the National Security Council, consisting of advisers to the President, the Director of Central Intelligence was appointed by the President with the consent of the Senate and removable only by the President.[135]

The second factor to be kept clear in this major issue between Hillenkoetter and his critics is closely related to the first. Both the statement in the Dulles Report with regard to supervision of the Agency's budget and expenditures and Hillenkoetter's comment in reply were incomplete.

The Report recognized that Congress and the Bureau of the Budget had given satisfactory support to the Agency; the Bureau had assigned the Agency's proposals to a single official who was fully cleared for security. Both Congress and the Bureau had refrained from examining internal affairs of the Agency. The Survey Group thought this behavior good; it urged that the National Security Council should "continuously assure itself as to the proper management and operations" of the Agency, "serving as the informed sponsor of the Agency and the protector of its security."

No one could take exception to that exhortation. The Council should support as well as direct the Agency for which it was responsible to the President by Act of Congress. But the Report did not reach the heart of the matter. This was the accounting for the funds provided by Congress as approved by the Bureau of the Budget, particularly unvouchered funds. Hillenkoetter also stressed merely the fact that the official in the Bureau of the Budget had gone over the details and approved the

Agency's budget. There was another significant point to be established at this time.[136]

Officials from the Bureau of the Budget, members of the House and Senate, the legal officers of the Agency, and representatives of the Comptroller General, administrative watchdog for Congress, were all discussing the problems of budgeting, appropriating, and accounting in preparation for the "CIA Act of 1949." Vouchered funds of the Agency were to be accounted for under the cover of appropriations to the departments. It was unvouchered spending for secret purposes, lying beyond the normal jurisdiction of the General Accounting Office, that caused deliberation. These expenditures were not to be itemized in accounting. And yet there had to be some arrangement for their external control.[137]

The lawyers of the Agency had proposed in the spring of 1948, and the Comptroller General had accepted, a measure limiting unvouchered funds to such amonts as the National Security Council might approve. This suggestion gave way to another that the Director of the Budget should exercise the control. The Senate's committee did not favor the second proposal and, in its place, put the stipulation that confidential expenditures should be made by the Agency with the certificate of the Director of Central Intelligence as sufficient voucher.[138]

The Comptroller General could not approve so great a delegation of responsibility to the Director of Central Intelligence. But, in view of past relations with the Agency and its special needs, the Comptroller General withheld active opposition to the Senate's measure as it went from the Bureau of the Budget back to Congress in February 1949. When passed by Congress and approved by President Truman on June 20, the "CIA Act of 1949" provided that sums made available to the Agency "for objects of a confidential, extraordinary, or emergency nature" were to be expended and accounted for "solely on the certificate of the Director" as sufficient voucher. This was the power in the process of clarification when Hillenkoetter commented upon the Dulles Report in February 1949. It could not be diffused among his subordinates even under the terms of NSC 10-2.[139]

The third factor to be made clear was involved in the "neverending argument" between administrative officers and those in charge of operations. Hillenkoetter agreed that there should be physical segregation of covert operations. He went so far in fact as to declare that "administration has no voice in determining the substance of operational direction, guidance, and production, nor should it have." No doubt he was right, if he was referring merely to administrative support, provisions for equipment, personnel, and similar matters.

Hillenkoetter was wrong if he excluded himself, as apparently some hoped that he would. Policies, management, and performance were not to be isolated in practice, however well they might look in separate boxes on charts. Management in government as in business is concerned with both policy and performance. The Director of Central Intelligence and his executive assistants were concerned with the operations of the Agency. The pronouncement, then, in the Dulles Report, that administrative considerations had been allowed to guide and even control "intelligence policy" was a statement of fact. The conclusion that this had been done to the "detriment" of the policy was opinion requiring evidence for its support. This proof was not given in the Report.[140]

Hillenkoetter's comment upon his superiors in the National Security Council was respectful, but it was specific. It turned on the essential of the central intelligence organization, the authority or rather the lack of it in an agency which had heavy and diverse responsibilities. The Central Intelligence Agency was obligated not only to the Council from which it received its direction but also to the several departments and agencies in the Government which it was expected to serve. He put his finger exactly on the point and in doing so fixed attention also upon the greatest weakness in the Dulles Report.[141]

The Survey Group stated that the Agency did not have independent authority to coordinate intelligence activities; Congress had vested in the National Security Council "final responsibility to establish policies." And yet the Survey Group's conclusions and recommendations rested upon the assumption that the Agency had some power other than appeal and persuasion with which to put its suggestions into effect. The way out of the dilemma for the Survey Group was to declare that the Agency lacked "the right measure of leadership." There have been successful leaders without authority. They have usually led revolutions, with the sanction of force.[142]

Hillenkoetter remarked that the larger part of the Dulles Report was concerned with the Agency's function of coordination and its failure to attain the "optimum." He asserted that much had been accomplished. He thought that no gaps remained, although there was duplication still among the departmental agencies and the central organization. On this subject, he said, he was sure that members of the National Security Council having to do with the "unification of the armed services" would realize the difficulties which the Agency had encountered. It had a fourth obstacle, the Department of State.

Having made the point that he lacked authorization by his superiors in the National Security Council, Hillenkoetter did not belabor it. He developed the theme of the Dulles Report that coordination was to be achieved most effectively "by mutual agreement among the various agencies." He accepted the statement. It was valid. But it required compromise, and that required time. It was remarkable under the circumstances that so much had been accomplished since the operation began. He recalled the three months spent in the fall of 1947 upon the NSCIDs. He reminded his readers that differences between the Air Force and the Navy had delayed one directive for a year. He reminded them, too, how often he had heard in those discussions with the departmental chiefs of intelligence that "such procedure would violate the chain of command."[143]

Hillenkoetter might have added that the NSCIDs were but the continuation of the directives of the National Intelligence Authority and the Central Intelligence Group over which members of the Intelligence Advisory Board and their ad hoc committees had talked and talked throughout the preceding year and a half. He might have declared with Secretary Patterson that command is better than cooperation in time of war. The "cold war" with the Soviet Union and its satellites was certainly not peace.[144]

Hillenkoetter did not indulge himself as well as he might. Instead, he accepted the responsibility of the Agency under the National Security Act with respect to coordinating intelligence activities. Such coordination, he said, must be achieved by mutual agreement with the departments. Lacking explicit authority, he could not impose coordination upon them. Even if he had the authority, its exercise would not be desirable because of the tensions and resentments it would create. He did not need to recall the rancor which he had inherited from Vandenberg's demand that he be made "executive agent" of the departments. Hillenkoetter had experiences of his own to govern his thinking on this problem. It had changed little in two years.[145]

He discussed it again as he examined the statement of the Survey Group that he and his executive assistants did not understand their "mandate" at the head of the Central Intelligence Agency in the national intelligence system, nor have the ability to discharge that mandate. The Agency, he said, had not been created in a vacuum. It had to live with other intelligence services and the administrative agencies of the Government: the Bureau of the Budget, Civil Service Commission, General Accounting Office. One might like to enjoy theoretical conditions; one had to live with the realistic. It was gratifying that much progress had been made and more was in view.[146]

Hillenkoetter would not concede that his centralized organization and its policies had impeded "the essential intelligence functions" of the Agency, or even had the tendency to do so. Rather, he said, it avoided confusion, duplication of effort, inefficiency, and frictions which always attended when every component of an organization tried to be self-sufficient and to compete in the same things at the same time in the same sphere. In view of the fact that the Survey Group was urging him to "integrate," or reunite, offices which the Council in NSC 10-2 had required him to separate, Hillenkoetter's defense of his centralized administration was fair argument, even though he did not muster evidence at the moment to prove that the administration itself was not obstructing the flow of "coordinated national intelligence estimates" to the policymakers of the Government.[147]

There was no reply to the statement in the Dulles Report that Hillenkoetter and his associates lacked the ability to discharge their mandate. The taste in making such a declaration in the Report was questionable. To notice it would have been as bad. Superior officers are supposed to decide such matters, upon close observation of their subordinates in their work.

Hillenkoetter agreed with Dulles, Jackson, and Correa that continuity of tenure was essential in the office of the Director of Central Intelligence. The post could not be properly filled as a mere tour of duty between military assignments nor, for that matter, as a civilian berth between other political appointments. Changes of Directors, said Hillenkoetter, with the consequent shifts in the Agency made its employees uncertain of their jobs and therefore less effective. This result, he remarked with a bit of humor, had been noticeable in the fall just before the election; "literally dozens of rumors were extant in Washington" that one of the committee's members was to become Director of Central Intelligence as soon as the election was over. This was not the first suggestion of Allen W. Dulles for high office in the national system of intelligence.[148]

To the conclusion of the Survey Group that the best hope for the Agency lay in having a civilian as Director of Central Intelligence, Hillenkoetter replied by quoting at length from the Eberstadt Report. After all had been said, it came to a question of choosing the best available man. Whether he wore a cap or a hat should have little to do with fitness for the office. It was wise, as the Act of Congress provided, that the President should be free to pick and to keep the right man for the office without forcing him to suffer either the loss of the perquisites of his service if he were a military man or the jeopardy of dismissal for political reasons if he were a civilian. Hillenkoetter's personal opinion was that the Director should have military training and long tenure.[149]

To date in May 1953 there has been no tenure long enough to deserve credit for continuity. The first civilian has just taken over the office. It may amuse him to prove that he was correct when he declared with Jackson, Correa, and Blum that the best hope of the Agency for "continuity of service" and the greatest assurance of "independence of action" lay in having a civilian as Director of Central Intelligence.[150]

The Dulles Report asserted categorically that many able persons had left the Agency and few qualified persons had been attracted to it. Quality was uneven in the higher offices and few in them were "outstanding in intelligence work." To meet this subjective criticism, Hillenkoetter presented statistical tables, although he may have agreed with Mark Twain that there were lies and blasted lies, and then there were statistics. [one line deleted] Hillenkoetter submitted a statement of cases without giving names. For the whole personnel of the Agency and for all causes during 1948, the "turnover" averaged 1.6 percent per month, a lower rate than for most of the government agencies.

As for quality and distinction in intelligence, if scholarship and experience were criteria, then the Agency was "not totally devoid of capable people." The percentages of college degrees, training in foreign languages, military service, experience in intelligence, and foreign travel ran always better than fifty percent and sometimes over ninety. Perhaps the most significant fact was that 61 percent of the Agency's professional personnel had been in intelligence work for three years and 76 percent for at least two.[151]

Another error, said the Dulles Report, was the placement of military men on a relatively short "tour of duty" in so many of the key positions to the discouragement of competent civilians. To this Hillenkoetter's reply was that only one out of six assistant directors was a military man. Four of the six deputy assistant directors were from the services, but he justified that fact on the ground that the military services were both the greatest suppliers of information to the Agency and the greatest consumers of its product. The total number of military personnel in the Agency was [numbered deleted], less than 2 percent of the whole number of employees. He further weakened the argument of the Dulles Report by showing that it called for more military personnel in the Information Control Section of the Office of Special Operations. The point remained unanswered that the "three top positions" in the Agency were occupied by military men.[152]

The Dulles Report virtually took Hillenkoetter himself to task for the fact that the Agency had been "publicized as a secret intelligence organization." Though stating that "public dramatization" of espionage and other secret operations was an aftermath of war, that intelligence had become "a subject of general discussion" to which the exposure of interagency rivalries had contributed, and that articles had appeared in magazines and newspapers during the past year, the Report focused upon Bogotá.

There had been "a public airing" of secret intelligence before a Congressional committee. Damaging disclosures had been made regarding the "operating details" of secret activities conducted by the Agency. The Director of Central Intelligence was responsible under the National Security

328 INVESTIGATION, 1948–1949

Act "for protecting intelligence sources and methods from unauthorized disclosure." This mandate appeared to give him "authority to resist pressure for disclosure of secret information." If, however, in his relations with Congress or with other branches of the Government, such disclosure were sought from him, and he had any doubt whether he should comply, he should consult with the National Security Council.[153]

Hillenkoetter agreed that the Agency had been unfortunately publicized. The notoriety for the Agency had not been sought nor encouraged. In fact, it had been actively discouraged. By his special plea, various periodicals and newspapers, among them *Life, Time, Newsweek,* the *United States News,* and the *New York Herald-Tribune,* had refrained from publishing articles. But under existing conditions of press and radio it was impossible to conceal the activities of the Agency altogether. It was more practicable, he said, to allow its overt activities to draw off attention from its clandestine operations. He was quite willing to consult with the National Security Council when he had any doubts whether he should comply with requests that he disclose secret information.[154]

Before we pass from this question of the Director's responsibility to protect sources and methods of intelligence from unauthorized disclosure, we should note again certain facts in the episode of Bogotá. There was no "public airing" before the committee of Congress. It heard Hillenkoetter's account of the affair in closed session on Thursday, April 15, 1948. Representative Brown as chairman released the documents to the press, but not until they had been edited in the Agency for publication. If the public learned of the weakness in the directive of the Council with regard to "coordination" in foreign areas, NSCID-2, the public did so through the remarks of Brown about censorship and the State Department.[155]

Whether Hillenkoetter as Director of Central Intelligence, under the authorization of Congress itself, should have refused to give testimony before the committee of Congress in closed session, on the ground that he had to protect "intelligence sources and methods from unauthorized disclosure," is a moot question. In the past officials in the Executive Branch of the Government have refused to testify unless so directed by the President. More recently, it has seemed as though there were no immunity for such officials from the subpoena of Congress in the event that its committees saw fit to investigate.

The head of the Office of Collection and Dissemination, Mr. James M. Andrews, was the first of the assistant directors to submit his views on the Dulles Report. Since the Office had a variety of duties which were differently related to the general purpose of the Agency, the Survey Group proposed that they be reallocated according to their natures, whether static services of common concern or coordinating functions or administrative activities. Thus considered, the function of coordinating collection and dissemination with the departmental intelligence agencies might be joined to the coordinating activities of ICAPS in a new Coordination Division of the Agency. The services of the library, the index of materials, and the geographic register should then be placed in the new Research and Reports Division.

The Assistant Director of OCD reported to Hillenkoetter that the proposal of the Survey Group, in essence, was to divorce the reference services of the Office from its liaison work with the departments. The best reply to this seemingly logical proposal, said Mr. Andrews, was that the Agency had already tried it in practice and found it unsatisfactory. The "administrative void" thus created between the two functions worked to the injury of both. If an analyst in ORE called for a document from the State Department, it was clearly an interlibrary loan to be arranged by the library in OCD. But if the document proved to be subject to stringent classification, it was then the task of a liaison officer to make the arrangements. The two jobs were one and the same, but they required a different approach and treatment. Experience had proved that they were better handled under a single administration.[156]

Andrews observed that the Dulles Report would give the Contact Branch of OO and the Information Control Section of OSO a greater degree of autonomy in disseminating their reports. He did not think that their personnel had better knowledge of the "consumers" and their needs. He pointed to the danger in the practice of sending outside the Agency reports that might be withheld from ORE and OCD in the Agency. In regard to assigning the reference services to the new Research and Reports Division, Andrews called attention to the unsatisfactory situation which had preceded the removal of the Reference Center from ORE. Its services were useful both to offices in the Agency and to the departments, but in that work the old Reference Center had been "without adequate administrative understanding or support." The situation would be worse in the new Research and Reports Division. There would be an additional demand from the new Office of Scientific Intelligence. The reference services should be separate and common to all.

Hillenkoetter incorporated in his "Comments" the statement regarding the Office of Collection and Dissemination practically as Andrews had written it. OCD had many various techniques using unique machines; it was only on paper that the functions appeared unrelated. In fact, they seemed the "single and common end" of getting and storing information for those who needed it. The Office of Collection and Dissemination should not be broken as suggested in the Dulles Report.[157]

Acting as Assistant Director, Colonel John M. Sterling replied for the

Office of Operations on February 14. Hillenkoetter accepted the report of OO and incorporated it in the "Comments" as he had the statement from OCD. The Dulles Report concluded that the Office of Operations had three distinct activities with "no particular relation to each other." Sterling and Hillenkoetter showed at once that this initial conclusion was wrong. The Contact Branch, the Foreign Documents Branch, and the Foreign Broadcast Information Branch had the common function of collecting information by overt means. Their activities were closely associated by "collection teams" and "field installations" which, though operating independently, required common direction and administrative support from the Office of Operations in Washington. Intelligence obtained by overt means constituted, as the Dulles Report itself agreed, the great bulk of the information upon which the Government relied for determining its foreign policies.[158]

The Dulles Report recommended that the Contact Branch should be taken from OO and joined with the Office of Special Operations and the Office of Policy Coordination in a new Operations Division within the Central Intelligence Agency. The Foreign Documents Branch should go into the proposed Research and Reports Division. The Foreign Broadcast Information Branch, if retained in the Agency, should be administered by the Operations Division, with the product "currently available for analysis" in the new Research and Reports Division. There was much here to consider, and a good part of it did not appear on the surface.

Such a realignment of these services would destroy what coordination there was in the Agency for overt collection. Moreover, just as the Dulles Report stated, organizations, institutions, and individuals in the United States who were willing to deal openly with representatives of the Contact Branch would not "wish to be embroiled in *anything that resembles espionage*." [four lines deleted] There was no other good argument for consolidating the branch with the covert offices in the proposed Operations Division. [four lines deleted][159]

The Foreign Documents Branch should not be placed in the Research and Reports Division. It was a "central exploitation service" for documents, current publications, and translations used extensively by the departmental intelligence agencies, the Research and Development Board, and technical services of the Government. It should remain available to them all and not be restricted as an adjunct to the Agency's own projects in research. The Foreign Broadcast Information Branch also should remain a "service of common concern" primarily for the intelligence agencies but for other parts of the Government as well. It was so closely related to open functions and offices that it should not come under the administration of the Operations Division designed to supervise and control secret activities.

The "Comments" of the Agency took exception to the inference in the Dulles Report that the FBIB should engage in analysis and evaluation of its materials before distributing them. Such interpretation would require research facilities which existed in all of the departmental intelligence agencies. The duplication would delay transmission to the "consumer agencies." The value of the FBIB lay chiefly in the rapidity of its service.[160]

The real matter at issue was the proposed Operations Division. It went beyond the plan which Secretaries Forrestal and Lovett had discussed with Dulles in the presence of Souers and Blum on May 28, 1948. The new Division would control practically all collection by the Agency, both overt and clandestine, whether direct or incidental to other operations, except the production of the Foreign Documents Branch.[161]

Colonel Sterling, speaking for OO, recommended that until the Office of Policy Coordination were completely under the "operational control" of the Director of Central Intelligence, it should be held apart from any consolidation within the Agency. It should be treated "more as a probable source than a partner."[162]

On the same day, February 14, 1949, Mr. Frank G. Wisner, Assistant Director of Policy Coordination, advised Admiral Hillenkoetter that he agreed with the recommendation in the Dulles Report. The new Operations Division, furthermore, should operate as "a distinctly separate entity, having a considerable degree of autonomy within the Agency." It had been his "original conviction," said Wisner, that a very close degree of coordination between the three activities was "essential and inevitable." The new Operations Division would then be an enlarged and strengthened OPC.[163]

Acting Assistant Director of OSO since Colonel Galloway had left, Mr. Alan R. McCracken sent his report to Hillenkoetter on February 21. He did not know enough about the activities of the Contact Branch, he said, to state whether they could be brought to advantage under a clandestine office. But McCracken was sure that eventually OSO and OPC must combine. The overlap of their functions, he declared, would make independent operation and administration "completely impossible."[164]

Thus, Admiral Hillenkoetter had before him three varying opinions from the offices involved in the proposed reformation. It was not hard for him to decide what should happen if the Council were to let him have his way. The Contact Branch of OO did its work openly and therefore should not be assimilated into a covert organization. The Office of Special Operations and the Office of Policy Coordination should be integrated. They should never have been separated. Their functions had been in one office under NSC 4-A. It was NSC 10-2, he said, which stated explicitly that OPC should be autonomous in the Agency. He might have added that

NSC 10-2 required the Assistant Director of OPC to report directly to the Director of Central Intelligence. The Director, not his subordinate, was to decide the "maximum degree consistent with efficiency" to which OPC should operate independently within the Agency. The authority would remain so, unless the National Security Council changed its directive.[165]

Hillenkoetter concurred with all of the remaining recommendations of the Dulles Report on covert activities, except one. He rejected the suggestion that OSO should exercise greater control over the dissemination of its material. This, he said, would produce duplication which had already been sharply criticized. But he agreed that covert intelligence activities conducted by the Agency and other agencies in occupied areas should be reviewed to effect closer coordination. [one line deleted] OSO must give primary attention to training personnel; he commented at length upon the service as a profession. [four lines deleted]

The counterespionage activities of OSO should be increased and there should be closer liaison with the Federal Bureau of Investigation. This, said Hillenkoetter, was developing; but he gave no details of past experiences or future hopes with the FBI. Relations with the departmental intelligence agencies should be closer; "guidance" from the "consumers" should be strengthened by including representatives from the State Department and the armed services in the Information Control Section of OSO. But he pointed out again that this would increase the number of military personnel in the Agency, already criticized for being too much under military influence.[166]

The Director should assure himself that OSO was getting adequate information on the needs of the Government for current and strategic intelligence. This might be achieved through closer relations with the Secretaries of State and Defense. The Nuclear Energy Group had already been moved to the new Office of Scientific Intelligence. There should be better access to communications intelligence for OSO; it was being done. In this connection, he said, the comment of the Survey Group was "a trifle gratuitous." It admitted that it had not gone into the matter.[167]

NATIONAL INTELLIGENCE

The Agency's "principal defect," said the Dulles Report, was that "its direction, administrative organization, and performance" did not show sufficient appreciation of assigned functions in the "fields of intelligence coordination and the production of intelligence estimates." Since it was the Director's task to carry out the assignments of the Agency, the failure to do so was "necessarily a reflection of inadequacies of direction." In other words, Hillenkoetter was to blame.[168]

The question whether the Director of Central Intelligence could be held responsible for the failure of "intelligence coordination," from the Presidential Directive of January 22, 1946, to the Dulles Report on January 1, 1949, has been a major consideration in this study. We should set the general problem of coordination aside here as we examine more particularly the production of "national estimates."

The Dulles Report declared that the Office of Reports and Estimates in the Agency had been concerned with miscellaneous reports and summaries which "by no stretch of the imagination could be considered national estimates." One of the most experienced persons in the Agency held that the statement was correct. And yet he himself had made one estimate almost single-handedly and taken a leading part in the production of others which deserve credit for their scope, accuracy, and usefulness to the makers of national policy. If they were not "national estimates," there was need then for closer scrutiny of the term. It had developed from Donovan's concept of intelligence for "national policy and strategy."[169]

Some fifteen pages in the Dulles Report were given to a recapitulation of the provisions in the National Security Act regarding the correlation and evaluation of intelligence "relating to the national security"; the directives of the Council, NSCID 1 and NSCID 3, for the coordination of departmental intelligence and the concurrence or dissent of the departmental chiefs in the Intelligence Advisory Committee; "dominant interests" of the departments in the various fields of intelligence; the organization of the Office of Reports and Estimates in the Agency; and running commentary throughout to show that the responsibility of the Agency had not been adequately discharged.[170]

The concept of "national intelligence estimates" which underlay the Act of Congress and the directives of the Council, said the Dulles Report, was that of "an authoritative interpretation and appraisal" to serve the policymakers of the Government. A national estimate should "reflect the coordination of the best intelligence opinion." It should be compiled centrally by an agency both objective and disinterested. Its ultimate approval should rest upon the "collective responsibility" of the highest officials in the various intelligence agencies; presumably these were the chiefs of intelligence in the Intelligence Advisory Committee. It should command recognition throughout the Government as the best available and the most authoritative intelligence estimate.[171]

For this achievement, the estimate must have been based upon "all available information," as the Report declared; it must have been prepared with "full knowledge of our own plans" and in the light of "our own policy requirements." If so, then there was no completely "national" intelligence estimate to June 1953 when this was written. The armed services continued to withhold from the estimators in the Central Intelligence Agency "operational intelligence" and information on "our own" capabilities and intentions. The services themselves did not possess "all available information." The estimates of the Joint Intelligence Committee of the Joint Chiefs of Staff did not rest upon the "collective responsibility of the highest officials" in the various intelligence agencies. The Department of State was not represented in the Joint Intelligence Committee.[172]

The Intelligence Survey Group of the Council conceded in the Dulles Report that the Central Intelligence Agency had fallen short of such a concept of national estimates, in part for reasons which the Agency did not control. The principle did not yet have "established acceptance" in the Government. The departments depended upon their own estimates. The military establishment looked to the Joint Chiefs of Staff for coordination; they relied upon their Joint Intelligence Committee. Neither the State Department nor the Central Intelligence Agency participated in it as had the State Department, the Foreign Economic Administration, and OSS during the war.

The Dulles Report did not enlarge upon these facts. In all candor perhaps it should have done so at this point in its argument about national estimates against the administration of the Central Intelligence Agency. Instead, the Report declared that, although the task was more difficult because there was no general acceptance of the concept of national estimates, it was the "clear duty" of the Agency under the Act of Congress and the directives of the Council "to assemble and produce such coordinated and authoritative estimates."[173]

May it be stated once more that the Act and the NSCIDs gave the Director of Central Intelligence and the Agency duties and responsibilities for planning coordination, for correlating and evaluating intelligence, for performing services of "common concern," and other functions and duties "related to intelligence affecting the national security" as the National Security Council might from time to time direct. But neither Congress nor the Council as yet had given the Director and the Agency any power beyond appeal and persuasion. It may have been Hillenkoetter's duty to try to produce "coordinated national intelligence estimates." He had not yet been authorized to require submission of the departmental intelligence which was essential for correlation by the Agency; he could not even set priorities for such collection and delivery in the national interest. The Act of Congress merely stated that departmental intelligence should be "made available." In the case of the Federal Bureau of

Investigation, such intelligence was to be "available" to the Director of Central Intelligence upon his "written request" of the Director of the Federal Bureau of Investigation.[174]

The task of producing "coordinated and authoritative estimates" was not simply difficult under the existing statute and directives. It was impossible unless the departments and agencies came under the spell of the Director's appeal and persuasion or cooperated with the Agency of their own volition. The National Security Council, made of ranking advisers to the President, had the legal right to strengthen the directives to the Agency and, through the Secretaries of the departments, to put pressure on their intelligence services. Congress could revise the Act and empower the Director of Central Intelligence not only to inspect "the intelligence of the departments and agencies of the Government" but to requisition that intelligence for use in preparing "national intelligence estimates." If this were done, there would be "unification" beyond the conception of most who advocated it for the armed services. There might also be "civil war."[175]

The Dulles Group proposed that the Federal Bureau of Investigation should take part in producing these "coordinated and authoritative" national estimates. The Bureau should provide its domestic intelligence and should have a permanent seat in the reconstituted Intelligence Advisory Committee to collaborate with the Agency. The Dulles Group was more critical than the Eberstadt Committee because the relations between the FBI and the Agency were poor. The implication was that the Agency had been at fault.

The Agency should concern itself with coordinating domestic intelligence and counterintelligence. It should make recommendations to the National Security Council, even though the Act of Congress, as Donovan had originally counselled, forbade the Agency to have "internal-security functions." The Dulles Report found this no barrier to investigation by the Agency and advice to the Council. There was "no systematic way" of tapping the domestic intelligence of the FBI. Apparently it was the business of the Agency to find one which the Director of the Federal Bureau of Investigation would accept.[176]

Regardless of the merits in having a representative of the FBI participate in estimating, which J. Edgar Hoover himself seems to have questioned and eventually to have rejected for himself, preceding events had not proved that the Agency was any more at fault than the Bureau. Mr. Hoover, or his representative, had taken part in the original Intelligence Advisory Board and had withdrawn of his own accord. Hoover had promised on August 23, 1946, that the FBI would transmit foreign intelligence which it acquired in its domestic operations. It could transmit as well domestic intelligence which would help to produce national estimates. The provisions in the National Security Act protected the Bureau against the intrusion of the Agency into the Bureau's field of operations and guarded its intelligence against inspection without the consent of its own Director. But those provisions also left it up to the Director and his superior, the Attorney General, rather than to the Director of Central Intelligence, to see to it that such intelligence in the possession of the Federal Bureau of Investigation reached the producers of "coordinated and authoritative" national estimates. Hillenkoetter might request in writing, but discretion remained with Hoover by Act of Congress.[177]

In the minds of the Dulles Group, reorganization of the Agency's research and estimating was second only to the need for change in "principal personnel." There should be no more reports at random, without particular attention to the requirements of the policymaking persons who looked to the Agency for "coordinated and authoritative" intelligence. On this question the Dulles Group and the Eberstadt Committee were in close agreement, even to the use of parallel phraseology. There had been cooperation of staff members and exchange of ideas, though the two surveys did not coincide.[178]

The Dulles Report accepted the NSCIDs. They had been incorrectly interpreted and improperly applied. The Office of Reports and Estimates was performing a number of functions which were not truly related to the "coordination of national intelligence estimates." The Office was competing with the departmental agencies in production, rather than correlating their products. The research of ORE in fields where no department had a dominant interest, such as economic, technological, scientific, and related subjects, should be placed in a separate Research and Reports Division. It was a service of common concern. The Coordination Division, or reformed ICAPS, should study the scope of the new Research and Reports Division and determine the services which it should perform centrally in the national system of intelligence.[179]

The primary function of estimating, said the Dulles Report, should be allotted to a small Estimates Division. This group of highly selected individuals would rely upon the intelligence of the several agencies; but they should have direct access to sources if necessary to review the departmental contributions. The Estimates Division would prepare the "consolidated estimates" which should go for final action to the Intelligence Advisory Committee, with the Director of Central Intelligence as chairman. Thus, the Dulles Group would have prepared those "coordinated and authoritative" national intelligence estimates for which the Intelligence Advisory Committee should assume "collective responsibility." Special arrangements should be made for speeding the process in emergencies when the makers of policy required the estimates without delay.[180]

The Dulles Survey Group proposed that the Intelligence Advisory Committee should be "reconstituted" for this work of collaboration and collective responsibility with the Dirctor of Central Intelligence in estimating. Hillenkoetter had not been meeting regularly in recent months with the Committee as a body, although he often conferred with its members. Before we go on to the stir in ORE over the criticism of its estimating in the Dulles Report, we should consider the Intelligence Advisory Committee, which the Survey Group wished to have take more active part.[181]

It was not the Intelligence Advisory Board of the President's Directive and the first directive of the National Intelligence Authority. It was not the body which had endeavored to make "all" recommendations of the Director to the Authority pass through its own councils for advice and consent, in the days when the Central Intelligence Group was a "cooperative interdepartmental activity." Nor was the Intelligence Advisory Committee of the Dulles Report to be the same as that conceived by the framers of section 303 in the National Security Act, proposed to the National Security Council by Hillenkoetter on September 19 and approved by Forrestal on October 10, 1947. That body, as it was interpreted to Admiral Inglis and General Chamberlin by Forrestal on that notable occasion in December 1947 and constituted in NSCID 1, was a group of departmental intelligence chiefs who were advisers to the Director of Central Intelligence. They were not a governing board for their respective departments. The Agency was no longer a "cooperative interdepartmental activity" by direction of the President. It was an "independent agency" established by Act of Congress.[182]

Since then Hillenkoetter had come under fire from several quarters. The National Security Council had subjected him to guidance from the Department of State and the National Military Establishment with regard to clandestine operations other than secret intelligence. He would be further subjected to supervision and restraint by representatives of the Secretaries of State and Defense if the recommendation of the Dulles Group prevailed with the Council; the plan was to merge overt and secret collection with those clandestine operations and segregate them all to the point of creating an agency within the Agency. Nevertheless, the Director of Central Intelligence had survived every effort to put a governing board of departmental intelligence officers between him and the President and his advisers in the National Security Council.[183]

The powers granted to the Director in the President's Directive had been maintained in the Act of Congress. The Director was appointed by the President with the consent of the Senate, and he was responsible to the President directly through the Council. The President had a personal interest in the work of the Director. There was little or no chance that a committee of the departmental chiefs of intelligence could advise the Director on the internal management of the Agency, its financing, or its secret operations.[184]

The Dulles Report seems to have taken into account that collective responsibility for such matters was a thing of the past. All that remained for the departmental chiefs were the powers of advising the Director in regard to the intelligence activities of their departments and of collaborating with him in the production of "national intelligence estimates." This was the nature of the Intelligence Advisory Committee, which the Dulles Group proposed to reconstitute, and the extent of its collective responsibility.

The Dulles Report praised the work of an ad hoc committee following the "war scare" of March 1946. It was an example of good procedure in an emergency which the reconstituted Intelligence Advisory Committee would be expected to employ. The affair, precipitated by General Clay, was not so celebrated publicly as Bogotá, which came about the same time; but it deserves attention for what it revealed in regard to the investigations of the Survey Group and the effectiveness of interdepartmental estimating. The Dulles Report declared that it was an "exception to a rather general failure" in the Agency to coordinate departmental intelligence and to produce authoritative national estimates.[185]

Clay's message came from Germany on March 4. He had no specific evidence, he said, but he had a distinct "feeling" that the Soviet Union might resort to military action in the near future. This message was discussed in the War Department. By March 13 General Chamberlain, G-2, called a meeting of the chiefs of intelligence who were members of the Intelligence Advisory Committee. They decided to appoint a working committee to make a quick estimate of Soviet intentions for the next sixty days and report back to them. For practical purposes this was a meeting of the Intelligence Advisory Committee in an emergency, presumably with the consent of the Director though not at his instigation. The procedure of consultation was, as the Dulles Report said, "largely fortuitous."[186]

In any case, the ad hoc committee was appointed under the chairmanship of DeForest Van Slyck, a member of the Global Survey Group in the Agency. The committee submitted its paper in a few days. The departmental chiefs did not accept the full report but sent a short statement instead to the President on March 16. It carried the essential conclusion of the report, however; no reliable evidence indicated that the Soviet Union intended to resort to war within the next sixty days. Then the chiefs directed the ad hoc committee to continue its studies on the possibilities of Soviet conquest in Western Europe and the Near East. This the committee did through the summer into the fall, amplifying the judgments of ORE 1, as the air lift matched the Berlin blockade.[187]

Van Slyck and others who observed the work of the ad hoc committee were not so impressed as the Dulles Group with the effectiveness of this kind of coordinated estimating. In the operation which produced the estimate of April 2, the day after the Berlin blockade began, each departmental representative submitted a draft and Van Slyck then made the synthesis in a new draft. This was discussed, amended, and accepted as the final paper. But some days after it had been published as such the chief of intelligence in the Air Force insisted upon issuing a dissent. No evidence was marshalled in it to contradict the finding of the committee that the Soviet Union was not likely to resort to military action in 1948. Instead, the dissent of the Air Force remarked that "our Occidental approach to logic might well be diametrically opposed to that of the Oriental mind." There was also this statement: "The fluidity and momentum inherent in the immediate situation render an abrupt change in the present balance readily possible."[188]

According to Van Slyck's report to Hillenkoetter on December 23, 1948, the Office of Reports and Estimates never saw any estimate from the Air Force with regard to Soviet intentions after the preliminary draft, along with those of the other agencies, for the coordinated estimate of April 2. There was none from the Air Force that could be said to substantiate the possibility that the United States was likely to be involved in war. It was true, however, that representatives of the Air Force were "far more alarmist" than any of the others. It was also true that many observed a marked change of attitude after the Air Force had obtained its seventy groups. The suggestion from General Chamberlin that the estimate of April 2 should include a recommendation for universal military training was rejected by Van Slyck. It was irrelevant to the question whether or not the Soviet Union would resort to military action in 1948.

As he recorded his experiences with the ad hoc committee, Van Slyck stated that it was "virtually impossible" under existing circumstances to get a "completely objective" estimate from the "Service departments"; they were "unable to free themselves from the influences of departmental policy and budget interests." It was their tendency "too readily to translate capabilities into intentions" without giving due weight to political, economic, and psychological considerations of wide range. He had made these comments, he said, to representatives of the Eberstadt and the Dulles–Jackson committees in a number of interviews with regard to the necessity for an "independent, top-level agency such as CIA to make intelligence appreciations and estimates for the policymakers of the Government." The points were equally "applicable to the State Department." His convictions were so strong that he "would be prepared to restate these views under any circumstances."[189]

The responses to the Dulles Report within the Office of Reports and Estimates ranged from the frank to the specious to the bewildered and subservient, as might be expected in any group whose interests, fears, and antipathies were aroused. One gained the impression from reading their papers that some were angry and possibly dismayed, others pleased, none amused at the time; all were uncertain of what was going to happen next. The Assistant Director, Theodore Babbitt, had Lewis E. Stevens of his Policy and Planning Staff prepare the draft of an answer for ORE and called upon the chiefs of the geographical branches and the Global Survey Group for their opinions.[190]

The major line of cleavage among the opinions was that which we observed in Vandenberg's administration between the geographical branches and the Intelligence Staff. Led by the chief of the Western Europe Branch, S. A. Dulany Hunter, the heads of the geographical branches for the most part considered estimating to be the function of each one of them while working with the facts in his own area. Ludwell L. Montague, now head of the Global Survey Group, believed as he always had since the days of the Central Reports Staff that estimating was the function of a separate body. It should receive the knowledge of the geographical specialists. It might be composed of such persons. It should be representative of the several departmental interests. But the process was one of reflection; it must be separate from the process of accumulating the information. It must be consequent to and not simultaneous with the fact-finding. It was a quasi-judicial, an argumentative process.[191]

The draft by Stevens stated that the principal involved in the Estimates Division could be applied within the existing structure of ORE. They should add a "Central Research Group" organized upon a functional basis. Its product would be sent to the regional branches for "substantive review." Stevens was standing the idea of the Dulles Report on its head. He would reverse the usual process. He would centralize the research for information and decentralize the synthesis of it. In fact, he could have as many syntheses as there were regional branches in the Office.

Hunter endorsed the draft by Stevens, but thought it best to check such a departure in the synthesis of materials. The proposed Estimates Division would be commendable, said Hunter, if it were in constant touch with the units which served it—more certainly if it allowed the branches and groups to do the coordinating with the intelligence agencies of the departments. But Hunter would prefer an estimating division which was composed of men "continually in touch with groups specializing in their respective fields"—in short, the chiefs of the geographical branches. It seems fair to assume that the chief of the leading Western Europe Branch might be the chairman of such an Estimates Division, unless the Assistant Director himself took the responsibility.[192]

Neither Stevens's Central Research Group nor Hunter's Estimates Division appeared in the final draft of the comments on the Dulles Report by ORE. There had been a sharp meeting of the minds in a conference within the Office. Montague had stated again his convictions and his plan for the production of coordinated national intelligence estimates by a board of experts. Apparently he gained more support. Babbitt was not wholly opposed to Montague's ideas, although he himself preferred to develop the estimating board of the Agency within ORE around its Global Survey Group. It should be the nucleus, with panels of geographical specialists and economists and others taking part from time to time as the problem before the board required their assistance.[193]

The final draft of the comments by ORE, on February 14, 1949, stated that opinion in the Office was divided on the necessity or desirability of reorganizing it at that time. But if the proposed Estimates Division were made large enough to provide for its own research on a "relatively high level," the recommendation in the Dulles Report was workable; it might simplify the production of estimates. The proposed Research and Reports Division also could operate profitably if it had a unit for economic research as well as the existing Map Branch and other facilities. But ORE was opposed to considering these recommendations without making other changes. There should be corresponding rearrangements in the departmental intelligence agencies. The proposals of the Dulles Survey Group were premature until NSCID 1 and NSCID 3 had been revised. These directives were not so sound as the Dulles Report maintained. The relations of the Agency with the reconstituted Intelligence Advisory Board needed to be clarified. The responsibilities, categories, and priorities of production should be redetermined.[194]

The Dulles Report recommended that the final papers from the Estimates Division of the Agency should be submitted for discussion and approval by the reconstituted Intelligence Advisory Committee. Its members would then assume collective responsibility for these "coordinated national intelligence estimates" and submit them to the policymakers as the most authoritative estimates available. But the Dulles Report gave no provision in detail for the procedure in case there were substantial dissent from the conclusions of the majority in the Estimates Division; nor did the Report discuss the division of responsibility between the Agency and the dissenting departmental representative in such cases. A dissenter could hardly be held responsible for the estimate to which he objected.

The Report warned against "prejudice in the form of stubborn adherence to preconceived ideas" on the part of those who prepared the estimates and it expressed the hope that the Intelligence Advisory Committee would catch and correct such "distortions" and "prejudices." The Dulles Group hoped, too, that "prejudice on the part of the policymakers" would not blind them to the achievements of the intelligence services. If these shortcomings were avoided, then "sound intelligence estimates" could become "a pillar of strength for our national security."[195]

All of this was intelligent hoping, but it did not solve the problem of individual versus collective responsibility in the major operation of the Central Intelligence Agency, the production of intelligence for "national policy and strategy" as Donovan had urged from the start. The Director of Central Intelligence and the Agency would still be left without a sanction if the departments represented in the Intelligence Advisory Committee failed to share the task of correlating divergent opinions of the same facts. By this time there had been experience during Vandenberg's and Hillenkoetter's administrations to prove that such failure could happen. Joint estimates to which all parties of interest could give their assent without hesitance were certain to be reduced to innocuous commentaries of little use to the policymakers. The Eberstadt Committee had appropriately characterized such a failure in the Joint Intelligence Committee and shown the distressing consequences for the Central Intelligence Agency.[196]

Writing to Babbitt on January 31 and again on February 11, 1949, Montague approved the position taken in the Dulles Report with regard to national estimates. The position was sound in principle, he said, but it was "technically naive." The recommendations of the Report conformed with the original concept of the Central Intelligence Group during the first six months of 1946. Correction of subsequent mistakes could not be accomplished, however, by isolated reform in the Office of Reports and Estimates of the Agency. The entire system of intelligence in Washington should be reconstructed. The departmental agencies were as much to blame as the Agency for the failure of "coordination."

It required, to be effective, that ideas of the departmental agencies should be synthesized with other views on the subject and that the members of the Intelligence Advisory Committee should accept the "resultant estimate." They might alter it, but they should identify themselves with it and take responsibility for it. Merely "joint estimates" could not be effective. Dissents on substantial grounds were, of course, valuable to the policymakers. For truly national estimating Montague advocated, as he had in March and October 1946, a permanent full-time committee in the Agency to make the synthesis. It should represent the departments and work with "suitable procedural safeguards" under "authoritative leadership." He did not favor the idea of joint ad hoc committees which the Dulles Report commended for emergencies. Such committees were slow and uncertain. They would not be necessary with a permanent representative committee working full time in the Agency.[197]

Although Babbitt did not agree that members of the Intelligence Advisory Committee should be collectively responsible for the estimates of the Agency, he accepted the essentials in Montague's concept of coordinated national estimating and incorporated them in the comments of ORE upon the Dulles Report. Babbitt emphasized the responsibility of the Director of Central Intelligence and the Agency. The comments of ORE on February 14 placed that responsibility in realistic conjunction with Montague's plan for submitting a "resultant estimate" from the representative working committee in the Agency to the Intelligence Advisory Committee. The finished estimate was to be the sole responsibility of the Central Intelligence Agency even though the Intelligence Advisory Committee was unanimous in its concurrence. The production of Donovan's intelligence for "national policy and strategy" or Souers's "strategic and national policy" intelligence transcended the competence of the departmental intelligence services. It was the ultimate responsibility of the Director and the Central Intelligence Agency.[198]

There should be equally realistic treatment of dissents. They had of course to be bona fide dissents on substantial grounds relevant to the subject of discussion. But, more than that, the Agency should not be required to publish a dissent, for example, from the Navy on political grounds when the State Department, primarily concerned with political matters, concurred in the view which the Agency had taken in regard to the political aspects of the problem. This did not mean that such a dissent could not go to the policymakers in the National Security Council; it could do so through the Secretary of the department concerned. It could not obstruct the course of the Agency's national intelligence estimate through the Intelligence Advisory Committee to the Council.

Hillenkoetter adopted for the most part the comments of ORE on the Dulles Report. There was no "confusion" in the Agency between the functions of producing coordinated intelligence and of miscellaneous research and reporting. There had been unnecessary work done. Hillenkoetter accepted that criticism. But the Dulles Group itself seemed not to recognize that the Agency had a threefold responsibility. It was not only the agency to perform services of "common concern" to the departments and to produce the national intelligence estimates. It was also the intelligence facility of the National Security Council, the President, and such agencies as might be designated by them. Many of its "intelligence memoranda" were prepared in response to requests which did not want coordination. Often there was no time for it.[199]

The provisions in the National Security Act for the responsibility of the Agency to the Council and of the Council to the President should have made that fact evident. But there were still in 1949 members of the departmental intelligence services who believed that the Central Intelligence Agency was a "cooperative interdepartmental activity" subject to direction and control by the departments at the level of their chiefs of intelligence.[200]

Hillenkoetter noted that the Dulles Report did not comment upon the Agency's monthly "Review of the World Situation" for the Council, as the Report criticized the Agency's daily and weekly summaries for being "essentially political summaries" which duplicated the work of the State Department. He replied that these current intelligence reports were designed for the President and the Council. He might have said with equal force that the monthly review had been expressly requested of the Director of Central Intelligence for the first meeting of the National Security Council on September 26, 1947, when he was also instructed to attend its meetings as "observer and adviser." Under these circumstances it was hardly to be assumed that he was obliged to "coordinate" his views with those in the departmental intelligence services, even if he might have the time to do so, or that he should be much concerned if he duplicated the work of some other agency or department.[201]

Hillenkoetter recommended for the Agency that the directive of the Council concerning the production of intelligence, NSCID 3, should be revised. It was possible to suggest that the Council do so in order to reduce the independent reporting of the Director and to require that he "coordinate" with the departmental agencies even before making his oral statements at the request of the Council and the President. Hillenkoetter proposed, however, that NSCID 3 be strengthened to provide for "adequate treatment of the matter of priority" within the departmental agencies; they should give better support to the Central Intelligence Agency. There should be better allocation of responsibilities for production and clearer definition of the fields of common concern. It was, then, primarily for the Council to take action and improve the central intelligence system which Congress had authorized it to direct.[202]

As for the proposed Estimates Division, Hillenkoetter saw no need to create a new office apart from ORE. An "Estimates Group," as recommended by both the Dulles and the Eberstadt Reports, could be formed within ORE at the highest level. This would avoid the duplication of a special staff and researchers for the new office. The Estimates Group would obtain the "ultimate control and coordination of estimates" desired by the Dulles Group.[203]

The "Comments" of the Agency on the "Conclusions and Recommendations" of the Dulles Survey Group went to the National Security Council on February 28, 1949, with those of the Army and the Atomic Energy Commission. There soon followed others, which will be examined in the next chapter with the McNarney Report and subsequent actions of the National Security Council. There remained buried in the files of the Office of Reports and Estimates within the Central Intelligence Agency an appraisal of the situation by the chief of the Far East/Pacific Branch. It might have gone along, too, for the Council to ponder when examining the findings of its Intelligence Survey Group and the answers of the Agency.

Captain E. Watts of the Navy, on a tour of duty in the Agency, expressed his views with engaging candor. The "principal shortcomings of CIA," he said, were due primarily to "a lack of direction from NSC itself." In the three years of the Agency's existence it had been made "abundantly clear that individual departmental interests are not wholly subject to the erosive disintegration of time." The Director of Central Intelligence was "powerless himself to overcome this situation." The Council, on the other hand, was in a position "to correct by direction." The Dulles Report apparently failed to recognize "this basic evil." It placed "the responsibility for failure in the lap of the Director's office." Reorganizations such as proposed for the Office of Reports and Estimates would "actually hamper a progress" which had made "good strides even though at the pace of a turtle."[204]

Introduction to Chapter IX

Secretary of Defense Forrestal held the Dulles Report in high regard and favored the strengthening of the post of DCI and the degree of centralization it said was needed. He might have compelled his subordinates to make way for the reforms the Report advocated, as he had in the past. Alas, he was not to see it implemented. Plagued by mental illness, Forrestal resigned in March 1949 and committed suicide in May. Louis Johnson replaced Forrestal as Secretary of Defense, but lacked his predecessor's forcefulness to push through the reforms the Report advocated. Also, a personal feud between Johnson and Secretary of State Dean Acheson effectively froze progress.

As a result, implementing the Dulles Report fell back to the National Security Council. To help it decide what to do with the study it had commissioned, the NSC tasked General Joseph McNarney of the Army and Carlisle Humelsine from the State Department to review the Report and prepare recommendations for implementation. Darling writes that by this point the State Department was eager to rid itself of Hillenkoetter at almost any price and so let the Defense Department have its way on most issues during the development of the recommendations on implementation. Thus, McNarney took the lead in completing the review, which was submitted to the NSC on July 1, 1949.

McNarney was generally in agreement with the Dulles Report and recommended that the NSC implement its findings by directing the DCI to take appropriate action. Consistent with the Dulles Report, McNarney believed the highest priority should be given to fixing both the dissemination of information and the coordination of estimates, as well as merging the various offices responsible for covert action into a single organization. The NSC adopted the Dulles Report, as modified by McNarney, on July 7, 1949, and directed Hillenkoetter to begin implementing its recommendations. He was to report back to the Council within ninety days on matters concerning the internal organization of the CIA and within six months on the other matters.

Yet while Hillenkoetter went about implementing the Report's recommendations, officials within the intelligence bureaucracy continued to respond in the fashion that was by now well established: urge more studies, reiterate their departments' established positions in papers and meetings, and generally act as though not much had changed. The heads of the departmental intelligence organizations took the issuance of the Dulles Report as an occasion to state once again that the DCI should be subservient to the Intelligence Advisory Committee, rather than the other way around, and that the purview of the CIA should be nothing more than matters of "common concern"—that is, matters that were not the primary responsibility of at least one of the departmental intelligence services. (The exception was the FBI, whose unwillingness to support the IAC suggested that J. Edgar Hoover continued to believe that the FBI should itself be a central intelligence organization.)

One area covered by McNarney's report to the NSC is especially important, as it was a significant step in the evolution of national intelligence estimates. The Dulles Report recommended that community estimates be based on "collective responsibility," meaning that all of the leading intelligence community officials had to be willing to support a jointly issued estimate. This would have actually been a step backward; the Presidential Directive establishing the office of DCI in 1946 had made the Director responsible for estimates, though he was to ensure that dissenting views would be communicated to the President, if they existed. McNarney feared that collective responsibility would reduce community estimates to the lowest common denominator of agreement among agencies within the community. Hence, he recommended that the DCI continue to take personal responsibility for estimates but that each agency be allowed to express its dissents where appropriate.

This approach is essentially the one that has been followed up to the present day, although the way in which it has been implemented has varied somewhat. From the 1950s until the early 1980s National Intelligence Estimates presented a primary view, which was usually that of the DCI. If an agency wanted, it could add its own views in a footnote to the main text. In the 1980s the community adopted the practice of putting all views in the main text and then indicating in footnotes which agencies accepted a particular assessment. In either case, Darling believed that this process would not have prevailed if McNarney had not interceded in the Dulles Report's recommendations.

After his report was adopted by the NSC, McNarney continued to develop recommendations for the NSC in the area of covert action. A key concern was establishing a united Operations Division. McNarney studied the problem throughout the summer and presented his findings in July to the NSC, which accepted his proposals on August 4. Under his plan a new Operations Division would be responsible for covert action. It would be administered separately from other parts of the CIA, and State and Defense representatives would be included in its management structure to ensure that U.S. covert action would be coordinated with its overt defense and diplomatic policy. Even so, this plan for a new Operations Division was not implemented; as before, the State Department and Defense Department could not agree on a choice to head the new organization, and the CIA continued to be reluctant to be responsible for carrying out covert action. The OSO and OPC were merged within the CIA only later, in 1953.

IX

CHANGE, 1949-1950

FORRESTAL'S GUIDEBOOK

 Secretary Forrestal received the report of the Intelligence Survey Group as a "guidebook" for a "long time to come." He wrote to Dulles on February 24, 1949, that it was an example of how a report should be prepared. But Forrestal was not to live to see it applied. When the National Security Council determined what it should do about the recommendations of the Dulles Report as they had been shaped for action, Louis Johnson was Secretary of Defense in place of James Forrestal. The change was not fortunate for the Agency. Forrestal had done much of the pioneering in the union of the armed forces and the development of the central intelligence organization. He had acquired comprehension of those problems and their interrelationships through experience. Such knowledge was not to be expected of Johnson, who came relatively uninformed to the post as the "principal adviser" of the President with regard to matters pertaining to the national security.[1]

Johnson was not to be blamed for the lack of information. It is, though, a matter of more than interesting speculation what Forrestal would have done with the Dulles Report and the comments of the Agency had he remained in the office of the Secretary of Defense. There could not have been the feud with Secretary Acheson, which marred the effectiveness of Secretary Johnson in the office. At times the quarrel made it practically impossible for Admiral Hillenkoetter as Director of Central Intelligence to get the business of the Central Intelligence Agency through the National Security Council. The Secretaries of State and Defense were hardly on speaking terms. Animosity between Acheson and Johnson, however, did not keep the Department of State and the National Military Establishment from working together against Hillenkoetter's administration of the Agency.[2]

Secretary Johnson was too busy to read the Dulles Report or Hillenkoetter's comments. Instead, he asked General Joseph T. McNarney to study them for him and report. The result was the appointment of Carlisle H. Humelsine for the State Department and McNarney for the National Military Establishment to prepare recommendations to the Council. According to Admiral Hillenkoetter, Humelsine hardly said yes and he never said no. It was McNarney who did the work for what is known in the Agency as NSC 50, submitted by the Secretaries of State and Defense to the National Security Council on July 1, 1949. Souers for the Council, Armstrong from the State Department, and others attended some meetings.[3]

Admiral Souers recalled that the State Department was so eager to get rid of Hillenkoetter that it made concessions which it should not have given to the military establishment. When Souers took exception, he was told that he was defending "his man" Hillenkoetter. This was not true, he said, because he had not picked Hillenkoetter for the President. Souers was curious to know who had. He learned subsequently that it was Admiral Leahy.[4]

In fairness to General McNarney, he should not be called the "hatchet man" of Secretary Johnson. McNarney had been interested in intelligence during the days of OSS and had made a study of it together with Admiral Horne for Donovan. Nor is it fair to say that NSC 50 was just another report by Robert Blum because he served McNarney as he had Dulles. There was humor in the fact that Blum wrote comments upon his own observations. But the amusement was chiefly Blum's. McNarney was responsible for a report differing from and taking issue with the Dulles Report in specific instances. Humelsine may have been mute; not so other members of the State Department. The activities of Webb and Armstrong will appear shortly.[5]

FAMILIAR HEARINGS

It was to be expected that the departmental services would be heard on the Dulles Report because of their "common concern" in the central intelligence system. It was as fully to be expected that their representatives would take accustomed exceptions to the organization and performance of the Agency. By this time these opinions had become habitual, although the chiefs of intelligence in some instances had been changed. General Chamberlin had been replaced by General S. Leroy Irwin. General McDonald had given way to General Charles P. Cabell as Director of Intelligence for the Air Force. Admiral Inglis was still present to state his honest and stubborn case for a collective interdepartmental enterprise.[6]

The Atomic Energy Commission was the first to reply to Hillenkoetter's request that the members of the Intelligence Advisory Committe should comment for the National Security Council. Dr. Walter F. Colby wrote on February 24, 1949, opposing the suggestion that the Commission should be dropped from membership in the Intelligence Advisory Committee. Colby objected also to the statement in the Dulles Report that the role of AEC in intelligence was "a limited one and confined to a highly specialized field."[7]

The interest of the Commission in raw materials, export control, and military applications, said Colby, could not be called "highly limited." The importance of nuclear energy in the national defense could not be overemphasized. The Atomic Energy Commission should retain permanent membership in the Intelligence Advisory Committe especially since the Committee was to include with its advisory functions the "evaluation of final reports and estimates." Colby favored the reorganization within the Agency which brought the Nuclear Energy Group from the Office of Special Operations into the new Office of Scientific Intelligence. He was concerned only that there should be insulation for certain information which required clearance by AEC, and that it should have direct access to the work of the Nuclear Energy Group through special representation in the new Office. The Office of Special Operations, he said, needed as close liaison with AEC as with the armed services and the Department of State.[8]

General Irwin replied for the Army's Military Intelligence Division and General Staff on February 25. It was inappropriate for him to comment upon "the internal organization or administration of the Agency." He carefully avoided doing so and confined his remarks to those matters in which he believed the Army had an interest. It was notable but not surprising, therefore, to find General Irwin virtually agreeing with Admiral Hillenkoetter that the Dulles Report erred when it stated categorically that the Agency had not fully discharged its responsibility for coordinating the intelligence activities of the departmental agencies.[9]

Irwin's viewpoint, however, was not the same as Hillenkoetter's. To General Irwin the business of coordinating those activities belonged to the Intelligence Advisory Committee as a body. The Director of Central

Intelligence had no individual responsibility in the matter. The idea that he had such a mandate to control activities, said Irwin, was not sound; it was based on an interpretation of the Act of Congress not shared by the National Security Council. The various directives of the Council indeed proved the point, as General Irwin maintained. Whether the Council should have exercised its undoubted authority under the Act of Congress and should have given such a mandate to the Director of Central Intelligence is another question.

General Irwin did not discuss it. Instead, he declared that the Director of Central Intelligence had no part in the National Military Establishment and accordingly no mandate to supervise, direct, or control the intelligence agencies of the services. Their staffs were responsible to their own Chiefs of Staff and to the Secretaries. There Irwin left the argument. It could have been completed for him by those who held that the Secretaries themselves were collectively responsible in the National Security Council for issuing a mandate to the Director of Intelligence, just as they were individually responsible for directing their respective departments. They might have issued such an order from the Council if they wished the Director of Central Intelligence to do more than advise the several departmental chiefs of intelligence that they ought to coordinate their activities because they should avoid competition, repetition, and lack of enterprise.

General Irwin accepted the statement of the Dulles Report that more active efforts and better coordination were needed in scientific intelligence. The FBI should participate in the Intelligence Advisory Committee if the Attorney General and the Director of Central Intelligence so desired. But the Director of Central Intelligence should not be permanent chairman of the United States Communications Intelligence Board. In this Irwin agreed with Hillenkoetter. Membership seemed sufficient where decisions had to be unanimous. It was not until the fall of 1952 under the administration of General Smith that the Director of Central Intelligence became permanent chairman of USCIB.[10]

The idea of the Dulles Group that the Atomic Energy Commission and the Joint Intelligence Group under the Joint Chiefs of Staff should be dropped from permanent membership in the Intelligence Advisory Committee did not appeal to General Irwin. They should participate in the Advisory Committee; it should engage in the discussion and approval of national estimates. This opinion may appear surprising after one had read Irwin's statement that too much dependence for preparing estimates had been placed within the Agency upon personnel from the services. It seems odd to complain of using persons in one place and then to advocate the use of them in another for much the same purpose. But then General

Irwin was joining in the chorus; there had been confusion in the CIA with regard to national intelligence estimates and miscellaneous activities in research and reporting.

Irwin was also criticizing the Agency for preparing estimates without consultation in fields of "primary concern" to other agencies. He made this remark without considering whether some of those estimates, such as the review of the world situation for the National Security Council and certain intelligence memoranda, had been supplied on request from other agencies which did not expect the estimates to be held until coordinated among the several departmental intelligence services.[11]

It was significant that the Council in its meeting on January 6, 1949, instructed the Director of Central Intelligence to supplement the Agency's written reports on the world situation with monthly oral presentations of intelligence to the Council. There was no stipulation that the statements had to be coordinated among the departments before presentation. It was relevant to the criticism of the Agency that President Truman himself, in the meeting of the Council on April 21, 1949, commented upon the reports of the Council and the Agency as "one of the best means available to the President for obtaining coordinated advice as a basis for reaching decisions."[12]

On behalf of the Army, and military men generally, Major General Irwin, GSC, Director of Intelligence, did not concur in the statement of the Dulles Report that the intelligence agencies of the services should be staffed with specialists who concentrated upon intelligence over the major portion of their careers. His views were typical of professional soldiers who see in the command of troops the way to rank, preferment, and recognition. The most that Irwin would concede for the Military Intelligence Division was "semi-permanent specialization" by a "small percentage of senior officers." This concession was short, too, of the recommendations in the Eberstadt Report.[13]

Major General W. E. Todd, writing on March 3 for the Joint Chiefs of Staff as Deputy Director for Intelligence of the Joint Staff, took exception to the statement in the Dulles Report that representation of the Joint Staff on the Intelligence Advisory Committee was "largely duplicative" because there were so many other members of the armed services there. General Todd had attended the meetings of the Committee and knew its relationships with Vandenberg and Hillenkoetter as Directors of Central Intelligence; Todd maintained that he represented the Joint Chiefs of Staff rather than any service. He believed that such representation for the Joint Chiefs should not be reduced to "an ad hoc basis"; for the representative would be excluded from the Committee unless invited to attend. This, he said, would deprive the Joint Staff and the Joint Intelligence Committee under the Joint Chiefs of most of the benefits which they then derived from association with the Intelligence Advisory Committee.[14]

Participation in its meetings during the past year, Todd said, had enabled him to keep informed on matters of common interest and concern. It had also ensured that the estimates, plans, and policies of the Joint Intelligence Committee were "in harmony" with those which were "national in scope." Todd's reluctance to take part in the affairs of the Agency at the working level did not interfere now; he accepted the proposal in the Dulles Report that the Joint Intelligence Group of the Joint Staff should work in "close liaison" with the new Estimates Division in the Agency. He favored the idea that the representative of the Joint Chiefs of Staff in the Intelligence Advisory Committee should share in producing the "coordinated national intelligence estimates" for which the Dulles Group would have the members of the Committee take collective responsibility with the Director of Central Intelligence.[15]

Those who had followed Admiral Inglis's persistent efforts from the beginning of the Central Intelligence Group would expect him to read the Dulles Report for every justification of his "philosophy" that Central Intelligence should be a collective interdepartmental enterprise. They could not have been surprised when they saw his comments on March 4 for the National Security Council by way of the "Director, Central Intelligence Agency." It was significant that Inglis did not entitle Hillenkoetter Director of Central Intelligence; he was to Inglis only the head of the Agency. Hillenkoetter had no authority in the intelligence agencies of the departments; that, said Inglis, would be inconsistent with "normal command relations."[16]

Inglis did not propose that the Council should give such authority over the departmental chiefs of intelligence to the Director of Central Intelligence, even though he was by Act of Congress and by action of the Council itself adviser to the Council on matters of intelligence relating to the national security. Inglis stated, as he had before, that the Intelligence Advisory Committee, which the departmental chiefs composed, should participate in coordinating the intelligence activities of the various agencies. But now he made his position clearer than ever by declaring that the Intelligence Advisory Committee, having the responsibility collectively, should be given the collective authority to maintain that responsibility.[17]

The Secretaries in the National Security Council, in other words, should not exercise the authority. Nor should they delegate it to their own chief intelligence officers. They should assign it to their subordinate departmental chiefs of intelligence in the Advisory Committee. For this purpose Inglis would have the Council revise NSCID 1. The name of the Committee should be changed to Intelligence Coordinating Committee.

It should have power to forward its recommendations to the Council whether or not the Director of the Agency agreed. Although Inglis did not say so, this meant that, if he had his way, the judgment of James Forrestal, first Secretary of Defense, would be forgotten. The Intelligence Advisory Committee, by whatever name, would be the governing board of the Central Intelligence Agency.[18]

Admiral Inglis, Director of Naval Intelligence, must have known from his long familiarity with "normal command relations" that the power of decision had to be exercised somewhere. Sovereignty must reside either in the will of the despot or in the tyranny of the majority. It is futile to expect decisions of any moment from the concerted action of interested parties unless they are like-minded and their interests virtually coincide, as they seldom do. Inglis must have known, too, from his years of experience in the Intelligence Advisory Board and its successor, the Advisory Committee, that at best the system which he advocated was vulnerable to ceaseless conferring, stalling, reconsidering, and recourse to ad hoc studies for the sake not of information but of delay. These experiences he did not put before the National Security Council in his comments upon the Dulles Report.[19]

The conception of ICAPS which Inglis held was historically inaccurate. It had not originated as a staff of the Intelligence Advisory Board. Vandenberg had created it to replace the Central Planning Staff in the Group; ICAPS was to serve as his personal staff to work with the Intelligence Advisory Board so that the Board might be kept informed of his purposes and plans as Director of Central Intelligence. The members of ICAPS had been chosen from the armed services and the State Department to represent their interests and views. But the members of ICAPS had been responsible to the Director and not to the chiefs of intelligence in their respective services. It was the Intelligence Advisory Board which had vitiated ICAPS as an instrument of coordination by sending ad hoc committees to deal with it on every issue. This became such a habit that Hillenkoetter had suggested the Standing Committee. It saved at least the effort consumed in designating the same group of junior officers to serve as another ad hoc committee.[20]

Admiral Inglis would break up this dilatory practice. He would reform ICAPS as the "Coordinating Staff" of the Intelligence Coordinating Committee. A representative of the Director should be chairman of the Staff, but it should receive its instructions from the Committee. Inglis would frankly take the Staff away from the Director of the Agency and make it responsible to the departmental chiefs of intelligence in the Committee.[21]

Inglis favored placing all covert functions of the Agency under a single administrative division. It would improve security, he said; it might also be assumed that by inference he endorsed the plan of "policy guidance" in NSC 10-2 which was explicit in the proposed merger of OPC, OSO, and the Contact Branch of the Office of Operations. But, as Inglis made no comment on that possibility, it can be no more than a logical assumption. In view of his devotion to the concept of the Advisory Committee as a governing board for all matters of coordination, it would seem likely that he preferred to have the Advisory Committee supply also that "guidance" in covert operations, rather than to have special representatives of the State Department and the National Military Establishment serve as a Consultants Group for the purpose. Such an extension of authority to his Intelligence Coordinating Committee would have been consistent with his concept of the Central Intelligence Agency as a "cooperative interdepartmental activity."[22]

Inglis opposed the recommendation of the Dulles Group that there should be an Estimates Division. He did not think it necessary in order to review the specialized product of the departmental agencies and to prepare coordinated national intelligence estimates. Such a board of "review of reviews," he said, would be hard to staff and it would duplicate the functions which the Dulles Group expected the reconstituted Intelligence Advisory Committee to perform. His statement should remind us that he had objected to Montague's plan in 1946 for a chief and four assistants who should represent the departments in the Estimates Branch of the Central Reports Staff enlarged to become the Office of Reports and Estimates. Admiral Inglis was not one to waver from any position which he had taken originally with conviction.[23]

Inglis worked over again the question of whether or not the Director of Central Intelligence should be a civilian and came out with the familiar conclusion. The best man of course should be chosen, but the woods were not full of qualified civilians. In wartime Inglis would prefer, though he did not actually say, that the Agency should be under the orders of the Joint Chiefs of Staff. The Joint Intelligence Committee was studying the problem; as a member of the Committee he therefore would refrain from comment until the Joint Chiefs had acted upon the Committee's recommendations. It was a typically military reaction. Other committees were considering the matter, not the least of which was the civilian committee under Eberstadt's chairmanship for the Hoover Commission.[24]

One more commentator on the Dulles Report objected to the proposal that the Director of Central Intelligence should be made chairman of the United States Communications Intelligence Board. Inglis saw no reason for change from the practice of assigning the office annually in rotation.[25]

To ensure timely action in "crisis situations," said Inglis, the "echelons above the IAC" must be made fully aware that the Committee was prepared to handle the intelligence rapidly. Information received through "Eyes Only" messages and similar sources must be relayed expeditiously to the member of the Committee under the particular echelon. He wished an NSCID to that effect. One may doubt, however, that Admiral Inglis would have been willing to transmit as quickly and completely the "operational intelligence" which he had been so determined to keep from civilian estimators. Matters of "sole concern" to the National Military Establishment, he said, should be coordinated through the Joint Intelligence Committee of the Joint Chiefs of Staff. It still is difficult to persuade military men that civilians should know the "capabilities and intentions" of their own defensive forces. Such knowledge is nevertheless vital to the construction of effective national intelligence estimates.[26]

There was no paper on the Dulles Report from the Air Force. The comments which its Directorate of Intelligence had approved in detail went on March 1, 1949, to the office of Secretary Symington, and apparently no farther. No copy could be found for this study in the files of the Agency, nor with the comments of other departments in the minutes of the National Security Council. General Charles P. Cabell, Deputy Director of Central Intelligence, could not at first recall in August 1953 what had happened to his recommendations on the Dulles Report when he was Director of Intelligence in the Air Force. But he thought that he had taken a position more favorable to it than most, and he remembered that Admiral Hillenkoetter was not pleased.[27]

General Cabell was provoked by Hillenkoetter's neglect of the Intelligence Advisory Committee. Cabell therefore proposed that the Committee should be the advisory body of the National Security Council on "governmental intelligence problems." The Committee should have its "own procedures" including those for national intelligence estimates "in both routine and crisis situations." The Director of Central Intelligence might use this new Committee of the Council "to provide advice to him in the performance of his statutory duties." Cabell did not think that Congress would have to rewrite the National Security Act of 1947 in order to provide such an advisory board under section 303 of the Act. The duty of the Agency under section 102(d) to advise the Council on the "intelligence activities" of the departments and to make recommendations to the Council for the coordination of those activities, Cabell insisted, was not an exclusive function. The National Security Council could have other sources of advice and counsel.[28]

What the Secretary of the Air Force said in the meeting of the Council on April 7, 1949, when the Dulles Report was considered with Hillenkoetter's comments for the Agency and those of other departments, is not an available record. The minutes of the Council are statements of action and not of opinions and arguments. The remarks of its members are memoranda to the President and, if kept, are among his own papers. There were pencilled remarks upon the recommendations from the Directorate of Intelligence when they were returned without the Secretary's signature. Cabell's idea of a "National Security Council Intelligence Advisory Committee" was rejected. Among the marginal notes on the recommendations of the Directorate of Intelligence, Air Force, were: "The DCI should be the DCI. . . . Either the DCI should be something, or it all should be chucked."[29]

The comment on the Dulles Report from the State Department was not relayed through Hillenkoetter, Director of Central Intelligence. Notice was given that Armstrong would submit his views directly to the Secretary of State. Complying with the action of the Council on March 22, Under Secretary James E. Webb on April 4 stated the "basic issues" which according to the Department the Dulles Group had raised for consideration by the Council at its next meeting on April 7, 1949.[30]

These issues did not take Webb long to state. Nor did he leave ambiguity regarding the attitude of the Department. The Central Intelligence Agency was properly placed under the National Security Council in the structure of the Government. The Intelligence Advisory Committee was soundly conceived. Its advisory relationship with the Director of Central Intelligence was correct; it should participate more actively with the Director in coordinating intelligence activities and producing finished estimates. The allocation of responsibilities among the agencies with respect to coordination should be carried out under "the forthright leadership of CIA." In producing estimates for the President and the Council, the Agency should utilize the facilities of the members of the Intelligence Advisory Committee. They should assume collective responsibility for those estimates.

Webb did not say what the Director of Central Intelligence should do if there were no response from the several agencies to the "forthright leadership" of the Agency in the allocation of responsibilities. Nor did he indicate what should be done about the collective responsibility of members of the Intelligence Advisory Committee for a national estimate if a majority of them disagreed with the Director of Central Intelligence and they did not have the authority to override his opinion as Admiral Inglis wished.

Webb declared that the Director of the Federal Bureau of Investigation should be a member of the Intelligence Advisory Committee in order to improve the coordination of intelligence and security. Secret operations should be integrated with secret intelligence and the domestic exploitation of foreign intelligence in a "single self-administered office" within the

Central Intelligence Agency. And, finally, the Director of Central Intelligence should be a civilian. The President should be "invited to give his early consideration to a person of considerable stature and prominence, possessing the requisite qualifications of experience and willingness to serve." Perhaps Mr. Webb already had the person in mind. It was certain that as soon as the President discovered him Mr. Webb would have Admiral Hillenkoetter depart.[31]

MCNARNEY AT WORK

The Secretaries of State and Defense by order of the National Security Council were to have the benefit of consultation with the Departments of the Treasury and Justice in digesting the Dulles Report and making recommendations to the Council for action. Both departments had services concerned with foreigners entering the country and with matters of internal security. No evidence has been preserved in the file of the Agency on NSC 50 to show whether the Treasury gave any help to Humelsine, McNarney, and their staff; there was no great reason why the Treasury should do so, beyond its interest in apprehending smugglers. The Bureau of the Budget and the Comptroller General's Office were likely to be more useful in appraising the Dulles Report. But there was activity in the Department of Justice to make sure that no invasion occurred into the realm of J. Edgar Hoover. Admiral Souers recalled that Attorney General Tom Clark was vehement on the telephone against the Dulles Report as he read it. Souers was amused, in recollection, because Correa had been supposed to be the particular friend of the FBI by reason of his own service in the Department of Justice.[32]

Clark sent an elaborate statement to General McNarney in the Office of the Secretary of Defense as the General's report came under final discussion during May before going to the Council for action. If the Federal Bureau of Investigation, said Clark, became a member of the Intelligence Advisory Committee, NSCID 1 should be amended. It should not affect or change the duties and responsibilities of the Interdepartmental Intelligence Conference recently established; nor should it impair the jurisdiction of the FBI over domestic espionage, counterespionage, sabotage, subversion, and related matters affecting internal security.[33]

Clark and Hoover were not satisfied that the Act of Congress kept the Central Intelligence Agency from the field of internal security. Apparently they did not believe there was sufficient protection in requiring Hillenkoetter to ask in writing for Hoover's permission before anyone from the Agency could see the materials of intelligence which the Bureau collected in its pursuit of subversives.[34]

The Attorney General and the Director of the FBI really wanted more than protection. Clark proposed that the Interdepartmental Intelligence Conference, operating under NSC 17/4 as approved by the President on March 23, 1949, should have power of coordination. [seven lines deleted][35]

As set up by the Council, the Interdepartmental Intelligence Conference (IIC) and its companion, the Interdepartmental Committee on Internal Security (ICIS), were designed to exclude the Central Intelligence Agency. It was to have representation only upon invitation as an "ad hoc" member. The IIC, responsible for the "coordination of the investigation" of all domestic espionage, counterespionage, subversion, and "other related intelligence matters affecting internal security," was to consist of the Director of the FBI, the Chief of Naval Intelligence, the Director of the Army's Intelligence Division, and the Director of Intelligence for the Air Force. The ICIS, to handle other matters of internal security, would be composed of representatives from the Departments of State, the Treasury, Justice, and the National Military Establishment. Again there was no permanent membership for the Central Intelligence Agency. A representative of the National Security Council served both committees as an adviser, assistant, and observer and reporter for the Council. He was not to have any powers of instruction, direction, or supervision. Mr. J. Patrick Coyne, formerly with the FBI, was appointed to the office.[36]

Intelligence is inseparable from internal security. The directive of the Council itself specifically acknowledged the fact by referring to "other related intelligence matters affecting internal security." Moreover, security is not confined to the domestic scene; many affairs jeopardizing the internal security of the country have their origins far beyond the waterfront. Clandestine intelligence abroad, primarily the concern of the Central Intelligence Agency, has inescapable relationships with the detection of sabotage and subversion within this country. For this very reason, if no other, the Central Intelligence Agency should have constant representation in the interdepartmental body supposed to confer upon problems of internal security. But J. Edgar Hoover, though not displeased that security reached beyond the domestic scene, in fact quite willing to maintain outposts for the FBI in foreign countries, was not so willing to have the CIA participate as a regular member of the Interdepartmental Intelligence Conference or the Interdepartmental Committee on Internal Security.[37]

Further evidence that Clark and Hoover had no such desire or intention lay in Clark's statement to McNarney that the Dulles Group was wrong in thinking that the FBI did not gather intelligence and disseminate it as well as coordinate it through the IIC. [six lines deleted] This was not only an acknowledgement that intelligence and security were interrelated. It was an admission that Clark and Hoover thought of the FBI itself as a central intelligence organization.[38]

Careful study of Clark's memorandum to McNarney with NSC 17/4 could yield no other conclusion than that Clark and Hoover had overshot their mark in defending the FBI against possible encroachment by the Central Intelligence Agency. It is hard to believe that the Interdepartmental Intelligence Conference was authorized to extend its jurisdiction to functions which had been assigned primarily to the Agency by the Act of Congress. The IIC was intended to reconcile conflicting interpretations and activities, to prevent obstruction and interference through ignorance; it was to keep the FBI and the armed services reciprocally informed and interacting. The Conference and its companion, the ICIS, were not to usurp the established coordinating functions either of the Central Intelligence Agency or of the Intelligence Advisory Committee, any more than they were to invade the sacred precincts of Hoover's Bureau of Investigation.[39]

After a meeting of representatives from the Council and the military establishment with Hillenkoetter, McNarney's report was phrased in such a way that Clark and Hoover should have no fear. The FBI would not become too hampered and involved if Hoover accepted a permanent place in the Intelligence Advisory Committee. He might even take part in constructing the "crisis" estimates which the Dulles Group urged. This affair should recall Hoover's concern in 1946, and the progress of his thinking, when Vandenberg established the Contact Branch in the Office of Operations to obtain foreign intelligence within this country. It was Admiral Leahy, personal representative of the President, who seemed then to be successful in removing the tension.[40]

Hoover was reluctant to join the Intelligence Advisory Committee, even more so to engage in its national estimating. As Souers remarked to him, he was not equipped for that sort of work; he should take part in it only as an observer. He should participate in the coordination of intelligence activities. The Federal Bureau of Investigation, though hesitant and on occasion anxious to withdraw, had maintained until the fall of 1953, when this was written, its representation in the IAC and the subcommittees on the working level at the insistence of the Office of National Estimates. There was advantage in having a member of the FBI present to make its contribution should a matter in which it was interested suddenly appear during the discussion of a forthcoming estimate.[41]

With Clark and Hoover satisfied that the FBI was secure, that nothing in NSCID 1 as revised would alter NSC 17/4, there were no further departmental objections to having the National Security Council act upon the conclusions which McNarney drew from his study of the Dulles Report. As they differed in several instances from the recommendations of the Dulles Group, McNarney's proposals merit consideration at some length.

The Act of Congress was sound as approved by the President in 1947. There was no need for amendment. The location of the Central Intelligence Agency under the National Security Council was proper. In time of war certain functions and responsibilities of the Agency should be under military control. It only remained for the Director of Central Intelligence himself to establish "close liaison" with the two members of the Council upon whom the Agency chiefly depended, the Secretaries of State and Defense. It was a relationship which Hillenkoetter had recommended from the start and which Secretaries Lovett and Forrestal had favored. But it was one which the feud between Secretaries Acheson and Johnson was not making easy for Hillenkoetter to obtain.[42]

The McNarney Report endorsed as a "statement of principles" the conclusions of the Dulles Group that the CIA had not fully discharged its responsibility for coordinating intelligence activities. The Intelligence Advisory Committee should engage more actively both in such "continuing coordination" and in the "discussion and approval" of intelligence estimates. General McNarney did not accept General Irwin's view that the Director had no individual responsibility for coordination. McNarney agreed with the Dulles Group that Hillenkoetter should take "forthright initiative and leadership" in the Intelligence Advisory Committee. The McNarney Report recommended that NSCID 1 should be amended to further that accomplishment.

The directive should be revamped to make the Director of Central Intelligence a member of the Intelligence Advisory Committee and its chairman. Other members should be the Director of the Federal Bureau of Investigation, the chiefs of intelligence from the Departments of State, Army, Navy, and Air Force, the Joint Staff of the Joint Chiefs of Staff, and the Atomic Energy Commission. All might have representatives attend in their places. Any other agency concerned with the national security would be invited by the Director of Central Intelligence to send a representative whenever matters within its jurisdiction were to be discussed.

Admiral Hillenkoetter himself had suggested at the time of the adoption of NSCID 1 in December 1947 that the Director should be a member of the Intelligence Advisory Committee and its chairman. It would seem that a person in command should not be a member of the board which advised him. But the concept of the Advisory Committee was changing. The original idea had been that it should cooperate with the Director in making national estimates. The idea had fallen into disuse largely through reluctance or indifference on the part of responsible officers in the departments. If the Intelligence Advisory Committee were actually to develop now into such a cooperative estimating board, working with and sharing responsibility with the Director, there would be reason for him to be a member of that body. He would function then in much the same manner as the King in Council of British constitutional history. It is not apparent, however, that the original concept of the Intelligence Advisory Board had been recaptured in 1949 and placed uppermost in the minds of Hillenkoetter's critics. It is not easy to think of them as wishing to see him sit like a King in Council.[43]

General McNarney did not approve the recommendation in the Dulles Report that membership of the Atomic Energy Commission and the Joint Chiefs of Staff in the IAC should be abandoned. On the contrary, he tacitly accepted the arguments of Hillenkoetter, Colby, and Todd that the Commission and the Joint Chiefs should continue to have representation in the Advisory Committee. We should take note also that McNarney's revision of NSCID 1 retained the stipulation that the Committee should "advise the Director of Central Intelligence." There was no connotation of guidance or supervision; he was not to wait upon the consent of the Committee. General McNarney did not agree with Admiral Inglis that the IAC should become the Intelligence Coordinating Committee and take over the business of the Central Intelligence Agency as a "cooperative interdepartmental activity." Although McNarney did not say it in so many words, he was treating the CIA as an "independent agency" and the Director of Central Intelligence indisputably as its head.[44]

McNarney made this clearer still when he came to the recommendations of the Dulles Group concerning national intelligence estimates and dissents. He agreed with the Group that there had been "confusion" in the Agency, between its responsibility for "coordinated national intelligence estimates" and its responsibility for miscellaneous research and reporting. The Agency should interpret and follow the directives of the Council "so as to refrain as far as possible" from competition in producing "research intelligence estimates." But McNarney concurred in the conclusion of the Dulles Report with an exception; and it was a significant demurrer. He did not believe that the Director and the Intelligence Advisory Committee should be bound by "the concept of collective responsibility."

Coordinated national intelligence under such restriction, he said, would be inevitably reduced to "the lowest common denominator among the agencies concerned." The procedure to be adopted should permit the Director and the Committee to fulfill their "respective responsibilities" to the President and to the National Security Council. And this should be

"regardless of unanimous consent." McNarney proposed "concurrent sub-
missions." He recommended the revision of NSCID 1 to allow "substantially differing opinions" in place of "an agreed statement of substantial
dissent."[45]

It would appear that McNarney stood upon the ground which Vandenberg and Hillenkoetter had taken for their individual responsibility as
Directors of Central Intelligence. The Director, rather than the departmental chiefs in the Advisory Committee, was responsible. But it is hard
to find in the text of the McNarney Report any advance over previous
arrangements regarding that responsibility. The idea had been throughout the life of the Central Intelligence Group and of the Agency from the
President's Directive of January 22, 1946, up to this time that the Director
could submit his considered opinion as the estimate of the central intelligence organization. The only qualification was that he should also submit
any substantial dissent from that opinion by the representatives of the
departments. The makers of policy in the National Security Council or
elsewhere were free to take either estimate, or to rely on their own if they
wished. McNarney's proposal to allow several rather than one substantial
dissent loosened the requirements for coordinated intelligence estimates.
He had not found a new formula. The problem was still one of performance according to old principles.[46]

The Joint Intelligence Committee of the Joint Chiefs of Staff, including
civilian as well as military representation, had produced under the stress
of war national intelligence estimates worthy of the name. There were
many who felt the same urgency during the spring of 1949, but they were
not in command. Before another year had passed, conditions approximat-
ing the stress of war had returned. One contention is that, even so, there
were no national estimates properly coordinated and compounded from
departmental intelligence and other information until the advent of General Smith and the Office of National Estimates in the fall of 1950. The
opposing view, quite as effectively presented, is that if the estimates on
Korea which came from the Agency prior to the Communist invasion
below the 38th parallel were not constructed according to the Dulles or
the McNarney formulas, they were nevertheless national in scope. They
were in fact surprisingly accurate forecasts of events to come.[47]

The McNarney Report gathered from the conclusions and recommendations throughout the Dulles Report a list of particular questions which
the National Security Council should call to the attention of the Director
of Central Intelligence and the Intelligence Advisory Committee for "early
and sustained action." The Director should submit a progress report
within six months. The questions were scientific intelligence, domestic
intelligence, and counterintelligence related to national security, coordi-

nated estimates in crises, the allocation of responsibility for political summaries, the exploitation of foreign nationals within the United States, covert intelligence activities in occupied areas, the handling of "defectors," counterespionage abroad and at home. These topics, eight in all, were the subject of controversy among the Agency, the FBI, the Department of State, and the armed services throughout the remainder of Hillenkoetter's stay in office as Director of Central Intelligence. Many of them perplexed the administration of his successor, General Smith, and remained for Mr. Dulles to handle.[48]

General McNarney followed the lead of the Dulles Group to recommend specified changes in the internal organization of the Agency. The National Security Council, he said, should order the Director of Central Intelligence to report in ninety days how far he had gone with the changes. This was much more drastic than the manner of the Eberstadt Committee of the Hoover Commission in its report to Congress. One may question the interpretation of the National Security Act which both McNarney and the Dulles Group assumed in their specific proposals and peremptory suggestion of a limitation in time.[49]

Congress established the Central Intelligence Agency upon statutory foundations. Congress could have specified, but did not specify, the details of its internal construction. Instead, Congress stipulated that the Agency had the duty to perform particular functions under the direction of the National Security Council. Congress gave the Council implicit authority to create branches or divisions, committees, staffs, or offices within the Agency to exercise those functions. In the absence of express assignment by the Council of a function to this staff or to that office, or denial of the right to the Director, he had the right as head of the Agency to organize and reorganize its internal structure as he desired. The presumption was of course that he would keep the Council informed. Vandenberg had been assured that the Director would not have to go to the Council for instructions in detail. Although he was subject to supervision and direction by his superiors in the Council, how he organized and administered institutions within the Agency would be his own concern. Anyone who observed the arrangements and rearrangements more recently under General Smith could hardly deny the fact. Such matters of institution and procedure were his privilege.[50]

Even Secretary Royall for all practical purposes had admitted this right of the Director of Central Intelligence when he said that the Director should look to the Council for "broad directives." Royall had objected to the idea that the Council should delegate its authority to a subcommittee of itself; he had not opposed the thought that the Director of Central Intelligence should administer the internal organization of the Agency.

Royall had advocated that the Intelligence Advisory Committee should have autonomy because it represented the interests of the departments in the central intelligence system.[51]

Secretary Royall had not argued, as the Dulles Group proposed and McNarney agreed, that the Director of Central Intelligence should be ordered to reconstruct his own Interdepartmental Coordinating and Planning Staff to suit the departmental chiefs of intelligence; or to rearrange the Office of Collection and Dissemination within the Agency because some outsiders did not like the way in which it was functioning; or to split the Office of Reports and Estimates into new formations because others thought them desirable; or to move the Foreign Documents Branch from the Office of Operations to the proposed Research and Reports Division; or to gather the Office of Special Operations, the Office of Policy Coordination, and the Contact Branch of the Office of Operations into one large division of operations. McNarney did not agree with the Dulles Group on placing the Foreign Broadcast Information Branch in that large semi-autonomous division. McNarney also remarked that there might be other methods of organization which would accomplish the same objectives.[52]

All of these proposals were matters of suggestion to the Council and, in the absence of directives from the Council, of voluntary acceptance by the Director of Central Intelligence. Hillenkoetter had no doubt of the mandate to the Intelligence Survey Group to make suggestions. In fact, he had been among the first to propose that there should be such an investigation and report to the National Security Council. He had cooperated with the Dulles Group. It was supposed to take him into its full confidence, as it did not. There was no question of the right to suggest changes, including the removal of the Director.

Nor was there any question of the right of the National Security Council under stipulations in sections 102 and 303 of the National Security Act of 1947 to issue directives to the Central Intelligence Agency and its head, the Director of Central Intelligence. The right to direct him perhaps could be extended so far as to give the Council power to dictate whether the Director should employ women rather than men as secretaries in his outer office, if one may use a trivial example to fix the point. The expectation was obvious. The Council would seldom if ever have recourse to directives in small detail. Even though it had such power, it would not exercise the power. It would confine itself, as Royall proposed, to "broad directives" regarding major institutions and policies.

On the other hand, it was certain that the National Security Council could not grant functions to the Agency nor direct actions by the Agency beyond the intentions of Congress. Any usurpation by the Council could be stopped short the moment the committees of Congress came to the business of appropriating the funds, vouchered or unvouchered, which were involved in those activities. There were bounds to the Council's right of direction over the Central Intelligence Agency.

The Director of Central Intelligence, moreover, was appointed by the President with the consent of the Senate. The National Security Council had the power to direct the Director of Central Intelligence but not to remove him from office. Only the President could do that. If the President should favor action by the Director of Central Intelligence which the Council did not approve, the situation would obviously be unpleasant but the Secretaries in the Council would be able to do little about it.

The Director of Central Intelligence was close to them in rank and distinction within the hierarchy of the Government. Souers was fully aware of this when he urged Hillenkoetter to drop the practice of signing his papers as Rear Admiral and to use his title as Director of Central Intelligence. He was at least equal to the Under Secretaries of the departments. He was by Act of Congress the equal of the Joint Chiefs of Staff among the advisers of the President and the National Security Council.[53]

There was no question at all that the Director of Central Intelligence was superior in position and prestige to the departmental chiefs of intelligence who were his advisers in the Intelligence Advisory Committee and were supposed to cooperate with him in producing national intelligence estimates. This could have been one reason why they sought to bring him down to their level in the Intelligence Advisory Committee, if not below it as the executive officer of an agency which they would direct from the Intelligence Advisory Committee as a governing board.

In language that was diplomatic but without equivocation, General McNarney disagreed with the Dulles Group regarding the "understanding" and "the ability" of the directing staff in the Agency. There were "important defects," he said, in the organization and the operations of CIA, but the conclusions of the Dulles Report were "too sweeping." There had been too little time for the Hillenkoetter administration to develop an effective organization. There was "a lack of common understanding" in regard to the "respective missions of CIA and the departmental intelligence agencies." If this was an indictment, it was to be shared by the departmental authorities with the responsible officers of the Agency. McNarney recommended that the National Security Council view the conclusions and recommendations of the Dulles Report with these comments in mind.[54]

He did not think that there were too many military men in the Agency, nor that they discouraged its civilians unnecessarily. Continuity of service was essential, but the Director did not have to be a civilian to ensure it. Independence of action could be obtained with "a service man or a foreign service officer" if he were either retired from his service or given the directorship of the Agency as his "final tour of active duty." McNarney proposed only that the Council should call these considerations with regard to the Director of Central Intelligence to the attention of the President. Others in the Agency should be left to the Director.

The Dulles Report, following up the publicity which Hillenkoetter and the Agency had received from Representative Brown and others at the time of Bogotá, proposed that the Director when in doubt should consult the Council regarding the disclosure of secret information and should divert public attention to the coordinating activities of the Agency. McNarney concurred but declared that all publicity was undesirable; he opposed the procedure recommended by the Dulles Report unless it was unavoidable. He urged that the Director should prepare new directives for the Council covering these matters and should submit the directives in thirty days. McNarney's view could be taken to support Hillenkoetter's position quite as much as that of the Dulles Survey Group, Walter Lippmann, Thomas E. Dewey, or any other critic of Hillenkoetter's handling of the Bogotá affair.[55]

General McNarney joined Admiral Hillenkoetter, General Irwin, and Admiral Inglis in opposing the recommendation of the Dulles Group that the Director of Central Intelligence should be made permanent chairman of the United States Communications Intelligence Board. The rotating chairmanship was working satisfactorily. It seemed undesirable to make a change.[56]

Regarding the comments in the Dulles Report on the intelligence agencies of the armed services and the Department of State, the McNarney Report had only to repeat the decisions in the military establishment and the Department. They were not answerable to the Council. The State Department concurred with the Dulles Group with respect to reorganizing its intelligence staff and designating a high officer to maintain close relations with the Central Intelligence Agency. Those recommendations were to be put into effect. The National Military Establishment also agreed in the general conclusions of the Dulles Report on its intelligence services, but with one decided reservation. The Establishment would continue assigning qualified personnel to intelligence duties, though they had no previous experience. Rotation should remain the rule, with efforts "to attract the highest type of personnel." Military men were not yet willing to concentrate upon intelligence "over the major portion of their careers." It seemed evident that they would remain unwilling until forces available in military life, other than attraction, were applied.[57]

Several recommendations of the Dulles Report on "operating problems related to clandestine activities" received McNarney's approval, as they had Hillenkoetter's acceptance. [two lines deleted] The departmental agencies should be brought closer to OSO. It should receive better guidance from its "consumers"; for this purpose representatives of those agencies might be included in appropriate sections of the Office. To this particular point Hillenkoetter had mildly objected on the ground that military personnel would be increased when the Dulles Group was charging that the Agency already had too many. McNarney, and Hillenkoetter, agreed with the Dulles Group that the Director of Central Intelligence should assure himself that the operating services of the CIA received adequate guidance on the "current and strategic and policy needs of the Government." And those services should have access to communications intelligence to the fullest extent required for guidance in their operations and more effective counterespionage.[58]

McNarney recommended that the Council approve these proposals concerning the clandestine activities of the Agency. The Director of Central Intelligence should carry them out "with the assistance of the other departments and agencies concerned." The Director should report to the Council upon "any difficulties encountered." This last recommendation offered an interesting prospect.[59]

It was possible that the departmental intelligence services might be subject to closer inspection by the Director of Central Intelligence than they had yet experienced. It was possible, but no more likely, that the Council would take action against the departmental intelligence services if the Director of Central Intelligence reported his difficulties with them.[60]

The Council in fact was not used to pressing the services for action in favor of the Agency against their wishes. The Secretary of Defense, though given "general direction, authority, and control" over the National Military Establishment in the National Security Act of 1947, did not have the prestige and respect as yet really to do more than admonish the departments and advise the President that they should be ordered to conform. The Secretaries of the departments were not inclined to issue unpopular directives, much less to enforce them. It was easier to turn to the Director of Central Intelligence and instruct him to exert "forthright initiative and leadership" in coordinating the activities of the departments. If he did not have the authority, he did have the responsibility; he could take the initiative and hope for response to his leadership. If he did not succeed, he would be a good whipping boy.[61]

Assured that the development of Central Intelligence was the underlying purpose of the President's Directive of 1946 and the Act of Congress which replaced it in 1947, one must conclude from the minutes of meetings, memoranda, letters, and reports, which constitute a voluminous record, that the chiefs of intelligence were always deliberate, often obstinate, and usually disposed to block the efforts of the Director of Central Intelligence for the accomplishment of the purpose. How willful the misunderstanding was on the part of the departmental agencies is to be decided by each reader of the record for himself according to his own temper. It took, anyway, more time than Admiral Hillenkoetter was allowed in office to establish "common understanding" on matters of common concern.[62]

There still are differences of opinion and performance. Such matters as "agreed activities" in clandestine operations abroad, the "capabilities and intentions" of our own country, "operational intelligence" of the armed services, "domestic intelligence and counterintelligence" under the jurisdiction of the Federal Bureau of Investigation, and others delay the millenium. When it comes, the central intelligence service and the departmental intelligence services will cooperate in "common understanding." Then perhaps "coordination" will no longer mean coercion to some and frustration to others. The American people will have a national system of intelligence.

ACTION BY THE COUNCIL

With Dean Acheson, Secretary of State, presiding and Under Secretary Stephen Early attending in place of Louis Johnson, Secretary of Defense, the National Security Council adopted the recommendations of the Dulles Survey Group on July 7, 1949, as those recommendations had been reconsidered and modified in the McNarney Report. There was one exception to be explained presently. The Treasury was represented at this meeting of the Council by Under Secretary Edward H. Foley. There was no one present for the Department of Justice and its FBI.[63]

Clark and Hoover had gained many of their points elsewhere. The revised NSCID 1 was ready for issue by the Council on this date. There remained only an exchange of notes between Clark and Souers for the Attorney General to accept the membership in the reconstituted Intelligence Advisory Committee on behalf of the Federal Bureau of Investigation and to make sure that its functions under section 102 of the National Security Act of 1947 and NSC 17/4 were not impaired. The IIC and the ICIS would continue their operations in the fields of internal security. But it was agreed that the Intelligence Advisory Committee, with the FBI in its membership, should do the coordinating whenever the problems of domestic and of foreign intelligence were mingled. Hoover conceded again, as he had in the fall of 1946, that foreign intelligence was concerned with intelligence activities in this country such as the exploitation of foreign nationality groups, refugees, and "defectors."[64]

Details in regard to "defectors," however, were not settled until well into the following year [seven lines deleted]. The Agency was to seek guidance from and keep in close touch with the appropriate departments. Further specification cannot detain us here. The Intelligence Advisory Committee and the Federal Bureau of Investigation were obviously expected to work with the Agency as smoothly and as quietly as possible in so delicate a matter.

[two lines deleted] The agency with primary responsibility, therefore, was the Federal Bureau of Investigation for purposes of "internal security." The Central Intelligence Agency came into the action when acquiring "foreign intelligence." Such allocation was not, however, to "preclude joint exploitation"; it was to be encouraged wherever feasible. [one line deleted] It looked good on paper. Members of both establishments will admit nevertheless that statements of procedure are easier to obtain than performances according to them, especially when the participants think of themselves as competitors rather than as partners in the endeavor.[65]

The decision of the Council on July 7, 1949, with respect to the McNarney Report was elaborated in separate memoranda from the office of the Executive Secretary to the Director of Central Intelligence and to the Intelligence Advisory Committee. Souers wrote to Hillenkoetter on July 7 that he was directed to carry out the recommendations of the Survey Group in regard to "operating problems relating to clandestine activities" as listed in NSC 50. He was to report any difficulties encountered.[66]

Hillenkoetter was already trying to solve those problems by the steady method of working with the parties of interest as best he could. It had not been his policy in 1947 to press for his right of inspection in departmental activities as the chief intelligence officer or executive agent of the Secretaries in the Council. It was not his policy now. Hillenkoetter knew as well as anyone else that even a President's purposes could suffer from attrition and sabotage within the departmental services and agencies of the Government. This was the last that he heard from the Council on the subject. He had no order to report in so many days. A search of the record has not discovered that he ever reported on these matters.[67]

Other directives from the Council, sent by Lay on July 8, set time limits upon Hillenkoetter's execution and report. He was to take up with the Intelligence Advisory Committee the "particular intelligence questions" in the McNarney Report and answer within six months. He was to attend to the "organization of the Central Intelligence Agency," excepting the separate administration for the proposed operations division, and report in ninety days. To frame new directives regarding "the security of information and avoidance of publicity" he was given a month.[68]

In order that we may not lose sight of the last instruction in discussing the more controversial matters upon which Hillenkoetter was to act, let us follow it here to its conclusion. He laid drafts of the new directives before the Intelligence Advisory Committee. But he was unable to get unanimous approval within the month, and so he informed Souers in advance of the next meeting of the Council on August 4. At that time the Council authorized the Director to defer submission of the new directives until its next meeting. It was not, however, until after the meeting on January 5, 1950, that NSCID 11 and NSCID 12 were approved by the National Security Council.[69]

The first of these directives, pertaining to the security of sources and methods of intelligence, authorized the departments and agencies of the Government to determine their own channels of "authorization to release any such information." The Director of Central Intelligence no longer was (if he ever had been) responsible for protecting "sources and methods" other than those of the Central Intelligence Agency itself. His duty was to coordinate the policies concerning such protection, within the limits set by section 102 of the National Security Act of 1947, except when the Council had made provision, as in the case of the Federal Bureau of Investigation.[70]

Overt information from a clandestine source was not to be purveyed if doing so revealed its source. The Director of Central Intelligence and other intelligence chiefs should be guided by the principle that covert information should go only to officials who required the knowledge. The last paragraph of the directive was dutiful, but it was also futile. Any reference to the Central Intelligence Agency, it said, should emphasize that the Agency coordinated intelligence rather than engaged in secret activities. The restriction was useless so long as agents of other countries picked up information about those activities and put that information into the newspapers and radio broadcasts of the world.

The second directive, NSCID 12, required all departments and agencies represented in the Intelligence Advisory Committee to prevent the unauthorized disclosure for publication of any information concerning intelligence and intelligence activities. The head of each establishment was to determine his "channel for granting such authorization as may be necessary." All other executive establishments should be advised that the above statements were an expression of policy on the part of the National Security Council.

If the Director of Central Intelligence had doubt whether he should comply with a request for the disclosure of classified information, he should refer the question to the National Security Council. The directive contained no further reference to such cases as the one which had given rise to the criticism of Hillenkoetter in the Dulles Report for the exposure of Bogotá. Disclosures before committees of Congress presumably were authorized disclosures about which the Director of Central Intelligence would have no doubt unless they were forbidden by the President.[71]

As for the "organization of the Central Intelligence Agency," the Council had agreed on July 7, 1949, with McNarney and Hillenkoetter that the Foreign Broadcast Information Branch should not be included in the merger of OSO, OPC, and the Contact Branch of OO. But the Council, possibly in deference to Hillenkoetter's comments, did not immediately accept the proposal of the Dulles Group, endorsed by McNarney, that the new Operations Division should have a "separate administration" within the Agency. This exception was referred to the Secretaries of State and Defense for further study. Humelsine and McNarney were named again. McNarney reported on July 22. Souers forwarded his paper to the members of the Council three days later and invited the Attorney General to take part when the report should come up for consideration. Clark neither attended nor sent a representative to the meeting of the Council on August 4.[72]

McNarney's paper of July 22 on separate administrative services of support in the Agency shows that he conferred with Hillenkoetter and two of his assistant directors who would be responsible for carrying out the recommendations; presumably they were Colonel Robert A. Schow of OSO and Mr. Frank G. Wisner of OPC. From previous exchanges of opinion between Hillenkoetter and Wisner, the assumption is fair that their ideas still were at variance. Having given full weight to the views of the Director and his assistants, said McNarney, the representatives of the Secretaries of State and Defense reaffirmed the recommendation of the Dulles–Jackson–Correa Committee that the proposed Operations Division should have a "separate administration."[73]

The endorsement was not, however, so complete an acceptance of the State Department's interpretation of the power of guidance in NSC 10-2 as one might think. McNarney went into the problem of administrative support with care. There was marked silence upon Hillenkoetter's objection that decentralization of supporting services ran counter to his responsibility for certifying unvouchered expenditures.[74]

McNarney found separate administrative organizations for overt and covert offices particularly desirable in handling these matters: the management of personnel (except clerical help in headquarters) including recruitment and security; travel abroad, reproducing and photocopying, storage and warehousing for clandestine materials; fiscal, accounting, and budgetary functions including the management and control of confidential funds; the administration of contracts where they involved clandestine matters; and related administrative business requiring close relationship and knowledge on the part of the smallest number of officials to ensure flexibility and security for the operations.

But McNarney recommended that certain other functions should be kept in the central administrative office of the Agency. These were the obvious matters of housing, ordinary supplies, and transportation in this country. With them were legal services even for clandestine operations. This reservation alone indicated that McNarney did not believe in complete autonomy for the Operations Division within the Agency, subject to "guidance" from the Departments of State and Defense and receiving merely cover and services of support in the Agency. The law officers of the Director would have a considerable amount of supervision and control over the operations of the new Division.[75]

McNarney said nothing about the power of the Director himself to require an accounting of the smallest project by his subordinate in charge of covert operations. The Director of Central Intelligence might not be able to overrule the wishes of the Departments of State and Defense upon appeal to the Council from their "guidance." So long as the President kept the Director in office, however, he could hold the Assistant Director of Covert Operations in check. Congress allotted unvouchered funds to the Agency for accounting "solely on the certificate of the Director."[76]

The Council accepted McNarney's view of the "separate administration" for the proposed Operations Division in the Agency on August 4 and ordered Hillenkoetter to expedite and complete the merger of OSO, OPC, and the Contact Branch within ninety days. He was ready on August 31 with a plan of consolidation which had been accepted among the interested parties in the Agency. A preliminary suggestion had gone, on August 16, to Mr. George F. Kennan in the State Department, Major General James H. Burns in the Office of the Secretary of Defense, apparently acting in place of General McNarney, and to Colonel Ivan D. Yeaton, representative of the Joint Chiefs of Staff. It would seem that they were functioning as the consultants to OPC on behalf of the Secretaries of State and Defense under NSC 10-2.[77]

Admiral Hillenkoetter issued a general order on September 20, 1949, to reorganize his system of budgeting, disbursing, and accounting in conformity with the directive of the National Security Council that there should be separate administrative services for the overt and covert offices in the Agency. Budgeting for the whole Agency remained a centralized staff function under the Executive Director. Overt and covert support staffs were now created to separate their respective fiscal and financial affairs, their personnel and supporting services.[78]

Under this arrangement, once the Assistant Director of Special Operations or of Policy Coordination received his portion of the unvouchered funds, he was in charge of their specific budgeting and disbursement within his Office; their accounting and internal auditing were to be done apart from those of any other office. Certification of the unvouchered funds, however, and the external audit conducted in the Agency by representatives from the General Accounting Office and the Comptroller General remained the concern of the Director of Central Intelligence. This arrangement continued until it was changed on December 1, 1950, in the administration of General Smith. The change supported Hillenkoetter's opinion that budgetary, fiscal, and financial matters should be under central control.[79]

There is no point at this juncture in explaining the details of the plan for the Operations Division. It did not go into effect. As Hillenkoetter remembered the episode, neither the State Department nor the Department of Defense wished to approve the other party's candidate for the office of Assistant Director of the Operations Division. The State Department did not want Colonel Schow, who held the senior position as head of OSO, the older Office in the Agency. The armed services would not accept Mr. Wisner, head of OPC. And so there was no merger and no creation of an enlarged OPC under the guidance of representatives of the Secretaries of State and Defense. Hillenkoetter continued to direct the collection of secret intelligence as he had before the departure of Colonel Galloway. The Contact Branch, much to the satisfaction of many who worked on it, remained a part of the overt Office of Operations. It was there, as this account was written in August 1953, after the Offices of Special Operations and of Policy Coordination had gone into the process of "integration."[80]

Souers advised the Director of Central Intelligence and the Intelligence Advisory Committee on July 7, 1949, that the Council wished them to follow McNarney's commentary upon the recommendations of the Dulles Group concerning the coordination of intelligence activities and the production of national estimates as a "statement of principles." Souers spoke in the same memorandum of the vote by the Council that the Director should report within six months upon "particular intelligence questions," among them the matter of emergency estimating. Lay repeated this directive in his memorandum on the following day. Together these instructions provided an opportunity for Hillenkoetter's opponents and gave him a task that was to endure for more than six months.[81]

As we enter this contest over principles steeped in bitterness, we should keep always in mind that General McNarney did not accept the argument of the Dulles Report for "collective responsibility." On the contrary, McNarney favored the individual responsibility of the Director of Central Intelligence, provided there were statements of "substantially differing opinions." He gave his support to Vandenberg and Hillenkoetter rather than to William H. Jackson. This fact should be kept clear in the heat of the ensuing discussion, or there will be distortion.[82]

STATE'S FOUR PAPERS

The State Department seized the opportunity. At the meeting of the Intelligence Advisory Committee on July 22, 1949, W. Park Armstrong announced that the Department was endeavoring to isolate four or five problems which involved the Advisory Committee; they were to be distinguished from the internal affairs of the Agency. Except for the facts that the personalities were different and specific issues had changed, one could have been in the fall of 1945, when the Bureau of the Budget called for coordinating committees and laid the groundwork for McCormack's plan in the Department of State. There was little doubt who would endeavor to take the lead in the Intelligence Advisory Committee as Armstrong unfolded the four "problems." A fifth, regarding guidance to the Agency from the departments, was not necessary. Armstrong abandoned it. The four would suffice.[83]

The four were presented to Admiral Hillenkoetter on August 2, 1949, for distribution among the representatives of the departments and the Agency. The State Department believed, said Armstrong, that the "aspects of NSC 50" which were portrayed in these papers "should be implemented at the earliest feasible time." If Hillenkoetter agreed, they could be placed on the "IAC agenda." The titles of the four papers were: Coordination of Intelligence Activities, Production of National Intelligence, Research and Reports, Political Summaries. It is hardly necessary to examine them in every detail. Certain leads and arguments will reveal their direction and their purpose.[84]

The first paper rehearsed the old arguments whether ICAPS was or was not representative of the departments from which its members came to the Agency. Could it serve as a "joint staff" for the Director and the Advisory Committee? Or should the Standing Committee instead of ICAPS do the work for the Advisory Committee? The real issue was whether the Director of Central Intelligence or the Intelligence Advisory Committee should dominate in coordinating "intelligence activities."

In favoring the opinion that the Advisory Committee should refer the problems of coordination to the Standing Committee, Armstrong's writer in the State Department made an insinuation on the shortcomings of the Agency that might have seemed novel to General McNarney. The CIA should recognize that "coordination also implies assistance to the agencies"; they ought to be helped in meeting their responsibilities by "temporary assignments of personnel." It was reminiscent of Lovell's desire in 1946 for editorial assistance from CIG with his huge Defense Project. But one could hardly imagine that any departmental intelligence agency under normal conditions would be eager for assignments of personnel from CIA, however temporary. Departmental antipathy toward inspection was great.[85]

In his second paper Armstrong got to the business of producing national intelligence. He paid little attention to McNarney's principle that the Director and the Advisory Committee were not to be bound by "collective responsibility." Armstrong proposed that the IAC should "discuss and approve" all national intelligence estimates on which there was substantial disagreement among the agencies. There could be no objections to his idea that the Advisory Committee should discuss the estimates. This was the major purpose of having representatives of the departments share in making authoritative "coordinated national intelligence estimates." But to have them "approve" all estimates on which there was "substantial disagreement among the agencies" was either needless or it was absurd.

If the formula meant that the dissenting members of the Committee should approve an estimate from which they had dissented, it was nonsense. If the formula simply meant that the remaining members should approve, it was unnecessary. They would approve what they had accepted in the course of the discussion.

There was a third possibility. If the formula meant that no estimate could pass without unanimous consent on the part of the departmental members in the Intelligence Advisory Committee, then the Director of Central Intelligence would stand alone in dissent. Nevertheless, his opinion would be that of the Central Intelligence Agency of which he was head by Act of Congress. The makers of policy, it may be said again, could take his opinion, adopt the estimate of the Advisory Committee, or use their own judgment.

In the third paper Armstrong returned to ideas which he had expressed in the fall of 1947. He had advocated then that the Agency should vigorously inspect the work of other intelligence services and engage in little

research and evaluation of its own; it should rely upon "finished departmental intelligence" and confine itself to the production of national estimates. He endorsed now the Estimates Division proposed by the Dulles
Group for that purpose. Aside from national intelligence, he said, the
Agency should produce reports "only in fields of common concern." The
telltale point was that it should do so as prescribed by the Director "on the
advice of the IAC." If he received no advice upon a matter, the presumption was that the Agency's new Research and Reports Division would
produce no report.[86]

To go back to the beginning and start over, Armstrong suggested that
ICAPS should prepare for "consideration in IAC" recommendations on
the "delineations of fields of common concern." This should be done "on a
priority basis." Surely Armstrong knew from heresay regarding the trials
of his predecessors, Langer and Eddy, if not from his own experience
with the NSCIDs, that the "fields of common concern" had been bounded
and much trampled since 1946. But the idea made a good point for talk.
Perhaps that was its purpose.[87]

The fourth paper raised again the question which Secretary Byrnes had
taken straight to President Truman. Should the Agency produce daily and
weekly summaries of events when the State Department was already
issuing political reviews and other agencies were engaged in similar enterprises? President Truman had welcomed the reports from the Agency and
praised the service from time to time. He had gained a reputation, within
and without the Agency, for being one of the few who did read the summaries. But Armstrong saw more than gratification of the President in this
matter of "political summaries." There should be another study, this time
by ICAPS, and recommendations for "consideration by the IAC" on the
allocation of responsibility. It was a "difficult problem," he said, involving
information which was "in part intelligence and in part operational."
Again it is fair to point out that the departmental intelligence services so
far had been conveying to the Central Intelligence Agency little that they
considered "staff intelligence" or "operational intelligence" belonging to
themselves only.[88]

Coincident with Armstrong's "Four Papers," to take advantage of the
actions by the National Security Council on the McNarney Report, there
appeared a significant study of the Office of Reports and Estimates,
known in the Agency as the Reitzel Report. Its origins were distinct.
Captain Winecoff, formerly deputy to Babbitt in ORE and now Executive
for Hillenkoetter, urged that they should discover what was the "mission"
of the Office. They should go to the original documents to learn what
kinds of estimates they were supposed to make and what reports they
should file. They needed a "blueprint."[89]

The committee appointed for the task was familiar with the Dulles Report and possibly with the Eberstadt Report. But Reitzel and his associates had been working since May without knowledge of McNarney's efforts and report. Though aware of the State Department's activities and interests, they were not conversant with Armstrong's immediate aims. The Reitzel Report was relatively free from interdepartmental influence. It was rather the product of the divergence and conflict which had beset the Office since its creation in the summer of 1946 and harassed the preparation of the comments from the Office to Hillenkoetter on the Dulles Report. For simplicity's sake, this cleavage may be ascribed to the antipathy which seems inherent in every situation where specialists are obliged to accept judgments from others who are not necessarily expert but are unusually experienced.[90]

The Reitzel Report went to Theodore Babbitt, Assistant Director for Reports and Estimates, on July 19, 1949. It was entitled "Analysis of ORE Production, with Conclusions, First Report." There never was another, opinion in the Agency has it, for good reasons. One of them appears to have been that Babbitt preferred an organization of the estimating system different from either the Estimates Division (which the Dulles Group proposed and Armstrong endorsed) or a modification of the Global Survey Group in the Agency (which Reitzel himself had in mind).[91]

Babbitt had directed the committee on May 4, 1949, to review the production of ORE to see if its effort corresponded with its "mission." This was clearly in response to the charge in the Dulles Report that there had been "confusion." Reitzel and his associates went to the directives of the Council and the Agency. They did not return to the original administrative order by Montague on August 7, 1946, setting up the Office of Research and Evaluation for General Vandenberg under the authorization of the Fifth Directive of the National Intelligence Authority. As Reitzel recalled in 1953, his failure to do so was deliberate. Montague was in the center of the quarrel. His plan for a national estimating board was at issue. And so the committee endeavored to get beneath the structure of the controversy to its bedrock.[92]

For that very reason, the omission was in error. The administrative order of August 7, 1946, showed exactly what were the foundations of the Office of Reports and Estimates. Moreover, the order made clear that the work of the geographical specialists in "strategic and national policy intelligence" was originally to be subject to direction and coordination by the Central Reports staff, composed of experienced men. It was not a question of whether one group was abler than the other. It was essential to the whole process of estimating that there should be reflection upon the findings of the specialists, and that such reconsideration should be concentrated in one board of estimators. Specialists of course could be members of such a board of review. Final estimating should not be dispersed among several boards working by chance in concert, as often at cross-purposes and incompletely informed.[93]

For reasons of policy in the summer of 1949 Reitzel saw fit to leave out of his report any reference to plans or actions prior to the Act of Congress establishing the National Security Council and placing the Central Intelligence Agency under its jurisdiction. Technically he was correct in reporting that no adequate definition of an "ORE mission" existed under the directives of the Council and the Agency. He was justified in saying that NSCID 3 did not make explicit statement of the "relevant parts in the form of a mission for ORE." But it would seem that he went too far in stating that the Office was "without an authoritative frame of reference" to plan, guide, and appraise its production. NSCID 3 was legally "authoritative." It did not "spell out" details, to be sure; it left those to reasoned interpretation by the responsible officers in the Agency. The function of the Council, if Royall's view is accepted, was not to give specific order on small matters but to issue "broad directives" on affairs of major import.[94]

The proper criticism in the Reitzel Report was not so much criticism of authority, or lack of it, as of internal policy and administration. The Agency had authority to produce national intelligence. It did not have power to compel the coordination of departmental intelligence activities. It had only the power to advise the Council and to recommend action in regard to matters of coordination.[95]

The Reitzel Report elaborated upon "patterns of production," which had been turned from the original design of "current intelligence" and "strategic and national policy intelligence" for a restricted audience of policymakers to a wide range of general intelligence for lesser uses. The pressures had come from external demands upon the Office of Reports and Estimates and from competition within it among the branches and groups. The inference was apparent that a stronger will should have been exerted in the Office to prevent haphazard, unrelated, and inconsequential reporting. Babbitt looked back upon the situation ruefully. He knew, he said, that he should have been "tougher" than he was.[96]

At the time Babbitt was not affected by the Reitzel Report so much as by the open criticism of ORE in Armstrong's "Four Papers" for the State Department. As one who had spent some time in its Office of Intelligence Research before coming to the Agency to head the Office of Reports and Estimates on the nomination of the State Department, Babbitt was familiar with situations and personalities in both places. He was aware, too, from a report which he had signed shortly after arriving in the Agency during the summer of 1947, that the Department of State was remiss in its "coordinating" with the Office of Reports and Estimates. The record showed that the Department delayed more than any of the armed services. It was rather more galling, then, to be charged with confusion and ineptitude by the State Department than by the Department of Defense.[97]

Babbitt wrote to Hillenkoetter on August 15, 1949, that he was in "fundamental disagreement with the general principles" underlying Armstrong's proposals. Armstrong assumed that the National Security Council had approved specifically the realignments in the Agency recommended by the Dulles Report. The fact was that the Council had accepted McNarney's Report as NSC 50, and McNarney had recognized that there were other ways than those of the Dulles Report for reaching the same objectives. Armstrong had stated that the NSCIDs were adequate. Babbitt submitted that NSCID 1 and NSCID 3 both should be strengthened.[98]

He was ready with another NSCID 1 on policies, duties, and responsibilities. It should identify all categories of intelligence requirements and allocate responsibilities for collection and production throughout the intelligence system of the Government. ORE would have the "continuing interchange" of intelligence and unevaluated information between the departmental services and the Agency include "operational" information and any which was to be given "special security handling." In the latter case, each service would arrange promptly with the Director of Central Intelligence for the proper safeguards. And the ORE proposal would have each service upon specific request from the Director give "first priority" to the requirements of the Agency. The cumbersome method of NSCID 4 for determining priority of "national intelligence objectives" in the staff of the National Security Council would be superseded. From the marginal notes on his copy Prescott Childs, chief of ICAPS, appears to have thought the proposed revision of NSCID 1 too strong. It was withdrawn on October 3 before Hillenkoetter's report to the Council. Even so, it was good to have stress put directly upon real weaknesses in the existing procedure.[99]

Babbitt declared that NSCID 1 and NSCID 3 not only did not provide adequate priority in departmental support for the Agency but made no mention of the Agency's role as the intelligence service of the National Security Council, which in fact it was according to law whether or not the members of the departmental intelligence services ever thought so. Babbitt objected to definition of national intelligence as solely "integrated departmental intelligence." The Agency itself, he might have added, made significant contributions to that integration from its secret collection of intelligence abroad.

Armstrong's misinterpretations, said Babbitt, led him to believe that the Agency should not enter into the negotiations with the Intelligence Advisory Committee which Armstrong desired. Armstrong's ideas about changes in the organization of the Agency might not materialize. NSC 50 did not require that they should. The Agency did not have to establish an Estimates Division. The Office of Reports and Estimates was preparing recommendations for Hillenkoetter to consider in regard to the responsibilities of the Office and the production of intelligence. The Director might prefer those recommendations. In the meantime, the Standing Committee of the Intelligence Advisory Committee should take up the proposed revisions of NSCID 1 and NSCID 3 for report to the Advisory Committee. ORE would have a revision of NSCID 3 on production to submit shortly.

At the next meeting of the Intelligence Advisory Committee on August 19 Babbitt's recommendations were disregarded and Armstrong's "Four Papers" were referred in their entirety to the Standing Committee. The crux of the matter, as Prescott Childs, chief of ICAPS, reported it to Hillenkoetter, was that the State Department wanted ORE to leave the field of major research to its own Office of Intelligence Research. The Agency should have only "a very small research staff" to support its small Estimates Division. Until the National Security Council settled the issue, there would always be friction and duplication. The State Department also felt that it alone was the authority on political intelligence; no matter who asked for political information from the Agency, he should be advised to go to the State Department. Childs thought one man could correct that impression if he wished. President Truman had informed Secretary Byrnes that the daily summary of the Central Intelligence Group was information which the President needed, and so it was intelligence to him.[100]

Out of the reference of the "Four Papers" to the Standing Committee came a development that was not happy for Armstrong and the State Department. The members of the Standing Committee from the Department of Defense separated from the representatives of the State Department, Atomic Energy Commission, and Federal Bureau of Investigation to prepare a memorandum of their views in common. This they presented to the Standing Committee on September 8. As soon as Colonel Booth, representing the State Department, understood that they were in agreement, he remarked that the meeting was finished. They were "all set." "We still like ours best," he said, "so we have a definite split to put before the IAC."[101]

The members of the Standing Committee from the Department of Defense considered the internal organization of the Agency to be "the sole responsibility" of the Director of Central Intelligence. The matter of an Estimates Division, therefore, was not appropriate for action by the Standing Committee or by the Intelligence Advisory Committee itself unless the Director asked for its advice. The original proposals of the State Department should be referred with all pertinent data to ICAPS for a comprehensive report. ICAPS should consist of full-time members supplied by the members of the IAC, but it should be under the direction of and responsible to the Director of Central Intelligence. It should do the staff work for the IAC and its Standing Committee and perform such other functions as the Director of Central Intelligence should direct. After this defeat Colonel Booth might continue to argue that ICAPS could not serve two masters. There was little for Armstrong to do except await the comprehensive study by ICAPS and Hillenkoetter's report to the Council on his progress with the instructions in NSC 50.[102]

Before Hillenkoetter made this report to the Council, he called upon the Office of Reports and Estimates for another recording of the evidence that cooperation between the Intelligence Advisory Committee and the Central Intelligence Agency had failed. The compilation which he received on September 30, 1949, was arranged in three parts: those obstacles which resulted from departmental policy; failures of action by the departmental services; and failures on their part in coordinating reports and estimates from the Agency. Statements of particular cases were given in each category.[103]

The NSCIDs themselves were examples of the restrictions and reservations placed upon the Agency by the departments. In addition they failed to meet their obligations in amount of material or of time for the Agency to develop the resulting intelligence. They withheld information of value for estimates upon one justification or another according to their own interpretations of the directives. They did not advise the Agency as soon as they had completed their research and production and were ready to proceed with cooperative estimating. They delayed over their concurrences and dissents. They introduced matters of departmental policy having little or nothing to do with cases in question. The outstanding example which followed General Clay's premonition of war in March 1948 has been given in the preceding chapter to show the effect upon the Dulles Survey Group.[104]

Hillenkoetter had now in October 1949 to report to the National Security Council progress in establishing better relationships with the departmental intelligence services. Their chiefs sat in the Intelligence Advisory Committee. The Committee was expected in some quarters to take the lead and become the body of consent as well as of advice to the Director of Central Intelligence.

Introduction to Chapter X

Hillenkoetter made his first progress report to the National Security Council on October 10, 1949. In an aside Darling notes that, prior to the presentation of the report, Lawrence Houston and Walter Pforzheimer in the CIA's Office of General Counsel had prepared materials that would have given Hillenkoetter the legal and legislative analysis that would have supported him in an attempt to assert his authority if he chose to do so. Houston and Pforzheimer had reviewed the legislative history establishing the office of DCI and the CIA, demonstrating that Congress had clearly intended that the Director was to be the coordinator of intelligence and that the CIA was to have access to all intelligence data that it required to carry out its mission. They prepared two memoranda for Hillenkoetter that would have provided the basis for revising NSCID 1 and 3 to clarify this authority. Darling suggests that, had Hillenkoetter pressed his case, the President would have supported him. Nevertheless, the DCI proved reluctant to take on the rest of the community and did not act.

In his first report Hillenkoetter did not present any requests for action from the NSC. Instead, he presented his plan for consolidating the covert action community, which he had passed to the State Department and Defense Department for comment. He had also reorganized the financial system of the Agency to separate the finances of covert and overt operations. The issue of the production of national intelligence was left unresolved.

Hillenkoetter's second report to the NSC in December 1949 responded to the particular intelligence questions posed by McNarney. In response to the first of these, whether the intelligence community was equipped to deal with new scientific issues such as atomic energy, Hillenkoetter reported that he had established an Office of Scientific Intelligence and an interdepartmental Scientific Intelligence Committee in October 1949. In response to McNarney's concerns with the coordination of domestic and foreign counterintelligence operations, Hillenkoetter was able to report that the FBI had accepted membership in the IAC.

Still, the question of national estimates proved to be a problem. Hillenkoetter bypassed the suggestions of the Dulles Report, which would have required him to take control of national estimates by fighting for control of the interagency process within the Intelligence Advi-

sory Committee. Instead, Hillenkoetter tried to reorganize the Office of
Reports and Estimates within the CIA to provide him with an independent capability to produce national intelligence. The new ORE
Estimates Production Board was composed of the chiefs of the geographical and functional divisions within the office. This Board would
participate in the production and review of estimates before they were
sent to IAC for coordination. Darling suggests that this proposal still
fell short because the resulting estimates would not truly be
community-wide assessments and because it still left the question of
the DCI's relationship to the IAC unanswered.

A group of State Department and Defense Department officials tried
to fill the vacuum. The study came to be known as the "Webb Plan,"
after Under Secretary of State James Webb, who sponsored it. In reality, though, it was written mainly by General John Magruder, the
former OSS Deputy Director for Intelligence and Director of the War
Departments's SSU.

One will remember that Magruder had been responsible for some of
the original proposals that led to the creation of the CIA, acknowledging the need for centralized national intelligence; even so, the Webb
Plan would have effectively placed national estimating under the control of the IAC. Under the plan a National Intelligence Group would be
established under the IAC. It would serve as the top level of review
over a National Estimates Staff and a Current Intelligence Staff, which
would produce the intelligence. The DCI would only have the power to
veto the IAC's decisions. In an interview with Darling, Magruder said
that he had become so convinced that the CIA under Hillenkoetter
would be unable to produce true national intelligence estimates that he
believed that his proposal was the only solution. The Webb Plan was
submitted to the DCI on July 7, 1950.

Before this study reached Hillenkoetter, the Korean War had begun
and Hillenkoetter consequently asked to return to duty in the Navy. By
the fall of 1950 Hillenkoetter was ready to return to a line command.
Darling's judgment of Hillenkoetter's tenure is that, although he had
the legal right to take charge of the national intelligence system, he
was defeated by the opposition of the organizations within the community on which he depended. To make matters worse, the NSC had
given the DCI and the CIA the written authority they required, but
then failed to support them in implementing these directives.

Hillenkoetter was succeeded by General Walter B. Smith. Even before he assumed office, Houston apprised him of the problems besetting the office of DCI and the CIA. Smith appointed William Jackson, who had participated in writing the Dulles Report, as his Deputy Director, and the two of them went on the offensive in the reorganization of the CIA.

Smith's solution for the policy impasse over covert action was to say that there were "too many lawyers" in the process and to suspend all deliberation over the various directives that were being developed to define the relationships among the CIA, the military services, and the State Department. Instead, Smith put in place a set of informal arrangements under which OPC would be responsible for covert action and would keep the Defense Department apprised of its activities. He also discarded the 1948 interpretation of NSC 10-2, which had stipulated that control over covert action would pass to the military services during wartime.

Smith dealt with the problem of coordinating national estimates directly. Under his plan the Intelligence Advisory Council would take collective responsibility for estimates, but the estimates themselves would be developed by a staff under the direction of the DCI. This Office of National Estimates (ONE), which was to be concerned exclusively with producing national estimates, was established on November 13, 1950. The office, writes Darling, consisted of a National Estimates Board, a panel of "gurus" with broad expertise; an Estimates Staff, comprised of technical experts to support the members of the Estimates Board in drafting estimates; and a support staff.

This system survived until the early 1970s. The Intelligence Advisory Council was later renamed the U.S. Intelligence Board (USIB) and, still later, the National Foreign Intelligence Board (NFIB). The National Estimates Board was soon known as the Board of National Estimates (BNE), and the Estimates Staff became synonymous with ONE itself. In October 1973 William Colby (DCI from 1973 to 1976) dissolved the BNE and ONE. The Board was replaced with a looser structure of National Intelligence Officers, each specializing in a particular subject. Estimates were drafted by various offices within the community on an ad hoc basis, rather than by a single CIA office.

How Smith was able to implement these changes to the degree he did and why he was successful when his predecessors were not is the subject of the next volume in the DCI Historical Series (forthcoming from the Pennsylvania State University Press). Darling does point out, though, that Smith was more forceful than Hillenkoetter and had more political access than Vandenberg. He also points out that he had worked with Souers to gain personal access to the President and suggests that he was able to work very effectively with the new Secretary of Defense, fellow general George Marshall. Moreover, the crisis atmosphere of the Korean War probably suppressed much of the bureaucratic haggling. Darling's study nevertheless reminds us how departmental and service resistance to a centralized intelligence authority can threaten the effectiveness of the CIA as an instrument of government.

X

DECISIONS, 1950

RESTRAINT FROM CHOICE

 Admiral Hillenkoetter was well informed before he made his first report of progress in compliance with the Council's actions of July 7, 1949, on the McNarney Report. In addition to the record from ORE of its difficulties with the departmental intelligence services, he had a special report from Willard Machle, his Assistant Director of Scientific Intelligence, and advice from his legal officers.

Machle aggressively assigned elsewhere, with supporting evidence, the inability of the Office of Scientific Intelligence to accomplish its "mission." It was due to the indifference and obstruction of the departmental services. He urged that a new directive from the Council should force the departments to recognize the intent of the National Security Act and give proper authorization to the Central Intelligence Agency. The power which had been granted to Vandenberg by the National Intelligence Authority on February 12, 1947, said Machle, should be restored; Hillenkoetter should be the "agent" of the secretaries in the Council; the idea must be eliminated that the Intelligence Advisory Committee was the "Board of Directors" of the Central Intelligence Agency. Machle distracted his audience somewhat from his primary grievance, the recalcitrance of the departments, by including the Office of Special Operations in his criticism at this time.[1]

Houston and Pforzheimer in the General Counsel's Office prepared two memoranda for Hillenkoetter to consider with the proposed revisions of NSCID 1 on the duties and responsibilities of the Agency and of NSCID 3 regarding the production of intelligence. The first of these papers, dated

September 27, 1949, explained the legal responsibilities of the Agency under the National Security Act of 1947 and stated the intentions of Congress as they were understood by Houston and Pforzheimer. Both had been actively engaged as officers of the Agency with representatives of the Army and Navy, the President, and members of Congress in drafting the statute.[2]

Whatever subsequent interpretations and uncertainties from inadequate wording there might be, the intent of Congress, they said, was clear and unchanged. Congress intended to create an independent intelligence agency to perform the functions set forth in the Act. Proof of this intent could be found in the fact that whenever anything went wrong with the Agency or questions arose, as in the Bogotá affair, Congress held the Director personally responsible and looked no further. Congress intended to have the National Security Council exercise only the "broadest type of guidance." The day-to-day operations of the Agency were in the hands of the Director. Congress had placed him and the Agency under the direction of the National Security Council for two important reasons. One was that the President was too busy to give adequate personal attention to the needs of the Agency and should not be burdened. The Agency, however, could not be left in a "vacuum." It was in fact a part of the executive system. Thus, the other reason was that the Agency should be placed where it could answer to the President and his Secretaries, especially to the Secretaries of State and Defense whose departments were the "primary users" of the material which the Agency provided. Congress did not intend that they should govern every move of the Agency. They should "set certain broad patterns and directives for the Agency to follow."

Congress had clearly established duties and functions for the Agency. It was certain that the duty of advising the Council concerning the intelligence activities of the departments meant that the Director as head of the Agency could give positive advice on the "inadequacies, gaps, and overlaps" in the entire field of foreign intelligence. The fact that other intelligence agencies were "loath to accept such a concept" did not alter the fact that such supervisory power lay within the function of the Central Intelligence Agency.

For the same ultimate purpose Congress had given the Director and the Agency the duty of making recommendations for the coordination of departmental intelligence activities. Again that such recommendations had been reduced in "joint papers" to compromises with the departmental services, compromises which lacked effectiveness, did not alter the fact that Congress had given the Agency the power to make "positive and aggressive recommendations for improvement of all intelligence activities relative to the national security." The remark was double-edged. It cut the pretensions of the departmental chiefs of intelligence. It told Hillen-koetter that he had the permission of Congress and of the President to speak his mind to the Council as he pleased in regard to the national system of intelligence. If he refrained, it was not from lack of authorization by Congress, but from choice.

Houston and Pforzheimer turned then to the duty of the Agency to correlate, evaluate, and disseminate intelligence relating to the national security. There was no question, they declared, as to what Congress intended in this matter. In placing the burden of correlating and evaluating such intelligence upon the Agency, Congress meant the Agency to have the raw material necessary to perform the function. Representative Judd had stated in the course of the debate on July 19, 1947, that all intelligence relating to the national security developed by the agencies of the Government must be made available to the Director of Central Intelligence.

The scope of the word "national" was indisputable. The special provision for the consent of the Director of the FBI did not mean that he should withhold any of the information which the FBI possessed, but that its operations in the field of internal security should be safe from inspection. The right of the Agency to inspect all other intelligence materials to the extent recommended by the Council and approved by the President showed most clearly that the purpose of Congress was to have the Agency receive all of the information which it needed to perform its functions. Here the Council had vitiated the intent of Congress. The Council had stipulated in NSCID 1 that the Director could inspect such materials of intelligence only by arrangement with the head of the departmental intelligence service concerned. The directive of the Council should be revised to give the Director and the Agency proper working control where Congress meant them to have it.

The second paper from the General Counsel's Office, which reached its third draft on October 13, after Hillenkoetter had made his first report on progress to the Council, went more into detail with regard to the devices and rationalizations which the departments employed to withhold information from the Central Intelligence Agency. The memorandum was designed to accompany the revisions of NSCID 1 and NSCID 3 to be submitted by the Agency to the National Security Council.[3]

The departmental intelligence services were not only holding out "operational" information and "eyes only" reports and denying the Agency materials which required "special security handling"; they also were resorting to intelligence memoranda plausibly serving their purposes alone which nevertheless carried overtones of value to estimating in the Agency. They invoked the "third agency rule." It was reasonable to say that they were willing to release information to the Agency, but they could not allow it to pass the information along to another intelligence service, particularly to a foreign service; and so they should not let the Agency have the information in the first place. It was reasonable, but it was also to the great disadvantage of national estimating in the Central Intelligence Agency. And then there were the practices of questioning whether the Agency would find a piece of information useful and of delaying deliveries to the Agency. It had no power to commandeer intelligence. It could only request. There was not even an effective system of priorities for delivery, though the departmental services might be willing to deliver, when they got around to it. The result was that materials arrived eventually, but often after they had lost their greatest usefulness to the Agency in preparing its estimates for the National Security Council and the President.

The two memoranda from Houston and Pforzheimer gave to Hillenkoetter the arguments and the conclusions with which to send the proposed revisions of NSCID 1 and NSCID 3 to the National Security Council. He might take the offensive against critics in the Departments of State and Defense. He might follow up the actions of the Council on McNarney's Report with further recommendations that were his right under the Act of Congress whether or not members of the Intelligence Advisory Committee enjoyed the prospect. They would have more influence perhaps than he upon the Secretaries of the departments who sat in the Council. It did not follow that they would have greater persuasion with the President. Mr. Truman had told Hillenkoetter frequently that the Agency was his own intelligence service, and again and again that he was looking to Hillenkoetter to get information for him. Hillenkoetter was not to care what the members of the IAC thought.[4]

Admiral Hillenkoetter did not choose to take the offensive at this time. He preferred, as he had in the summer of 1946, to do without the practices of an executive agent and to await better conditions for Central Intelligence. He and his associates were endeavoring to profit from their experiences and from constructive criticism. It was his nature and his training to carry out orders even if he did not agree with them. It was not his character to jump to conclusions that others were stalking him. It seemed necessary on occasion to tell him that they were. It was, after all has been thought and said of him, a matter of timing for Hillenkoetter with regard to the welfare of the Agency. His own appears not to have been absorbing to him. It was his reward when he left the Agency to find in the usual letter of thanks from the President a remark that was not so common. He had performed his duties, said Truman, "in a manner designed to serve the national interest rather than that of any particular group."[5]

REPLIES TO THE STATE DEPARTMENT

Hillenkoetter had made the preparations necessary for consolidating the Office of Special Operations, the Office of Policy Coordination, and the Contact Branch of the Office of Operations in a new Operations Division. He had submitted his plan to the Department of State and Defense. It remained for them to consider the changes in NSC 10-2 which were involved and to agree upon the man whom they would like to see at the head of the Division. Hillenkoetter had reorganized the financial and fiscal work of the Agency in accordance with McNarney's second report on July 22, so that there should be separate covert and overt support staffs. ICAPS had been renamed the Coordination, Operations, and Policy Staff and given more duties within the Agency; for one, it was to work with the management staff on improvement programs in the annual budgeting of the Agency. But, Hillenkoetter reported to the Council, he still considered ICAPS responsible only to the Director of Central Intelligence, even though it was a joint staff and devoted to "interdepartmental coordination."[6]

Hillenkoetter did not approve the establishment of a Coordination Division comparable to the Operations Division. He preferred to leave the Office of Collection and Dissemination as it was, an independent "housekeeping" office performing centralized services. It was neither necessary nor desirable to involve those functions with "policy planning" as the Dulles Group had advised. Some appropriate place would be found in the Agency for the Foreign Documents Branch which would be left out of the new Operations Division. The Foreign Broadcast Information Branch, as McNarney had agreed, would not be included in it. Hillenkoetter did not say what he would do with the Office of Operations when the proposed consolidation of overt collection and secret collection with covert operations had been accepted by the State and Defense Departments. In fact, he did not have to break up the Office of Operations. The plan for the Operations Division did not succeed.

This first report of progress went to the Council on October 10. Hillenkoetter made no request for action. He was informing the Council of what had been done in response to its instructions of July 7 and within the discretion which it had given to him. But Under Secretary Webb did not allow the event to pass without comment on December 13 to Souers, Executive Secretary of the Council. It would be helpful, wrote Webb, if the Director were to explain further the organization which he planned in accordance with the recommendations of the Dulles Survey Group as

approved in the McNarney Report with respect to estimating and research. Hillenkoetter had not accepted the proposal of an Estimates Division separate from a Research and Reports Division. He believed that
other methods would accomplish the same objectives. Good estimates, he
said, should be closely tied with research. He reported that ORE was
reorganizing.[7]

Webb wished particularly to know how the Agency would meet the
requirements of NSC 50 concerning national estimates. It seems apparent that he already knew. The plan which Hillenkoetter submitted in his
report of progress on December 27 was well within his rights under NSC
50. But it was not the organization for reports and estimates which the
Dulles Group had urged and which some members of the Agency with
the most experience in central intelligence had endorsed. Nor was it the
plan which Hillenkoetter had advanced in his comments on the Dulles
Report to the Council in the preceding February. The plan which
Hillenkoetter had accepted from ORE since the argument had begun
over Armstrong's "Four Papers" and Reitzel had made his report to Babbitt laid the Agency open to renewed attack from the Departments of
State and Defense.[8]

Close upon Secretary Webb's inquiry of December 13, ICAPS, known
now as COAPS, submitted the comprehensive report on "State's Four
Papers" which the members of the Standing Committee from the Department of Defense had proposed in September. The Intelligence Advisory
Committee had finally agreed in November, although it weakened the
prestige of the IAC to concede that a staff responsible to the Director of
Central Intelligence, rather than to the Advisory Committee itself, should
make such a report.[9]

Every bid in Armstrong's "Four Papers" for supervision and control over
the Agency was rebuffed by COAPS. It should do the staff work on all
problems brought to the attention of the Intelligence Advisory Committee. With adequate staff study there would be no need to submit items for
the agenda to the Standing Committee before their consideration by the
IAC; matters should be referred to the Standing Committee by the IAC in
order to speed up "the attainment of interdepartmental views on interdepartmental issues." This would preclude those minor disputes between the Agency and individual members of the IAC which had contributed to the debate and the delay in the councils of the Advisory Board and
its ad hoc committees.[10]

The advice that the Agency ought to fulfill its coordinating responsibility for programs of research through the proposed Estimates Division was
gratuitous. Other departments and agencies of the Government were not
to tell the Agency what its internal organization should be. That was the

concern of the Director of Central Intelligence until the Council should instruct him to do otherwise. Similar suggestions in "State's Four Papers" had the same reception. When COAPS came to the familiar statement that the Agency should have free access to the plans and programs of the other intelligence agencies subject to "overall departmental regulation," the answer for the Central Intelligence Agency dispensed with all sham. The IAC members should instruct their respective organizations that such regulation should mean "only the *security* regulations" in each case.

The Agency would be glad to take the responsibility for "active liaison," but it would have to be on the understanding that there would be "free access" to the plans and programs of the departmental agencies and "free flow" of their materials. This interrelationship was in fact essential to a national system of intelligence. By the same token, the Agency would endeavor to effect coordination with "positive action," after receiving guarantees of "full cooperation" from the departmental agencies. Here once more was the issue in its simplest terms. The concepts of "forthright initiative and leadership" and of "full cooperation" were magnificent to contemplate. Their accomplishment was hopeless without a sanction.[11]

To Armstrong's suggestion that the Agency should refer to the departmental services all requests for intelligence other than national intelligence, COAPS replied that departmental estimates were usually limited to the viewpoints of the departments concerned. Such estimates would not necessarily meet the requirements of the original requestor. The Central Intelligence Agency had a responsibility to him which would not be discharged by merely calling upon another intelligence service for the production of an estimate. The IAC agencies should realize that the CIA had been placed in the "Executive Structure" to enable it to prepare national intelligence estimates objectively, without the necessity of referring or deferring to established policy. For this reason the Agency had responsibility for producing estimates even in the "fields of dominant interest" which had been allocated to the departments.

It was a contention with intrinsic merit. But it was not one to gratify the State Department, which was striving to retain political intelligence for itself. Nor would it please the Department of Defense whose armed services were jealous of their "operational" intelligence and determined to keep military estimating within the Joint Intelligence Committee of the Joint Chiefs of Staff.[12]

As for the proposal that the Central Intelligence Agency should assist the departmental services in meeting their responsibilities, in some cases including temporary assignments of personnel, COAPS declared that such "coordination" was unsound in general application. Lovell's Defense Project, which had grown into the program of National Intelligence Surveys, was not to be considered a precedent. It was an exception to the "normal operating practices of CIA." The Agency was the recipient of financial allotments from the departments rather than the dispenser of funds. It should be understood that, whenever the Agency did give financial assistance to an "IAC agency," the aid was for a *"particular purpose"*; the Agency did not prepare, could not properly prepare, a budget to take care of anything but "contingency" cases of this nature.

On reading this protest, one could not but recall why covert psychological warfare, though subject to remote control by the Secretary of State, had been assigned to the Agency under NSC 4-A. It was in large part because the Agency not only afforded cover but had unvouchered funds from Congress to be accounted for solely on the certificate of the Director of Central Intelligence.[13]

The Agency could not accept the statement in Armstrong's second paper that national intelligence applied only to intelligence which was interdepartmental in substance. If COAPS agreed, it would weaken the principle that the Agency was an independent instrument of government created by Act of Congress. The Central Intelligence Group may have been a "cooperative interdepartmental activity," but the Central Intelligence Agency was an institution created by Congress and endowed by Congress with definite functions. These had not been detailed and refined in the National Security Act; they were particular and definite nonetheless. Departmental intelligence was designated and set apart in the Act of Congress.[14]

The Agency was given the right to have access to that departmental intelligence in order to correlate and evaluate intelligence relating to the national security. There was no statement in the Act that the Agency could have access to no other information than departmental intelligence. The correct interpretation, on the contrary, was that the Agency should have other sources of intelligence; it did so when it performed "additional services of common concern" and engaged in "other functions and duties" as the Council from time to time might direct. The production of national intelligence was the business of the Director of Central Intelligence in accordance with NSCID 1. He was not obliged to conduct it as the Intelligence Advisory Committee might see fit to advise him. COAPS summarily rejected the recommendation from the State Department because it failed to recognize "the responsibilities imposed by law."[15]

The IAC agencies should recognize that national intelligence was not simply editing and joining departmental products. It was the result of evaluation and analysts transcending the "competency, capacity, and policies" of any department. Duplication, within reasonable bounds, was more a "blessing than a curse." Duplication among the departmental intelligence services themselves was as much to be apprehended and deplored. COAPS urged again that the IAC agencies themselves should expedite the "free flow" of departmental information to the Central Intelligence Agency.

They should give up the idea that, except in "crisis situations," no step should be taken by the Agency in preparing national estimates before consultation with the departmental agencies. In short, they should abandon their notion that the Intelligence Advisory Committee was a "Board of Directors" responsible for the "content of CIA's products"—the National Intelligence Estimates. They did not have the right to stop an estimate on which there was "substantial disagreement." They might dissent. They did not have collective responsibility.

Armstrong's provision in his third paper that, aside from national intelligence, the Agency should produce intelligence reports only in fields of common concern "on the advice of the IAC" was too restrictive upon the Agency and the Director of Central Intelligence. Worse than that, the provision was contrary to the Act of Congress. Neither the Director nor the Intelligence Advisory Committee could set aside the obligation of the Director to comply with requests from the President and the National Security Council, whether or not those requests pertained to matters of "common concern." It was the function of the President and the Council to decide what related to "national security." Doubtless Armstrong did not suppose that the Council could issue a directive authorizing the Director and the Advisory Committee to set aside the Council's own obligations under the Act of Congress. His suggestion, however, gave room for that supposition and subjected itself to question. COAPS rejected the recommendation.

Then came the definition of "common concern." It was easy to say that such fields of activity were those which did not fall wholly within the responsibility of any one department or agency. It was quite another problem to draw the lines around those areas. The best coordination, said COAPS, was not achieved by "delineation" of the fields. The precedent of the Scientific Intelligence Committee just created for interdepartmental planning and coordination seemed applicable to economic matters. COAPS proposed that the Director of Central Intelligence should establish a similar Economic Intelligence Committee.[16]

The recommendation in Armstrong's fourth paper that there should be study and recommendation to the Intelligence Advisory Committee on "political summaries" did not detain COAPS. The daily and weekly summaries of the Agency were based upon the Department of State's materials, but they were issued as current intelligence, the only reports of that nature designed primarily for the President and the National Security Council. The inference was clear. The summaries were not usurping functions of another agency. If those for whom they were designed no longer had use for them, they could readily be abandoned without further study by an ad hoc committee and pondering in the Intelligence Advisory Committee.

Hillenkoetter's second report of progress to the National Security Council on December 27 followed the barrage which COAPS had laid upon "State's Four Papers." Hillenkoetter took up as they were listed in McNarney's Report the "particular intelligence questions" requiring an answer from the Director of Central Intelligence within six months.

On scientific intelligence Hillenkoetter could say that the Office of Scientific Intelligence had been established in January 1949 as the Dulles and Eberstadt Reports were completed. And, with the concurrence of the Intelligence Advisory Committee, the interdepartmental Scientific Intelligence Committee had been created on October 28, 1949, to "plan, support, and coordinate" the production of scientific intelligence as it affected national security. He made no prophecy as to the successful outcome of its enterprise.[17]

This permanent committee to expedite the acquisition of scientific intelligence of every sort had been delayed five months. Much time had gone into expatiation upon the special safeguards and unique requirements of the departmental intelligence services. The chief cause of hesitation and delay appears, however, to have been unwillingness to have the Scientific Intelligence Committee and its ad hoc working groups bound by regulations of the Director of Central Intelligence. The Committee should be free to set its own problems; it should report to the Intelligence Advisory Committee, that is, to the departmental chiefs of intelligence among whom the DCI was only chairman. The formula which finally passed all obstructions was that problems which could not be solved in the Scientific Intelligence Committee would be referred, "with appropriate recommendations, to the DCI for consideration by the Intelligence Advisory Committee."[18]

The Federal Bureau of Investigation, said Hillenkoetter, had accepted membership in the Intelligence Advisory Committee to coordinate domestic intelligence and related matters with foreign intelligence. The Office of Special Operations in the Agency was working closely with the FBI. As for "crisis situations" and the estimating with regard to them in which the FBI was expected to participate, Hillenkoetter reported that a written understanding of February 2, 1949, with members of the IAC had yet to be incorporated in a directive. The matter had recently been referred to the National Security Council after a meeting of the Intelligence Advisory Committee in which no agreement on the method of issuing the directive had been reached.

A directive on the subject had been sent to the departmental agencies. But, as in previous cases, they would not accept a directive from the Director of Central Intelligence; and so the Army's proposal had been referred on December 19 to the Council. Souers submitted a memorandum on "crisis situations" on December 22; the National Security Council amended NSCID 1 on January 19, 1950. A new paragraph stipulated that, whenever any member of the Intelligence Advisory Committee obtained information which indicated an impending crisis, he should immediately furnish the other members of the Committee with the information, and the Director of Central Intelligence should convene the Committee. As soon as the Director received the views of the members, he should promptly prepare and disseminate the national intelligence estimate, with the substantially differing opinions. Thus, the National Security Council completed for the time being the reaction which had begun with Clay's "war scare" in March 1948. It was the only revision of NSCID 1 in January 1950, although the knowledge was general that the directive was satisfactory neither to officers in the Agency nor to its critics in the Department of State and Defense.[19]

Hillenkoetter also had something to say about "political summaries." The Agency must continually and systematically report on current developments, as the intelligence facility of the Council and the President. Each departmental agency was authorized to produce current publications required for its own needs. On the exploitation of foreign nations, groups, and individuals, he went into more detail to show the monitoring by the Foreign Broadcast Information Division of foreign radio broadcasts within the United States, the continuing survey of foreign language publications and their foreign correspondents, and groups which were being handled by the [one word deleted] regional offices of the Agency in the large cities of the country.

Individual aliens were coming under the Agency's observation in collaboration with the FBI. Action was being taken with the Intelligence Division of the Army to obtain closer coordination of secret intelligence in occupied areas of the Far East and Europe. Defectors had been a matter of importance for more than a year. Hillenkoetter looked to the time when the proposed NSCIDs on this delicate problem should be in operation. Meanwhile, a "pro tem interdepartmental working committee" was in charge. The Office of Special Operations was striving for better counterespionage and closer liaison with the FBI. From these matters on which he could report little more than persistent efforts to improve the performance of the Agency, Hillenkoetter turned to the plans for which the State Department seemed most impatient.

Webb's inquiry of December 13 drew from Hillenkoetter on December

27 an explicit statement of his purposes and arrangements to meet the requirement of the Council that he should change the system of estimating in the Agency. He did not adopt the suggestions in the Dulles Report of a small Estimates Division and a separate Research and Reports Division engaging primarily in economic investigation. Hillenkoetter chose other means, as NSC 50 allowed, to reach the same objectives.

Hillenkoetter preferred to reorganize the Office of Reports and Estimates and to retain both functions of research and estimating under the control of a single officer responsible to him. The Assistant Director would be chairman of an Estimates Production Board composed of the chiefs of the geographical and functional divisions within ORE. The Board was to advise the Assistant Director on programs for producing intelligence and on the essential priorities; it was to recommend the scope and the "terms of reference" for national intelligence estimates; and it was to participate in the production and the "final substantive review" of such estimates before they went to the Intelligence Advisory Committee for coordination.

At first glance it may appear that the Estimates Production Board would be a real board of correlation and synthesis from whose thinking upon evidence from every possible source would emerge national estimates. But other features in the plan for ORE indicated that the Estimates Production Board was not likely to become such a body of final review. Each regional division in ORE was to have its own estimates staff supported by regional, analytical, and research branches. They were to afford "separate facilities for high-level estimates." Each staff would produce "national intelligence estimates" within its own area.

These estimates would not go directly to the Intelligence Advisory Committee. They would pass through the Estimates Production Board on the way. But they were not likely to receive more than a cursory examination as they passed. They certainly would not undergo the scrutiny, appraisal, and detached judgment that a board of "final substantive review" should be expected to give them. The Estimates Production Board was to be composed of the chiefs of the geographical and functional divisions whose estimates staffs had just produced the so-called national intelligence estimates. One should not try one's own case.

The realignment of ORE furthermore contained the Central Research Group which had appeared for a time in the "Comments of ORE" on the Dulles Report, only to disappear before the paper was submitted to Hillenkoetter on February 14, 1949. This Group now consisted of the Map Division, the old Basic Intelligence Group (renamed the National Intelligence Survey Division), and the Plans and Policy Staff. It looked very much like realignments on paper to give pleasure to interested persons.

That it would become the research center of the Office and of the Agency, or rival the Office of Intelligence Research in the Department of State, was problematical. Hillenkoetter did not say.[20]

WEBB AND MAGRUDER

Using the major theme of "cooperation" in national estimating, the Departments of State and Defense moved to the offensive in the spring of 1950 on higher ground. Sponsored by Under Secretary of State Webb, a staff study largely written by General Magruder on assignment for the Secretary of Defense was to go directly to the National Security Council, of course after Admiral Hillenkoetter had seen it and had an opportunity to express his views. Hillenkoetter was wide open to such an attack. The arrangement in the Agency for an Estimates Production Board had fallen short of the Estimates Group which Hillenkoetter announced in his "Comments on the Dulles Report" in February 1949. Babbitt, Assistant Director of Reports and Estimates, had not yet made the Global Survey Group the nucleus of a single national estimates board with geographical and functional specialists taking part as their knowledge became essential. He had not reached for the ideal which he had in mind. To do so might have required resignations in the Office which he was not prepared to ask.[21]

Instead, there had been what amounted to surrender within the Agency to the principle of dispersion. There were many estimating boards, each working in a limited geographical or functional province. Nor was the Central Research Group equipped for the task, except perhaps in the production of the encyclopedic "National Intelligence Surveys" of conditions reaching from yesterday into the historic past. There was no adequate provision in such a group for sweeping research into the conditions of the present indispensable in the production of national estimates. Possibly the research staffs of the geographical divisions might have supplied that dynamic investigation, but the presumption was that they were occupied with the needs of the respective estimates staffs.

The Estimates Production Board and the Central Research Group did not promise correlation and syntheses of widely gathered materials, the concerted thinking which the advocates of central intelligence had right to expect. Moreover, there was immediate proof of weakness within the Office of Reports and Estimates. The Estimates Production Board did not handle the "program of production" effectively. A committee, known from its chairman as the Stout Committee, made a report to show that such a program was essentially the task of a single authority. Although the idea of a single officer was implicit, the Stout Report recommended a representative committee. Presumably it would reach decisions by a majority vote. But four members of the Stout Committee held in dissent that the several heads of the geographical and functional divisions in the Office, individually, were the ones to decide what estimates should be produced. Unless there were superhuman coincidence of opinion, there would be about as many estimates undertaken simultaneously as there were heads of divisions. The chances of coordination would be as slim within the Agency as without. The resulting estimates might be of national importance. They were not so likely to be national in scope.[22]

Talk persisted in the Agency that the Estimates Production Board was subterfuge, that there was no real intention to have a single board of coordination and final review. This opinion assumes that Hillenkoetter, Babbitt, and others in ORE did not take the inquiries and recommendations of the Dulles Survey Group seriously or think that the National Security Council would follow up the McNarney Report with decisive action. Some warned at the time that heads would roll from the guillotine unless something were done to end the "confusion" of which the Office was accused and there were efforts to produce coordinated national estimates.[23]

Whatever may be said, the record of behavior then and candid recollections since show that both Hillenkoetter and Babbitt took the investigators seriously, endeavored to aid them, and sought improvement from their findings. The record has shown, too, that both men knew the reluctance, the resistance, and obstruction which they often met in dealing with the departmental intelligence services. They were not inclined to yield to that opposition. It was on behalf of these agencies that the Departments of State and Defense now launched as sharp an attack as had been made upon the central intelligence organization since the days when Magruder took the beating for Donovan in the Joint Intelligence Committee of the Joint Chiefs of Staff.[24]

It was ironic that the man who had done so much to advance Central Intelligence both with constructive ideas and in active participation should become the architect of a plan running so far from his original thinking. John Magruder would of course not concede that it did. No one who knew him could doubt the sincerity of his purpose. He himself said, and his smile vanished as he said it, that he undertook the staff study and made so determined an effort to get it adopted by the National Security Council because he was convinced that the Agency under Hillenkoetter's direction was not going to produce national estimates. It should be compelled to do so, even if it had to be turned into merely another intelligence service in the conglomerate structure of the Government. If Magruder saw, he did not admit that after the Acts of Congress in 1947 and 1949 the change could not be made without returning to Congress for organic legislation. One thing is to be said before proceeding further: Hillenkoetter appreciated the rare quality of the man and held no grudge, though he was equally determined to tell Magruder that in this endeavor he was wrong.[25]

The Webb Plan, revealing at many points the military thoughts and expressions to which Magruder was accustomed, would take national estimating away from ORE and deposit it in the custody of the Intelligence Advisory Committee. With this seizure Magruder planned also to have the Advisory Committee take charge of current intelligence. The new devices by which he would strip existing divisions and branches in the Agency were designed to defer to the ultimate responsibility of the Director of Central Intelligence to the President and his National Security Council under the Act of Congress. That the devices would have so operated in practice is doubtful.[26]

The location of the National Intelligence Group proposed by Magruder reflected the system in which the Joint Intelligence Group of the Joint Staff came under the Joint Intelligence Committee of the Joint Chiefs of Staff, as provided in the National Security Act of 1947 amended in 1949. The National Intelligence Group (NIG) was to be an organic part of the Agency. It should consist of one hundred persons, not more than twenty of whom could be detailed from any departmental agency. The Director of Central Intelligence should provide the necessary authorizations and reimbursement for the civilian personnel. He should also provide space for additional military personnel which might be assigned. The NIG would be divided into a National Estimates Staff (NES) and a Current Intelligence Staff (CIS).[27]

These staffs were to do the work on detail for the Intelligence Advisory Committee, cooperating with each other whenever their problems were related. It was the Intelligence Advisory Committee to which Magruder gave attention. The specification of its functions told the story. They ranged over the field of intelligence. The military membership, as it always had, coincided with that of the Joint Intelligence Committee of the Joint Chiefs of Staff; the civilian members were the representatives of the State Department, the Atomic Energy Commission, the Federal Bureau of Investigation again since July 7, 1949, and any other agencies invited because their interests were involved in the pending discussion. The Director of Central Intelligence was a member of the Advisory Committee and its chairman. But if the ideas in Magruder's "staff study" prevailed, the IAC would take over most of the Director's functions under the Act of

1947. He would be only the general manager for a board of directors, though he was always burdened with responsibility to the higher authority in the National Security Council.[28]

Magruder would have the Intelligence Advisory Committee engage in the following activities, presumably by a majority vote. It could hardly function otherwise. It should initiate national intelligence requirements, advise the DCI on the desirability and feasibility of national estimates and studies which he might initiate, and review the drafts of those estimates and studies by the National Estimates Staff.

The IAC should maintain contact through its chairman, the DCI, with the staff of the National Security Council and the planning agencies of the Government. It should do so in order to be "cognizant at all times of contemplated high-level negotiations, plans, or projects which should be soundly based on national intelligence estimates." Here Magruder was nodding dangerously, if he wrote it. Estimators are supposed to supply policymakers with the substance for their decision before the event of it rather than afterwards. The sequence has to be guarded closely or the "most authoritative" coordinated national intelligence estimate may become not the evidence from which a policy is constructed but the stuffing which rounds it out.[29]

Magruder, or his writer, stipulated also that the Intelligence Advisory Committee should maintain "close liaison" with the Joint Intelligence Committee in order that projects for estimates in the two bodies might be coordinated and "appropriate parts" of national estimates might be integrated with joint estimates. This liaison would not be hard to obtain in view of the fact that military membership in both committees was identical. It was significant that Magruder did not provide for the reverse process of integrating the estimates of JIC with the national estimates of the Intelligence Advisory Committee. Until that was done, no product of the IAC could be truly national.

It was reported in June 1953 that with NSC 140/1, an appraisal of the vulnerability of the United States to Soviet attack from the air in which our own "capabilities and intentions" were taken into account, the first "net estimate" had been obtained. It apparently was one of the first, if not the first, to approximate the wishes of the Dulles Group for an authoritative coordinated national intelligence estimate.[30]

The Webb Plan stated further that the Intelligence Advisory Committee should keep under "continuing review" all critical current intelligence in order to be prepared "to draw national significant conclusions" from that intelligence. Such conclusions should be recommended without delay to the DCI for transmission to "key executive officials." Nothing was said about his having any discretion in the matter, though clearly by the Act of

Congress as head of the Central Intelligence Agency he had the duty and the responsibility of disseminating national intelligence to the proper officials of the Government.

The plan gave to the IAC the power to recommend to the DCI the nature and specifications of current summaries and reports. The IAC was to tell him what "special intelligence products" he should have prepared in "recognized fields of common interest." The Advisory Committee henceforth should be responsible for conducting all discussions with foreign intelligence agencies regarding combined estimates.

To make the new order complete, the Intelligence Advisory Committee should move into "permanent headquarters" provided by the Central Intelligence Agency, so that the full-time representatives of the departmental chiefs of intelligence who constituted the IAC might be "conveniently located" near the National Intelligence Group and its facilities. All CIA offices having "intelligence resources" were to contribute to the requirements of the National Estimates Staff and the Current Intelligence Staff according to the principles governing federal agencies outside of the CIA. Except for the National Intelligence Group, no offices of the Agency would produce intelligence in fields of "common concern" unless directed by the National Security Council.

Other members of the Intelligence Advisory Committee, declared the Webb Plan, were responsible in no less degree than the Director of Central Intelligence to support "with their full resources" the mechanism for accomplishing national intelligence objectives. But the plan called for no action on the part of anybody if they did not give that support.

"Until the emergence of a national estimate or study from the IAC," it said, "collective responsibility is inescapable under the Act of 1947." As a statement of moral principle, perhaps this was correct. But nowhere in the National Security Act of 1947 or its amendment in 1949 may be found, outside of the implicit authority of the National Security Council under the President, authorization for any other officer or body to force compliance on the part of the departments and other agencies of the Government sharing in the privileges and obligations of the national intelligence system. The Director of Central Intelligence certainly did not have that power of compulsion.

The statutory responsibility of the Director of Central Intelligence, according to the Webb Plan, would become operative only when the heads of the federal intelligence agencies had discharged their obligations. Until then he was one of their number, chairman of their meetings as the Intelligence Advisory Committee, but subject to the will of the majority if there emerged a majority. The idea that such a body of competitors could reach decisions of strength and moment unanimously was still in the realm of fantasy. When, however, these heads of the several agencies had final drafts of national estimates or studies and recommended them to the Director of Central Intelligence, then the Director became responsible. It was, from that instant, for him alone to give the "final approval and dissemination" to those estimates and studies.

Thus, Magruder would allow the Director of Central Intelligence to exercise a veto over the Intelligence Advisory Committee. It is inconceivable that the Director would be obliged to take sole responsibility for an estimate or study in which he himself did not believe. He might suspect or know for a fact through his own sources of secret information that the departmental chiefs of intelligence had not completely fulfilled their obligations; that they had not delivered all of the intelligence available to them, whether "operational" or for "eyes only" or requiring "special secret handling." They could not be forced to deliver. They could only be criticized for failing to do so. Under such conditions it was practical to talk of decision and dissent. It was not proper to say that the Director of Central Intelligence, regardless of personal convictions, had ultimate responsibility to the National Security Council and the President.

Webb sent Magruder's study to Hillenkoetter on July 7, 1950. The Departments of State and Defense proposed to submit it to the National Security Council at an early date. "Naturally," said Webb, "they would want very much to have" Hillenkoetter's comments upon the study before they did. It arrived in the Agency after the North Koreans had crossed the 38th parallel and were driving before them the South Koreans and such American forces as could be rushed into the peninsula from Japan. It was not certain that reinforcements for the United Nations would arrive from the United States and elsewhere soon enough or with strength enough to hold Pusan. ORE was gasping with everyone else but was expected to produce estimates as fast as they were demanded whether or not they could be fully coordinated.[31]

The Estimates Production Board and its related geographical divisions, whatever their merits in other respects, lacked the compactness and flexibility to work swiftly and with decisiveness under such trying conditions. Babbitt summoned representatives from the geographical and functional divisions and from the Global Survey Group to form under his chairmanship a Special Staff. In most cases the men were those who stood second in the organization of their respective offices. This choice left the heads of the offices to their administrative duties. It saved Babbitt as well from the hard feeling which would have risen if he had put some heads of offices on and kept others off the Special Staff. Moreover, it gave him a staff which he could devote exclusively to estimating. Its members were released from other duties during the emergency.[32]

How well the Special Staff in ORE would have succeeded in making coordinated national estimates is good speculation. Though brought together in an emergency, its experienced estimators might have made the transition from the feverish uncertainty of the summer of 1950 to more stable conditions. They might have won the cooperation of the chiefs of departmental intelligence on the Intelligence Advisory Committee. The Special Staff might have proved its worth. It was given neither time nor situation for the development. Not only were the Departments of State and Defense pressing their own Webb Plan in the midst of the Korean War, but the administration came into the controversy over the Central Intelligence Agency. In the end it set aside the Webb Plan, but did so in a way to make the retention of ORE difficult, let alone the development of any of its promising institutions.

Admiral Hillenkoetter had served more than three years as Director. He had requested return to active duty in the Navy. He had been under investigation and criticism most of his term in the Agency. Regardless of the merits in his case, it was considered time for a "strong man," and the man was at hand. President Truman selected him without counselling from others. He had been ambassador in Moscow. He "knew the Russians." He had served in Europe as General Eisenhower's Chief of Staff. Before that he had been Secretary to the Combined Chiefs of Staff in close touch with the Office of Strategic Services and General Donovan. He did not want to be Director of Central Intelligence.[33]

General Walter B. Smith would appeal to the public as the man in the emergency. Admiral Hillenkoetter would stay until General Smith could take charge. In the meantime, Admiral Hillenkoetter for himself would match every thrust in the Webb Plan for departmental intelligence agencies with a sharper jab on behalf of the Central Intelligence Agency. He would not profit from the effort. General Smith might. As Hillenkoetter talked in December 1952 about those last weeks in the Agency during the summer and fall of 1950, there was evident amusement and some pleasure in the recollection.[34]

Houston, General Counsel for Hillenkoetter, gave the Webb Plan a critical reading. His marginal notes narrowed Magruder's specifications for the Intelligence Advisory Committee to functions of advice. It was not supposed to be a body of consent. Houston confined the issue to one of conflict between the Intelligence Advisory Committee and the Director of Central Intelligence, as it always had been. He had aided in drafting the statute during 1946 and 1947. He had heard Forrestal's interpretation and admonition to General Chamberlin and Admiral Inglis in December 1947.[35]

Adhering to this restriction of the issue, Houston therefore objected to all features of the plan involving internal changes. They might of course be made if the Director saw fit to adopt the suggestions. It was not the intention of Congress that the Council should spend time on such matters. If, for example, the Director wanted to establish so cumbersome a device as the National Intelligence Group, he might; but the inference was that he should not do so. Certainly it would be good if the Government could obtain "integration" of the best intelligence. But it should be done by a single responsible agency such as Congress expected the Central Intelligence Agency to be and the sponsors of the Webb Plan did not intend.

The scrutiny of the plan was convincing. Magruder should not be given personal offense if it could be avoided. But it was provoking that, at a time when the Agency was endeavoring to improve, the critics of the Hillenkoetter administration should have chosen to make demands beyond legal rights. The Council might add to the "duties and functions" of the Central Intelligence Agency under the Acts of 1947 and 1949 as the Council itself from time to time should direct. But the Council could not take away functions which Congress had assigned to the Agency and its responsible head, the Director of Central Intelligence. Congress had no intention that the Intelligence Advisory Committee should have administrative powers over the Agency. On the contrary, Congress had deliberately included section 303 of the Act of 1947 to give the Director of Central Intelligence the option of choosing advisers as he wished. He was not required by the Act of Congress to have any advisers. As a matter of tactics in the contest with the Departments of State and Defense, therefore, the officers of the Agency decided to match extreme with extreme.[36]

Hillenkoetter directed Babbitt, head of ORE, to prepare comments with COAPS and the Executive. In a series of meetings almost daily Babbitt (Assistant Director for Reports and Estimates), Shannon (Acting Executive), Childs (Chief of COAPS), Machle (Assistant Director for Scientific Intelligence), and Houston (General Counsel) prepared a reply to Webb's letter of July 7, with an accompanying proposal of a new NSCID 1 on the duties and responsibilities of the Agency. When the reply and directive were sent to Webb on July 26, they gave him a positive program for the improvement of national estimating which he so much desired. It was, though, a program to extend the jurisdiction of the Agency and to strengthen the powers of direction, management, and inspection which had been inherent in the responsibilities of the Director of Central Intelligence since the President's Directive of January 22, 1946. Even the critics of Hillenkoetter could not dispute that the Council might issue orders to the departmental intelligence agencies upon the recommendation of the DCI, if the secretaries who were the Council wished to give those orders. The fun would begin when they undertook to see to it that the orders were obeyed in their own departments.[37]

Rather unexpected assistance had come to the Agency from Louis Johnson, Secretary of Defense. Hillenkoetter's advisers were not hesitant in quoting him to Webb, Under Secretary of State. Atomic energy intelligence had been under discussion between the Director of Central Intelligence and the Intelligence Advisory Committee in June. The Secretary of State had accepted the recommendations from the Director and the Advisory Committee to the National Security Council. The Secretary of Defense lingered over them to comment upon the responsibilities of the Director and his relationships with the departmental intelligence agencies.

Johnson reiterated that the Act of 1947 placed the responsibility upon the Director of Central Intelligence for coordinating intelligence activities in atomic energy, general science, economic conditions, and others. The Director could not effect that coordination, however, without "aggressive leadership on his part and wholehearted support by the heads of departmental agencies and their principal intelligence units overseas." Hillenkoetter was to take some blame regarding leadership, but the chiefs of departmental intelligence should have as much. Johnson did not concede that an "elaborate committee structure" was desirable. He believed that it was the result of "interbureau rivalries" rather than of objective study. Final responsibility for coordinating the collection of materials as well as its processing, he said, "should rest squarely" in the Central Intelligence Agency. With the responsibility should go corresponding authority. It was "ambiguous and obscured in the present interlocking committee structure."[38]

Thus supported by the Secretary of Defense, Hillenkoetter and his advisers in the Agency asked Secretary Webb to remember that the principle of collective responsibility had no basis in the Acts of Congress. Moreover, it had been expressly disavowed by the National Security Council when adopting McNarney's Report as NSC 50. The Director of Central Intelligence was solely responsible by law. Duties were not to be imposed upon the departmental agencies exceeding "their legal responsibilities and actual competence." A new NSCID 1 was attached for Webb's information. In it he would find "the minimum authorities necessary to enable this Agency to fulfill its statutory responsibilities." The directive would establish also "the responsibilities of the departmental agencies in support of national intelligence."[39]

The authorities of the Agency and the responsibilities of the departments, which Webb should think over, went to the other extreme from the proposals in his "staff study." The decisions, orders, and directives concerning the intelligence activities of the Government which came from the

Director of Central Intelligence should be considered as emanating from the members of the National Security Council. He would be their executive agent as General Vandenberg had insisted. The Director or his representatives should make "surveys and inspections" of departmental intelligence "activities and facilities" as he deemed necessary in connection with his duty to advise the Council. The Director would have the authority which he had once possessed under the President's Directive of January 22, 1946, to inspect departmental operations as well as their materials of intelligence. The Central Intelligence Agency should function under the Director of Central Intelligence as the "intelligence facility" of the National Security Council and the President of the United States.

In accordance with section 303 of the Act of 1947 as amended, the Director of Central Intelligence might appoint such advisory committees as he deemed necessary in carrying out the functions of the Agency. If the Council listened now to Hillenkoetter rather than to Magruder and Webb, there would be no Intelligence Advisory Committee taking on administrative as well as advisory functions for the Agency.

Other provisions in the new "basic directive" followed this principle consistently through the details of coordination, collection, production, and dissemination of intelligence. The departments and agencies of the Government would have responsibilities to the Central Intelligence Agency. They should make available "all intelligence, intelligence information, and other information" in their possession useful for "intelligence purposes." This formula covered every kind of information. But in addition the new directive would require specifically that the "third agency rule" should be abrogated so far as the Central Intelligence Agency was concerned. Finally, its "commitments and deadlines" should be imperative. When the Director made a specific request, each department or agency should give his requirements for collection, for production, and for comments on reports and estimates of the Central Intelligence Agency "first priority."

Such was the nature of the letter and the proposed directive which Admiral Hillenkoetter approved and sent to Under Secretary Webb on July 26. The instructions within the Agency the next day were that there should be no discussion outside unless it had "the personal approval of the Director." On August 3 Webb acknowledged Hillenkoetter's letter with its enclosures. The Department of State had not had an opportunity to study the documents, said Webb, or to discuss Hillenkoetter's comments with the Department of Defense. It did appear, however, on preliminary reading that the "joint proposals" which they had submitted to him had been misconstrued.[40]

Wisner, Assistant Director for Policy Coordination, had written on July

27 to Babbitt, Assistant Director of Reports and Estimates, that his office concurred in the staff study "as presented." The Office of Policy Coordination would continue, said Wisner, to provide the Office of Special Operations or the Office of Operations for processing and disseminating any "intelligence information" which was collected as a "byproduct of its normal operations." The original of Mr. Wisner's letter, signed by him, was given to Admiral Hillenkoetter on August 2. The plan for consolidating OSO, OPC, and the Contact Branch of OO had been in suspense by this time for nearly a year.[41]

A revised "staff study" with minor changes came to the Agency on August 14. Hillenkoetter directed Houston to examine the proposal from the departments and eliminate the features objectionable to "our theory" of the Director's responsibilities. Houston did so and sent his draft to General Magruder. Magruder asked for a conference. Thereupon Hillenkoetter and Houston met with Magruder on Monday, August 21, to discuss the whole matter. Magruder accepted Houston's changes concerning advice by the Intelligence Advisory Committee. And finally Magruder agreed to the statement in the revised draft that national intelligence should be produced only by the Central Intelligence Agency; the Director had "the direct and sole responsibility for such production." He would not be bound by any concept of collective responsibility.

When Magruder accepted this statement, he abandoned for all practical purposes the position which he had taken in the Webb Plan on behalf of the Intelligence Advisory Committee. It mattered little that Hillenkoetter might keep the suggestion of a National Intelligence Group, subdivided into a National Estimating Staff and a Current Intelligence Staff, for presentation to the National Security Council "at the earliest opportunity," as Magruder apparently desired. The staffs would be ultimately responsible to the Director of Central Intelligence within the Central Intelligence Agency. But the whole matter had become academic by the first of September.[42]

General Smith on August 23 had called upon Houston, General Counsel of the Agency, to give him in writing a statement of the major problems which he should have to meet. Admiral Souers, as special adviser to the President, had informed Hillenkoetter that no commitments or agreements affecting the Agency should be completed prior to the arrival of the new Director. This information Houston passed on to Magruder as he forwarded, on September 13, twenty copies of the draft to which they had agreed. The draft made an interesting study of the fundamental conflict in the national system of intelligence. It was not, however, the plan which Houston preferred to recommend to General Smith; neither was it the one which the General would adopt.[43]

ADVICES TO SMITH

Smith's general counsel told him with candor and a minimum of words that his problems were the same as Vandenberg's and Hillenkoetter's. In coordinating the intelligence activities of the departments as provided by the Acts of Congress, Smith would find that the Intelligence Advisory Committee acted as if it were a board of directors. This result Houston attributed to the nature of the directives from the National Security Council rather than, as he might have, to the persistance of the departmental chiefs of intelligence in the Advisory Committee. The fact that the Director was required by the Council to submit dissenting opinions with his recommendations, however, did not transform the dissenters into a governing board over the Director of Central Intelligence. The Council itself had that function.[44]

The individual chiefs of intelligence had always been able to submit their opinions to the Council through their respective Secretaries—that is, if the Secretaries chose to relay those opinions. On occasion the Secretary of a department might not favor the ideas of this director of intelligence. Then, of course, the ideas might not reach the National Security Council. As a practical matter it was not likely that a departmental chief of intelligence would make it the business of his office to force such opinions through to the Council by way of his right of dissent in the Intelligence Advisory Committee. That he disagreed with his Secretary, though, and held his views off the record would doubtless be well enough known and repeated; they were likely to reach the Council regardless of his reluctance to advance or the Secretary's intention to thwart them. Only the historian of the event would be pressed at a later date to discover just what had happened.[45]

Houston told Smith that the recommendations which went to the Concil were not recommendations from the Agency as contemplated by the law. They were "watered-down compromises" in an attempt to gain the complete support of the Advisory Committee. In other words, for the sake of harmony in the effort to develop common responsibility among the departmental intelligence services and the Central Intelligence Agency in the national system of intelligence, Hillenkoetter had refrained from exercising the power which Congress had given to him. He could have made recommendations to the Council as he saw fit whether or not members of the Intelligence Advisory Committee severally or as a body disagreed with him.

It was the Director's legal right. That he should have exercised it in the face of the resistance which both Vandenberg and Hillenkoetter had to endure was a separate question for General Smith to examine. One possible conclusion from the criticisms in the Dulles Report available to Smith was that Hillenkoetter should have assumed the "forthright initiative and leadership" which McNarney advocated. Hillenkoetter, then, would have told the departmental chiefs of intelligence that he was advising the National Security Council and the President according to his own judgment; he was sending along their "substantially differing opinions" simply because he had to do so. The Council could decide. The procedure would have heightened antagonisms as comparable action by Vandenberg had angered his Intelligence Advisory Board. The procedure might have dried up sources of intelligence that were already sluggish from departmental antipathies for Central Intelligence. General Smith had the choice.[46]

Smith would find the Agency encountering difficulties in its production of estimates, said Houston, because the departmental services customarily withheld "operational" information, "eyes only" materials, and others restricted by special provisions for security. The Agency could not enforce its requests for collection nor establish priorities. The "third agency rule" continued to work against the Agency. There was, said Houston putting it mildly, "a failure of spontaneous dissemination" of certain information to the Central Intelligence Agency.

When he came to estimating, Smith would discover that he was handicapped not only by these obstructions in the flow of information to the Agency but also by departmental procedures in concurrence and dissent. The process of coordination might take months and result in a compromise of questionable usefulness. Departmental bias and budgetary interests often affected deliberation upon the facts in a case. Dissents were frequently "unsubstantial, quibbling, or reflective of departmental policy."

The IAC agencies, said Houston, resisted the grant of authority to the Agency to issue directives in the general field of intelligence and in their own areas particularly, on the ground that such action violated "the concept of command channels." One might add that the National Security Council itself had yet to support the Agency fully with the power which Congress had given to the Council. It could issue directives or commands which were to be obeyed in the several departments represented upon the Council. It had a collective responsibility with potential sanction. The actions of the Council were advices to the President. He had but to issue an executive order to bring into full force a directive of the Council which had been authorized by Congress.[47]

In Houston's opinion, the status of the Agency in relation to the President and the Council must be redefined and clarified. Relations with the Department of Justice and the FBI especially concerning "defectors" must be improved. The difficulties which NSC 10-2 had created in the field of "unconventional warfare" must be eliminated; particularly, the Departments of State and Defense should not have "policy control" over the Agency. The clandestine operations of the Agency should not be separated in two offices within the Agency; this division created "serious problems of efficiency, efficacy, and, above all, security."

The failure to coordinate the collection of overt intelligence in the field was due in part to competition among the departments, but there was a lack of planning and action by the Agency. Nuclear energy and other special subjects had their own problems. General Smith would also have to give urgent thought at any moment to the relations of the Agency with the Joint Chiefs of Staff in the event of war. The desperate situation in Korea would seem to have proved that the moment had arrived.

The solution for all of these problems, said Houston in conclusion, lay in a grant of adequate authority to the Director of Central Intelligence and the Agency by the National Security Council and the President. The time had come to "achieve the necessary coordination by direction." It was time for command. There no longer was any point to reliance upon a "spirit of cooperation and good will."

Other advices to Smith came from Babbitt, Montague, and Van Slyck in the Office of Reports and Estimates, by way of a response to the oral request of the new Deputy Director of Central Intelligence. Hillenkoetter left the place vacant after the departure of General Wright and managed the affairs of the Director's office with the aid only of his executive, Winecoff and then Shannon. The new Deputy Director, William H. Jackson, was uniquely chosen and placed. He was in position to put into effect, as General Smith agreed, the recommendations of the Dulles Report for which Jackson himself was in large part responsible and which General McNarney had not wholly accepted. In NSC 50 the Council had left discretion with Hillenkoetter concerning internal changes. He had not seen fit to carry out the wishes of the Dulles Group for an Estimates Division. Smith and Jackson now might have the institution they desired.

It certainly was not to be the arrangement for estimating which ORE was promoting before the Korean War forced Babbitt to create the Special Staff. Nor was it to be the device which Magruder had labored to establish in the Webb Plan. The system which Smith and Jackson were eventually to adopt was a modification of the Estimates Branch that Montague had proposed to Souers in the spring of 1946 for the Central Reports Staff and had tried unsuccessfully to establish for Vandenberg in the Office of Reports and Estimates. The departmental intelligence services had defeated Montague's purposes then. If Houston's judgment of their procedures were correct, Smith and Jackson would have trouble with such coordination and control of estimating now.[48]

The response of Babbitt, Montague, and Van Slyck to the request of Jackson on October 7, 1950, was in the name of all three. But internal evidence shows that it was drawn for the most part from the thinking and the experience of Montague. They warned Jackson in clearest fashion at the start that the "end in view" could not be accomplished by reorganization within the Agency alone. There would have to be "complementary action" by the departmental intelligence services, supplying adequate "research support" and a "cooperative attitude."[49]

From past experiences it was fair to say that both would be hard to get. There would have to be more insistence on the part of the Secretaries in the Council and the President than had been used heretofore. The departmental chiefs of intelligence would have to give Smith support which neither Vandenberg nor Hillenkoetter had enjoyed. We should recall that Admiral Souers made arrangements for General Smith to meet regularly with President Truman. Hillenkoetter had gone frequently to the White House. But now the Secretaries of the departments and their chiefs of intelligence were to observe a steady proceeding in which they might not share. Its subjects of conversation they might never know.[50]

Babbitt, Montague, and Van Slyck told Jackson that their proposal for an Office of Estimates and an Office of Research to work with it should not be put into effect until the departmental services had reasonably met the requirements for research and cooperation. It was especially important to be certain that the Office of Intelligence Research in the Department of State was prepared to support the effort of the Agency. One final point had to be "absolutely clear" before there was any use in adopting the proposal. The "patent defect of a joint committee system" must be avoided.

All those who were concerned must understand that the Director of Central Intelligence "at his level" and the Assistant Director, Office of Estimates, within his jurisdiction had the power of decision. Once they had heard all of the pertinent evidence and argument, the decision was theirs with respect to both form and content of an estimate. Other parties of interest, representatives of the departments, retained the right of "divergent views" when those views related to "substantial issues" and served to "increase the reader's comprehension of the problem." But it was then only. Such an interpretation of collective responsibility for national estimates was not Jackson's concept of the right procedure in the fall of 1945, nor was it so stated in the Dulles Report. It was doubtful that Jackson would agree in October 1950 without some qualification.[51]

In any event, Babbitt, Montague, and Van Slyck submitted their proposal on October 10 [two lines deleted]. Babbitt, Montague, and Van Slyck wanted to recruit "senior personnel" of superior ability which the Agency did not have in sufficient number. There should be a full-time Coordination and Liaison Staff composed of representatives of the Department of State, War, Navy, and Air Force; a member of the Agency's Office of Research or part-time representation of its components; a Staff Assistant for the Agency on the staff of the National Security Council; and similar representatives of the Agency with the Office of the Secretary of Defense and the Joint Intelligence Group under the Joint Chiefs of Staff. With these officers there should be an Executive Secretariat.

The functions of this Coordination and Liaison Staff would be to represent the interests of the departments in the Estimates Office of the Agency, on the one hand, and, on the other, the interests of that Office in the departmental intelligence agencies. The Staff should aid the Assistant Director with the program for producing estimates, with formulating the "terms of reference" for particular estimates and the requests for research, in obtaining timely and effective compliance, and in reviewing the estimates prior to their submission to the Director and the Intelligence Advisory Committee. It would be the final duty of this Staff to secure the concurrence of the Advisory Committee, or at least "dissent in the light of joint consideration." The hope was that "direct and informal consultation" in the British manner would succeed where formal exchange of views had failed to bring separate and often competitive interests together. A fairly concerted effort might produce truly national estimates with a minimum of dissent.

It is to be especially noted that the proposed Staff would contain a member of the Agency who served also on the staff of the National Security Council. Babbitt, Montague, and Van Slyck were dissatisfied with representation of the Agency on the Council's staff by the chief of ICAPS. To them he had insulated ORE from the Council. At best his usefulness was secondhand. He had not kept the two institutions in close touch. At times he had taken sides against the Office rather than helped to accomplish its purposes. Sherman Kent had commented in his report to Hillenkoetter on ORE during February 1948 that the Office as an estimating body was too removed from its sources of foreign intelligence and from the users of its material. The situation had not been much improved since then, so far as it concerned relations with the working staff of the Council. The remedy for Babbitt, Montague, and Van Slyck was to replace the chief of ICAPS with a representative from ORE, or its successor in estimating. He should participate in the discussions of the Council's staff, not as an occasional alternate as Montague himself had been, but as a regular attendant.[52]

Babbitt, Montague, and Van Slyck would have a Current Intelligence Division within the new Office of Estimates. It should produce the daily summary, edit and publish other reviews, have custody of "sensitive material," and maintain the "situation room" and the "off-hours watch." There should be five Regional Divisions in the Office—American, North Atlantic, East European, Southern, and Far Eastern. These divisions would contain senior analysts qualified to appraise current information and the products of research. They should discern trends and anticipate developments. With such "surveillance" of current affairs, they would produce the estimates falling within their "divisional competence." They should also provide the expert participation necessary in "task groups" formed to make estimates of broader scope.

There should be a Functional Division of scientists, economists, and geographers not confined to a region. And there should be a General Division in the Office of Estimates where could be found a small number of analysts with "broad competence rather than particular specialization." Babbitt, Montague, and Van Slyck would have Smith and Jackson rely upon these exceptional persons for the ability to ascertain the interrelationships between two or more divisions of the Office and the leadership in the task groups which should deal with those problems.

Another request from Jackson, Deputy Director, brought advice on the revision of NSC 10-2 for the advantage of General Smith. Houston had told him that control of covert operations by the Departments of State and Defense should be eliminated. A drafting committee of Houston and Pforzheimer from the General Counsel's Office and Wisner, Assistant Director in charge of OPC, prepared a list of changes. The phrase "in time of peace" should be deleted; the authority of the Director of Central Intelligence over covert operations should be unquestioned in war as well as peace. Then it should be expressly stated that the Central Intelligence Agency was to plan and conduct those operations. The activity existed in the Agency; there should be no implication that a new office had to be created for the purpose.[53]

The paragraphs stipulating that the Secretary of State should nominate the Assistant Director but that he should report directly to the Director of Central Intelligence ought to be removed from NSC 10-2. The first was in derogation of the Director's authority over the Agency. The second was unnecessary. Moreover, it impaired the authority of the Director, for it implied autonomy and separation in the conduct of those clandestine operations.

Houston, Pforzheimer, and Wisner proposed that the Director of Central Intelligence alone should be responsible for seeing that covert operations were consistent with foreign and military policies and with overt activities. The requirements that he should work "through designated representatives" of the Secretaries of State and Defense and that he should take his disagreements with them to the National Security Council were "unduly restrictive" upon the Director. And he should be free without consulting an intermediary to deal directly with the Joint Chiefs of Staff when making plans for covert operations in time of war.

The paragraph in NSC 10-2 on wartime planning and covert operations in military theaters presented "the greatest difficulties." Any change of language would raise "a host of questions" concerning the interrelationships of the Agency, the Joint Chiefs, and the theater commanders, not to mention the Department of State. Houston, Pforzheimer, and Wisner therefore recommended that they should not attempt a draft of this section; the Director of Central Intelligence should endeavor "forthwith to formulate the appropriate concepts" with the Joint Chiefs of Staff and the Departments of State and Defense. Regarding the section on economic warfare, however, they did have specific and definitive recommendations. It should not state that such covert operations were to be under the guidance of the departments and agencies responsible for planning economic warfare. They were "not competent to guide the actual conduct" of covert operations. They should plan in coordination with the Agency. But the Agency should conduct "all such covert operations." This was the responsibility of the Director of Central Intelligence.

THE GENERAL'S REFORMS

The incoming Director of Central Intelligence did not take the advice of Houston, Pforzheimer, and Wisner regarding NSC 10-2. General Smith came to other conclusions on covert operations. He is said to have remarked in his first meeting with the Intelligence Advisory Committee that there were "too many lawyers." Instead of accepting their advice, Smith reached agreement with the Departments of State and Defense. General Marshall was now Secretary of Defense in place of Louis Johnson. The understanding was that no further consideration would be given to the proposed changes in the directives of the Council, either those recommended in the Agency or the scheme upon which General Magruder had labored for Webb, Under Secretary of State. It is to be noted again that

Admiral Souers, personal adviser to President Truman on matters pertaining to the national security, had arranged that the President's own choice to succeed Admiral Hillenkoetter as Director of Central Intelligence should have direct and regular access to the President himself.[54]

General Smith gave oral instructions to Wisner, Assistant Director in charge of OPC. He was to notify the representatives of the Departments of State and Defense and the Joint Chiefs of Staff with whom he did business that the "Memorandum of Interpretation" dated August 12, 1948, and entitled "Implementation of NSC 10-2" was no longer applicable or effective "in the light of altered circumstances." What those circumstances were did not appear in Wisner's written report on October 12. One of them certainly was that General Smith, and no longer Admiral Hillenkoetter, was Director of Central Intelligence. Hillenkoetter had signed the "Memorandum of Interpretation" on August 6, 1948. His view of it has been discussed in Chapter VII of this study. Admiral Souers's interpretation of the purposes and procedures under NSC 10-2, rather than Admiral Hillenkoetter's, was about to come into effect.[55]

General Smith told Mr. Wisner to say that there was no immediate necessity for revising NSC 10-2 in order to make the Office of Policy Coordination fully responsive to Smith's authority and command. Smith acknowledged the propriety and desirability of having OPC continue to receive "advice and policy guidance" (Wisner's words) from the Departments of State and Defense. But there should be no mistaking that the advice and guidance would come not only "in theory" but "in fact" to the Agency; it would not pass directly from the departments to the Office. Both Kennan and Hillenkoetter would have been interested to know that the autonomy which had been planned for the Office of Special Projects was to be so curtailed.[56]

Wisner's report to Smith on October 12 stated that it would be Wisner's responsibility to keep the General fully informed upon all matters "worthy" of his attention. The difference between determining what was "important" enough to tell Admiral Hillenkoetter and deciding what was less than "worthy" of Smith's attention remained Wisner's peculiarly personal anxiety. The chances seemed good that the new regime would allow him a narrower margin of error.[57]

Eight days later General Smith gave much the same information to the departmental chiefs of intelligence in his first meeting with the Intelligence Advisory Committee. The fact that he did was significant. There was no need to tell the chiefs of intelligence in order to inform their departments. Mr. Wisner had done so. Such covert operations as those in which OPC engaged were not the concern of departmental intelligence officers. Black propaganda, economic manipulation, sabotage, and other subversive practices abroad were instruments of "unorthodox warfare" as General Donovan aptly said; but they were not conducted by the intelligence services of the Armed Forces and the Department of State, or the Atomic Energy Commission, or the Federal Bureau of Investigation in the Department of Justice. Advice and guidance regarding such practices had come to the Agency from the interested departments through representatives specially chosen and assigned to the task, and not through the Intelligence Advisory Committee. Hillenkoetter and Wright had considered those operations, with the financial affairs of the Agency, to be matters which they should not discuss with the departmental chiefs of intelligence.[58]

In speaking of OPC at his first meeting with the Intelligence Advisory Committee, General Smith gave the impression that he would take its members into his counsel with regard to problems of the Agency generally, that he would talk with the departmental chiefs on matters other than those of their immediate concern. He told them further that he did not intend to consolidate the Office of Special Operations, which engaged in secret collection and counterespionage, with the Office of Policy Coordination conducting other clandestine operations, and with the Contact Branch of the Office of Operations, which obtained overt intelligence. The merger, he said, was neither practical nor advisable at this time. He believed that the coordination of these offices, as recommended by the Dulles Report and directed in NSC 50, could be achieved by more effective cooperation without actual merger.

He had stated his opinion orally to the Council on October 12 and had received its approval. In other words, the National Security Council had virtually rescinded its action of August 4, 1949. Following General McNarney's second report on July 22, 1949, urging separate administrative support for the covert activities of the Agency, the Council had directed Hillenkoetter against his expressed wishes to proceed with the consolidation of the offices, including the Contact Branch. The minutes of Smith's first meeting with the Intelligence Advisory Committee, written from the notes of Jackson, did not record that Smith relayed these facts to the departmental chiefs, or his conversations with Jackson about the plan of the Dulles Survey Group, or the fact that the departments themselves had stalled the merger of the Offices more than a year. But then it must have been common knowledge by this time.[59]

General Cabell, Director of Intelligence for the Air Force, was pleased with the new attitude toward the Intelligence Advisory Committee. He had been so dissatisfied with Hillenkoetter's treatment of it that he had proposed a new NSCID 1 to provide for an Intelligence Advisory Committee of the National Security Council on "governmental intelligence problems." But Cabell might also have remarked that Smith did not ask the Committee for advice before proceeding. Smith told the Committee what he had done.[60]

In regard to financial problems of the Agency, General Smith felt as free as General Vandenberg was, and Admiral Hillenkoetter as well, to make changes without consulting the Intelligence Advisory Committee. It could not be said that the problems were unrelated to "governmental intelligence problems" and therefore of no conceivable interest or concern to the departmental chiefs of intelligence. It could be said that the chiefs had never been influential enough in their own departments to make a protest stick on the record because the Director of the Central Intelligence Agency had not taken them into his counsel about the management of the Agency's funds.[61]

It is evident that the chiefs of intelligence were practical men when they had no footing. They knew that, although the funds came to the Agency through appropriations for their departments, Congress marked the money from the beginning for the use of the Agency on the Director's responsibility. They understood that Congress had its own ways of holding him accountable through the Comptroller General and the General Accounting Office. General Smith continued Hillenkoetter's policy of centralized administration over fiscal and financial matters, gathering them all into one Finance Office under a Comptroller who in turn was responsible to a Deputy Director of Administration.[62]

The Operations Division which the Dulles Group proposed, the Council directed Hillenkoetter to establish, and Smith postponed was not so easily obtained as the Finance Office. The Dulles Report recommended that the covert offices and the Contact Branch should be "integrated"; they should be under the "common control of a single directing head" who should be one of the principal assistants to the Director of Central Intelligence. But more than a year was to lapse after another inquiry and survey in the spring of 1951 by Jackson himself as Deputy Director before that "integration" or "merger" of the Office of Special Operations and the Office of Policy Coordination approached accomplishment.[63]

The account of the process belongs more properly in the next historical chapter on Central Intelligence. The reports of it current when this was written in September 1953 were that it seemed more like a collision than a merger. The philosophical concept which goes by the name of "integration" was remote from the facts. Mr. Wisner, however, was Deputy Director (Plans), the "single directing head" under the Director of Central Intelligence.

The transformation of COAPS into an office under an Assistant Director undeniably responsible to the Director of Central Intelligence was swift and easy. Vandenberg's ICAPS, designed to be his working staff of representatives from the departments who could explain the views of the Director of Central Intelligence to the chiefs of intelligence in the Intelligence Advisory Board, had been thwarted by the chiefs themselves. They had insisted upon setting up ad hoc committees to explore and debate with ICAPS in every instance and report back to the Board as if there were no familiarity with the subject, even though it might be threadbare.[64]

Hillenkoetter had received the same treatment, notwithstanding the fact that in pursuit of harmony he abandoned the position which Vandenberg had gained as "executive agent" for the Secretaries in the National Intelligence Authority. Hillenkoetter tried to improve the situation by suggesting that the usual appointees to the ad hoc committees should become a Standing Committee available for any discussion with ICAPS at the moment of alarm without wondering whether they were on their way to the right blaze.[65]

The Standing Committee had not served, however, to expedite deliberations. Rather it had increased difficulties perceptibly by raising the question whether a matter should be referred from the Intelligence Advisory Committee by way of the Director to his ICAPS become COAPS, or from the Director by way of the Advisory Committee to its Standing Committee, or some other interchange. In short, the whole procedure had become ridiculous, and almost everybody knew it. The principle of representation was vestigial except as an annoyance to those who had come to COAPS from departments particularly exasperated with the Director of Central Intelligence.[66]

James Q. Reber, nominated by Armstrong in the State Department to replace Prescott Childs when he finished his term of office at the head of COAPS, saw at once the fallacy in its organization by representation and the uselessness in having so many military men on the staff. It did not take three to express the military mind as distinguished from the civilian way of thinking. The intricate details of the Navy's case to be separated from that of the Army or the Air Force, for example, should be presented anyway by specialists and technical experts brought into the discussion of specific matters or issues. Reber came to the chairmanship of COAPS, as was traditional, from the Department of State. But there was no good reason why he should remain on that "payroll" during his stay in the Agency. While here he was obviously supposed to be the loyal servant of the Director of Central Intelligence and to carry out the Director's instructions, even though his own ideas might be different.

Reber expressed his opinions of the fallacy and weakness in COAPS to Jackson, Deputy Director, and found that both Jackson and Smith agreed with him. By a general order on December 13, 1950, Reber became

Acting Assistant Director for Intelligence Coordination and, in consequence of his office, Secretary to the Intelligence Advisory Committee. A
single officer with a supporting staff of assistants chosen as he recommended, and not because they were representatives of departments, had
taken the place of ICAPS and its successor, COAPS, as the coordinating
facility of the Central Intelligence Agency in its intelligence activities
with the departments and other agencies of the Government. No one
seems to have mourned the departure of COAPS nor to have regretted
much that General Smith did not install the Coordinating Division which
the Dulles Group had proposed.[67]

Once General Smith had decided to create the division or office for
estimating recommended in the Dulles Report, it was a relatively simple
matter to segregate the research elements in the old Office of Reports and
Estimates as a nucleus for the new Office of Research and Reports. It
would support the Office of National Estimates and take care of other
services of "common concern" to the departments and agencies of the
Government, such as the National Intelligence Surveys which had begun
with the Defense Project of 1946. Colonel Lovell's idea that the United
States Government should know everything to be known about the Soviet
Union and its satellites thus had grown until the Central Intelligence
Agency was on the point of establishing a separate office to engage primarily in economic research and to concentrate that effort almost exclusively
upon the Union of Soviet Socialist Republics and its dependent states.[68]

The Office of Research and Reports came into existence on December
1, 1950, by "Regulation No. 70." Theodore Babbitt was left in charge for a
while. The new head, Max Millikan, took office as Assistant Director on
January 16, 1951. Millikan found that twenty-four different agencies of
the Government were studying "foreign economies." The problem of their
correlation had been understood by the previous administration of the
Agency. The memorandum from COAPS of December 30, 1949, on the
State Department's "Four Papers re NSC 50" had suggested an interdepartmental Economic Intelligence Committee similar to the Scientific Intelligence Committee recently established. The National Security
Council adopted the recommendation on March 3, 1950, and instructed
the Agency to make a study and report in collaboration with other agencies concerned.[69]

It had not been accomplished during the summer of 1950. The delay was
caused in large part by the Korean War, which burst upon the Agency as
upon every other instrument of the Government. It could be that absorption with the campaign of the Departments of State and Defense to force
the Webb Plan through to the Council at that time had as much to do with
delaying the report from ORE on interdepartmental coordination of eco-

nomic research. It is certain that other agencies did not give to their collaboration more than their habitual interest and effort in such enterprises. In any case, it was not until May 31, 1951, that Jackson submitted the report to the Council for the Agency. The Council established the Economic Intelligence Committee on June 22, 1951, by NSCID 15. The Assistant Director, Office of Research and Reports in the Agency, was to be its chairman. Millikan sent a progress report on July 11, 1951, as requested to Jackson, Deputy Director of Central Intelligence.[70]

Before leaving the Agency, Babbitt had another conference with Jackson on the ills and needs of the Central Intelligence Agency. As Babbitt remembered later, General Smith found that in the reorganization the necessary provision for current intelligence had failed to appear. Babbitt, Montague, and Van Slyck had proposed to take care of the daily summary, the situation room, and the twenty-four-hour watch in the Agency, as it participated in the Interdepartmental Watch Committee at the Pentagon. General Smith wanted such institutions in the Agency, but not in the new Office of National Estimates.[71]

Jackson called a meeting to consider having an office under another Assistant Director. Babbitt, asked to give his opinion, stated that such an Office of Current Intelligence would have to employ a staff of at least seventy persons. Jackson protested that Babbitt wanted to "bring ORE in the back door." Babbitt replied that he did. The Office of Current Intelligence was established on January 11, 1951. [one line deleted] Kingman Douglass, [one line deleted] who had been largely responsible for developing the Office of Operations, returned to the Agency on January 19, 1951, to become Assistant Director for Current Intelligence.[72]

General Smith's central purpose, second only, if that, to his determination that OPC should be under his command, was to bring the departmental chiefs of intelligence into active cooperation with the Central Intelligence Agency, under his direction. The last statement is not to be set aside. It seems quite evident that Smith and Jackson gave the matter thought. The Agency and the Intelligence Advisory Committee must have "forthright initiative and leadership," as McNarney declared. Admiral Hillenkoetter had been so often charged with lacking those attributes that anyone succeeding him as Director of Central Intelligence had no recourse but to sound the tocsin.[73]

Smith's associates in the "cooperative interdepartmental activity" which Souers had begun for President Truman in 1946, and Congress had made into an "independent agency" in 1947, could have been reminded of the fact that their predecessors on the Advisory Board and the Committee had been persistently remiss. It was true that they had tried often to check the development of Central Intelligence. But their successors evidently were not to be told so at this time. They should be summoned to positive effort. Smith told them in the meeting on October 20, 1950, that the Intelligence Advisory Committee "must be geared for rapid cooperative work"; it therefore must include "the best intelligence brains in the nation." The warning and the complimentary exhortation did not ricochet unnoticed. They were included in the minutes of the meeting written from Jackson's notes. They were in those taken by Colonel Howze, who attended for the Department of the Army that day.[74]

Jackson prepared for the first meeting of General Smith with the Intelligence Advisory Committee. Assuming that as chief of COAPS he would supply the brief for Smith, Reber drew up a statement and took it to Jackson. In it Reber proposed that the Director should "*use* the mechanism" of the Advisory Committee. Reber meant that it should actually be put to work and hard work, if possible; he outlined a course of action for the production of estimates which, he remarked in 1953, was much like that eventually adopted. But apparently Jackson was irked by Reber's venture. Jackson made it known that he himself would take care of the General's meeting with the departmental chiefs. Anyhow, Reber did not attend. Jackson took the notes, which he later dictated. Reber then put them in order for multigraphing and circulation.[75]

After explaining his action in regard to OPC, General Smith came to the real business of the meeting with the Intelligence Advisory Committee. He read at length, and Jackson quoted in the minutes, from a paper which Jackson had written as a letter to Walter Lippmann upon "The Responsibility of the Central Intelligence Agency for National Intelligence Estimates." This memorandum recapitulated the provisions in the National Security Act of 1947 for correlating and evaluating national intelligence and for departmental intelligence, and it repeated in much the same form and phrasing the essential points on the subject in the Dulles Report.[76]

There was missing that notable provision which appeared in the draft of the first directive of the National Intelligence Authority in February 1946 and failed to survive. Jackson made no specific mention of the necessity that the departmental intelligence services should supply information on the "capabilities and intentions" of the United States if the estimators were to give truly "national intelligence" to the makers of national policy. But then no one could reasonably expect Smith and Jackson in their first meeting with the departmental chiefs to make a statement so critical of the Armed Forces. Smith had to be content in 1950, as had Souers in 1946, with asserting that a national intelligence estimate ought to "reflect the coordination" of the best intelligence opinion based on "all available" information. It was so in 1953, although there seemed to be indication that "net estimates" had begun to appear in the National Security Council.[77]

Jackson repeated in this paper his formula that "ultimate approval" should rest upon the "collective responsibility" of the highest intelligence officers in the various departmental services. The corrected version of the minutes for October 20, 1950, had the word "responsibility" lined out and replaced by the word "judgment." According to Reber, it was General Smith who made the change. Collective judgment is a different concept from collective responsibility, nearer the views of General McNarney in NSC 50 and of Admiral Souers. Souers held that the Director should have individual responsibility "based on coordinated effort."[78]

As General Smith worked upon national estimates with the Intelligence Advisory Committee, he realized more and more, he said, that they were collectively responsible. It might have been clearer if he had said that theirs was a common responsibility. There is no evidence that he gave up the individual responsibility of the Director of Central Intelligence. It was his duty by Act of Congress just as "substantially differing opinions" were the right of the departmental chiefs of intelligence under the directive of the National Security Council.[79]

Following Smith's presentation of Jackson's paper on October 20, there was "general assent" in the Intelligence Advisory Committee that, as Jackson had written, the Central Intelligence Agency had by law the "independent right" to produce national intelligence estimates. But as a "practical matter" they could not be obtained without the "collaboration of experts in many fields" and the "cooperation" of the departments. General Smith then announced that he proposed to have an Office of National Estimates; it would be the heart of the Agency and of the national machinery for intelligence. The accompanying Office of Research and Reports would confine its activities to specific assignments by directives of the National Security Council as services of "common concern."

Mr. Jackson interposed the familiar point of the Dulles Survey Group. In the past ORE had produced national estimates and miscellaneous reports to the confusion of both function and product. The inference was that production now in separate offices would keep reports distinct from estimates; there would be no confusion or blur. One should not suppress the counterpoint that research has to accompany estimating closely. That two assistant directors could keep them together better than one assistant director would seem open to query.[80]

To obtain the "collaboration" of experts and the "cooperation" of the departments, General Smith intended that the Intelligence Advisory Committee should work at estimating as it had not worked heretofore. Babbitt, Montague, and Van Slyck had proposed a representative Coordination and Liaison Staff in the Agency. General Smith called upon the Intelligence Advisory Committee itself to take the responsibility for "an intelligence plan, or more specifically, a list of required national estimates in order of priority." Moreover, the departmental chiefs of intelligence in the Committee, though their junior officers might do the digging, should be responsible in particular estimates for determining "a frame of reference and the assumptions" upon which the estimate was based. The Office of National Estimates should then produce the first draft and look after its modification and development through discussion among the interested agencies until the estimate went to the Intelligence Advisory Committee for final discussion and approval or statements of dissent.

For "crisis estimates" General Smith wished to summon special meetings of the Intelligence Advisory Committee such as had prepared a series of estimates for President Truman before his journey to confer with General MacArthur on Wake Island. It was agreed that the Advisory Committee should get down to business at once. The next meeting was scheduled for the following Wednesday, October 25. The subject of discussion would be "the frame of reference and assumptions" for an estimate on the situation in Indo-China.

Colonel Howze, reporting the session of October 20, 1950, for the Army, took note that General Smith wanted a "panel of five or six individuals" in the new estimating office to constitute the "top brains." This was a reflection of the statement by Babbitt, Montague, and Van Slyck that ORE did not have adequate personnel for the work. General Smith, said Howze, was "looking hard for a retired General or Admiral" to head the organization. Smith tried to get Admiral Stevens, who had been Naval Attaché in Moscow. Smith also remarked that he was anxious to have General Huebner become a member of the panel, possibly head of the Office.[81]

It was natural that General Smith should turn to former associates when seeking able men for important places in his administration. Apparently he was persuaded by Mr. Jackson, or by his own reconsideration of the problem, however, to invite a civilian to head the Office of National Estimates, which he was determined to make the heart of the national system of intelligence. General Smith summoned William L. Langer back to public service from retirement after years of active participation, first in the Office of Strategic Services with General Donovan and then in the Department of State which he had represented on the Intelligence Advisory Board.[82]

The Office of National Estimates came formally into existence on November 13, 1950, by a general order announcing the appointment of Langer as Assistant Director for National Estimates. The Office was organized in three major parts: the National Estimates Board, the Estimates Staff, and the Support Staff. Upon the Board under Langer's chairmanship General Smith placed, "personally and individually" selected by himself, experts in the fields of "strategy, political science, economics, and other social sciences" and individuals with the "broadest of experience in the field of intelligence at the highest level."[83]

Among them were Lieutenant General Huebner, Vice Admiral Bieri, and Professors Sontag and Kent. Kent, in line to succeed Langer, was qualified by his experience in the Research and Analysis Branch of OSS during the war as well as by his study of *Strategic Intelligence*. Montague and Van Slyck came to the National Estimates Board from the shambles of ORE. They had stood from the beginning for coordinated national estimating, on the one hand, against the departmental chiefs of intelligence and, on the other, against the heads of the geographical divisions within the Agency.[84]

The Estimates Staff under Langer's direction was to be a group of officers chosen for their competence to support the National Estimates Board. Although they were not selected as representatives of the departments, their functions were much like those which Babbitt, Montague, and Van Slyck would have assigned to the Coordination and Liaison Staff for the preparation of estimates with the departmental intelligence organizations. The "draft estimates" should be the responsibility of a General Group of the Estimates Staff. Expert knowledge would come from the Specialist Group of the Staff. Individuals would be given particular tasks. There would be special assignments such as those to the staff of the National Security Council and to the Watch Committee in the Pentagon and to the Joint Staff of the Joint Chiefs of Staff. In addition to this internal organization, the Office should have a Panel of Consultants, persons like George Kennan and Vannevar Bush, who would confer with members of the National Estimating Board on the most important estimates.[85]

As Langer reviewed the situation after the first eight months, the Office of National Estimates was discharging its responsibilities primarily through the National Estimates Board. It directed the production of national intelligence estimates. The action included setting the priorities which General Smith had intended that the Advisory Committee should determine. Once the Advisory Committee had approved the scheduling, or the Estimates Board had decided upon the urgency, the Office of National Estimates was "more appropriately identified" as an integral part of the "interagency mechanism" in producing a given estimate. Cooperation between the National Estimates Board and the several intelligence organizations of the Departments of State and Defense, said Langer, was now complete. Meetings occurred at every stage in the progress of the estimates from the "statement of the problem" to the final draft for submission to the Intelligence Advisory Committee.

Langer did not think that he had brought about the great change. The procedure, he said, was "not wholly dissimilar" from that which the Agency had employed before the Office of National Estimates had been established. The "important advance" was that "*active cooperation had displaced reluctant and marginal participation.*" The emphasis was Langer's. The result, as he saw it, was that "top policymakers" now attached "real importance" to the estimates which were produced. This had not formerly been so. As an example, he said, G-2 had dispatched to General Ridgway at once the contents of a special estimate on "possible Communist objectives" in proposing a cease-fire in Korea. The Secretary of State on the same day made an "urgent appeal" for the same estimate.[86]

The solution may have been found as counsel for Smith had suggested. The General saw the President often. Could word have gone around that at last there was "a grant of adequate authority" for this instrument of government? Uncertainty over Korea gave General Smith decided advantage. Now the Director of Central Intelligence could use "coordination by direction." He did not have to rely upon "a spirit of cooperation and good will" in preparing the national system of intelligence for war.[87]

Appendix A: Chronology

1940

July–August: First Donovan mission to Europe

December–March 1941: Second Donovan mission to Europe

1941

Spring–Fall: Establishment of Foreign Information Service, Research and Analysis Branch, Visual Presentation Branch, Oral Intelligence Service, undercover collection, [several words deleted] special activities K & L funds (subversive operations)

June 10: Donovan's memorandum to the President proposing the creation of the Service of Strategic Information

June 25: Presidential order appointing Donovan Coordinator of Strategic Information

July 11: Presidential order creating Office of Coordinator of Information

Fall: Creation of Army–Navy Joint Intelligence Committee

December 22: Donovan's paper on the British Commando system

1942

March: Joint Psychological Warfare Committee created by Joint Chiefs of Staff (JCS)

June 13: Presidential order creates Office of Strategic Services (OSS) and places it under JCS

June 21: JCS reorganizes Joint Psychological Warfare Committee, with Donovan as chairman

August 25: Magruder submits "Proposed Plan for Joint Intelligence Bureau"

December 22: JCS abolishs Joint Psychological Warfare Committee and gives its functions to OSS; JCS defines OSS' intelligence functions

1943

Winter: JCS creates Joint Intelligence Collection Agencies

January 19: JCS supports Army and Navy position regarding release of information to OSS

July 30: Magruder states his ideas on permanent U. S. intelligence system to JCS Executive Secretary

September 17: Donovan gives details of his plan to General Walter B. Smith

October 27: JCS makes final revision of intelligence functions of OSS

1944

Fall: Joint Intelligence Staff (JIS) produces "services plan" and "civilian plan" for permanent national intelligence service

November 18: Donovan submits to President final draft of his plan for "permanent worldwide intelligence service"

December 22: Joint Intelligence Committee (JIC) begins work of perfecting "services" and "civilian" plans and produces its plan within a week

December 26: Donovan leaves for Europe having rejected "services plan" and accepted most of the "civilian plan"

1945

January 9: White House conference; Truman decides in favor of JCS plan and picks Souers to become first DCI

January 18: Joint Strategic Survey Committee's Report accepts JIC plan as superior to Donovan's project

February 9: Leak to the press of Donovan's plan and JIC plan

April 5–May 16: Donovan's exchanges of letters with departmental Secretaries concerning proposed new intelligence agency

May 25, 27: Wartime commanders reply to inquiry of House Appropriations Committee concerning use of OSS in Pacific area

August 25: Bureau of the Budget advises Donovan that continuation of OSS is unlikely

Fall: State Department plan

September 19: JCS revives its plan and sends it to Secretaries of War and Navy

September 20: End of OSS by Presidential order; Research and Analysis and Presentation Branches go to the State Department, all other activities to the War Department where the Strategic Services Unit (SSU) is established; Truman directs Byrnes to take the lead in developing a comprehensive foreign intelligence system and to form an interdepartmental group to make plans; Bureau of the Budget presents its plan for a new intelligence organization; Bureau of the Budget, *Report on Intelligence and Security Activities of the Government*

October 16: Forrestal, Patterson, Byrnes meet and agree that any central intelligence agency should report to them rather than to the President

October 22: Patterson (War) appoints Lovett Committee to recommend plan for Central Intelligence; Eberstadt Report published, including section on military intelligence

October–December: State–War–Navy working committee formulates plan for permanent intelligence system

November 3: Lovett committee reports

November 14: William H. Jackson [several words deleted] submits plan for permanent central intelligence organization

November–December: State Department plan

1946

January 22: Souers takes office as DCI (remaining until June 10, 1946); President's Directive establishes Central Intelligence Group (CIG)

February–March: Interdepartmental committee studies problem and recommends that SSU should be partly liquidated and partly taken over by CIG

February 5: National Intelligence Authority (NIA) begins (and operates until September 20, 1947); first NIA meeting

February 8: NIA Directive 1—"Policy and Procedures Governing the Central Intelligence Group"; NIA Directive 2—"Organization and Functions of the Central Intelligence Group"

February 26: "White House Bill" for National Security Council (NSC) and Central Intelligence Agency (CIA) released to press; bill for National Defense Establishment sent to Congress

March 4: CIG Administrative Order organizing Central Reports Staff (CRS); Colonel J. R. Lovell, Military Intelligence Service, proposes Defense Project to get all information on USSR

March 30: NIA Directive 3—"NIA Views on Proposed Executive Order 'Directing the Cooperation of Government Agencies in the Coordination of Foreign Intelligence Activities of the United States' "

April 2: NIA Directive 4—"Policy on Liquidation of SSU"

June 7: Souers's final report as DCI

June 10: Vandenberg takes office as DCI (remaining until May 1, 1947)

July 19: Office of Reports and Estimates (ORE) replaces (CRS)

Summer–mid-October: Liquidation of SSU except for those personnel, undercover agents, and foreign stations taken over by CIG

July 8: NIA Directive 5—"Functions of the DCI"

July 11: Galloway replaces Fortier as Assistant Director for Special Operations

July 20: Vandenberg abolishes Central Planning Staff (CPS); Vandenberg establishes the Interdepartmental Coordinating and Planning Staff (ICAPS)

July 26: NIA Directive 6—"Provision for Coordinating the Acquisition of Foreign Publications"

[one entry deleted]

October 1: Establishment of contact control register and CIG field offices for foreign intelligence from domestic sources

1947

January 2: NIA Directive 7—"Coordination of Collection Activities"

January 10: Vandenberg–Bush agreement for cooperation concerning scientific intelligence

January 20: Wright becomes Executive and Deputy Director

February 12: NIA defines concept of national intelligence; ninth meeting of the NIA; Vandenberg receives authority as "executive agent"; NIA Directive 8—"National Intelligence Requirements: China"

February 17: Hillenkoetter approved as DCI by President and NIA

February 18: Transfer of intelligence division of the Manhatten Engineer District to CIG

March 28: Establishment of Nuclear Energy Group in the Scientific Branch of ORE

April 18: NIA Directive 9—"Coordination of Intelligence Activities, Related Foreign Atomic Developments and Potentialities"

May 1: Hillenkoetter takes office as DCI (remaining until October 7, 1950)

June 26: Last meeting of NIA

July 26: National Security Act becomes law; effective date of NSC

[one entry deleted]

September 16: NIA Directive 11—"Action by the Intelligence Advisory Board on Matters Submitted to the NIA"

September 20: Hillenkoetter takes office as DCI under the National Security Act

September 26: First meeting of NSC

October 31: State Department withdraws its representative from the Joint Intelligence Committee and Joint Intelligence Staff, considering the DCI and CIA the proper channel for joint action between State and the Joint Chiefs

December 8: Meeting of Hillenkoetter with Forrestal, the Secretaries, and their intelligence chiefs, State Department representative, and Souers; Forrestal backs Hillenkoetter in his concept of a strong directorship

December 12: National Security Council Intelligence Directive (NSCID) 1—"Duties and Responsibilities"; NSCID 4—"National Intelligence Objectives"; NSCID 5—"Espionage and Counterespionage Operations"; NSCID 6—"Foreign Wireless and Radio Monitoring"

December 17: NSC Action 4-A—"Assignment of Conduct of Covert Psychological Operations against the Communist Powers to the Central Intelligence Agency"

December 22: Hillenkoetter instructs Colonel Galloway, Assistant Director in the Office of Special Operations, to organize a "Foreign Information Branch"; this became the Special Procedures Group, for false publications, black radio, etc. (U.S. origin concealed)

1948

January 13: NSC establishes the Intelligence Survey Group (Dulles–Jackson–Correa Committee, or "Dulles Group"); NSCID 2—"Coordination of Collection Activities Abroad"; NSCID 3—"Coordination of Intelligence Production"

February–March: Departmental statements of resistance to and/or cooperation with Dulles Group, which by the terms of Souers's memorandum was to examine departmental intelligence organizations

February 5: DCI Directive 4/1—"National Intelligence Objectives"

February 9: Report on CIA to Hillenkoetter by Sherman Kent

February 12: NSCID 7—"Domestic Exploitation"

February 13: Souers's memorandum to Dulles Group authorizing them to proceed with survey of CIA

[one entry deleted]

March 5: DCI Directive 1/1—"Procedures for the Intelligence Advisory Committee"

March 30: Pan-American Conference opens in Bogotá

April 9: Assassination of Jorge Gaitan in Bogotá; beginning of Bogotá riots

April 12: Hillenkoetter accepts Atomic Energy Commission plan for improving evaluation of foreign atomic energy intelligence

May 3: Interim Report No. 1 by Dulles Group [several words deleted]

May 13: Interim Report No. 2 by Dulles Group ("Secret Intelligence and Covert Operations")

May 25: NSCID 8—"Biographical Data on Foreign Scientific and Technological Personalities"

June–September: Eberstadt Committee investigation of CIA, hearings, and report

June 18: NSC 10-2—"Organization of Covert Psychological Operations"; this added sabotage, demolitions, evacuation, aid to guerrilla action and underground resistance to functions given under NSC 4-A

July 1: NSCID 9—"Communications Intelligence"

July 8: DCI Directive 3/1—"Standard Operating Procedures for Departmental Participation in the Production and Coordination of National Intelligence"

September 1: Establishment of Office of Policy Coordination by CIA General Order, to conform with terms of NSC 10-2

September 13: DCI Directive 3/2—"Policy Governing Departmental Concurrences in National Intelligence Reports and Estimates"

October 25: DCI Directive 2/1—"Implementation of Coordination of Collection Plan"

December 31: Establishment of Office of Scientific Intelligence

1949

January 1: Dulles Group Report appears

January 18: NSCID 10—"Collection of Foreign Scientific and Technological Data"

February 24: Atomic Energy Commission comments on Dulles Report

February 25: Army comments on Dulles Report

February 28: Hillenkoetter's "Comments" on Dulles Report sent to NSC

March 1: Air Force comments on Dulles Report

March 3: JSC comments on Dulles Report

March 4: Navy comments on Dulles Report

April 4: State Department comments on Dulles Report

June 20: CIA Act of 1949 becomes law

July 1: McNarney Report submitted to NSC

July 7: NSC decides that new Operations Division in CIA (merger of Office of Special Operations, Office of Policy Coordination, Contact Branch of Office of Operations) shall not include Foreign Broadcast Information Branch and appoints McNarney to study and report on Dulles recommendation for "separate administration" within CIA for Operations Division; NSC 50 (Security Council adoption of Dulles Survey Group recommendations as reconsidered and modified in McNarney Report); NSCID 1 (revised)—"Duties and Responsibilities"

July 19: Reitzel Report to Babbitt (Assistant Director of ORE)—"Analysis of ORE Production, with Conclusions, First Report"

July 22: McNarney reports, reaffirming "separate administration" idea

August 2: State's "Four Papers" presented to Hillenkoetter (State believed the aspects of NSC 50 portrayed in these papers should be implemented at earliest feasible time)—"Coordination of Intelligence Activities"; "Production of National Intelligence"; "Research and Reports"; "Political Summaries"

August 4: NSC orders creation of proposed Operations Division with "separate administration"

September 20: CIA General Order reorganizing CIA fiscal procedures to conform with "separate administration" idea (Operations Division plan never went into effect)

October 1: ICAPS renamed the Coordination, Operations, and Policies Staff (COAPS) and given more duties in CIA

October 10: Hillenkoetter's first progress report to NSC according to Council Directive of July 7, 1949

October 28: Establishment of interdepartmental Scientific Intelligence Committee; DCI Directive 3/3—"Scientific Intelligence"

December 27: Hillenkoetter's second progress report

1950

January 6: NSCID 11—"Security of Information and Intelligence Sources and Methods"; NSCID 12—"Avoidance of Publicity Concerning the Intelligence Agencies of the U. S. Government"

January 19: NSCID 1 (revised)—"Duties and Responsibilities"

[one entry deleted]

March 3: NSC adopts COAPS recommendation for establishment of interdepartmental Economic Intelligence Committee

[one entry deleted]

March 7: Stout Committee Report

May 1: Webb Staff Study, emphasizing major theme of "cooperation" in national estimating

July 7: Hillenkoetter receives Webb Staff Study

[one entry deleted]

July 26: CIA reply to Webb Staff Study, proposing strengthening of CIA jurisdiction and powers concerning estimating

August 15: Inter-Agency Operating Procedure No. 3—"Nongovernmental Visitors Interested in Intelligence Matters"

August 29: Houston memorandum to Smith describing CIA problems and making recommendations

September 28: DCI Directive 4/2—"Priority List of Critical National Intelligence Objectives"

October 5: Houston, Pforzheimer, Wisner recommendations for Smith to Jackson for revision of NSC 10-2

October 7: Smith takes office as DCI (remaining until February 26, 1953)

October 10: ORE recommendations to Smith concerning estimates production problems

October 20: Smith, with NSC approval of October 12, informs Intelligence Advisory Committee that he will not create the Operations Division

November 13: Establishment of the Office of National Estimates

December 1: Establishment of the Office of Research and Reports from research elements in old ORE

December 13: Office of Intelligence Coordination (CIA) replaces COAPS

1951

January 11: Establishment of Office of Current Intelligence

June 22: NSCID 15 (corrected)—"Coordination and Production of Foreign Economic Intelligence"; this establishes the interdepartmental Economic Intelligence Committee

1953

February 26: Dulles takes office as DCI

March 7: NSCID 16—"Foreign Language Publications"

Appendix B:
Memoranda on the Historical
Review Program

Central Intelligence Agency

Washington, D.C. 20505

18 June 1985

MEMORANDUM FOR ALL EMPLOYEES

SUBJECT: Historical Review Program

    1.   In October 1983, when the Senate Select Committee on Intelligence took up a bill to permit the Director of Central Intelligence (DCI) to exempt certain CIA files from search under the Freedom of Information Act (FOIA), Senator David Durenberger wrote to me about an issue highlighted by the Agency's work with the Committee. This issue was the need to make more declassified Agency materials available to historians. "As historians write the definitive works on the post-World War II era," Senator Durenberger wrote, "it is terribly important that their studies be based on as full a record as possible, consistent with the need to protect our national security." He therefore urged me to establish procedures for reviewing and declassifying some of the material in files not covered by the bill's exemptions. Recognizing that such a program would be a burden for the Agency, he offered to lead the effort to provide budgetary support for new positions to be devoted to this project.

    2.   I share Senator Durenberger's views on the need for an accurate historical record, and on 4 October 1983 I wrote him stating, "If Congress is willing to provide the resources, I am prepared to institute a new program of selective declassification review of those materials we believe would be of greatest historical interest and most likely to result in declassification of useful information."

    3.   The agreement by this exchange of letters envisioned an Agency Historical Review Program organized after the passage of the prospective CIA Information Act and using additional resources Congress would provide for this purpose. I had already asked the Chief of the History Staff, however, to explore a program to release historical materials from the World War II period. As a result of this initiative, the Agency took steps to transfer to the National Archives its entire holdings of declassified World War II Office of Strategic Services (OSS) permanent records, a large collection of major historical importance. This transfer began a year ago and up to now the National Archives has received and opened to public research approximately 800 cubic feet of these declassified OSS records. As I wrote to Senator Durenberger in June 1984, this transfer constitutes "an important first step in implementing the selective declassification program I promised to initiate last October."

    4.   In October 1984 Congress passed the CIA Information Act, which relieves the Agency from the burden of searching certain designated files in response to FOIA requests. The Agency's commitment to a Historical

Review Program and its release of OSS records played an important role in the passage of this new Act by reassuring Congress and the public that, in light of the Act's FOIA exemptions, the Agency will undertake new efforts to declassify and transfer to the National Archives historically significant CIA records. Continuing Congressional interest in historians having access to CIA records is evident in the Act's requirement that the DCI, after consulting with the Archivist of the United States, the Librarian of Congress, and representative historians, submit a report to four Congressional committees by 1 June 1985 on the feasibility of conducting a program for the systematic review, declassification, and release to the public of CIA information of historical value.

5. In my report to Congress of 29 May 1985 on the Historical Review Program, I stated that this kind of review is feasible, and described the program that we have established to carry it out. The Agency's consultations with those officials and historians specified by the CIA Information Act proved extraordinarily helpful, and their findings are appended to my report to Congress. Balancing the Agency's statutory duty to protect intelligence sources and methods with legitimate public interest in CIA records, this new program is designed to make significant historical information available without risking damage to national security. As I reported to Congress, this program has my strong support and we are determined to make it succeed.

6. As Senator Durenberger promised, Congress has provided CIA with ten additional positions to support the Historical Review Program which will be described in a forthcoming headquarters regulation. I have assigned principal responsibility for the program to the Office of Information Services (OIS) in the Directorate of Administration, with advice and support from the History Staff in the Office of the DCI. The Classification Review Division of OIS will coordinate closely with Agency components in reviewing documents of historical significance in order to declassify those that no longer require protection. The program is beginning with the review of the Agency's oldest records, which with the transfer of our declassified OSS records are those of CIA's postwar predecessor organizations, namely, the Strategic Services Unit (SSU) of 1945-1946 and the Central Intelligence Group (CIG) of 1946-1947.

7. Although some time will be needed to find out how well the Historical Review Program will work in practice, I believe that it has been established on a sound footing. I am hopeful that this program will make possible a more accurate record and fuller understanding of our Nation's history since World War II.

William J. Casey
Director of Central Intelligence

DISTRIBUTION: ALL EMPLOYEES (1-6)

29 December 1989

MEMORANDUM FOR ALL EMPLOYEES

SUBJECT: Historical Review Program

1.   In a recent visit to the National Archives, I presented
the Archivist of the United States, Dr. Don W. Wilson, with the
declassified version of <u>The Central Intelligence Agency: An
Instrument of Government, to 1950</u>. This 1,000-page history,
written in 1951-1953 by CIA's first Chief Historian,
Dr. Arthur B. Darling, is the first CIA document to be declassified and transferred to the National Archives for release to
the public under the Agency's Historical Review Program. After
our meeting at the National Archives, Dr. Wilson and I jointly
presented a copy of this history to President Bush, who has
described Dr. Darling, under whom he studied at Phillips
Academy, Andover, as his favorite teacher. I have also sent
copies of this history to the chairmen of the two congressional
intelligence committees.

2.   Other records will follow this transfer, and I have
assured the Archivist of the United States of my own strong
support for CIA's commitment to the Historical Review Program.
This program resulted from the passage by Congress of the CIA
Information Act of 1984, which relieved the Agency from the
burden of searching certain designated operational files in
response to Freedom of Information Act requests. At the
request of Congress, and with our earlier declassification of
the Office of Strategic Services records as precedent, the
Agency agreed to undertake new efforts to declassify and
transfer historically significant CIA records to the National
Archives.

3.   The Historical Review Program has been established in
the Office of Information Technology (OIT), Directorate of
Administration. Balancing the Agency's statutory duty to
protect intelligence sources and methods with legitimate public
interest in CIA records, this program is designed to make
significant historical information available without risking
damage to national security. As our first transfer indicates,
the program has begun with the review of the Agency's oldest
records. The Classification Review Branch in OIT, with the

advice and support of the History Staff in the Office of the
DCI, coordinates closely with Agency components to declassify
suitable documents while assuring the security of those
documents that still require protection.

4. Although this is a challenging program to carry out,
I am gratified by the way that all parts of the Agency, and
especially the Directorates of Operations and Intelligence,
have cooperated in getting the program under way. As part of
our accountability to the American people, the Historical
Review Program will make possible a more accurate record and
fuller understanding of CIA's role in our nation's history.
I ask all of you to give this program your fullest measure of
support.

William H. Webster
Director of Central Intelligence

DISTRIBUTION: ALL EMPLOYEES (1-6)

N.B. "ALL EMPLOYEES (1-6)" signifies that one copy of an
issuance is available for circulation for each six
employees within a specific component. (See HR 5-2.)

Notes

Chapter I

1. A. F. Tyler, *The Foreign Policy of James G. Blaine*, 1927, Ch. VII, pp. 165–90, and the records of the conference cited in the bibliography.

2. A. T. Mahan, *Mahan on Naval Warfare*, 1944, pp. 100–12.

3. Bureau of the Budget, *Report on Intelligence and Security Activities of the Government*, Sept. 20, 1945, p. 2. See below, pp. 107, 292–94, 332–34, 395–98.

4. T. Paine, *Common Sense*, in *Writings*, ed. M. D. Conway, 1894, Vol. 1, pp. 88–89.

5. D. Webster, *Writings* (National Edition), 1903, Vol. XV, p. 191. For discussion of national security at the time of the Act of Congress in 1947, see below, pp. 181–82.

6. W. J. Donovan to A. B. Darling, Feb. 17, 1953.

7. Bureau of the Budget, *Report on Intelligence*, p. 5.

8. Henry L. Stimson to A. B. Darling, June 1940, quoting Churchill's cable.

9. Foreword by William J. Donovan, *War Report, Office of Strategic Services*, cited hereafter as *OSS War Report*.

10. *New York Times*, Aug. 20–23, 1940.

11. W. J. Donovan to A. B. Darling, Feb. 17, 1953.

12. *OSS War Report*, Vol. I, pp. 6–7, 259–60, 289–90.

13. W. J. Donovan to W. B. Smith, Sept. 17, 1943.

14. *OSS War Report*, Vol. I, p. 260.

15. Ibid., pp. 7–8, 261–62. Donovan insisted that the order was revised, not withdrawn.

16. W. J. Donovan to A. B. Darling, Feb. 17, 1953.

17. H. F. Gosnell, "Relationship between Planning and Intelligence in Overseas Propaganda," pp. 5–6. Paper prepared for the Bureau of the Budget, Jan. 31, 1944

(OSS Archives File #8 COI, Exhibits, Vol. I). See *Congressional Record* for July 11, 1941 (Gosnell paper).

18. W. O. Hall, memorandum of Aug. 28, 1941, on "Functional Confusion in the Office for Coordinator of Information." Paper prepared for the Bureau of the Budget, cited by H. F. Gosnell in "Relationship between Planning and Intelligence in Overseas Propaganda," pp. 10–11.

19. W. J. Donovan to A. B. Darling, Feb. 17, 1953.

20. Sherman Miles to Chief of Staff, July 7, 1941 (*OSS War Report,* Vol. I, pp. 10–14); Sherman Miles to Chief of Staff, Sept. 5, 1941 (*OSS War Report,* Vol. I, p. 292); W. J. Donovan to the President, Oct. 10, 1941 (*OSS War Report,* Vol. I, p. 293).

21. Charles Seymour to A. B. Darling, Jan. 17 and 23, 1952.

22. *OSS War Report,* Vol. I, pp. 70, 72–73, 262, 294. Paper on the Commandos (OSS Archives File #8A COI, Exhibits, Vol. II).

23. C. D. Dillon, "Military Conditions of the War—The Joint Chiefs of Staff," in F. Eberstadt, *Report to Secretary Forrestal,* Oct. 22, 1945, Vol. II, Ch. 2, p. 57; *OSS War Report,* Vol. I, pp. 20–21.

24. *OSS War Report,* Vol. I, pp. 274–82. For Roosevelt's advice to Donovan against placing the OSS under the Joint Chiefs of Staff, see J. Magruder to A. B. Darling, Jan. 8, 1953.

25. *OSS War Report,* Vol. I, pp. 266, 277, 279–81. H. F. Gosnell, "Relationship between Planning and Intelligence in Overseas Propaganda," pp. 33–34.

26. *OSS War Report,* Vol. I, pp. 98–99, 105, 330, 367–84.

27. W. J. Donovan to A. B. Darling, Feb. 17, 1953.

28. *OSS War Report,* Vol. I, pp. 105, 379–83.

29. Ibid., p. 384.

30. Ibid., pp. 372, 382.

31. Admiral Leahy to Elmer Davis, Dec. 22, 1942; Davis to J. G. Rogers, Feb. 11, 1943 (OSS Archives File: Advisory Committee).

32. *OSS War Report,* Vol. I, pp. 381, 383, 398, 414. See below, pp. 157, 383–84.

33. Sherman Miles to Chief of Staff, Sept. 5, 1941 (*OSS War Report,* Vol. I, p. 292); W. J. Donovan to the President, Oct. 10, 1941 (*OSS War Report,* Vol. I, p. 293); L. L. Montague to A. B. Darling, April 1, 1952.

34. *OSS War Report,* Vol. I, pp. 379 (Dec. 23, 1942), 394 (April 4, 1943), 413 (Oct. 27, 1943).

35. W. J. Donovan to A. B. Darling, Feb. 17, 1953.

36. J. Magruder to A. B. Darling, Feb. 26, 1952.

37. W. J. Donovan to the Joint Intelligence Committee, Oct. 22, 1942 (OSS Archives File: JIC).

38. J. Magruder to W. J. Donovan, Jan. 8, 1943 (OSS Archives File: JIC).

39. See pp. 78–81, 198–99, 201–3, 405–6.

40. *OSS War Report,* Vol. I, p. 182; "Intelligence," in F. Eberstadt, *Report to Secretary Forrestal,* Oct. 22, 1945, Vol. III, Ch. 2, p. 159. See below, pp. 180–82.

41. Warner Paper (OSS Archives File: JIC).

42. W. H. Jackson, *The British Intelligence System,* July 1945, pp. 4–10.

43. Warner Paper (OSS Archives File: JIC); L. L. Montague to A. B. Darling, in conversation, Feb. 26, 1952.

44. J. Magruder to W. J. Donovan, Sept. 11, 1943 (Ms File JM-311).

45. See pp. 93, 101, 105, 107–10, 127–32.

46. L. L. Montague to A. B. Darling, in conversation, Feb. 26, 1952.

47. See pp. 257 (and note), 417–18.

48. *OSS War Report,* Vol. I, pp. 63–65, 198, 202.

49. Ibid., pp. 179–88.

50. Ibid., pp. 188, 197–98.

51. W. J. Donovan to A. B. Darling, Feb. 17, 1953.

52. OSS–SOE Agreements 27 (OSS Archives File, Safe #5, Drawer 2); S. Kent to A. B. Darling, Feb. 1, 1952.

53. OSS–SOE Agreements 27.

54. W. H. Jackson, *Coordination of Intelligence Functions and the Organization of Secret Intelligence in the British Intelligence System* (Top Secret), Office of Strategic Services, July 1945. See below, pp. 119–20.

55. See pp. 145–47.

56. *OSS War Report,* Vol. I, pp. 61, 170.

57. Ibid., p. 173. See below, pp. 309–10.

58. *OSS War Report,* Vol. II, p. 445; W. J. Donovan to A. B. Darling, Feb. 17, 1953. See below, pp. 38–39.

59. R. Patterson to J. Forrestal, March 5, 1946 (SWNCC 304 File). For the State–War–Navy Coordinating Committee, see pp. 250–56.

60. J. Magruder to A. B. Darling, Feb. 26, 1952.

61. J. Magruder to W. J. Donovan, "Proposed Plan for Joint Intelligence Bureau," Aug. 25, 1942 (Ms File JM-311).

62. J. Magruder to Col. C. R. Peck, JCS, July 30, 1943.

63. W. J. Donovan to W. B. Smith, Sept. 17, 1943; J. Magruder to A. B. Darling, Jan. 8, 1953.

64. See pp. 410–21.

65. See pp. 32–38; also pp. 179–80. The quotation is from a cable, April 11, 1945, to Buxton and Cheston (OSS Archives File: OSS–CIA–A–2).

66. "The Basis for a Permanent, World-Wide Intelligence Service," Oct. 5, 1944 (OSS Archives File 12733).

67. Ibid., p. 2 (for discussion of "individual versus collective responsibility" in estimating).

68. For the order of June 13, 1942, see pp. 10–11. Pencilled memorandum from General Magruder, Nov. 22, 1944 (OSS Archives File 12733: Permanent Intelligence Service).

69. OSS Archives File 12733: Permanent Intelligence Service. See below, pp. 47–48.

70. State Plan, Sept. 30, 1944 (OSS Archives File 12733: Need for CIA). For subsequent activities of the State Department, see below, pp. 49–56.

71. W. J. Donovan to F. D. Roosevelt, Oct. 31, 1944 (OSS Archive File 12733: Permanent Intelligence Service).

72. W. J. Donovan to A. B. Darling, Feb. 17, 1953.

73. W. J. Donovan to F. D. Roosevelt, Nov. 7, 1944 (OSS Archives File 12733 U: OSS–CIA Principles).

74. Report by Louis M. Ream to W. J. Donovan, Nov. 7, 1944 (OSS Archives File 12733). See pp. 120–27 (Vandenberg and Hoover in Aug. 1946).

75. W. J. Donovan to F. D. Roosevelt, Nov. 18, 1944 (OSS Archives File 12733 G).

76. W. J. Donovan to F. D. Roosevelt, Nov. 18, 1944, with directive enclosed (OSS Archives File 12733 G).

77. Executive Order of 1944 (Proposed), "Directive to the Director of Strategic Services on Functions of the Office of Strategic Services."

78. Pencilled memorandum from General Magruder, Nov. 22, 1944 (OSS Archives File 12733: Permanent Intelligence Service).

79. W. J. Donovan to Isador Lubin, Nov. 29, 1944 (OSS Archives File: OSS–CIA–A–1).

80. See pp. 70–74.

81. L. L. Montague to A. B. Darling, Feb. 15, 1952. (At that time Montague was a senior member of the Joint Intelligence Staff.) J. S. Lay, Jr., to A. B. Darling, April 3, 1952. (Lay was Secretary of the Joint Intelligence Committee.)

82. S. E. Gleason, Jr., to A. B. Darling, Feb. 19, 1952; S. E. Gleason, Jr., to W. J. Donovan, Feb. 15, 1945 (OSS Archives File 12733: Permanent Intelligence Service).

83. Minutes of the 121st meeting, Dec. 22, 1944 (OSS Archives File: JIS Series).

84. Services Plan (JIC 239/1); L. L. Montague to A. B. Darling, Feb. 15, 1952.

85. Civilian Plan (JIC 239/2). See charts in the file (JIS Series 96).

86. W. J. Donovan to President Roosevelt, Dec. 26, 1944 (File: Development of Central Intelligence Theory, General Counsel's Office, Item No. 3).

87. JSSC, Jan. 18, 1945 (OSS Archives File: Director's Safe, Dr. 1, JIS Series 96).

88. See pp. 191–92.

89. L. L. Montague to A. B. Darling, Feb. 26, 1952.

90. JIC 239/5 was withdrawn by order of the Joint Chiefs of Staff on February 15, 1945. For the purposes of this study, JIC 239/5 is the plan of the Joint Chiefs shown in columnar comparison with the Donovan plan in OSS Archives File 12733 C: Suggestions.

91. JIC 239/5 (OSS Archives File 12733 C: Suggestions).

92. JSSC Report, Jan. 18, 1945, p. 6 (OSS Archives File: JIS Series 96).

93. JSSC Report, Jan. 18, 1945, p. 4 (OSS Archives File: JIS Series 96).

94. S. W. Souers to A. B. Darling, Jan. 30, 1952; W. J. Donovan to A. B. Darling, Feb. 17, 1953.

95. *Chicago Tribune* and *Washington Times Herald,* Feb. 9, 1945.

96. OSS Archives File: OSS–CIA–A–1; Director's Safe, Dr. 1, JIS Series 96.

97. OSS Archives File: OSS–CIA–A–1.

98. OSS Archives File 12733 U: OSS–CIA Principles.

99. The original from Secretary Stimson, May 1, 1945, is in OSS Archives File: OSS–CIA–A–2.

100. J. Magruder to W. J. Donovan, May 2, 1945 (Ms File JM-311).

101. Cable from W. J. Donovan, April 11, 1945 (OSS Archives File: OSS–CIA–A–2).

102. W. J. Donovan to H. L. Stimson, May 16, 1945 (OSS Archives File: OSS–CIA–A–2).

103. Admiral Leahy to Hon. Clarence Cannon, May 25 and 27, 1945 (OSS Archives File: Budget 1946).

104. For comments by W. J. Donovan, see his interview with A. B. Darling, Feb. 17, 1953.

105. H. D. Smith to W. J. Donovan, July 17 and Aug. 25, 1945 (OSS Archives File 17, 204: Budget 1947).

106. W. J. Donovan to S. Roseman, Sept. 4, 1945 (OSS Archives File 12733 U: OSS–CIA Principles).

107. Report of General Magruder to Secretary Lovett, Oct. 26, 1945 (File: Development of Central Intelligence Theory, General Counsel's Office); *OSS War Report*, Vol. I (Observations, Chart, p. 166); J. B. Reston quoted from *New York Times*, Dec. 9, 1951.

108. President Truman to General Donovan, Sept. 20, 1945 (*OSS War Report*, Vol. I, p. 450); Executive Order (*OSS War Report*, Vol. I, p. 448).

Chapter II

1. W. J. Donovan to H. D. Smith, Aug. 25, 1945 (OSS Archives File 12733 U: OSS–CIA Principles); J. G. Coughlin's memorandum, Aug. 21, 1945, and G. Bateson's report, Aug. 18, 1945 (OSS Archives File 12733 C: Suggestions).

2. Memorandum from J. Magruder to W. J. Donovan, May 2, 1945 (Ms File JM-311, Tab B).

3. H. S. Aldrich to R. J. Riddell, Sept. 5, 1945 (OSS Archives File 12733 U: OSS–CIA Principles).

4. Bureau of the Budget, *Report on Intelligence and Security Activities of the Government,* Sept. 20, 1945. This report was credited to George Schwarzwalder and Donald Stone by Robert A. Lovett in his remarks to the Secretaries on November 14, 1945. See above, p. 8.

5. S. M. Robinson to Secretary of Navy, Oct. 4, 1945 (File: Souers's Papers—these papers are in the Historical Collection); W. D. Puleston to F. J. Horne, Sept. 22, 1945 (File: Souers's Papers). See above, pp. 24–25.

6. Bureau of the Budget, *Report on Intelligence,* p. 22.

7. President Truman to Secretary Byrnes, Sept. 20, 1945 (File: NIA Plans, State).

8. Executive Order, Sept. 20, 1945 (*OSS War Report,* Vol. I, pp. 448–49); J. Magruder to R. A. Lovett, *Report on Intelligence Matters,* Oct. 26, 1945 (File:

CIA, SSU 5743, General Counsel's Office). For W. J. Donovan to S. Rosenman, Sept. 4, 1945, see above, p. 40. W. J. Donovan to H. D. Smith, Sept. 13, 1945 (OSS Archives File 12733 C: Suggestions).

9. Public Law 358, 78th Congress, Section 213.

10. W. D. Leahy to Secretary of War and Secretary of Navy, Sept. 19, 1945; Secretaries to the President, Sept. 19, 1945 (File: NIA Plans, State).

11. James Forrestal, *Diary,* 1951, p. 101; Sherman Kent, "Prospects for the National Intelligence Service," *Yale Review,* Oct. 1946.

12. W. D. Leahy to Secretary of War and Secretary of Navy, Sept. 19, 1945; memorandum on "Establishment of a Central Intelligence Service upon Liquidation of OSS" (File: NIA Plans, State). See above, pp. 33–34. W. D. Leahy to A. B. Darling, July 3, 1952.

13. "Creation of an Office of Foreign Intelligence," Sept. 30, 1944 (OSS Archives File 12733 D: Need for CIA). See above, p. 26.

14. D. Acheson to A. McCormack, Oct. 1, 1945; Secretary's Staff Committee, *Report on Development of a National Intelligence Program,* Nov. 15, 1945.

15. S. W. Souers to A. B. Darling, Jan. 30, 1952. See above, pp. 29–30.

16. T. B. Inglis to the Aide to the Secretary of the Navy, Oct. 10, 1945 (File: Souers's Papers); Forrestal, *Diary,* 1951, p. 101.

17. Meeting of the Secretaries of State, War, and Navy, Nov. 14, 1945 (File: Souers's Papers).

18. T. B. Inglis to E. J. King, Nov. 30, 1945 (File: Souers's Papers).

19. A. McCormack, *Report on Comparison of Plans for Coordinated or Centralized Intelligence,* Nov. 19, 1945.

20. See p. 46. A. McCormack, memorandum for the Secretary of War and the Secretary of the Navy, Dec. 15, 1945 (File: NIA Plans, State).

21. See pp. 183–85, 188, 404–6.

22. McCormack, *Report on Comparison of Plans.*

23. See pp. 44–45.

24. A. F. Tyler, *The Foreign Policy of James G. Blaine,* 1927, pp. 165–90, and the records of the conference cited in the bibliography.

25. For the provision in the Lovett Report, see pp. 66–67.

26. A. McCormack, memorandum of Dec. 15, 1945 (File: NIA Plans, State).

27. *OSS War Report,* Vol. I, pp. 398, 418 (Ch. I/18).

28. See pp. 11–13.

29. A. McCormack, *Report on Reconciliation of Plans for Coordination of Foreign Intelligence,* Nov. 26, 1945; memorandum of Dec. 10, 1945 (File: NIA Plans, State).

30. McCormack, *Report on Comparison of Plans;* Donovan's memorandum of June 10, 1941, on "Establishment of Service of Strategic Information" (*OSS War Report,* Vol. I, pp. 259–60).

31. F. Eberstadt, *Unification of the War and Navy Departments and Postwar Organization for National Security,* report to Hon. James Forrestal, 79th Congress, 1st Session, Senate Committee on Naval Affairs, Oct. 22, 1945, pp. 3–14.

32. S. W. Souers to A. B. Darling, Jan. 25, 1952.

33. S. W. Souers, "Military Intelligence," Ch. II in Vol. III, *Studies of the Eberstadt Report to Secretary Forrestal*, Oct. 22, 1945.

34. See p. 15. See below for subsequent discussion of civilian membership in it, pp. 154–60, 232–39.

35. Souers, "Military Intelligence."

36. *Washington Post*, March 17, 1952.

37. President Truman's letter to Secretary Byrnes, Sept. 20, 1945; R. P. Patterson to J. F. Byrnes, Sept. 29, 1945 (File: NIA Plans, State).

38. R. P. Patterson to H. S. Truman, Oct. 22, 1945 (File: CIA Papers, OSS).

39. T. B. Inglis to Forrestal's aide, Oct. 10, 1945 (File: Souers's Papers); report of Robert A. Lovett, Nov. 3, 1945.

40. W. H. Jackson to J. Forrestal, Nov. 14, 1945 (File: CIA–IAC Miscellaneous, 1946–1950).

41. W. H. Jackson to A. B. Darling, March 15, 1952.

42. See pp. 145–47.

43. See pp. 332–36, 397–98, 417–18.

44. J. Magruder to R. A. Lovett, Oct. 20, 1945.

45. Ibid.

46. Report by J. Magruder to R. A. Lovett, Oct. 26, 1945 (File: CIA, SSU 5743, General Counsel's Office), Part II, pp. 1–3. For the extraordinary estimate following the "war scare" in the spring of 1948, see below, pp. 338–40. For Magruder's opinion in 1950, see below, p. 396.

47. See p. 58.

48. Magruder's report to Lovett, Part II, pp. 5–6; J. Magruder to A. B. Darling, Jan. 8, 1953.

49. For ORE 22–48 and the dissent from the Air Force, see p. 339.

50. See pp. 34–35.

51. Magruder's report to Lovett, Part II, p. 16.

52. J. Magruder to R. A. Lovett, Oct. 31, 1945 (File: CIA Papers, Oct. 1, 1945).

53. J. Magruder to A. B. Darling, Jan. 8, 1953; report of Robert A. Lovett, p. 3.

54. See p. 57.

55. Meeting of the Secretaries of State, War, and Navy, Nov. 14, 1945 (File: Souers's Papers).

56. Ibid.; W. H. Jackson to J. Forrestal, Nov. 14, 1945.

57. S. W. Souers to A. B. Darling, in conversation, Jan. 30 and June 30, 1952; McCormack's memorandum on National Intelligence Authority, Dec., 15, 1945 (File: NIA Plans, State).

58. J. Magruder to Major General R. C. Smith, Dec. 27, 1945 (File: CIA Papers, Oct. 1, 1945).

59. For Nimitz on OSS, see p. 38.

60. Memorandum for the Secretary of the Navy on the National Intelligence Authority (File: Souers's Papers, Op23); W. D. Leahy to A. B. Darling, July 3, 1952.

61. S. W. Souers to A. B. Darling, June 30, 1952; draft of letter to Byrnes after McCormack's plan of Dec. 15, 1945 (File: Souers's Papers); memorandum in Souers's *Diary,* Jan. 3, 1946 (File: Souers's Papers).

62. S. W. Souers to A. B. Darling, April 23, 1952.

63. S. W. Souers to A. B. Darling, Jan. 25, 1952; J. Byrnes, "Speaking Frankly," 1947.

64. President's Directive of Jan. 22, 1946 (File: CIA, SSU 5743, General Counsel's Office); S. W. Souers to A. B. Darling, Jan. 25, 1952. See above, p. 33.

65. JIS Series 96, JIC 239/3, p. 13.

66. S. W. Souers to A. B. Darling, Jan. 25, 1952.

67. See pp. 120–21, 180–82, 307–8.

68. For the action of the National Security Council with regard to the Federal Bureau of Investigation at the time of the McNarney Report, July 1, 1949, see pp. 356–59.

Chapter III

1. S. W. Souers to A. B. Darling, Jan. 30, 1952. See above, pp. 56–57.

2. NIA Directive 1, Feb. 8, 1946.

3. CIG Directive 2, March 13, 1946; memorandum by the Director of Central Intelligence; NIA Directive 3, March 30, 1946.

4. Memorandum for the record, May 23, 1946 (File: CPS Organizations and Functions CIG).

5. NIA Directive 1, Feb. 8, 1946.

6. CIG Directive 8, April 29, 1946.

7. S. W. Souers to A. B. Darling, April 16, 1952.

8. S. W. Souers and J. S. Lay, Jr., to A. B. Darling, April 3 and 16, 1952; L. L. Montague to A. B. Darling, April 18, 1952. For the right of inspection under further discussion, see below, p. 185. S. W. Souers to A. B. Darling, June 30, 1952.

9. S. W. Souers to A. B. Darling, April 3, 1952.

10. NIA Directive 1, Feb. 8, 1946.

11. See pp. 282–83. NIA Directive 1, Feb. 8, 1946, Article 3, p. 2. See above, pp. 62–63.

12. See pp. 132–33, 198–99, 373–74.

13. NIA Meeting 1, Feb. 5, 1946.

14. S. W. Souers to A. B. Darling, April 3 and 16, 1952.

15. NIA Directive 2, Feb. 8, 1946; Central Planning Staff Procedure Memorandum 7, March 4, 1946 (File: CIG 6.04 ICAPS).

16. CIG Directive 3, March 15, 1946.

17. CIG Directive 3, March 15, 1946, and CIG Directive 4, March 19, 1946. For subsequent events concerning the Joint Army–Navy Intelligence Surveys, see below, pp. 146–47.

18. H. S. Vandenberg to S. W. Souers, Feb. 12, 1946; CIG Directive 1, Enclosure B, Feb. 12, 1946.

19. IAB Meeting 4, May 9, 1946, Item 2 on the Agenda (File: NIA and IAB Meetings, General Counsel's Office); CIG Directive 1/1, April 26, 1946; CIG Directive 1/2, May 8, 1946; CIG Directive 2, March 5, 1946.

20. See p. 127, for the eventual location of the Service in the Office of Operations. Enclosure to CIG Directive 1/3, June 4, 1946.

21. CPS Planning Directive 40, June 6, 1946 (File: CIG 6.04); CIG Directive 10, "Index of U. S. Residents' Foreign Intelligence Information," May 31, 1946; CIG Directive 11, "Survey of Exploitation of American Business Concerns with Connections Abroad as Sources of Foreign Intelligence Information," June 4, 1946. [Dates for these two CIG directives appear to be inconsistent with the date given for CIG Directive 10 below, Ch. IV, notes 1, 6, 7, and 15.]

22. Memorandum from C. E. Olsen to H. S. Vandenberg, July 19, 1946 (File: CPS 6.04).

23. The files of the Central Planning Staff have been placed in the Records Center of the Agency.

24. CIG Directive 9, May 9, 1946; CPS Planning Directive 9, March 11, 1946 (File: CPS, Development of Intelligence on USSR); Francis Parkman, memorandum to Acting Chief, CPS, April 25, 1946, on "Request for Editorial Assistance on Defense Project"—Lovell's memorandum, March 4, 1946 (File: CPS, Development of Intelligence on USSR); CIG Directive 8, April 29, 1946 (File: CPS, Development of Intelligence on USSR).

25. S. Kent to A. B. Darling, in conversation, April 22, 1952.

26. S. Kent to A. B. Darling, in conversation, April 22, 1952.

27. CPS Planning Directive 9, March 11, 1946 (File: CPS, Development of Intelligence on USSR).

28. See pp. 21, 62–66.

29. Francis Parkman, memorandum to Acting Chief, CPS, April 25, 1946 (File: CPS, Development of Intelligence on USSR).

30. G. S. Jackson, Paper No. 3, "The 'Defense Project,' First Post-War Experiment in Cooperative Interdepartmental Intelligence Production," May 20, 1952.

31. John M. Maury to G. S. Jackson, May 29, 1952 (Paper No. 3, telephone conversation with Maury regarding the Defense Project).

32. Minutes of CIG Council Meeting 1, March 18, 1946 (File: Central Reports Staff); L. L. Montague to A. McCormack, Jan. 14, 1946 (File: Souers's Papers).

33. Administrative Order 3, March 4, 1946, "Activation of Central Reports Staff" (File: Central Reports Staff). See below, pp. 141–43, 342–43, 375–77.

34. See pp. 29–33, 130–31. L. L. Montague to A. McCormack, Jan. 14, 1946, p. 2 (File: Souers's Papers).

35. See pp. 417–20.

36. L. L. Montague, memorandum to S. W. Souers, April 16, 1946 (File: CPS Organizations and Functions CIG); L. L. Montague, memorandum to S. W. Souers, April 15, 1946 (File: Central Reports Staff).

37. L. L. Montague to S. W. Souers, March 15, 1946 (File: Central Reports Staff).

38. S. W. Souers to A. B. Darling, June 30, 1952.

39. L. L. Montague to A. McCormack, Jan. 14, 1946 (File: Souers's Papers); NIA Directive 2, Feb. 5, 1946.

40. L. L. Montague to S. W. Souers, April 16, 1946 (File: CPS Organizations and Functions CIG).

41. L. L. Montague to S. W. Souers, April 16, 1946 (File: CPS Organizations and Functions CIG).

42. Minutes of CIG Council Meeting 1, March 18, 1946.

43. W. B. Goggins to S. W. Souers, May 13, 1946.

44. J. S. Lay, Jr., memorandum to S. W. Souers, March 28, 1946; minutes of IAB Meeting 3, April 8, 1946 (File: NIA and IAB Meetings, General Counsel's Office). See below, pp. 129–30.

45. J. S. Lay, Jr., to H. S. Vandenberg, June 18, 1946; E. Wright to A. B. Darling, April 10, 1953.

46. See pp. 46–47.

47. J. Magruder to the Executive to the Assistant Secretary of War, Jan. 19, 1946 (OSS Archives File: SSU World Coverage).

48. L. R. Houston, memorandum for the Deputy Director, Jan. 30, 1952; L. R. Houston to A. B. Darling, April 11, 1952. OSS Archives—these documents are now in the Agency's "Records Integration" under the Deputy Director, Plans. See J. M. Scott, *History and Development of the Centralized Operational Records for the Clandestine Services, 1948–1952*, Oct. 16, 1952.

49. Magruder to Major General S. LeRoy Irwin, Jan. 15, 1946 (OSS Archives File: SSU World Coverage); S. LeRoy Irwin, memorandum for the Assistant Secretary of War, Jan. 28, 1946.

50. Fortier Report, March 14, 1946, pp. 9, 13.

51. J. Magruder to Secretary of War, Feb. 4, 1946 (OSS Archives File: SSU World Coverage); memorandum by J. Magruder, "Establishment of Clandestine Collection Service for Foreign Intelligence," Feb. 14, 1945 (OSS Archive File: SSU World Coverage).

52. CIG Directive 3, March 15, 1946; W. H. Harris to L. J. Fortier, "Personnel and Expenditures," March 22, 1946.

53. Fortier Report.

54. Minutes of the Fortier Committee, Feb. 20 to March 6, 1946 (RI Top Secret File, Deputy Director, Plans); L. R. Houston to A. B. Darling, April 11, 1952.

55. Fortier Report, pp. 20 and 21.

56. Fortier Report, p. 14; W. W. Quinn to W. L. Langer, "State Department Cables," June 3, 1946; W. L. Langer to W. W. Quinn, June 17, 1946; W. W. Quinn to H. S. Vandenberg, "Access to State Department Intelligence Cables," June 24, 1947.

57. See pp. 49–61, 118–19.

58. S. W. Souers to A. B. Darling, April 16, 1952. "Initial Outline Plan for World Coverage by SSU" (OSS Archives File: SSU World Coverage).

59. NIA Directive 3, March 30, 1946 (NIA Directives, NIA Numbered Papers, IAB Memoranda File in General Counsel's Office); NIA Directive 4, April 2, 1946 (NIA Directives, NIA Numbered Papers, IAB Memoranda File in General Counsel's Office).

60. CIG Directive 6, April 8, 1946, Enclosure A Memo for Director, SSU, from Acting Secretary of War, April 3, 1946 (File 310: CIG Directives).

61. L. R. Houston to A. B. Darling, April 30, 1952.

62. Economy Act of 1933, 73rd Congress, 1st Session.

63. See p. 188 for the effect of the National Security Act of 1947.

64. NIA Directive 1, Feb. 8, 1946, p. 1.

65. Minutes of IAB Meeting 1, Feb. 4, 1946 (File: NIA and IAB Meetings, General Counsel's Office).

66. Minutes of IAB Meeting 1, March 26, 1946, p. 2 (File: NIA and IAB Meetings, General Counsel's Office).

67. Minutes of IAB Meeting 3, April 8, 1946 (File: NIA and IAB Meetings, General Counsel's Office).

68. See pp. 110–11. G. S. Jackson, Paper No. 1, "Organizational Development of the Office of Reports and Estimates, 1946–1950," April 10, 1952.

69. Minutes of IAB Meeting 4, May 9, 1946, p. 4 (File: NIA and IAB Meetings, General Counsel's Office).

70. CIG Directive 8, May 9, 1946. [This directive should be numbered 9; cf. note 24 above.] Minutes of IAB Meeting 8, Oct. 1, 1946 (File: NIA and IAB Meetings, General Counsel's Office).

71. Minutes of IAB Meeting 5, June 10, 1946, p. 1 (File: NIA and IAB Meetings, General Counsel's Office).

72. S. W. Souers to A. B. Darling, April 16, 1952.

73. "Digest of Progress Report on the Central Intelligence Group by Admiral Souers," June 7, 1946. The stencil is preserved in the Historical Collection. No copy from it has been found.

74. "Digest"; E. Wright to A. B. Darling, April 10, 1953.

75. L. R. Houston to H. S. Vandenberg, June 13, 1946.

76. "Digest."

Chapter IV

1. CIG Directive 10, June 20, 1946; S. W. Souers to A. B. Darling, April 16, 1952; W. D. Leahy to A. B. Darling, July 3, 1952; H. S. Vandenberg to A. B. Darling, March 17, 1952.

2. Minutes of IAB Meeting 3, April 8, 1946. The minutes of the Intelligence Advisory Board and of the National Intelligence Authority are in a collection kept by the General Counsel's Office.

3. NIA Directive 1, Feb. 8, 1946, p. 1. See above, pp. 24–25, 76.

4. H. S. Vandenberg to A. B. Darling, March 17, 1952.

5. NIA Directive 1, Feb. 8, 1946, p. 1.

6. CIG Directive 10, June 20, 1946, Appendix B, p. 7.

7. NIA Directive 4, June 29, 1946; H. F. Cunningham to Chief, CPS, June 24, 1946, regarding comments on CIG Directive 10, June 20, 1946.

8. See pp. 223–24.

9. Minutes of IAB Meeting 6, June 28, 1946 (File: NIA and IAB Meetings, General Counsel's Office).

10. Fortier Report, March 14, 1946, p. 4; minutes of IAB Meeting 6, June 28, 1946 (File: NIA and IAB Meetings, General Counsel's Office); NIA Directive 5, July 8, 1946. For Research and Analysis, COI and OSS, see above, pp. 15–17.

11. For the Russell Plan of Feb. 25, 1946, in the State Department, see the Historical Collection (File: CIG 6.05, R&E).

12. D. Van Slyck to A. B. Darling, Jan. 10, 1952, and April 21, 1953; E. K. Wright to A. B. Darling, April 10, 1953.

13. NIA Directive 5, June 28, 1946, p. 2. For the criticism of Hillenkoetter on this score in the Dulles Report, see below, pp. 324–25, 359–60.

14. Draft of NIA Directive 5 dated June 28, 1946.

15. CIG Directive 10, June 20, 1946; NIA Directive 5, July 8, 1946. See above, p. 90.

16. Minutes of NIA Meeting 4, July 17, 1946 (File: NIA and IAB Meetings, General Counsel's Office). See above, pp. 63–66, 89–92.

17. See pp. 33–34, 51–56.

18. L. R. Houston to H. S. Vandenberg, June 13, 1946. See above, pp. 104–5.

19. See pp. 139–40.

20. Minutes of NIA Meeting 4, July 17, 1946 (File: NIA and IAB Meetings, General Counsel's Office). For J. Magruder to W. J. Donovan on an independent directorate, see above, pp. 43–44.

21. H. S. Vandenberg to the Secretaries, July 30, 1946 (File 210: Budgets, Appropriations, Allotments).

22. Letter from the Secretaries to the Comptroller General, Sept. 5, 1946 (File 210: Budgets, Appropriations, Allotments); H. S. Vandenberg to A. B. Darling, March 17, 1952.

23. See pp. 45–46, 49–51.

24. Administrative Order 53, Jan. 20, 1947 (File: CIG 6.03); E. K. Wright to A. B. Darling, April 10, 1953; W. H. Jackson to A. B. Darling, March 15, 1952.

25. Army Order, W. W. Quinn to S. B. L. Penrose, July 17, 1946 (File: CIG 6.03). For NSCID 5, see below, pp. 221–22. For the Army's activities in 1951, see L. B. Kirkpatrick, memorandum for the Director of Central Intelligence, Nov. 30, 1951, on "Agreed Activities under NSCID 5"; a photocopy of this document is in the Historical Collection, File Records Integration–Foreign Intelligence.

26. D. H. Galloway to Executive Officer, CIG, July 29, 1946 (File: CIG 6.03).

27. E. K. Wright to A. B. Darling, May 28, 1953; order to OSO of Oct. 25 signed by Colonel W. H. Harris, Executive for Personnel and Administration.

28. H. S. Vandenberg to A. B. Darling, March 17, 1952.

29. W. H. Harris to Assistant Executive Director and Assistant Director for Special Operations, July 31, 1946; H. S. Vandenberg, memorandum for the Secretary of War, Sept. 12, 1946, and accompanying papers; W. W. Quinn to H. C. Petersen, April 11, 1947; H. S. Vandenberg to H. C. Petersen, April 11, 1947. These papers are in File: CIG 6.03.

30. H. S. Vandenberg to C. A. Willoughby, Nov. 27, 1946 (File: CIG 6.03, Special Operations).

31. For MacArthur, see pp. 38–39. H. S. Vandenberg to C. A. Willoughby, Nov. 27, 1946 (File: CIG 6.03, Special Operations).

32. K. Douglass and W. H. Jackson to H. S. Vandenberg, Aug. 10, 1946.

33. W. H. Jackson to A. B. Darling, March 15, 1952; K. Douglass to A. B. Darling, April 2 and May 28, 1952.

34. W. W. Quinn to D. H. Galloway, Aug. 16, 1946 (File: RI/FI); E. K. Wright to H. S. Vandenberg, Aug. 19, 1946 (File: RI/FI).

35. K. Douglass and W. H. Jackson to H. S. Vandenberg, Aug. 10, 1946, pp. 15–16.

36. W. H. Jackson to A. B. Darling, March 15, 1952; L. L. Montague to Chief, ICAPS, "Intelligence Estimates Prepared by the Central Intelligence Group," Oct. 16, 1946.

37. K. Douglass and W. H. Jackson to H. S. Vandenberg, Aug. 10, 1946, p. 11; W. M. Scott to W. W. Quinn, April 30, 1946 (File: RI/FI).

38. The Douglass–Jackson Report, Aug. 10, 1946, pp. 14–18. See below, pp. 154–60.

39. H. S. Vandenberg to A. B. Darling, March 17, 1952.

40. Minutes of NIA Meetings 5 and 7, Aug. 7 and Sept. 25, 1946 (File: NIA and IAB Meetings, General Counsel's Office).

41. Fortier Report, p. 12.

42. H. S. Vandenberg to A. B. Darling, March 17, 1952. For Hoover, Clark, and NSC 17/4, see below, pp. 356–59.

43. For the earlier period, see *History of the Office of Operations* (Historical Collection).

44. Ibid., Ch. II, "History of the Contact Division," pp. 4–6.

45. First draft of CIG Directive 12 by H. S. Vandenberg, July 22, 1946 (File: CIG 12).

46. H. F. Cunningham to D. H. Galloway, Aug. 14, 1946 (File: CIG 12).

47. K. Douglass to H. S. Vandenberg, Aug. 26, 1946, p. 2 (File: CIG 12).

48. Ibid.

49. Minutes of IAB Meeting 7, Aug. 26, 1946 (File: NIA and IAB Meetings, General Counsel's Office); H. F. Cunningham, to Secretary, NIA, Aug. 27, 1946 (File: CIG 12).

50. CIG Directive 12/1, Aug. 21, 1946; CIG Directive 12/2, Aug. 27, 1946.

51. NIA Directive 1, Section 3, Feb. 8, 1946.

52. CIG Directive 15, Oct. 1, 1946.

53. *History of the Office of Operations*, p. 7.

54. J. E. Hoover to H. S. Vandenberg, Aug. 23, 1946 (File: CIG 12); J. E. Hoover to W. D. Leahy, Aug. 23, 1946 (File: CIG 12); President's Directive, Jan. 22, 1946, p. 2.

55. J. E. Hoover to W. D. Leahy, Aug. 23, 1946 (File: CIG 12); W. D. Leahy to J. E. Hoover, Sept. 4, 1946 (File: CIG 12).

56. J. S. Lay, Jr., to H. S. Vandenberg, Sept. 3, 1946 (File: CIG 12).

57. J. E. Hoover to H. S. Vandenberg, Sept. 5 and 23, 1946 (File: CIG 12); draft of CIG Directive 12/3, undated; minutes of IAB Meeting 8, Oct. 1, 1946 (File: NIA and IAB Meetings, General Counsel's Office); CIG Directive 15, Oct. 1, 1946.

58. K. Douglass to A. B. Darling, April 1 and May 28, 1952. For Donovan's use of American business and travel, see above, pp. 9 and 18. For further light on General Sibert's appointment, see R. Helms to A. B. Darling, Nov. 10, 1952. For Foreign Documents Branch, see *History of the Office of Operations*, Ch. IV.

59. NIA Directive 5, July 8, 1946.

60. For Donovan's perception, see p. 7. For Souers's statement, see p. 104.

61. CIG Administrative Order 3, March 4, 1946. See above, p. 90.

62. H. S. Vandenberg to J. F. Byrnes, July 31, 1946 (File: CIG 6.05, R&E).

63. L. L. Montague to A. B. Darling, April 1 and 11, June 12, 1952.

64. CIG Directive 14, July 19, 1946.

65. ORE Administrative Order 1, Aug. 7, 1946.

66. ORE 1, "Soviet Foreign and Military Policy," Copy 37, July 23, 1946. G. S. Jackson, Paper No. 12, "Review of Formal Reports and Estimates Produced under the Central Intelligence Group and Agency, 1946 to mid-1948," Nov. 26, 1952, p. 2.

67. ORE 1.

68. See p. 57 for comment on the Joint Intelligence Committee. Also see pp. 87–92 for the plan in the Central Reports Staff.

69. CIG Directive 16, Oct. 14, 1946.

70. Minutes of IAB Meeting 9, Oct. 31, 1946, p. 4 (File: NIA and IAB Meetings, General Counsel's Office).

71. L. L. Montague to D. Edgar, Oct. 16, 1946.

72. CIG Directive 16/1, Oct. 26, 1946; Administrative Order 32, Nov. 1, 1946.

73. Minutes of IAB Meeting 9, Oct. 31, 1946 (File: NIA and IAB Meetings, General Counsel's Office).

74. L. L. Montague to H. S. Vandenberg, April 15, 1947. For Vandenberg's action, see below, pp. 153–54.

75. L. L. Montague to Eddy, Chamberlin, Inglis, McDonald, Aug. 11, 1947.

76. ORE 17, May 31, 1947; T. Babbitt to R. H. Hillenkoetter, July 16, 1947. The incoming Assistant Director of ORE signed a report on July 16, 1947, on the failure of coordination; see below, pp. 377–79.

77. Galloway's inquiry of Aug. 1, 1946, cited in memorandum of L. L. Montague to D. Edgar, Aug. 7, 1946.

78. J. K. Huddle to H. S. Vandenberg, Dec. 31, 1946 (Progress Reports, Research and Evaluation).

79. L. L. Montague to A. B. Darling, April 1 and 11, June 12, 1952.

80. Ibid.

81. Montague's memorandum, May 1947.

82. G. P. Simons, "Some Considerations of Organizational Defects Imposing Qualitative and Quantitative Restrictions on the Output of Intelligence Material in Office of Reports and Estimates, and Recommendations for Their Correction," memorandum to S. A. Dulany Hunter, April 15, 1947 (Historical Collection). L. L. Montague to A. B. Darling, June 11, 1952.

83. See the preceding footnote.

84. L. L. Montague to J. K. Huddle, April 17, 1947; L. L. Montague to A. B. Darling, June 12, 1952.

85. G. P. Simons to S. A. Dulany Hunter, April 21, 1947, p. 2.

86. Montague's memorandum, May 1947.

87. G. S. Jackson, Paper No. 1, "Organizational Development of the Office of Reports and Estimates, 1946–1950," April 10, 1952. For the resurrection of Montague and Van Slyck, see below, pp. 406–7, 420.

88. NIA Directive 1, Feb. 8, 1946.

89. L. L. Montague to A. B. Darling, April 11, 1952.

90. H. S. Vandenberg to A. B. Darling, March 17, 1952; CIG Directive 14, July 19, 1946; Administrative Order 6, July 22, 1946. For reorganization of ICAPS later, see below, p. 205.

91. J. S. Lay, Jr., to the Director of Central Intelligence, April 25, 1946.

92. ICAPS "Box" in the chart of July 22, 1946.

93. Change 2, Administrative Order 6, Aug. 12, 1946.

94. D. Edgar to Acting Assistant Directors for Collection, Research and Evaluation, Dissemination, July 26, 1946 (File: CIG 6.04).

95. D. Edgar to Acting Assistant Director, Office of Research and Evaluation (Publication Review File, CIG Weekly and Daily); Office of Dissemination, Dissemination Study No. 1, July 31, 1946.

96. D. Edgar to E. K. Wright, Jan. 7, 1947 (File: CIG 6.05, R&E).

97. D. Edgar to Assistant Director for Reports and Estimates, Jan. 13, 1947.

98. L. L. Montague to Assistant Director, R&E, Dec. 17, 1946.

99. Jackson, "Organizational Development."

100. Memorandum from L. L. Montague to Assistant Director, R&E, Jan. 29, 1947.

101. For Souers's opinions, see pp. 82–87.

102. L. L. Montague to J. K. Huddle, March 11, 1947, Tab A.

103. L. L. Montague to J. K. Huddle, March 11, 1947, Tab B. For Souers's "Progress Report," see above, pp. 104–5.

104. D. Edgar to R. H. Hillenkoetter, June 18, 1947 (File: CIG 6.05); E. K. Wright to Chief, ICAPS, March 25, 1947 (File: CIG 6.05).

105. D. Edgar to E. Watts, June 25, 1947 (File: Interdepartmental Coordinating and Planning Staff); G. S. Jackson to A. B. Darling, in conversation, June 20, 1952.

106. See pp. 24–25, 58–59.

107. L. L. Montague to J. K. Huddle, Jan. 19, 1947.

108. L. T. Shannon to D. Edgar, Oct. 14 and 21, 1946 (File: ICAPS Weekly Reports).

109. S. Edwards to D. Edgar, Dec. 31, 1946.

110. S. Edwards to D. Edgar for "DCI ONLY," Dec. 31, 1946 (File: ICAPS Weekly Reports).

111. CIG Directive 13, Sept. 17, 1946, Enclosure. See above, pp. 82–87.

112. Minutes of IAB Meeting 8, Oct. 1, 1946 (File: NIA and IAB Meetings, General Counsel's Office).

113. See p. 85. D. Edgar to Assistant Director, ORE, Oct. 2, 1946 (File: ICAPS); G. S. Jackson, Paper No. 3, "The 'Defense Project,' First Post-War Experiment in Cooperative Interdepartmental Intelligence Production," May 20, 1952; minutes of IAB Meeting 8, Oct. 1, 1946 (File: NIA and IAB Meetings, General Counsel's Office).

114. Minutes of IAB Meeting 9, Oct. 31, 1946. See above, pp. 132–33.

115. CIG Directive 18, Oct. 25, 1946; W. A. Eddy to DCI, Oct. 18, 1946. For scientific intelligence, see below, pp. 161–65, 227–32.

116. CIG Directive 18/1, Oct. 28, 1946.

117. See preceding footnote.

118. CIG Directive 18/2, Nov. 21, 1946; minutes of IAB Meeting 11, Nov. 26, 1946 (File: NIA and IAB Meetings, General Counsel's Office).

119. For "Bogotá," see pp. 240–44.

120. Minutes of IAB Meeting 12, Dec. 17, 1946.

121. Minutes of the ad hoc committee, Dec. 3, 1946 (File: CIG 18). For the continued struggle over this subject in Hillenkoetter's time, see below, pp. 224–25.

122. CIG Directive 18, Jan. 23, 1947. [The number of this directive must be incorrect: cf. note 115 above.] There is conflicting evidence regarding the date of the meeting. It appears to have been December 17 rather than December 20.

123. CIG Directive 18/3, Dec. 16, 1946; minutes of IAB Meeting 12, Dec. 17, 1946.

124. For the Dominican affair in 1947 and Bogotá in 1948, see below, pp. 223, 240–44.

125. NIA Directive 7, Jan. 2, 1947.

126. See p. 153.

127. See above, pp. 100–101, 119–20.

128. J. K. Huddle to D. Edgar, Oct. 1, 1946 (File: ICAPS).

129. Minutes of IAB Meeting 10, Nov. 7, 1946 (File: NIA and IAB Meetings, General Counsel's Office).

130. CIG Directive 19, Oct. 30, 1946.

131. H. S. Vandenberg to S. J. Chamberlin, Jan. 23, 1947 (File: CIG 319).

132. H. S. Vandenberg to S. J. Chamberlin, Jan. 23, 1947. For the President's Directive, see above, pp. 70–71.

133. Minutes of NIA Meeting 9, Feb. 12, 1947 (File: NIA and IAB Meetings, General Counsel's Office).

134. See pp. 25, 58, 147. L. L. Montague to Chief, ICAPS, Oct. 28, 1946.

135. For Leahy's statement, see p. 114.

136. Minutes of NIA Meeting 9, Feb. 12, 1947 (File: NIA and IAB Meetings, General Counsel's Office).

137. CIG Directive 24, March 12, 1947; NIA Directive 11, Sept. 16, 1947. For Hillenkoetter, see below, pp. 198–205.

138. For Marshall and Donovan, see p. 15. For Leahy, Patterson, and Forrestal, see pp. 47–48. See p. 167.

139. See p. 47.

140. CIG Directive 15, Sept. 18, 1946.

141. H. S. Vandenberg to T. B. Inglis, Sept. 4, 1946 (File: CIG 15).

142. D. Edgar to H. S. Vandenberg, Sept. 12, 1946; James S. Lay, Jr., to H. S. Vandenberg, Sept. 18, 1946.

143. C. W. Clarke to W. M. Adams, Sept. 25, 1946 (File: CIG 15).

144. W. M. Adams to D. Edgar, Sept. 27, 1946 (File: CIG 15).

145. Minutes of NIA Meeting 7, Sept. 25, 1946 (File: NIA and IAB Meetings, General Counsel's Office); H. S. Vandenberg to A. B. Darling, March 17, 1952.

146. Minutes of NIA Meeting 7.

147. Minutes of IAB Meeting 8, Oct. 1, 1946 (File: NIA and IAB Meetings, General Counsel's Office).

148. Minutes of Meeting 10, Nov. 7, 1946 (File: NIA and IAB Meetings, General Counsel's Office); T. B. Inglis to R. H. Hillenkoetter, July 17, 1946. The memorandum of the Chief of Naval Operations was numbered JCS 1569/2. Brigadier General R. C. Partridge gave permission, on July 10, 1952, to examine in the Pentagon his series of papers of the Joint Chiefs of Staff.

149. Minutes of IAB Meeting 10, Nov. 7, 1946 (File: NIA and IAB Meetings, General Counsel's Office).

150. For the National Intelligence Authority, see pp. 70–71.

151. Minutes of NIA Meeting 9, Feb. 12, 1947 (File: NIA and IAB Meetings, General Counsel's Office).

152. JCS 1569 Series (file in the Pentagon).

153. See below, pp. 232–39. For Donovan on military deputies, see the interview with him, Feb. 17, 1953.

154. *History of the Office of Scientific Intelligence,* May 9, 1952, pp. 5–6 and Tab A; H. W. Dix, *Technical Section SI: History,* Feb. 9, 1945; H. W. Dix to W. J. Donovan, Sept. 4, 1945 (File 12733 C).

155. See pp. 42, 47–48. Status of Projects, March 18 and 25, 1946. *New York Times,* Aug. 2, 1946.

156. E. K. Wright to S. J. Chamberlin, Aug. 12, 1946 (File: NIA 6–9).

157. Minutes of NIA Meeting 6, Aug. 21, 1946 (File: NIA 6–9). A Digest of the Act establishing the Atomic Energy Commission was prepared in the Legislative Counsel's Office for Vandenberg. A summary dated September 24, 1946, is in the Historical Collection. L. R. Groves to the Atomic Energy Commission, Nov. 21, 1946 (File: Scientific-Technical Intelligence).

158. W. D. Leahy to H. S. Truman, Aug. 21, 1946 (File: NIA 6–9); W. D. Leahy

to Secretaries of State, War, Navy, and H. S. Vandenberg, Aug. 23, 1946 (File: NIA 6–9).

159. R. L. Clark to A. B. Darling, in conversation, July 28, 1952. Mr. Clark, Deputy Assistant Director, Office of Scientific Intelligence, served under Vannevar Bush on the Joint Research and Development Board. A. T. Waterman, Director of the National Science Foundation, was deputy to Karl Compton during the war in the field service of the Office of Scientific Research and Development.

160. ORE 3/1, Oct. 31, 1946; minutes of meeting of Technical Advisors, Joint Research and Development Board, Nov. 20, 1946.

161. See pp. 43–44. W. J. Donovan, article in *Life,* Sept. 30, 1946; J. Gunther, "Inside CIA: The Story of Our Spy Network," *Look,* Aug. 12, 1952.

162. Minutes of IAB Meeting 10, Nov. 7, 1946, pp. 4–6 (File: NIA and IAB Meetings, General Counsel's Office).

163. Minutes of the meeting of the Technical Advisors to the Policy Council, Dec. 12, 1946.

164. Agreement of H. S. Vandenberg and V. Bush, Jan. 10, 1947.

165. H. S. Vandenberg to V. Bush, March 13, 1947 (File: RLB–CIG Relationship). See below, pp. 227–28.

166. Minutes of NIA Meeting 9, Feb. 12, 1947 (File: NIA and IAB Meetings, General Counsel's Office); NIA Directive 9, April 18, 1947.

167. E. K. Wright to Assistant Director for Reports and Estimates, March 28, 1947 (File: CIG 6.05). For scientific intelligence in Hillenkoetter's administration, see below, pp. 227–32. For the news of the Eberstadt Committee and the Dulles Group, see pp. 295–96, 316, 332.

Chapter V

1. See p. 15.

2. *Hearings before the Committee on Military Affairs,* U.S. Senate, 79th Congress, 1st Session, pp. 30–48.

3. See p. 20.

4. F. Eberstadt, *Unification of the War and Navy Departments and Postwar Organization for National Security,* report to Hon. James Forrestal, Secretary of the Navy, Oct. 22, 1945, p. 6.

5. See pp. 34–35.

6. *Hearings,* pp. 2–4.

7. See pp. 22–25. W. D. Leahy to A. B. Darling, July 3, 1952.

8. See pp. 32–34, 198–205.

9. W. B. Goggins to S. W. Souers, May 8, 1946, regarding S. 2102.

10. Souers's Report, June 7, 1946; L. R. Houston to H. S. Vandenberg, June 13, 1946.

11. Independent Offices Appropriation Act of 1945; see above, p. 47.

12. L. R. Houston to A. B. Darling, in conversation, June 6, 1952.

13. See pp. 78–79; "Bill for the Establishment of a Central Intelligence Agency" (File 606: CIA Legislation).

14. See pp. 34–35.

15. L. R. Houston to A. B. Darling, July 16, 1952. See above, pp. 107–8 (NIA Directive 5).

16. Clippings in "Merger File," Legislative Counsel's Office; *Hearings,* pp. 155–56. For K. Douglass and W. H. Jackson, see above, pp. 119–20.

17. R. Patterson and J. Forrestal to H. S. Truman, Jan. 16, 1947. Photocopy of *New York Times,* Jan. 17, 1947, in Legislative Counsel's Office.

18. L. R. Houston and W. L. Pforzheimer were also present at this conference. W. L. Pforzheimer, "Memorandum for the Record," Jan. 23, 1947. For H. S. Vandenberg and the Board, see above, pp. 153–54.

19. For Parkman's criticism, see p. 169. Pforzheimer, "Memorandum."

20. The bearing of this suggestion upon the Agency's covert operations may be observed below in Ch. VII, pp. 253–54.

21. For Vandenberg and the Advisory Board, see pp. 107–12. Pforzheimer, "Memorandum."

22. E. K. Wright to C. M. Clifford, Jan. 28, 1947; W. L. Pforzheimer to A. B. Darling, July 16, 1952.

23. E. K. Wright to C. S. Murphy, Jan. 27, 1947.

24. H. J. Ford, *Washington and His Colleagues: A Chronicle of the Rise and Fall of Federalism,* 1918, pp. 42–51. S. 758 (Gurney), Public Law 253, 80th Congress, 1st Session.

25. E. K. Wright to C. M. Clifford, Jan. 28, 1947; W. L. Pforzheimer to A. B. Darling, in conversation, July 24, 1952. For later enactment regarding the Deputy Director, see Public Law 15, 83rd Congress, April 4, 1953.

26. See pp. 198–205.

27. W. L. Pforzheimer to A. B. Darling, July 16 and 29, 1952.

28. W. L. Pforzheimer, "Memorandum for the Record," June 12, 1947.

29. Statement of Lt. Gen. Hoyt S. Vandenberg, Director of Central Intelligence, before the Armed Services Committee of the U.S. Senate on S. 758, "The National Security Act of 1947," April 29, 1947.

30. W. L. Pforzheimer, "Memorandum for the Record," April 29, 1947.

31. W. D. Leahy to A. B. Darling, July 3, 1952; excerpts from testimony by Gen. Dwight D. Eisenhower, May 7, 1947.

32. CBS broadcast, June 10, 1947; W. L. Pforzheimer, "Memorandum for the Record," June 12, 1947; C. S. Cheston to C. Gurney, June 2, 1947.

33. W. J. Donovan, "Intelligence: Key to Defense," *Life,* Sept. 30, 1946. See above, pp. 163–64. H. S. Vandenberg to the House Committee on Expenditures in the Executive Departments, *Secret Hearings on H.R. 2319, Unification of the Armed Forces,* p. 40.

34. W. L. Pforzheimer, drafted amendment, July 2, 1947; C. S. Cheston to C. Gurney, June 2, 1947; R. H. Hillenkoetter to C. Gurney, June 3, 1947.

35. W. D. Leahy to A. B. Darling, June 3, 1952; R. H. Hillenkoetter to A. B. Darling, Oct. 24 and Dec. 2, 1952; S. W. Souers to A. B. Darling, June 30 and Sept. 8, 1952.

36. House Committee, *Secret Hearings*, June 27, 1947, pp. 7–8. A photocopy of these *Secret Hearings* is in the Office of the Legislative Counsel. See above, pp. 123–25, for the resistance of the Army and Navy to the establishment of the Contact Branch in the Office of Operations.

37. *Secret Hearings*, pp. 70–117, at 77, 91, 111; for NIA Directive 1, see above, pp. 78–82. For NIA Directive 5, see above, pp. 107–15.

38. *Secret Hearings*, pp. 127–35, at 132, 130. For the remark of Admiral Inglis, see pp. 161–62. *New York Times*, article by Anthony Leviero, May 21, 1947. For comment on this special service in the Army, see E. K. Wright to A. B. Darling, May 28, 1953, pp. 3–4; R. H. Hillenkoetter to A. B. Darling, Dec. 2, 1952, p. 19.

39. See p. 15.

40. *Secret Hearings*, pp. 150–51 for Dulles's statement and pp. 159–61 for Inglis's points. For McCormack, see above, pp. 51–56.

41. *Secret Hearings*, pp. 24–27.

42. *Secret Hearings*, p. 33. W. L. Pforzheimer and L. R. Houston to A. B. Darling, in conversation, July 16, 1952. For the British system, see W. H. Jackson, *Coordination of Intelligence Functions and the Organization of Secret Intelligence in the British Intelligence System,* July 1945; W. H. Jackson to A. B. Darling, March 15, 1952; Douglass–Jackson Report, Aug. 10, 1946. See above, pp. 120–21.

43. S. 758 sponsored by Senator Chan Gurney.

44. Public Law 253, 80th Congress, 1st Session; J. Forrestal, statement on June 10, 1947.

45. T. B. Inglis, in *Secret Hearings*, p. 162. See above, pp. 5–6.

46. President's Directive of Jan. 22, 1946; Public Law 253, 80th Congress, 1st Session.

47. Public Law 253, Section 102d(3).

48. See p. 34 for the origin of the duty to protect sources close to military operations.

49. National Security Act of 1947, Section 102e.

50. W. L. Pforzheimer to A. B. Darling, Aug. 1 and 29, 1952.

51. L. R. Houston to R. H. Hillenkoetter, Sept. 25, 1947; L. R. Houston to A. B. Darling, in conversation, Feb. 13, 1953.

52. See pp. 72 and 110 (NIA Directive 5). For NSCID 5, see below, pp. 221–22.

53. See pp. 247–50.

54. L. R. Houston to R. H. Hillenkoetter, Sept. 25, 1947; L. R. Houston to A. B. Darling, in conversation, Feb. 13, 1953.

55. National Security Act of 1947, Section 303a, p. 14.

56. G. C. Marshall, R. P. Patterson, J. Forrestal, W. D. Leahy to the Comptroller General of the United States, July 1, 1947; L. R. Houston, "Memorandum for the Files," Sept. 5, 1947; L. R. Houston to R. H. Hillenkoetter, Nov. 14, 1947; memo-

randum for his assistants by R. H. Hillenkoetter, Dec. 16, 1947. Those memoranda are from File 606, CIA Legislation, in General Counsel's Office.

57. Marshall et al. to the Comptroller General.

58. See pp. 240–44, pp. 338–40 (Clay); W. L. Pforzheimer to A. B. Darling, in conversation, April 2, 1953.

59. L. R. Houston to A. B. Darling, April 21, 1953.

60. Public Law 110, 81st Congress, 1st Session.

61. Public Law 216, 81st Congress, 1st Session; Public Law 110, 81st Congress, 1st Session.

62. L. Warren to W. B. Smith, Nov. 21, 1951; L. R. Houston to A. B. Darling, Nov. 28, 1951. For closer examination of Public Law 110, see the "Text and Explanation," Oct. 10, 1952, prepared in the General Counsel's Office.

Chapter VI

1. S. W. Souers to A. B. Darling, June 30 and July 1, 1952; W. D. Leahy to A. B. Darling, July 3, 1952.

2. The quotation is from Admiral Leahy as he read from his diary to A. B. Darling on July 3, 1952; R. H. Hillenkoetter to A. B. Darling, Oct. 22 and 24, Dec. 2, 1952; W. J. Donovan to A. B. Darling, Feb. 17, 1953.

3. Leahy's diary as read to A. B. Darling, July 3, 1952. See above, p. 160.

4. CIG Directive 24, March 12, 1947. See above, p. 154.

5. See pp. 178–79.

6. A. W. Dulles, "Germany's Underground," 1947; L. L. Montague to A. B. Darling, Sept. 22, 1952. See above, p. 51 for Lovett's recommendation and p. 179 for Dulles's testimony in *Secret Hearings* of the House Committee.

7. See p. 182. William Hillman, *Mr. President*, 1952, pp. 14–15. For Leahy on the State Department, see his interview with A. B. Darling, July 3, 1952. For Leahy's antipathies, see S. W. Souers to A. B. Darling, July 1, 1952.

8. See p. 158.

9. R. H. Hillenkoetter to A. B. Darling, Oct. 24, 1952.

10. See the Preamble of the Constitution.

11. R. H. Hillenkoetter to C. Gurney, June 3, 1947; W. D. Leahy to A. B. Darling, July 3, 1952; L. L. Montague to A. B. Darling, Sept. 22, 1952.

12. The National Security Act of 1947, Public Law 253, 80th Congress, 1st Session, Section 303; L. R. Houston, memorandum to the Director on "IAB Procedures," July 29, 1947; letter of farewell to H. S. Vandenberg from the Intelligence Advisory Board, May 29, 1947, written by Admiral Inglis (File: CIG 6.024, Executive for Advisory Council).

13. R. H. Hillenkoetter to A. B. Darling, Oct. 22 and 24, Dec. 2, 1952. See above, pp. 188–89. National Security Act of 1947, Section 102d(1). See below, pp. 218–20 for NSCID 1.

14. See p. 165.

15. R. Helms to A. B. Darling, Nov. 10, 1952.

16. "History of the Contact Division," Ch. II of *History of the Office of Operations*. R. Helms to A. B. Darling, Nov. 10, 1952. See above, pp. 27–28. W. H. Jackson, *Survey of Office of Policy Coordination* (Executive Registry File).

17. See pp. 145–54.

18. IAB 1, "Coordination of Intelligence Production," April 21, 1947.

19. IAB 2, "Amendment of the Definition of Strategic and National Policy Intelligence," May 9, 1947; T. B. Inglis to Director of Central Intelligence, March 10, 1947 (File: IAB 2). For further comment at the time this chapter was written, see S. Kent to A. B. Darling, Oct. 7, 1952. W. J. Donovan, memorandum on "Establishment of Service of Strategic Information," June 10, 1941; W. J. Donovan to the President, Nov. 18, 1944 (*OSS War Report*, Vol. I, pp. 259, 442); memorandum from Chief, Intelligence Staff, ORE, to Chief, ICAPS, Oct. 28, 1946, on "Strategic and National Policy Intelligence." See above, p. 25, quoting from "The Basis for a Permanent, World-Wide Intelligence Service," Oct. 5, 1944.

20. CIG Directive 24, March 12, 1947.

21. T. B. Inglis to Director of Central Intelligence, Feb. 20, 1947; CIG Directive 24/1, May 13, 1947. See above, p. 72. Regarding the Director's control of financial matters, see R. H. Hillenkoetter to A. B. Darling, Oct. 22 and 24, Dec. 12, 1952; E. K. Wright to A. B. Darling, April 10, 1953.

22. The rosters of meetings have been compared for the above statement. See above, p. 154.

23. Minutes of IAB Meeting 13, May 15, 1947, pp. 3–4 (File: NIA and IAB Meetings, General Counsel's Office).

24. NIA Directive 1, Feb. 8, 1946.

25. The authority of J. Forrestal's view is R. H. Hillenkoetter's statement in the minutes of IAB Meeting 14, July 17, 1947, p. 5 (File: NIA and IAB Meetings, General Counsel's Office).

26. Minutes of NIA Meeting 4, July 7, 1946, p. 2. See above, p. 153. W. D. Leahy to A. B. Darling, July 3, 1952. For General Smith and the Intelligence Advisory Committee, see S. Kent to A. B. Darling, Oct. 7, 1952.

27. Minutes of NIA Meeting 10, June 26, 1947 (File: NIA and IAB Meetings, General Counsel's Office).

28. R. H. Hillenkoetter to A. B. Darling, Dec. 2, 1952.

29. See pp. 179–80, 182.

30. For Chamberlin's statement, on July 17, 1947, see minutes of IAB Meeting 14, p. 11. See above, p. 182, for Inglis in the *Secret Hearings*.

31. Minutes of IAB Meeting 14, July 17, 1947, p. 12 (File: NIA and IAB Meetings, General Counsel's Office).

32. See pp. 199–201 for IAB Meeting 14. See pp. 59 and 107–8.

33. Minutes of IAB Meeting 15, July 31, 1947; minutes of IAB Meeting 16, Sept. 11, 1947; National Security Act of 1947, Section 310b.

34. Report of the ad hoc committee, Aug. 12, 1947; CIG Directive 24/2.

35. NIA Directive 5, July 8, 1946, para. 3, p. 2; minutes of IAB Meeting 16, Sept. 11, 1947. See below, pp. 221–22, for NSCID 5.

36. September 20, 1947, was the day on which Hillenkoetter actually took office under the National Security Act. See the memorandum of Oct. 10, 1947 (File: CIG 6.024, Executive for Advisory Council). September 16, 1947, was the date of issue of NIA Directive 11; the Authority went out of existence on September 20. See National Security Act, Section 102f.

37. R. H. Hillenkoetter to A. B. Darling, Oct. 24 and Dec. 1, 1952.

38. R. H. Hillenkoetter to Secretaries, Sept. 11, 1947 (Executive Registry File: CIG-6 Organization, March 1, 1947, through Nov. 1947).

39. See p. 183.

40. W. C. Ford, Acting Director of Central Intelligence, to the Secretaries of War and the Navy, Aug. 22, 1947 (Executive Registry File: CIG 6 Organization, March 1, 1947, through Nov. 1947); R. H. Hillenkoetter to the Intelligence Advisory Board, Sept. 18, 1947 (File: ICAPS Organization).

41. R. H. Hillenkoetter to the National Security Council, Sept. 19, 1947. (Original memorandum is in NSC File: CIA-5-1947; also a copy is in the Historical Collection.) R. H. Hillenkoetter to M. J. Connelly, Secretary to the President, Sept. 24, 1947 (File: Hillenkoetter's Memoranda). See below, pp. 245–47, regarding psychological warfare.

42. L. R. Houston to the Director, July 29, 1947.

43. NSC File: CIA-5-1947. Notes taken from the records of the Council are in the card box, Historical Collection. Transcriptions could not be made.

44. R. A. Lovett, memorandum to R. H. Hillenkoetter, Sept. 23, 1947, was found in NSC File: CIA-5-1947.

45. The first meeting of the National Security Council. See its *Policies of the Government of the United States of America Relating to the National Security,* Vol. I, p. 73, Appendix B. J. S. Lay, Jr., memorandum for the Director of Central Intelligence, Sept. 26, 1947 (Executive Registry File: National Security Council; also in NSC File: CIA-5-1947).

47. R. H. Hillenkoetter to National Security Council, Oct. 17, 1947 (Executive Registry File: National Security Council). There are pencilled notes on the copy of Royall's memorandum in NSC File: CIA-5-1947 to show that Hillenkoetter was urged to withdraw his suggestion. See below, pp. 362–65, for further discussion of Royall and the internal management of the Agency.

48. S. W. Souers to A. B. Darling, Nov. 4, 1952.

49. R. H. Hillenkoetter to A. B. Darling, Oct. 24, 1952, p. 13.

50. The replies of the Secretaries are in NSC File: CIA-5-1947. Permission was given to examine them on September 12, 1952.

51. K. C. Royall to S. W. Souers through Secretary Forrestal, Nov. 26, 1947; memorandum by J. H. Ohly, Nov. 28, 1947. Both are in NSC File: CIA-5-1947.

52. National Security Council to the Director of Central Intelligence, Dec. 3, 1947 (Executive Registry File: National Security Council); R. H. Hillenkoetter to A. B. Darling, Dec. 2, 1952.

53. D. Edgar to the Assistant Director for Special Operations, Oct. 15, 1947 (File: NSCID, Correspondence Concerning). For the NIAs, see above, pp. 78–82. For the Fortier Report, see above, pp. 96–98.

54. R. H. Hillenkoetter, letter of Oct. 9, 1947, on the "Initial Security Council Directive to CIA" is referred to in Armstrong's letter to Hillenkoetter of Oct. 29, 1947, and in Hillenkoetter's reply to Armstrong of Nov. 3, 1947. The latter are in File: NSCID, Correspondence Concerning.

55. See p. 140. W. P. Armstrong, Jr., to R. H. Hillenkoetter, Oct. 29, 1947 (File: NSCID, Correspondence Concerning); L. R. Houston to A. B. Darling, Nov. 6, 1952. For the President's Directive, see above, pp. 71–72.

56. NIA Directive 5, July 8, 1946, para. 2.

57. See pp. 151–53.

58. R. H. Hillenkoetter to W. P. Armstrong, Jr., Nov. 3, 1947, written by D. Edgar, ICAPS, Oct. 31, 1947 (File: NSCID, Correspondence Concerning).

59. P. Childs was now head of ICAPS. Memorandum confirming telephone call of Nov. 13, 1947, by P. Childs (File: NSCID, Correspondence Concerning).

60. National Security Act of 1947, Section 102f(1).

61. Minutes of the IAB Meeting, Nov. 20, 1947, p. 4 (File: NIA and IAB Meetings, General Counsel's Office).

62. See pp. 145–54.

63. See pp. 102, 146. Admiral Inglis attended almost every meeting of the Intelligence Advisory Board from the first one on February 4, 1946.

64. For General Chamberlin at the meeting on November 20, see the minutes, pp. 3, 6–7.

65. The ad hoc committee consisted of E. P. Mussett, E. J. Treacy, R. K. Davis, M. B. Booth, W. C. Trueheart, and R. F. Innis.

66. For Admiral Gingrich's remark, see minutes of the meeting, Nov. 20, 1947, p. 5. See minutes of IAB Meeting 14, July 17, 1947, for inclusion of the Atomic Energy Commission.

67. Copies of the drafts and revisions are in NSC Files: NSCID 17 Mill, 1, 7, and others. Other papers are in the Agency's files, now with the Historical Collection. As neither collection is complete, it has been necessary to refer to both.

68. Stenotyped report of the meeting on Dec. 8, 1947, p. 15. See also NSC File: NSCID 17-1.

69. For the origin and development of the right of inspection, see pp. 34, 72, 79.

70. ICAPS to members of ad hoc committee, Nov. 25, 1947; E. K. Wright to members of the Intelligence Advisory Board, Dec. 2, 1947. These memoranda are in File: NSCID, Correspondence Concerning.

71. Stenotyped report of the meeting on Dec. 8, 1947.

72. See p. 183.

73. R. H. Hillenkoetter to A. B. Darling, Dec. 2, 1952, pp. 14–15.

74. For the relation to scientific intelligence, see p. 230. Vannevar Bush to the Secretary of Defense, Dec. 5, 1947 (the original is in NSC File: CIA-5-1947).

75. D. Z. Beckler to R. L. Clark, Dec. 2, 1947; R. L. Clark to V. Bush, Dec. 3, 1947. These memoranda are in File 825: Scientific-Technical Intelligence.

76. Stenotyped report of the meeting on Dec. 8, 1947, p. 5. For IAB Meeting 14, see above, p. 202. Minutes of IAB Meeting 14, p. 11; minutes of the meeting on Nov. 20, pp. 6–7.

77. L. R. Houston to A. B. Darling, Oct. 14, 1952; stenotyped report, Dec. 8, 1947, pp. 8, 45 (bottom).

78. Stenotyped report, Dec. 8, 1947, p. 5.

79. Memorandum to the Executive Secretary of the National Security Council, Dec. 9, 1947. This document is in NSC File: NSCID 17 Mill and CIA-5-1947. A search did not uncover it in the files of the Executive Registry of the Agency.

80. NSCID 1, Dec. 12, 1947. See NSC File: NSCID 17-1 for the original and subsequent revisions.

81. See pp. 80–81.

82. See pp. 360–61. For NSCID 1 as revised, July 7, 1949, see the Historical Collection.

83. See pp. 126–27.

84. See pp. 156, 239.

85. NSCID 4, Dec. 12, 1947 (NSC File: NSCID 17-4).

86. NSCID 6, Dec. 12, 1947 (NSC File: NSCID 17-6); "History of the Foreign Broadcast Information Division, 1940–1952," Ch. III of *History of the Office of Operations*.

87. See pp. 63, 111, 181.

88. NSCID 5, Dec. 12, 1947; draft of Nov. 24, 1947; J. B. Sherman to P. Childs, Dec. 10, 1947. NSC File: NSCID 17 has no folder for NSCID 5; the papers were found in the Agency.

89. See pp. 118–19. For the situation in 1951, see the memorandum from L. B. Kirkpatrick to General Smith (File: Records Integration–Foreign Intelligence, Historical Collection).

90. See pp. 123–25. S. W. Souers to A. B. Darling, Sept. 8, 1952; J. Forrestal to the Secretaries of the Navy and the Air Force, Jan. 3, 1948 (File: NSCID, Correspondence Concerning); NSC File: NSCID 17-2 and 3; also NSC File: CIA-5-1947 containing papers relevant to the controversy from Sept. 12 to Sept. 25, 1947.

91. R. H. Hillenkoetter to A. B. Darling, Oct. 22 and 24, 1952; R. H. Hillenkoetter to W. P. Armstrong, S. J. Chamberlin, T. B. Inglis, G. C. McDonald, Oct. 16, 1947.

92. D. Edgar to D. H. Galloway, ICAPS draft, Oct. 14, 1947. It was much the same on October 30, 1947.

93. CIG Directive 18, Oct. 25, 1946; NIA Directive 7, Jan. 2, 1947. See above, p. 150.

94. NSCID 2, Jan. 13, 1948.

95. NSCID 3, Jan. 13, 1948.

96. S. Kent and A. B. Darling, in conversation, Oct. 7, 1952.

97. NSC File: NSCID 17-7; NSCID 7, Feb. 12, 1948; W. C. Ford to E. L. Sibert, March 1, 1948.

98. S. J. Chamberlin to R. H. Hillenkoetter, Jan. 27, 1948; R. H. Hillenkoetter to S. J. Chamberlin, Feb. 2, 1948. Both memoranda are in File: NSCID 7.

99. NSCID 7, Feb. 12, 1948. For K. Douglass, see above, pp. 122–23.

100. For the texts of these last directives from the National Security Council, see the Historical Collection. Regarding NSCID 9 of July 1, 1948, Admiral Souers, Assistant to the President for matters of security, advised on September 8, 1952, that the affairs of the United States Communications Intelligence Board in detail did not seem to him essential to this study of the Central Intelligence Agency.

101. For Vandenberg's agreement with Bush, see p. 165.

102. R. H. Wise to Chief, ICAPS, Aug. 21, 1947 (File 825: Scientific-Technical Intelligence).

103. K. T. Compton to J. Forrestal, July 31, 1947 (File 825: Scientific-Technical Intelligence).

104. R. H. Hillenkoetter to J. Forrestal, Aug. 18, 1947 (File 825: Scientific-Technical Intelligence).

105. S. Edwards to Colonel Seeman, April 14, 1947.

106. E. K. Wright to A. B. Darling, April 10 and May 28, 1953.

107. S. W. Souers, report for the Atomic Energy Commission, July 1, 1947. Access to this report was given on November 24, 1952, by Roy B. Snapp, Secretary of the Commission.

108. Minutes of IAB Meeting 14, July 17, 1947, p. 16; memorandum for the National Intelligence Authority from U.S. Atomic Energy Commission, July 7, 1947.

109. R. H. Hillenkoetter to L. L. Strauss, April 12, 1948 (File 825: Scientific-Technical Intelligence).

110. R. H. Hillenkoetter, memorandum of Nov. 6, 1947; draft of proposed Joint Nuclear Energy Intelligence Committee, Oct. 29, 1947; T. B. Inglis to R. H. Hillenkoetter, Jan. 2, 1948. These memoranda are in File: CIA 7.02. V. Bush to J. Forrestal, Dec. 5, 1947; R. L. Clark to V. Bush, Dec. 3, 1947; D. Z. Beckler to R. L. Clark, Dec. 2, 1947. These memoranda are in File 825: Scientific-Technical Intelligence.

111. See p. 216. See pp. 295–96 for Dr. Brode's work in 1948.

112. R. H. Hillenkoetter to T. Babbitt, March 3, 1948 (File: DIG 6.05, Reports and Estimates).

113. See p. 309.

114. R. H. Hillenkoetter to L. L. Strauss, April 12, 1948 (File 825: Scientific-Technical Intelligence).

115. See pp. 295–96 having to do with the Eberstadt Report, p. 309 with the Dulles Group, and pp. 316–19 with biological warfare.

116. JCS 1569/4, May 16, 1947; Appendix D, Feb. 21, 1947. Access to these papers in the Pentagon was given by Brigadier General Richard C. Partridge on July 10, 1952.

117. Donald Edgar, Chief of ICAPS, made the preliminary suggestion for the

Agency on June 27, 1947. CIG draft, Joint Intelligence Committee, July 1, 1947; D. Edgar to R. H. Hillenkoetter, July 7, 1947; R. H. Hillenkoetter to the Joint Chiefs of Staff, July 8, 1947.

118. CIG draft, Joint Intelligence Committee, July 1, 1947.

119. See the texts of the President's Directive of Jan. 22, 1946, and Public Law 110, 81st Congress.

120. R. H. Hillenkoetter to W. A. Eddy, S. J. Chamberlin, T. B. Inglis, G. C. McDonald, July 11, 1947.

121. For the Montague plan in which these representatives of the departmental agencies in the Office of Reports and Estimates were to function as an estimating group, see pp. 89, 132–33. L. L. Montague to A. B. Darling, Oct. 30, 1952.

122. T. B. Inglis to R. H. Hillenkoetter, July 17, 1947. See above, p. 160.

123. L. L. Montague to A. B. Darling, in conversation, Oct. 30, 1952.

124. See pp. 287, 360–62.

125. G. C. McDonald to R. H. Hillenkoetter, July 25, 1947 (File: JCS, JIC, JIS Charters).

126. National Security Act of 1947, Public Law 253, Sections 102d, 211.

127. R. H. Hillenkoetter to the Joint Chiefs of Staff, Aug. 7, 1947 (File: JCS, JIC, JIS Charters).

128. National Security Act of 1947, Section 303; W. P. Armstrong to R. H. Hillenkoetter, Nov. 5, 1947. See above, p. 205.

129. R. H. Hillenkoetter to A. M. Gruenther, Nov. 14, 1947 (File: Hillenkoetter's Memoranda); minutes of the meetings on Nov. 20 and Dec. 8, 1947.

130. P. Childs to R. H. Hillenkoetter, Feb. 10, 1948 (File: NSCID, Correspondence Concerning); L. L. Montague to A. B. Darling, Oct. 30, 1952.

131. R. H. Hillenkoetter to A. B. Darling, Oct. 24 and Dec. 2, 1952; L. L. Montague to A. B. Darling, Oct. 30, 1952. See above, pp. 14–15, for Donovan's and Magruder's experiences.

132. R. H. Hillenkoetter to A. B. Darling, Dec. 2, 1952.

133. JCS 1569/7, Dec. 4, 1947 (JCS Files, Pentagon); L. L. Montague to A. B. Darling, Oct. 30, 1952.

134. R. H. Hillenkoetter to W. P. Armstrong, Jr. (written by P. Childs and E. K. Wright), Dec. 26, 1947.

135. A. M. Gruenther to R. H. Hillenkoetter, Dec. 12, 1947 (NSC File: NSCID 17-1).

136. NSC File: NSCID 17-1. The memorandum by Souers was penciled on the margin of his copy of the memorandum from Gruenther to Hillenkoetter, Dec. 12, 1947.

137. The Office of National Estimates was established following the Dulles Report. See below, pp. 419–20.

138. *New York Times*, April 13, 1948. See above, pp. 120–21.

139. *New York Herald Tribune*, April 16, 1948.

140. W. L. Pforzheimer to R. H. Hillenkoetter, April 19, 1948 (CIA News Clippings); WINX reported in *Washington Post*, April 19, 1948.

141. April 16, 1948, copy in CIA News Clippings, Jan.–June 1948 (Pforz-heimer's file).

142. April 10, 1948, copy in CIA News Clippings, Jan.–June 1948 (Pforz-heimer's file); R. H. Hillenkoetter to A. B. Darling, Dec. 2, 1952.

143. *New York Times,* April 16, 1948.

144. J. F. Devlin, paper on the Bogotá Riots, April 1948 (File: Bogotá Riots, April 1948).

145. Harriman's statement reported in *New York Times,* April 22, 1948; Devlin, paper on the Bogotá Riots.

146. R. H. Hillenkoetter to A. B. Darling, Oct. 24, 1952. See above, p. 223. See p. 148 for Vandenberg and CIA 18, NIA Directive 7. F. Kuhn, Jr., *Washington Post,* April 16, 1948. *New York Sun,* April 16, 1948.

147. R. H. Hillenkoetter to A. B. Darling, statements of Oct. 24, pp. 19–21, and Dec. 2, 1952, p. 22.

148. Public Law 253, 80th Congress, Section 102(2–3).

149. R. H. Hillenkoetter to A. B. Darling, Oct. 24, 1952, pp. 19–21.

150. See pp. 223–24, 309.

151. *New York Herald Tribune,* April 20, 1948.

152. Members of Subcommittee of the House: C. Hoffman, Representative of Michigan, A. McCormack, Representative of Massachusetts. Statement to the press, April 16, p. 2 (CIA News Clippings, Jan.–June 1948). R. H. Hillenkoetter to W. P. Armstrong, S. J. Chamberlin, T. B. Inglis, G. C. McDonald, Oct. 16, 1947 (File: CIG 20.03, Cuba).

153. NSC File, p. 13 (CIA 1948–5).

154. Statement to the press, April 16, p. 3 (CIA News Clippings, Jan.–June 1948); *Newsweek,* April 26, 1948.

Chapter VII

1. The copy of the directive of December 17, 1947, in the file of the Agency, Executive Registry, NSC 4 Series, is marked "Copy No. 1 of 2 Copies." A note in the file of the National Security Council, Official Minutes, Tab B, Meeting 4, December 17, 1947, shows that a third copy went to Mr. Kennan. The official minutes of the Council are in the Office of the Executive Secretary. R. H. Hillenkoetter to A. B. Darling, Oct. 22 and Dec. 2, 1952; S. W. Souers to A. B. Darling, Dec. 9, 1952; J. S. Lay, Jr., to A. B. Darling, Dec. 17 and 18, 1952, March 17 and June 26, 1953; NSC 11, Nov. 14, 1947, *Policies of the Government of the United States of America Relating to the National Security,* Vol. I, p. 73; comment by P. Childs, May 3, 1948 (file from Executive Registry tabbed "NSC 4 Series").

2. See pp. 34–35. For "Policy and Methods of Black Propaganda Against Germany," Supreme Headquarters Allied Expeditionary Force, Nov. 10, 1944, see Historical Collection.

3. *New York Times,* Sept. 18, 1947.

4. For Vandenberg on German intelligence, see p. 122. W. J. Donovan to R. H. Hillenkoetter, Sept. 18, 1947 (File D).

5. E. K. Wright to R. H. Hillenkoetter, Nov. 4, 1947. For Donovan on the Director of Central Intelligence, see above, pp. 25–27, 179–80.

6. See pp. 197–98. For the Dominican affair, see papers in the Historical Collection. For Section 303, National Security Act of 1947, see above, pp. 188–89, 205–6.

7. L. R. Houston to R. H. Hillenkoetter, Sept. 25, 1947. See above, pp. 187–88, and National Security Act of 1947, Section 102d(4-5).

8. NSC, *Policies*, Vol. I, p. 73. Minutes of NSC Meeting 2, Nov. 14, 1947, Tab B, report of Oct. 15 on position of the United States regarding Italy. Access given at request of Admiral Souers. Draft of Nov. 25, 1947, NSC 4 Series.

9. J. S. Lay, Jr., and S. W. Souers to A. B. Darling, Dec. 17 and 18, 1952; reference by Lay to NSC 1/1. See *Policies*, Vol. I, pp. 11–13, 79. Congress adopted the Marshall Plan on April 3, 1948.

10. See pp. 187–88. National Security Act of 1947, Section 102d(5).

11. The Psychological Strategy Board was established on April 4, 1951.

12. National Security Act of 1947, Section 102d(1–5).

13. J. S. Lay, Jr., to A. B. Darling, Dec. 18, 1952.

14. See pp. 179–80.

15. See p. 20. SWNCC was formed by an exchange of letters among the Secretaries of War, State, and Navy, on November 29 and December 1, 1944. It became SANACC by a similar exchange on November 4, 1947, as the Air Force gained representation. It was terminated on June 30, 1949, by an announcement (No. 100) from the Department of State. SAWACC 304/15 and "Brief History," Jan. 21, 1948.

16. Plan of MID, G-2, in SWNCC File. SANACC 304/15, p. 89.

17. SWNCC 304/1, Dec. 10, 1946, p. 23 (SWNCC File).

18. See p. 158.

19. SWNCC 304/1, Dec. 10, 1946, pp. 7–8.

20. NSC 1, Oct. 15, 1946; *Policies*, Vol. I, pp. 11–13.

21. SWNCC 304/1, Dec. 10, 1946, p. 3, before revision on Sept. 30, 1947.

22. SWNCC 304/6, Sept. 30, 1947, p. 54 (SWNCC File).

23. S. W. Souers to A. B. Darling, Dec. 9, 1952; R. H. Hillenkoetter to A. B. Darling, Dec. 2, 1952.

24. R. H. Hillenkoetter to S. W. Souers, Sept. 24, 1947 (original in NSC File: NSC 10-OSP, Executive Secretary's Office).

25. Memorandum by J. S. Lay, Jr., in pencil in NSC File: NSC 10-OSP.

26. D. H. Galloway to R. H. Hillenkoetter, May 29, 1947 (SWNCC, Advisory Council); R. H. Hillenkoetter to A. B. Darling, Oct. 22 and Dec. 2, 1952. The quotation is from R. H. Hillenkoetter's paper of Oct. 24, 1952, pp. 17–19.

27. J. H. Halversen to R. H. Hillenkoetter, Oct. 15, 1947; R. H. Hillenkoetter to SWNCC, Oct. 22, 1947.

28. SWNCC 304/10, Nov. 3, 1947. Copy 31 is in NSC File: NSC 10-OSP.

29. See pp. 204–5.

468 Notes to Chapter VII

30. The critique by J. S. Lay, Jr., Nov. 3, 1947, is in NSC File: NSC 10-OSP.

31. S. W. Souers to A. B. Darling, Sept. 8, 1952.

32. S. W. Souers to A. B. Darling, Nov. 4, 1952; Central Intelligence Agency Act of 1949, Public Law 110, 81st Congress.

33. Memorandum of J. S. Lay, Jr., Nov. 3, 1947, in NSC File: NSC 10-OSP.

34. For the War Council, see the National Security Act of 1947, Section 210. E. K. Wright to R. H. Hillenkoetter, Nov. 4, 1947. Minutes of NSC Meeting 2, Nov. 14, 1947 (file in the Executive Secretary's Office). Access given at request of Admiral Souers.

35. SANACC 304/11, Nov. 7, 1947; S. W. Souers to A. B. Darling, Dec. 9, 1952; NSC 11, *Policies*, Vol. I, pp. 36–37; S. W. Souers to the Council, Nov. 25, 1947 (File: NSC 4 Series).

36. R. H. Hillenkoetter to S. W. Souers, Nov. 13, 1947, regarding SANACC 304/11; Wright's copy is in RI File 100-120-1. Departmental Regulation 132.10, "Office of International Information and Cultural Affairs (OIC): (Effective 12-31-45)," in *Department of State Bulletin*, Vol. XIV (Jan. 6–June 30, 1946), p. 42. "U. S. Information and Educational Exchange Act of 1948," Jan. 27, 1948, Public Law 402, 80th Congress, 2nd Session.

37. Minutes of NSC Meeting 4, Dec. 17, 1947 (file in Executive Secretary's Office); NSC 1/1, advice to the President on Italy, Oct. 15, 1947; minutes of NSC Meeting 2, Nov. 14, 1947, Tab B; *Policies*, p. 11; J. S. Lay, Jr., to A. B. Darling, Dec. 17, 1952.

38. *Washington Post*, Jan. 9, 1953; James Reston, *New York Times*, Jan. 11, 1953. The commission under the chairmanship of William H. Jackson reported to President Eisenhower on June 30, 1953. For some discussion of its recommendations, see the interviews and conversations with L. R. Houston, General Counsel, in the Historical Collection. The date of the discussion was July 23, 1953.

39. R. H. Hillenkoetter to A. B. Darling, Dec. 2, 1952.

40. Draft of Nov. 25, 1947, "Notes by the Executive Secretary to the National Security Council on Psychological Operations."

41. Revised paper, Dec. 17, 1947 (Executive Registry File: NSC 4 Series).

42. See pp. 223–24. E. K. Wright to P. Childs, Dec. 8, 1947, regarding coordination in the field (Executive Registry File: NSC 4 Series); R. H. Hillenkoetter to S. W. Souers, Dec. 15, 1947 (written by Wright).

43. Memorandum 1 by P. Childs, Dec. 2, 1947.

44. For the meeting with Forrestal, see pp. 208–9. E. K. Wright to P. Childs, Dec. 2, 1947 (Executive Registry File: NSC 4 Series).

45. P. Childs to E. K. Wright, Dec. 5, 1947; proposed note by S. W. Souers to the NSC, Dec. 4, 1947; proposed directive to R. H. Hillenkoetter by S. W. Souers, Dec. 4, 1947.

46. S. W. Souers to the NSC, Dec. 16, 1947 (File: NSC 4 Series).

47. NSC Directive of Dec. 17, 1947, to R. H. Hillenkoetter.

48. Minutes of NSC Meeting 4, Tab B, Related Papers (file in the Executive Secretary's Office); S. W. Souers to A. B. Darling, Dec. 9, 1952.

49. R. H. Hillenkoetter to A. B. Darling, Dec. 2, 1952. See documents in the

Historical Collection from the "Chronos" of the Special Procedures Group. The "Chronos" is in Records Integration–Foreign Intelligence of the Agency.

50. S. W. Souers to A. B. Darling, Dec. 9, 1952. See above, p. 215.

51. NSC Directive of Dec. 17, 1947 to R. H. Hillenkoetter, p. 2.

52. S. W. Souers to A. B. Darling, Dec. 9, 1952.

53. E. H. Hillenkoetter to A. B. Darling, Dec. 2, 1952.

54. See pp. 249–50. For control by the Intelligence Advisory Committee, see pp. 216–17.

55. R. H. Hillenkoetter to D. H. Galloway, Dec. 22, 1947 (Executive Registry File: NSC 4 Series); SPG "Chronos."

56. [citation deleted]

57. T. G. Cassady through D. H. Galloway to R. H. Hillenkoetter, Aug. 4, 1948, p. 3 (File: SPG "Chronos"); R. H. Hillenkoetter to A. B. Darling, Dec. 1, 1952.

58. H. T. Orville to T. G. Cassady, April 7, 1948; progress report for the period ending April 30, 1948, from R. E. Dulin to D. H. Galloway, May 12, 1948; T. G. Cassady to R. E. Dulin, April 27, 1948. These memoranda are in File: SPG "Chronos."

59. R. H. Hillenkoetter to A. B. Darling, Dec. 2, 1952.

60. T. G. Cassady to R. E. Dulin, April 27, 1948 (File: SPG "Chronos").

61. Evidence in the "Chronos" of the Special Procedures Group.

62. T. G. Cassady to R. E. Dulin, April 27, 1948 (File: SPG "Chronos"); R. H. Hillenkoetter to A. B. Darling, Dec. 2, 1952.

63. J. Forrestal to Executive Secretary, National Security Council, March 26, 1948 (Executive Registry File: NSC 4 Series). For Bogotá, see above, pp. 240–44.

64. G. V. Allen, letter dated June 8, 1948 (Executive Registry File: NSC 4 Series); R. H. Hillenkoetter to A. B. Darling, Dec. 2, 1952.

65. S. W. Souers to the National Security Council, April 26, 1948 (Executive Registry File: NSC 4 Series).

66. R. E. Dulin to D. H. Galloway, May 12, 1948; quote from R. J. Williams to T. G. Cassady, July 24, 1948. These memoranda are in File: SPG "Chronos." S. W. Souers to A. B. Darling, Dec. 9, 1952.

67. R. L. Campbell to Captain Austin, Office of Chief of Naval Operations, April 16, 1948 (file in the Executive Secretary's Office); P. Childs, memorandum for discussion with the NSC staff, May 3, 1948 (Executive Registry File: NSC 4 Series); NSC Staff Meeting, April 19, 1948, record in NSC 10-OSP (file in the Executive Secretary's Office).

68. "Inauguration of Organized Political Warfare," May 4, 1948 (file in the Executive Secretary's Office); proposed NSC Directive, "Director of Special Studies," May 4, 1948 (Executive Registry File: NSC 10 Series).

69. T. G. Cassady to R. E. Dulin, Aril 27, 1948 (File: SPG "Chronos").

70. "Inauguration of Organized Political Warfare"; "Director of Special Studies."

71. R. H. Hillenkoetter, memorandum for Executive Secretary, NSC, regarding "Director of Special Studies," May 5, 1948; R. H. Hillenkoetter to A. B. Darling, Dec. 2, 1952.

72. See pp. 307–8.

73. R. H. Hillenkoetter to A. B. Darling, Dec. 2, 1952.

74. [citation deleted]

75. S. W. Souers to A. B. Darling, Sept. 8, 1952; R. H. Hillenkoetter to S. W. Souers, May 11, 1948 (NSC File: NSC 10-OSP).

76. [citation deleted]

77. National Security Act of 1947, Sections 102d(5), 101.

78. A. W. Dulles to S. W. Souers, May 13, 1948 (NSC File: NSC 10-OSP); Interim Report No. 2, "Relations between Secret Operations and Secret Intelligence," May 13, 1948 (NSC File: NSC 10-OSP); R. H. Hillenkoetter to A. B. Darling, Dec. 2, 1952, p. 20.

79. Cite the Dulles Report, p. 131. See below, pp. 310–11. Meeting, April 30, 1948 (Blum's File 6236/18, Executive Secretary's Office). See above, pp. 60–62.

80. *Policies*, p. 74, for NSC 47; R. H. Hillenkoetter to S. W. Souers, May 24, 1948 (Executive Registry File: NSC 10 Series).

81. See pp. 240–44.

82. R. Blum to A. B. Darling, March 10, 1953.

83. Memorandum of a meeting in Forrestal's office on May 28, 1948, in NSC 10-OSP under date of June 1, 1948 (Executive Secretary's Office).

84. S. W. Souers to the National Security Council, June 2, 1948. For Marshall and Royall, see above, pp. 260–61.

85. R. H. Hillenkoetter to S. W. Souers, June 4, 1948 (NSC File: NSC 10-OSP).

86. Ibid.

87. J. S. Lay, Jr., to R. H. Hillenkoetter, June 7, 1948 (NSC File: NSC 10-OSP).

88. For changes made by the staff, see J. S. Lay, Jr., to the consultants, June 11, 1948 (NSC File: NSC 10-OSP).

89. Two letters of R. H. Hillenkoetter to J. S. Lay, Jr., June 9, 1948 (Executive Registry File: NSC 10 Series).

90. W. H. Jackson, Deputy Director of Central Intelligence, memorandum to the Director, May 24, 1951 (*Survey of Office of Policy Coordination*, Vol. I, pp. 2, 6–7); R. H. Hillenkoetter to A. B. Darling, Oct. 24, 1952, pp. 21–22. For Hillenkoetter's views on budgeting and financial controls, see his "Comments" on the Dulles Report, discussed below in Ch. VIII, pp. 320–23.

91. Army Paper, June 15, 1948; D. C. Fahey to J. S. Lay, Jr., June 15, 1948; NSC 10-1, June 15, 1948, Copy 22. These memoranda are in NSC File: NSC 10-OSP.

92. M. K. Ruddock to E. K. Wright, Aug. 25, 1948 (File: SPG "Chronos II"). See below, pp. 331–32.

93. NSC 10-2, June 18, 1948. Amendment regarding theater commanders. Memorandum from J. S. Lay, Jr., April 16, 1951.

94. NSC 10-2 3d(1).

95. See pp. 321–22.

96. S. W. Souers to A. B. Darling, Dec. 9, 1952.

97. R. H. Hillenkoetter to A. B. Darling, Oct. 22 and Dec. 2, 1952. Executive

Registry File: NSC 50, "Comments by the Central Intelligence Agency on the Dulles Report."

98. R. H. Hillenkoetter to A. B. Darling, Dec. 2, 1952; G. Kennan to A. W. Dulles, April 30, 1948, as reported by R. Blum (NSC File 6236-18).

99. T. G. Cassady to D.K.E. Bruce, June 11, 1948 (File: SPG "Chronos").

100. R. J. Williams to T. G. Cassady, July 24, 1948; T. G. Cassady to R. H. Hillenkoetter, July 30 and Aug. 4, 1948; T. G. Cassady to D. H. Galloway, Aug. 6, 1948. These memoranda are in File: SPG "Chronos." J. E. Baker to A. B. Darling, in conversation, July 1, 1953.

101. R. J. Williams to T. G. Cassady, July 24, 1948; T. G. Cassady to D. H. Galloway, Aug. 6, 1948. These memoranda are in File: SPG "Chronos."

102. J. E. Baker to A. B. Darling, in conversation, July 1, 1953.

103. Minutes of NSC Meeting 18, Aug. 19, 1948. Documents in Tab C in NSC File: NSC 10-OSP.

104. R. H. Hillenkoetter to A. B. Darling, Oct. 22 and 24, Dec. 2, 1952. Minutes of NSC Meeting 18, Aug. 19, 1948. Documents in Tab C in NSC File: NSC 10-OSP.

105. R. H. Hillenkoetter to A. B. Darling, Dec. 2, 1952.

106. See pp. 352–53.

107. R. Blum to A. B. Darling, March 10, 1953.

108. General Order 10, Aug. 27, 1948; T. G. Cassady to D. H. Galloway, Aug. 6, 1948 (File: SPG "Chronos").

109. "History of the Contact Division," Ch. II of *History of the Office of Operations*, p. 101; W. E. Little, *History of the Office of Policy Coordination*, June 26, 1951; C. F. Von Kann, "Draft Progress Report: OPC," Dec. 26, 1951 (Historical Collection).

110. General Order 11, Sept. 14, 1948; F. P. Bishop, "Historical Notes: Budget and Finance Activities" May 8, 1952, pp. 10–14; R. H. Hillenkoetter, "Comments" on the Dulles Report, pp. 3, 5, Section 3c. See below, pp. 321–33.

111. F. G. Wisner to R. H. Hillenkoetter, Feb. 14, 1949. "Comments" on the Dulles Report (Executive Registry File: Dulles–Jackson–Correa Survey). See below, pp. 321–22.

112. See pp. 319–20.

113. See pp. 321–22, 371–72.

Chapter VIII

1. NIA Directive 1, Feb. 8, 1946. See above, pp. 69–71.

2. S. Kent to A. B. Darling, Oct. 7, 1952.

3. J. F. Neck, Executive Secretary for Hoover, to R. H. Hillenkoetter, April 16, 1948 (Eberstadt Committee File).

4. See pp. 57–58. Actively interested with Eberstadt in the study of the Cen-

tral Intelligence Agency were Raymond B. Allen, President of the University of Washington, Hanson W. Baldwin of the *New York Times,* John J. McCloy, at that time President of the International Bank for Reconstruction and Development, and Frederick A. Middlebush, President of the University of Missouri. R. Blum to Dulles, Correa, and Jackson, July 21, 1948 (NSC File 6236-3).

5. W. L. Pforzheimer, memorandum of April 2, 1953.

6. W. S. Smith, "Progress Report," April 23, 1953.

7. See pp. 240–44.

8. See pp. 167–68. R. Blum, memorandum of committee meetings (NSC File 6236-8). For NSC 10-2 and OPC, see above, pp. 273–81.

9. R. H. Hillenkoetter to A. B. Darling, Oct. 24, 1952, pp. 17–19, and Dec. 2, 1952, p. 18. See above, pp. 156–57, 217. S. W. Souers to A. B. Darling, Sept. 8 and Dec. 9, 1952.

10. See pp. 73–74, 182–83. For the issue of political intelligence in Vandenberg's regime, see above, pp. 125–27.

11. See p. 58. Eberstadt Report, pp. 43–44. See pp. 175–76.

12. Eberstadt Report, p. 44. For the NIA, see above, pp. 71–74.

13. For General Chamberlin on "chain of command," see pp. 201–2.

14. *Washington Post,* March 29, 1953.

15. Eberstadt Report, p. 32. For Inglis's argument, see above, pp. 201–2. For NSCID 1, see the minutes of the meetings of Nov. 20 and Dec. 8, 1947, p. 52.

16. Eberstadt Report, pp. 32–33. See pp. 144–45, 205.

17. The concept of the "best diagonal" has come from R. W. Emerson, *Journals,* 1909–1914, Vol. VII, p. 197.

18. Eberstadt Report, pp. 33–35.

19. R. H. Hillenkoetter to the Eberstadt Committee, Sept. 10, 1948, minutes, p. 65 (Eberstadt Committee File: Commission on Organization of the Executive Branch of the Government).

20. For Hoover and Vandenberg, see pp. 125–27.

21. Eberstadt Report, p. 57; R. H. Hillenkoetter to A. B. Darling, Oct. 24 and Dec. 2, 1952. For OPC, see above, pp. 273–81.

22. For Hillenkoetter's own plan of May 24, 1948, see pp. 269–70. Eberstadt Report, pp. 46–47. For Dulles and Kennan on secret intelligence and covert operations, see above, pp. 263–64.

23. For Jackson's ideas in 1945, see pp. 60–61.

24. See p. 270. Chart regarding Deputy Director (Plans), March 20, 1953, "Organization and Functions, Central Intelligence Agency Regulation No. 1-100." W. H. Jackson, *Survey of Office of Policy Coordination,* Vol. I; *Survey of Office of Policy Coordination,* Appendix, Vol. II.

25. Eberstadt Report, pp. 37–38, 52–53.

26. See pp. 120, 232–39. Eberstadt Report, pp. 52–53.

27. Eberstadt Report, pp. 35, 38.

28. Eberstadt Report, pp. 41–42.

29. Eberstadt Report, pp. 42–43.

30. L. R. Houston to R. H. Hillenkoetter, Sept. 2, 1948; statement by E. K.

Wright, Sept. 9, 1948, in minutes, p. 9 (Executive Registry File: Eberstadt Committee); Eberstadt Report, p. 39.

31. For Souers's recommendations in the Eberstadt Report of 1945 to J. Forrestal, see pp. 57–59.

32. Eberstadt Report, pp. 39–41. See below, pp. 298–308.

33. Eberstadt Report, pp. 51–52.

34. For Donovan to Rosenman, Sept. 4, 1945, see p. 40.

35. Eberstadt Report, pp. 49–51; E. K. Wright to A. B. Darling, April 10, 1953.

36. T. Smith to A. W. Dulles, Oct. 14, 1948 (NSC File 6236-2).

37. For the Estimates Branch, see pp. 87–88. For the Intelligence Staff, see pp. 135–38.

38. Sherman Kent, *Strategic Intelligence for American World Policy*, 1949, pp. 81, 102.

39. Eberstadt Report, pp. 52–53.

40. For Donovan's principles, see pp. 25–27. Dulles Report, pp. 76–78; W. L. Langer, "Progress Report," Office of National Estimates, July 9, 1951.

41. See pp. 309–10.

42. Eberstadt Report, pp. 48, 37. For Hillenkoetter's centralized control of budgeting and expenditure, see above, pp. 280–81, and below, pp. 321–23.

43. See pp. 164–65, 216–17. *History of the Office of Scientific Intelligence*, May 9, 1952, p. 9; S. W. Souers, *Report on Atomic Energy Intelligence*, July 1, 1947. Access to this report was granted for the Atomic Energy Commission by Roy B. Snapp, Secretary, Nov. 24, 1952. E. K. Wright to A. B. Darling, April 10, 1953.

44. See pp. 227–32. For the Becker Report, consult the Office of Scientific Intelligence.

45. Eberstadt Report, pp. 55–56.

46. Eberstadt Report, pp. 53–55.

47. For the enabling bill and the CIA Act of 1949, see p. 191. For previous arrangements, see pp. 113–15. Eberstadt Report, p. 58.

48. For Houston's letter for Hillenkoetter to Eberstadt on Sept. 14, 1948, see Executive Registry File: Eberstadt Committee, Commission on Organization of Executive Branch.

49. *Washington Post,* April 15, 1953, article by the Alsops.

50. Eberstadt Report, pp. 59–60.

51. Eberstadt Report, pp. 60, 40.

52. For psychological warfare, see pp. 272–73. For Bogotá, see pp. 240–44. For the internal organization of the Agency, see pp. 373–75, 386–87, 395–97.

53. For NIA Directive 1, see pp. 78–82.

54. R. H. Hillenkoetter to A. B. Darling, Oct. 22 and Dec. 2, 1952.

55. S. W. Souers to A. B. Darling, Sept. 8 and Nov. 4, 1952.

56. For Souers as the first Director, see pp. 75–77.

57. For the origin of CIG, see pp. 70–74. For Forrestal on the Intelligence Advisory Committee, see pp. 215–16.

58. For the NSCIDs, see pp. 218–26. For NSC 4A, see pp. 245–47.

59. [one line deleted] W. H. Jackson to A. B. Darling, March 15, 1952; R. Blum to A. B. Darling, March 10, 1953; *Armed Force,* Oct. 18, 1947, in Historical Collection; R. Blum to J. H. Ohly, Nov. 21, 1947 (NSC File: CIA-5-1947).

60. These papers by Lay, Blum, and Ohly are in the file of the National Security Council, CIA-5-1947.

61. For Action No. 25, see National Security Council, *Policies,* Vol. I, p. 66; R. H. Hillenkoetter to S. Kent, Dec. 23, 1947, and Jan. 21, 1948; S. Kent to R. H. Hillenkoetter, Jan. 16, 1948.

62. S. Kent to R. H. Hillenkoetter, memorandum on ORE, Feb. 9, 1948; S. Kent to A. B. Darling, Nov. 21, 1952.

63. The pencilled memorandum is in the Executive Registry File.

64. Report of Jan. 16, 1948, on Allen W. Dulles, unsigned (NSC File: CIA Survey Group 5–8); S. W. Souers to A. B. Darling, June 30, 1952.

65. For Dewey's activity, see p. 24.

66. S. W. Souers to A. B. Darling, June 30, 1952; report on Correa, Jan. 16 (NSC File: CIA Survey Group 5–8). See above, pp. 51–56.

67. Report on Jackson, Jan. 16 (NSC File: CIA Survey Group 5–8); R. Blum to J. Forrestal, Feb. 2, 1948 (NSC File 6236-9). For Jackson's letter to Forrestal, Nov. 14, 1945, see above, pp. 60–62.

68. R. Blum to J. H. Ohly, Feb. 12, 1948 (NSC File 6236-10). See above, Chs. IV and VI.

69. *Washington Post,* April 21, 1953.

70. See pp. 327–29. Resolution of the Council, Jan. 13, 1948, printed in the Dulles Report, p. 166.

71. Blum's conversation with Souers, Feb. 20, 1948 (NSC File 6236-10).

72. Blum's conversation with Hillenkoetter and Wright, Feb. 20, 1948 (NSC File 6236-10). For Cassady, see above, pp. 262–65.

73. S. W. Souers to Dulles, Correa, and Jackson, Feb. 26, 1948 (Executive Registry File: Dulles–Jackson–Correa Survey). Some of the staff reports are in NSC File 6236.

74. J. Forrestal to S. W. Souers, March 3, 1948; S. W. Souers, memorandum for the Secretary of State, March 8, 1948 (NSC File: CIA Survey Group 5–8). The second meeting of the Survey Group was held on February 23 in Forrestal's office. Those present besides Forrestal were Souers, Jackson, and Blum, but not Dulles and Correa. Memorandum in NSC File 6236-8.

75. For the War Council, see the National Security Act of 1947, Section 210. S. W. Souers to G. C. Marshall, March 8, 1948 (NSC File: CIA Survey Group 5–8).

76. J. L. Sullivan to S. W. Souers, March 10, 1948; G. C. Marshall to S. W. Souers, March 12, 1948 (NSC File: CIA Survey Group 5–8). See Ch. III in the Dulles Report.

77. S. W. Souers to National Security Council, April 7, 1948 (NSC File: CIA Survey Group 5–8). L. Denfeld to S. W. Souers, April 16, 1948 (Executive Registry File: Dulles–Jackson–Correa Survey).

78. Dulles Report, p. 139. For the Eberstadt Report, see pp. 285–98.

79. R. Blum, memorandum of meetings (NSC File 6236-8).

80. The memorandum of March 12 has not been found, but there is a reference to it in the memorandum of April 12, 1948 (NSC File 6236-2). R. Blum, paper on ICAPS, March 18, 1948 (NSC File 6236-15). For Galloway's removal, see above, p. 271.

81. For Sibert, see pp. 120, 127. R. Blum, memorandum to W. H. Jackson, March 31, 1948 (NSC File 6236-3).

82. R. Blum, memorandum of meetings, April 3, 1948 (NSC File 6236-8); R. Blum to A. B. Darling, March 10, 1953; S. W. Souers to A. B. Darling, June 30 and Sept. 8, 1952. For the directive of Dec. 17, 1947, see above, pp. 256–62.

83. For Jackson's view in 1945, see pp. 60–62; his letter of Nov. 14, 1945, p. 4. For Kennan to Allen Dulles on April 30, 1948, see above, p. 266.

84. For representatives of G-2 in Congress, see pp. 180–82. Magruder's Report, pp. 63–65; the Donovan Plan, pp. 7–10, 43–44. For Interim Report No. 2, see p. 269. Dulles Report, pp. 117–122.

85. R. Blum to W. H. Jackson, April 12, 1948 (NSC File 6236-3); R. Blum to Dulles, Correa, and Jackson, April 12, 1948 (NSC File 6236-2).

86. R. H. Hillenkoetter to A. B. Darling, Oct. 22 and 24, 1952; E. K. Wright to A. B. Darling, April 10, 1953; security clearance for the Survey Group, May 12, 1948 (NSC File 6236-12). For Action No. 25 by the Council on Jan. 13, 1948, see the Dulles Report, p. 166. For the removal of Galloway, see above, p. 271.

87. R. Blum, minutes of meetings, April 3, 1948 (NSC File 6236-8). See File 6236-17 for a memorandum by Blum on Strauss, March 29, 1948. For the agreement of Strauss and Hillenkoetter, April 12, 1948, see above, p. 232. Dulles Report, pp. 30, 88–90, 114–115.

88. [citation deleted]

89. See pp. 242–44.

90. [citation deleted]

91. A copy of this report, Interim Report No. 1, is in the Executive Registry File: Dulles–Jackson–Correa Survey. The quotations above are from pp. 4, 5, and 8.

92. E. K. Wright to S. W. Souers, May 7, 1948 (Executive Registry File: Dulles–Jackson–Correa Survey).

93. S. W. Souers, memorandum for the National Security Council, Aug. 19, 1948 (Executive Registry File: Dulles–Jackson–Correa Survey).

94. R. Blum to A. W. Dulles, April 20, 1948 (NSC File 6236-2). See above, pp. 240–44. R. Blum to A. B. Darling, March 10, 1953.

95. Ch. VI in Kent's book; S. Kent to A. B. Darling, Nov. 21, 1952.

96. R. Blum to W. H. Jackson, April 23, 1948 (NSC File 6236-3). For reports by Larocque and Sprague, see NSC File 6236-15.

97. See pp. 263–64, 268–69. R. Blum, memorandum for the file, meeting of Kennan, Davies, and Villard with Dulles and Blum, April 30, 1948 (NSC File 6236-18).

98. See pp. 270–71. R. Blum, memorandum for Dulles, Correa, Jackson, June 4, 1948 (NSC File 6236-2); R. Blum to A. B. Darling, March 10, 1953.

99. R. Blum, memorandum for Jackson, June 9, 1948 (NSC File 6236-3).

100. Dulles Report, pp. 4–5, 135–38; R. Blum, memorandum on the IAC, June 10, 1948 (NSC File 6236-15).

101. For Robert Patterson on command, see pp. 166–67.

102. See pp. 60–62.

103. A transcript of Jackson's paper for Forrestal is in the Historical Collection.

104. W. H. Jackson, interview with major General Bolling and Colonel Carter Clarke, June 14, 1948 (NSC File 6236-3).

105. See pp. 156–57. For the action of the Joint Chiefs of Staff, see pp. 232–39.

106. W. H. Jackson, interview with Bolling and Clarke; statements of Bolling and Clarke, Nov. 22 and 23, 1948 (NSC File 6236-11).

107. W. H. Jackson, interview with General Gruenther, June 15, 1948 (NSC File 6236-3).

108. For the discussion in the 121st meeting of the Joint Intelligence Committee, Dec. 22, 1944, see pp. 29–32.

109. National Security Act of 1947, Section 102d(3).

110. W. H. Jackson, interview with T. Babbitt, June 15, 1948 (NSC File 6236-3); T. Babbitt to A. B. Darling, March 13, 1953.

111. W. H. Jackson, interview with W. P. Armstrong, Jr., June 15, 1948 (NSC File 6236-3). See above, pp. 145–51, 209–11. Sprague's report on OIR, June 30, 1948, is in NSC File 6236-15. Dulles Report, Ch. III.

112. R. Blum to J. Forrestal, June 15, 1948 (NSC File 6236-9); R. Blum to A. W. Dulles, June 22, 1948 (NSC File 6236-2).

113. R. Blum to W. H. Jackson, July 24, 1948 (NSC File 6236-3).

114. E. K. Wright to A. B. Darling, April 10, 1953. For Cassady and Galloway, see above, pp. 262–65.

115. A. W. Dulles to S. W. Souers, July 12, 1948 (NSC File: CIA Survey Group 5-8).

116. J. Forrestal to S. W. Souers, May 22, 1948 (NSC File: CIA Survey Group 5-8); J. Forrestal to R. H. Hillenkoetter, May 22, 1948.

117. R. H. Hillenkoetter to J. Forrestal, May 28, 1948.

118. Ibid.

119. W. Machle, "Inability of OSI to Accomplish Its Mission," Sept. 29, 1949. For R. H. Hillenkoetter's experiences, 1947–1948, see above, pp. 227–32.

120. Machle's Report, Sept. 29, 1949, Enclosure I, Tab B.

121. Ibid., Enclosure IV, Tab B.

122. See pp. 123–27, 198–205.

123. Machle's Report, Sept. 29, 1949, Enclosure II, Tab B.

124. H. Baldwin, articles on Central Intelligence, *New York Times*, July 20–25, 1948. See above, p. 300.

125. For Bogotá, see pp. 240–44.

126. P. Childs to J. S. Lay, Jr., no date (NSC File: CIA Survey Group 5-8); R. Blum to W. H. Jackson, July 24, 1948 (NSC File 6236-3). See above, p. 298. Eberstadt Report, p. 40.

127. R. Blum to W. H. Jackson, Oct. 16, 1948 (NSC File 6236-3).

128. Minutes on the formal hearings and written statements are in NSC File

6236-11. R. H. Hillenkoetter to A. W. Dulles, Nov. 17, 1948 (Executive Registry File: Dulles–Jackson–Correa Survey).

129. R. H. Hillenkoetter to A. B. Darling, Oct. 24 and Dec. 2, 1952.

130. Dulles Report, p. 135. See above, pp. 307–8.

131. Dulles Report, pp. 32, 38, 11. See above, pp. 279–80.

132. For financial arrangements in Vandenberg's administration, see pp. 112–15. R. H. Hillenkoetter, "Comments," pp. 3, 5.

133. Hillenkoetter, "Comments," pp. 12, 5; F. P. Bishop, "Historical Notes: Budget and Finance Activities," May 8, 1952, p. 11.

134. F. G. Wisner to R. H. Hillenkoetter, Feb. 14, 1949, "Comments on the Dulles Report"; A. McCracken to R. H. Hillenkoetter, Feb. 21, 1949, "Comments on the Dulles Report." These memoranda are in Executive Registry File: Dulles–Jackson–Correa Survey. Bishop, "Historical Notes," p. 10–14. General Order 24, Sept. 20, 1949. For the order of 1948, see above, pp. 280–81.

135. Hillenkoetter, "Comments," pp. 3–4; National Security Act of 1947, Section 102a; Dulles Report, pp. 33–34.

136. Hillenkoetter, "Comments," p. 11.

137. See pp. 173–76.

138. L. R. Houston, memoranda to the files, Feb. 7, 1949 (File 606:CIA Legislation), and March 11, 1949 (File 210: Budgets, Appropriations, Allotments). These files are in the General Counsel's Office.

139. CIA Act of 1949, Section 10b. For NSC 10-2, see above, pp. 265–81. Hillenkoetter, "Comments," pp. 3–4.

140. Dulles Report, p. 11.

141. Hillenkoetter, "Comments," p. 2; Dulles Report, p. 41.

142. Dulles Report, pp. 2–4, 5–6, 12, 26–27, 135–36, 146, 149; L. R. Houston, memorandum to R. H. Hillenkoetter, May 7, 1948 (File 606: CIA Legislation).

143. Hillenkoetter, "Comments," pp. 1–2; Dulles Report, p. 5.

144. For the NSCIDs, see pp. 209–26. For R. P. Patterson, see above, pp. 166–67. Eberstadt Report, p. 41.

145. Dulles Report, p. 63; Hillenkoetter, "Comments," p. 14. See above, p. 154. For the relation to covert operations, see above, pp. 247–50.

146. Dulles Report, pp. 135, 138; Hillenkoetter, "Comments," p. 40; R. H. Hillenkoetter to A. B. Darling, Dec. 2, 1952.

147. Dulles Report, pp. 136–38; Hillenkoetter, "Comments," pp. 40–41.

148. Dulles Report, pp. 136–38; Hillenkoetter, "Comments," p. 41. See above, pp. 51, 302.

149. See pp. 175–76. L. R. Houston to R. H. Hillenkoetter, Sept. 2, 1948; Hillenkoetter, "Comments," pp. 42–45; R. H. Hillenkoetter to A. B. Darling, Dec. 2, 1952.

150. Dulles Report, p. 138.

151. Dulles Report, p. 38; Hillenkoetter, "Comments," pp. 5–9.

152. Dulles Report, pp. 37, 39, 113, 130; Hillenkoetter, "Comments," p. 10.

153. Dulles Report, pp. 34–35; National Security Act of 1947, Section 102d(3).

154. Hillenkoetter, "Comments," pp. 11, 13.

155. For origin of the responsibility, see p. 170. For the record of the hearing, see NSC File: CIA-5-1948. W. Pforzheimer to A. B. Darling, Jan. 30, 1953. For the story of Bogotá, see above, pp. 240–44. Dulles Report, pp. 31, 48–49, 63–64.

156. J. M. Andrews to R. H. Hillenkoetter, Feb. 7, 1949 (Executive Registry File: Dulles–Jackson–Correa Survey).

157. Hillenkoetter, "Comments," pp. 17, 49.

158. J. M. Sterling to R. H. Hillenkoetter, Feb. 14, 1949 (Executive Registry File: Dulles–Jackson–Correa Survey); Dulles Report, pp. 96, 104–6; Hillenkoetter, "Comments," p. 29.

159. J.B.L. Reeves to A. B. Darling, March 16, 1953.

160. Hillenkoetter, "Comments," p. 31.

161. See pp. 270–71.

162. J. M. Sterling to R. H. Hillenkoetter, Feb. 14, 1949, p. 2 (Executive Registry File: Dulles–Jackson–Correa Survey).

163. The original of Wisner's letter is in Executive Registry File: Dulles–Jackson–Correa Survey. For the agreement of Aug. 6, 1948, see above, pp. 279–80.

164. A. McCracken to R. H. Hillenkoetter, Feb. 21, 1949 (Executive Registry File: Dulles–Jackson–Correa Survey).

165. Hillenkoetter, "Comments," pp. 34–38. See above, pp. 272–75. For General Smith's action in Oct. 1950, see below, pp. 410–13.

166. For the FBI, see pp. 120–22, 356–59, 367–68.

167. Hillenkoetter, "Comments," p. 38.

168. Dulles Report, p. 11.

169. Dulles Report, p. 6; L. L. Montague to T. Babbitt, Jan. 31, 1949. For ORE, see above, pp. 130–32. G. S. Jackson, Paper Nos. 8 and 9, "Origin and Nature of the 'CIA Review of the World Situation'," and "Analysis of Estimates Contained in the 'CIA Review of the World Situation'," Sept. 1947–Jan. 1950. See above, pp. 23–26.

170. Dulles Report, pp. 65–81; NSC Intelligence Directive 1, "Duties and Responsibilities," revised Jan. 19, 1950; NSC Intelligence Directive 3, "Coordination of Intelligence Production," Jan. 13, 1948.

171. Dulles Report, pp. 68–69.

172. See pp. 235–36.

173. Dulles Report, pp. 26–70. For OSS during the war, see above, pp. 10–20.

174. National Security Act of 1947, Sections 102d and 102e; L. R. Houston to R. H. Hillenkoetter, May 7, 1948 (File 606: CIA Legislation).

175. National Security Act of 1947, Section 102e. For unification, see above, pp. 185–86. S. Kent to A. B. Darling, Oct. 7, 1952.

176. Dulles Report, pp. 63–64, 58, 69–70; National Security Act of 1947, Section 102d(3). For the Eberstadt Report, see above, p. 288.

177. S. W. Souers to A. B. Darling, Nov. 6, 1952, p. 43; P. Borel to A. B. Darling, July 30, 1953. See above, pp. 125–27. National Security Act of 1947, Section 102e.

178. For this parallel phrasing, compare the Eberstadt Report, p. 51, with the Dulles Report, p. 73.

179. Dulles Report, pp. 65, 81.

180. Dulles Report, pp. 77, 81.

181. Dulles Report, pp. 43–45, 63, 81; R. H. Hillenkoetter to A. B. Darling, Oct. 11, 1952, p. 3.

182. See pp. 70–74, 79–82, 183–89, 218–20.

183. For NSC 10-2, see pp. 273–81. Dulles Report, p. 129.

184. R. H. Hillenkoetter to A. B. Darling, Oct. 22 and 24, 1952; E. K. Wright to A. B. Darling, April 10, 1953. For the terms of the Act, see above, pp. 183–89.

185. Dulles Report, pp. 74–75. From D. Van Slyck's Report to R. H. Hillenkoet-ter: [(a) deleted] (b) "The Strategic Value to the USSR of the Conquest of Western Europe and the Near East (to Cairo) Prior to 1950" (ORE 58-48), July 30, 1948; [(c) deleted] (d) "Appendices to ORE 58-48," Oct. 27, 1948 [one line of note (d) deleted] File: G. S. Jackson, Paper No. 16, May 21, 1953, note of the "March War Scare" of 1948.

186. D. Van Slyck to R. H. Hillenkoetter, Dec. 23, 1948; Dulles Report, p. 75.

187. Special Evaluation No. 27, March 16, 1948. For ORE 1, see pp. 130–32.

188. L. L. Montague to T. Babbitt, Jan. 31, 1949. [one line deleted] Comments by the Director of Intelligence, USAF, and the Director of Naval Intelligence.

189. D. Van Slyck to R. H. Hillenkoetter, Dec. 23, 1948. For the reflection of Van Slyck's views on the Eberstadt Report, see above, p. 304.

190. T. Babbitt to A. B. Darling, March 13, 1953. Stevens's draft of February 8, 1949, marked "S/PP," was obtained from the file in the Office of Research and Reports. It and the accompanying papers are now in the Historical Collection.

191. See pp. 87–89, 131–34.

192. S.A.D. Hunter to T. Babbitt, comments on "Draft Comments on Dulles Report," Feb. 9, 1949. This document is in the file of the present Office of Research and Reports.

193. L. L. Montague to A. B. Darling, March 23, 1953; T. Babbitt to A. B. Darling, March 13, 1953; D. Van Slyck to A. B. Darling, April 21, 1953, pp. 8–9.

194. "ORE Comments," p. 7 (Executive Registry File: Dulles–Jackson–Correa Survey); Dulles Report, p. 81.

195. Dulles Report, pp. 79–81.

196. See p. 292. Eberstadt Report, p. 40.

197. L. L. Montague to T. Babbitt, Jan. 31 and Feb. 11, 1949. See above, pp. 87–89, 131–34.

198. See pp. 27, 58, 71–72. T. Babbitt to A. B. Darling, March 13, 1953; "ORE Comments," pp. 2, 7–8 (Executive Registry File: Dulles–Jackson–Correa Survey). For the definition of national intelligence estimates accepted by the National Intelligence Authority, see above, p. 154.

199. Hillenkoetter, "Comments," pp. 17–18, 27; Dulles Report, p. 81; G. S. Jackson, Paper No. 11, "Note on the Intelligence Memorandum (IM) Series, 1948–1950."

200. See pp. 305–6. National Security Act of 1947, Sections 101, 102, and 303.

201. Hillenkoetter, "Comments," pp. 25–27. For the origin of the daily summary, see above, pp. 81–82. National Security Council, *Policies*, pp. 73, 89; G. S. Jackson, Paper No. 11.

202. Hillenkoetter, "Comments," p. 20.

203. Hillenkoetter, "Comments," pp. 51–52 and Enclosure C. For Eberstadt's recommendation, see above, pp. 293–95.

204. E. Watts to T. Babbitt, Feb. 9, 1949.

Chapter IX

1. NSC File 6236-2.

2. L. R. Houston to A. B. Darling, Nov. 6, 1952; R. H. Hillenkoetter to A. B. Darling, Dec. 2, 1952, pp. 20–21.

3. R. H. Hillenkoetter to A. B. Darling, Dec. 2, 1952, p. 23; S. W. Souers to A. B. Darling, Nov. 6, 1952, p. 42.

4. See pp. 193–94. See the interviews with Souers and with Leahy, June 20, July 1, and July 3, 1952.

5. See p. 11.

6. C. P. Cabell to A. B. Darling, Aug. 7, 1953.

7. Dulles Report, pp. 61–63.

8. Dulles Report, pp. 9–10; W. F. Colby to R. H. Hillenkoetter, Feb. 24, 1949 (Executive Registry File: NSC 50 Series).

9. R. H. Hillenkoetter, "Comments," p. 14; Irwin's Report (Executive Registry File: NSC 50 Series).

10. Hillenkoetter, "Comments," pp. 15–16; Dulles Report, p. 63; S. W. Souers to A. B. Darling, Nov. 4, 1952, p. 41.

11. Irwin's Report, p. 5 (Executive Registry File: NSC 50 Series).

12. National Security Council, *Policies,* Vol., II, p. 108.

13. Dulles Report, p. 149; J. Magruder to A. B. Darling, Jan. 8, 1953. For the Eberstadt Report, see above, pp. 285–98. Eberstadt Report, pp. 39–40.

14. Dulles Report, p. 61; W. E. Todd, paper, pp. 2–3.

15. See pp. 238–39. Dulles Report, p. 81.

16. See p. 217. T. B. Inglis, memorandum for S. W. Souers, March 4, 1949 (Executive Registry File: Dulles–Jackson–Correa Survey).

17. National Security Act of 1947, Section 102d; Action of the Council No. 1(b), Sept. 26, 1947; National Security Council, *Policies*, p. 46; minutes of the first meeting of the Intelligence Advisory Committee. These files are in the Executive Secretary's Office.

18. See pp. 218–20.

19. See p. 200. S. Kent to A. B. Darling, March 25 and Oct. 7, 1952.

20. H. S. Vandenberg to A. B. Darling, March 17, 1952. See above, pp. 138–40, 205.

21. T. B. Inglis, memorandum for S. W. Souers, March 4, 1949, pp. 6–7 (Executive Registry File: Dulles–Jackson–Correa Survey).

22. T. B. Inglis, memorandum for S. W. Souers, March 4, 1949, p. 8 (Executive Registry File: Dulles–Jackson–Correa Survey); Dulles Report, pp. 99–100, 116–17, 134. For NSC 10-2, see above, pp. 273–81. For Inglis's concept of the Group and the Agency, see above, pp. 100–102, 198–99, 234–35.

23. See pp. 88–89, 131–32.

24. Dulles Report, p. 136. See above, pp. 289–91.

25. Dulles Report, p. 63.

26. T. B. Inglis to S. W. Souers, March 4, 1949 (Executive Registry File: Dulles–Jackson–Correa Survey). For references to operational intelligence, see above, pp. 198–99, 202, 235, 239. For NIA Directive 1, see above, p. 80.

27. Executive Registry Files: Dulles–Jackson–Correa Survey and NSC 50 Series; minutes of NSC Meeting 37, April 7, 1949 (Executive Secretary's Office); C. P. Cabell to A. B. Darling, Aug. 7 and Sept. 17, 1953; Air Staff Summary with attachments, March 1, 1949.

28. C. P. Cabell to A. B. Darling, Sept. 17, 1953; "Annex" to "Comments on the Dulles Report," Air Staff Summary, March 1, 1949; National Security Act of 1947 as amended in 1949.

29. Minutes of NSC Meeting 37, April 7, 1949 (Executive Secretary's Office); S. W. Souers to A. B. Darling, Sept. 8 and Nov. 4, 1952; Air Staff Summary with attachments, March 1, 1949.

30. J. E. Webb to S. W. Souers, April 4, 1949, NSC Action No. 198 (Executive Registry File: NSC 50 Series).

31. Ibid.

32. Action No. 202, NSC Meeting 37, April 7, 1949 (Executive Secretary's Office); NSC 17, "Report on the Internal Security of the United States," June 28, 1948, written by J. Patrick Coyne, former chief of the FBI's Internal Security Division and temporary consultant on the staff of the National Security Council for the purpose (Executive Registry File: NSC 50 Series); S. W. Souers to A. B. Darling, Nov. 6, 1952.

33. T. Clark to J. T. McNarney, May 27, 1949 (Executive Registry File: NSC 50 Series). The copy in the file of the Agency does not reveal the author of this memorandum. Hoover or an associate, however, may be considered likely.

34. For the Act of 1947, see p. 175.

35. These items were 2, 3, 5, 7 and 8 in the McNarney Report, Section 4a, pp. 4–5.

36. Minutes of NSC Meeting 36, March 22, 1949 (Executive Secretary's Office); NSC 17/4, March 23, 1949 (Executive Registry File).

37. See pp. 125–27. S. W. Souers to A. B. Darling, Nov. 6, 1952.

38. Dulles Report, pp. 57–58; T. Clark to J. T. McNarney, May 27, 1949 (Executive Registry File: NSC 50 Series).

39. For the charters of IIC and ICIS, see National Security Council, *Policies*, Vol. II, pp. 89–94.

40. See pp. 335–36. N. E. Halaby to R. H. Hillenkoetter, June 2, 1949. The

482   Notes to Chapter IX

representatives were Coyne for Souers and Halaby for McNarney. S. W. Souers to A. B. Darling, Nov. 6, 1952; Dulles Report, pp. 75–76.

41. S. W. Souers to A. B. Darling, Nov. 6, 1952, p. 43; P. Borel to A. B. Darling, July 30, 1953.

42. McNarney Report, p. 7, para. 5. See above, pp. 200–201.

43. T. P. Taswell-Langmead, *English Constitutional History,* 10th edn. 1946, pp. 683–89; McNarney Report, p. 2. See above, pp. 214–15, 285–86. For the original idea, see above, pp. 100–105. L. L. Montague to A. B. Darling, Nov. 6, 1953.

44. See pp. 336–37. See pp. 79–81 for the definitions at the time of the first directive of the National Intelligence Authority, Feb. 8, 1946. For Hillenkoetter's "Comments," see pp. 316–32.

45. McNarney Report, pp. 7–8 (Executive Registry File: NSC 50 Series). There is a photocopy in the Historical Collection, File Records Integration–Foreign Intelligence. For NSCID 1 as originally drafted, see above, pp. 218–20. S. Kent to A. B. Darling, March 25 and Oct. 7, 1952.

46. For Vandenberg's position, see pp. 131–33. For Hillenkoetter's position, see pp. 218–20. H. S. Vandenberg to A. B. Darling, March 17, 1952; R. H. Hillenkoetter to A. B. Darling, Dec. 2, 1952.

47. G. S. Jackson, Paper No. 14, "The Record of Central Intelligence before 1951 with respect to the Korean War, July 14, 1953." [three lines deleted] ORE 15-48, "The Current Situation in Korea," March 18, 1948; ORE 44-48, "Prospects for Survival of the Republic of Korea," Oct. 28, 1948. [two lines deleted] ORE 3-49, "Consequences of U. S. Troop Withdrawal from Korea in Spring 1949," Feb. 28, 1949. [two lines deleted]

48. McNarney Report, pp. 4–7.

49. See pp. 283–85.

50. See p. 173.

51. See pp. 207–9.

52. McNarney Report, pp. 9–10.

53. S. W. Souers to A. B. Darling, Nov. 4, 1952. See above, pp. 183–89.

54. McNarney Report, pp. 14–15.

55. Dulles Report, p. 35. See above, pp. 309–11.

56. See pp. 240–43.

57. Dulles Report, Chs. XI and XII; McNarney Report, p. 16. For the Eberstadt Report on intelligence as a career, see above, pp. 291–92.

58. Hillenkoetter, "Comments," pp. 34–38. See above, pp. 308–9.

59. McNarney Report, p. 13.

60. For the right of inspection, see p. 185.

61. National Security Act of 1947, Section 202(2).

62. R. H. Hillenkoetter to A. B. Darling, Oct. 24, 1952, pp. 5–9; McNarney Report, p. 15.

63. Minutes of NSC Meeting 43 (Executive Secretary's Office).

64. For NSCID 1 as revised, July 7, 1949, see the Historical Collection. T. Clark to S. W. Souers, July 15, 1949; S. W. Souers to IIC and ICIS, July 18, 1949;

minutes of NSC Meeting 43; National Security Council, *Policies*, Vol. II, p. 91. For the settlement of 1946 regarding the Office of Operations, see above, pp. 125–27.

65. [citation deleted]

66. S. W. Souers to R. H. Hillenkoetter, July 7, 1949, para. 9a of NSC 50.

67. For Vandenberg's position, see pp. 132–33. For Hillenkoetter's revocation, see pp. 218–20. For Souers on the point of sabotage, see p. 76.

68. J. S. Lay, Jr., to R. H. Hillenkoetter, July 8, 1949 (Executive Registry File: NSC 50 Series).

69. *Policies*, Vol. III, pp. 104–6, 113. NSCID 11 and NSCID 12 dated Jan. 6, 1950.

70. See p. 185.

71. For Bogotá, see pp. 240–44. For the criticism in the Dulles Report, see pp. 309–11.

72. For Hillenkoetter's views on the "separate administration" and other discussion, see pp. 321–22. For the provisions in the CIA Act of 1949 approved by the President on June 20, 1949, see pp. 191–92. Minutes of NSC Meeting 44, Aug. 4, 1949 (Executive Secretary's Office); S. W. Souers to Tom C. Clark, July 25, 1949 (copy with the minutes of Meeting 44).

73. See pp. 321–22. J. T. McNarney to S. W. Souers, July 22, 1949 (Executive Registry File: NSC 50 Series).

74. For NSC 10-2, see pp. 274–81. For Hillenkoetter's objection, see pp. 320–23.

75. J. T. McNarney to S. W. Souers, July 22, 1949 (Executive Registry File: NSC 50 Series.

76. Public Law 110, Section 10c, 81st Congress, June 20, 1949.

77. Minutes of NSC Meeting 44, Aug. 4, 1949 (Executive Secretary's Office); R. H. Hillenkoetter, memorandum of Aug. 16, 1949 (Executive Registry File: NSC 50 Series); "Proposed Organization of Office to Conduct Clandestine Operations," Aug. 30, 1949; R. A. Schow and F. G. Wisner to R. H. Hillenkoetter, Aug. 31, 1949 (Executive Registry File: NSC 50 Series).

78. General Order 24, Sept. 20, 1949; F. P. Bishop, "Historical Notes: Budget and Finance Activities," p. 14.

79. F. P. Bishop to A. B. Darling, in conversation, Aug. 7, 1953; F. P. Bishop, "Historical Notes," pp. 16–17 regarding Regulation No. 70 of Dec. 1, 1950, on the Finance Office and the Comptroller reporting directly to the Deputy Director for Administration.

80. R. H. Hillenkoetter to A. B. Darling, Dec. 2, 1952, p. 24; J. Larocque and J.B.B. Reeves to A. B. Darling, Nov. 17, 1952, and March 16, 1953; W. H. Jackson, *Survey of Office of Policy Coordination*, 2 vols. (Executive Registry File).

81. S. W. Souers, memorandum of July 7, 1949; J. S. Lay, Jr., memorandum of July 8, 1949; McNarney Report, pp. 3, 5, 8.

82. McNarney Report, pp. 8, 17. For the position of Vandenberg and Hillenkoetter, see above, pp. 107, 225. H. S. Vandenberg to A. B. Darling, March 15, 1952; R. H. Hillenkoetter to A. B. Darling, Dec. 2, 1952. For Jackson's position, see above, pp. 60–62, 312–13.

83. W. P. Armstrong, Jr., to R. H. Hillenkoetter, Aug. 2, 1949 (File: State, "Four Problems," NSC 50 Series). For the Bureau of the Budget and the McCormack plan, see above, pp. 44–47, 51–56. P. Childs, memorandum for the Assistant Directors, Aug. 3, 1948.

84. W. P. Armstrong, Jr., to R. H. Hillenkoetter, Aug. 2, 1949.

85. For the Defense Project, see pp. 82–87.

86. W. P. Armstrong, Jr., to R. H. Hillenkoetter, Oct. 29, 1947 (File: NSCID, Correspondence Concerning). See above, pp. 209–11. W. P. Armstrong, Jr., to R. H. Hillenkoetter, Aug. 2, 1949, enclosing the "four papers."

87. For Langer on primary and secondary interests, see pp. 107–9. For Vandenberg and CIG Directive 12, July 29, 1946, see pp. 219–20.

88. For Byrnes and the daily summary, see pp. 81–82. For previous studies by OCD, see pp. 141–45.

89. P. Borel to A. B. Darling, Aug. 24, 1953; G. S. Jackson, Paper No. 2, "Controversies within the Office of Reports and Estimates, 1948–1950."

90. W. Reitzel to A. B. Darling, March 27, 1953. For the controversy during Vandenberg's administration, see above, pp. 129–38. For the comments of ORE to Hillenkoetter, see above, pp. 339–45.

91. T. Babbitt to A. B. Darling, March 13, 1953; W. Reitzel to A. B. Darling, March 27, 1953. The Reitzel Report is in the Historical Collection on loan from the Office of Research and Reports (DIR, ORR, 2214 M Building).

92. For NIA Directive 5, see pp. 107–11.

93. For ORE Administrative Order 1, Aug. 7, 1946, see pp. 128–30, 135–38. For the Central Reports Staff under Souers and Montague, see pp. 87–89.

94. For Royall's view, see p. 207. For Souers on internal organization and matters of policy, see the interview with him, Nov. 6, 1952, p. 44.

95. National Security Act of 1947, Public Law 253, Section 102d(1–3) 80th Congress, July 26, 1947.

96. Reitzel Report, p. 407, Tabs B and C for documentation; D. Van Slyck to A. B. Darling, Jan. 10, 1952; T. Babbitt to A. B. Darling, March 13, 1953.

97. T. Babbitt to A. B. Darling, March 13, 1953. For the report of July 16, 1947, see above, pp. 133–34.

98. T. Babbitt to R. H. Hillenkoetter, Aug. 15, 1949, on "Implementation of NSC 50" (File: State, "Four Problems," NSC 50 Series); McNarney Report, p. 10.

99. Proposed revision of NSCID 1, Aug. 12, 1949 (File: State, "Four Problems," NSC 50 Series).

100. P. Childs to R. H. Hillenkoetter, Aug. 31, 1949 (File: State, "Four Problems," NSC 50 Series); memorandum for the Standing Committee from the representatives of the Department of Defense, Sept. 8, 1949. For Truman to Byrnes, see above, p. 82.

101. Minutes of the Standing Committee's Meeting, Sept. 8, 1949 (File: State, "Four Problems," NSC 50 Series).

102. Report on State's "Four Problems" from all Standing Committee Members except State's, Sept. 23, 1949 (File: State, "Four Problems," NSC 50 Series).

103. T. Babbitt to R. H. Hillenkoetter, Sept. 30, 1949, on "IAC Cooperation with CIA." For reports on previous occasions, see above, pp. 133–37.

104. For the NSCIDs, see pp. 218–26. For the "war scare" and the ad hoc estimating of 1948, see pp. 161–62.

Chapter X

1. W. Machle to R. H. Hillenkoetter, Sept. 29, 1949, memorandum on "Inability of OSI to Accomplish Its Mission." For the authorization of Vandenberg and its revocation at the request of Hillenkoetter, see above, pp. 161–65, 200–201.

2. See pp. 186–89. L. R. Houston and W. L. Pforzheimer to the Executive, Sept. 27, 1949.

3. W. L. Pforzheimer, memorandum to the Chief of COAPS, P. Childs, with accompanying "Memorandum for the National Security Council," 3rd draft, Oct. 13, 1949 (memoranda in the Office of General Counsel, File: NSCID 1, "Duties and Responsibilities").

4. R. H. Hillenkoetter to A. B. Darling, Oct. 24, 1952, p. 6, and Dec. 2, 1952, p. 4.

5. For the situation in the summer of 1946, see pp. 199–201. R. H. Hillenkoetter to A. B. Darling, Oct. 24 and Dec. 2, 1952; H. Truman to R. H. Hillenkoetter, Oct. 10, 1950, as shown to A. B. Darling, Dec. 2, 1952.

6. For NSC 10/2, June 18, 1948, see pp. 273–76. For General Order 24, Sept. 20, 1949, see p. 322. R. H. Hillenkoetter, memorandum for the Executive Secretary, Oct. 7, 1949 (Executive Registry File: NSC 50 Series).

7. S. W. Souers, memorandum for the National Security Council, Oct. 10, 1949; J. E. Webb to S. W. Souers, Dec. 13, 1949 (Executive Registry File: NSC 50 Series).

8. For Hillenkoetter's "Comments," Feb. 28, 1949, see p. 345. Dulles Report, Chs. V and VI.

9. Report on the "four papers" submitted to the Director of Central Intelligence, memorandum for the members of the Intelligence Advisory Committee, Dec. 21, 1949, submitted by R. H. Hillenkoetter, Dec. 30, 1949 (Executive Registry File: NSC 50 Series).

10. See pp. 150–54.

11. G. S. Jackson, Paper No. 5, "Aspects of the Problem of Inter-Agency Exchange of Information in the Period 1946–1950."

12. See pp. 145–48, 238–39.

13. See pp. 190–91, 280–81.

14. See pp. 184–85.

15. For NSCID 1, see pp. 218–20.

16. For NSCID 15 and the establishment of the Economic Intelligence Committee, see p. 416.

486   Notes to Chapter X

17. R. H. Hillenkoetter, memorandum for the Executive Secretary, National Security Council, Dec. 27, 1949 (Executive Registry File: NSC 50 Series).

18. W. Machle to R. H. Hillenkoetter, Sept. 29, 1949, memorandum on "Inability of OSI to Accomplish Its Mission," and Enclosure II, pp. 2–4; S. L. Irwin to R. H. Hillenkoetter regarding proposed "DCI 3/3," Sept. 28, 1949; R. H. Hillenkoetter, memorandum to members of the Intelligence Advisory Committee on "Scientific Intelligence," Oct. 6, 1949; "DCI 3/3" as adopted on Oct. 28, 1949.

19. For previous DCIs, see pp. 218–19, 221, 222. See the text of NSCID 1, para. 6, Jan. 19, 1950. For Clay's "war scare" and the ad hoc estimating, see above, pp. 338–40.

20. For the comments of ORE in Feb. 1949, see pp. 340–41.

21. J. Magruder to A. B. Darling, Nov. 18, 1952. See above, pp. 341–45. T. Babbitt to A. B. Darling, March 13, 1953.

22. Report of the (ORE) Committee on a Comprehensive Production Plan (Stout Report), March 7, 1950; G. S. Jackson, Paper No. 2, "Controversies within the Office of Reports and Estimates, 1948–1950."

23. D. Van Slyck to A. B. Darling, April 21, 1953.

24. R. H. Hillenkoetter to A. B. Darling, Oct. 24 and Dec. 2, 1952; T. Babbitt to A. B. Darling, March 13, 1953. For Magruder and the Joint Intelligence Committee in Jan. 1943, see above, pp. 14–15.

25. For Magruder's contribution to the Donovan plan, see pp. 20–22. J. Magruder to A. B. Darling, Nov. 18, 1952, and Jan. 8, 1953; R. H. Hillenkoetter to A. B. Darling, Dec. 2, 1952, pp. 24–26; L. R. Houston to A. B. Darling, April 21 and Aug. 19, 1953.

26. Staff Study, "Production of National Intelligence," May 1, 1950 (copy in File: Webb Staff Study, Historical Collection).

27. National Security Act of 1949, Public Law 253, 80th Congress, Section 212; National Security Act of 1949, Public Law 216, 81st Congress, Section 7c.

28. For the elimination of civilian membership from the Joint Intelligence Committee of the Joint Chiefs of Staff, see pp. 232–34.

29. Dulles Report, p. 81.

30. W. H. Jackson, Chairman, *Report to the President on International Information Activities*, June 30, 1953, p. 3.

31. J. E. Webb to R. H. Hillenkoetter, July 7, 1950 (File: NSCID 1, "Duties and Responsibilities").

32. T. Babbitt, Order No. 15, July 2, 1950; Order No. 18, Aug. 3, 1950; Instruction No. 27, July 12, 1950 (File: ORE, Special Staff Papers, Miscellaneous); G. S. Jackson, Paper No. 1, "Organizational Development of the Office of Reports and Estimates, 1946–1950."

33. S. W. Souers to A. B. Darling, Sept. 8, 1952. For Smith and Donovan, see above, pp. 22–23.

34. R. H. Hillenkoetter to A. B. Darling, Dec. 2, 1952.

35. L. R. Houston, marginal notes on the Staff Study made after July 7, 1950 (File: NSCID 1, "Duties and Responsibilities"). See above, pp. 171, 174, 188–89, 198–201, 215–16.

36. See pp. 188–89. National Security Act of 1947, Section 102d(5); R. H. Hillenkoetter to A. B. Darling, Dec. 2, 1952. For possible reorganization of the Agency by the President, see W. L. Pforzheimer to A. B. Darling, June 26, 1953.

37. T. Babbitt to Executive, CIA and COAPS, July 11, 1950 (File: Webb Staff Study). Copies went to the Assistant Directors of other offices in the Agency. For the meetings, see L. R. Houston to A. B. Darling, Aug. 19, 1953. For the President's Directive, Jan. 22, 1946, see above, pp. 70–73.

38. J. S. Lay, Jr., Executive Secretary, memorandum for the Director of Central Intelligence on atomic energy intelligence, advance draft, July 19, 1950. The quotations from Secretary Johnson's comments are in this paper (File: Webb Staff Study).

39. R. H. Hillenkoetter to J. E. Webb, July 26, 1950, enclosing comments on the Staff Study and Basic NSCID (File: Webb Staff Study).

40. L. T. Shannon, Acting Executive, memorandum for each Assistant Director and Staff Chief, July 27, 1950; J. E. Webb to R. H. Hillenkoetter, Aug. 3, 1950 (the original is in File: Webb Staff Study).

41. F. G. Wisner to T. Babbitt, July 27, 1950 (copy in File: NSCID 1, "Duties and Responsibilities"). Upon this copy is the notation in ink by L. T. Shannon, Acting Executive, that the original went to the Director on August 2, 1950.

42. L. R. Houston to P. Childs, Sept. 1, 1950, and to R. H. Hillenkoetter, Sept. 11, 1950; L. R. Houston to A. B. Darling, April 21 and Aug. 19, 1953.

43. L. R. Houston to W. B. Smith, Aug. 29, 1950; L. R. Houston to J. Magruder, Sept. 13, 1950; J. Magruder to A. B. Darling, Jan. 8, 1953.

44. L. R. Houston, memorandum for Lieutenant General W. B. Smith, Aug. 29, 1950.

45. For the Air Forces and the Dulles Report, see pp. 354–55.

46. Dulles Report, pp. 60, 135–38; McNarney Report, p. 2. The quotation is from NSCID 1, July 7, 1949. See above, pp. 359–61.

47. For discussion of this point, see pp. 220–21, 285–87, 333–37, 362–64, 366–67.

48. See pp. 87–92, 131–33.

49. T. Babbitt, L. L. Montague, and D. Van Slyck to W. H. Jackson, "Plan for a CIA Office of Estimates," Oct. 10, 1950 (File: Souvenirs of G/GS).

50. S. W. Souers to A. B. Darling, June 30, 1952, p. 23; R. H. Hillenkoetter to A. B. Darling, Oct. 22, 1952, p. 2, and Oct. 24, 1952, p. 6. For the Director as the personal intelligence officer of the President, see above, pp. 70, 188–89.

51. T. Babbitt to A. B. Darling, March 13, 1953, pp. 2–3; L. L. Montague to A. B. Darling, Sept. 22, 1952. For Kent's report, see above, pp. 301–2.

52. L. R. Houston, W. L. Pforzheimer, F. G. Wisner to W. H. Jackson, Deputy Director, Oct. 5, 1950 (Executive Registry File: NSC 10 Series); text of NSCID 1, June 18, 1948, in Historical Collection.

53. For Jackson's proposal to Forrestal in Nov. 1945, see pp. 61–62. For his views as a member of the Dulles Group, see pp. 312–13. Dulles Report, pp. 77, 81.

54. Minutes of meeting, Intelligence Advisory Committee, Oct. 20, 1950, written from W. H. Jackson's notes; J. Q. Reber to A. B. Darling, Sept. 22, 1953. For

Magruder and the Webb Staff Study, see above, p. 393. J. Magruder to A. B. Darling, Nov. 18, 1952; S. W. Souers to A. B. Darling, June 30 and Sept. 8, 1952.

55. F. G. Wisner to W. B. Smith, Oct. 12, 1950. For the "Memorandum of Interpretation," see above, pp. 277–80. The quotations in the text above are from Wisner's report; Smith's instructions were oral.

56. F. G. Wisner to W. B. Smith, Oct. 12, 1950. For Kennan and Hillenkoetter, see above, p. 263.

57. See p. 278.

58. Minutes of meeting, Jackson's notes, Oct. 20, 1950. For Donovan's views, see above, pp. 7–8. W. J. Donovan to A. B. Darling, Feb. 17, 1953; E. K. Wright to A. B. Darling, April 10 and May 28, 1953.

59. Minutes of meeting, Intelligence Advisory Committee, Jackson's notes, Oct. 20, 1950. For McNarney's second report, July 22, 1949, see above, pp. 370–71. National Security Council, Action No. 237, *Policies,* Vol. II, p. 109, and Vol. III, p. 99 (Meeting 69, Oct. 12); minutes of NSC Meeting 44, Aug. 4, 1949. For Hillenkoetter's action regarding the merger of the covert offices, see above, pp. 371–72.

60. C. P. Cabell to A. B. Darling, Aug. 7 and Sept. 17, 1953. See above, pp. 354–55.

61. For Vandenberg and the working fund, see pp. 113–15. For the Acts of Congress regarding the finances of the Agency, see pp. 189–90, 191–92. For Hillenkoetter and expenditures, see pp. 320–23.

62. CIA Regulation No. 60, Dec. 1, 1950; E. R. Saunders, "Progress Report to the Deputy Director (Administration)," Nov. 6, 1951; F. P. Bishop, "Historical Notes: Budget and Finance Activities," p. 16 (a copy of the "Progress Report" is attached).

63. Dulles Report, pp. 100, 116, 134; W. H. Jackson, *Survey of Office of Policy Coordination* (Executive Registry File).

64. For Vandenberg, ICAPS, and the Board, see pp. 138–40.

65. For Hillenkoetter's proposal, see p. 205.

66. P. Childs, memorandum for COAPS on the State Department's "Four Papers regarding NSC 50," p. 23; National Security Council, Action No. 282, *Policies,* Vol. III, pp. 99, 113. See above, p. 389.

67. For ORE in the summer of 1950, see p. 399. W. H. Jackson, memorandum for the Executive Secretary, National Security Council, on "Appraisal of Foreign Economic Intelligence Requirements . . . ," May 31, 1951, with attachments; M. Millikan, "Progress Report," July 11, 1951, and the "Role of ORR in Economic Intelligence," Aug. 1, 1951.

68. T. Babbitt to A. B. Darling, March 13, 1953; Smith, "Progress Report," April 23, 1952 (Executive Registry File: NSC 50 series).

69. T. Babbitt to A. B. Darling, March 13, 1953; E. Beattie, "Report on OCI," Dec. 13, 1951 (Historical Collection).

70. For the Standing Committee, see p. 374.

71. J. Q. Reber to A. B. Darling, Sept. 22, 1953; Dulles Report, pp. 5, 9, 62.

72. Dulles Report, pp. 6–7, 77. For the Defense Project, see above, pp. 82–87, 146–47.

73. For McNarney's statement in NSC 50 and the exception which he took to the accusation of Hillenkoetter, see pp. 364–65.

74. Intelligence Advisory Committee, minutes of meeting, Oct. 20, 1950, dictated from notes by Jackson, before correction and organization for circulation; notes on IAC meeting, Oct. 20, 1950, rough draft, signed by Colonel Howze.

75. J. Q. Reber to A. B. Darling, Sept. 22, 1953.

76. Minutes of meeting on Oct. 20, 1950, pp. 3–4.

77. For NIA Directive 1, see pp. 78–82. For the "net estimate," NSC 140/1, "current appraisal of vulnerability to Soviet attack," see pp. 257–58, 260. W. H. Jackson, *Report to the President on International Information Activities,* June 30, 1953, p. 3. For Smith's cautious approach to a similar problem, "Interrelationship between Intelligence and Operational Planning," see his "Progress Report," April 23, 1952, p. 4.

78. For Jackson's view in Nov. 1945, see pp. 60–62. W. H. Jackson to J. Forrestal, Nov. 14, 1945; minutes of meeting, Oct. 20, 1950, Jackson's notes, as corrected for multigraphing; J. Q. Reber to A. B. Darling, Sept. 22, 1953; McNarney Report, July 1, 1949, p. 8; S. W. Souers to A. B. Darling, Jan. 25, 1952.

79. J. Q. Reber to A. B. Darling, Sept. 22, 1953; NSCID 1 as revised on July 7, 1949.

80. Minutes of meeting, Oct. 20, 1950, Jackson's notes, pp. 4–5; Dulles Report, pp. 6, 71–72. For discussion of the "confusion" in the Office of Reports and Estimates, see above, pp. 332–33, 336, 343–44.

81. Minutes of meeting, Oct. 20, 1950; notes by Colonel Howze, GSC.

82. J. Q. Reber to A. B. Darling, Sept. 22, 1953. For Langer, Vandenberg, and the IAB, see above, pp. 108–9.

83. W. L. Langer to W. H. Jackson, "Activities of the Office of National Estimates," July 9, 1951.

84. S. Kent, *Strategic Intelligence for American World Policy,* 1949. For Montague and Van Slyck, see above, pp. 137–38, 332–33, 338–40, 342–43.

85. For Kennan as a consultant of the National Security Council regarding psychological warfare, see pp. 245–46, 266. For Bush and the Agency, see pp. 216, 226–31.

86. W. L. Langer to W. H. Jackson, July 9, 1951, pp. 5–6.

87. L. R. Houston to W. B. Smith, Aug. 29, 1950.

Index

sents in reports of, 134–35; Dulles Report investigation of, 338–43; Eberstadt Report's comments on, 288; friction within, 135–38, 197–98; Hillenkoetter's reorganization of, 392; Intelligence Advisory Committee and, 395; intelligence collection in China, 151–52; Joint Chiefs of Staff and, 234–39; McNarney Report assessment of, 363; Reitzel Report on, 375–78; Scientific Branch, 227–32; scientific intelligence collection, 163–65, 197–98; Smith's reform of, 415–16; State Department report on, 377–80
Office of Research, 407
Office of Research and Evaluation (CIG): ICAPS and, 140–45; origins of, 101; research and estimation procedures, 129–30
Office of Research and Reports, 375, 415–21
Office of Scientific Intelligence, 390; Eberstadt Committee assessment of, 317–18; Machle Report and, 381–82; Nuclear Energy Group and, 348
Office of Scientific Research and Development, 161–63
Office of Special Operations (OSO): Central Planning Staff disposition, 148; consolidation plans for, 385–93; Dulles Report assessment of, 315–16, 329–32; evaluations of reports and estimates, 135–36; FBI operations and, 197–98, 391–92; foreign intelligence activity, 222; friction with OO, 197–98; McNarney Report assessment of, 363, 370–73; organization of, 118–21; origins of, 114–15; Smith's reform proposals and, 412; Webb/Magruder Report and, 403
Office of Special Projects, 272
Office of Strategic Services (OSS), 1942–1945: civilian intelligence operations and, 235–36; development of, 10–20; Joint Intelligence Committee and, 290–91; liquidation of, 38–41; military planning and intelligence, 155; propaganda planning by, 251; Research and Analysis Branch, 15–17, 98; restrictions on, 12–13; scientific intelligence, 87–88; Secret Intelligence Branch of, 15

Office of War Information (OWI), 1941–1945; foreign information service and, 10; operations of, 12, 43; propaganda planning by, 251
Ohly, John H., 300–301, 303–4
Olsen, Captain C.E., 307
operational intelligence vs. national intelligence, 27–28
Operations Advisory Board (Committee), 271–73; Office of Policy Coordination and, 274–75
Operations Division: McNarney Report proposal for, 370, 372–73; proposals for, 385–93, 413–15
Operations Groups, 20
Oral Intelligence Unit (COI), 9
"ORE 1" estimate, 130–36
overt operations: CIG and, 115–27; Dulles Report findings on, 330–31; McNarney Report recommendations on, 370–71

Pan-American Union, 4, 54
"panel of guidance" concept: covert operations planning, 258–62, 271–72; Office of Policy Coordination and, 274–75
Parkman, Francis, 169, 173
Patterson, Robert P., 20, 47–51; Atomic Energy Commission files, 153–54; on CIG funding, 113–15; Congressional hearings on CIA, 176, 178; creation of national defense council, 172; DCI powers assessed, 201; military planning and intelligence, 155, 157–60; national security concerns, 166–67; permanent intelligence system proposal, 47–51; psychological warfare discussed, 250; scientific intelligence collection, 162–63; Strategic Services Unit disposition, 99; War Department stand on central intelligence, 59
Peace Conference (Paris, 1946), 85
Pearl Harbor: Intelligence Center at, 193–94; intelligence operations and, 15, 61
Pearson, Drew, 276–77
Penrose, Stephen B. L., 118
Pentagon Watch Committee, 420
Perkins, Frances, 36
permanent joint intelligence system (1944–1945): Bateson opposition to, 42–43; Bureau of the Budget proposal for,